SONGS OF THREE CENTURIES.

EDITED BY

JOHN GREENLEAF WHITTIER.

BOSTON:
HOUGHTON, MIFFLIN AND COMPANY.
The Riverside Press, Cambridge.
1883.

PREFACE.

IT would be doing injustice to the compiler of this volume to suppose that his work implied any lack of appreciation of the excellent anthologies already published in this country. Dana's "Household Book of Poetry" is no misnomer ; and the honored names of Bryant and Emerson are a sufficient guaranty for "Parnassus" and the "Library of Song." With no thought of superseding or even of entering into direct competition with these large and valuable collections, it has been my design to gather up in a comparatively small volume, easily accessible to all classes of readers, the wisest thoughts, rarest fancies, and devoutest hymns of the metrical authors of the last three centuries. To use Shelley's definition of poetry, I have endeavored to give something like "a record of the best thoughts and happiest moments of the best and happiest minds." The plan of my work has compelled me to confine myself, in a great measure, to the lyrical productions of the authors quoted, and to use only the briefer poems of the old dramatists and such voluminous writers as Spenser, Milton, Dryden, Cowper, Pope, Byron, Scott, Wordsworth, and the Brownings. Of course, no anthology, however ample its extracts, could do justice to the illimitable genius of Shakespeare.

It is possible that it may be thought an undue prominence has been given to the poetry of the period beginning with Cowper and reaching down to Tennyson and his living contemporaries. But it must be considered that the last century has been prolific in song; and, if Shakespeare and Milton still keep their unapproachable position, "souls like stars that dwell apart," there can be little doubt that the critical essayist of the twentieth century will make a large advance upon the present estimate, not only of Cowper and Burns, but of Wordsworth, Coleridge, Shelley, Keats, Browning, Tennyson, and Emerson.

It will be seen that the middle of the sixteenth century is the earliest date of my citations. The great name of Chaucer does not appear ; and some of the best of the early ballad poetry of England and Scotland has been reluctantly omitted. James I., whose Queen's Quhair has hidden his kingly crown under the poet's garland, William Dunbar, and Sackville, Earl of Dorset, may well be thought worthy of a place in any collection of English verse, but the language and rhythm of these writers render them wellnigh unintelligible to the ordinary reader.

The selections I have made indicate, in a general way, my preferences; but I have not felt at liberty to oppose my own judgment or prejudice to the best critical authorities, or to attempt a reversal of the verdicts of Time. It would be too much to hope that I have, in all cases, made the best possible exposition of an author's productions. Judging from my own experience in looking over selected poems, I cannot doubt that my readers will often have occasion to question the wisdom of my choice, and regret the omission of favorite pieces. It is rarely that persons of equal capacity for right judging can be found to coincide entirely in regard to the merits of a particular poem. The canons of criticism are by no means fixed and infallible; and the fashion of poetry, like that of the world, "passeth away." Not only every age, but every reader, holds the right of private judgment. It would be difficult for any literary inquisitor-general to render a good reason for condemning as a heretic the man who finds the "Castle of Indolence" pleasanter reading than the "Faerie Queene," who prefers Cowper to Dryden, Scott to Byron, and Shelley to Scott, who passes by Moore's "Lalla Rookh" to take up Clough's "Bothie of Tober-na Vuolich," who thinks Emerson's "Threnody" better than Milton's "Lycidas," and who would not exchange a good old ballad or a song of Burns for the stateliest of epics.

The considerable space which I have given to American authors will, I trust, find its justification in the citations from their writings. The poetical literature of our country can scarcely be said to have a longer date than that of a single generation. As a matter of fact, the very fathers of it are still living. It really commenced with Bryant's "Thanatopsis" and Dana's "Buccaneer." The grave, philosophic tone, chaste simplicity of language, freedom of versification, and freshness and truth of illustration, which marked the former poem, and the terse realism of the "Buccaneer," with its stern pictures of life and nature drawn with few strokes sharp and vigorous as those of Retzsch's outlines, left the weak imitators of an artificial school without an audience. All further attempts to colonize the hills and pastures of New England from old mythologies were abandoned; our boys and girls no longer figured in impossible pastorals. If we have no longer ambitious Columbiads and Conquests of Canaan, we have at least truth and nature, wit and wisdom, in Bryant's "Robert of Lincoln," Emerson's "Humblebee," Lowell's "Courtin'," and "The One-Hoss Shay" of Holmes.

In dealing with contemporary writers I have found myself embarrassed by the very large number of really noticeable poems, many of which, although in my own estimation vastly better than those of some of the old versifiers whose age and general reputation have secured them a place in this volume, I have been compelled to omit solely from lack of space. The future gleaner in the fields over which I have passed will doubtless find many an ungarnered sheaf quite as well worth preserving as these I have gathered within the scanty limits of my compendium. The rare humorists of our time, especially such poets as Holmes and Lowell, can be only partially represented in these necessarily brief selections.

It may be observed that the three divisions of the book do not strictly correspond to the headings which indicate them, — the first, for instance, beginning before Shakespeare and ending somewhat after Milton. It is difficult to be quite exact in such classifications; and as it seemed desirable to make their number as small as possible, I trust the few leading names mentioned may serve to characterize the periods they accompany with a sufficient degree of accuracy. Pope was doubtless the great master of what is sometimes spoken of as artificial verse, shaping the mould of poetic thought for his own and the succeeding generation; but as Dryden stands in point of time nearer to the colossal name which closes the first period of English song, he has been chosen as a representative of the second, in connection and contrast with Burns, who, in his vigorous rebound from the measured pomp of rhymed heroics to the sturdiest and homeliest Scottish simplicity, gave to the modern lyric its inspiration, striking for the age the musical pitch of true and tender emotion, as decidedly as Wordsworth has touched for it the key-note of the thoughtful harmonies of natural and intellectual beauty. Tennyson undoubtedly stands at the head of all living singers, and his name might well serve as the high-water mark of modern verse; but as our volume gives a liberal space to American authorship, I have ventured to let the name of the author of "Evangeline" represent, as it well may, the present poetic culture of our English-speaking people at home and abroad.

While by no means holding myself to a strict responsibility as regards the sentiment and language of the poems which make up this volume, and while I must confess to a large tolerance of personal individuality manifesting itself in widely varying forms of expression, I have still somewhat scrupulously endeavored to avoid in my selections everything which seemed liable to the charge of irreverence or questionable morality. In this respect the poetry of the last quarter of a century, with a few exceptions, has been noteworthy for purity of thought and language, as well as for earnestness and religious feeling. The Muse of our time is a free but profoundly reverent inquirer; it is rarely found in "the seat of the scorner." If it does not always speak in the prescribed language of creed and formula, its utterances often give evidence of fresh communion with that Eternal Spirit whose responses are never in any age or clime withheld from the devout questioner.

My great effort has been to make a thoroughly readable book. With this in view I have not given tedious extracts from dull plays and weary epics, but have gathered up the best of the old ballads and short, time-approved poems, and drawn largely from contemporary writers and the waifs and estrays of unknown authors. I have also, as a specialty of the work, made a careful selection of the best hymns in our language. I am prepared to find my method open to criticism from some quarters, but I have catered not so much for the scholarly few as for the great mass of readers to whose "snatched leisure" my brief lyrical selections would seem to have a special adaptation.

It only remains for me to acknowledge the valuable suggestions and aid I have received from various sources during the preparation of this volume, and especially the essential assistance I have had from Lucy Larcom of Beverly Farms, to whose services I have before been indebted in the compilation of "Child Life."

J. G. W.

Amesbury, 9th mo., 1875.

CONTENTS.

FROM SHAKESPEARE TO MILTON.

FROM DRYDEN TO BURNS.

FROM WORDSWORTH TO LONGFELLOW.

LIST OF AUTHORS.

FROM SHAKESPEARE TO MILTON.

From Shakespeare to Milton.

LORD THOMAS VAUX.

[1510 – 1557.]

THOUGHT.

When all is done and said,
  In the end this shall you find:
He most of all doth bathe in bliss
  That hath a quiet mind;
And, clear from worldly cares,
  To deem can be content
The sweetest time in all his life
  In thinking to be spent.

The body subject is
  To fickle Fortune's power,
And to a million of mishaps
  Is casual every hour;
And Death in time doth change
  It to a clod of clay;
When as the mind, which is divine,
  Runs never to decay.

Companion none is like
  Unto the mind alone,
For many have been harmed by speech, —
  Through thinking, few, or none.
Fear oftentimes restraineth words,
  But makes not thoughts to cease;
And he speaks best, that hath the skill
  When for to hold his peace.

Our wealth leaves us at death,
  Our kinsmen at the grave:
But virtues of the mind unto
  The heavens with us we have;
Wherefore, for virtue's sake,
  I can be well content
The sweetest time of all my life
  To deem in thinking spent.

THOMAS STERNHOLD.

[Died 1549.]

MAJESTY OF GOD.

The Lord descended from above,
  And bowed the heavens most high,
And underneath his feet he cast
  The darkness of the sky.

On cherubim and seraphim
  Full royally he rode,
And on the wings of mighty winds
  Came flying all abroad.

He sat serene upon the floods,
  Their fury to restrain;
And he, as sovereign Lord and King,
  For evermore shall reign.

HENRY HOWARD, EARL OF SURREY.

[1515 – 1547.]

NO AGE CONTENT WITH HIS OWN ESTATE.

Laid in my quiet bed,
  In study as I were,
I saw within my troubled head
  A heap of thoughts appear.

And every thought did show
  So lively in mine eyes,
That now I sighed, and then I smiled,
  As cause of thoughts did rise.

I saw the little boy,
  In thought how oft that he
Did wish of God, to scape the rod,
  A tall young man to be.

The young man eke that feels
  His bones with pains opprest,
How he would be a rich old man,
  To live and lie at rest:

The rich old man that sees
  His end draw on so sore,
How he would be a boy again,
  To live so much the more.

Whereat full oft I smiled,
  To see how all these three,
From boy to man, from man to boy,
  Would chop and change degree:

And musing thus, I think,
  The case is very strange,
That man from wealth, to live in woe,
  Doth ever seek to change.

Thus thoughtful as I lay,
  I saw my withered skin,
How it doth show my dented thews,
  The flesh was worn so thin;

And eke my toothless chaps,
  The gates of my right way,
That opes and shuts as I do speak,
  Do thus unto me say:

"The white and hoarish hairs,
  The messengers of age,
That show, like lines of true belief,
  That this life doth assuage;

"Bid thee lay hand, and feel
  Them hanging on my chin.
The which do write two ages past,
  The third now coming in.

"Hang up, therefore, the bit
  Of thy young wanton time;
And thou that therein beaten art,
  The happiest life define."

Whereat I sighed, and said,
  "Farewell my wonted joy!
Truss up thy pack, and trudge from me,
  To every little boy;

"And tell them thus from me,
  Their time most happy is,
If to their time they reason had,
  To know the truth of this."

SIR THOMAS WYATT.

[1503 - 1542.]

PLEASURE MIXED WITH PAIN.

VENOMOUS thorns that are so sharp and keen
  Bear flowers, we see, full fresh and fair of hue:
Poison is also put in medicine,
  And unto man his health doth oft renew.
The fire that all things eke consumeth clean,
  May hurt and heal: then if that this be true,
I trust some time my harm may be my health,
Since every woe is joinéd with some wealth.

A DESCRIPTION OF SUCH A ONE AS HE WOULD LOVE.

A FACE that should content me wondrous well,
Should not be fair, but lovely to behold
With gladsome cheer, all grief for to expel;
With sober looks so would I that it should
Speak without words, such words as none can tell;
The tress also should be of crispéd gold.
With wit and these, might chance I might be tied,
And knit again with knot that should not slide.

CHRISTOPHER MARLOWE.

[1564 - 1593.]

THE PASSIONATE SHEPHERD TO HIS LOVE.

COME live with me, and be my love,
And we will all the pleasures prove,
That valleys, groves, and hills and fields,
Wood or steepy mountain yields.

And we will sit upon the rocks,
Seeing the shepherds feed their flocks

By shallow rivers, to whose falls
Melodious birds sing madrigals.

And I will make thee beds of roses,
And a thousand fragrant posies;
A cap of flowers and a kirtle,
Embroidered all with leaves of myrtle;

A gown made of the finest wool,
Which from our pretty lambs we pull;
Fair linéd slippers for the cold,
With buckles of the purest gold;

A belt of straw and ivy buds,
With coral clasps and amber studs:
And if these pleasures may thee move,
Come live with me, and be my love.

The shepherd swains shall dance and sing,
For thy delight, each May-morning:
If these delights thy mind may move,
Then live with me, and be my love.

SIR WALTER RALEIGH.

[1552–1618.]

THE NYMPH'S REPLY.

If all the world and love were young,
And truth in every shepherd's tongue,
These pretty pleasures might me move
To live with thee, and be thy love.

Time drives the flocks from field to fold,
When rivers rage and rocks grow cold;
And Philomel becometh dumb,
The rest complain of cares to come.

The flowers do fade, and wanton fields
To wayward winter reckoning yields;
A honey tongue, a heart of gall,
Is fancy's spring, but sorrow's fall.

Thy gowns, thy shoes, thy beds of roses,
Thy cap, thy kirtle, and thy posies,
Soon break, soon wither, soon forgotten,
In folly ripe, in reason rotten.

Thy belt of straw and ivy buds,
Thy coral clasps and amber studs,—
All these in me no means can move
To come to thee and be thy love.

But could youth last, and love still breed,
Had joys no date, nor age no need,
Then these delights my mind might move
To live with thee and be thy love.

THE PILGRIM.

Give me my scallop-shell of quiet,
My staff of faith to walk upon;
My scrip of joy, immortal diet;
My bottle of salvation;
My gown of glory (hope's true gauge),
And thus I'll take my pilgrimage.
Blood must be my body's 'balmer,
Whilst my soul, a quiet Palmer,
Travelleth towards the land of Heaven;
No other balm will there be given.
Over the silver mountains,
Where spring the nectar fountains,
There will I kiss the bowl of bliss,
And drink mine everlasting fill
Upon every milken hill;
My soul will be a-dry before,
But after, it will thirst no more.
Then, by that happy, blissful day,
More peaceful pilgrims I shall see,
That have cast off their rags of clay,
And walk apparelled fresh, like me.

THE SOUL'S ERRAND.

Go, soul, the body's guest,
Upon a thankless errand!
Fear not to touch the best,
The truth shall be thy warrant:
Go, since I needs must die,
And give the world the lie.

Go, tell the court it glows,
And shines like rotten wood;
Go, tell the church it shows
What's good, and doth no good:
If church and court reply,
Then give them both the lie.

Tell potentates they live
Acting by others' actions;
Not loved unless they give,
Not strong but by their factions:
If potentates reply,
Give potentates the lie.

Tell men of high condition
That rule affairs of state,

Their purpose is ambition,
Their practice only hate:
And if they once reply,
Then give them all the lie.

Tell them that brave it most,
They beg for more by spending,
Who in their greatest cost,
Seek nothing but commending:
And if they make reply,
Then give them all the lie.

Tell zeal it lacks devotion,
Tell love it is but lust,
Tell time it is but motion,
Tell flesh it is but dust:
And wish them not reply,
For thou must give the lie.

Tell age it daily wasteth,
Tell honor how it alters,
Tell beauty how she blasteth,
Tell favor how she falters:
And as they shall reply,
Give every one the lie.

Tell wit how much it wrangles
In tickle points of niceness;
Tell wisdom she entangles
Herself in over-wiseness:
And when they do reply,
Straight give them both the lie.

Tell physic of her boldness,
Tell skill it is pretension,
Tell charity of coldness,
Tell law it is contention:
And as they do reply,
So give them still the lie.

Tell fortune of her blindness,
Tell nature of decay,
Tell friendship of unkindness,
Tell justice of delay:
And if they will reply,
Then give them all the lie.

Tell arts they have no soundness,
But vary by esteeming;
Tell schools they want profoundness,
And stand too much on seeming:
If arts and schools reply,
Give arts and schools the lie.

Tell faith it 's fled the city;
Tell how the country erreth;
Tell, manhood shakes off pity;
Tell, virtue least preferreth:
And if they do reply,
Spare not to give the lie.

So when thou hast, as I
Commanded thee, done blabbing,
Although to give the lie
Deserves no less than stabbing,
Yet stab at thee who will,
No stab the soul can kill.

SIR PHILIP SIDNEY.

[1554 – 1586.]

SONNETS.

WITH how sad steps, O Moon! thou climb'st the skies,
How silently, and with how wan a face!
What may it be, that even in heavenly place
That busy Archer his sharp arrows tries?
Sure, if that long with love acquainted eyes
Can judge of love, thou feel'st a lover's case;
I read it in thy looks, thy languished grace
To me that feel the like thy state descries.
Then, even of fellowship, O Moon, tell me,
Is constant love deemed there but want of wit?
Are beauties there as proud as here they be?
Do they above love to be loved, and yet
Those lovers scorn whom that love doth possess?
Do they call virtue there ungratefulness?

COME, Sleep, O Sleep, the certain knot of peace,
The baiting-place of wit, the balm of woe,
The poor man's wealth, the prisoner's release,
The indifferent judge between the high and low.
With shield of proof shield me from out the prease
Of those fierce darts, Despair at me doth throw;
O make in me those civil wars to cease!
I will good tribute pay, if thou do so.

Take thou of me smooth pillows, sweetest bed;
A chamber deaf to noise and blind to light;
A rosy garland, and a weary head.
And if these things, as being thine by right,
Move not thy heavy grace, thou shalt in me
Livelier than elsewhere Stella's image see.

MATTHEW ROYDON.

LAMENT FOR ASTROPHEL (SIR PHILIP SIDNEY).

You knew, — who knew not Astrophel?
That I should live to say I knew,
And have not in possession still! —
Things known permit me to renew.
Of him you know his merit such
I cannot say — you hear — too much.

Within these woods of Arcady
He chief delight and pleasure took;
And on the mountain Partheny,
Upon the crystal liquid brook,
The muses met him every day, —
Taught him to sing, and write, and say.

When he descended down the mount
His personage seemed most divine;
A thousand graces one might count
Upon his lovely, cheerful eyne.
To hear him speak, and see him smile,
You were in Paradise the while.

A sweet, attractive kind of grace;
A full assurance given by looks;
Continual comfort in a face;
The lineaments of gospel books:
I trow that countenance cannot lie
Whose thoughts are legible in the eye.

Above all others this is he
Who erst approvéd in his song,
That love and honor might agree,
And that pure love will do no wrong.
Sweet saints, it is no sin or blame
To love a man of virtuous name.

Did never love so sweetly breathe
In any mortal breast before:
Did never muse inspire beneath
A poet's brain with finer store.
He wrote of love with high conceit
And beauty reared above her height.

EDMUND SPENSER.

[1553 - 1599.]

ANGELIC MINISTRY.

And is there care in Heaven? And is there love
In heavenly spirits to these creatures base,
That may compassion of their evils move?
There is, — else much more wretched were the case
Of men than beasts: but O the exceeding grace
Of highest God, that loves his creatures so,
And all his works with mercy doth embrace,
That blessed angels he sends to and fro,
To serve to wicked man, to serve his wicked foe!

How oft do they their silver bowers leave,
To come to succor us that succor want!
How oft do they with golden pinions cleave
The flitting skies, like flying pursuivant,
Against foul fiends to aid us militant!
They for us fight, they watch and duly ward,
And their bright squadrons round about us plant;
And all for love and nothing for reward;
O, why should heavenly God to men have such regard?

THE TRUE WOMAN.

Thrice happy she that is so well assured
Unto herself, and settled so in heart,
That neither will for better be allured,
Ne fears to worse with any chance to start,
But like a steady ship doth strongly part
The raging waves, and keeps her course aright;
Ne ought for tempest doth from it depart,
Ne ought for fairer weather's false delight.

Such self-assurance need not fear the spite
Of grudging foes, ne favor seek of friends;
But in the stay of her own steadfast might,
Neither to one herself or other bends.
Most happy she that most assured doth rest,
But he most happy who such one loves best.

FROM THE EPITHALAMIUM.

Open the temple-gates unto my love.
Open them wide that she may enter in,
And all the posts adorn as doth behove,
And all the pillars deck with garlands trim,
For to receive this saint with honor due,
That cometh in to you.
With trembling steps and humble reverence
She cometh in before the Almighty's view:
Of her, ye virgins! learn obedience,
When so ye come into these holy places,
To humble your proud faces.
Bring her up to the high altar, that she may
The sacred ceremonies there partake,
The which do endless matrimony make;
And let the roaring organs loudly play
The praises of the Lord, in lively notes,
The whiles with hollow throats
The choristers the joyous anthems sing,
That all the woods may answer, and their echo ring.

Behold whiles she before the altar stands,
Hearing the holy priest that to her speaks,
And blesses her with his two happy hands,
How red the roses flush up in her cheeks!
And the pure snow, with goodly vermeil stain,
Like crimson dyed in grain,
That even the angels, which continually
About the sacred altar do remain,
Forget their service, and about her fly,
Oft peeping in her face, that seems more fair
The more they on it stare;
But her sad eyes, still fastened on the ground,
Are governed with goodly modesty,
That suffers not one look to glance awry,
Which may let in a little thought unsound.
Why blush ye, Love! to give to me your hand,
The pledge of all your band?
Sing, ye sweet angels! Alleluia sing,
That all the woods may answer, and your echo ring.

UNA AND THE LION.

One day, nigh weary of the irksome way,
From her unhasty beast she did alight;
And on the grass her dainty limbs did lay
In secret shadow, far from all men's sight;
From her fair head her fillet she undight,
And laid her stole aside: her angel's face,
As the great eye of heaven, shinéd bright,
And made a sunshine in a shady place;
Did never mortal eye behold such heavenly grace.

It fortunéd, out of the thickest wood,
A ramping lion rushéd suddenly,
Hunting full greedy after savage blood;
Soon as the royal virgin he did spy,
With gaping mouth at her ran greedily,
To have at once devoured her tender corse;
But to the prey when as he drew more nigh,
His bloody rage assuagéd with remorse,
And, with the sight amazed, forgot his furious force.

Instead thereof he kissed her weary feet,
And licked her lily hands with fawning tongue,
As he her wrongéd innocence did weet.
O how can beauty master the most strong,
And simple truth subdue avenging wrong!
Whose yielded pride and proud submission,
Still dreading death, when she had markéd long,
Her heart 'gan melt in great compassion,
And drizzling tears did shed for pure affection.

The lion would not leave her desolate,
But with her went along, as a strong guard
Of her chaste person, and a faithful mate
Of her sad troubles, and misfortunes hard.
Still, when she slept, he kept both watch and ward;
And, when she waked, he waited diligent,
With humble service to her will prepared:
From her fair eyes he took commandment,
And ever by her looks conceivéd her intent.

THE HOUSE OF RICHES.

THAT house's form within was rude and strong,
Like an huge cave hewn out of rocky clift,
From whose rough vault the ragged breaches hung
Embossed with massy gold of glorious gift,
And with rich metal loaded every rift,
That heavy ruin they did seem to threat;
And over them Arachne high did lift
Her cunning web, and spread her subtle net,
Enwrappéd in foul smoke and clouds more black than jet.

Both roof, and floor, and walls, were all of gold,
But overgrown with dust and old decay,
And hid in darkness, that none could behold
The hue thereof: for view of cheerful day
Did never in that house itself display,
But a faint shadow of uncertain light;
Such as a lamp whose life does fade away;
Or as the Moon, clothéd with cloudy night,
Does show to him that walks in fear and sad affright.

In all that room was nothing to be seen
But huge great iron chests, and coffers strong,
All barred with double bends, that none could ween
Them to enforce by violence or wrong;
On every side they placéd were along.
But all the ground with sculls was scatteréd
And dead men's bones, which round about were flung;
Whose lives, it seeméd, whilome there were shed,
And their vile carcasses now left unburiéd.

THE BOWER OF BLISS.

THERE the most dainty paradise on ground
Itself doth offer to his sober eye,
In which all pleasures plenteously abound,
And none does others' happiness envy;
The painted flowers, the trees upshooting high,
The dales for shade, the hills for breathing space,
The trembling groves, the crystal running by;
And that which all fair works doth most aggrace,
The art, which all that wrought, appearéd in no place.

One would have thought (so cunningly the rude
And scornéd parts were mingled with the fine)
That nature had for wantonness ensued
Art, and that art at nature did repine;
So striving each the other to undermine,
Each did the other's work more beautify;
So differing both in wills, agreed in fine:
So all agreed through sweet diversity,
This garden to adorn with all variety.

Eftsoons they heard a most melodious sound,
Of all that might delight a dainty ear,
Such as at once might not on living ground,
Save in this paradise be heard elsewhere:
Right hard it was for wight which did it hear,
To read what manner music that might be:
For all that pleasing is to living ear,
Was there consorted in one harmony;
Birds, voices, instruments, winds, waters, all agree.

The joyous birds, shrouded in cheerful shade,
Their notes unto the voice attempered sweet;
The angelical soft trembling voices made
To the instruments divine respondence meet;
The silver sounding instruments did meet
With the base murmur of the water's fall:
The water's fall with difference discreet,
Now soft, now loud, unto the wind did call:
The gentle warbling wind low answeréd to all.

ROBERT SOUTHWELL.

[1560–1595.]

CONTENT AND RICH.

I DWELL in grace's courts,
  Enriched with virtue's rights;
Faith guides my wit, love leads my will,
  Hope all my mind delights.

In lowly vales I mount
  To pleasure's highest pitch,
My simple dress sure honor brings,
  My poor estate is rich.

My conscience is my crown,
  Contented thoughts my rest;
My heart is happy in itself;
  My bliss is in my breast.

Enough, I reckon wealth;
  A mean, the surest lot,
That lies too high for base contempt,
  Too low for envy's shot.

My wishes are but few,
  All easy to fulfil;
I make the limits of my power
  The bounds unto my will.

I have no hopes but one,
  Which is of heavenly reign:
Effects attained, or not desired,
  All lower hopes refrain.

I feel no care of coin,
  Well-doing is my wealth:
My mind to me an empire is,
  While grace affordeth health.

I clip high-climbing thoughts,
  The wings of swelling pride:
Their fate is worst, that from the height
  Of greater honor slide.

Silk sails of largest size
  The storm doth soonest tear:
I bear so low and small a sail
  As freeth me from fear.

I wrestle not with rage
  While fury's flame doth burn;
It is in vain to stop the stream
  Until the tide doth turn.

But when the flame is out,
  And ebbing wrath doth end,
I turn a late-enragéd foe
  Into a quiet friend;

And, taught with often proof,
  A tempered calm I find
To be most solace to itself,
  Best cure for angry mind.

Spare diet is my fare,
  My clothes more fit than fine;
I know I feed and clothe a foe
  That, pampered, would repine.

I envy not their hap
  Whom favor doth advance:
I take no pleasure in their pain
  That have less happy chance.

To rise by others' fall
  I deem a losing gain:
All states with others' ruins built
  To ruins run amain.

No change of fortune's calms
  Can cast my comforts down:
When fortune smiles, I smile to think
  How quickly she will frown;

And when, in froward mood,
  She proved an angry foe,
Small gain I found to let her come,
  Less loss to let her go.

ALEXANDER HUME.

[About 1599.]

A SUMMER'S DAY.

THE time so tranquil is and clear,
  That nowhere shall ye find,
Save on a high and barren hill,
  An air of passing wind.

All trees and simples, great and small,
  That balmy leaf do bear,
Than they were painted on a wall,
  No more they move or stir.

The ships becalmed upon the seas,
  Hang up their sails to dry;
The herds, beneath the leafy trees,
  Among the flowers they lie.

Great is the calm, for everywhere
The wind is settling down:
The smoke goes upright in the air,
From every tower and town.

What pleasure, then, to walk and see,
Along a river clear,
The perfect form of every tree
Within the deep appear:

The bells and circles on the waves,
From leaping of the trout;
The salmon from their creels and caves
Come gliding in and out.

O sure it were a seemly thing,
While all is still and calm,
The praise of God to play and sing,
With trumpet and with shalm!

All laborers draw home at even,
And can to others say,
"Thanks to the gracious God of heaven,
Who sent this summer day."

SIR JOHN DAVIES.

[1570-1626.]

THE SOUL.

AGAIN, how can she but immortal be,
When with the motions of both will and wit
She still aspireth to eternity,
And never rests till she attain to it?

Water in conduit-pipes can rise no higher
Than the well-head from whence it first doth spring:
Then, since to eternal God she doth aspire,
She cannot be but an eternal thing.

"All moving things to other things do move
Of the same kind, which shows their nature such";
So earth falls down, and fire doth mount above,
Till both their proper elements do touch.

And as the moisture which the thirsty earth
Sucks from the sea to fill her empty veins,
From out her womb at last doth take a birth,
And runs a lymph along the grassy plains:

Long doth she stay, as loth to leave the land
From whose soft side the first did issue make;
She tastes all places, turns to every hand,
Her flowery banks unwilling to forsake.

Yet Nature so her streams doth lead and carry,
As that her course doth make no final stay,
Till she herself unto the Ocean marry,
Within whose watery bosom first she lay.

Even so the soul, which in this earthly mould
The spirit of God doth secretly infuse,
Because at first she doth the earth behold,
And only this material world she views.

At first her mother Earth she holdeth dear,
And doth embrace the world, and worldly things.
She flies close by the ground and hovers here,
And mounts not up with her celestial wings:

Yet under heaven she cannot light on aught
That with her heavenly nature doth agree;
She cannot rest, she cannot fix her thought,
She cannot in this world contented be.

For who did ever yet, in honor, wealth,
Or pleasure of the sense, contentment find?
Who ever ceased to wish when he had wealth?
Or having wisdom was not vexed in mind?

Then as a bee, which among weeds doth fall,
Which seem sweet flowers with lustre fresh and gay,
She lights on that and this, and tasteth all;
But pleased with none, doth rise and soar away.

So when the soul finds here no true content,
And like Noah's dove can no sure footing take,
She doth return from whence she first was sent,
And flies to Him that first her wings did make.

So while the virgin soul on earth doth stay,
She, wooed and tempted in ten thousand ways,
By these great powers which on the earth bear sway,
The wisdom of the world, wealth, pleasure, praise:

With these sometimes she doth her time beguile,
These do by fibs her fantasy possess;
But she distastes them all within a while,
And in the sweetest finds a tediousness;

But if upon the world's Almighty King
She once doth fix her humble, loving thought;
Who by his picture drawn in every thing,
And sacred messages, her love hath sought;

Of him she thinks she cannot think too much;
This honey tasted still, is ever sweet;
The pleasure of her ravished thought is such,
As almost here she with her bliss doth meet.

But when in heaven she shall his essence see,
This is her sovereign good, and perfect bliss,
Her longings, wishings, hopes, all finished be,
Her joys are full, her motions rest in this.

There is she crowned with garlands of content;
There doth she manna eat, and nectar drink:
That presence doth such high delights present,
As never tongue could speak, nor heart could think.

THOMAS NASH.

[1564-1600.]

CONTENTMENT.

I NEVER loved ambitiously to climb,
Or thrust my hand too far into the fire.
To be in heaven sure is a blessed thing,
But, Atlas-like, to prop heaven on one's back
Cannot but be more labor than delight.
Such is the state of men in honor placed:
They are gold vessels made for servile uses;
High trees that keep the weather from low houses,
But cannot shield the tempest from themselves.
I love to dwell betwixt the hills and dales,
Neither to be so great as to be envied,
Nor yet so poor the world should pity me.

WILLIAM DRUMMOND.

[1585-1649.]

THE LESSONS OF NATURE.

OF this fair volume which we World do name
If we the sheets and leaves could turn with care,
Of him who it corrects, and did it frame,
We clear might read the art and wisdom rare:

Find out his power which wildest powers doth tame,
His providence extending everywhere,
His justice which proud rebels doth not spare,
In every page, no period of the same.

But silly we, like foolish children, rest
Well pleased with colored vellum, leaves of gold,
Fair dangling ribbons, leaving what is best,
On the great writer's sense ne'er taking hold;

Or if by chance we stay our minds on aught,
It is some picture on the margin wrought.

SIR HENRY WOTTON.

[1568 - 1639.]

TO HIS MISTRESS, THE QUEEN OF BOHEMIA.

You meaner beauties of the night,
That poorly satisfy our eyes
More by your number than your light!
You common people of the skies!
What are you, when the sun shall rise?

You curious chanters of the wood,
That warble forth dame Nature's lays,
Thinking your voices understood
By your weak accents! what 's your praise
When Philomel her voice shall raise?

You violets that first appear,
By your pure purple mantles known,
Like the proud virgins of the year,
As if the spring were all your own!
What are you, when the rose is blown?

So, when my mistress shall be seen
In form and beauty of her mind;
By virtue first, then choice, a Queen!
Tell me, if she were not designed
The eclipse and glory of her kind?

THE GOOD MAN.

How happy is he born and taught,
That serveth not another's will;
Whose armor is his honest thought,
And simple truth his utmost skill!

Whose passions not his masters are,
Whose soul is still prepared for death,
Untied unto the worldly care
Of public fame, or private breath;

Who envies none that chance doth raise,
Or vice; who never understood
How deepest wounds are given by praise;
Nor rules of state, but rules of good;

Who hath his life from rumors freed,
Whose conscience is his strong retreat;
Whose state can neither flatterers feed,
Nor ruin make oppressors great;

Who God doth late and early pray,
More of his grace than gifts to lend;
And entertains the harmless day
With a religious book or friend:

This man is freed from servile bands,
Of hope to rise, or fear to fall;
Lord of himself, though not of lands;
And having nothing, yet hath all.

LADY ELIZABETH CAREW

[About 1613.]

REVENGE OF INJURIES.

The fairest action of our human life
Is scorning to revenge an injury;
For who forgives without a further strife,
His adversary's heart to him doth tie;
And 't is a firmer conquest truly said,
To win the heart, than overthrow the head.

If we a worthy enemy do find,
To yield to worth it must be nobly done;
But if of baser metal be his mind,
In base revenge there is no honor won.
Who would a worthy courage overthrow?
And who would wrestle with a worthless foe?

We say our hearts are great, and cannot yield;
Because they cannot yield, it proves them poor:
Great hearts are tasked beyond their power but seld;
The weakest lion will the loudest roar.
Truth's school for certain doth this same allow;
High-heartedness doth sometimes teach to bow.

A noble heart doth teach a virtuous scorn: —
To scorn to owe a duty overlong;
To scorn to be for benefits forborne;
To scorn to lie; to scorn to do a wrong;
To scorn to bear an injury in mind;
To scorn a free-born heart slave-like to bind.

But if for wrongs we needs revenge must have,
Then be our vengeance of the noblest kind.
Do we his body from our fury save,
And let our hate prevail against his mind?
What can 'gainst him a greater vengeance be,
Than make his foe more worthy far than he?

SAMUEL DANIEL.

[1562-1619.]

FROM AN EPISTLE TO THE COUNTESS OF CUMBERLAND.

He that of such a height hath built his mind,
And reared the dwelling of his thoughts so strong,
As neither fear nor hope can shake the frame
Of his resolvéd powers; nor all the wind
Of vanity or malice pierce to wrong
His settled peace, or to disturb the same:
What a fair seat hath he, from whence he may
The boundless wastes and wilds of man survey?

And with how free an eye doth he look down
Upon these lower regions of turmoil?
Where all the storms of passions mainly beat
On flesh and blood: where honor, power, renown,
Are only gay afflictions, golden toil;
Where greatness stands upon as feeble feet,
As frailty doth; and only great doth seem
To little minds, who do it so esteem.

He looks upon the mightiest monarch's wars
But only as on stately robberies;
Where evermore the fortune that prevails
Must be the right: the ill-succeeding mars
The fairest and the best faced enterprise.
Great pirate Pompey lesser pirates quails:
Justice, he sees (as if seducéd), still
Conspires with power, whose cause must not be ill.

And whilst distraught ambition compasses,
And is encompassed; whilst as craft deceives,
And is deceived: whilst man doth ransack man,
And builds on blood, and rises by distress;
And the inheritance of desolation leaves
To great-expecting hopes: he looks thereon,
As from the shore of peace, with unwet eye,
And bears no venture in impiety.

Thus, madam, fares that man, that hath prepared
A rest for his desires; and sees all things
Beneath him; and hath learned this book of man,
Full of the notes of frailty; and compared
The best of glory with her sufferings:
By whom, I see, you labor all you can
To plant your heart; and set your thoughts as near
His glorious mansion, as your powers can bear.

Which, madam, are so soundly fashionéd
By that clear judgment, that hath carried you
Beyond the feeble limits of your kind,
As they can stand against the strongest head
Passion can make; inured to any hue
The world can cast: it cannot cast that mind
Out of her form of goodness, that doth see
Both what the best and worst of earth can be.

Which makes, that whatsoever here befalls,
You in the region of yourself remain:
Where no vain breath of the impudent molests
That hath secured within the brazen walls

Of a clear conscience, that (without all stain)
Rises in peace, in innocency rests;
Whilst all that Malice from without procures
Shows her own ugly heart, but hurts not yours.

And whereas none rejoice more in revenge,
Than women use to do; yet you well know,
That wrong is better checked by being contemned,
Than being pursued; leaving to him to avenge,
To whom it appertains. Wherein you show
How worthily your clearness hath condemned
Base malediction, living in the dark,
That at the rays of goodness still doth bark.

Knowing the heart of man is set to be
The centre of this world, about the which
These revolutions of disturbances
Still roll; where all the aspects of misery
Predominate: whose strong effects are such,
As he must bear, being powerless to redress:
And that unless above himself he can
Erect himself, how poor a thing is man.

WILLIAM BYRD.

[1540–1623.]

MY MIND TO ME A KINGDOM IS.

My mind to me a kingdom is;
  Such perfect joy therein I find
As far exceeds all earthly bliss
  That God or Nature hath assigned;
Though much I want that most would have,
Yet still my mind forbids to crave.

Content I live; this is my stay, —
  I seek no more than may suffice.
I press to bear no haughty sway;
  Look, what I lack my mind supplies.
Lo! thus I triumph like a king,
Content with that my mind doth bring.

I see how plenty surfeits oft,
  And hasty climbers soonest fall;
I see that such as sit aloft
  Mishap doth threaten most of all.
These get with toil, and keep with fear;
Such cares my mind could never bear.

No princely pomp nor wealthy store,
  No force to win the victory,
No wily wit to salve a sore,
  No shape to win a lover's eye, —
To none of these I yield as thrall;
For why, my mind despiseth all.

Some have too much, yet still they crave;
  I little have, yet seek no more.
They are but poor, though much they have;
  And I am rich with little store.
They poor, I rich; they beg, I give;
They lack, I lend; they pine, I live.

I laugh not at another's loss,
  I grudge not at another's gain;
No worldly wave my mind can toss;
  I brook that is another's bane.
I fear no foe, nor fawn on friend;
I loathe not life, nor dread mine end.

I joy not in no earthly bliss;
  I weigh not Crœsus' wealth a straw;
For care, I care not what it is;
  I fear not fortune's fatal law;
My mind is such as may not move
For beauty bright, or force of love.

I wish but what I have at will;
  I wander not to seek for more;
I like the plain, I climb no hill;
  In greatest storms I sit on shore,
And laugh at them that toil in vain
To get what must be lost again.

I kiss not where I wish to kill;
  I feign not love where most I hate;
I break no sleep to win my will;
  I wait not at the mighty's gate.
I scorn no poor, I fear no rich;
I feel no want, nor have too much.

The court nor cart I like nor loathe;
  Extremes are counted worst of all;
The golden mean betwixt them both
  Doth surest sit, and fears no fall;
This is my choice; for why, I find
No wealth is like a quiet mind.

My wealth is health and perfect ease;
  My conscience clear my chief defence;
I never seek by bribes to please,
  Nor by desert to give offence.
Thus do I live, thus will I die;
Would all did so as well as I!

WILLIAM SHAKESPEARE.

[1564–1616.]

SONGS.

ARIEL'S SONG.

WHERE the bee sucks, there lurk I;
In a cowslip's bell I lie;
There I couch when owls do cry;
On the bat's back I do fly.
After summer merrily,
Merrily, merrily, shall I live now,
Under the blossom that hangs on the
    bough.

THE FAIRY TO PUCK.

OVER hill, over dale,
Thorough bush, thorough brier,
Over park, over pale,
Thorough flood, thorough fire,
I do wander everywhere,
Swifter than the moon's sphere.
And I serve the Fairy Queen,
To dew her orbs upon the green;
The cowslips tall her pensioners be,
In their gold coats spots you see, —
Those be rubies, fairy favors;
In those freckles live their savors.
I must go seek some dew-drops here,
And hang a pearl in every cowslip's ear.

AMIENS'S SONG.

BLOW, blow, thou winter wind,
Thou art not so unkind
  As man's ingratitude;
Thy tooth is not so keen,
Because thou art not seen,
  Although thy breath be rude.

Freeze, freeze, thou bitter sky,
That dost not bite so nigh
  As benefits forgot:
Though thou the waters warp,
Thy sting is not so sharp
  As friend remembered not.

A SEA DIRGE.

FULL fathom five thy father lies:
  Of his bones are coral made;
Those are pearls that were his eyes:
  Nothing of him that doth fade,
But doth suffer a sea-change
Into something rich and strange.
Sea-nymphs hourly ring his knell:
Hark! now I hear them, —
  Ding, dong, bell.

HARK! HARK! THE LARK!

HARK! hark! the lark at heaven's gate
    sings,
  And Phœbus 'gins arise,
His steeds to water at those springs
  On chaliced flowers that lies;
And winking Mary-buds begin
  To ope their golden eyes;
With everything that pretty bin;
  My lady sweet, arise.

UNDER THE GREENWOOD-TREE.

UNDER the greenwood-tree
Who loves to lie with me,
And tune his merry note
Unto the sweet bird's throat,
Come hither, come hither, come hither;
    Here shall he see
    No enemy,
But winter and rough weather.

Who doth ambition shun,
And loves to live i' the sun,
Seeking the food he eats,
And pleased with what he gets,
Come hither, come hither, come hither!
    Here shall he see
    No enemy,
But winter and rough weather.

DIRGE FOR FIDELE.

FEAR no more the heat o' the sun,
Nor the furious winter's rages;
Thou thy worldly task hast done,
Home art gone, and ta'en thy wages:

Golden lads and girls all must,
As chimney-sweepers, come to dust.

Fear no more the frown o' the great,
Thou art past the tyrant's stroke;
Care no more to clothe, and eat;
To thee the reed is as the oak:
The sceptre, learning, physic, must
All follow this, and come to dust.

Fear no more the lightning flash,
Nor the all-dreaded thunder-stone;
Fear not slander, censure rash;
Thou hast finished joy and moan:
All lovers young, all lovers must
Consign to thee, and come to dust.

No exorciser harm thee!
Nor no witchcraft charm thee!
Ghost unlaid forbear thee!
Nothing ill come near thee!
Quiet consummation have;
And renownéd be thy grave.

SONNETS.

When in disgrace with fortune and men's eyes,
I all alone beweep my outcast state,
And trouble deaf heaven with my bootless cries,
And look upon myself, and curse my fate,
Wishing me like to one more rich in hope,
Featured like him, like him with friends possessed,
Desiring this man's art, and that man's scope,
With what I most enjoy contented least;
Yet in these thoughts myself almost despising,
Haply I think on thee, — and then my state
(Like to the lark at break of day arising
From sullen earth) sings hymns at heaven's gate;
For thy sweet love remembered, such wealth brings,
That then I scorn to change my state with kings.

When to the sessions of sweet silent thought
I summon up remembrance of things past,
I sigh the lack of many a thing I sought,
And with old woes new wail my dear time's waste:
Then can I drown an eye, unused to flow,
For precious friends hid in death's dateless night,
And weep afresh love's long-since-cancelled woe,
And moan the expense of many a vanished sight.
Then can I grieve at grievances foregone,
And heavily from woe to woe tell o'er
The sad account of fore-bemoanéd moan,
Which I new pay as if not paid before.
But if the while I think on thee, dear friend,
All losses are restored, and sorrows end.

That time of year thou mayst in me behold
When yellow leaves, or none, or few, do hang
Upon those boughs which shake against the cold,
Bare ruined choirs, where late the sweet birds sang.
In me thou seest the twilight of such day,
As after sunset fadeth in the west,
Which by and by black night doth take away,
Death's second self, that seals up all in rest.
In me thou seest the glowing of such fire,
That on the ashes of his youth doth lie,
As the death-bed whereon it must expire,
Consumed with that which it was nourished by.
This thou perceiv'st, which makes thy love more strong,
To love that well which thou must leave erelong.

They that have power to hurt and will do none,
That do not do the thing they most do show,
Who, moving others, are themselves as stone,
Unmovéd, cold, and to temptation slow;
They rightly do inherit heaven's graces,
And husband nature's riches from expense;

They are the lords and owners of their faces,
Others but stewards of their excellence.
The summer's flower is to the summer sweet,
Though to itself it only live and die;
But if that flower with base infection meet,
The basest weed outbraves his dignity:
For sweetest things turn sourest by their deeds;
Lilies that fester smell far worse than weeds.

Alas, 'tis true, I have gone here and there,
And made myself a motley to the view,
Gored mine own thoughts, sold cheap what is most dear,
Made old offences of affections new.
Most true it is, that I have looked on truth
Askance and strangely; but, by all above,
These blenches gave my heart another youth,
And worse essays proved thee my best of love.
Now all is done, save what shall have no end:
Mine appetite I never more will grind
On newer proof, to try an older friend,
A God in love, to whom I am confined.
Then give me welcome, next my heaven the best,
Even to thy pure and most most loving breast.

Let me not to the marriage of true minds
Admit impediments. Love is not love
Which alters when it alteration finds,
Or bends with the remover to remove;
O no; it is an ever-fixéd mark,
That looks on tempests, and is never shaken;
It is the star to every wandering bark,
Whose worth 's unknown, although his height be taken.
Love 's not Time's fool, though rosy lips and cheeks
Within his bending sickle's compass come;
Love alters not with his brief hours and weeks,
But bears it out even to the edge of doom.
If this be error, and upon me proved,
I never writ, nor no man ever loved.

No! Time, thou shalt not boast that I do change:
Thy pyramids built up with newer might
To me are nothing novel, nothing strange;
They are but dressings of a former sight.
Our dates are brief, and therefore we admire
What thou dost foist upon us that is old;
And rather make them born to our desire,
Than think that we before have heard them told.
Thy registers and thee I both defy,
Not wondering at the present nor the past;
For thy records and what we see do lie,
Made more or less by thy continual haste:
This I do vow, and this shall ever be,
I will be true, despite thy scythe and thee.

BEN JONSON.

[1574–1637.]

THE NOBLE NATURE.

It is not growing like a tree
In bulk, doth make man better be;
Or standing long an oak, three hundred year,
To fall a log at last, dry, bald, and sere:
A lily of a day
Is fairer far in May,
Although it fall and die that night,—
It was the plant and flower of Light.
In small proportions we just beauties see;
And in short measures life may perfect be.

SONG OF HESPERUS.

Queen, and huntress, chaste and fair,
Now the sun is laid to sleep,
Seated in thy silver chair,
State in wonted manner keep:
Hesperus entreats thy light,
Goddess excellently bright.

Earth, let not thy envious shade
Dare itself to interpose;
Cynthia's shining orb was made
Heaven to clear, when day did close:
Bless us then with wishéd sight,
Goddess excellently bright.

Lay thy bow of pearl apart,
And thy crystal shining quiver;
Give unto the flying hart
Space to breathe, how short soever:
Thou that makest a day of night,
Goddess excellently bright.

ON LUCY, COUNTESS OF BEDFORD.

This morning, timely rapt with holy fire,
I thought to form unto my zealous Muse,
What kind of creature I could most desire,
To honor, serve, and love; as poets use,
I meant to make her fair, and free, and wise,
Of greatest blood, and yet more good than great;
I meant the day-star should not brighter rise,
Nor lend like influence from his lucent seat.
I meant she should be courteous, facile, sweet,
Hating that solemn vice of greatness, pride;
I meant each softest virtue there should meet,
Fit in that softer bosom to reside.
Only a learned and a manly soul
I purposed her; that should, with even powers,
The rock, the spindle, and the shears control
Of Destiny, and spin her own free hours.
Such when I meant to feign, and wished to see,
My Muse bade, Bedford write, and that was she.

THE SWEET NEGLECT.

Still to be neat, still to be drest,
As you were going to a feast:
Still to be powdered, still perfumed:
Lady, it is to be presumed,
Though art's hid causes are not found,
All is not sweet, all is not sound.

Give me a look, give me a face,
That makes simplicity a grace;
Robes loosely flowing, hair as free:
Such sweet neglect more taketh me,
Than all the adulteries of art,
That strike mine eyes, but not my heart.

HOW NEAR TO GOOD IS WHAT IS FAIR!

How near to good is what is fair!
Which we no sooner see,
But with the lines and outward air
Our senses taken be.
We wish to see it still, and prove
What ways we may deserve;
We court, we praise, we more than love,
We are not grieved to serve.

EPITAPH ON ELIZABETH L. H.

Wouldst thou hear what man can say
In a little?—reader, stay!
Underneath this stone doth lie
As much beauty as could die,—
Which in life did harbor give
To more virtue than doth live.
If at all she had a fault,
Leave it buried in this vault.
One name was Elizabeth,—
The other, let it sleep with death.
Fitter where it died to tell,
Than that it lived at all. Farewell!

UNKNOWN.

[Before 1649.]

LOVE WILL FIND OUT THE WAY.

Over the mountains,
And under the waves,
Over the fountains,
And under the graves,
Under floods which are deepest,
Which Neptune obey,
Over rocks which are steepest,
Love will find out the way.

Where there is no place
For the glow-worm to lie,
Where there is no place
For the receipt of a fly,
Where the gnat dares not venture,
Lest herself fast she lay,
If Love come he will enter,
And find out the way.

If that he were hidden,
And all men that are,
Were strictly forbidden
That place to declare;

Winds that have no abidings,
Pitying their delay,
Would come and bring him tidings,
And direct him the way.

If the earth should part him,
He would gallop it o'er;
If the seas should o'erthwart him,
He would swim to the shore.
Should his love become a swallow,
Through the air to stray,
Love will lend wings to follow,
And will find out the way.

There is no striving
To cross his intent,
There is no contriving
His plots to prevent;
But if once the message greet him,
That his true love doth stay,
If death should come and meet him,
Love will find out the way.

UNKNOWN.

[Before 1689.]

MAY-DAY SONG.

Remember us poor Mayers all!
And thus do we begin
To lead our lives in righteousness,
Or else we die in sin.

We have been rambling all the night,
And almost all the day;
And now returnéd back again,
We have brought you a branch of May.

A branch of May we have brought you,
And at your door it stands:
It is but a sprout,
But it 's well budded out
By the work of our Lord's hands.

The heavenly gates are open wide,
Our paths are beaten plain;
And if a man be not too far gone,
He may return again.

The moon shines bright, and the stars give a light,
A little before it is day;
So God bless you all, both great and small,
And send you a joyful May!

UNKNOWN.

[Before 1649.]

BEGONE DULL CARE!

Begone dull care!
I prithee begone from me:
Begone dull care!
Thou and I can never agree.
Long while thou hast been tarrying here,
And fain thou wouldst me kill;
But i' faith, dull care,
Thou never shalt have thy will.

Too much care
Will make a young man gray;
Too much care
Will turn an old man to clay.
My wife shall dance, and I will sing,
So merrily pass the day;
For I hold it is the wisest thing,
To drive dull care away.

Hence, dull care,
I 'll none of thy company;
Hence, dull care,
Thou art no pair for me.
We 'll hunt the wild boar through the wold,
So merrily pass the day;
And then at night, o'er a cheerful bowl,
We 'll drive dull care away.

BISHOP RICHARD CORBETT.

[1582 - 1635.]

FAREWELL TO THE FAIRIES.

Farewell rewards and fairies!
Good housewifes now may say,
For now foul sluts in dairies
Do fare as well as they.
And though they sweep their hearths no less
Than maids were wont to do;
Yet who of late, for cleanliness,
Finds sixpence in her shoe?

Lament, lament, old Abbeys,
The fairies' lost command;
They did but change priests' babies,
But some have changed your land;
And all your children sprung from thence
Are now grown Puritans;

Who live as changelings ever since,
  For love of your domains.

At morning and at evening both,
  You merry were and glad,
So little care of sleep or sloth
  These pretty ladies had;
When Tom came home from labor,
  Or Cis to milking rose,
Then merrily went their tabor,
  And nimbly went their toes.

Witness those rings and roundelays
  Of theirs, which yet remain,
Were footed in Queen Mary's days
  On many a grassy plain;
But since of late Elizabeth,
  And later, James came in,
They never danced on any heath
  As when the time hath been.

By which we note the fairies
  Were of the old profession,
Their songs were Ave-Maries,
  Their dances were procession:
But now, alas! they all are dead,
  Or gone beyond the seas;
Or farther for religion fled;
  Or else they take their ease.

A tell-tale in their company
  They never could endure,
And whoso kept not secretly
  Their mirth, was punished sure;
It was a just and Christian deed,
  To pinch such black and blue:
O, how the commonwealth doth need
  Such justices as you!

UNKNOWN.

[Before 1649.]

ROBIN GOODFELLOW.

From Oberon, in fairy-land,
  The king of ghosts and shadows there,
Mad Robin I, at his command,
  Am sent to view the night-sports here.
    What revel rout
    Is kept about,
  In every corner where I go,
    I will o'ersee,
    And merry be,
  And make good sport, with ho, ho, ho!

More swift than lightning can I fly
  About this airy welkin soon,
And, in a minute's space, descry
  Each thing that's done below the moon.
    There 's not a hag
    Or ghost shall wag,
  Or cry, 'ware goblins! where I go;
    But Robin I
    Their feasts will spy,
  And send them home with ho, ho, ho!

Whene'er such wanderers I meet,
  As from their night-sports they trudge home,
With counterfeiting voice I greet,
  And call them on with me to roam:
    Through woods, through lakes;
    Through bogs, through brakes;
  Or else, unseen, with them I go.
    All in the nick,
    To play some trick,
  And frolic it, with ho, ho, ho!

Sometimes I meet them like a man,
  Sometimes an ox, sometimes a hound;
And to a horse I turn me can,
  To trip and trot about them round.
    But if to ride
    My back they stride,
  More swift than wind away I go,
    O'er hedge and lands,
    Through pools and ponds,
  I hurry, laughing, ho, ho, ho!

When lads and lasses merry be,
  With possets and with junkets fine;
Unseen of all the company,
  I eat their cakes and sip their wine!
    And, to make sport,
    I puff and snort:
  And out the candles I do blow:
    The maids I kiss,
    They shriek—Who 's this?
  I answer naught but ho, ho, ho!

Yet now and then, the maids to please,
  At midnight I card up their wool;
And, while they sleep and take their ease,
  With wheel to threads their flax I pull.
    I grind at mill
    Their malt up still;
  I dress their hemp; I spin their tow;
    If any wake,
    And would me take,
  I wend me, laughing, ho, ho, ho!

When any need to borrow aught,
  We lend them what they do require:
And for the use demand we naught;
  Our own is all we do desire.
    If to repay
    They do delay,
  Abroad amongst them then I go,
    And night by night,
    I them affright,
  With pinchings, dreams, and ho, ho,
    ho!

When lazy queans have naught to do,
  But study how to cog and lie;
To make debate and mischief too,
  'Twixt one another secretly:
    I mark their gloze,
    And it disclose
  To them whom they have wrongéd so:
    When I have done
    I get me gone,
  And leave them scolding, ho, ho,
    ho!

When men do traps and engines set
  In loopholes, where the vermin creep,
Who from their folds and houses get
  Their ducks and geese, and lambs and
    sheep;
    I spy the gin,
    And enter in,
  And seem a vermin taken so;
    But when they there
    Approach me near,
  I leap out laughing, ho, ho, ho!

By wells and rills, in meadows green,
  We nightly dance our heyday guise;
And to our fairy king and queen,
  We chant our moonlight minstrelsies.
    When larks 'gin sing,
    Away we fling;
  And babes new-born steal as we go;
    And elf in bed
    We leave in stead,
  And wend us laughing ho, ho, ho!

From hag-bred Merlin's time, have I
  Thus nightly revelled to and fro;
And for my pranks men call me by
  The name of Robin Goodfellow.
    Fiends, ghosts, and sprites,
    Who haunt the nights,
  The hags and goblins do me know;
    And beldames old
    My feats have told,
  So vale, vale; ho, ho, ho!

UNKNOWN.

[Before 1649.]

EDOM O' GORDON.

It fell about the Martinmas,
  When the wind blew shrill and cauld,
Said Edom o' Gordon to his men,
  "We maun draw to a hauld.

"And whatna hauld sall we draw to,
  My merry men and me?
We will gae to the house of the Rodes,
  To see that fair ladye."

The lady stood on her castle wa',
  Beheld baith dale and down;
There she was aware of a host of men
  Came riding towards the town.

"O see ye not, my merry men a',
  O see ye not what I see?
Methinks I see a host of men;
  I marvel who they be."

She weened it had been her lovely lord,
  As he cam' riding hame;
It was the traitor, Edom o' Gordon,
  Wha recked nor sin nor shame.

She had nae sooner buskit hersell,
  And putten on her gown,
Till Edom o' Gordon an' his men
  Were round about the town.

They had nae sooner supper set,
  Nae sooner said the grace,
But Edom o' Gordon an' his men
  Were lighted about the place.

The lady ran up to her tower-head,
  As fast as she could hie,
To see if by her fair speeches
  She could wi' him agree.

"Come doun to me, ye lady gay,
  Come doun, come doun to me;
This night sall ye lig within mine arms,
  To-morrow my bride sall be."

"I winna come down, ye fause Gordon,
  I winna come down to thee;
I winna forsake my ain dear lord, —
  And he is na far frae me."

"Gie owre your house, ye lady fair,
Gie owre your house to me;
Or I sall burn yoursell therein,
But and your babies three."

"I winna gie owre, ye fause Gordon,
To nae sic traitor as thee;
And if ye burn my ain dear babes,
My lord sall mak' ye dree.

"Now reach my pistol, Glaud, my man,
And charge ye weel my gun;
For, but an I pierce that bluidy butcher,
My babes, we been undone!"

She stood upon her castle wa',
And let twa bullets flee:
She missed that bluidy butcher's heart,
And only razed his knee.

"Set fire to the house!" quo' fause Gordon,
Wud wi' dule and ire:
"Fause ladye, ye sall rue that shot
As ye burn in the fire!"

"Wae worth, wae worth ye, Jock, my man!
I paid ye weel your fee;
Why pu' ye out the grund-wa' stane,
Lets in the reek to me?

"And e'en wae worth ye, Jock, my man!
I paid ye weel your hire;
Why pu' ye out the grund-wa' stane,
To me lets in the fire?"

"Ye paid me weel my hire, ladye,
Ye paid me weel my fee:
But now I 'm Edom o' Gordon's man, —
Maun either do or dee."

O then bespake her little son,
Sat on the nurse's knee:
Says, "O mither dear, gie owre this house,
For the reek it smothers me."

"I wad gie a' my goud, my bairn,
Sae wad I a' my fee,
For ae blast o' the western wind,
To blaw the reek frae thee."

O then bespake her daughter dear, —
She was baith jimp and sma':
"O row' me in a pair o' sheets,
And tow me o'er the wa'!"

They row'd her in a pair o' sheets,
And tow'd her owre the wa';
But on the point o' Gordon's spear
She gat a deadly fa'.

O bonnie, bonnie was her mouth,
And cherry were her cheeks,
And clear, clear was her yellow hair,
Whereon the red blood dreeps.

Then wi' his spear he turned her owre;
O gin her face was wan!
He said, "Ye are the first that e'er
I wished alive again."

He cam' and lookit again at her;
O gin her skin was white!
"I might hae spared that bonnie face
To hae been some man's delight."

"Busk and boun, my merry men a',
For ill dooms I do guess; —
I cannot look on that bonnie face
As it lies on the grass."

"Wha looks to freits, my master dear,
Its freits will follow them;
Let it ne'er be said that Edom o' Gordon
Was daunted by a dame."

But when the ladye saw the fire
Come flaming o'er her head,
She wept, and kissed her children twain,
Says, "Bairns, we been but dead."

The Gordon then his bugle blew,
And said, "Awa', awa'!
This house o' the Rodes is a' in a flame;
I hauld it time to ga'."

And this way lookit her ain dear lord,
As he came owre the lea;
He saw his castle a' in a lowe,
Sae far as he could see.

"Put on, put on, my wighty men,
As fast as ye can dri'e!
For he that 's hindmost o' the thrang
Sall ne'er get good o' me."

Then some they rade, and some they ran,
Out-owre the grass and bent;
But ere the foremost could win up,
Baith lady and babes were brent.

And after the Gordon he is gane,
Sae fast as he might dri'e;
And soon i' the Gordon's foul heart's blude
He 's wroken his fair ladye.

UNKNOWN.

TAKE THY AULD CLOAK ABOUT THEE.

In winter, when the rain rained cauld,
 And frost and snow were on the hill,
And Boreas with his blasts sae bâuld
 Was threat'ning all our kye to kill;
Then Bell, my wife, wha loves not strife,
 She said to me right hastilie,
"Get up, gudeman, save Crummie's life,
 And take thy auld cloak about thee!

"Cow Crummie is a useful cow,
 And she is come of a good kin';
Aft has she wet the bairnies' mou',
 And I am laith that she should pine:
Get up, gudeman, it is fu' time!
 The sun shines frae the lift sae hie;
Sloth never made a gracious end, —
 Gae, take thy auld cloak about thee!"

"My cloak was once a gude gray cloak,
 When it was fitting for my wear;
But now it 's scantly worth a groat,
 For I hae worn 't this thirty year:
Let 's spend the gear that we hae won,
 We little ken the day we 'll dee;
Then I 'll be proud, since I hae sworn
 To hae a new cloak about me."

"In days when our King Robert reigned,
 His breeches cost but half a crown;
He said they were a groat too dear,
 And ca'd the tailor thief and loun.
He was the king that wore the crown,
 And thou the man of low degree:
It 's pride puts a' the country down,
 Sae take thy auld cloak about thee!"

"O Bell, my wife, why dost thou flout?
 Now is now, and then was then.
Seek anywhere the world throughout,
 Thou ken'st not clowns from gentlemen.
They are clad in black, green, yellow, and gray,
 Sae far above their ain degree:
Once in my life I 'll do as they,
 For I 'll have a new cloak about me."

"Gudeman, I wot it 's thirty year
 Sin' we did ane anither ken,
And we hae had atween us twa
 Of lads and bonnie lasses ten;
Now they are women grown and men,
 I wish and pray weel may they be:
If thou wilt prove a good husband,
 E'en take thy auld cloak about thee."

Bell, my wife, she loves not strife,
 But she will rule me if she can:
And oft, to lead a quiet life,
 I 'm forced to yield, though I 'm gudeman.
It 's not for a man with a woman to threape
 Unless he first give o'er the plea:
As we began so will we leave,
 And I 'll take my auld cloak about me.

UNKNOWN.

THE BARRING O' THE DOOR.

It fell about the Martinmas time,
 And a gay time it was than,
When our gudewife got puddings to make,
 And she boiled them in the pan.

The wind sae cauld blew east and north,
 It blew into the floor:
Quoth our gudeman to our gudewife,
 "Gae out and bar the door!"

"My hand is in my huswif's kap,
 Gudeman, as ye may see;
An' it should nae be barred this hundred year,
 It 's no be barred for me."

They made a paction 'tween them twa,
 They made it firm and sure,
That the first word whae'er should speak
 Should rise and bar the door.

Then by there came twa gentlemen
 At twelve o'clock at night;
And they could neither see house nor hall,
 Nor coal nor candle light.

And first they ate the white puddings,
 And then they ate the black;
Though muckle thought the gudewife to hersel',
 Yet ne'er a word she spak'.

Then said the one unto the other,
 "Here, man, tak' ye my knife!

Do ye tak' aff the auld man's beard,
And I 'll kiss the gudewife."

"But there 's nae water in the house,
And what shall we do than?"
"What ails ye at the puddin' broo
That boils into the pan?"

O, up then started our gudeman,
And an angry man was he:
"Will ye kiss my wife before my een,
And scaud me wi' puddin' bree?"

Then up and started our gudewife,
Gied three skips on the floor:
"Gudeman, ye 've spoken the foremost word,—
Get up and bar the door!"

THOMAS CAREW.

[1589-1639.]

HE THAT LOVES A ROSY CHEEK.

He that loves a rosy cheek,
Or a coral lip admires,
Or from starlike eyes doth seek
Fuel to maintain his fires;
As old Time makes these decay,
So his flames must waste away.

But a smooth and steadfast mind,
Gentle thoughts, and calm desires,
Hearts with equal love combined,
Kindle never-dying fires;—
Where these are not, I despise
Lovely cheeks or lips or eyes.

WILLIAM BROWNE.

[1590-1645.]

THE SIRENS' SONG.

Steer hither, steer your wingéd pines,
All beaten mariners:
Here lie undiscovered mines,
A prey to passengers:
Perfumes far sweeter than the best
That make the phœnix urn and nest:
Fear not your ships,
Nor any to oppose you save our lips:
But come on shore,
Where no joy dies till love has gotten more.

For swelling waves our panting breasts,
Where never storms arise,
Exchange; and be awhile our guests:
For stars, gaze on our eyes.
The compass, love shall hourly sing,
And, as he goes about the ring,
We will not miss
To tell each point he nameth with a kiss.

SONG.

Shall I tell you whom I love?
Hearken then awhile to me,
And if such a woman move
As I now shall versify,
Be assured, 't is she, or none,
That I love, and love alone.

Nature did her so much right,
As she scorns the help of art,
In as many virtues dight
As e'er yet embraced a heart.
So much good so truly tried,
Some for less were deified.

Wit she hath, without desire
To make known how much she hath;
And her anger flames no higher
Than may fitly sweeten wrath.
Full of pity as may be,
Though perhaps not so to me.

Reason masters every sense,
And her virtues grace her birth:
Lovely as all excellence,
Modest in her most of mirth:
Likelihood enough to prove
Only worth could kindle love.

Such she is; and if you know
Such a one as I have sung,—
Be she brown, or fair, or so,
That she be but somewhile young,—
Be assured, 't is she, or none,
That I love, and love alone.

SIR ROBERT AYTON.

[1570–1638.]

FAIR AND UNWORTHY.

I do confess thou 'rt smooth and fair,
And I might have gone near to love thee,
Had I not found the lightest prayer
That lips could speak, had power to move thee:
But I can let thee now alone,
As worthy to be loved by none.

I do confess thou 'rt sweet; yet find
Thee such an unthrift of thy sweets,
Thy favors are but like the wind,
That kisses everything it meets;
And since thou canst with more than one,
Thou 'rt worthy to be kissed by none.

The morning rose that untouched stands
Armed with her briers, how sweetly smells!
But plucked and strained through ruder hands,
No more her sweetness with her dwells,
But scent and beauty both are gone,
And leaves fall from her, one by one.

Such fate, erelong, will thee betide,
When thou hast handled been awhile, —
Like sere flowers to be thrown aside:
And I will sigh, while some will smile,
To see thy love for more than one
Hath brought thee to be loved by none.

WILLIAM STRODE.

[1600–1644.]

MUSIC.

O lull me, lull me, charming air!
My senses rock with wonder sweet:
Like snow on wool thy fallings are;
Soft, like a spirit's, are thy feet!
Grief who need fear
That hath an ear?
Down let him lie
And slumbering die,
And change his soul for harmony!

THOMAS HEYWOOD.

[About 1640.]

GOOD-MORROW.

Pack clouds away, and welcome day,
With night we banish sorrow;
Sweet air, blow soft; mount, larks, aloft,
To give my love good-morrow.
Wings from the wind to please her mind,
Notes from the lark I 'll borrow;
Bird, prune thy wing; nightingale, sing,
To give my love good-morrow.

Wake from thy nest, robin redbreast;
Sing, birds, in every furrow;
And from each hill let music shrill
Give my fair love good-morrow.
Blackbird and thrush in every bush,
Stare, linnet, and cock-sparrow;
You pretty elves, among yourselves,
Sing my fair love good-morrow.

SEARCH AFTER GOD.

I sought thee round about, O thou my God!
In thine abode.
I said unto the earth, "Speak, art thou he?"
She answered me,
"I am not." I inquired of creatures all,
In general,
Contained therein. They with one voice proclaim
That none amongst them challenged such a name.

I asked the seas and all the deeps below,
My God to know;
I asked the reptiles and whatever is
In the abyss, —
Even from the shrimp to the leviathan
Inquiry ran;
But in those deserts which no line can sound,
The God I sought for was not to be found.

I asked the air if that were he! but lo!
It told me "No."
I from the towering eagle to the wren
Demanded then
If any feathered fowl 'mongst them were such;
But they all, much

Offended with my question, in full choir,
Answered, "To find thy God thou must look higher."

I asked the heavens, sun, moon, and stars; but they
Said, "We obey
The God thou seekest." I asked what eye or ear
Could see or hear,—
What in the world I might descry or know
Above, below;
With an unanimous voice, all these things said,
"We are not God, but we by him were made."

I asked the world's great universal mass
If that God was;
Which with a mighty and strong voice replied,
As stupefied, —
"I am not he, O man! for know that I
By him on high
Was fashioned first of nothing; thus instated
And swayed by him by whom I was created."

I sought the court; but smooth-tongued flattery there
Deceived each ear;
In the thronged city there was selling, buying,
Swearing, and lying;
I' the country, craft in simpleness arrayed,
And then I said, —
"Vain is my search, although my pains be great;
Where my God is there can be no deceit."

A scrutiny within myself I then
Even thus began:
"O man, what art thou?" What more could I say
Than dust and clay, —
Frail, mortal, fading, a mere puff, a blast,
That cannot last;
Enthroned to-day, to-morrow in an urn,
Formed from that earth to which I must return?

I asked myself what this great God might be
That fashioned me.
I answered: The all-potent, sole, immense,
Surpassing sense;
Unspeakable, inscrutable, eternal,
Lord over all;
The only terrible, strong, just, and true,
Who hath no end, and no beginning knew.

He is the well of life, for he doth give
To all that live
Both breath and being; he is the Creator
Both of the water,
Earth, air, and fire. Of all things that subsist
He hath the list, —
Of all the heavenly host, or what earth claims,
He keeps the scroll, and calls them by their names.

And now, my God, by thine illumining grace,
Thy glorious face
(So far forth as it may discovered be)
Methinks I see;
And though invisible and infinite,
To human sight
Thou, in thy mercy, justice, truth, appearest,
In which, to our weak sense, thou comest nearest.

O, make us apt to seek and quick to find,
Thou, God, most kind!
Give us love, hope, and faith, in thee to trust,
Thou, God, most just!
Remit all our offences, we entreat,
Most good! most great!
Grant that our willing, though unworthy quest
May, through thy grace, admit us 'mongst the blest.

HENRY KING.

[1591-1669.]

SIC VITA.

Like to the falling of a star,
Or as the flights of eagles are;
Or like the fresh spring's gaudy hue,
Or silver drops of morning dew;

Or like a wind that chafes the flood,
Or bubbles which on water stood:
Even such is man, whose borrowed light
Is straight called in, and paid to-night.
The wind blows out, the bubble dies;
The spring entombed in autumn lies;
The dew dries up, the star is shot;
The flight is past, — and man forgot.

ELEGY.

Sleep on, my love, in thy cold bed,
Never to be disquieted!
My last good night! Thou wilt not wake
Till I thy fate shall overtake;
Till age, or grief, or sickness must
Marry my body to that dust
It so much loves, and fill the room
My heart keeps empty in thy tomb.

Stay for me there! I will not fail
To meet thee in that hollow vale.
And think not much of my delay:
I am already on the way,
And follow thee with all the speed
Desire can make, or sorrow breed.
Each minute is a short degree,
And every hour a step towards thee.
At night, when I betake to rest,
Next morn I rise nearer my west
Of life, almost by eight hours' sail,
Than when sleep breathed his drowsy gale.
Thus from the sun my vessel steers,
And my day's compass downward bears:
Nor labor I to stem the tide
Through which to thee I swiftly glide.

'T is true, with shame and grief I yield,
Thou, like the van, first took'st the field,
And gotten hast the victory,
In thus adventuring to die
Before me, whose more years might crave
A just precedence in the grave.
But hark! my pulse, like a soft drum,
Beats my approach, tells thee I come:
And slow howe'er my marches be,
I shall at last sit down by thee.

The thought of this bids me go on,
And wait my dissolution
With hope and comfort. Dear, forgive
The crime, — I am content to live
Divided, with but half a heart,
Till we shall meet, and never part.

MARQUIS OF MONTROSE.

[1612 – 1650.]

I'LL NEVER LOVE THEE MORE.

My dear and only love, I pray
  That little world of thee
Be governed by no other sway
  But purest monarchy:
For if confusion have a part,
  Which virtuous souls abhor,
I 'll call a synod in my heart,
  And never love thee more.

As Alexander I will reign,
  And I will reign alone;
My thoughts did evermore disdain
  A rival on my throne.
He either fears his fate too much,
  Or his deserts are small,
Who dares not put it to the touch,
  To gain or lose it all.

JAMES SHIRLEY.

[1596 – 1666.]

DEATH THE LEVELLER.

The glories of our blood and state
  Are shadows, not substantial things;
There is no armor against fate;
  Death lays his icy hand on kings:
      Sceptre and crown
      Must tumble down,
And in the dust be equal made
With the poor crooked scythe and spade.

Some men with swords may reap the field,
  And plant fresh laurels where they kill;
But their strong nerves at last must yield;
  They tame but one another still:
      Early or late
      They stoop to fate,
And must give up their murmuring breath
When they, pale captives, creep to death.

The garlands wither on your brow;
  Then boast no more your mighty deeds;
Upon Death's purple altar now
  See where the victor-victim bleeds:

Your heads must come
To the cold tomb;
Only the actions of the just
Smell sweet, and blossom in their dust.

EDWARD HERBERT, (EARL OF CHERBURY.)

[1581 - 1648.]

CELINDA.

Walking thus towards a pleasant grove,
Which did, it seemed, in new delight
The pleasures of the time unite
To give a triumph to their love, —
They stayed at last, and on the grass
Reposéd so as o'er his breast
She bowed her gracious head to rest,
Such a weight as no burden was.
Long their fixed eyes to heaven bent,
Unchangéd they did never move,
As if so great and pure a love
No glass but it could represent.
"These eyes again thine eyes shall see,
Thy hands again these hands infold,
And all chaste pleasures can be told,
Shall with us everlasting be.
Let then no doubt, Celinda, touch,
Much less your fairest mind invade;
Were not our souls immortal made,
Our equal loves can make them such."

SIR THOMAS BROWNE.

[1605 - 1682.]

EVENING HYMN.

The night is come; like to the day,
Depart not thou, great God, away.
Let not my sins, black as the night,
Eclipse the lustre of thy light.
Keep in my horizon: for to me
The sun makes not the day, but thee.
Thou whose nature cannot sleep,
On my temples sentry keep:
Guard me 'gainst those watchful foes,
Whose eyes are open while mine close.
Let no dreams my head infest
But such as Jacob's temples blest.
Whilst I do rest, my soul advance;
Make my sleep a holy trance:
That I may, my rest being wrought,
Awake into some holy thought,
And with as active vigor run
My course, as doth the nimble sun.
Sleep is a death; O, make me try,
By sleeping, what it is to die:
And as gently lay my head
On my grave as now my bed.
Howe'er I rest, great God, let me
Awake again at last with thee.
And thus assured, behold I lie
Securely, or to wake or die.
These are my drowsy days; in vain
I do now wake to sleep again:
O, come that hour when I shall never
Sleep thus again, but wake forever.

RICHARD CRASHAW.

[1605 - 1650.]

WISHES.

Whoe'er she be,
That not impossible She
That shall command my heart and me;

Where'er she lie,
Locked up from mortal eye
In shady leaves of destiny,

Till that ripe birth
Of studied Fate stand forth,
And teach her fair steps to our earth;

Till that divine
Idea take a shrine
Of crystal flesh, through which to shine:

— Meet you her, my Wishes,
Bespeak her to my blisses,
And be ye called, my absent kisses.

I wish her beauty
That owes not all its duty
To gaudy tire, or glist'ring shoe-tie:

Something more than
Taffeta or tissue can,
Or rampant feather, or rich fan.

A face that 's best
By its own beauty drest,
And can alone command the rest:

A face made up
Out of no other shop
Than what Nature's white hand sets ope.

Sydneian showers
Of sweet discourse, whose powers
Can crown old Winter's head with flowers.

Whate'er delight
Can make day's forehead bright
Or give down to the wings of night.

Soft silken hours,
Open suns, shady bowers;
'Bove all, nothing within that lowers.

Days, that need borrow
No part of their good morrow
From a fore-spent night of sorrow:

Days, that in spite
Of darkness, by the light
Of a clear mind are day all night.

Life, that dares send
A challenge to his end;
And when it comes, says, "Welcome, friend."

I wish her store
Of worth may leave her poor
Of wishes; and I wish — no more.

— Now, if Time knows
That Her, whose radiant brows
Weave them a garland of my vows;

Her that dares be
What these lines wish to see:
I seek no further, it is She.

'T is She, and here
Lo! I unclothe and clear
My wishes' cloudy character.

Such worth as this is
Shall fix my flying wishes,
And determine them to kisses.

Let her full glory,
My fancies, fly before ye;
Be ye my fictions: — but her story.

SIR RICHARD LOVELACE.

[1618-1658.]

TO ALTHEA.

When love with unconfinéd wings
Hovers within my gates,
And my divine Althea brings
To whisper at my grates;
When I lie tangled in her hair,
And fettered to her eye,
The birds that wanton in the air
Know no such liberty.

Stone walls do not a prison make,
Nor iron bars a cage;
Minds innocent and quiet take
That for a hermitage:
If I have freedom in my love,
And in my soul am free, —
Angels alone that soar above
Enjoy such liberty.

TO LUCASTA.

Tell me not, sweet, I am unkind,
That from the nunnery
Of thy chaste breast, and quiet mind,
To war and arms I fly.

True: a new mistress now I chase,
The first foe in the field;
And with a stronger faith embrace
A sword, a horse, a shield.

Yet this inconstancy is such,
As you too shall adore;
I could not love thee, dear, so much,
Loved I not honor more.

ROBERT HERRICK.

[1591-1674.]

TO DAFFODILS.

Fair Daffodils, we weep to see
You haste away so soon:
As yet the early-rising sun
Has not attained his noon:
Stay, stay,

Until the hasting day
Has run
But to the even song;
And, having prayed together, we
Will go with you along.

We have short time to stay as you,
We have as short a spring;
As quick a growth to meet decay,
As you, or anything.
We die,
As your hours do, and dry
Away
Like to the summer's rain,
Or as the pearls of morning's dew,
Ne'er to be found again.

TO BLOSSOMS.

Fair pledges of a fruitful tree,
Why do ye fall so fast?
Your date is not so past,
But you may stay yet here awhile,
To blush and gently smile,
And go at last.

What! were ye born to be
An hour or half's delight,
And so to bid good-night?
'T was pity Nature brought ye forth
Merely to show your worth,
And lose you quite.

But you are lovely leaves, where we
May read how soon things have
Their end, though ne'er so brave;
And after they have shown their pride,
Like you, awhile, they glide
Into the grave.

TO KEEP A TRUE LENT.

Is this a fast, to keep
The larder lean,
And clean
From fat of veals and sheep?

Is it to quit the dish
Of flesh, yet still
To fill
The platter high with fish?

Is it to fast an hour,
Or rag'd to go,
Or show
A downcast look, and sour?

No: 't is a fast to dole
Thy sheaf of wheat,
And meat,
Unto the hungry soul.

It is to fast from strife,
From old debate
And hate;
To circumcise thy life.

To show a heart grief-rent;
To starve thy sin,
Not bin:
And that 's to keep thy Lent.

GEORGE HERBERT.

[1593-1633.]

VIRTUE.

Sweet Day, so cool, so calm, so bright,
The bridal of the earth and sky,
The dew shall weep thy fall to-night;
For thou must die.

Sweet Rose, whose hue, angry and brave,
Bids the rash gazer wipe his eye,
Thy root is ever in its grave,
And thou must die.

Sweet Spring, full of sweet days and roses,
A box where sweets compacted lie,
My music shows ye have your closes,
And all must die.

Only a sweet and virtuous soul,
Like seasoned timber, never gives;
But though the whole world turn to coal,
Then chiefly lives.

THE FLOWER.

How fresh, O Lord, how sweet and clean
Are thy returns! e'en as the flowers in spring;
To which, besides their own demesne,
The late-past frosts tributes of pleasure bring.
Grief melts away
Like snow in May,
As if there were no such cold thing.

Who would have thought my shrivelled heart
Could have recovered greenness? It was gone
Quite under ground; as flowers depart
To see their mother-root, when they have blown;
Where they together,
All the hard weather,
Dead to the world, keep house unknown.

These are thy wonders, Lord of power,
Killing and quickening, bringing down to hell
And up to heaven in an hour;
Making a chiming of a passing bell.
We say amiss,
This or that is:
Thy word is all, if we could spell.

O that I once past changing were,
Fast in thy Paradise, where no flower can wither!
Many a spring I shoot up fair
Offering at heaven, growing and groaning thither;
Nor doth my flower
Want a spring-shower,
My sins and I joining together.

But while I grow in a straight line,
Still upwards bent, as if heaven were mine own,
Thy anger comes, and I decline:
What frost to that? what pole is not the zone
Where all things burn,
When thou dost turn,
And the least frown of thine is shown?

And now in age I bud again,
After so many deaths I live and write;
I once more smell the dew and rain,
And relish versing: O my only Light,
It cannot be
That I am he
On whom thy tempests fell all night.

These are thy wonders, Lord of love,
To make us see we are but flowers that glide;
Which when we once can find and prove,
Thou hast a garden for us, where to bide.
Who would be more,
Swelling through store,
Forfeit their Paradise by their pride.

REST.

When God at first made man,
Having a glass of blessings standing by,
"Let us," said he, "pour on him all we can:
Let the world's riches, which disperséd lie,
Contract into a span."

So strength first made a way;
Then beauty flowed; then wisdom, honor, pleasure:
When almost all was out, God made a stay,
Perceiving that alone, of all his treasure,
Rest in the bottom lay.

"For if I should," said he,
"Bestow this jewel also on my creature,
He would adore my gifts instead of me,
And rest in nature, not the God of nature;
So both should losers be.

"Yet let him keep the rest,
But keep them with repining restlessness:
Let him be rich and weary, that at least,
If goodness lead him not, yet weariness
May toss him to my breast."

HENRY VAUGHAN.

[1614-1695.]

THE BIRD.

Hither thou com'st. The busy wind all night
Blew through thy lodging, where thy own warm wing
Thy pillow was. Many a sullen storm,
For which coarse man seems much the fitter born,
Rained on thy bed
And harmless head;

And now, as fresh and cheerful as the light,
Thy little heart in early hymns doth sing
Unto that Providence whose unseen arm
Curbed them, and clothed thee well and warm.
All things that be praise Him; and had
Their lesson taught them when first made.

So hills and valleys into singing break;
And though poor stones have neither speech nor tongue,

While active winds and streams both run
and speak,
Yet stones are deep in admiration.
Thus praise and prayer here beneath the
sun
Make lesser mornings, when the great
are done.

For each inclosèd spirit is a star
Inlightning his own little sphere,
Whose light, though fetcht and borrowèd
from far,
Both mornings makes and evenings
there.

But as these birds of light make a land
glad,
Chirping their solemn matins on each
tree;
So in the shades of night some dark
fowls be,
Whose heavy notes make all that hear
them sad.

The turtle then in palm-trees mourns,
While owls and satyrs howl;
The pleasant land to brimstone turns,
And all her streams grow foul.

Brightness and mirth, and love and faith,
all fly,
Till the day-spring breaks forth again
from high.

THEY ARE ALL GONE.

THEY are all gone into the world of light,
And I alone sit lingering here!
Their very memory is fair and bright,
And my sad thoughts doth clear.

It glows and glitters in my cloudy breast,
Like stars upon some gloomy grove,
Or those faint beams in which this hill
is drest
After the sun's remove.

I see them walking in an air of glory,
Whose light doth trample on my days;
My days, which are at best but dull and
hoary,
Mere glimmering and decays.

O holy hope! and high humility, —
High as the heavens above!

These are your walks, and you have
showed them me
To kindle my cold love.

Dear, beauteous death, — the jewel of the
just, —
Shining nowhere but in the dark!
What mysteries do lie beyond thy dust,
Could man outlook that mark!

He that hath found some fledged bird's
nest may know,
At first sight, if the bird be flown;
But what fair dell or grove he sings in
now,
That is to him unknown.

And yet, as angels in some brighter
dreams
Call to the soul when man doth sleep,
So some strange thoughts transcend our
wonted themes,
And into glory peep.

If a star were confined into a tomb,
Her captive flames must needs burn
there;
But when the hand that lockt her up
gives room,
She'll shine through all the sphere.

O Father of eternal life, and all
Created glories under thee!
Resume thy spirit from this world of
thrall
Into true liberty!

Either disperse these mists, which blot
and fill
My perspective still as they pass;
Or else remove me hence unto that hill
Where I shall need no glass.

GEORGE WITHER.

[1588-1667.]

FOR ONE THAT HEARS HIMSELF MUCH PRAISED.

MY sins and follies, Lord! by thee
From others hidden are,
That such good words are spoke of me,
As now and then I hear;

For sure if others knew me such,
  Such as myself I know,
I should have been dispraised as much
  As I am praisèd now.

The praise, therefore, which I have heard,
  Delights not so my mind,
As those things make my heart afeard,
  Which in myself I find:
And I had rather to be blamed,
  So I were blameless made,
Than for much virtue to be famed,
  When I no virtues had.

Though slanders to an innocent
  Sometimes do bitter grow,
Their bitterness procures content,
  If clear himself he know.
And when a virtuous man hath erred,
  If praised himself he hear,
It makes him grieve, and more afeard,
  Than if he slandered were.

Lord! therefore make my heart upright,
  Whate'er my deeds do seem;
And righteous rather in thy sight,
  Than in the world's esteem.
And if aught good appear to be
  In any act of mine,
Let thankfulness be found in me,
  And all the praise be thine.

COMPANIONSHIP OF THE MUSE.

She doth tell me where to borrow
Comfort in the midst of sorrow;
Makes the desolatest place
To her presence be a grace,
And the blackest discontents
Be her fairest ornaments.
In my former days of bliss,
Her divine skill taught me this,
That from everything I saw
I could some invention draw,
And raise pleasure to her height,
Through the meanest object's sight,
By the murmur of a spring,
Or the least bough's rustlëing.
By a daisy, whose leaves spread,
Shut when Titan goes to bed;
Or a shady bush or tree,
She could more infuse in me,
Than all nature's beauties can
In some other wiser man.
By her help I also now
Make this churlish place allow
Some things that may sweeten gladness,
In the very gall of sadness.
The dull loneness, the black shade,
That these hanging vaults have made;
The strange music of the waves,
Beating on these hollow caves;
This black den which rocks emboss,
Overgrown with eldest moss;
The rude portals that give light
More to terror than delight;
This my chamber of neglect,
Walled about with disrespect,—
From all these, and this dull air,
A fit object for despair,
She hath taught me by her might
To draw comfort and delight.
Therefore, thou best earthly bliss,
I will cherish thee for this.
Poesy, thou sweet'st content
That e'er heaven to mortals lent:
Though they as a trifle leave thee,
Whose dull thoughts cannot conceive thee;
Though thou be to them a scorn,
That to naught but earth are born,—
Let my life no longer be
Than I am in love with thee!

ANDREW MARVELL.

[1620–1678.]

THOUGHTS IN A GARDEN.

How vainly men themselves amaze,
To win the palm, the oak, or bays:
And their incessant labors see
Crowned from some single herb or tree,
Whose short and narrow-vergéd shade
Does prudently their toils upbraid;
While all the flowers and trees do close,
To weave the garlands of repose.

Fair Quiet, have I found thee here,
And Innocence, thy sister dear?
Mistaken long, I sought you then
In busy companies of men.
Your sacred plants, if here below,
Only among these plants will grow.

Society is all but rude
To this delicious solitude.

No white nor red was ever seen
So amorous as this lovely green.
Fond lovers, cruel as their flame,
Cut in these trees their mistress' name.
Little, alas, they know or heed,
How far these beauties her exceed!
Fair trees! where'er your barks I wound,
No name shall but your own be found.

What wondrous life is this I lead!
Ripe apples drop about my head.
The luscious clusters of the vine
Upon my mouth do crush their wine.
The nectarine, and curious peach,
Into my hands themselves do reach.
Stumbling on melons, as I pass,
Insnared with flowers, I fall on grass.
Meanwhile the mind from pleasure less
Withdraws into its happiness, —
The mind, that ocean where each kind
Does straight its own resemblance find;
Yet it creates transcending these,
Far other worlds and other seas;
Annihilating all that 's made
To a green thought in a green shade.
Here at the fountain's sliding foot,
Or at some fruit-tree's mossy root,
Casting the body's vest aside,
My soul into the boughs does glide;
There, like a bird, it sits and sings,
Then whets and claps its silver wings,
And, till prepared for longer flight,
Waves in its plumes the various light.

Such was the happy garden state,
While man there walked without a mate:
After a place so pure and sweet,
What other help could yet be meet!
But 't was beyond a mortal's share
To wander solitary there:
Two paradises are in one,
To live in paradise alone.

How well the skilful gardener drew
Of flowers and herbs this dial new!
Where, from above, the milder sun
Does through a fragrant zodiac run:
And, as it works, the industrious bee
Computes its time as well as we.
How could such sweet and wholesome hours
Be reckoned, but with herbs and flowers?

THE BERMUDAS.

Where the remote Bermudas ride
In the ocean's bosom unespied,
From a small boat that rowed along,
The listening winds received this song:
"What should we do but sing His praise
That led us through the watery maze
Where he the huge sea monsters racks,
That lift the deep upon their backs,
Unto an isle so long unknown,
And yet far kinder than our own?
He lands us on a grassy stage,
Safe from the storms and prelates' rage.
He gave us this eternal spring
Which here enamels everything,
And sends the fowls to us in care,
On daily visits through the air.
He hangs in shades the orange bright,
Like golden lamps in a green night,
And does in the pomegranates close
Jewels more rich than Ormus shows.
He makes the figs our mouths to meet,
And throws the melons at our feet,
With apples, plants of such a price,
No tree could ever bear them twice.
With cedars, chosen by his hand,
From Lebanon he stores the land;
And makes the hollow seas that roar,
Proclaim the ambergris on shore.
He cast (of which we rather boast)
The gospel's pearl upon our coast;
And in these rocks for us did frame
A temple where to sound his name.
O, let our voice his praise exalt,
Till it arrive at heaven's vault,
Which then perhaps rebounding may
Echo beyond the Mexic bay."

Thus sang they in the English boat
A holy and a cheerful note;
And all the way, to guide their chime,
With falling oars they kept the time.

JOHN MILTON.

[1608–1674.]

HYMN ON THE NATIVITY.

It was the winter wild,
While the heaven-born child
All meanly wrapt in the rude manger lies;
Nature, in awe of him,

Had doffed her gaudy trim,
With her great Master so to sympathize:
It was no season then for her
To wanton with the sun, her lusty paramour.

Only with speeches fair
She wooes the gentle air,
To hide her guilty front with innocent snow;
And on her naked shame,
Pollute with sinful blame,
The saintly veil of maiden-white to throw;
Confounded, that her Maker's eyes
Should look so near upon her foul deformities.

But he, her fears to cease,
Sent down the meek-eyed Peace:
She, crowned with olive green, came softly sliding
Down through the turning sphere,
His ready harbinger,
With turtle wing the amorous clouds dividing;
And, waving wide her myrtle wand,
She strikes a universal peace through sea and land.

No war or battle's sound
Was heard the world around:
The idle spear and shield were high uphung;
The hookéd chariot stood
Unstained with hostile blood;
The trumpet spake not to the arméd throng;
And kings sat still with awful eye,
As if they surely knew their sovereign lord was by.

But peaceful was the night,
Wherein the Prince of Light
His reign of peace upon the earth began:
The winds, with wonder whist,
Smoothly the waters kissed,
Whispering new joys to the mild ocean,
Who now hath quite forgot to rave,
While birds of calm sit brooding on the charméd wave.

The stars, with deep amaze,
Stand fixed in steadfast gaze,
Bending one way their precious influence;
And will not take their flight,
For all the morning light,
Or Lucifer had often warned them thence;
But in their glimmering orbs did glow,
Until their Lord himself bespake, and bid them go.

And, though the shady gloom
Had given day her room,
The sun himself withheld his wonted speed,
And hid his head for shame,
As his inferior flame
The new-enlightened world no more should need;
He saw a greater sun appear
Than his bright throne, or burning axletree, could bear.

The shepherds on the lawn,
Or ere the point of dawn,
Sat simply chatting in a rustic row;
Full little thought they then
That the mighty Pan
Was kindly come to live with them below;
Perhaps their loves, or else their sheep,
Was all that did their silly thoughts so busy keep.

When such music sweet
Their hearts and ears did greet,
As never was by mortal fingers strook,
Divinely warbled voice
Answering the stringéd noise,
As all their souls in blissful rapture took:
The air, such pleasure loath to lose,
With thousand echoes still prolongs each heavenly close.

Nature, that heard such sound,
Beneath the hollow round
Of Cynthia's seat, the airy region thrilling,
Now was almost won,
To think her part was done,
And that her reign had here its last fulfilling;
She knew such harmony alone
Could hold all heaven and earth in happier union.

At last surrounds their sight
A globe of circular light,
That with long beams the shame-faced night arrayed;
The helméd cherubim,

And sworded seraphim,
Are seen in glittering ranks with wings displayed,
Harping in loud and solemn quire,
With unexpressive notes, to Heaven's new-born heir.

Such music as 't is said
Before was never made,
But when of old the sons of morning sung,
While the Creator great
His constellations set,
And the well-balanced world on hinges hung,
And cast the dark foundations deep,
And bid the weltering waves their oozy channel keep.

Ring out, ye crystal spheres,
Once bless our human ears,
If ye have power to touch our senses so;
And let your silver chime
Move in melodious time;
And let the bass of Heaven's deep organ blow;
And, with your ninefold harmony,
Make up full concert to the angelic symphony.

For, if such holy song
Enwrap our fancy long,
Time will run back, and fetch the age of gold;
And speckled Vanity
Will sicken soon and die,
And leprous Sin will melt from earthly mould;
And Hell itself will pass away,
And leave her dolorous mansions to the peering day.

Yea, Truth and Justice then
Will down return to men,
Orbed in a rainbow; and, like glories wearing,
Mercy will sit between,
Throned in celestial sheen,
With radiant feet the tissued clouds down steering;
And Heaven, as at some festival,
Will open wide the gates of her high palace hall.

But wisest Fate says no,
This must not yet be so;
The babe yet lies in smiling infancy,
That on the bitter cross
Must redeem our loss,
So both himself and us to glorify:
Yet first, to those ychained in sleep,
The wakeful trump of doom must thunder through the deep,

With such a horrid clang
As on Mount Sinai rang,
While the red fire and smouldering clouds outbrake;
The aged earth aghast,
With terror of that blast,
Shall from the surface to the centre shake;
When, at the world's last session,
The dreadful Judge in middle air shall spread his throne.

And then at last our bliss,
Full and perfect is,
But now begins; for, from this happy day,
The old dragon, underground,
In straiter limits bound,
Not half so far casts his usurpéd sway;
And, wroth to see his kingdom fail,
Swinges the scaly horror of his folded tail.

The oracles are dumb;
No voice or hideous hum
Runs through the archéd roof in words deceiving.
Apollo from his shrine
Can no more divine,
With hollow shriek the steep of Delphos leaving.
No nightly trance, or breathéd spell,
Inspires the pale-eyed priest from the prophetic cell.

The lonely mountains o'er,
And the resounding shore,
A voice of weeping heard and loud lament;
From haunted spring and dale,
Edged with poplar pale,
The parting Genius is with sighing sent;
With flower-inwoven tresses torn,
The nymphs in twilight shade of tangled thickets mourn.

In consecrated earth,
And on the holy hearth,
The Lars and Lemures mourn with midnight plaint.
In urns and altars round,

A drear and dying sound
  Affrights the Flamens at their service quaint;
And the chill marble seems to sweat,
While each peculiar power foregoes his wonted seat.

Peor and Baälim
Forsake their temples dim
  With that twice-battered God of Palestine;
And mooned Ashtaroth,
Heaven's queen and mother both,
  Now sits not girt with tapers' holy shine;
The Libyac Hammon shrinks his horn;
In vain the Tyrian maids their wounded Thammuz mourn.

And sullen Moloch, fled,
Hath left in shadows dread
  His burning idol all of blackest hue:
In vain with cymbals' ring
They call the grisly king,
  In dismal dance about the furnace blue:
The brutish gods of Nile as fast,
Isis, and Orus, and the dog Anubis, haste.

Nor is Osiris seen
In Memphian grove or green,
  Trampling the unshowered grass with lowings loud;
Nor can he be at rest
Within his sacred chest,
  Naught but profoundest hell can be his shroud;
In vain with timbrelled anthems dark
The sable-stoléd sorcerers bear his worshipped ark.

He feels from Judah's land
The dreaded infant's hand,
  The rays of Bethlehem blind his dusky eyne;
Nor all the gods beside
Longer dare abide,
  Not Typhon huge ending in snaky twine;
Our babe, to show his Godhead true,
Can in his swaddling bands control the damnéd crew.

So, when the sun in bed,
Curtained with cloudy red,
  Pillows his chin upon an orient wave,
The flocking shadows pale
Troop to the infernal jail,
  Each fettered ghost slips to his several grave;
And the yellow-skirted fays
Fly after the night-steeds, leaving their moon-loved maze.

But see, the Virgin blest
Hath laid her babe to rest;
  Time is our tedious song should here have ending:
Heaven's youngest-teeméd star
Hath fixed her polished car,
  Her sleeping Lord with handmaid lamp attending;
And all about the courtly stable
Bright-harnessed angels sit in order serviceable.

SONNETS.

ON ARRIVING AT THE AGE OF TWENTY-THREE.

How soon hath Time, the subtle thief of youth,
  Stolen on his wing my three-and-twentieth year!
  My hasting days fly on with full career,
  But my late spring no bud or blossom showeth.
Perhaps my semblance might deceive the truth,
  That I to manhood am arrived so near,
  And inward ripeness doth much less appear,
  That some more timely-happy spirits endu'th.
Yet, be it less or more, or soon or slow,
  It shall be still in strictest measure even
  To that same lot, however mean or high,
Toward which Time leads me, and the will of Heaven;
  All is, if I have grace to use it so,
  As ever in my great Taskmaster's eye.

ON HIS BLINDNESS.

When I consider how my light is spent,
  Ere half my days in this dark world and wide,
  And that one talent, which is death to hide,
Lodged with me useless, though my soul more bent
To serve therewith my Maker, and present

My true account, lest he returning chide;
"Doth God exact day-labor, light denied?"
I fondly ask: but Patience, to prevent
That murmur, soon replies, "God doth not need
Either man's work or his own gifts: who best
Bear his mild yoke, they serve him best: his state
Is kingly; thousands at his bidding speed,
And post o'er land and ocean without rest;
They also serve who only stand and wait."

THOMAS ELWOOD.

[1639-1713.]

PRAYER.

Unto the glory of thy Holy Name,
Eternal God! whom I both love and fear,
Here bear I witness that I never came
Before thy throne and found thee loath to hear,
But, ever ready with an open ear.
And though sometimes thou seem'st thy face to hide
As one that hath his love withdrawn from me,
'T is that my faith may to the full be tried,
And I thereby may only better see
How weak I am when not upheld by Thee.

RICHARD BAXTER.

[1615-1691.]

RESIGNATION.

Lord, it belongs not to my care,
Whether I die or live:
To love and serve thee is my share,
And this thy grace must give.
If life be long, I will be glad,
That I may long obey;
If short, yet why should I be sad
To soar to endless day?

Christ leads me through no darker rooms
Than he went through before;
He that into God's kingdom comes
Must enter by his door.
Come, Lord, when grace has made me meet
Thy blessed face to see;
For if thy work on earth be sweet,
What will thy glory be?

Then shall I end my sad complaints,
And weary, sinful days;
And join with the triumphant saints
That sing Jehovah's praise.
My knowledge of that life is small,
The eye of faith is dim;
But 't is enough that Christ knows all,
And I shall be with him.

SIR ROGER L'ESTRANGE.

[1616-1704.]

IN PRISON.

Beat on, proud billows; Boreas, blow;
Swell, curlèd waves, high as Jove's roof;
Your incivility doth show
That innocence is tempest proof;
Though surly Nereus frown, my thoughts are calm;
Then strike, Affliction, for thy wounds are balm.

That which the world miscalls a jail
A private closet is to me;
Whilst a good conscience is my bail,
And innocence my liberty:
Locks, bars, and solitude together met,
Make me no prisoner, but an anchoret.

I, whilst I wisht to be retired,
Into this private room was turned;
As if their wisdoms had conspired
The salamander should be burned;
Or like those sophists, that would drown a fish,
I am constrained to suffer what I wish.

The cynic loves his poverty;
The pelican her wilderness;
And 't is the Indian's pride to be
Naked on frozen Caucasus:

Contentment cannot smart; stoics we see
Make torments easier to their apathy.

These manacles upon my arm
I as my mistress' favors wear;
And for to keep my ankles warm
I have some iron shackles there:
These walls are but my garrison; this cell,
Which men call jail, doth prove my citadel.

I 'm in the cabinet lockt up,
Like some high-prizèd margarite,
Or, like the Great Mogul or Pope,
Am cloistered up from public sight:
Retiredness is a piece of majesty,
And thus, proud sultan, I 'm as great as thee.

Here sin for want of food must starve,
Where tempting objects are not seen;
And these strong walls do only serve
To keep vice out, and keep me in:
Malice of late 's grown charitable sure;
I 'm not committed, but am kept secure.

So he that struck at Jason's life,
Thinking t' have made his purpose sure,
By a malicious friendly knife
Did only wound him to a cure.
Malice, I see, wants wit; for what is meant
Mischief, ofttimes proves favor by the event.

Have you not seen the nightingale,
A prisoner like, coopt in a cage,
How doth she chant her wonted tale,
In that her narrow hermitage?
Even then her charming melody doth prove
That all her bars are trees, her cage a grove.

I am that bird, whom they combine
Thus to deprive of liberty;
But though they do my corps confine,
Yet maugre hate, my soul is free:
And though immured, yet can I chirp, and sing
Disgrace to rebels, glory to my king.

My soul is free as ambient air,
Although my baser part 's immured,
Whilst loyal thoughts do still repair
T' accompany my solitude:
Although rebellion do my body bind,
My king alone can captivate my mind.

EDMUND WALLER.

[1605-1687.]

OLD AGE AND DEATH.

The seas are quiet when the winds give o'er;
So calm are we when passions are no more.
For then we know how vain it was to boast
Of fleeting things, too certain to be lost.

Clouds of affection from our younger eyes
Conceal that emptiness which age descries.
The soul's dark cottage, battered and decayed,
Lets in new light through chinks that time has made.

Stronger by weakness, wiser men become,
As they draw near to their eternal home.
Leaving the old, both worlds at once they view,
That stand upon the threshold of the new.

ABRAHAM COWLEY.

[1618-1667.]

OF MYSELF.

This only grant me, that my means may lie
Too low for envy, for contempt too high.
Some honor I would have,
Not from great deeds, but good alone;
The unknown are better than ill known:
Rumor can ope the grave.
Acquaintance I would have, but when 't depends
Not on the number, but the choice, of friends.

Books should, not business, entertain the light,
And sleep, as undisturbed as death, the night.
My house a cottage more
Than palace ; and should fitting be
For all my use, no luxury.
My garden painted o'er
With Nature's hand, not Art's; and pleasures yield,
Horace might envy in his Sabine field.

Thus would I double my life's fading space;
For he that runs it well twice runs his race.
And in this true delight,
These unbought sports, this happy state,
I would not fear, nor wish, my fate;
But boldly say each night,
To-morrow let my sun his beams display,
Or in clouds hide them; I have lived to-day.

LIBERTY.

WHERE honor or where conscience does not bind,
No other law shall shackle me;
Slave to myself I will not be:
Nor shall my future actions be confined
By my own present mind.
Who by resolves and vows engaged does stand
For days that yet belong to Fate,
Does, like an unthrift, mortgage his estate
Before it falls into his hand.
The bondman of the cloister so
All that he does receive does always owe;
And still as time comes in, it goes away,
Not to enjoy, but debts to pay.
Unhappy slave ! and pupil to a bell!
Which his hour's work, as well as hours, does tell!
Unhappy to the last, the kind releasing knell.

FROM DRYDEN TO BURNS.

FROM DRYDEN TO BURNS.

JOHN DRYDEN.

[1631 – 1701.]

SONG FOR SAINT CECILIA'S DAY, 1687.

FROM harmony, from heavenly harmony,
This universal frame began:
When Nature underneath a heap
Of jarring atoms lay,
And could not heave her head,
The tuneful voice was heard from high,
Arise, ye more than dead!
Then cold, and hot, and moist, and dry
In order to their stations leap,
And music's power obey.
From harmony, from heavenly harmony,
This universal frame began:
From harmony to harmony
Through all the compass of the notes it ran,
The diapason closing full in man.

What passion cannot music raise and quell?
When Jubal struck the chorded shell
His listening brethren stood around,
And, wondering, on their faces fell
To worship that celestial sound.
Less than a God they thought there could not dwell
Within the hollow of that shell
That spoke so sweetly and so well.
What passion cannot music raise and quell?

The trumpet's loud clangor
Excites us to arms,
With shrill notes of anger
And mortal alarms.
The double double double beat
Of the thundering drum
Cries, "Hark! the foes come;
Charge, charge, 't is too late to retreat!"

The soft complaining flute
In dying notes discovers
The woes of hopeless lovers,
Whose dirge is whispered by the warbling lute.

Sharp violins proclaim
Their jealous pangs and desperation,
Fury, frantic indignation,
Depth of pains, and height of passion,
For the fair, disdainful dame.

But O, what art can teach,
What human voice can reach,
The sacred organ's praise?
Notes inspiring holy love,
Notes that wing their heavenly ways
To mend the choirs above.

Orpheus could lead the savage race,
And trees uprooted left their place,
Sequacious of the lyre:
But bright Cecilia raised the wonder higher;
When to her organ vocal breath was given,
An angel heard, and straight appeared, —
Mistaking earth for heaven!

GRAND CHORUS.

As from the power of sacred lays
The spheres began to move,
And sung the great Creator's praise
To all the blest above;
So when the last and dreadful hour
This crumbling pageant shall devour,
The trumpet shall be heard on high,
The dead shall live, the living die,
And music shall untune the sky.

UNDER MILTON'S PICTURE.

THREE Poets, in three distant ages born,
Greece, Italy, and England did adorn.
The first in loftiness of thought surpassed;
The next in majesty; in both the last.
The force of Nature could no further go;
To make a third, she joined the former two.

CHARACTER OF A GOOD PARSON.

A PARISH priest was of the pilgrim train;
An awful, reverend, and religious man.
His eyes diffused a venerable grace,
And charity itself was in his face.
Rich was his soul, though his attire was poor
(As God hath clothed his own ambassador);
For such, on earth, his blessed Redeemer bore.
Of sixty years he seemed; and well might last
To sixty more, but that he lived too fast,
Refined himself to soul, to curb the sense,
And made almost a sin of abstinence.
Yet had his aspect nothing of severe,
But such a face as promised him sincere.
Nothing reserved or sullen was to see;
But sweet regards, and pleasing sanctity.
Mild was his accent, and his action free.
With eloquence innate his tongue was armed;
Though harsh the precept, yet the people charmed.
For, letting down the golden chain from high,
He drew his audience upward to the sky:
And oft with holy hymns he charmed their ears
(A music more melodious than the spheres);
For David left him, when he went to rest,
His lyre; and after him he sung the best.
He bore his great commission in his look;
But sweetly tempered awe, and softened all he spoke.
He preached the joys of heaven and pains of hell,
And warned the sinner with becoming zeal;
But on eternal mercy loved to dwell.
He taught the gospel rather than the law;
And forced himself to drive; but loved to draw.
For fear but freezes minds; but love, like heat,
Exhales the soul sublime, to seek her native seat.
To threats the stubborn sinner oft is hard,
Wrapped in his crimes, against the storm prepared;
But when the milder beams of mercy play,
He melts, and throws his cumbrous cloak away.
Lightning and thunder (heaven's artillery)
As harbingers before the Almighty fly:
Those but proclaim his style, and disappear;
The stiller sounds succeed, and God is there.

REASON.

DIM as the borrowed beams of moon and stars
To lonely, weary, wandering travellers,
Is reason to the soul: and as on high,
Those rolling fires discover but the sky,
Not light us here; so reason's glimmering ray
Was lent, not to assure our doubtful way,
But guide us upward to a better day.
And as those nightly tapers disappear
When day's bright lord ascends our hemisphere;
So pale grows reason at religion's sight.—
So dies, and so dissolves in supernatural light.

THOMAS KEN.

[1637–1711.]

MORNING HYMN.

AWAKE, my soul, and with the sun
Thy daily course of duty run;
Shake off dull sloth, and joyful rise
To pay thy morning sacrifice.

Wake, and lift up thyself, my heart,
And with the angels bear thy part,

Who all night long unwearied sing
High praises to the eternal King.

All praise to Thee, who safe hast kept,
And hast refreshed me whilst I slept;
Grant, Lord, when I from death shall wake,
I may of endless light partake.

Lord, I my vows to thee renew;
Disperse my sins as morning dew;
Guard my first springs of thought and will,
And with thyself my spirit fill.

Direct, control, suggest, this day,
All I design, or do, or say;
That all my powers, with all their might,
In thy sole glory may unite.

Praise God, from whom all blessings flow;
Praise him, all creatures here below;
Praise him above, ye heavenly host;
Praise Father, Son, and Holy Ghost.

JOSEPH ADDISON.

[1672–1719.]

HYMN.

How are thy servants blest, O Lord!
How sure is their defence!
Eternal Wisdom is their guide,
Their help Omnipotence.

In foreign realms and lands remote,
Supported by thy care,
Through burning climes I passed unhurt,
And breathed in tainted air.

Thy mercy sweetened every toil,
Made every region please;
The hoary Alpine hills it warmed,
And smoothed the Tyrrhene seas.

Think, O my soul, devoutly think,
How, with affrighted eyes,
Thou saw'st the wide extended deep
In all its horrors rise.

Confusion dwelt in every face,
And fear in every heart;
When waves on waves, and gulfs on gulfs,
O'ercame the pilot's art.

Yet then from all my griefs, O Lord,
Thy mercy set me free,
Whilst in the confidence of prayer,
My faith took hold on thee.

For, though in dreadful whirls we hung,
High on the broken wave,
I knew thou wert not slow to hear,
Nor impotent to save.

The storm was laid, the winds retired
Obedient to thy will;
The sea, that roared at thy command,
At thy command was still.

In midst of dangers, fears, and death,
Thy goodness I'll adore,
And praise thee for thy mercies past,
And humbly hope for more.

My life, if thou preserv'st my life,
Thy sacrifice shall be;
And death, if death must be my doom,
Shall join my soul to thee.

PARAPHRASE OF PSALM XXIII.

THE Lord my pasture shall prepare,
And feed me with a shepherd's care;
His presence shall my wants supply,
And guard me with a watchful eye;
My noonday walks he shall attend,
And all my midnight hours defend.

When in the sultry glebe I faint,
Or on the thirsty mountain pant,
To fertile vales and dewy meads
My weary, wandering steps he leads,
Where peaceful rivers, soft and slow,
Amid the verdant landscape flow.

Though in the paths of death I tread,
With gloomy horrors overspread,
My steadfast heart shall fear no ill;
For thou, O Lord, art with me still:
Thy friendly crook shall give me aid,
And guide me through the dreadful shade.

Though in a bare and rugged way,
Through devious lonely wilds I stray,
Thy bounty shall my wants beguile,
The barren wilderness shall smile,
With sudden greens and herbage crowned,
And streams shall murmur all around.

ALEXANDER POPE.

[1688 - 1744.]

THE UNIVERSAL PRAYER.

FATHER of all! in every age,
  In every clime adored,
By saint, by savage, and by sage,
  Jehovah, Jove, or Lord!

Thou great First Cause, least understood,
  Who all my sense confined
To know but this, that thou art good,
  And that myself am blind;

Yet gave me, in this dark estate,
  To see the good from ill;
And, binding nature fast in fate,
  Left free the human will.

What conscience dictates to be done,
  Or warns me not to do,
This teach me more than hell to shun,
  That more than heaven pursue.

What blessings thy free bounty gives
  Let me not cast away;
For God is paid when man receives:
  To enjoy is to obey.

Yet not to earth's contracted span
  Thy goodness let me bound,
Or think thee Lord alone of man,
  When thousand worlds are round.

Let not this weak, unknowing hand
  Presume thy bolts to throw,
And deal damnation round the land
  On each I judge thy foe.

If I am right, thy grace impart
  Still in the right to stay;
If I am wrong, O, teach my heart
  To find that better way!

Save me alike from foolish pride,
  Or impious discontent,
At aught thy wisdom has denied,
  Or aught thy goodness lent.

Teach me to feel another's woe,
  To hide the fault I see;
That mercy I to others show,
  That mercy show to me.

Mean though I am, not wholly so,
  Since quickened by thy breath;
O, lead me wheresoe'er I go,
  Through this day's life or death.

This day be bread and peace my lot;
  All else beneath the sun
Thou know'st if best bestowed or not,
  And let thy will be done!

To thee, whose temple is all space, —
  Whose altar, earth, sea, skies, —
One chorus let all beings raise!
  All Nature's incense rise!

HAPPINESS.

O HAPPINESS! our being's end and aim!
Good, pleasure, ease, content! whate'er thy name;
That something still, which prompts the eternal sigh;
For which we bear to live or dare to die;
Which still so near us, yet beyond us lies,
O'erlooked, seen double by the fool, and wise.
Plant of celestial seed! if dropped below,
Say, in what mortal soil thou deign'st to grow?
Fair opening to some court's propitious shrine,
Or deep with diamonds in the flaming mine?
Twined with the wreaths Parnassian laurels yield,
Or reaped in iron harvests of the field?
Where grows? — where grows it not? If vain our toil,
We ought to blame the culture, not the soil:
Fixed to no spot is happiness sincere,
'T is nowhere to be found, or everywhere.
  Ask of the learned the way, the learned are blind;
This bids to serve, and that to shun mankind:
Some place the bliss in action, some in ease;
Those call it pleasure, and contentment these:
Some, sunk to beasts, find pleasure end in pain;
Some, swelled to gods, confess e'en virtue vain:
Or indolent, to each extreme they fall, —

To trust in everything, or doubt of all.
Who thus define it, say they more or less
Than this, that happiness is happiness?
Take nature's path, and mad opinion's leave;
All states can reach it, and all heads conceive;
Obvious her goods, in no extremes they dwell;
There needs but thinking right and meaning well;
And mourn our various portions as we please,
Equal is common sense and common ease.
Remember, man, "The Universal Cause
Acts not by partial, but by general laws";
And makes what happiness we justly call
Subsist not in the good of one, but all.
There 's not a blessing individuals find,
But some way leans and hearkens to the kind;
No bandit fierce, no tyrant mad with pride,
No caverned hermit rests self-satisfied:
Who most to shun or hate mankind pretend,
Seek an admirer, or would fix a friend:
Abstract what others feel, what others think,
All pleasures sicken, and all glories sink:
Each has his share; and who would more obtain
Shall find the pleasure pays not half the pain.
Order is Heaven's first law; and, this confessed,
Some are, and must be, greater than the rest,
More rich, more wise: but who infers from hence
That such are happier shocks all common-sense.
Heaven to mankind impartial we confess,
If all are equal in their happiness:
But mutual wants this happiness increase;
All nature's difference keeps all nature's peace.
Condition, circumstance, is not the thing;
Bliss is the same in subject or in king,
In who obtain defence or who defend,
In him who is or him who finds a friend;
Heaven breathes through every member of the whole
One common blessing, as one common soul.
But fortune's gifts if each alike possessed,
And all were equal, must not all contest?
If then to all men happiness was meant,
God in externals could not place content.
Fortune her gifts may variously dispose,
And these be happy called, unhappy those;
But Heaven's just balance equal will appear,
While those are placed in hope, and these in fear;
Not present good or ill, the joy or curse,
But future views of better or of worse.
O sons of earth, attempt ye still to rise,
By mountains piled on mountains, to the skies?
Heaven still with laughter the vain toil surveys,
And buries madmen in the heaps they raise.
Know, all the good that individuals find,
Or God and nature meant to mere mankind,
Reason's whole pleasure, all the joys of sense,
Lie in three words, health, peace, and competence.

ALLAN RAMSAY.

[1685-1758.]

SONG.

Farewell to Lochaber, farewell to my Jean,
Where heartsome with thee I have mony a day been:
To Lochaber no more, to Lochaber no more,
We 'll maybe return to Lochaber no more.
These tears that I shed they are a' for my dear,
And not for the dangers attending on weir;
Though borne on rough seas to a far bloody shore,
Maybe to return to Lochaber no more!

Though hurricanes rise, and rise every wind,
No tempest can equal the storm in my mind;
Though loudest of thunders on louder waves roar,
That 's naething like leaving my love on the shore.
To leave thee behind me my heart is sair pained,
But by ease that 's inglorious no fame can be gained:
And beauty and love 's the reward of the brave;
And I maun deserve it before I can crave.

Then glory, my Jeany, maun plead my excuse;
Since honor commands me, how can I refuse?
Without it I ne'er can have merit for thee,
And losing thy favor I 'd better not be.
I gae then, my lass, to win honor and fame,
And if I should chance to come glorious hame,
I 'll bring a heart to thee with love running o'er,
And then I 'll leave thee and Lochaber no more.

JOHN GAY.

[1688 – 1732.]

THE PAINTER WHO PLEASED NOBODY AND EVERYBODY.

Lest men suspect your tale untrue,
Keep probability in view.
The traveller, leaping o'er those bounds,
The credit of his book confounds.
Who with his tongue hath armies routed
Makes even his real courage doubted:
But flattery never seems absurd;
The flattered always takes your word:
Impossibilities seem just;
They take the strongest praise on trust.
Hyperboles, though ne'er so great,
Will still come short of self-conceit.
So very like a painter drew,
That every eye the picture knew;
He hit complexion, feature, air,
So just, the life itself was there.
No flattery with his colors laid,
To bloom restored the faded maid;
He gave each muscle all its strength,
The mouth, the chin, the nose's length.
His honest pencil touched with truth,
And marked the date of age and youth.
He lost his friends, his practice failed;
Truth should not always be revealed;
In dusty piles his pictures lay,
For no one sent the second pay.
Two bustos, fraught with every grace,
A Venus' and Apollo's face,
He placed in view; resolved to please,
Whoever sat, he drew from these,
From these corrected every feature,
And spirited each awkward creature.
All things were set; the hour was come,
His pallet ready o'er his thumb.
My lord appeared; and seated right
In proper attitude and light,
The painter looked, he sketched the piece,
Then dipped his pencil, talked of Greece,
Of Titian's tints, of Guido's air;
"Those eyes, my lord, the spirit there
Might well a Raphael's hand require,
To give them all their native fire;
The features fraught with sense and wit,
You 'll grant are very hard to hit;
But yet with patience you shall view
As much as paint and art can do.
Observe the work." My lord replied:
"Till now I thought my mouth was wide;
Besides, my nose is somewhat long;
Dear sir, for me, 't is far too young."
"Oh! pardon me," the artist cried,
"In this the painters must decide.
The piece even common eyes must strike,
I warrant it extremely like."
My lord examined it anew;
No looking-glass seemed half so true.
A lady came; with borrowed grace
He from his Venus formed her face.
Her lover praised the painter's art;
So like the picture in his heart!
To every age some charm he lent;
Even beauties were almost content.
Through all the town his art they praised;
His custom grew, his price was raised.
Had he the real likeness shown,
Would any man the picture own?
But when thus happily he wrought,
Each found the likeness in his thought.

JOHN BYROM.

[1691 - 1763.]

CARELESS CONTENT.

I AM content, I do not care,
  Wag as it will the world for me;
When fuss and fret was all my fare,
  It got no ground as I could see:
So when away my caring went,
I counted cost, and was content.

With more of thanks and less of thought,
  I strive to make my matters meet;
To seek what ancient sages sought,
  Physic and food in sour and sweet:
To take what passes in good part,
And keep the hiccups from the heart.

With good and gentle-humored hearts,
  I choose to chat where'er I come,
Whate'er the subject be that starts;
  But if I get among the glum,
I hold my tongue to tell the truth,
And keep my breath to cool my broth.

For chance or change of peace or pain,
  For Fortune's favor or her frown,
For lack or glut, for loss or gain,
  I never dodge nor up nor down;
But swing what way the ship shall swim,
Or tack about with equal trim.

I suit not where I shall not speed,
  Nor trace the turn of every tide;
If simple sense will not succeed,
  I make no bustling, but abide;
For shining wealth or scaring woe,
I force no friend, I fear no foe.

Of ups and downs, of ins and outs,
  Of they 're i' the wrong, and we 're i' the right,
I shun the rancors and the routs;
  And wishing well to every wight,
Whatever turn the matter takes,
I deem it all but ducks and drakes.

With whom I feast I do not fawn,
  Nor if the folks should flout me, faint;
If wonted welcome be withdrawn,
  I cook no kind of a complaint:
With none disposed to disagree,
But like them best who best like me.

Not that I rate myself the rule
  How all my betters should behave;
But fame shall find me no man's fool,
  Nor to a set of men a slave:
I love a friendship free and frank,
And hate to hang upon a hank.

Fond of a true and trusty tie,
  I never loose where'er I link;
Though if a business budges by,
  I talk thereon just as I think;
My word, my work, my heart, my hand,
Still on a side together stand.

If names or notions make a noise,
  Whatever hap the question hath,
The point impartially I poise,
  And read or write, but without wrath;
For should I burn, or break my brains,
Pray, who will pay me for my pains?

I love my neighbor as myself,
  Myself like him too, by his leave;
Nor to his pleasure, power, or pelf
  Came I to crouch, as I conceive:
Dame Nature doubtless has designed
A man the monarch of his mind.

Now taste and try this temper, sirs;
  Mood it and brood it in your breast;
Or if ye ween, for worldly stirs,
  That man does right to mar his rest,
Let me be deft, and debonair,
I am content, I do not care.

JAMES THOMSON.

[1700 - 1748.]

FROM THE "CASTLE OF INDOLENCE."

  IN lowly dale, fast by a river's side,
  With woody hill o'er hill encompassed round,
  A most enchanting wizard did abide,
  Than whom a friend more fell is nowhere found.
  It was, I ween, a lovely spot of ground:
  And there a season atween June and May,
  Half pranked with spring, with summer half imbrowned,
  A listless climate made, where, sooth to say,
No living wight could work, nor caréd even for play.

Was naught around but images of rest:
Sleep-soothing groves, and quiet lawns between;
And flowery beds that slumberous influence kest,
From poppies breathed; and beds of pleasant green,
Where never yet was creeping creature seen.
Meantime unnumbered glittering streamlets played,
And hurléd everywhere their waters sheen;
That, as they bickered through the sunny glade,
Though restless still themselves, a lulling murmur made.

Joined to the prattle of the purling rills,
Were heard the lowing herds along the vale,
And flocks loud bleating from the distant hills,
And vacant shepherds piping in the dale;
And now and then sweet Philomel would wail,
Or stock-doves plain amid the forest deep,
That drowsy rustled to the sighing gale;
And still a coil the grasshopper did keep;
Yet all these sounds yblent inclinéd all to sleep.

Full in the passage of the vale above,
A sable, silent, solemn forest stood,
Where naught but shadowy forms was seen to move,
As Idlesse fancied in her dreamy mood:
And up the hills, on either side, a wood
Of blackening pines, aye waving to and fro,
Sent forth a sleepy horror through the blood;
And where this valley winded out below,
The murmuring main was heard, and scarcely heard, to flow.

A pleasing land of drowsy-head it was,
Of dreams that wave before the half-shut eye:
And of gay castles in the clouds that pass,
Forever flushing round a summer sky:
There eke the soft delights, that witchingly
Instil a wanton sweetness through the breast,
And the calm pleasures, always hovered nigh;
But whate'er smacked of noyance or unrest
Was far, far off expelled from this delicious nest.

A HYMN.

THESE, as they change, Almighty Father, these
Are but the varied God. The rolling year
Is full of thee. Forth in the pleasing spring
Thy beauty walks, thy tenderness and love.
Wide flush the fields; the softening air is balm;
Echo the mountains round; the forest smiles;
And every sense, and every heart, is joy.
Then comes thy glory in the summer months,
With light and heat refulgent. Then thy sun
Shoots full perfection through the swelling year;
And oft thy voice in dreadful thunder speaks,
And oft at dawn, deep noon, or falling eve,
By brooks and groves, in hollow-whispering gales.
Thy bounty shines in autumn unconfined,
And spreads a common feast for all that lives.
In winter awful thou! with clouds and storms
Around thee thrown, tempest o'er tempest rolled,
Majestic darkness! On the whirlwind's wing,
Riding sublime, thou bid'st the world adore,
And humblest nature with thy northern blast.

Mysterious round! what skill, what force divine,
Deep felt, in these appear! a simple train,
Yet so delightful mixed, with such kind art,
Such beauty and beneficence combined;
Shade, unperceived, so softening into shade;
And all so forming an harmonious whole;
That, as they still succeed, they ravish still.
But wandering oft, with brute unconscious gaze,
Man marks not thee, marks not the mighty hand,
That, ever busy, wheels the silent spheres;
Works in the secret deep; shoots, steaming, thence
The fair profusion that o'erspreads the spring;
Flings from the sun direct the flaming day;
Feeds every creature; hurls the tempests forth;
And, as on earth this grateful change revolves,
With transport touches all the springs of life.
Nature, attend! join every living soul,
Beneath the spacious temple of the sky,
In adoration join; and, ardent, raise
One general song! To him, ye vocal gales,
Breathe soft, whose spirit in your freshness breathes:
O, talk of him in solitary glooms;
Where, o'er the rock, the scarcely waving pine
Fills the brown shade with a religious awe!
And ye, whose bolder note is heard afar,
Who shake the astonished world, lift high to heaven
The impetuous song, and say from whom you rage.
His praise, ye brooks, attune, ye trembling rills;
And let me catch it as I muse along.
Ye headlong torrents, rapid and profound;
Ye softer floods, that lead the humid maze
Along the vale; and thou, majestic main,
A secret world of wonders in thyself,
Sound his stupendous praise, whose greater voice
Or bids you roar, or bids your roarings fall.
Soft roll your incense, herbs, and fruits, and flowers,
In mingled clouds to him, whose sun exalts,
Whose breath perfumes you, and whose pencil paints.
Ye forests bend, ye harvests wave, to him;
Breathe your still song into the reaper's heart,
As home he goes beneath the joyous moon.
Ye that keep watch in heaven, as earth asleep
Unconscious lies, effuse your mildest beams,
Ye constellations, while your angels strike,
Amid the spangled sky, the silver lyre.
Great source of day! best image here below
Of thy Creator, ever pouring wide,
From world to world, the vital ocean round,
On Nature write with every beam his praise.
The thunder rolls: be hushed the prostrate world;
While cloud to cloud returns the solemn hymn.
Bleat out afresh, ye hills; ye mossy rocks,
Retain the sound; the broad responsive low,
Ye valleys, raise; for the great Shepherd reigns,
And his unsuffering kingdom yet will come.
Ye woodlands all, awake: a boundless song
Burst from the groves; and when the restless day,
Expiring, lays the warbling world asleep,
Sweetest of birds! sweet Philomela, charm
The listening shades, and teach the night his praise.
Ye chief, for whom the whole creation smiles,
At once the head, the heart, and tongue of all,
Crown the great hymn! in swarming cities vast,
Assembled men to the deep organ join

The long-resounding voice, oft breaking clear,
At solemn pauses, through the swelling bass;
And, as each mingling flame increases each,
In one united ardor rise to heaven.
Or if you rather choose the rural shade,
And find a fane in every sacred grove,
There let the shepherd's flute, the virgin's lay,
The prompting seraph, and the poet's lyre,
Still sing the God of seasons, as they roll.
For me, when I forget the darling theme,
Whether the blossom blows, the summer ray
Russets the plain, inspiring autumn gleams,
Or winter rises in the blackening east,
Be my tongue mute, my fancy paint no more,
And, dead to joy, forget my heart to beat!
Should fate command me to the farthest verge
Of the green earth, to distant barbarous climes,
Rivers unknown to song, — where first the sun
Gilds Indian mountains, or his setting beam
Flames on the Atlantic isles, — 't is naught to me:
Since God is ever present, ever felt,
In the void waste, as in the city full;
And where he vital breathes, there must be joy.
When even at last the solemn hour shall come,
And wing my mystic flight to future worlds,
I cheerful will obey; there, with new powers,
Will rising wonders sing: I cannot go
Where Universal Love not smiles around,
Sustaining all yon orbs, and all their suns;
From seeming evil still educing good,
And better thence again, and better still,
In infinite progression. But I lose
Myself in him, in light ineffable!
Come then, expressive Silence, muse his praise.

JOHN DYER.

[1700 - 1758.]

GRONGAR HILL.

Silent nymph, with curious eye!
Who, the purple eve, dost lie
On the mountain's lonely van,
Beyond the noise of busy man,
Painting fair the form of things,
While the yellow linnet sings,
Or the tuneful nightingale
Charms the forest with her tale, —
Come, with all thy various hues,
Come and aid thy sister Muse.
Now, while Phœbus, riding high,
Gives lustre to the land and sky,
Grongar Hill invites my song, —
Draw the landscape bright and strong;
Grongar, in whose mossy cells
Sweetly musing Quiet dwells;
Grongar, in whose silent shade,
For the modest Muses made,
So oft I have, the evening still,
At the fountain of a rill,
Sat upon a flowery bed,
With my hand beneath my head,
While strayed my eyes o'er Towy's flood,
Over mead and over wood,
From house to house, from hill to hill,
Till Contemplation had her fill.
About his checkered sides I wind,
And leave his brooks and meads behind,
And groves and grottos where I lay,
And vistas shooting beams of day.
Wide and wider spreads the vale,
As circles on a smooth canal.
The mountains round, unhappy fate!
Sooner or later, of all height,
Withdraw their summits from the skies,
And lessen as the others rise.
Still the prospect wider spreads,
Adds a thousand woods and meads;
Still it widens, widens still,
And sinks the newly risen hill.
Now I gain the mountain's brow;
What a landscape lies below!
No clouds, no vapors intervene;
But the gay, the open scene
Does the face of Nature show,
In all the hues of heaven's bow!
And, swelling to embrace the light,
Spreads around beneath the sight.
Old castles on the cliffs arise,

Proudly towering in the skies;
Rushing from the woods, the spires
Seem from hence ascending fires;
Half his beams Apollo sheds
On the yellow mountain-heads,
Gilds the fleeces of the flocks,
And glitters on the broken rocks.
Below me trees unnumbered rise,
Beautiful in various dyes:
The gloomy pine, the poplar blue,
The yellow beech, the sable yew,
The slender fir that taper grows,
The sturdy oak with broad-spread boughs;
And beyond the purple grove,
Haunt of Phyllis, queen of love!
Gaudy as the opening dawn,
Lies a long and level lawn,
On which a dark hill, steep and high,
Holds and charms the wandering eye.
Deep are his feet in Towy's flood:
His sides are clothed with waving wood,
And ancient towers crown his brow,
That cast an awful look below;
Whose ragged walls the ivy creeps,
And with her arms from falling keeps;
So both a safety from the wind
In mutual dependence find.
'T is now the raven's bleak abode;
'T is now the apartment of the toad;
And there the fox securely feeds;
And there the poisonous adder breeds,
Concealed in ruins, moss, and weeds;
While, ever and anon, there fall
Huge heaps of hoary mouldered wall.
Yet Time has seen, — that lifts the low
And level lays the lofty brow, —
Has seen this broken pile complete,
Big with the vanity of state.
But transient is the smile of Fate!
A little rule, a little sway,
A sunbeam in a winter's day,
Is all the proud and mighty have
Between the cradle and the grave.
And see the rivers how they run,
Through woods and meads, in shade and sun,
Sometimes swift, sometimes slow, —
Wave succeeding wave, they go
A various journey to the deep,
Like human life to endless sleep!
Thus is Nature's vesture wrought,
To instruct our wandering thought:
Thus she dresses green and gay,
To disperse our cares away.
Ever charming, ever new,
When will the landscape tire the view!
The fountain's fall, the river's flow;
The woody valleys, warm and low;
The windy summit, wild and high,
Roughly rushing on the sky;
The pleasant seat, the ruined tower,
The naked rock, the shady bower;
The town and village, dome and farm, —
Each gives each a double charm,
As pearls upon an Ethiop's arm.
See on the mountain's southern side,
Where the prospect opens wide,
Where the evening gilds the tide;
How close and small the hedges lie!
What streaks of meadow cross the eye!
A step methinks may pass the stream,
So little distant dangers seem;
So we mistake the Future's face,
Eyed through Hope's deluding glass;
As yon summits, soft and fair,
Clad in colors of the air,
Which to those who journey near,
Barren, brown, and rough appear;
Still we tread the same coarse way,
The present 's still a cloudy day.
O, may I with myself agree,
And never covet what I see;
Content me with an humble shade,
My passions tamed, my wishes laid;
For while our wishes wildly roll,
We banish quiet from the soul:
'T is thus the busy beat the air,
And misers gather wealth and care.
Now, even now, my joys run high,
As on the mountain-turf I lie;
While the wanton Zephyr sings,
And in the vale perfumes his wings;
While the waters murmur deep;
While the shepherd charms his sheep;
While the birds unbounded fly,
And with music fill the sky,
Now, even now, my joys run high.
Be full, ye courts; be great who will;
Search for Peace with all your skill:
Open wide the lofty door,
Seek her on the marble floor.
In vain you search; she is not there!
In vain you search the domes of Care!
Grass and flowers Quiet treads,
On the meads and mountain-heads,
Along with Pleasure, close allied,
Ever by each other's side;
And often, by the murmuring rill,
Hears the thrush, while all is still
Within the groves of Grongar Hill.

WILLIAM HAMILTON.

[1704–1754.]

THE BRAES OF YARROW.

Busk ye, busk ye, my bonny bonny bride,
Busk ye, busk ye, my winsome marrow!
Busk ye, busk ye, my bonny bonny bride,
And think nae mair on the Braes of Yarrow.

"Where gat ye that bonny bonny bride?
Where gat ye that winsome marrow?"
I gat her where I darena weil be seen,
Pu'ing the birks on the Braes of Yarrow.

Weep not, weep not, my bonny bonny bride,
Weep not, weep not, my winsome marrow!
Nor let thy heart lament to leave
Pu'ing the birks on the Braes of Yarrow.

"Why does she weep, thy bonny bonny bride?
Why does she weep, thy winsome marrow?
And why dare ye nae mair weil be seen,
Pu'ing the birks on the Braes of Yarrow?"

Lang maun she weep, lang maun she, maun she weep,
Lang maun she weep with dule and sorrow,
And lang maun I nae mair weil be seen,
Pu'ing the birks on the Braes of Yarrow.

For she has tint her lover lover dear,
Her lover dear, the cause of sorrow,
And I hae slain the comeliest swain
That e'er pu'ed birks on the Braes of Yarrow.

Why runs thy stream, O Yarrow, Yarrow, red?
Why on thy braes heard the voice of sorrow?
And why yon melancholious weeds
Hung on the bonny birks of Yarrow?

What's yonder floats on the rueful rueful flude?
What's yonder floats? O dule and sorrow!
'T is he, the comely swain I slew
Upon the duleful Braes of Yarrow.

Wash, O, wash his wounds, his wounds in tears,
His wounds in tears with dule and sorrow,
And wrap his limbs in mourning weeds,
And lay him on the Braes of Yarrow.

Then build, then build, ye sisters sisters sad,
Ye sisters sad, his tomb with sorrow,
And weep around in waeful wise,
His helpless fate on the Braes of Yarrow.

Curse ye, curse ye his useless useless shield,
My arm that wrought the deed of sorrow,
The fatal spear that pierced his breast,
His comely breast, on the Braes of Yarrow.

Did I not warn thee not to lo'e,
And warn from fight, but to my sorrow;
O'er rashly bauld a stronger arm
Thou met'st, and fell on the Braes of Yarrow.

Sweet smells the birk, green grows, green grows the grass,
Yellow on Yarrow bank the gowan,
Fair hangs the apple frae the rock,
Sweet the wave of Yarrow flowan.

Flows Yarrow sweet? as sweet, as sweet flows Tweed,
As green its grass, its gowan as yellow,
As sweet smells on its braes the birk,
The apple frae the rock as mellow.

Fair was thy love, fair fair indeed thy love,
In flowery bands thou him didst fetter;
Though he was fair and weil beloved again,
Than me he never lo'ed thee better.

Busk ye, then busk, my bonny bonny bride,
Busk ye, busk ye, my winsome marrow!
Busk ye, and lo'e me on the banks of Tweed,
And think nae mair on the Braes of Yarrow.

"How can I busk a bonny bonny bride,
How can I busk a winsome marrow,
How lo'e him on the banks of Tweed,
That slew my love on the Braes of Yarrow?

"O Yarrow fields! may never never rain
Nor dew thy tender blossoms cover,
For there was basely slain my love,
My love, as he had not been a lover.

"The boy put on his robes, his robes of green,
His purple vest, 't was my ain sewing;
Ah! wretched me! I little little kenned
He was in these to meet his ruin.

"The boy took out his milk-white milk-white steed,
Unheedful of my dule and sorrow,
But e'er the to-fall of the night
He lay a corpse on the Braes of Yarrow.

"Much I rejoiced that waeful waeful day;
I sang, my voice the woods returning,
But lang ere night the spear was flown
That slew my love, and left me mourning.

"What can my barbarous barbarous father do,
But with his cruel rage pursue me?
My lover's blood is on thy spear,
How canst thou, barbarous man, then woo me?

"My happy sisters may be, may be proud;
With cruel and ungentle scoffin,
May bid me seek on Yarrow Braes
My lover nailéd in his coffin.

"My brother Douglas may upbraid, upbraid,
And strive with threatening words to move me,
My lover's blood is on thy spear,
How canst thou ever bid me love thee?

"Yes, yes, prepare the bed, the bed of love,
With bridal sheets my body cover,
Unbar, ye bridal maids, the door,
Let in the expected husband lover.

"But who the expected husband husband is?
His hands, methinks, are bathed in slaughter.
Ah me! what ghastly spectre 's yon,
Comes in his pale shroud, bleeding after?

"Pale as he is, here lay him, lay him down,
O, lay his cold head on my pillow;
Take aff, take aff these bridal weeds,
And crown my careful head with willow.

"Pale though thou art, yet best, yet best beloved,
O, could my warmth to life restore thee!
Ye 'd lie all night between my breasts,
No youth lay ever there before thee.

"Pale pale, indeed, O lovely lovely youth,
Forgive, forgive so foul a slaughter,
And lie all night between my breasts,
No youth shall ever lie there after."

Return, return, O mournful mournful bride,
Return and dry thy useless sorrow:
Thy lover heeds naught of thy sighs,
He lies a corpse on the Braes of Yarrow.

ISAAC WATTS.

[1674–1748.]

THE HEAVENLY LAND.

THERE is a land of pure delight,
Where saints immortal reign;
Infinite day excludes the night,
And pleasures banish pain.

There everlasting spring abides,
And never-withering flowers;
Death, like a narrow sea, divides
This heavenly land from ours.

Sweet fields beyond the swelling flood
Stand dressed in living green;
So to the Jews old Canaan stood,
While Jordan rolled between.

But timorous mortals start and shrink
To cross this narrow sea,
And linger shivering on the brink,
And fear to launch away.

O, could we make our doubts remove,
These gloomy doubts that rise,
And see the Canaan that we love
With unbeclouded eyes, —

Could we but climb where Moses stood,
And view the landscape o'er,
Not Jordan's stream, nor death's cold flood,
Should fright us from the shore.

PHILIP DODDRIDGE.

[1702-1751.]

YE GOLDEN LAMPS OF HEAVEN, FAREWELL!

Ye golden lamps of heaven, farewell,
With all your feeble light!
Farewell, thou ever-changing moon,
Pale empress of the night!

And thou, refulgent orb of day,
In brighter flames arrayed;
My soul, that springs beyond thy sphere,
No more demands thy aid.

Ye stars are but the shining dust
Of my divine abode;
The pavement of those heavenly courts
Where I shall see my God.

There all the millions of his saints
Shall in one song unite;
And each the bliss of all shall view,
With infinite delight.

CHARLES WESLEY.

[1708-1788.]

JESUS, LOVER OF MY SOUL.

Jesus, lover of my soul,
Let me to thy bosom fly,
While the nearer waters roll,
While the tempest still is high:
Hide me, O my Saviour, hide,
Till the storm of life be past;
Safe into the haven guide,
O, receive my soul at last!

Other refuge have I none,
Hangs my helpless soul on thee;
Leave, ah! leave me not alone,
Still support and comfort me:
All my trust on thee is stayed,
All my help from thee I bring;
Cover my defenceless head
With the shadow of thy wing.

Thou, O Christ, art all I want;
More than all in thee I find:
Raise the fallen, cheer the faint,
Heal the sick, and lead the blind:
Just and holy is thy name,
I am all unrighteousness;
False and full of sin I am,
Thou art full of truth and grace.

Plenteous grace with thee is found,
Grace to cover all my sin;
Let the healing streams abound,
Make and keep me pure within:
Thou of life the fountain art;
Freely let me take of thee;
Spring thou up within my heart,
Rise to all eternity.

AUGUSTUS M. TOPLADY.

[1740-1778.]

LOVE DIVINE, ALL LOVE EXCELLING.

Love divine, all love excelling,
Joy of heaven to earth come down;
Fix in us thy humble dwelling,
All thy faithful mercies crown;
Jesus, thou art all compassion!
Pure, unbounded love thou art;
Visit us with thy salvation,
Enter every trembling heart.

Breathe, O, breathe thy loving Spirit
Into every troubled breast;
Let us all in thee inherit,
Let us find the promised rest;
Take away the love of sinning,
Alpha and Omega be;
End of faith, as its beginning,
Set our hearts at liberty.

Come, almighty to deliver,
Let us all thy life receive;
Suddenly return, and never,
Never more thy temples leave:
Thee we would be always blessing,
Serve thee as thy hosts above;
Pray and praise thee without ceasing,
Glory in thy precious love.

Finish then thy new creation,
Pure, unspotted may we be;
Let us see thy great salvation
Perfectly restored by thee:
Changed from glory into glory,
Till in heaven we take our place!
Till we cast our crowns before thee,
Lost in wonder, love, and praise.

SAMUEL JOHNSON.

[1709 - 1784.]

ON THE DEATH OF DR. LEVETT.

CONDEMNED to hope's delusive mine,
As on we toil from day to day,
By sudden blasts, or slow decline,
Our social comforts drop away.

Well tried through many a varying year,
See Levett to the grave descend,
Officious, innocent, sincere,
Of every friendless name the friend.

Yet still he fills affection's eye,
Obscurely wise and coarsely kind;
Nor, lettered arrogance, deny
Thy praise to merit unrefined.

When fainting nature called for aid,
And hovering death prepared the blow,
His vigorous remedy displayed
The power of art without the show.

In misery's darkest cavern known,
His useful care was ever nigh,
Where hopeless anguish poured his groan,
And lonely want retired to die.

No summons mocked by chill delay,
No petty gain disdained by pride;
The modest wants of every day
The toil of every day supplied.

His virtues walked their narrow round,
Nor made a pause, nor left a void;
And sure the Eternal Master found
The single talent well employed.

The busy day, the peaceful night,
Unfelt, uncounted, glided by;
His frame was firm, his powers were bright,
Though now his eightieth year was nigh.

Then with no fiery throbbing pain,
No cold gradations of decay,
Death broke at once the vital chain,
And freed his soul the nearest way.

WILLIAM SHENSTONE.

[1714 - 1763.]

THE SCHOOLMISTRESS.

HER cap, far whiter than the driven snow,
Emblem right meet of decency does yield:
Her apron dyed in grain, as blue, I trowe,
As is the harebell that adorns the field:
And in her hand, for sceptre, she does wield
Tway birchen sprays; with anxious fear entwined,
With dark distrust, and sad repentance filled;
And steadfast hate, and sharp affliction joined,
And fury uncontrolled, and chastisement unkind.

A russet stole was o'er her shoulders thrown;
A russet kirtle fenced the nipping air:
'T was simple russet, but it was her own;
'T was her own country bred the flock so fair,
'T was her own labor did the fleece prepare;
And, sooth to say, her pupils, ranged around,
Through pious awe, did term it passing rare;
For they in gaping wonderment abound,
And think, no doubt, she been the greatest wight on ground.

Albeit ne flattery did corrupt her truth,
Ne pompous title did debauch her ear;
Goody, good-woman, gossip, n' aunt forsooth,
Or dame, the sole additions she did hear;
Yet these she challenged, these she held right dear:
Ne would esteem him act as mought behove,
Who should not honored eld with these revere:

For never title yet so mean could prove,
But there was eke a mind which did that title love.

One ancient hen she took delight to feed,
The plodding pattern of the busy dame;
Which, ever and anon, impelled by need,
Into her school, begirt with chickens, came!
Such favor did her past deportment claim:
And, if Neglect had lavished on the ground
Fragment of bread, she would collect the same;
For well she knew, and quaintly could expound,
What sin it were to waste the smallest crumb she found.

Herbs too she knew, and well of each could speak
That in her garden sipped the silvery dew;
Where no vain flower disclosed a gaudy streak;
But herbs for use, and physic, not a few,
Of gray renown, within those borders grew:
The tufted basil, pun-provoking thyme,
Fresh baum, and marygold of cheerful hue;
The lowly gill, that never dares to climb;
And more I fain would sing, disdaining here to rhyme.

Yet euphrasy may not be left unsung,
That gives dim eyes to wander leagues around,
And pungent radish, biting infant's tongue,
And plantain ribbed, that heals the reaper's wound,
And marjoram sweet, in shepherd's posy found,
And lavender, whose spikes of azure bloom
Shall be, erewhile, in arid bundles bound,
To lurk amidst the labors of her loom,
And crown her kerchiefs clean with mickle rare perfume.

THOMAS GRAY.

[1716-1771.]

ELEGY WRITTEN IN A COUNTRY CHURCHYARD.

The curfew tolls the knell of parting day,
The lowing herd winds slowly o'er the lea;
The ploughman homeward plods his weary way,
And leaves the world to darkness and to me.

Now fades the glimmering landscape on the sight,
And all the air a solemn stillness holds,
Save where the beetle wheels his droning flight,
And drowsy tinklings lull the distant folds;

Save that from yonder ivy-mantled tower
The moping owl does to the moon complain
Of such as, wandering near her secret bower,
Molest her ancient solitary reign.

Beneath those rugged elms, that yew-tree's shade,
Where heaves the turf in many a mouldering heap,
Each in his narrow cell forever laid,
The rude forefathers of the hamlet sleep.

The breezy call of incense-breathing morn,
The swallow twittering from the straw-built shed,
The cock's shrill clarion, or the echoing horn,
No more shall rouse them from their lowly bed.

For them no more the blazing hearth shall burn,
Or busy housewife ply her evening care;
No children run to lisp their sire's return,
Or climb his knees the envied kiss to share.

Oft did the harvest to their sickle yield,
Their furrow oft the stubborn glebe has broke;

How jocund did they drive their team afield!
How bowed the woods beneath their sturdy stroke!

Let not Ambition mock their useful toil,
Their homely joys, and destiny obscure;
Nor Grandeur hear with a disdainful smile
The short and simple annals of the poor.

The boast of heraldry, the pomp of power,
And all that beauty, all that wealth e'er gave,
Await alike the inevitable hour;—
The paths of glory lead but to the grave.

Nor you, ye proud, impute to these the fault,
If memory o'er their tomb no trophies raise,
Where through the long-drawn aisle and fretted vault
The pealing anthem swells the note of praise.

Can storied urn or animated bust
Back to its mansion call the fleeting breath?
Can Honor's voice provoke the silent dust,
Or Flattery soothe the dull, cold ear of Death?

Perhaps in this neglected spot is laid
Some heart once pregnant with celestial fire;
Hands that the rod of empire might have swayed,
Or waked to ecstasy the living lyre:

But Knowledge to their eyes her ample page,
Rich with the spoils of time, did ne'er unroll;
Chill Penury repressed their noble rage,
And froze the genial current of the soul.

Full many a gem of purest ray serene
The dark, unfathomed caves of ocean bear;
Full many a flower is born to blush unseen,
And waste its sweetness on the desert air.

Some village Hampden, that with dauntless breast
The little tyrant of his fields withstood;
Some mute, inglorious Milton here may rest;
Some Cromwell, guiltless of his country's blood.

The applause of listening senates to command,
The threats of pain and ruin to despise,
To scatter plenty o'er a smiling land,
And read their history in a nation's eyes,

Their lot forbade: nor circumscribed alone
Their growing virtues, but their crimes confined;
Forbade to wade through slaughter to a throne,
And shut the gates of mercy on mankind;

The struggling pangs of conscious truth to hide,
To quench the blushes of ingenuous shame,
Or heap the shrine of luxury and pride
With incense kindled at the Muse's flame.

Far from the madding crowd's ignoble strife
Their sober wishes never learned to stray;
Along the cool, sequestered vale of life
They kept the noiseless tenor of their way.

Yet even these bones from insult to protect,
Some frail memorial still erected nigh,
With uncouth rhymes and shapeless sculpture decked,
Implores the passing tribute of a sigh.

Their name, their years, spelt by the unlettered Muse,
The place of fame and elegy supply;
And many a holy text around she strews,
That teach the rustic moralist to die.

For who, to dumb forgetfulness a prey,
This pleasing, anxious being e'er resigned,
Left the warm precincts of the cheerful day,
Nor cast one longing, lingering look behind?

On some fond breast the parting soul relies,
Some pious drops the closing eye requires;

E'en from the tomb the voice of Nature cries,
E'en in our ashes live their wonted fires.

For thee, who, mindful of the unhonored dead,
Dost in these lines their artless tale relate;
If chance, by lonely contemplation led,
Some kindred spirit shall inquire thy fate,

Haply some hoary-headed swain may say:
"Oft have we seen him at the peep of dawn,
Brushing with hasty steps the dews away,
To meet the sun upon the upland lawn;

"There at the foot of yonder nodding beech,
That wreathes its old, fantastic roots so high,
His listless length at noontide would he stretch,
And pore upon the brook that babbles by.

"Hard by yon wood, now smiling as in scorn,
Muttering his wayward fancies, he would rove;
Now drooping, woful-wan, like one forlorn,
Or crazed with care, or crossed in hopeless love.

"One morn I missed him on the customed hill,
Along the heath, and near his favorite tree;
Another came,—nor yet beside the rill,
Nor up the lawn, nor at the wood was he;

"The next, with dirges due, in sad array,
Slow through the church-way path we saw him borne;—
Approach and read (for thou canst read) the lay
Graved on the stone beneath yon aged thorn."

THE EPITAPH.

Here rests his head upon the lap of earth,
A youth to fortune and to fame unknown;
Fair Science frowned not on his humble birth,
And Melancholy marked him for her own.

Large was his bounty, and his soul sincere;
Heaven did a recompense as largely send:
He gave to Misery (all he had) a tear;
He gained from Heaven ('t was all he wished) a friend.

No further seek his merits to disclose,
Or draw his frailties from their dread abode:
(There they alike in trembling hope repose,)
The bosom of his Father and his God.

ODE ON A DISTANT PROSPECT OF ETON COLLEGE.

Ye distant spires, ye antique towers,
That crown the watery glade,
Where grateful Science still adores
Her Henry's holy shade;
And ye, that from the stately brow
Of Windsor's heights the expanse below
Of grove, of lawn, of mead survey;
Whose turf, whose shade, whose flowers among
Wanders the hoary Thames along
His silver-winding way!

Ah, happy hills! ah, pleasing shade!
Ah, fields beloved in vain!
Where once my careless childhood strayed,
A stranger yet to pain:
I feel the gales that from ye blow
A momentary bliss bestow,
As, waving fresh their gladsome wing,
My weary soul they seem to soothe,
And, redolent of joy and youth,
To breathe a second spring.

Say, Father Thames, for thou hast seen
Full many a sprightly race,
Disporting on thy margent green,
The paths of pleasure trace,
Who foremost now delight to cleave
With pliant arm thy glassy wave?
The captive linnet which inthrall?
What idle progeny succeed
To chase the rolling circle's speed,
Or urge the flying ball?

While some, on earnest business bent,
  Their murmuring labors ply
'Gainst graver hours, that bring constraint
  To sweeten liberty,
Some bold adventurers disdain
The limits of their little reign,
And unknown regions dare descry:
  Still as they run, they look behind;
  They hear a voice in every wind,
And snatch a fearful joy.

Gay hope is theirs, by fancy fed,
  Less pleasing when possessed;
The tear forgot as soon as shed,
  The sunshine of the breast.
Theirs buxom health of rosy hue,
Wild wit, invention ever new,
And lively cheer of vigor born;
  The thoughtless day, the easy night,
  The spirits pure, the slumbers light,
That fly the approach of morn.

Alas! regardless of their doom,
  The little victims play;
No sense have they of ills to come,
  Nor care beyond to-day;
Yet see how all around them wait
The ministers of human fate,
And black Misfortune's baleful train.
  Ah! show them where in ambush stand,
  To seize their prey, the murtherous band;
Ah, tell them they are men!

These shall the fury passions tear,
  The vultures of the mind,
Disdainful Anger, pallid Fear,
  And Shame, that skulks behind;
Or pining Love shall waste their youth,
Or Jealousy with rankling tooth,
That inly gnaws the secret heart;
  And Envy wan, and faded Care,
  Grim-visaged, comfortless Despair,
And Sorrow's piercing dart.

Ambition this shall tempt to rise,
  Then whirl the wretch from high,
To bitter Scorn a sacrifice,
  And grinning Infamy.
The stings of Falsehood those shall try,
And hard Unkindness' altered eye,
That mocks the tear it forced to flow;
  And keen Remorse with blood defiled,
  And moody Madness laughing wild
Amid severest woe.

Lo! in the vale of years beneath
  A grisly troop are seen,—
The painful family of Death,
  More hideous than their queen:
This racks the joints, this fires the veins,
That every laboring sinew strains,
Those in the deeper vitals rage:
  Lo! Poverty, to fill the band,
  That numbs the soul with icy hand;
And slow-consuming Age.

To each his sufferings: all are men,
  Condemned alike to groan;
The tender for another's pain,
  The unfeeling for his own.
Yet, ah! why should they know their fate,
Since sorrow never comes too late,
And happiness too swiftly flies!
  Thought would destroy their paradise.
  No more; where ignorance is bliss,
'T is folly to be wise.

WILLIAM COLLINS.

[1720–1756.]

DIRGE IN CYMBELINE.

To fair Fidele's grassy tomb
  Soft maids and village hinds shall bring
Each opening sweet of earliest bloom,
  And rifle all the breathing spring.

No wailing ghost shall dare appear
  To vex with shrieks this quiet grove;
But shepherd lads assemble here,
  And melting virgins own their love.

No withered witch shall here be seen,
  No goblins lead their nightly crew;
But female fays shall haunt the green,
  And dress thy grave with pearly dew.

The redbreast oft at evening hours
  Shall kindly lend his little aid,
With hoary moss and gathered flowers
  To deck the ground where thou art laid.

When howling winds and beating rain
  In tempest shake the sylvan cell,
Or midst the chase upon the plain,
  The tender thought on thee shall dwell.

Each lonely scene shall thee restore,
For thee the tear be duly shed;
Beloved till life can charm no more,
And mourned till Pity's self be dead.

ODE TO EVENING.

If aught of oaten stop or pastoral song
May hope, chaste Eve, to soothe thy modest ear,
Like thy own solemn springs,
Thy springs, and dying gales, —

O nymph reserved, while now the bright-haired Sun
Sits in yon western tent, whose cloudy skirts,
With braid ethereal wove,
O'erhang his wavy bed:

Now air is hushed, save where the weak-eyed bat,
With short, shrill shriek flits by on leathern wing;
Or where the beetle winds
His small but sullen horn,

As oft he rises midst the twilight path,
Against the pilgrim borne in heedless hum;
Now teach me, maid composed,
To breathe some softened strain,

Whose numbers, stealing through thy darkening vale,
May not unseemly with its stillness suit;
As, musing slow, I hail
Thy genial, loved return!

For when thy folding-star arising shows
His paly circlet, at his warning lamp,
The fragrant Hours, and Elves
Who slept in buds the day,

And many a Nymph who wreathes her brows with sedge,
And sheds the freshening dew, and, lovelier still,
The pensive Pleasures sweet,
Prepare thy shadowy car.

Then let me rove some wild and heathy scene;
Or find some ruin midst its dreary dells,
Whose walls more awful nod
By thy religious gleams.

Or, if chill, blustering winds, or driving rain,
Prevent my willing feet, be mine the hut
That from the mountain's side
Views wilds, and swelling floods,

And hamlets brown, and dim-discovered spires;
And hears their simple bell, and marks o'er all
Thy dewy fingers draw
The gradual, dusky veil.

While Spring shall pour his showers, as oft he wont,
And bathe thy breathing tresses, meekest Eve!
While Summer loves to sport
Beneath thy lingering light;

While sallow Autumn fills thy lap with leaves;
Or Winter, yelling through the troublous air,
Affrights thy shrinking train,
And rudely rends thy robes, —

So long, regardful of thy quiet rule,
Shall Fancy, Friendship, Science, smiling Peace,
Thy gentlest influence own,
And love thy favorite name!

JAMES MERRICK.

[1720 - 1769.]

THE CHAMELEON.

Oft has it been my lot to mark
A proud, conceited, talking spark,
With eyes that hardly served at most
To guard their master 'gainst a post;
Yet round the world the blade has been,
To see whatever could be seen.
Returning from his finished tour,
Grown ten times perter than before;
Whatever word you chance to drop,
The travelled fool your mouth will stop:
"Sir, if my judgment you 'll allow—
I 've seen — and sure I ought to know."
So begs you 'd pay a due submission,
And acquiesce in his decision.

Two travellers of such a cast,
As o'er Arabia's wilds they passed,
And on their way, in friendly chat,
Now talked of this, and then of that,
Discoursed awhile, 'mongst other matter,
Of the chameleon's form and nature.
"A stranger animal," cries one,
"Sure never lived beneath the sun:
A lizard's body, lean and long,
A fish's head, a serpent's tongue,
Its foot with triple claw disjoined;
And what a length of tail behind!
How slow its pace! and then its hue—
Who ever saw so fine a blue?"
"Hold there," the other quick replies;
"'T is green, I saw it with these eyes,
As late with open mouth it lay,
And warmed it in the sunny ray;
Stretched at its ease the beast I viewed,
And saw it eat the air for food."
"I 've seen it, sir, as well as you,
And must again affirm it blue;
At leisure I the beast surveyed
Extended in the cooling shade."
"'T is green, 't is green, sir, I assure ye."
"Green!" cries the other in a fury;
"Why, sir, d' ye think I 've lost my eyes?"
"'T were no great loss," the friend replies;
"For if they always serve you thus,
You 'll find them but of little use."
So high at last the contest rose,
From words they almost came to blows:
When luckily came by a third;
To him the question they referred,
And begged he 'd tell them, if he knew,
Whether the thing was green or blue.
"Sirs," cries the umpire, "cease your pother;
The creature 's neither one nor t' other.
I caught the animal last night,
And viewed it o'er by candlelight;
I marked it well, 't was black as jet—
You stare—but, sirs, I 've got it yet,
And can produce it."—"Pray, sir, do;
I 'll lay my life the thing is blue."
"And I 'll be sworn, that when you 've seen
The reptile, you 'll pronounce him green."
"Well, then, at once to ease the doubt,"
Replies the man, "I 'll turn him out;
And when before your eyes I 've set him,
If you don't find him black, I 'll eat him."
He said; and full before their sight
Produced the beast, and lo!—'t was white.
Both stared; the man looked wondrous wise—
"My children," the chameleon cries
(Then first the creature found a tongue),
"You all are right, and all are wrong:
When next you talk of what you view,
Think others see as well as you;
Nor wonder if you find that none
Prefers your eyesight to his own."

OLIVER GOLDSMITH.

[1728-1774.]

FROM "THE DESERTED VILLAGE."

SWEET was the sound, when oft, at evening's close
Up yonder hill the village murmur rose;
There, as I passsed with careless steps and slow,
The mingling notes came softened from below;
The swain responsive as the milkmaid sung,
The sober herd that lowed to meet their young;
The noisy geese that gabbled o'er the pool,
The playful children just let loose from school;
The watch-dog's voice that bayed the whispering wind,
And the loud laugh that spoke the vacant mind,—
These all in sweet confusion sought the shade,
And filled each pause the nightingale had made.
But now the sounds of population fail,
No cheerful murmurs fluctuate in the gale,
No busy steps the grass-grown footway tread,
But all the bloomy flush of life is fled.
All but yon widowed, solitary thing,
That feebly bends beside the plashy spring;
She, wretched matron, forced in age, for bread,
To strip the brook with mantling cresses spread,
To pick her wintry fagot from the thorn,
To seek her nightly shed, and weep till morn;

She only left of all the harmless train,
The sad historian of the pensive plain.

Near yonder copse, where once the garden smiled,
And still where many a garden flower grows wild,
There, where a few torn shrubs the place disclose,
The village preacher's modest mansion rose.
A man he was to all the country dear,
And passing rich with forty pounds a year;
Remote from towns he ran his godly race,
Nor e'er had changed, nor wished to change, his place;
Unpractised he to fawn, or seek for power,
By doctrines fashioned to the varying hour;
Far other aims his heart had learned to prize,
More skilled to raise the wretched than to rise.
His house was known to all the vagrant train,
He chid their wanderings, but relieved their pain;
The long-remembered beggar was his guest,
Whose beard descending swept his aged breast;
The ruined spendthrift, now no longer proud,
Claimed kindred there, and had his claims allowed;
The broken soldier, kindly bade to stay,
Sat by his fire, and talked the night away;
Wept o'er his wounds, or tales of sorrow done,
Shouldered his crutch, and showed how fields were won.
Pleased with his guests, the good man learned to glow,
And quite forgot their vices in their woe;
Careless their merits or their faults to scan,
His pity gave ere charity began.

Thus to relieve the wretched was his pride,
And even his failings leaned to virtue's side:
But in his duty prompt at every call,
He watched and wept, he prayed and felt for all;
And, as a bird each fond endearment tries
To tempt its new-fledged offspring to the skies,
He tried each art, reproved each dull delay,
Allured to brighter worlds, and led the way.

Beside the bed where parting life was laid,
And sorrow, guilt, and pain by turns dismayed,
The reverend champion stood. At his control,
Despair and anguish fled the struggling soul;
Comfort came down the trembling wretch to raise,
And his last, faltering accents whispered praise.

At church, with meek and unaffected grace,
His looks adorned the venerable place;
Truth from his lips prevailed with double sway,
And fools, who came to scoff, remained to pray.
The service past, around the pious man,
With steady zeal, each honest rustic ran;
Even children followed, with endearing wile,
And plucked his gown, to share the good man's smile.
His ready smile a parent's warmth expressed,
Their welfare pleased him, and their cares distressed;
To them his heart, his love, his griefs, were given,
But all his serious thoughts had rest in heaven.
As some tall cliff, that lifts its awful form,
Swells from the vale, and midway leaves the storm,
Though round its breast the rolling clouds are spread,
Eternal sunshine settles on its head.

Beside yon straggling fence that skirts the way,
With blossomed furze unprofitably gay,
There, in his noisy mansion, skilled to rule,
The village master taught his little school.
A man severe he was, and stern to view;
I knew him well, and every truant knew:

Well had the boding tremblers learned to trace
The day's disasters in his morning face;
Full well they laughed, with counterfeited glee,
At all his jokes, for many a joke had he;
Full well the busy whisper, circling round,
Conveyed the dismal tidings when he frowned.
Yet he was kind, or if severe in aught,
The love he bore to learning was in fault.
The village all declared how much he knew;
'T was certain he could write, and cipher too;
Lands he could measure, times and tides presage,
And even the story ran that he could gauge;
In arguing, too, the parson owned his skill,
For, even though vanquished, he could argue still;
While words of learned length and thundering sound
Amazed the gazing rustics ranged around;
And still they gazed, and still the wonder grew
That one small head could carry all he knew.

But past is all his fame. The very spot
Where many a time he triumphed is forgot.
Near yonder thorn, that lifts its head on high,
Where once the sign-post caught the passing eye,
Low lies that house where nut-brown draughts inspired,
Where gray-beard mirth and smiling toil retired,
Where village statesmen talked with looks profound,
And news much older than their ale went round.
Imagination fondly stoops to trace
The parlor splendors of that festive place:
The whitewashed wall; the nicely sanded floor;
The varnished clock that clicked behind the door;
The chest, contrived a double debt to pay,
A bed by night, a chest of drawers by day;
The pictures placed for ornament and use;
The twelve good rules; the royal game of goose;
The hearth, except when winter chilled the day,
With aspen boughs and flowers and fennel gay;
While broken teacups, wisely kept for show,
Ranged o'er the chimney, glistened in a row.

Vain, transitory splendors! could not all
Reprieve the tottering mansion from its fall?
Obscure it sinks, nor shall it more impart
An hour's importance to the poor man's heart;
Thither no more the peasant shall repair
To sweet oblivion of his daily care;
No more the farmer's news, the barber's tale,
No more the woodman's ballad shall prevail;
No more the smith his dusky brow shall clear,
Relax his ponderous strength, and lean to hear.
The host himself no longer shall be found
Careful to see the mantling bliss go round;
Nor the coy maid, half willing to be prest,
Shall kiss the cup to pass it to the rest.

THOMAS PERCY.

[1728-1811.]

THE FRIAR OF ORDERS GRAY.

It was a friar of orders gray
  Walked forth to tell his beads,
And he met with a lady fair,
  Clad in a pilgrim's weeds.

"Now Christ thee save, thou reverend friar!
  I pray thee tell to me,
If ever at yon holy shrine
  My true-love thou didst see."

"And how should I know your true-love
  From many another one?"
"Oh! by his cockle hat, and staff,
  And by his sandal shoon;

"But chiefly by his face and mien,
  That were so fair to view,
His flaxen locks that sweetly curled,
  And eyes of lovely blue."

"O lady, he is dead and gone!
  Lady, he 's dead and gone!
And at his head a green grass turf,
  And at his heels a stone.

"Within these holy cloisters long
  He languished, and he died,
Lamenting of a lady's love,
  And 'plaining of her pride.

"Here bore him barefaced on his bier
  Six proper youths and tall;
And many a tear bedewed his grave
  Within yon kirkyard wall."

"And art thou dead, thou gentle youth?
  And art thou dead and gone?
And didst thou die for love of me?
  Break, cruel heart of stone!"

"O, weep not, lady, weep not so;
  Some ghostly comfort seek:
Let not vain sorrow rive thy heart,
  Nor tears bedew thy cheek."

"O do not, do not, holy friar,
  My sorrow now reprove;
For I have lost the sweetest youth
  That e'er won lady's love.

"And now, alas! for thy sad loss
  I 'll evermore weep and sigh;
For thee I only wished to live,
  For thee I wish to die."

"Weep no more, lady, weep no more;
  Thy sorrow is in vain:
For violets plucked, the sweetest shower
  Will ne'er make grow again.

"Our joys as wingéd dreams do fly;
  Why then should sorrow last?
Since grief but aggravates thy loss,
  Grieve not for what is past."

"O, say not so, thou holy friar!
  I pray thee say not so;
For since my true-love died for me,
  'T is meet my tears should flow.

"And will he never come again?
  Will he ne'er come again?
Ah, no! he is dead, and laid in his grave,
  Forever to remain.

"His cheek was redder than the rose, —
  The comeliest youth was he;
But he is dead and laid in his grave,
  Alas! and woe is me."

"Sigh no more, lady, sigh no more,
  Men were deceivers ever;
One foot on sea and one on land,
  To one thing constant never.

"Hadst thou been fond, he had been false,
  And left thee sad and heavy;
For young men ever were fickle found,
  Since summer trees were leafy."

"Now say not so, thou holy friar,
  I pray thee say not so;
My love he had the truest heart, —
  O, he was ever true!

"And art thou dead, thou much-loved youth,
  And didst thou die for me?
Then farewell home; forevermore
  A pilgrim I will be.

"But first upon my true-love's grave
  My weary limbs I 'll lay,
And thrice I 'll kiss the green grass turf
  That wraps his breathless clay."

"Yet stay, fair lady, rest awhile
  Beneath this cloister wall;
The cold wind through the hawthorn blows,
  And drizzly rain doth fall."

"O, stay me not, thou holy friar,
  O stay me not, I pray;
No drizzly rain that falls on me
  Can wash my fault away."

"Yet stay, fair lady, turn again,
  And dry those pearly tears;
For see, beneath this gown of gray
  Thy own true-love appears.

"Here, forced by grief and hopeless love,
  These holy weeds I sought;
And here, amid these lonely walls,
  To end my days I thought.

"But haply, for my year of grace
  Is not yet passed away,

Might I still hope to win thy love,
  No longer would I stay."

"Now farewell grief, and welcome joy
  Once more unto my heart;
For since I 've found thee, lovely youth,
  We nevermore will part."

WILLIAM COWPER.

[1731-1800.]

LOSS OF THE ROYAL GEORGE.

Toll for the brave!
  The brave that are no more!
All sunk beneath the wave
  Fast by their native shore!

Eight hundred of the brave,
  Whose courage well was tried,
Had made the vessel heel,
  And laid her on her side.

A land-breeze shook the shrouds
  And she was overset;
Down went the Royal George,
  With all her crew complete.

Toll for the brave!
  Brave Kempenfelt is gone;
His last sea-fight is fought,
  His work of glory done.

It was not in the battle;
  No tempest gave the shock;
She sprang no fatal leak,
  She ran upon no rock.

His sword was in its sheath,
  His fingers held the pen,
When Kempenfelt went down
  With twice four hundred men.

Weigh the vessel up,
  Once dreaded by our foes!
And mingle with our cup
  The tear that England owes.

Her timbers yet are sound,
  And she may float again,
Full charged with England's thunder,
  And plough the distant main.

But Kempenfelt is gone,
  His victories are o'er;
And he and his eight hundred
  Shall plough the wave no more.

LINES TO MY MOTHER'S PICTURE.

O that those lips had language! Life has passed
With me but roughly since I heard thee last.
Those lips are thine,—thy own sweet smile I see,
The same that oft in childhood solaced me;
Voice only fails, else how distinct they say,
"Grieve not, my child; chase all thy fears away!"
The meek intelligence of those dear eyes
(Blest be the art that can immortalize,
The art that baffles time's tyrannic claim
To quench it!) here shines on me still the same.
  Faithful remembrancer of one so dear,
O welcome guest, though unexpected here!
Who bid'st me honor with an artless song,
Affectionate, a mother lost so long.
I will obey, not willingly alone,
But gladly, as the precept were her own;
And, while that face renews my filial grief,
Fancy shall weave a charm for my relief,
Shall steep me in Elysian revery,
A momentary dream that thou art she.
  My mother! when I learned that thou wast dead,
Say, wast thou conscious of the tears I shed?
Hovered thy spirit o'er thy sorrowing son,
Wretch even then, life's journey just begun?
Perhaps thou gav'st me, though unfelt, a kiss;
Perhaps a tear, if souls can weep in bliss—
Ah, that maternal smile! it answers—Yes.
I heard the bell tolled on thy burial day,
I saw the hearse that bore thee slow away,
And, turning from my nursery window, drew
A long, long sigh, and wept a last adieu!
But was it such? It was. Where thou art gone,
Adieus and farewells are a sound unknown.
May I but meet thee on that peaceful shore,

The parting words shall pass my lips no more!
Thy maidens, grieved themselves at my concern,
Oft gave me promise of thy quick return;
What ardently I wished I long believed,
And, disappointed still, was still deceived;
By expectation every day beguiled,
Dupe of to-morrow even from a child.
Thus many a sad to-morrow came and went,
Till, all my stock of infant sorrows spent,
I learned at last submission to my lot;
But, though I less deplored thee, ne'er forgot.
Where once we dwelt our name is heard no more,
Children not thine have trod my nursery floor;
And where the gardener Robin, day by day,
Drew me to school along the public way,
Delighted with my bawble coach, and wrapped
In scarlet mantle warm, and velvet capped,
'T is now become a history little known,
That once we called the pastoral house our own.
Short-lived possession! but the record fair,
That memory keeps of all thy kindness there,
Still outlives many a storm that has effaced
A thousand other themes less deeply traced.
Thy nightly visits to my chamber made,
That thou mightst know me safe and warmly laid, —
All this, and, more endearing still than all,
Thy constant flow of love, that knew no fall,
Ne'er roughened by those cataracts and breaks
That humor interposed too often makes, —
All this, still legible in memory's page,
And still to be so to my latest age,
Adds joy to duty, makes me glad to pay
Such honors to thee as my numbers may;
Perhaps a frail memorial, but sincere,
Not scorned in heaven, though little noticed here.
Could Time, his flight reversed, restore the hours
When, playing with thy vesture's tissued flowers,
The violet, the pink, and jessamine,
I pricked them into paper with a pin,
(And thou wast happier than myself the while,
Wouldst softly speak, and stroke my head, and smile,) —
Could those few pleasant days again appear,
Might one wish bring them, would I wish them here?
I would not trust my heart, — the dear delight
Seems so to be desired, perhaps I might.
But no, — what here we call our life is such,
So little to be loved, and thou so much,
That I should ill requite thee to constrain
Thy unbound spirit into bonds again.
Thou, as a gallant bark from Albion's coast
(The storms all weathered and the ocean crossed)
Shoots into port at some well-havened isle,
Where spices breathe and brighter seasons smile;
There sits quiescent on the floods, that show
Her beauteous form reflected clear below,
While airs impregnated with incense play
Around her, fanning light her streamers gay, —
So thou, with sails how swift! hast reached the shore,
Where tempests never beat, nor billows roar;
And thy loved consort, on the dangerous tide
Of life, long since has anchored by thy side.
But me, scarce hoping to attain that rest,
Always from port withheld, always distressed, —
Me howling blasts drive devious, tempest-tossed,
Sails ripped, seams opening wide, and compass lost;
And day by day some current's thwarting force
Sets me more distant from a prosperous course.
Yet O, the thought that thou art safe, and he! —
That thought is joy, arrive what may to me.
My boast is not that I deduce my birth

From loins enthroned, and rulers of the earth;
But higher far my proud pretensions rise, —
The son of parents passed into the skies.
And now, farewell! — Time, unrevoked, has run
His wonted course, yet what I wished is done.
By contemplation's help, not sought in vain,
I seem to have lived my childhood o'er again, —
To have renewed the joys that once were mine
Without the sin of violating thine;
And while the wings of Fancy still are free,
And I can view this mimic show of thee,
Time has but half succeeded in his theft, —
Thyself removed, thy power to soothe me left.

MYSTERIES OF PROVIDENCE.

God moves in a mysterious way
His wonders to perform;
He plants his footsteps in the sea,
And rides upon the storm.

Deep in unfathomable mines
Of never-failing skill,
He treasures up his bright designs,
And works his sovereign will.

Ye fearful saints, fresh courage take!
The clouds ye so much dread
Are big with mercy, and shall break
In blessings on your head.

Judge not the Lord by feeble sense,
But trust him for his grace;
Behind a frowning providence
He hides a smiling face.

His purposes will ripen fast,
Unfolding every hour;
The bud may have a bitter taste,
But sweet will be the flower.

Blind unbelief is sure to err,
And scan his works in vain;
God is his own interpreter,
And he will make it plain.

WILLIAM JULIUS MICKLE.

[1734-1788.]

THE MARINER'S WIFE.

And are ye sure the news is true?
And are ye sure he 's weel?
Is this a time to think o' wark?
Mak haste, lay by your wheel;
Is this the time to spin a thread,
When Colin 's at the door?
Reach down my cloak, I 'll to the quay,
And see him come ashore.
For there 's nae luck about the house,
There 's nae luck at a';
There 's little pleasure in the house
When our gudeman 's awa'.

And gie to me my bigonet,
My bishop's satin gown;
For I maun tell the baillie's wife
That Colin 's in the town.
My Turkey slippers maun gae on,
My stockings pearly blue;
It 's a' to pleasure our gudeman,
For he 's baith leal and true.

Rise, lass, and mak a clean fireside,
Put on the muckle pot;
Gie little Kate her button gown,
And Jock his Sunday coat;
And mak their shoon as black as slaes,
Their hose as white as snaw;
It 's a' to please my ain gudeman,
For he 's been lang awa'.

There 's twa fat hens upo' the coop,
Been fed this month and mair;
Mak haste and thraw their necks about,
That Colin weel may fare;
And mak our table neat and clean,
Let everything look braw,
For wha can tell how Colin fared
When he was far awa'?

Sae true his heart, sae smooth his speech,
His breath like caller air;
His very foot has music in 't
As he comes up the stair.
And will I see his face again?
And will I hear him speak?
I 'm downright dizzy wi' the thought,
In troth I 'm like to greet!

The cauld blasts o' the winter wind,
That thirlèd through my heart,

They 're a' blawn by, I hae him safe,
Till death we 'll never part;
But what puts parting in my head?
It may be far awa'!
The present moment is our ain,
The neist we never saw.

Since Colin 's weel, and weel content,
I hae nae mair to crave;
And gin I live to keep him sae,
I 'm blest aboon the lave.
And will I see his face again?
And will I hear him speak?
I 'm downright dizzy wi' the thought,
In troth I 'm like to greet.
For there 's nae luck about the house,
There 's nae luck at a';
There 's little pleasure in the house
When our gudeman 's awa'.

JAMES BEATTIE.

[1735-1803.]

THE HERMIT.

At the close of the day, when the hamlet is still,
And mortals the sweets of forgetfulness prove,
When naught but the torrent is heard on the hill,
And naught but the nightingale's song in the grove,
'T was thus, by the cave of the mountain afar,
While his harp rung symphonious, a hermit began;
No more with himself or with nature at war,
He thought as a sage, though he felt as a man:

"Ah! why, all abandoned to darkness and woe,
Why, lone Philomela, that languishing fall?
For spring shall return, and a lover bestow,
And sorrow no longer thy bosom inthrall.
But, if pity inspire thee, renew the sad lay,—
Mourn, sweetest complainer, man calls thee to mourn;
O, soothe him whose pleasures like thine pass away!
Full quickly they pass, — but they never return.

"Now, gliding remote on the verge of the sky,
The moon, half extinguished, her crescent displays;
But lately I marked when majestic on high
She shone, and the planets were lost in her blaze.
Roll on, thou fair orb, and with gladness pursue
The path that conducts thee to splendor again!
But man's faded glory what change shall renew?
Ah, fool! to exult in a glory so vain!

"'T is night, and the landscape is lovely no more.
I mourn, but, ye woodlands, I mourn not for you;
For morn is approaching your charms to restore,
Perfumed with fresh fragrance, and glittering with dew.
Nor yet for the ravage of winter I mourn, —
Kind nature the embryo blossom will save;
But when shall spring visit the mouldering urn?
O, when shall day dawn on the night of the grave?

"'T was thus, by the glare of false science betrayed,
That leads to bewilder, and dazzles to blind,
My thoughts wont to roam from shade onward to shade,
Destruction before me, and sorrow behind.
'O pity, great Father of light,' then I cried,
'Thy creature, who fain would not wander from thee!
Lo, humbled in dust, I relinquish my pride;
From doubt and from darkness thou only canst free!'

"And darkness and doubt are now flying away;
No longer I roam in conjecture forlorn.

So breaks on the traveller, faint and astray,
The bright and the balmy effulgence of morn.
See truth, love, and mercy in triumph descending,
And nature all glowing in Eden's first bloom!
On the cold cheek of death smiles and roses are blending,
And beauty immortal awakes from the tomb."

JOHN LANGHORNE.

[1735-1779.]

THE DEAD.

Of them who, wrapt in earth so cold,
  No more the smiling day shall view,
Should many a tender tale be told,
  For many a tender thought is due.

Why else the o'ergrown paths of time
  Would thus the lettered sage explore,
With pain these crumbling ruins climb,
  And on the doubtful sculpture pore?

Why seeks he with unwearied toil,
  Through Death's dim walks to urge his way,
Reclaim his long-asserted spoil,
  And lead oblivion into day?

'T is nature prompts, by toil or fear,
  Unmoved, to range through Death's domain;
The tender parent loves to hear
  Her children's story told again!

MRS. THRALE.

[1740-1822.]

THE THREE WARNINGS.

The tree of deepest root is found
Least willing still to quit the ground;
'T was therefore said by ancient sages,
  That love of life increased with years
So much, that in our latter stages,
When pains grow sharp and sickness rages,
  The greatest love of life appears.
This great affection to believe,
Which all confess, but few perceive,
If old assertions can't prevail,
Be pleased to hear a modern tale.

When sports went round, and all were gay,
On neighbor Dodson's wedding-day,
Death called aside the jocund groom
With him into another room,
And, looking grave, "You must," says he,
"Quit your sweet bride, and come with me."
"With you! and quit my Susan's side?
With you!" the hapless husband cried;
"Young as I am, 't is monstrous hard!
Besides, in truth, I'm not prepared:
My thoughts on other matters go;
This is my wedding-day, you know."

What more he urged I have not heard,
  His reasons could not well be stronger;
So Death the poor delinquent spared,
  And left to live a little longer.
Yet calling up a serious look,
His hour-glass trembled while he spoke.
"Neighbor," he said, "farewell! no more
Shall Death disturb your mirthful hour:
And further, to avoid all blame
Of cruelty upon my name,
To give you time for preparation,
And fit you for your future station,
Three several warnings you shall have,
Before you 're summoned to the grave;
Willing for once I'll quit my prey,
  And grant a kind reprieve,
In hopes you'll have no more to say,
But when I call again this way,
  Well pleased the world will leave."
To these conditions both consented,
And parted perfectly contented.

What next the hero of our tale befell,
How long he lived, how wise, how well,
How roundly he pursued his course,
And smoked his pipe, and stroked his horse,
  The willing muse shall tell:
He chaffered, then he bought and sold,
Nor once perceived his growing old,
  Nor thought of Death as near:
His friends not false, his wife no shrew,
Many his gains, his children few,

He passed his hours in peace.
But while he viewed his wealth increase,
While thus along life's dusty road
The beaten track content he trod,
Old Time, whose haste no mortal spares,
Uncalled, unheeded, unawares,
Brought on his eightieth year.
And now, one night, in musing mood,
As all alone he sate,
The unwelcome messenger of Fate
Once more before him stood.

Half killed with anger and surprise,
"So soon returned!" Old Dodson cries.
"So soon, d' ye call it!" Death replies;
"Surely, my friend, you 're but in jest!
Since I was here before
'T is six-and-thirty years at least,
And you are now fourscore."

"So much the worse," the clown rejoined;
"To spare the aged would be kind:
However, see your search be legal;
And your authority, — is 't regal?
Else you are come on a fool's errand,
With but a secretary's warrant.
Beside, you promised me three warnings,
Which I have looked for nights and mornings;
But for that loss of time and ease
I can recover damages."

"I know," cries Death, "that at the best
I seldom am a welcome guest;
But don't be captious, friend, at least:
I little thought you 'd still be able
To stump about your farm and stable:
Your years have run to a great length;
I wish you joy, though, of your strength!"

"Hold," says the farmer, "not so fast!
I have been lame these four years past."
"And no great wonder," Death replies:
"However, you still keep your eyes;
And sure to see one's loves and friends
For legs and arms would make amends."
"Perhaps," says Dodson, "so it might,
But latterly I 've lost my sight."
"This is a shocking tale, 't is true;
But still there 's comfort left for you:
Each strives your sadness to amuse;
I warrant you hear all the news."
"There 's none," cries he; and if there were,
I 'm grown so deaf, I could not hear."
"Nay, then," the spectre stern rejoined,
"These are unjustifiable yearnings:
If you are lame, and deaf, and blind,
You 've had your three sufficient warnings;
So come along, no more we 'll part."
He said, and touched him with his dart.
And now Old Dodson, turning pale,
Yields to his fate, — so ends my tale.

ANNA L. BARBAULD.

[1743–1825.]

THE SABBATH OF THE SOUL.

Sleep, sleep to-day, tormenting cares,
Of earth and folly born;
Ye shall not dim the light that streams
From this celestial morn.

To-morrow will be time enough
To feel your harsh control;
Ye shall not violate, this day,
The Sabbath of my soul.

Sleep, sleep forever, guilty thoughts;
Let fires of vengeance die;
And, purged from sin, may I behold
A God of purity!

THE DEATH OF THE VIRTUOUS.

Sweet is the scene when virtue dies!
When sinks a righteous soul to rest,
How mildly beam the closing eyes,
How gently heaves the expiring breast!

So fades a summer cloud away,
So sinks the gale when storms are o'er,
So gently shuts the eye of day,
So dies a wave along the shore.

Triumphant smiles the victor brow,
Fanned by some angel's purple wing; —
Where is, O grave! thy victory now?
And where, insidious death! thy sting?

Farewell, conflicting joys and fears,
Where light and shade alternate dwell!

How bright the unchanging morn appears; —
Farewell, inconstant world, farewell!

Life's labor done, as sinks the day,
Light from its load the spirit flies;
While heaven and earth combine to say,
"Sweet is the scene when virtue dies!"

LIFE.

LIFE! I know not what thou art,
But know that thou and I must part;
And when, or how, or where we met,
I own to me 's a secret yet.

Life! we 've been long together
Through pleasant and through cloudy weather;
'T is hard to part when friends are dear, —
Perhaps 't will cost a sigh, a tear;
—Then steal away, give little warning,
Choose thine own time;
Say not Good Night, — but in some brighter clime
Bid me Good Morning.

SUSANNA BLAMIRE.

[1747 - 1794.]

WHAT AILS THIS HEART O' MINE?

WHAT ails this heart o' mine?
What ails this watery ee?
What gars me a' turn pale as death
When I take leave o' thee?
When thou art far awa',
Thou 'lt dearer grow to me;
But change o' place and change o' folk
May gar thy fancy jee.

When I gae out at e'en,
Or walk at morning air,
Ilk rustling bush will seem to say,
I used to meet thee there.
Then I 'll sit down and cry,
And live aneath the tree,
And when a leaf fa's i' my lap,
I 'll ca' 't a word frae thee.

I 'll hie me to the bower
That thou wi' roses tied,
And where wi' mony a blushing bud
I strove myself to hide.
I 'll doat on ilka spot
Where I ha'e been wi' thee;
And ca' to mind some kindly word,
By ilka burn and tree.

JOHN LOGAN.

[1748 - 1788.]

TO THE CUCKOO.

HAIL, beauteous stranger of the grove!
Thou messenger of spring!
Now heaven repairs thy rural seat,
And woods thy welcome sing.

What time the daisy decks the green,
Thy certain voice we hear;
Hast thou a star to guide thy path,
Or mark the rolling year?

Delightful visitant! with thee
I hail the time of flowers,
And hear the sound of music sweet
From birds among the bowers.

The school-boy, wandering through the wood
To pull the primrose gay,
Starts, the new voice of spring to hear,
And imitates thy lay.

What time the pea puts on the bloom,
Thou fliest thy vocal vale,
An annual guest in other lands,
Another spring to hail.

Sweet bird! thy bower is ever green,
Thy sky is ever clear;
Thou hast no sorrow in thy song,
No winter in thy year!

O, could I fly, I 'd fly with thee!
We 'd make, with joyful wing,
Our annual visit o'er the globe,
Companions of the spring.

YARROW STREAM.

THY banks were bonnie, Yarrow stream,
When first on thee I met my lover;
Thy banks how dreary, Yarrow stream,
When now thy waves his body cover!

Forever now, O Yarrow stream,
Thou art to me a stream of sorrow;
For never on thy banks shall I
Behold my love, — the flower of Yarrow!

He promised me a milk-white horse,
To bear me to his father's bowers;
He promised me a little page,
To squire me to his father's towers.

He promised me a wedding-ring,
The wedding-day was fixed to-morrow;
Now he is wedded to his grave,
Alas! a watery grave in Yarrow!

Sweet were his words when last we met,
My passion as I freely told him;
Clasped in his arms, I little thought
That I should nevermore behold him.

Scarce was he gone, I saw his ghost, —
It vanished with a shriek of sorrow;
Thrice did the Water Wraith ascend,
And give a doleful groan through Yarrow!

His mother from the window looked,
With all the longing of a mother;
His little sister, weeping, walked
The greenwood path to meet her brother.

They sought him east, they sought him
  west,
They sought him all the forest thorough;
They only saw the clouds of night,
They only heard the roar of Yarrow!

No longer from thy window look, —
Thou hast no son, thou tender mother!
No longer walk, thou lovely maid, —
Alas! thou hast no more a brother!

No longer seek him east or west,
No longer search the forest thorough,
For, murdered in the night so dark,
He lies a lifeless corpse in Yarrow!

The tears shall never leave my cheek;
No other youth shall be my marrow;
I 'll seek thy body in the stream,
And there with thee I 'll sleep in Yarrow!

The tear did never leave her cheek:
No other youth became her marrow;
She found his body in the stream,
And with him now she sleeps in Yarrow.

UNKNOWN.

BONNIE GEORGE CAMPBELL.

Hie upon Hielands,
  And low upon Tay,
Bonnie George Campbell
  Rade out on a day.
Saddled and bridled
  And gallant rade he;
Hame came his gude horse,
  But never came he.

Out came his auld mither
  Greeting fu' sair,
And out came his bonnie bride
  Rivin' her hair.
Saddled and bridled
  And booted rade he;
Toom hame came the saddle,
  But never came he.

"My meadow lies green,
  And my corn is unshorn;
My barn is to build,
  And my babie 's unborn."
Saddled and bridled
  And booted rade he;
Toom hame came the saddle,
  But never came he!

UNKNOWN.

WALY, WALY, BUT LOVE BE BONNY.

O, waly, waly up the bank,
  And waly, waly down the brae,
And waly, waly yon burnside,
  Where I and my love wont to gae.
I leaned my back unto an aik,
  And thought it was a trusty tree,
But first it bowed, and syne it brak',
  Sae my true love did lightly me.

O, waly, waly, but love is bonny,
  A little time while it is new;
But when 't is auld, it waxeth cauld,
  And fades away like morning dew.
O, wherefore should I busk my head?
  Or wherefore should I kame my hair?
For my true love has me forsook,
  And says he 'll never love me mair.

Now Arthur-Seat shall be my bed,
  The sheets shall ne'er be filled by me;

Saint Anton's well shall be my drink,
Since my true love 's forsaken me,
Martinmas wind, when wilt thou blaw,
And shake the green leaves off the tree?
O gentle death! when wilt thou come?
For of my life I am weary.

'T is not the frost that freezes fell,
Nor blowing snow's inclemency;
'T is not sic cauld that makes me cry,
But my love's heart grown cauld to me.
When we came in by Glasgow town,
We were a comely sight to see;
My love was clad in the black velvet,
And I mysel' in cramasie.

But had I wist, before I kissed,
That love had been so ill to win,
I 'd locked my heart in a case of gold,
And pinned it with a silver pin.
And O, if my young babe were born,
And set upon the nurse's knee,
And I mysel' were dead and gane,
Wi' the green grass growing over me!

UNKNOWN.

LADY MARY ANN.

O, Lady Mary Ann looked o'er the castle wa',
She saw three bonnie boys playing at the ba',
The youngest he was the flower amang them a':
My bonnie laddie 's young, but he 's growin' yet.

"O father, O father, an' ye think it fit,
We 'll send him a year to the college yet:
We 'll sew a green ribbon round about his hat,
And that will let them ken he 's to marry yet."

Lady Mary Ann was a flower in the dew,
Sweet was its smell, and bonnie was its hue,
And the langer it blossomed the sweeter it grew;
For the lily in the bud will be bonnier yet.

Young Charlie Cochran was the sprout of an aik,
Bonnie and blooming and straight was its make,
The sun took delight to shine for its sake;
And it will be the brag o' the forest yet.

The summer is gone when the leaves they were green,
And the days are awa' that we hae seen,
But far better days I trust will come again;
For my bonnie laddie 's young, but he 's growing yet.

UNKNOWN.

THE BOATIE ROWS.

O, weel may the boatie row,
And better may she speed;
And liesome may the boatie row
That wins the bairnies' bread.
The boatie rows, the boatie rows,
The boatie rows indeed;
And weel may the boatie row
That wins the bairnies' bread.

I coost my line in Largo Bay,
And fishes I catched nine;
'T was three to boil and three to fry,
And three to bait the line.
The boatie rows, the boatie rows,
The boatie rows indeed,
And happy be the lot o' a'
Wha wishes her to speed.

O, weel may the boatie row,
That fills a heavy creel,
And cleeds us a' frae tap to tae,
And buys our parritch meal.
The boatie rows, the boatie rows,
The boatie rows, indeed,
And happy be the lot o' a'
That wish the boatie speed.

When Jamie vowed he wad be mine,
And wan frae me my heart,
O, muckle lighter grew my creel —
He swore we 'd never part.
The boatie rows, the boatie rows,
The boatie rows fu' weel;
And muckle lighter is the load
When love bears up the creel.

My kurtch I put upo' my head,
  And dressed mysel' fu' braw;
I trow my heart was dough and wae,
  When Jamie gade awa'.
But weel may the boatie row,
  And lucky be her part,
And lightsome be the lassie's care
  That yields an honest heart.

UNKNOWN.

GLENLOGIE.

Threescore o' nobles rade up the king's ha',
But bonnie Glenlogie 's the flower o' them a',
Wi' his milk-white steed and his bonnie black e'e,
"Glenlogie, dear mither, Glenlogie for me!"

"Haud your tongue, daughter, ye 'll get better than he."
"O, say nae sae, mither, for that canna be;
Though Doumlie is richer and greater than he,
Yet if I maun tak him, I 'll certainly dee.

"Where will I get a bonnie boy, to win hose and shoon,
Will gae to Glenlogie, and come again soon?"
"O, here am I a bonnie boy, to win hose and shoon,
Will gae to Glenlogie and come again soon."

When he gaed to Glenlogie, 't was "Wash and go dine";
'T was "Wash ye, my pretty boy, wash and go dine."
"O, 't was ne'er my father's fashion, and it ne'er shall be mine
To gar a lady's errand wait till I dine.

"But there is, Glenlogie, a letter for thee."
The first line that he read, a low laugh gave he;
The next line that he read, the tear blindit his e'e;
But the last line that he read, he gart the table flee.

"Gar saddle the black horse, gar saddle the brown;
Gar saddle the swiftest steed e'er rade frae a town":
But lang ere the horse was drawn and brought to the green,
O, bonnie Glenlogie was twa mile his lane.

When he came to Glenfeldy's door, little mirth was there;
Bonnie Jean's mother was tearing her hair.
"Ye 're welcome, Glenlogie, ye 're welcome," said she, —
"Ye 're welcome, Glenlogie, your Jeanie to see."

Pale and wan was she, when Glenlogie gaed ben,
But red and rosy grew she, whene'er he sat down;
She turned awa' her head, but the smile was in her e'e,
"O, binna feared, mither, I 'll maybe no dee."

UNKNOWN.

JOHN DAVIDSON.

John Davidson and Tib his wife
  Sat toastin' their taes ae night,
When somethin' started on the fluir
  An' blinkéd by their sight.

"Guidwife!" quo' John, "did ye see that mouse?
  Whar sorra was the cat?"
"A mouse?" — "Ay, a mouse." — "Na, na, Guidman,
  It wasna a mouse, 't was a rat."

"Oh, oh! Guidwife, to think ye 've been
  Sae lang about the house
An' no to ken a mouse frae a rat!
  Yon wasna a rat, but a mouse!"

"I 've seen mair mice than you, Guidman,
  An' what think ye o' that?

Sae haud your tongue an' say nae mair, —
I tell ye 't was a rat."

"*Me* haud my tongue for *you*, Guidwife!
I 'll be maister o' this house, —
I saw it as plain as een could see,
An' I tell ye 't was a mouse!"

"If you 're the maister o' the house,
It 's I 'm the mistress o' 't;
An' I ken best what 's i' the house, —
Sae I tell ye 't was a rat."

"Weel, weel, Guidwife, gae mak the brose,
An' ca' it what ye please."
Sae up she gat an' made the brose,
While John sat toastin' his taes.

They suppit an' suppit an' suppit the brose,
An' aye their lips played smack;
They suppit an' suppit an' suppit the brose
Till their lugs began to crack.

"Sic fules we were to fa' out, Guidwife,
About a mouse." — "A what!
It 's a lee ye tell, an' I say again
It wasna a mouse, 't was a rat."

"Wad ye ca' me a leear to my very face?
My faith, but ye craw croose! —
I tell ye, Tib, I never will bear 't, —
'T was a mouse." — "'T was a rat." —
"'T was a mouse."

Wi' that she struck him ower the pow.
"Ye dour auld doit, tak' that!
Gae to your bed, ye cankered sumph!
'T was a rat." — "'T was a mouse!" —
"'T was a rat!"

She sent the brose-cup at his heels
As he hirpled ben the house;
But he shoved out his head as he steekit the door,
An' cried, "'T was a mouse, 't was a mouse!"

Yet when the auld carle fell asleep,
She paid him back for that,
An' roared into his sleepin' lug,
"'T was a rat, 't was a rat, 't was a rat!"

The deil be wi' me, if I think
It was a beast at all.
Next mornin', when she sweept the floor,
She found wee Johnie's ball!

RICHARD BRINSLEY SHERIDAN.

[1751 - 1816.]

HAD I A HEART FOR FALSEHOOD FRAMED.

HAD I a heart for falsehood framed,
I ne'er could injure you;
For though your tongue no promise claimed,
Your charms would make me true:
To you no soul shall bear deceit,
No stranger offer wrong;
But friends in all the aged you 'll meet,
And lovers in the young.

For when they learn that you have blest
Another with your heart,
They 'll bid aspiring passion rest,
And act a brother's part.
Then, lady, dread not here deceit,
Nor fear to suffer wrong;
For friends in all the aged you 'll meet,
And brothers in the young.

THOMAS CHATTERTON.

[1752 - 1770.]

THE MINSTREL'S SONG IN ELLA.

O, SING unto my roundelay!
O, drop the briny tear with me!
Dance no more at holiday,
Like a running river be.
My love is dead,
Gone to his death-bed,
All under the willow-tree.

Black his hair as the winter night,
White his neck as the summer snow,
Ruddy his face as the morning light;
Cold he lies in the grave below.
My love is dead,
Gone to his death-bed,
All under the willow-tree.

Sweet his tongue as throstle's note,
Quick in dance as thought was he;
Deft his tabor, cudgel stout;
O, he lies by the willow-tree!
My love is dead,
Gone to his death-bed,
All under the willow-tree.

Hark! the raven flaps his wing
  In the briered dell below;
Hark! the death-owl loud doth sing
  To the nightmares as they go.
    My love is dead,
    Gone to his death-bed,
    All under the willow-tree.

See! the white moon shines on high;
  Whiter is my true-love's shroud,
Whiter than the morning sky,
  Whiter than the evening cloud.
    My love is dead,
    Gone to his death-bed,
    All under the willow-tree.

Here, upon my true-love's grave,
  Shall the garish flowers be laid,
Nor one holy saint to save
  All the sorrows of a maid.
    My love is dead,
    Gone to his death-bed,
    All under the willow-tree.

With my hands I 'll bind the briers
  Round his holy corse to gre;
Elfin-fairy, light your fires,
  Here my body still shall be.
    My love is dead,
    Gone to his death-bed,
    All under the willow-tree.

Come with acorn cup and thorn,
  Drain my heart's blood all away;
Life and all its good I scorn,
  Dance by night, or feast by day.
    My love is dead,
    Gone to his death-bed,
    All under the willow-tree.

Water-witches, crowned with reytes,
  Bear me to your deadly tide.
I die—I come—my true-love waits.
  Thus the damsel spake, and died.

GEORGE CRABBE.

[1754-1832.]

ISAAC ASHFORD.

Next to these ladies, but in naught allied,
A noble peasant, Isaac Ashford, died.
Noble he was, contemning all things mean,
His truth unquestioned and his soul serene:
Of no man's presence Isaac felt afraid;
At no man's question Isaac looked dismayed:
Shame knew him not, he dreaded no disgrace;
Truth, simple truth, was written in his face;
Yet while the serious thought his soul approved,
Cheerful he seemed, and gentleness he loved;
To bliss domestic he his heart resigned,
And with the firmest, had the fondest mind.
Were others joyful, he looked smiling on,
And gave allowance where he needed none;
Good he refused with future ill to buy,
Nor knew a joy that caused reflection's sigh.
A friend to virtue, his unclouded breast
No envy stung, no jealousy distressed
(Bane of the poor! it wounds their weaker mind
To miss one favor which their neighbors find);
Yet far was he from stoic pride removed;
He felt humanely, and he warmly loved.
I marked his action when his infant died,
And his old neighbor for offence was tried;
The still tears, stealing down that furrowed cheek,
Spoke pity plainer than the tongue can speak.
If pride were his, 't was not their vulgar pride
Who, in their base contempt, the great deride;
Nor pride in learning, though my clerk agreed,
If fate should call him, Ashford might succeed;
Nor pride in rustic skill, although we knew
None his superior, and his equals few:
But if that spirit in his soul had place,
It was the jealous pride that shuns disgrace;
A pride in honest fame, by virtue gained,
In sturdy boys to virtuous labors trained;
Pride in the power that guards his country's coast,
And all that Englishmen enjoy and boast;
Pride in a life that slander's tongue defied,
In fact, a noble passion, misnamed pride.
  He had no party's rage, no sectary's whim;

Christian and countryman was all with him,
True to his church he came, no Sunday-shower
Kept him at home in that important hour;
Nor his firm feet could one persuading sect
By the strong glare of their new light direct:—
"On hope, in mine own sober light, I gaze,
But should be blind and lose it in your blaze."
In times severe, when many a sturdy swain
Felt it his pride, his comfort, to complain,
Isaac their wants would soothe, his own would hide,
And feel in that his comfort and his pride.
At length he found, when seventy years were run,
His strength departed and his labor done;
When, save his honest fame, he kept no more;
But lost his wife and saw his children poor.
'T was then a spark of — say not discontent —
Struck on his mind, and thus he gave it vent:
"Kind are your laws ('t is not to be denied)
That in yon house for ruined age provide,
And they are just; when young, we give you all,
And then for comforts in our weakness call.
Why then this proud reluctance to be fed,
To join your poor and eat the parish-bread?
But yet I linger, loath with him to feed
Who gains his plenty by the sons of need:
He who, by contract, all your paupers took,
And gauges stomachs with an anxious look:
On some old master I could well depend;
See him with joy and thank him as a friend;
But ill on him who doles the day's supply,
And counts our chances who at night may die:
Yet help me, Heaven! and let me not complain
Of what befalls me, but the fate sustain."
Such were his thoughts, and so resigned he grew;
Daily he placed the workhouse in his view!
But came not there, for sudden was his fate,
He dropt expiring at his cottage-gate.
I feel his absence in the hours of prayer,
And view his seat, and sigh for Isaac there;
I see no more those white locks thinly spread
Round the bald polish of that honored head;
No more that awful glance on playful wight
Compelled to kneel and tremble at the sight,
To fold his fingers all in dread the while,
Till Mister Ashford softened to a smile;
No more that meek and suppliant look in prayer,
Nor the pure faith (to give it force) are there: . . . .
But he is blest, and I lament no more,
A wise good man contented to be poor.

SAMUEL ROGERS.

[1763-1855.]

A WISH.

MINE be a cot beside the hill;
A bee-hive's hum shall soothe my ear;
A willowy brook that turns a mill,
With many a fall shall linger near.

The swallow, oft, beneath my thatch
Shall twitter from her clay-built nest;
Oft shall the pilgrim lift the latch,
And share my meal, a welcome guest.

Around my ivied porch shall spring
Each fragrant flower that drinks the dew;
And Lucy, at her wheel, shall sing
In russet gown and apron blue.

The village-church among the trees,
Where first our marriage-vows were given,
With merry peals shall swell the breeze,
And point with taper spire to heaven.

ITALIAN SONG.

DEAR is my little native vale,
The ring-dove builds and murmurs there;
Close by my cot she tells her tale
To every passing villager.

The squirrel leaps from tree to tree,
And shells his nuts at liberty.

In orange groves and myrtle bowers,
That breathe a gale of fragrance round,
I charm the fairy-footed hours
With my loved lute's romantic sound;
Of crowns of living laurel weave
For those that win the race at eve.

The shepherd's horn at break of day,
The ballet danced in twilight glade,
The canzonet and roundelay
Sung in the silent greenwood shade:
These simple joys that never fail
Shall bind me to my native vale.

ROBERT BURNS.

[1759-1796.]

OF A' THE AIRTS THE WIND CAN BLAW.

Of a' the airts the wind can blaw,
I dearly like the west;
For there the bonnie lassie lives,
The lassie I lo'e best.
There wild woods grow, and rivers row,
And monie a hill 's between;
But day and night my fancy's flight
Is ever wi' my Jean.

I see her in the dewy flowers,
I see her sweet and fair;
I hear her in the tunefu' birds,
I hear her charm the air;
There 's not a bonnie flower that springs
By fountain, shaw, or green, —
There 's not a bonnie bird that sings,
But minds me o' my Jean.

MARY MORISON.

O Mary, at thy window be!
It is the wished, the trysted hour!
Those smiles and glances let me see,
That make the miser's treasure poor:
How blithely wad I bide the stoure,
A weary slave frae sun to sun,
Could I the rich reward secure,
The lovely Mary Morison.

Yestreen when to the trembling string
The dance gaed through the lighted ha',
To thee my fancy took its wing,
I sat, but neither heard nor saw.
Though this was fair, and that was braw,
And yon the toast of a' the town,
I sighed, and said amang them a',
"Ye are na Mary Morison."

O Mary, canst thou wreck his peace
Wha for thy sake wad gladly dee?
Or canst thou break that heart of his,
Whase only faut is loving thee?
If love for love thou wilt na gie,
At least be pity to me shown;
A thought ungentle canna be
The thought o' Mary Morison.

HIGHLAND MARY.

Ye banks and braes and streams around
The castle o' Montgomery,
Green be your woods, and fair your flowers,
Your waters never drumlie!
There simmer first unfauld her robes
And there the langest tarry!
For there I took the last fareweel
O' my sweet Highland Mary.

How sweetly bloomed the gay green birk,
How rich the hawthorn's blossom,
As underneath their fragrant shade
I clasped her to my bosom!
The golden hours on angel wings
Flew o'er me and my dearie;
For dear to me as light and life
Was my sweet Highland Mary.

Wi' monie a vow and locked embrace
Our parting was fu' tender;
And pledging aft to meet again,
We tore ourselves asunder;
But, O, fell Death's untimely frost,
That nipt my flower sae early!
Now green 's the sod, and cauld 's the clay,
That wraps my Highland Mary!

O pale, pale now, those rosy lips
I aft hae kissed sae fondly!
And closed for aye the sparkling glance
That dwelt on me sae kindly!
And mouldering now in silent dust
That heart that lo'ed me dearly!
But still within my bosom's core
Shall live my Highland Mary.

TO MARY IN HEAVEN.

Thou lingering star, with lessening ray,
That lov'st to greet the early morn,
Again thou usherest in the day
My Mary from my soul was torn.
O Mary! dear, departed shade!
Where is thy place of blissful rest?
Seest thou thy lover lowly laid?
Hear'st thou the groans that rend his breast?

That sacred hour can I forget,
Can I forget the hallowed grove,
Where by the winding Ayr we met
To live one day of parting love?
Eternity will not efface
Those records dear of transports past;
Thy image at our last embrace!
Ah! little thought we 't was our last!

Ayr, gurgling, kissed his pebbled shore,
O'erhung with wild woods, thickening green;
The fragrant birch, and hawthorn hoar,
Twined amorous round the raptured scene.
The flowers sprang wanton to be pressed,
The birds sang love on every spray,
Till too, too soon, the glowing west
Proclaimed the speed of wingéd day.

Still o'er these scenes my memory wakes,
And fondly broods with miser care;
Time but the impression deeper makes,
As streams their channels deeper wear.
My Mary! dear, departed shade!
Where is thy place of blissful rest?
Seest thou thy lover lowly laid?
Hear'st thou the groans that rend his breast?

A VISION.

As I stood by yon roofless tower,
Where the wa'-flower scents the dewy air,
Where the howlet mourns in her ivy bower,
And tells the midnight moon her care.

The winds were laid, the air was still,
The stars they shot alang the sky;
The fox was howling on the hill,
And the distant-echoing glens reply.

The stream, adown its hazelly path,
Was rushing by the ruined wa's,
Hasting to join the sweeping Nith,
Whase distant roaring swells and fa's.

The cauld blue north was streaming forth
Her lights, wi' hissing, eerie din;
Athort the lift they start and shift,
Like fortune's favors, tint as win.

By heedless chance I turned mine eyes,
And by the moon-beam, shook, to see
A stern and stalwart ghaist arise,
Attired as minstrels wont to be.

Had I a statue been o' stane,
His darin look had daunted me:
And on his bonnet graved was plain,
The sacred posy—Libertie!

And frae his harp sic strains did flow,
Might roused the slumbering dead to hear;
But O, it was a tale of woe,
As ever met a Briton's ear!

He sang wi' joy his former day,
He weeping wailed his latter times;
But what he said it was nae play,
I winna ventur 't in my rhymes.

A BARD'S EPITAPH.

Is there a whim-inspiréd fool,
Owre fast for thought, owre hot for rule,
Owre blate to seek, owre proud to snool,
Let him draw near,
And owre this grassy heap sing dool,
And drap a tear.

Is there a bard of rustic song,
Who, noteless, steals the crowds among,
That weekly this area throng,
O, pass not by!
But with a frater-feeling strong,
Here heave a sigh.

Is there a man whose judgment clear
Can others teach the course to steer,
Yet runs himself life's mad career,
Wild as the wave;
Here pause, and, thro' the starting tear,
Survey this grave.

This poor inhabitant below
Was quick to learn and wise to know,

And keenly felt the friendly glow,
And softer flame;
But thoughtless follies laid him low,
And stained his name!

Reader, attend, — whether thy soul
Soars fancy's flights beyond the pole,
Or darkling grubs this earthly hole,
In low pursuit;
Know prudent, cautious self-control
Is wisdom's root.

ELEGY ON CAPTAIN MATTHEW HENDERSON.

He 's gane, he 's gane! he 's frae us torn,
The ae best fellow e'er was born!
Thee, Matthew, Nature's sel shall mourn
By wood and wild,
Where, haply, Pity strays forlorn,
Frae man exiled.

Ye hills, near neebors o' the starns,
That proudly cock your cresting cairns!
Ye cliffs, the haunts of sailing yearns
Where echo slumbers!
Come join, ye Nature's sturdiest bairns,
My wailing numbers!

Mourn, ilka grove the cushat kens!
Ye haz'lly shaws and briery dens!
Ye burnies, wimplin down your glens,
Wi' toddlin din,
Or foaming strang, wi' hasty stens,
Frae lin to lin.

Mourn, little harebells o'er the lea;
Ye stately foxgloves fair to see;
Ye woodbines hanging bonnilie,
In scented bow'rs;
Ye roses on your thorny tree,
The first o' flow'rs.

At dawn, when every grassy blade
Droops with a diamond at its head,
At ev'n, when beans their fragrance shed,
I' th' rustling gale,
Ye maukins whiddin thro' the glade,
Come join my wail.

Mourn, ye wee songsters o' the wood;
Ye grouse that crap the heather bud;
Ye curlews calling thro' a clud;
Ye whistling plover;
And mourn, ye whirring paitrick brood;
He 's gane forever!

Mourn, sooty coots, and speckled teals;
Ye fisher herons, watching eels;
Ye duck and drake, wi' airy wheels
Circling the lake;
Ye bitterns, till the quagmire reels,
Rair for his sake.

Mourn, clam'ring craiks at close o' day,
'Mang fields o' flow'ring claver gay;
And when ye wing your annual way
Frae our cauld shore,
Tell thae far warlds, wha lies in clay,
Wham we deplore.

Ye howlets, frae your ivy bow'r,
In some auld tree, or eldritch tow'r,
What time the moon, wi' silent glow'r,
Sets up her horn,
Wail thro' the dreary midnight hour
Till waukrife morn.

O rivers, forests, hills, and plains!
Oft have ye heard my canty strains;
But now, what else for me remains
But tales of woe?
And frae my een the drapping rains
Maun ever flow.

Mourn, Spring, thou darling of the year!
Ilk cowslip cup shall kep a tear;
Thou, Summer, while each corny spear
Shoots up its head.
Thy gay, green, flow'ry tresses shear
For him that 's dead!

Thou, Autumn, wi' thy yellow hair,
In grief thy sallow mantle tear!
Thou, Winter, hurling thro' the air
The roaring blast,
Wide o'er the naked world declare
The worth we 've lost!

Mourn him, thou Sun, great source of light;
Mourn, Empress of the silent night!
And you, ye twinkling starnies bright,
My Matthew mourn!
For through your orbs he 's ta'en his flight,
Ne'er to return.

O Henderson; the man! the brother!
And art thou gone, and gone forever!
And hast thou crost that unknown river,
Life's dreary bound!
Like thee, where shall I find another,
The world around?

Go to your sculptured tombs, ye Great,
In a' the tinsel trash o' state!

But by thy honest turf I 'll wait,
Thou man of worth!
And weep the ae best fellow's fate
E'er lay in earth.

LADY ANNE BARNARD.

[1705-1825.]

AULD ROBIN GRAY.

When the sheep are in the fauld, and the kye come hame,
And a' the weary warld to sleep are gane;
The waes o' my heart fa' in showers frae my ee,
While my gudeman lies sound by me.

Young Jamie lo'ed me weel, and socht me for his bride;
But saving a croun, he had naething else beside;
To mak that croun a pund, my Jamie gaed to sea;
And the croun and the pund they were baith for me.

He hadna been gane a twelvemonth and a day,
When my father brak his arm, and the cow was stown awa:
My mither she fell sick, —my Jamie was at sea,
And auld Robin Gray cam' a-courtin' me.

My father couldna work, and my mother couldna spin;
I toiled day and nicht, but their bread I couldna win;
Auld Rob maintained them baith, and, wi' tears in his ee',
Said, "Jeannie, for their sakes, will ye na marry me?"

My heart it said nay, for I looked for Jamie back;
But the wind it blew high, and the ship it was a wrack;
The ship it was a wrack—why didna Jamie dee?
Or why do I live to say, Wae 's me?

My father urged me sair: my mither didna speak;
But she lookit in my face till my heart was like to break;
They gied him my hand, though my heart was in the sea;
And auld Robin Gray was gudeman to me.

I hadna been a wife a week but only four,
When, mournfu' as I sat on the stane at my door,
I saw my Jamie's wraith, for I couldna think it he,
Till he said, "I 'm come home, love, to marry thee."

O, sair did we greet, and muckle say of a'!
I gie'd him but ae kiss, and bade him gang awa':
I wish I were dead! but I 'm no like to dee;
And why do I live to cry, Wae 's me?

I gang like a ghaist, and I carena to spin;
I daurna think on Jamie, for that wad be a sin;
But I 'll do my best a gude wife to be,
For auld Robin Gray, he is kind to me.

WILLIAM BLAKE.

[1757-1827.]

THE TIGER.

Tiger! Tiger! burning bright,
In the forests of the night;
What immortal hand or eye
Could frame thy fearful symmetry?

In what distant deeps or skies
Burned the fire of thine eyes?
On what wings dare he aspire?
What the hand dare seize the fire?

And what shoulder, and what art,
Could twist the sinews of thine heart?
And when thy heart began to beat,
What dread hand? and what dread feet?

What the hammer, what the chain?
In what furnace was thy brain?
What the anvil? what dread grasp
Dare its deadly terrors clasp?

When the stars threw down their spears,
And watered heaven with their tears,

Did he smile his work to see?
Did He, who made the Lamb, make thee?

Tiger! Tiger! burning bright,
In the forests of the night,
What immortal hand or eye
Dare frame thy fearful symmetry?

TO THE MUSES.

Whether on Ida's shady brow
  Or in the chambers of the East,
The chambers of the sun, which now
  From ancient melodies have ceased;

Whether in Heaven ye wander fair,
  Or the green corners of the earth,
Or the blue regions of the air,
  Where the melodious winds have birth,

Whether on crystal rocks ye rove,
  Beneath the bosom of the sea,
Wandering in many a coral grove,
  Fair Nine, forsaking Poetry,

How have you left the ancient lore
  That bards of old engaged in you!
The languid strings do scarcely move,
  The sound is forced, the notes are few.

JOANNA BAILLIE.

[1762-1831.]

THE GOWAN GLITTERS ON THE SWARD.

The gowan glitters on the sward,
  The lav'rock 's in the sky,
And Collie on my plaid keeps ward,
  And time is passing by.
    O, no! sad and slow,
      And lengthened on the ground;
    The shadow of our trysting bush
      It wears so slowly round.

My sheep-bells tinkle frae the west,
  My lambs are bleating near;
But still the sound that I love best,
  Alack! I canna hear.
    O, no! sad and slow,
      The shadow lingers still;
    And like a lanely ghaist I stand,
      And croon upon the hill.

I hear below the water roar,
  The mill wi' clacking din,
And Lucky scolding frae the door,
  To ca' the bairnies in.
    O, no! sad and slow,
      These are nae sounds for me;
    The shadow of our trysting bush
      It creeps sae drearily.

I coft yestreen, frae chapman Tam,
  A snood o' bonnie blue,
And promised, when our trysting cam',
  To tie it round her brow.
    O, no! sad and slow,
      The mark it winna' pass;
    The shadow o' that dreary bush
      Is tethered on the grass.

O now I see her on the way!
  She 's past the witch's knowe;
She 's climbing up the brownies brae;
  My heart is in a lowe,
    O, no! 't is not so,
      'T is glamrie I hae seen;
    The shadow o' that hawthorn bush
      Will move nae mair till e'en.

My book o' grace I 'll try to read,
  Though conned wi' little skill;
When Collie barks I 'll raise my head,
  And find her on the hill.
    O, no! sad and slow,
      The time will ne'er be gane;
    The shadow o' our trysting bush
      Is fixed like ony stane.

LADY CAROLINE NAIRN.

[1766-1845.]

THE LAND O' THE LEAL.

I 'm wearin' awa', Jean,
Like snaw in a thaw, Jean,
I 'm wearin' awa'
  To the Land o' the Leal.
There 's nae sorrow there, Jean,
There 's neither cauld nor care, Jean,
The day is ever fair
  In the Land o' the Leal.

You 've been leal and true, Jean,
Your task is ended noo, Jean,
And I 'll welcome you
  To the Land o' the Leal.

Then dry that tearfu' ee, Jean;
My soul langs to be free, Jean;
And angels wait on me
To the Land o' the Leal.

Our bonnie bairn 's there, Jean,
She was baith gude and fair, Jean,
And we grudged her sair
To the Land o' the Leal!
But sorrow 's self wears past, Jean,
And joy 's a comin' fast, Jean,
The joy that 's aye to last,
In the Land o' the Leal.

A' our friends are gane, Jean;
We 've lang been left alane, Jean;
But we 'll a' meet again
In the Land o' the Leal.
Now fare ye weel, my ain Jean!
This world's care is vain, Jean!
We 'll meet, and aye be fain
In the Land o' the Leal.

ROBERT BLOOMFIELD.

[1766–1823.]

THE SOLDIER'S RETURN.

How sweet it was to breathe that cooler air,
And take possession of my father's chair!
Beneath my elbow, on the solid frame,
Appeared the rough initials of my name,
Cut forty years before! The same old clock
Struck the same bell, and gave my heart a shock
I never can forget. A short breeze sprung,
And while a sigh was trembling on my tongue,
Caught the old dangling almanacs behind,
And up they flew like banners in the wind;
Then gently, singly, down, down, down they went,
And told of twenty years that I had spent
Far from my native land. That instant came
A robin on the threshold; though so tame,
At first he looked distrustful, almost shy,
And cast on me his coal-black steadfast eye,
And seemed to say, — past friendship to renew, —
"Ah ha! old worn-out soldier, is it you?"
While thus I mused, still gazing, gazing still,
On beds of moss spread on the window-sill,
I deemed no moss my eyes had ever seen
Had been so lovely, brilliant, fresh, and green,
And guessed some infant hand had placed it there,
And prized its hue, so exquisite, so rare.
Feelings on feelings mingling, doubling rose;
My heart felt everything but calm repose;
I could not reckon minutes, hours, nor years,
But rose at once, and bursted into tears;
Then, like a fool, confused, sat down again,
And thought upon the past with shame and pain;
I raved at war and all its horrid cost,
And glory's quagmire, where the brave are lost.
On carnage, fire, and plunder long I mused,
And cursed the murdering weapons I had used.
Two shadows then I saw, two voices heard,
One bespoke age, and one a child's appeared.
In stepped my father with convulsive start,
And in an instant clasped me to his heart.
Close by him stood a little blue-eyed maid;
And stooping to the child, the old man said,
"Come hither, Nancy, kiss me once again;
This is your uncle Charles, come home from Spain."
The child approached, and with her fingers light
Stroked my old eyes, almost deprived of sight.
But why thus spin my tale, — thus tedious be?
Happy old soldier! what 's the world to me?

JANE ELLIOTT.

[1781 - 1849.]

LAMENT FOR FLODDEN.

I 'VE heard them lilting at our ewe-milking,
Lasses a' lilting before dawn o' day;
But now they are moaning on ilka green loaning—
The Flowers of the Forest are a' wede away.

At bughts, in the morning, nae blythe lads are scorning,
Lasses are lonely and dowie and wae;
Nae daffin', nae gabbin', but sighing and sabbing,
Ilk ane lifts her leglin and hies her away.

In har'st, at the shearing, nae youths now are jeering,
Bandsters are lyart, and runkled, and gray;
At fair or at preaching, nae wooing, nae fleeching—
The Flowers of the Forest are a' wede away.

At e'en, in the gloaming, nae younkers are roaming
'Bout stacks wi' the lasses at bogle to play;
But ilk ane sits drearie, lamenting her dearie—
The Flowers of the Forest are weded away.

Dool and wae for the order, sent our lads to the Border!
The English, for ance, by guile wan the day;
The Flowers of the Forest, that fought aye the foremost,
The prime of our land, are cauld in the clay.

We 'll hear nae mair lilting at the ewe-milking;
Women and bairns are heartless and wae;
Sighing and moaning on ilka green loaning—
The Flowers of the Forest are a' wede away.

ROBERT TANNAHILL.

[1774 - 1810.]

THE MIDGES DANCE ABOON THE BURN.

THE midges dance aboon the burn;
The dews begin to fa';
The paitricks down the rushy holm
Set up their e'ening ca'.
Now loud and clear the blackbird's sang
Rings through the briery shaw,
While flitting gay the swallows play
Around the castle wa'.

Beneath the golden gloamin' sky
The mavis mends her lay;
The redbreast pours his sweetest strains,
To charm the ling'ring day;
While weary yaldrins seem to wail
Their little nestlings torn,
The merry wren, frae den to den,
Gaes jinking through the thorn.

The roses fauld their silken leaves,
The foxglove shuts its bell;
The honeysuckle and the birk
Spread fragrance through the dell.
Let others crowd the giddy court
Of mirth and revelry,
The simple joys that Nature yields
Are dearer far to me.

THE BRAES O' BALQUHITHER.

LET us go, lassie, go,
To the braes o' Balquhither,
Where the blae-berries grow
'Mang the bonnie Highland heather;
Where the deer and the roe,
Lightly bounding together,
Sport the lang summer day
On the braes o' Balquhither.

I will twine thee a bower
By the clear siller fountain,
And I 'll cover it o'er
Wi' the flowers of the mountain;
I will range through the wilds,
And the deep glens sae drearie,
And return wi' the spoils
To the bower o' my dearie.

When the rude wintry win'
Idly raves round our dwelling,

And the roar of the linn
  On the night breeze is swelling,
So merrily we 'll sing,
  As the storm rattles o'er us,
Till the dear shieling ring
  Wi' the light lilting chorus.

Now the summer 's in prime
  Wi' the flowers richly blooming,
And the wild mountain thyme
  A' the moorlands perfuming;
To our dear native scenes
  Let us journey together,
Where glad innocence reigns
  'Mang the braes o' Balquhither.

WILLIAM R. SPENCER.

[1770 - 1834.]

TO THE LADY ANNE HAMILTON.

Too late I stayed, forgive the crime,
  Unheeded flew the hours;
How noiseless falls the foot of Time
  That only treads on flowers!

What eye with clear account remarks
  The ebbing of his glass,
When all its sands are diamond sparks
  That dazzle as they pass!

Ah! who to sober measurement
  Time's happy swiftness brings,
When birds of Paradise have lent
  Their plumage to its wings?

JAMES GLASSFORD.

[1772 - .]

THE DEAD WHO HAVE DIED IN THE LORD.

Go, call for the mourners, and raise the lament,
Let the tresses be torn, and the garments be rent;
But weep not for him who is gone to his rest,
Nor mourn for the ransomed, nor wail for the blest.
The sun is not set, but is risen on high,
Nor long in corruption his body shall lie;
Then let not the tide of thy griefs overflow,
Nor the music of heaven be discord below;
Rather loud be the song, and triumphant the chord,
Let us joy for the dead who have died in the Lord.

Go, call for the mourners, and raise the lament,
Let the tresses be torn, and the garments be rent;
But give to the living thy passion of tears,
Who walk in this valley of sadness and fears;
Who are pressed by the combat, in darkness are lost,
By the tempest are beat, on the billows are tossed:
O, weep not for those who shall sorrow no more,
Whose warfare is ended, whose trial is o'er;
Let the song be exalted, triumphant the chord,
And rejoice for the dead who have died in the Lord.

JOSEPH BLANCO WHITE.

[1775 - 1841.]

NIGHT AND DEATH.

Mysterious night! when our first parent knew
  Thee from report Divine, and heard thy name,
  Did he not tremble for this lovely frame,
This glorious canopy of light and blue?
Yet, 'neath a curtain of translucent dew,
Bathed in the rays of the great setting flame,
Hesperus, with the host of heaven, came,
And lo! creation widened in man's view.
Who could have thought such darkness lay concealed
  Within thy beams, O sun! or who could find,
Whilst fly, and leaf, and insect stood revealed,
  That to such countless orbs thou mad'st us blind?

Why do we, then, shun death with anxious strife?
If light can thus deceive, wherefore not life?

JOHN LEYDEN.

[1775–1811.]

ODE TO AN INDIAN GOLD COIN.

WRITTEN IN CHERICAL, MALABAR.

Slave of the dark and dirty mine!
What vanity has brought thee here?
How can I love to see thee shine
So bright, whom I have bought so dear?—
The tent-ropes flapping lone I hear,
For twilight converse, arm in arm;
The jackal's shriek bursts on mine ear
Whom mirth and music wont to charm.

By Chérical's dark wandering streams,
Where cane-tufts shadow all the wild,
Sweet visions haunt my waking dreams
Of Teviot loved while still a child,
Of castled rocks stupendous piled
By Esk or Eden's classic wave,
Where loves of youth and friendship smiled,
Uncursed by thee, vile yellow slave!

Fade, day-dreams sweet, from memory fade!—
The perished bliss of youth's first prime,
That once so bright on fancy played,
Revives no more in after time.
Far from my sacred natal clime,
I haste to an untimely grave;
The daring thoughts that soared sublime
Are sunk in ocean's southern wave.

Slave of the mine! thy yellow light
Gleams baleful as the tomb-fire drear.
A gentle vision comes by night
My lonely widowed heart to cheer;
Her eyes are dim with many a tear,
That once were guiding stars to mine:
Her fond heart throbs with many a fear!
I cannot bear to see thee shine.

For thee, for thee, vile yellow slave,
I left a heart that loved me true!
I crossed the tedious ocean-wave,
To roam in climes unkind and new.
The cold wind of the stranger blew
Chill on my withered heart: the grave
Dark and untimely met my view,—
And all for thee, vile yellow slave!

Ha! comest thou now so late to mock
A wanderer's banished heart forlorn,
Now that his frame the lightning shock
Of sun-rays tipt with death has borne?
From love, from friendship, country, torn,
To memory's fond regrets the prey,
Vile slave, thy yellow dross I scorn!
Go mix thee with thy kindred clay!

SIR HUMPHRY DAVY.

[1778–1829.]

WRITTEN AFTER RECOVERY FROM A DANGEROUS ILLNESS.

Lo! o'er the earth the kindling spirits pour
The flames of life that bounteous nature gives;
The limpid dew becomes the rosy flower,
The insensate dust awakes, and moves, and lives.

All speaks of change: the renovated forms
Of long-forgotten things arise again;
The light of suns, the breath of angry storms,
The everlasting motions of the main,—

These are but engines of the Eternal will,
The One Intelligence, whose potent sway
Has ever acted, and is acting still,
Whilst stars, and worlds, and systems all obey;

Without whose power, the whole of mortal things
Were dull, inert, an unharmonious band,
Silent as are the harp's untunéd strings
Without the touches of the poet's hand.

A sacred spark created by His breath,
The immortal mind of man His image bears;
A spirit living 'midst the forms of death,
Oppressed but not subdued by mortal cares;

A germ, preparing in the winter's frost
To rise, and bud, and blossom in the spring;
An unfledged eagle by the tempest tossed,
Unconscious of his future strength of wing;

The child of trial, to mortality
And all its changeful influences given;
On the green earth decreed to move and die,
And yet by such a fate prepared for heaven.

Soon as it breathes, to feel the mother's form
Of orbéd beauty through its organs thrill,
To press the limbs of life with rapture warm,
And drink instinctive of a living rill;

To view the skies with morning radiance bright,
Majestic mingling with the ocean blue,
Or bounded by green hills, or mountains white,
Or peopled plains of rich and varied hue;

The nobler charms astonished to behold,
Of living loveliness,—to see it move,
Cast in expression's rich and varied mould,
Awakening sympathy, compelling love;

The heavenly balm of mutual hope to taste,
Soother of life, affliction's bliss to share;
Sweet as the stream amidst the desert waste,
As the first blush of arctic daylight fair;

To mingle with its kindred, to descry
The path of power; in public life to shine;
To gain the voice of popularity,
The idol of to-day, the man divine;

To govern others by an influence strong
As that high law which moves the murmuring main,
Raising and carrying all its waves along,
Beneath the full-orbed moon's meridian reign;

To scan how transient is the breath of praise,
A winter's zephyr trembling on the snow,
Chilled as it moves; or, as the northern rays,
First fading in the centre, whence they flow.

To live in forests mingled with the whole
Of natural forms, whose generations rise,
In lovely change, in happy order roll,
On land, in ocean, in the glittering skies;

Their harmony to trace; the Eternal cause
To know in love, in reverence to adore;
To bend beneath the inevitable laws,
Sinking in death, its human strength no more!

Then, as awakening from a dream of pain,
With joy its mortal feelings to resign;
Yet all its living essence to retain,
The undying energy of strength divine!

To quit the burdens of its earthly days,
To give to nature all her borrowed powers,—
Ethereal fire to feed the solar rays,
Ethereal dew to glad the earth with showers.

GEORGE CROLY.

[1780-1860.]

CUPID GROWN CAREFUL.

THERE was once a gentle time
When the world was in its prime;
And every day was holiday,
And every month was lovely May.
Cupid then had but to go
With his purple wings and bow;

And in blossomed vale and grove
Every shepherd knelt to love.

Then a rosy, dimpled cheek,
And a blue eye, fond and meek;
And a ringlet-wreathen brow,
Like hyacinths on a bed of snow:
And a low voice, silver sweet,
From a lip without deceit;
Only those the hearts could move
Of the simple swains to love.

But that time is gone and past,
Can the summer always last?
And the swains are wiser grown,
And the heart is turned to stone,
And the maiden's rose may wither;
Cupid 's fled, no man knows whither.
But another Cupid 's come,
With a brow of care and gloom:
Fixed upon the earthly mould,
Thinking of the sullen gold;
In his hand the bow no more,
At his back the household store,
That the bridal gold must buy:
Useless now the smile and sigh:
But he wears the pinion still,
Flying at the sight of ill.

O, for the old true-love time,
When the world was in its prime!

HENRY KIRKE WHITE.

[1785-1806.]

TO THE HERB ROSEMARY.

Sweet-scented flower! who 'rt wont to bloom
On January's front severe,
And o'er the wintry desert drear
To waft thy waste perfume!
Come, thou shalt form my nosegay now,
And I will bind thee round my brow;
And as I twine the mournful wreath,
I 'll weave a melancholy song:
And sweet the strain shall be and long,
The melody of death.

Come, funeral flower! who lov'st to dwell
With the pale corpse in lonely tomb,
And throw across the desert gloom
A sweet decaying smell.
Come, press my lips, and lie with me
Beneath the lowly alder-tree,
And we will sleep a pleasant sleep,
And not a care shall dare intrude,
To break the marble solitude
So peaceful and so deep.

And hark! the wind-god, as he flies,
Moans hollow in the forest trees,
And sailing on the gusty breeze,
Mysterious music dies.
Sweet flower! that requiem wild is mine,
It warns me to the lonely shrine,
The cold turf altar of the dead;
My grave shall be in yon lone spot,
Where as I lie, by all forgot,
A dying fragrance thou wilt o'er my ashes shed.

TO AN EARLY PRIMROSE.

Mild offspring of a dark and sullen sire!
Whose modest form, so delicately fine,
Was nursed in whirling storms,
And cradled in the winds.

Thee, when young Spring first questioned Winter's sway,
And dared the sturdy blusterer to the fight,
Thee on this bank he threw
To mark his victory.

In this low vale, the promise of the year,
Serene, thou openest to the nipping gale,
Unnoticed and alone,
Thy tender elegance.

So virtue blooms, brought forth amid the storms
Of chill adversity; in some lone walk
Of life she rears her head,
Obscure and unobserved;

While every bleaching breeze that on her blows
Chastens her spotless purity of breast,
And hardens her to bear
Serene the ills of life.

THE STAR OF BETHLEHEM.

WHEN marshalled on the nightly plain,
The glittering host bestud the sky;
One star alone, of all the train,
Can fix the sinner's wandering eye.

Hark! hark! to God the chorus breaks,
From every host, from every gem:
But one alone the Saviour speaks,
It is the Star of Bethlehem.

Once on the raging seas I rode,
The storm was loud, the night was dark,
The ocean yawned, and rudely blowed
The wind that tossed my foundering bark.

Deep horror then my vitals froze,
Death-struck, I ceased the tide to stem;
When suddenly a star arose, —
It was the Star of Bethlehem.

It was my guide, my light, my all,
It bade my dark forebodings cease;
And through the storm and dangers' thrall,
It led me to the port of peace.

Now safely moored, my perils o'er,
I'll sing, first in night's diadem,
Forever and forevermore
The Star!—the Star of Bethlehem!

HERBERT KNOWLES.

[1798-1827.]

LINES WRITTEN IN RICHMOND CHURCHYARD, YORKSHIRE.

"It is good for us to be here; if thou wilt, let us make here three tabernacles; one for thee, and one for Moses, and one for Elias." — MATT. xvii. 4.

METHINKS it is good to be here;
If thou wilt, let us build — but for whom?
Nor Elias nor Moses appear,
But the shadows of eve that encompass the gloom,
The abode of the dead and the place of the tomb.

Shall we build to Ambition? O, no!
Affrighted, he shrinketh away;
For, see! they would pin him below,
In a small narrow cave, and, begirt with cold clay,
To the meanest of reptiles a peer and a prey.

To Beauty? ah, no!—she forgets
The charms which she wielded before—
Nor knows the foul worm that he frets
The skin which but yesterday fools could adore,
For the smoothness it held, or the tint which it wore.

Shall we build to the purple of Pride—
The trappings which dizen the proud?
Alas! they are all laid aside;
And here's neither dress nor adornment allowed,
But the long winding-sheet and the fringe of the shroud.

To Riches? alas! 't is in vain;
Who hid, in their turn have been hid:
The treasures are squandered again;
And here in the grave are all metals forbid,
But the tinsel that shines on the dark coffin-lid.

To the pleasures which Mirth can afford, —
The revel, the laugh, and the jeer?
Ah! here is a plentiful board!
But the guests are all mute as their pitiful cheer,
And none but the worm is a reveller here.

Shall we build to Affection and Love?
Ah, no! they have withered and died,
Or fled with the spirit above;
Friends, brothers, and sisters are laid side by side,
Yet none have saluted, and none have replied.

Unto Sorrow?—The dead cannot grieve;
Not a sob, not a sigh meets mine ear,
Which compassion itself could relieve!
Ah! sweetly they slumber, nor hope, love, nor fear,—
Peace, peace is the watchword, the only one here!

Unto Death, to whom monarchs must bow?
Ah, no! for his empire is known,
And here there are trophies enow!
Beneath—the cold dead, and around—the dark stone,
Are the signs of a sceptre that none may disown!

The first tabernacle to Hope we will build,
And look for the sleepers around us to rise;
The second to Faith, which insures it fulfilled;
And the third to the Lamb of the great sacrifice,
Who bequeathed us them both when he rose to the skies.

FROM WORDSWORTH TO LONGFELLOW.

FROM WORDSWORTH TO LONGFELLOW.

WILLIAM WORDSWORTH.

[1770-1850.]

INTIMATIONS OF IMMORTALITY

FROM RECOLLECTIONS OF EARLY CHILDHOOD.

THERE was a time when meadow, grove, and stream,
The earth, and every common sight,
To me did seem
Apparelled in celestial light,
The glory and the freshness of a dream.
It is not now as it hath been of yore;—
Turn wheresoe'er I may,
By night or day,
The things which I have seen I now can see no more.

The rainbow comes and goes,
And lovely is the rose;
The moon doth with delight
Look round her when the heavens are bare;
Waters on a starry night
Are beautiful and fair;
The sunshine is a glorious birth:
But yet I know, where'er I go,
That there hath passed away a glory from the earth.

Now, while the birds thus sing a joyous song,
And while the young lambs bound
As to the tabor's sound,
To me alone there came a thought of grief;
A timely utterance gave that thought relief,
And I again am strong.

The cataracts blow their trumpets from the steep,—
No more shall grief of mine the season wrong:
I hear the echoes through the mountains throng,
The winds come to me from the fields of sleep,
And all the earth is gay;
Land and sea
Give themselves up to jollity,
And with the heart of May
Doth every beast keep holiday;—
Thou child of joy,
Shout round me, let me hear thy shouts, thou happy shepherd boy!

Ye blessèd creatures, I have heard the call
Ye to each other make; I see
The heavens laugh with you in your jubilee;
My heart is at your festival,
My head hath its coronal,
The fulness of your bliss, I feel—I feel it all.
O evil day! if I were sullen
While Earth herself is adorning,
This sweet May morning,
And the children are culling,
On every side,
In a thousand valleys far and wide,
Fresh flowers; while the sun shines warm,
And the babe leaps up on his mother's arm:—
I hear, I hear, with joy I hear!
—But there's a tree, of many one,
A single field which I have looked upon,—
Both of them speak of something that is gone;

The pansy at my feet
Doth the same tale repeat.
Whither is fled the visionary gleam?
Where is it now, the glory and the dream?

Our birth is but a sleep and a forgetting:
The soul that rises with us, our life's star,
Hath had elsewhere its setting,
And cometh from afar;
Not in entire forgetfulness,
And not in utter nakedness,
But trailing clouds of glory, do we come
From God, who is our home:
Heaven lies about us in our infancy!
Shades of the prison-house begin to close
Upon the growing boy;
But he beholds the light, and whence it flows,—
He sees it in his joy.
The youth who daily farther from the east
Must travel, still is Nature's priest,
And by the vision splendid
Is on his way attended;
At length the man perceives it die away,
And fade into the light of common day.

Earth fills her lap with pleasures of her own;
Yearnings she hath in her own natural kind,
And even with something of a mother's mind,
And no unworthy aim,
The homely nurse doth all she can
To make her foster-child, her inmate man,
Forget the glories he hath known,
And that imperial palace whence he came.

Behold the child among his new-born blisses,
A six years' darling of a pygmy size!
See where mid work of his own hand he lies,
Fretted by sallies of his mother's kisses,
With light upon him from his father's eyes!
See, at his feet, some little plan or chart,
Some fragment from his dream of human life,
Shaped by himself with newly learnéd art,—
A wedding or a festival,
A mourning or a funeral,—
And this hath now his heart,
And unto this he frames his song:
Then will he fit his tongue
To dialogues of business, love, or strife;
But it will not be long
Ere this be thrown aside,
And with new joy and pride
The little actor cons another part;
Filling from time to time his humorous stage
With all the persons, down to palsied age,
That Life brings with her in her equipage;
As if his whole vocation
Were endless imitation.

Thou, whose exterior semblance doth belie
Thy soul's immensity;
Thou best philosopher, who yet dost keep
Thy heritage; thou eye among the blind,
That, deaf and silent, read'st the eternal deep,
Haunted forever by the eternal mind,—
Mighty prophet! Seer blest!
On whom those truths do rest
Which we are toiling all our lives to find,
In darkness lost, the darkness of the grave;
Thou, over whom thy immortality
Broods like the day, a master o'er a slave,
A presence which is not to be put by;
Thou little child, yet glorious in the might
Of heaven-born freedom, on thy being's height,
Why with such earnest pains dost thou provoke
The years to bring the inevitable yoke,
Thus blindly with thy blessedness at strife?
Full soon thy soul shall have her earthly freight,
And custom lie upon thee with a weight
Heavy as frost, and deep almost as life!

O joy! that in our embers
Is something that doth live;
That Nature yet remembers
What was so fugitive!
The thought of our past years in me doth breed
Perpetual benediction: not indeed
For that which is most worthy to be blest;
Delight and liberty, the simple creed
Of childhood, whether busy or at rest,
With new-fledged hope still fluttering in his breast:—

Not for these I raise
The song of thanks and praise;
But for those obstinate questionings
Of sense and outward things,
Fallings from us, vanishings,
Blank misgivings of a creature
Moving about in worlds not realized,
High instincts before which our mortal nature
Did tremble like a guilty thing surprised:
But for those first affections,
Those shadowy recollections,
Which, be they what they may,
Are yet the fountain light of all our day,
Are yet a master light of all our seeing;
Uphold us, cherish, and have power to make
Our noisy years seem moments in the being
Of the eternal silence: truths that wake,
To perish never;
Which neither listlessness, nor mad endeavor,
Nor man nor boy,
Nor all that is at enmity with joy,
Can utterly abolish or destroy!
Hence, in a season of calm weather,
Though inland far we be,
Our souls have sight of that immortal sea
Which brought us hither;
Can in a moment travel thither,
And see the children sport upon the shore,
And hear the mighty waters rolling evermore.

Then, sing, ye birds, sing, sing a joyous song!
And let the young lambs bound
As to the tabor's sound!
We, in thought, will join your throng,
Ye that pipe and ye that play,
Ye that through your hearts to-day
Feel the gladness of the May!
What though the radiance which was once so bright
Be now forever taken from my sight;
Though nothing can bring back the hour
Of splendor in the grass, of glory in the flower, —
We will grieve not, rather find
Strength in what remains behind;
In the primal sympathy
Which, having been, must ever be;
In the soothing thoughts that spring
Out of human suffering;
In the faith that looks through death,
In years that bring the philosophic mind.

And O ye fountains, meadows, hills, and groves,
Forebode not any severing of our loves!
Yet in my heart of hearts I feel your might;
I only have relinquished one delight,
To live beneath your more habitual sway.
I love the brooks which down their channels fret,
Even more than when I tripped lightly as they;
The innocent brightness of a new-born day
Is lovely yet;
The clouds that gather round the setting sun
Do take a sober coloring from an eye
That hath kept watch o'er man's mortality;
Another race hath been, and other palms are won.
Thanks to the human heart by which we live,
Thanks to its tenderness, its joys and fears,
To me the meanest flower that blows can give
Thoughts that do often lie too deep for tears.

THE DAFFODILS.

I WANDERED lonely as a cloud
That floats on high o'er vales and hills,
When all at once I saw a crowd,
A host of golden daffodils,
Beside the lake, beneath the trees,
Fluttering and dancing in the breeze.

Continuous as the stars that shine
And twinkle on the Milky Way,
They stretched in never-ending line
Along the margin of a bay:
Ten thousand saw I at a glance,
Tossing their heads in sprightly dance.

The waves beside them danced, but they
Outdid the sparkling waves in glee:
A poet could not but be gay
In such a jocund company!
I gazed — and gazed — but little thought
What wealth the show to me had brought;

For oft, when on my couch I lie
In vacant or in pensive mood,
They flash upon that inward eye
Which is the bliss of solitude:
And then my heart with pleasure fills;
And dances with the daffodils.

TO THE CUCKOO.

O BLITHE new-comer! I have heard,
I hear thee, and rejoice:
O cuckoo! shall I call thee bird,
Or but a wandering voice?

While I am lying on the grass
Thy twofold shout I hear;
From hill to hill it seems to pass,
At once far off and near.

Though babbling only to the vale
Of sunshine and of flowers,
Thou bringest unto me a tale
Of visionary hours.

Thrice welcome, darling of the spring!
Even yet thou art to me
No bird, but an invisible thing,
A voice, a mystery;

The same whom in my school-boy days
I listened to; that cry
Which made me look a thousand ways,
In bush and tree and sky.

To seek thee did I often rove
Through woods and on the green;
And thou wert still a hope, a love;
Still longed for, never seen!

And I can listen to thee yet;
Can lie upon the plain
And listen, till I do beget
That golden time again.

O blessèd bird! the earth we pace
Again appears to be
An unsubstantial, fairy place
That is fit home for thee!

A MEMORY.

THREE years she grew in sun and shower;
Then Nature said, "A lovelier flower
On earth was never sown:
This child I to myself will take;
She shall be mine, and I will make
A lady of my own.

"Myself will to my darling be
Both law and impulse; and with me
The girl, in rock and plain,
In earth and heaven, in glade and bower,
Shall feel an overseeing power
To kindle or restrain.

"She shall be sportive as the fawn,
That wild with glee across the lawn
Or up the mountain springs;
And hers shall be the breathing balm,
And hers the silence and the calm,
Of mute insensate things.

"The floating clouds their state shall lend
To her; for her the willow bend;
Nor shall she fail to see
E'en in the motions of the storm
Grace that shall mould the maiden's form
By silent sympathy.

"The stars of midnight shall be dear
To her; and she shall lean her ear
In many a secret place,
Where rivulets dance their wayward round,
And beauty born of murmuring sound
Shall pass into her face.

"And vital feelings of delight
Shall rear her form to stately height,
Her virgin bosom swell;
Such thoughts to Lucy I will give
While she and I together live
Here in this happy dell."

Thus Nature spake. The work was done—
How soon my Lucy's race was run!
She died, and left to me
This heath, this calm and quiet scene;
The memory of what has been,
And nevermore will be.

SHE WAS A PHANTOM OF DELIGHT.

SHE was a phantom of delight
When first she gleamed upon my sight;
A lovely apparition, sent
To be a moment's ornament;
Her eyes as stars of twilight fair;
Like twilight's, too, her dusky hair;
But all things else about her drawn
From May-time and the cheerful dawn;
A dancing shape, an image gay,
To haunt, to startle, and waylay.

I saw her upon nearer view,
A spirit, yet a woman too!
Her household motions light and free,
And steps of virgin liberty;
A countenance in which did meet
Sweet records, promises as sweet;

A creature not too bright or good
For human nature's daily food,
For transient sorrows, simple wiles,
Praise, blame, love, kisses, tears, and smiles.

And now I see with eye serene
The very pulse of the machine;
A being breathing thoughtful breath,
A traveller between life and death;
The reason firm, the temperate will,
Endurance, foresight, strength, and skill;
A perfect woman, nobly planned
To warn, to comfort, and command;
And yet a spirit still, and bright
With something of an angel light.

YARROW UNVISITED.

From Stirling Castle we had seen
The mazy Forth unravelled;
Had trod the banks of Clyde and Tay,
And with the Tweed had travelled;
And when we came to Clovenford,
Then said my "winsome Marrow,"
"Whate'er betide, we 'll turn aside,
And see the Braes of Yarrow."

"Let Yarrow folk, frae Selkirk town,
Who have been buying, selling,
Go back to Yarrow, 't is their own,
Each maiden to her dwelling!
On Yarrow's banks let herons feed,
Hares couch, and rabbits burrow!
But we will downward with the Tweed,
Nor turn aside to Yarrow.

"There 's Galla Water, Leader Haughs,
Both lying right before us;
And Dryburgh, where with chiming Tweed
The lintwhites sing in chorus;
There 's pleasant Teviotdale, a land
Made blithe with plough and harrow:
Why throw away a needful day
To go in search of Yarrow?

"What 's Yarrow but a river bare,
That glides the dark hills under?
There are a thousand such elsewhere
As worthy of your wonder."
— Strange words they seemed of slight and scorn;
My true-love sighed for sorrow,
And looked me in the face, to think
I thus could speak of Yarrow!

"O, green," said I, "are Yarrow's holms,
And sweet is Yarrow flowing!
Fair hangs the apple frae the rock,
But we will leave it growing.
O'er hilly path and open strath
We 'll wander Scotland thorough;
But, though so near, we will not turn
Into the dale of Yarrow.

"Let beeves and home-bred kine partake
The sweets of Burn Mill meadow;
The swan on still Saint Mary's Lake
Float double, swan and shadow!
We will not see them; will not go
To-day, nor yet to-morrow;
Enough if in our hearts we know
There 's such a place as Yarrow.

"Be Yarrow stream unseen, unknown!
It must, or we shall rue it:
We have a vision of our own;
Ah! why should we undo it?
The treasured dreams of times long past,
We 'll keep them, winsome Marrow!
For when we 're there, although 't is fair,
'T will be another Yarrow!

"If care with freezing years should come,
And wandering seem but folly, —
Should we be loath to stir from home,
And yet be melancholy;
Should life be dull, and spirits low,
'T will soothe us in our sorrow
That earth has something yet to show,
The bonny holms of Yarrow!"

ON A PICTURE OF PEELE CASTLE IN A STORM.

Painted by Sir George Beaumont.

I was thy neighbor once, thou rugged pile!
Four summer weeks I dwelt in sight of thee:
I saw thee every day; and all the while
Thy form was sleeping on a glassy sea.

So pure the sky, so quiet was the air!
So like, so very like, was day to day!
Whene'er I looked, thy image still was there;
It trembled, but it never passed away.

How perfect was the calm! It seemed no sleep,
No mood, which season takes away, or brings:
I could have fancied that the mighty Deep
Was even the gentlest of all gentle things.

Ah! then if mine had been the painter's hand
To express what then I saw; and add the gleam,
The light that never was on sea or land,
The consecration, and the poet's dream, —

I would have planted thee, thou hoary pile,
Amid a world how different from this!
Beside a sea that could not cease to smile;
On tranquil land, beneath a sky of bliss.

A picture had it been of lasting ease,
Elysian quiet, without toil or strife;
No motion but the moving tide, a breeze;
Or merely silent Nature's breathing life.

Such, in the fond illusion of my heart,
Such picture would I at that time have made;
And seen the soul of truth in every part,
A steadfast peace that might not be betrayed.

So once it would have been, —'t is so no more;
I have submitted to a new control:
A power is gone, which nothing can restore;
A deep distress hath humanized my soul.

Not for a moment could I now behold
A smiling sea, and be what I have been:
The feeling of my loss will ne'er be old;
This, which I know, I speak with mind serene.

Then, Beaumont, Friend! who would have been the friend,
If he had lived, of him whom I deplore,
This work of thine I blame not, but commend;
This sea in anger, and that dismal shore.

O, 't is a passionate work!—yet wise and well,
Well chosen is the spirit that is here;
That hulk which labors in the deadly swell,
This rueful sky, this pageantry of fear!

And this huge castle, standing here sublime,
I love to see the look with which it braves—
Cased in the unfeeling armor of old time—
The lightning, the fierce wind, and trampling waves.

Farewell, farewell the heart that lives alone,
Housed in a dream, at distance from the kind!
Such happiness, wherever it be known,
Is to be pitied; for 't is surely blind.

But welcome fortitude, and patient cheer,
And frequent sights of what is to be borne!
Such sights, or worse, as are before me here:—
Not without hope we suffer and we mourn.

ODE TO DUTY.

Stern daughter of the voice of God!
O Duty! if that name thou love,
Who art a light to guide, a rod
To check the erring, and reprove;
Thou who art victory and law
When empty terrors overawe,
From vain temptations dost set free,
And calm'st the weary strife of frail humanity!

There are who ask not if thine eye
Be on them; who, in love and truth,
Where no misgiving is, rely
Upon the genial sense of youth:
Glad hearts! without reproach or blot;
Who do thy work, and know it not:
May joy be theirs while life shall last!
And thou, if they should totter, teach them to stand fast!

Serene will be our days and bright,
And happy will our nature be,
When love is an unerring light,
And joy its own security.
And blest are they who in the main
This faith, even now, do entertain:

Live in the spirit of this creed;
Yet find that other strength, according to their need.

I, loving freedom, and untried,
No sport of every random gust,
Yet being to myself a guide,
Too blindly have reposed my trust;
Full oft, when in my heart was heard
Thy timely mandate, I deferred
The task imposed, from day to day;
But thee I now would serve more strictly, if I may.

Through no disturbance of my soul,
Or strong compunction in me wrought,
I supplicate for thy control;
But in the quietness of thought:
Me this unchartered freedom tires;
I feel the weight of chance desires:
My hopes no more must change their name,
I long for a repose which ever is the same.

Stern lawgiver! yet thou dost wear
The Godhead's most benignant grace;
Nor know we anything so fair
As is the smile upon thy face.
Flowers laugh before thee on their beds,
And fragrance in thy footing treads;
Thou dost preserve the stars from wrong,
And the most ancient heavens, through thee, are fresh and strong.

To humbler functions, awful power!
I call thee: I myself commend
Unto thy guidance from this hour;
O, let my weakness have an end!
Give unto me, made lowly wise,
The spirit of self-sacrifice;
The confidence of reason give;
And, in the light of truth, thy bondman let me live!

TO SLEEP.

A FLOCK of sheep that leisurely pass by
One after one; the sound of rain, and bees
Murmuring; the fall of rivers, winds and seas,
Smooth fields, white sheets of water, and pure sky;—

I 've thought of all by turns, and still I lie
Sleepless; and soon the small birds' melodies
Must hear, first uttered from my orchard trees,
And the first cuckoo's melancholy cry.

Even thus last night, and two nights more I lay,
And could not win thee, Sleep! by any stealth:
So do not let me wear to-night away:
Without thee what is all the morning's wealth?
Come, blessèd barrier between day and day,
Dear mother of fresh thoughts and joyous health!

THE WORLD.

THE world is too much with us; late and soon,
Getting and spending, we lay waste our powers:
Little we see in nature that is ours;
We have given our hearts away, a sordid boon!
This sea that bares her bosom to the moon,
The winds that will be howling at all hours
And are up-gathered now like sleeping flowers,
For this, for everything, we are out of tune;
It moves us not. Great God! I 'd rather be
A pagan suckled in a creed outworn;
So might I, standing on this pleasant lea,
Have glimpses that would make me less forlorn,
Have sight of Proteus coming from the sea,
Or hear old Triton blow his wreathèd horn.

TO THE RIVER DUDDON.

I THOUGHT of thee, my partner and my guide,
As being passed away,—vain sympathies!
For backward, Duddon! as I cast my eyes,
I see what was, and is, and will abide:
Still glides the stream, and shall forever glide;
The form remains, the function never dies;

While we, the brave, the mighty, and the wise,
We men, who in our morn of youth defied
The elements, must vanish;—be it so!
Enough, if something from our hands have power
To live, and act, and serve the future hour;
And if, as toward the silent tomb we go,
Through love, through hope, and faith's transcendent dower,
We feel that we are greater than we know.

SIR WALTER SCOTT.

[1771-1832.]

YOUNG LOCHINVAR.

O, YOUNG Lochinvar is come out of the west,
Through all the wide Border his steed was the best;
And save his good broadsword he weapon had none,
He rode all unarmed, and he rode all alone.
So faithful in love, and so dauntless in war,
There never was knight like the young Lochinvar!

He stayed not for brake, and he stopped not for stone,
He swam the Esk River where ford there was none;
But, ere he alighted at Netherby gate,
The bride had consented, the gallant came late:
For a laggard in love, and a dastard in war,
Was to wed the fair Ellen of brave Lochinvar.

So boldly he entered the Netherby Hall,
'Mong bridesmen, and kinsmen, and brothers, and all!
Then spoke the bride's father, his hand on his sword,—
For the poor craven bridegroom said never a word,—
"O, come ye in peace here, or come ye in war,
Or to dance at our bridal, young Lord Lochinvar?"

"I long wooed your daughter, my suit you denied:
Love swells like the Solway, but ebbs like its tide!
And now am I come, with this lost love of mine,
To lead but one measure, drink one cup of wine!
There be maidens in Scotland more lovely by far,
That would gladly be bride to the young Lochinvar!"

The bride kissed the goblet; the knight took it up,
He quaffed off the wine, and he threw down the cup!
She looked down to blush, and she looked up to sigh,
With a smile on her lips and a tear in her eye.
He took her soft hand, ere her mother could bar,—
"Now tread we a measure!" said young Lochinvar.

So stately his form, and so lovely her face,
That never a hall such a galliard did grace!
While her mother did fret, and her father did fume,
And the bridegroom stood dangling his bonnet and plume,
And the bride-maidens whispered, "'T were better by far
To have matched our fair cousin with young Lochinvar!"

One touch to her hand, and one word in her ear,
When they reached the hall door, and the charger stood near,
So light to the croupe the fair lady he swung,
So light to the saddle before her he sprung.
"She is won! we are gone, over bank, bush, and scaur;
They'll have fleet steeds that follow!" quoth young Lochinvar.

There was mounting 'mong Græmes of the Netherby clan;
Fosters, Fenwicks, and Musgraves, they rode and they ran;
There was racing and chasing on Cannobie Lea,
But the lost bride of Netherby ne'er did they see!
So daring in love, and so dauntless in war,
Have ye e'er heard of gallant like young Lochinvar?

A SERENADE.

Ah! County Guy, the hour is nigh,
The sun has left the lea,
The orange-flower perfumes the bower,
The breeze is on the sea.
The lark, his lay who trilled all day,
Sits hushed his partner nigh;
Breeze, bird, and flower confess the hour,
But where is County Guy?

The village maid steals through the shade
Her shepherd's suit to hear;
To Beauty shy, by lattice high,
Sings high-born Cavalier.
The star of Love, all stars above,
Now reigns o'er earth and sky,
And high and low the influence know,—
But where is County Guy?

SONG.

"A weary lot is thine, fair maid,
A weary lot is thine!
To pull the thorn thy brow to braid,
And press the rue for wine!
A lightsome eye, a soldier's mien,
A feather of the blue,
A doublet of the Lincoln-green,—
No more of me you knew,
My love!
No more of me you knew.

"This morn is merry June, I trow,—
The rose is budding fain;
But she shall bloom in winter snow
Ere we two meet again."
He turned his charger as he spake,
Upon the river shore;
He gave his bridle-reins a shake,
Said, "Adieu forevermore,
My love!
And adieu forevermore."

LAY OF THE IMPRISONED HUNTSMAN.

My hawk is tired of perch and hood,
My idle greyhound loathes his food,
My horse is weary of his stall,
And I am sick of captive thrall.
I wish I were as I have been,
Hunting the hart in forests green,
With bended bow and bloodhound free,
For that 's the life is meet for me.

I hate to learn the ebb of time
From yon dull steeple's drowsy chime,
Or mark it as the sunbeams crawl,
Inch after inch, along the wall.
The lark was wont my matins ring,
The sable rook my vespers sing;
These towers, although a king's they be,
Have not a hall of joy for me.

No more at dawning morn I rise,
And sun myself in Ellen's eyes,
Drive the fleet deer the forest through,
And homeward wend with evening dew;
A blithesome welcome blithely meet,
And lay my trophies at her feet,
While fled the eve on wing of glee,—
That life is lost to love and me!

THE TROSACHS.

The western waves of ebbing day
Rolled o'er the glen their level way;
Each purple peak, each flinty spire,
Was bathed in floods of living fire.
But not a setting beam could glow
Within the dark ravines below,
Where twined the path, in shadow hid,
Round many a rocky pyramid,
Shooting abruptly from the dell
Its thunder-splintered pinnacle;
Round many an insulated mass,
The native bulwarks of the pass,
Huge as the tower which builders vain
Presumptuous piled on Shinar's plain.
Their rocky summits, split and rent,
Formed turret, dome, or battlement,
Or seemed fantastically set
With cupola or minaret,
Wild crests as pagod ever decked,
Or mosque of Eastern architect.
Nor were these earth-born castles bare,
Nor lacked they many a banner fair;
For, from their shivered brows displayed,
Far o'er the unfathomable glade,
All twinkling with the dew-drop sheen,

The brier-rose fell in streamers green,
And creeping shrubs of thousand dyes,
Waved in the west-wind's summer sighs.

Boon nature scattered, free and wild,
Each plant or flower, the mountain's child.
Here eglantine embalmed the air,
Hawthorn and hazel mingled there;
The primrose pale, and violet flower,
Found in each cliff a narrow bower;
Foxglove and nightshade, side by side,
Emblems of punishment and pride,
Grouped their dark hues with every stain,
The weather-beaten crags retain.
With boughs that quaked at every breath,
Gray birch and aspen wept beneath;
Aloft, the ash and warrior oak
Cast anchor in the rifted rock;
And higher yet, the pine-tree hung
His shattered trunk, and frequent flung,
Where seemed the cliffs to meet on high,
His boughs athwart the narrowed sky.
Highest of all, where white peaks glanced,
Where glistening streamers waved and danced,
The wanderer's eye could barely view
The summer heaven's delicious blue;
So wondrous wild, the whole might seem
The scenery of a fairy dream.
Onward, amid the copse 'gan peep
A narrow inlet, still and deep,
Affording scarce such breadth of brim,
As served the wild-duck's brood to swim;
Lost for a space, through thickets veering,
But broader when again appearing.
Tall rocks and tufted knolls their face
Could on the dark-blue mirror trace;
And farther as the hunter strayed,
Still broader sweep its channels made.
The shaggy mounds no longer stood,
Emerging from entangled wood,
But, wave-encircled, seemed to float,
Like castle girdled with its moat;
Yet broader floods extending still,
Divide them from their parent hill,
Till each, retiring, claims to be
An islet in an inland sea.

And now, to issue from the glen,
No pathway meets the wanderer's ken,
Unless he climb, with footing nice,
A far-projecting precipice.
The broom's tough roots his ladder made,
The hazel saplings lent their aid;
And thus an airy point he won,
Where, gleaming with the setting sun,
One burnished sheet of living gold,
Loch-Katrine lay beneath him rolled;
In all her length far winding lay,
With promontory, creek, and bay,
And islands that, empurpled bright,
Floated amid the livelier light;
And mountains, that like giants stand,
To sentinel enchanted land.
High on the south, huge Ben-venue
Down to the lake in masses threw
Crags, knolls, and mounds, confusedly hurled,
The fragments of an earlier world;
A wildering forest feathered o'er
His ruined sides and summit hoar,
While on the north, through middle air,
Ben-an heaved high his forehead bare.

From the steep promontory gazed
The stranger, raptured and amazed,
And "What a scene were here," he cried,
"For princely pomp or churchman's pride!
On this bold brow, a lordly tower;
In that soft vale, a lady's bower;
On yonder meadow, far away,
The turrets of a cloister gray;
How blithely might the bugle-horn
Chide, on the lake, the lingering morn!
How sweet, at eve, the lover's lute,
Chime, when the groves are still and mute!
And when the midnight moon should lave
Her forehead in the silver wave,
How solemn on the ear would come
The holy matins' distant hum,
While the deep peal's commanding tone
Should wake, in yonder islet lone,
A sainted hermit from his cell,
To drop a bead with every knell, —
And bugle, lute, and bell, and all,
Should each bewildered stranger call
To friendly feast and lighted hall."

CORONACH.

He is gone on the mountain,
He is lost to the forest,
Like a summer-dried fountain,
When our need was the sorest.
The font reappearing
From the rain-drops shall borrow;
But to us comes no cheering,
To Duncan no morrow!

The hand of the reaper
Takes the ears that are hoary,

But the voice of the weeper
Wails manhood in glory.
The autumn winds, rushing,
Waft the leaves that are searest;
But our flower was in flushing,
When blighting was nearest.

Fleet foot on the correi,
Sage counsel in cumber,
Red hand in the foray,
How sound is thy slumber!
Like the dew on the mountain,
Like the foam on the river,
Like the bubble on the fountain,
Thou art gone, and forever.

HYMN OF THE HEBREW MAID.

When Israel, of the Lord beloved,
Out from the land of bondage came,
Her father's God before her moved,
An awful guide in smoke and flame.
By day, along the astonished lands,
The cloudy pillar glided slow;
By night, Arabia's crimsoned sands
Returned the fiery column's glow.

There rose the choral hymn of praise,
And trump and timbrel answered keen;
And Zion's daughters poured their lays,
With priest's and warrior's voice between.
No portents now our foes amaze, —
Forsaken Israel wanders lone;
Our fathers would not know thy ways,
And thou hast left them to their own.

But, present still, though now unseen,
When brightly shines the prosperous day,
Be thoughts of thee a cloudy screen,
To temper the deceitful ray.
And O, when stoops on Judah's path
In shade and storm the frequent night,
Be thou, long-suffering, slow to wrath,
A burning and a shining light!

Our harps we left by Babel's streams, —
The tyrant's jest, the Gentile's scorn;
No censer round our altar beams,
And mute are timbrel, trump, and horn.
But thou hast said, The blood of goats,
The flesh of rams, I will not prize, —
A contrite heart, and humble thoughts,
Are mine accepted sacrifice.

CHRISTMAS-TIME.

Heap on more wood! — the wind is chill;
But let it whistle as it will,
We 'll keep our Christmas merry still.
Each age has deemed the new-born year
The fittest time for festal cheer:
Even heathen yet, the savage Dane
At Iol more deep the mead did drain;
High on the beach his galleys drew,
And feasted all his pirate crew;
Then in his low and pine-built hall,
Where shields and axes decked the wall,
They gorged upon the half-dressed steer;
Caroused in seas of sable beer;
While round, in brutal jest, were thrown
The half-gnawed rib and marrow-bone,
Or listened all, in grim delight,
While scalds yelled out the joys of fight.
Then forth in frenzy would they hie,
While wildly loose their red locks fly;
And, dancing round the blazing pile,
They make such barbarous mirth the while,
As best might to the mind recall
The boisterous joys of Odin's hall.

And well our Christian sires of old
Loved when the year its course had rolled,
And brought blithe Christmas back again,
With all his hospitable train.
Domestic and religious rite
Gave honor to the holy night:
On Christmas eve the bells were rung;
On Christmas eve the mass was sung;
That only night, in all the year,
Saw the stoled priest the chalice rear.
The damsel donned her kirtle sheen;
The hall was dressed with holly green;
Forth to the wood did merry-men go,
To gather in the mistletoe.
Then opened wide the baron's hall
To vassal, tenant, serf, and all;
Power laid his rod of rule aside,
And Ceremony doffed his pride.
The heir, with roses in his shoes,
That night might village partner choose;
The lord, underogating, share
The vulgar game of "post and pair."
All hailed, with uncontrolled delight
And general voice, the happy night
That to the cottage, as the crown,
Brought tidings of salvation down.

The fire, with well-dried logs supplied,
Went roaring up the chimney wide;

The huge hall-table's oaken face,
Scrubbed till it shone the day to grace,
Bore then upon its massive board
No mark to part the squire and lord.
Then was brought in the lusty brawn,
By old blue-coated serving-man ;
Then the grim boar's head frowned on high,
Crested with bays and rosemary.
Well can the green-garbed ranger tell
How, when, and where the monster fell;
What dogs before his death he tore,
And all the baiting of the boar.
The wassail round, in good brown bowls,
Garnished with ribbons, blithely trowls.
There the huge sirloin reeked; hard by
Plum-porridge stood, and Christmas pie;
Nor failed old Scotland to produce,
At such high-tide, her savory goose.
Then came the merry maskers in,
And carols roared with blithesome din;
If unmelodious was the song,
It was a hearty note, and strong.
Who lists may in their mumming see
Traces of ancient mystery;
White skirts supplied the masquerade,
And smutted cheeks the visors made:
But, O, what maskers richly dight
Can boast of bosoms half so light!
England was merry England, when
Old Christmas brought his sports again.
'T was Christmas broached the mightiest ale;
'T was Christmas told the merriest tale;
A Christmas gambol oft could cheer
The poor man's heart through half the year.

SAMUEL TAYLOR COLERIDGE.

[1772-1834.]

GENEVIEVE.

All thoughts, all passions, all delights,
Whatever stirs this mortal frame,
All are but ministers of Love,
And feed his sacred flame.

Oft in my waking dreams do I
Live o'er again that happy hour,
When midway on the mount I lay
Beside the ruined tower.

The moonshine stealing o'er the scene
Had blended with the lights of eve;
And she was there, my hope, my joy,
My own dear Genevieve!

She leaned against the arméd man,
The statue of the arméd knight;
She stood and listened to my lay,
Amid the lingering light.

Few sorrows hath she of her own,
My hope! my joy! my Genevieve!
She loves me best, whene'er I sing
The songs that make her grieve.

I played a soft and doleful air,
I sang an old and moving story, —
An old rude song, that suited well
That ruin wild and hoary.

She listened with a flitting blush,
With downcast eyes and modest grace;
For well she knew, I could not choose
But gaze upon her face.

I told her of the Knight that wore
Upon his shield a burning brand;
And that for ten long years he wooed
The Lady of the Land.

I told her how he pined: and ah!
The deep, the low, the pleading tone
With which I sang another's love
Interpreted my own.

She listened with a flitting blush,
With downcast eyes, and modest grace;
And she forgave me, that I gazed
Too fondly on her face.

But when I told the cruel scorn
That crazed that bold and lovely Knight,
And that he crossed the mountain-woods,
Nor rested day nor night;

That sometimes from the savage den,
And sometimes from the darksome shade,
And sometimes starting up at once
In green and sunny glade,

There came and looked him in the face
An angel beautiful and bright;
And that he knew it was a Fiend,
This miserable Knight!

And that unknowing what he did,
He leaped amid a murderous band,
And saved from outrage worse than death,
The Lady of the Land;

And how she wept, and clasped his knees;
And how she tended him in vain;
And ever strove to expiate
The scorn that crazed his brain;

And that she nursed him in a cave,
And how his madness went away,
When on the yellow forest-leaves
A dying man he lay;

— His dying words — but when I reached
That tenderest strain of all the ditty,
My faltering voice and pausing harp
Disturbed her soul with pity!

All impulses of soul and sense
Had thrilled my guileless Genevieve;
The music and the doleful tale,
The rich and balmy eve;

And hopes, and fears that kindle hope,
An undistinguishable throng,
And gentle wishes long subdued,
Subdued and cherished long.

She wept with pity and delight,
She blushed with love, and virgin shame;
And like the murmur of a dream,
I heard her breathe my name.

Her bosom heaved, — she stepped aside,
As conscious of my look she stept, —
Then suddenly, with timorous eye,
She fled to me and wept.

She half enclosed me with her arms,
She pressed me with a meek embrace;
And, bending back her head, looked up,
And gazed upon my face.

'T was partly love, and partly fear,
And partly 't was a bashful art
That I might rather feel than see
The swelling of her heart.

I calmed her fears, and she was calm,
And told her love with virgin pride;
And so I won my Genevieve,
My bright and beauteous Bride.

HYMN BEFORE SUNRISE, IN THE VALE OF CHAMOUNI.

Hast thou a charm to stay the morning star
In his steep course? So long he seems to pause
On thy bald, awful head, O sovran Blanc!
The Arvé and Arveiron at thy base
Rave ceaselessly; but thou, most awful Form!
Risest from forth thy silent sea of pines
How silently! Around thee and above
Deep is the air, and dark, substantial, black,
An ebon mass: methinks thou piercest it
As with a wedge! But when I look again,
It is thine own calm home, thy crystal shrine,
Thy habitation from eternity!
O dread and silent Mount! I gazed upon thee,
Till thou, still present to the bodily sense,
Didst vanish from my thought: entranced in prayer
I worshipped the Invisible alone.
Yet, like some sweet beguiling melody,
So sweet we know not we are listening to it,
Thou, the meanwhile, wert blending with my thought,
Yea, with my life and life's own secret joy,
Till the dilating soul, enrapt, transfused,
Into the mighty vision passing, there,
As in her natural form, swelled vast to Heaven!
Awake, my soul! not only passive praise
Thou owest! not alone these swelling tears,
Mute thanks, and secret ecstasy! Awake,
Voice of sweet song! Awake, my heart, awake!
Green vales and icy cliffs, all join my hymn.
Thou first and chief, sole sovran of the vale!
O, struggling with the darkness all the night,
And visited all night by troops of stars,
Or when they climb the sky or when they sink, —
Companion of the morning star at dawn,
Thyself Earth's rosy star, and of the dawn
Co-herald, — wake, O, wake, and utter praise!
Who sank thy sunless pillars deep in earth?
Who filled thy countenance with rosy light?
Who made thee parent of perpetual streams?
And you, ye five wild torrents, fiercely glad!
Who called you forth from night and utter death,

From dark and icy caverns called you forth,
Down those precipitous, black, jagged rocks,
Forever shattered and the same forever?
Who gave you your invulnerable life,
Your strength, your speed, your fury, and your joy,
Unceasing thunder and eternal foam?
And who commanded (and the silence came),
Here let the billows stiffen and have rest?
Ye ice-falls! ye that from the mountain's brow
Adown enormous ravines slope amain, —
Torrents, methinks, that heard a mighty voice,
And stopped at once amid their maddest plunge!
Motionless torrents! silent cataracts!
Who made you glorious as the gates of Heaven
Beneath the keen full moon? Who bade the sun
Clothe you with rainbows? Who, with living flowers
Of loveliest blue, spread garlands at your feet? —
God! let the torrents, like a shout of nations,
Answer! and let the ice-plains echo, God!
God! sing, ye meadow-streams, with gladsome voice!
Ye pine-groves, with your soft and soul-like sounds!
And they too have a voice, yon piles of snow,
And in their perilous fall shall thunder, God!
Ye living flowers that skirt the eternal frost!
Ye wild goats sporting round the eagle's nest!
Ye eagles, playmates of the mountain-storm!
Ye lightnings, the dread arrows of the clouds!
Ye signs and wonders of the elements,
Utter forth God, and fill the hills with praise!
Thou, too, hoar Mount! with thy sky-pointing peaks,
Oft from whose feet the avalanche, unheard,
Shoots downward, glittering through the pure serene,
Into the depth of clouds that veil thy breast, —
Thou too again, stupendous Mountain! thou
That as I raise my head, awhile bowed low
In adoration, upward from thy base
Slow travelling with dim eyes suffused with tears,
Solemnly seemest like a vapory cloud
To rise before me — Rise, O, ever rise,
Rise like a cloud of incense from the Earth!
Thou kingly Spirit throned among the hills,
Thou dread ambassador from Earth to Heaven,
Great hierarch! tell thou the silent sky,
And tell the stars, and tell yon rising sun,
Earth, with her thousand voices, praises God.

CHRISTABEL.

PART I.

'T is the middle of night by the castle clock,
And the owls have awakened the crowing cock;
Tu-whit! tu-whoo!
And hark, again! the crowing cock,
How drowsily it crew.

Sir Leoline, the Baron rich,
Hath a toothless mastiff bitch;
From her kennel beneath the rock
She maketh answer to the clock,
Four for the quarters, and twelve for the hour;
Ever and aye, by shine and shower,
Sixteen short howls, not over-loud;
Some say, she sees my lady's shroud.

Is the night chilly and dark?
The night is chilly, but not dark.
The thin gray cloud is spread on high,
It covers but not hides the sky.
The moon is behind, and at the full;
And yet she looks both small and dull.
The night is chill, the cloud is gray;
'T is a month before the month of May,
And the Spring comes slowly up this way.

The lovely lady, Christabel,
Whom her father loves so well,
What makes her in the wood so late,
A furlong from the castle gate?
She had dreams all yesternight
Of her own betrothéd knight;

And she in the midnight wood will pray
For the weal of her lover that's far away.

She stole along, she nothing spoke,
The sighs she heaved were soft and low,
And naught was green upon the oak,
But moss and rarest mistletoe:
She kneels beneath the huge oak-tree,
And in silence prayeth she.

The lady sprang up suddenly,
The lovely lady, Christabel!
It moaned as near as near can be,
But what it is she cannot tell.
On the other side it seems to be
Of the huge, broad-breasted, old oak-tree.

The night is chill; the forest bare;
Is it the wind that moaneth bleak?
There is not wind enough in the air
To move away the ringlet curl
From the lovely lady's cheek, —
There is not wind enough to twirl
The one red leaf, the last of its clan,
That dances as often as dance it can,
Hanging so light, and hanging so high,
On the topmost twig that looks up at the sky.

Hush, beating heart of Christabel!
Jesu Maria, shield her well!
She folded her arms beneath her cloak,
And stole to the other side of the oak.
What sees she there?

There she sees a damsel bright,
Drest in a silken robe of white,
That shadowy in the moonlight shone.
The neck that made that white robe wan,
Her stately neck, and arms were bare;
Her blue-veined feet unsandalled were,
And wildly glittered here and there
The gems entangled in her hair.
I guess, 't was frightful there to see
A lady so richly clad as she, —
Beautiful exceedingly!

"Mary mother, save me now!"
Said Christabel; "and who art thou?"

The lady strange made answer meet,
And her voice was faint and sweet:
"Have pity on my sore distress,
I scarce can speak for weariness."
"Stretch forth thy hand, and have no fear!"
Said Christabel; "how camest thou here?"
And the lady, whose voice was faint and sweet,
Did thus pursue her answer meet:—

"My sire is of a noble line,
And my name is Geraldine:
Five warriors seized me yestermorn, —
Me, even me, a maid forlorn;
They choked my cries with force and fright,
And tied me on a palfrey white.
The palfrey was as fleet as wind,
And they rode furiously behind.
They spurred amain, their steeds were white,
And once we crossed the shade of night.
As sure as Heaven shall rescue me,
I have no thought what men they be;
Nor do I know how long it is
(For I have lain entranced, I wis)
Since one, the tallest of the five,
Took me from the palfrey's back,
A weary woman, scarce alive.
Some muttered words his comrades spoke:
He placed me underneath this oak;
He swore they would return with haste;
Whither they went I cannot tell —
I thought I heard, some minutes past,
Sounds as of a castle-bell.
Stretch forth thy hand" (thus ended she),
"And help a wretched maid to flee."

Then Christabel stretched forth her hand
And comforted fair Geraldine:
"O well, bright dame! may you command
The service of Sir Leoline;
And gladly our stout chivalry
Will he send forth, and friends withal,
To guide and guard you safe and free
Home to your noble father's hall."

She rose: and forth with steps they passed
That strove to be, and were not, fast.
Her gracious stars the lady blest,
And thus spake on sweet Christabel:
"All our household are at rest,
The hall as silent as the cell;
Sir Leoline is weak in health,
And may not well awakened be,
But we will move as if in stealth,
And I beseech your courtesy,
This night, to share your couch with me."

They crossed the moat, and Christabel
Took the key that fitted well;

A little door she opened straight,
All in the middle of the gate;
The gate that was ironed within and without,
Where an army in battle array had marched out.
The lady sank, belike through pain,
And Christabel with might and main
Lifted her up, a weary weight,
Over the threshold of the gate:
Then the lady rose again,
And moved, as she were not in pain.

So free from danger, free from fear,
They crossed the court: right glad they were.
And Christabel devoutly cried
To the lady by her side:
"Praise we the Virgin all divine
Who hath rescued thee from thy distress!"
"Alas, alas!" said Geraldine,
I cannot speak for weariness." —
So free from danger, free from fear,
They crossed the court: right glad they were.

Outside her kennel the mastiff old
Lay fast asleep, in moonshine cold.
The mastiff old did not awake,
Yet she an angry moan did make!
And what can ail the mastiff bitch?
Never till now she uttered yell
Beneath the eye of Christabel.
Perhaps it is the owlet's scritch;
For what can ail the mastiff bitch?

They passed the hall, that echoes still,
Pass as lightly as you will!
The brands were flat, the brands were dying,
Amid their own white ashes lying;
But when the lady passed, there came
A tongue of light, a fit of flame;
And Christabel saw the lady's eye,
And nothing else saw she thereby,
Save the boss of the shield of Sir Leoline tall,
Which hung in a murky old niche in the wall.
"O, softly tread!" said Christabel,
"My father seldom sleepeth well."

Sweet Christabel her feet doth bare,
And, jealous of the listening air,
They steal their way from stair to stair,
Now in glimmer, and now in gloom,
And now they pass the Baron's room,
As still as death with stifled breath!
And now have reached her chamber door;
And now doth Geraldine press down
The rushes of the chamber floor.

The moon shines dim in the open air,
And not a moonbeam enters here.
But they without its light can see
The chamber carved so curiously,
Carved with figures strange and sweet,
All made out of the carver's brain,
For a lady's chamber meet:
The lamp with twofold silver chain
Is fastened to an angel's feet.
The silver lamp burns dead and dim;
But Christabel the lamp will trim.
She trimmed the lamp, and made it bright,
And left it swinging to and fro,
While Geraldine, in wretched plight,
Sank down upon the floor below.

"O weary lady, Geraldine,
I pray you, drink this cordial wine!
It is a wine of virtuous powers;
My mother made it of wild flowers."

"And will your mother pity me,
Who am a maiden most forlorn?"
Christabel answered: "Woe is me!
She died the hour that I was born.
I have heard the gray-haired friar tell,
How on her death-bed she did say,
That she should hear the castle-bell
Strike twelve upon my wedding-day.
O mother dear! that thou wert here!"
"I would," said Geraldine, "she were!"
But soon with altered voice, said she:
"Off, wandering mother! Peak and pine!
I have power to bid thee flee."
Alas! what ails poor Geraldine?
Why stares she with unsettled eye?
Can she the bodiless dead espy?
And why with hollow voice cries she:
"Off, woman, off! this hour is mine, —
Though thou her guardian spirit be,
Off, woman, off! 'T is given to me."

Then Christabel knelt by the lady's side,
And raised to heaven her eyes so blue;
"Alas!" said she, "this ghastly ride, —
Dear lady! it hath wildered you!"
The lady wiped her moist cold brow,
And faintly said, "'T is over now!"

Again the wild-flower wine she drank:
Her fair large eyes 'gan glitter bright,

And from the floor whereon she sank
The lofty lady stood upright;
She was most beautiful to see,
Like a lady of a far countrée.

And thus the lofty lady spake:
"All they who live in the upper sky
Do love you, holy Christabel!
And you love them, and for their sake
And for the good which me befell,
Even I in my degree will try,
Fair maiden, to requite you well.
But now unrobe yourself; for I
Must pray, ere yet in bed I lie."

Quoth Christabel, "So let it be!"
And as the lady bade, did she.
Her gentle limbs did she undress,
And lay down in her loveliness.

But through her brain, of weal and woe
So many thoughts moved to and fro,
That vain it were her lids to close;
So half-way from the bed she rose,
And on her elbow did recline
To look at the Lady Geraldine.

Beneath the lamp the lady bowed,
And slowly rolled her eyes around;
Then drawing in her breath aloud,
Like one that shuddered, she unbound
The cincture from beneath her breast:
Her silken robe and inner vest
Dropt to her feet, and full in view,
Behold! her bosom and half her side,—
A sight to dream of, not to tell!
O, shield her! shield sweet Christabel!

Yet Geraldine nor speaks nor stirs;
Ah! what a stricken look was hers!
Deep from within she seems half-way
To lift some weight with sick assay,
And eyes the maid and seeks delay;
Then suddenly as one defied
Collects herself in scorn and pride,
And lay down by the maiden's side!—
And in her arms the maid she took,
Ah well-a-day!
And with low voice and doleful look,
These words did say:
"In the touch of this bosom there worketh a spell
Which is lord of thy utterance, Christabel!
Thou knowest to-night, and wilt know to-morrow
This mark of my shame, this seal of my sorrow;
But vainly thou warrest,
For this is alone in
Thy power to declare;
That in the dim forest
Thou heard'st a low moaning,
And found'st a bright lady, surpassingly fair:
And didst bring her home with thee in love and in charity,
To shield her and shelter her from the damp air."

THE CONCLUSION TO PART I.

It was a lovely sight to see
The Lady Christabel, when she
Was praying at the old oak-tree.
Amid the jagged shadows
Of mossy leafless boughs,
Kneeling in the moonlight,
To make her gentle vows;
Her slender palms together prest,
Heaving sometimes on her breast;
Her face resigned to bliss or bale,—
Her face, O, call it fair, not pale!
And both blue eyes more bright than clear,
Each about to have a tear.

With open eyes (ah, woe is me!)
Asleep, and dreaming fearfully,
Fearfully dreaming, yet, I wis,
Dreaming that alone which is—
O sorrow and shame! Can this be she,
The lady, who knelt at the old oak-tree?
And lo! the worker of these harms,
That holds the maiden in her arms,
Seems to slumber still and mild,
As a mother with her child.

A star hath set, a star hath risen,
O Geraldine! since arms of thine
Have been the lovely lady's prison.
O Geraldine! one hour was thine,—
Thou 'st had thy will! By tarn and rill,
The night-birds all that hour were still.
But now they are jubilant anew,
From cliff and tower, tu-whoo! tu-whoo!
Tu-whoo! tu-whoo! from wood and fell!
And see! the Lady Christabel
Gathers herself from out her trance;
Her limbs relax, her countenance
Grows sad and soft; the smooth thin lids
Close o'er her eyes; and tears she sheds,—
Large tears that leave the lashes bright!
And oft the while she seems to smile
As infants at a sudden light!

Yea, she doth smile, and she doth weep,
Like a youthful hermitess,
Beauteous in a wilderness,
Who, praying always, prays in sleep.
And, if she move unquietly,
Perchance, 't is but the blood so free,
Comes back and tingles in her feet.
No doubt she hath a vision sweet.
What if her guardian spirit 't were?
What if she knew her mother near?
But this she knows, in joys and woes,
That saints will aid if men will call;
For the blue sky bends over all!

PART II.

"EACH matin-bell," the Baron saith,
"Knells us back to a world of death."
These words Sir Leoline first said,
When he rose and found his lady dead:
These words Sir Leoline will say
Many a morn to his dying day!

And hence the custom and law began,
That still at dawn the sacristan,
Who duly pulls the heavy bell,
Five-and-forty beads must tell
Between each stroke, — a warning knell,
Which not a soul can choose but hear
From Bratha Head to Wyndermere.

Saith Bracy the bard, "So let it knell!
And let the drowsy sacristan
Still count as slowly as he can!
There is no lack of such, I ween,
As well fill up the space between.
In Langdale Pike and Witch's Lair,
And Dungeon-ghyll so foully rent,
With ropes of rock and bells of air
Three sinful sextons' ghosts are pent,
Who all give back, one after t' other,
The death-note to their living brother;
And oft, too, by the knell offended,
Just as their one! two! three! is ended,
The devil mocks the doleful tale
With a merry peal from Borodale."

The air is still! through mist and cloud
That merry peal comes ringing loud;
And Geraldine shakes off her dread,
And rises lightly from the bed;
Puts on her silken vestments white,
And tricks her hair in lovely plight,
And, nothing doubting of her spell,
Awakens the Lady Christabel.

"Sleep you, sweet lady Christabel?
I trust that you have rested well."

And Christabel awoke and spied
The same who lay down by her side, —
O, rather say, the same whom she
Raised up beneath the old oak-tree!
Nay, fairer yet! and yet more fair!
For she belike hath drunken deep
Of all the blessedness of sleep!
And while she spake, her look, her air,
Such gentle thankfulness declare,
That (so it seemed) her girded vests
Grew tight beneath her heaving breasts.
"Sure I have sinned!" said Christabel,
"Now Heaven be praised if all be well!"
And in low faltering tones, yet sweet,
Did she the lofty lady greet,
With such perplexity of mind
As dreams too lively leave behind.

So quickly she rose, and quickly arrayed
Her maiden limbs, and having prayed
That He who on the cross did groan
Might wash away her sins unknown,
She forthwith led fair Geraldine
To meet her sire, Sir Leoline.

The lovely maid and the lady tall
Are pacing both into the hall,
And pacing on through page and groom,
Enter the Baron's presence-room.

The Baron rose, and while he prest
His gentle daughter to his breast,
With cheerful wonder in his eyes,
The Lady Geraldine espies,
And gave such welcome to the same
As might beseem so bright a dame!

But when he heard the lady's tale,
And when she told her father's name,
Why waxed Sir Leoline so pale,
Murmuring o'er the name again,
Lord Roland de Vaux of Tryermaine?

Alas! they had been friends in youth;
But whispering tongues can poison truth;
And constancy lives in realms above,
And life is thorny, and youth is vain,
And to be wroth with one we love
Doth work like madness in the brain.
And thus it chanced, as I divine,
With Roland and Sir Leoline.
Each spake words of high disdain
And insult to his heart's best brother:
They parted, — ne'er to meet again!

But never either found another
To free the hollow heart from paining;—
They stood aloof, the scars remaining,
Like cliffs which had been rent asunder,
A dreary sea now flows between;
But neither heat nor frost nor thunder
Shall wholly do away, I ween,
The marks of that which once hath been.

Sir Leoline a moment's space
Stood gazing on the damsel's face,
And the youthful Lord of Tryermaine
Came back upon his heart again.

O, then the Baron forgot his age,
His noble heart swelled high with rage;
He swore by the wounds in Jesu's side
He would proclaim it far and wide
With trump and solemn heraldry,
That they who thus had wronged the dame
Were base as spotted infamy!
"And if they dare deny the same,
My herald shall appoint a week,
And let the recreant traitors seek
My tourney court, — that there and then
I may dislodge their reptile souls
From the bodies and forms of men!"
He spake: his eye in lightning rolls!
For the lady was ruthlessly seized; and he kenned
In the beautiful lady the child of his friend!

And now the tears were on his face,
And fondly in his arms he took
Fair Geraldine, who met the embrace,
Prolonging it with joyous look.
Which when she viewed, a vision fell
Upon the soul of Christabel,
The vision of fear, the touch and pain!
She shrunk and shuddered, and saw again—
(Ah, woe is me! Was it for thee,
Thou gentle maid! such sights to see?)
Again she saw that bosom old,
Again she felt that bosom cold,
And drew in her breath with a hissing sound:
Whereat the Knight turned wildly round,
And nothing saw but his own sweet maid,
With eyes upraised, as one that prayed.

The touch, the sight, had passed away,
And in its stead that vision blest,
Which comforted her after-rest
While in the lady's arms she lay,
Had put a rapture in her breast,
And on her lips and o'er her eyes
Spread smiles like light!
With new surprise,
"What ails then my beloved child?"
The Baron said. His daughter mild
Made answer, "All will yet be well!"
I ween, she had no power to tell
Aught else; so mighty was the spell.

Yet he who saw this Geraldine
Had deemed her sure a thing divine.
Such sorrow with such grace she blended,
As if she feared she had offended
Sweet Christabel, that gentle maid!
And with such lowly tones she prayed,
She might be sent without delay
Home to her father's mansion.
"Nay!
Nay, by my soul!" said Leoline.
"Ho! Bracy, the bard, the charge be thine!
Go thou, with music sweet and loud,
And take two steeds with trappings proud,
And take the youth whom thou lov'st best
To bear thy harp, and learn thy song,
And clothe you both in solemn vest,
And over the mountains haste along,
Lest wandering folk, that are abroad,
Detain you on the valley road.
And when he has crossed the Irthing flood,
My merry bard! he hastes, he hastes
Up Knorren Moor, through Halegarth Wood,
And reaches soon that castle good
Which stands and threatens Scotland's wastes.

"Bard Bracy! Bard Bracy! your horses are fleet,
Ye must ride up the hall, your music so sweet,
More loud than your horses' echoing feet!
And loud and loud to Lord Roland call,
Thy daughter is safe in Langdale hall!
Thy beautiful daughter is safe and free, —
Sir Leoline greets thee thus through me.
He bids thee come without delay
With all thy numerous array,
And take thy lovely daughter home;
And he will meet thee on the way
With all his numerous array
White with their panting palfreys' foam:
And by mine honor! I will say,
That I repent me of the day
When I spake words of fierce disdain
To Roland de Vaux of Tryermaine!—

For since that evil hour hath flown,
Many a summer's sun hath shone;
Yet ne'er found I a friend again
Like Roland de Vaux of Tryermaine."

The lady fell, and clasped his knees,
Her face upraised, her eyes o'erflowing;
And Bracy replied, with faltering voice,
His gracious hail on all bestowing!—
"Thy words, thou sire of Christabel,
Are sweeter than my harp can tell;
Yet might I gain a boon of thee,
This day my journey should not be,
So strange a dream hath come to me,
That I had vowed with music loud
To clear yon wood from thing unblest,
Warned by a vision in my rest!
For in my sleep I saw that dove,
That gentle bird, whom thou dost love,
And call'st by thy own daughter's name—
Sir Leoline! I saw the same
Fluttering, and uttering fearful moan,
Among the green herbs in the forest alone.
Which when I saw and when I heard,
I wondered what might ail the bird;
For nothing near it could I see,
Save the grass and green herbs underneath the old tree.

"And in my dream methought I went
To search out what might there be found;
And what the sweet bird's trouble meant,
That thus lay fluttering on the ground.
I went and peered, and could descry
No cause for her distressful cry;
But yet for her dear lady's sake
I stooped, methought, the dove to take,
When lo! I saw a bright green snake
Coilèd around its wings and neck,
Green as the herbs on which it couched.
Close by the dove's its head it crouched;
And with the dove it heaves and stirs,
Swelling its neck as she swelled hers!
I woke; it was the midnight hour,
The clock was echoing in the tower;
But though my slumber was gone by,
This dream it would not pass away,—
It seems to live upon my eye!
And thence I vowed this selfsame day,
With music strong and saintly song
To wander through the forest bare,
Lest aught unholy loiter there."

Thus Bracy said: the Baron the while
Half-listening heard him with a smile;
Then turned to Lady Geraldine,
His eyes made up of wonder and love,
And said in courtly accents fine,
"Sweet maid, Lord Roland's beauteous dove,
With arms more strong than harp or song,
Thy sire and I will crush the snake!"
He kissed her forehead as he spake,
And Geraldine, in maiden wise,
Casting down her large bright eyes,
With blushing cheek and courtesy fine
She turned her from Sir Leoline;
Softly gathering up her train,
That o'er her right arm fell again;
And folded her arms across her chest,
And couched her head upon her breast,
And looked askance at Christabel—
Jesu Maria, shield her well!

A snake's small eye blinks dull and shy,
And the lady's eyes they shrunk in her head,
Each shrunk up to a serpent's eye,
And with somewhat of malice, and more of dread,
At Christabel she looked askance!—
One moment—and the sight was fled!
But Christabel, in dizzy trance
Stumbling on the unsteady ground,
Shuddered aloud, with a hissing sound;
And Geraldine again turned round,
And like a thing that sought relief,
Full of wonder and full of grief,
She rolled her large bright eyes divine
Wildly on Sir Leoline.

The maid, alas! her thoughts are gone;
She nothing sees,—no sight but one!
The maid, devoid of guile and sin,
I know not how, in fearful wise
So deeply had she drunken in
That look, those shrunken serpent eyes,
That all her features were resigned
To this sole image in her mind,
And passively did imitate
That look of dull and treacherous hate!
And thus she stood in dizzy trance,
Still picturing that look askance
With forced unconscious sympathy
Full before her father's view,—
As far as such a look could be
In eyes so innocent and blue!
And when the trance was o'er, the maid
Pausèd awhile, and inly prayed:
Then falling at the Baron's feet,
"By my mother's soul do I entreat
That thou this woman send away!"
She said: and more she could not say:

For what she knew she could not tell,
O'ermastered by the mighty spell.

Why is thy cheek so wan and wild,
Sir Leoline? Thy only child
Lies at thy feet, thy joy, thy pride,
So fair, so innocent, so mild;
The same for whom thy lady died!
O, by the pangs of her dear mother,
Think thou no evil of thy child!
For her, and thee, and for no other,
She prayed the moment ere she died, —
Prayed that the babe for whom she died
Might prove her dear lord's joy and pride!
That prayer her deadly pangs beguiled,
Sir Leoline!
And wouldst thou wrong thy only child,
Her child and thine?

Within the Baron's heart and brain,
If thoughts like these had any share,
They only swelled his rage and pain,
And did but work confusion there.
His heart was cleft with pain and rage,
His cheeks they quivered, his eyes were wild.
Dishonored thus in his old age;
Dishonored by his only child,
And all his hospitality
To the wronged daughter of his friend,
By more than woman's jealousy
Brought thus to a disgraceful end. —
He rolled his eye with stern regard
Upon the gentle minstrel bard,
And said in tones abrupt, austere,
"Why, Bracy! dost thou loiter here?
I bade thee hence!" The bard obeyed;
And turning from his own sweet maid,
The aged knight, Sir Leoline,
Led forth the Lady Geraldine!

THE CONCLUSION TO PART II.

A LITTLE child, a limber elf,
Singing, dancing to itself,
A fairy thing with red round cheeks,
That always finds, and never seeks,
Makes such a vision to the sight
As fills a father's eyes with light;
And pleasures flow in so thick and fast
Upon his heart, that he at last
Must needs express his love's excess
With words of unmeant bitterness.
Perhaps 't is pretty to force together
Thoughts so all unlike each other;
To mutter and mock a broken charm,
To dally with wrong that does no harm.
Perhaps 't is tender too and pretty
At each wild word to feel within
A sweet recoil of love and pity.
And what if in a world of sin
(O sorrow and shame, should this be true!)
Such giddiness of heart and brain
Comes seldom save from rage and pain,
So talks as it 's most used to do.

ROBERT SOUTHEY.

[1774 - 1843.]

STANZAS.

MY days among the dead are passed;
Around me I behold,
Where'er these casual eyes are cast,
The mighty minds of old;
My never-failing friends are they,
With whom I converse day by day.

With them I take delight in weal,
And seek relief in woe;
And while I understand and feel
How much to them I owe,
My cheeks have often been bedewed
With tears of thoughtful gratitude.

My thoughts are with the dead; with them
I live in long-past years;
Their virtues love, their faults condemn,
Partake their hopes and fears,
And from their lessons seek and find
Instruction with an humble mind.

My hopes are with the dead; anon
My place with them will be,
And I with them shall travel on
Through all futurity:
Yet leaving here a name, I trust,
That will not perish in the dust.

THE INCHCAPE ROCK.

No stir in the air, no stir in the sea, —
The ship was as still as she could be;
Her sails from heaven received no motion,
Her keel was steady in the ocean.

Without either sign or sound of their shock
The waves flowed over the Inchcape Rock;

So little they rose, so little they fell,
They did not move the Inchcape Bell.

The good old Abbot of Aberbrothok
Had placed that bell on the Inchcape Rock;
On a buoy in the storm it floated and swung,
And over the waves its warning rung.

When the Rock was hid by the surges' swell,
The mariners heard the warning bell;
And then they knew the perilous Rock,
And blessed the Abbot of Aberbrothok.

The sun in heaven was shining gay,
All things were joyful on that day;
The sea-birds screamed as they wheeled around,
And there was joyance in their sound.

The buoy of the Inchcape Bell was seen
A darker speck on the ocean green;
Sir Ralph the Rover walked his deck,
And he fixed his eye on the darker speck.

He felt the cheering power of spring,
It made him whistle, it made him sing;
His heart was mirthful to excess,
But the Rover's mirth was wickedness.

His eye was on the Inchcape float;
Quoth he, "My men, put out the boat,
And row me to the Inchcape Rock,
And I'll plague the priest of Aberbrothok."

The boat is lowered, the boatmen row,
And to the Inchcape Rock they go;
Sir Ralph bent over from the boat,
And he cut the bell from the Inchcape float.

Down sank the bell, with a gurgling sound,
The bubbles rose and burst around;
Quoth Sir Ralph, "The next who comes to the Rock
Won't bless the Abbot of Aberbrothok."

Sir Ralph the Rover sailed away,
He scoured the seas for many a day;
And now, grown rich with plundered store,
He steers his course for Scotland's shore.

So thick a haze o'erspreads the sky
They cannot see the sun on high;
The wind hath blown a gale all day,
At evening it hath died away.

On the deck the Rover takes his stand,
So dark it is they see no land.
Quoth Sir Ralph, "It will be lighter soon,
For there is the dawn of the rising moon."

"Canst hear," said one, "the breakers roar?
For methinks we should be near the shore;
Now where we are I cannot tell,
But I wish I could hear the Inchcape Bell."

They hear no sound, the swell is strong;
Though the wind hath fallen, they drift along,
Till the vessel strikes with a shivering shock:
Cried they, "It is the Inchcape Rock!"

Sir Ralph the Rover tore his hair,
He cursed himself in his despair;
The waves rush in on every side,
The ship is sinking beneath the tide.

But even in his dying fear
One dreadful sound could the Rover hear,
A sound as if with the Inchcape Bell
The fiends below were ringing his knell.

BROUGH BELLS.

One day to Helbeck I had strolled,
Among the Crossfell Hills,
And, resting in the rocky grove,
Sat listening to the rills, —

The while to their sweet undersong
The birds sang blithe around,
And the soft west-wind awoke the wood
To an intermitting sound.

Louder or fainter, as it rose
Or died away, was borne
The harmony of merry bells
From Brough, that pleasant morn.

"Why are the merry bells of Brough,
My friend, so few?" said I;
"They disappoint the expectant ear,
Which they should gratify.

"One, two, three, four; one, two, three, four;
'T is still one, two, three, four:
Mellow and silvery are the tones;
But I wish the bells were more!"

"What! art thou critical?" quoth he;
  "Eschew that heart's disease
That seeketh for displeasure where
  The intent hath been to please.

"By those four bells there hangs a tale,
  Which being told, I guess,
Will make thee hear their scanty peal
  With proper thankfulness.

"Not by the Cliffords were they given,
  Nor by the Tuftons' line;
Thou hearest in that peal the crune
  Of old John Brunskill's kine.

"On Stanemore's side, one summer eve,
  John Brunskill sat to see
His herds in yonder Borrodale
  Come winding up the lea.

"Behind them, on the lowland's verge,
  In the evening light serene,
Brough's silent tower, then newly built
  By Blenkinsop, was seen.

"Slowly they came in long array,
  With loitering pace at will;
At times a low from them was heard,
  Far off, for all was still.

"The hills returned that lonely sound
  Upon the tranquil air:
The only sound it was which then
  Awoke the echoes there.

"'Thou hear'st that lordly bull of mine,
  Neighbor,' quoth Brunskill then:
'How loudly to the hills he crunes,
  That crune to him again!

"'Think'st thou if yon whole herd at once
  Their voices should combine,
Were they at Brough, that we might not
Hear plainly from this upland spot
  That cruning of the kine?'

"'That were a crune, indeed,' replied
  His comrade, 'which, I ween,
Might at the Spital well be heard,
  And in all dales between.

"'Up Mallerstang to Eden's springs,
The eastern wind upon its wings
  The mighty voice would bear;
And Appleby would hear the sound,
  Methinks, when skies are fair.'

"'Then shall the herd,' John Brunskill
    cried,
  'From yon dumb steeple crune;
And thou and I, on this hillside,
  Will listen to their tune.

"'So, while the merry Bells of Brough
  For many an age ring on,
John Brunskill will remembered be,
  When he is dead and gone,

"'As one who, in his latter years,
  Contented with enough,
Gave freely what he well could spare
  To buy the Bells of Brough.'

"Thus it hath proved: three hundred
    years
  Since then have passed away,
And Brunskill's is a living name
  Among us to this day."

"More pleasure," I replied, "shall I
  From this time forth partake,
When I remember Helbeck woods,
  For old John Brunskill's sake.

"He knew how wholesome it would be,
  Among these wild, wide fells
And upland vales, to catch, at times,
  The sound of Christian bells;—

"What feelings and what impulses
  Their cadence might convey
To herdsman or to shepherd-boy,
Whiling in indolent employ
  The solitary day;—

"That, when his brethren were convened
  To meet for social prayer,
He too, admonished by the call,
  In spirit might be there;—

"Or when a glad thanksgiving sound,
  Upon the winds of heaven,
Was sent to speak a nation's joy,
  For some great blessing given,—

"For victory by sea or land,
  And happy peace at length;
Peace by his country's valor won,
  And stablished by her strength;—

"When such exultant peals were borne
  Upon the mountain air,
The sound should stir his blood, and give
  An English impulse there."

Such thoughts were in the old man's mind,
When he that eve looked down
From Stanemore's side on Borrodale,
And on the distant town.

And had I store of wealth, methinks,
Another herd of kine,
John Brunskill, I would freely give,
That they might crune with thine.

CHARLES LAMB.

[1775 - 1834.]

THE HOUSEKEEPER.

The frugal snail, with forecast of repose,
Carries his house with him where'er he goes;
Peeps out,—and if there comes a shower of rain,
Retreats to his small domicile again.
Touch but a tip of him, a horn,—'t is well,—
He curls up in his sanctuary shell.
He 's his own landlord, his own tenant; stay
Long as he will, he dreads no Quarter Day.
Himself he boards and lodges; both invites
And feasts himself; sleeps with himself o' nights.
He spares the upholsterer trouble to procure
Chattels; himself is his own furniture,
And his sole riches. Wheresoe'er he roam,—
Knock when you will,—he 's sure to be at home.

THE OLD FAMILIAR FACES.

I have had playmates, I have had companions,
In my days of childhood, in my joyful school-days;
All, all are gone, the old familiar faces.

I have been laughing, I have been carousing,
Drinking late, sitting late, with my bosom cronies;
All, all are gone, the old familiar faces.

I loved a love once, fairest among women!
Closed are her doors on me now, I must not see her,—
All, all are gone, the old familiar faces.

I have a friend, a kinder friend has no man:
Like an ingrate, I left my friend abruptly;
Left him, to muse on the old familiar faces.

Ghost-like I paced round the haunts of my childhood,
Earth seemed a desert I was bound to traverse,
Seeking to find the old familiar faces.

Friend of my bosom, thou more than a brother,
Why wert not thou born in my father's dwelling?
So might we talk of the old familiar faces,—

How some they have died, and some they have left me,
And some are taken from me; all are departed;
All, all are gone, the old familiar faces.

HESTER.

When maidens such as Hester die,
Their place ye may not well supply,
Though ye among a thousand try,
With vain endeavor.

A month or more hath she been dead,
Yet cannot I by force be led
To think upon the wormy bed
And her together.

A springy motion in her gait,
A rising step, did indicate
Of pride and joy no common rate,
That flushed her spirit.

I know not by what name beside
I shall it call;—if 't was not pride,
It was a joy to that allied,
She did inherit.

Her parents held the Quaker rule,
Which doth the human feeling cool;
But she was trained in nature's school,
Nature had blessed her.

A waking eye, a prying mind,
A heart that stirs, is hard to bind;

A hawk's keen sight ye cannot blind,
Ye could not Hester.

My sprightly neighbor, gone before
To that unknown and silent shore,
Shall we not meet, as heretofore,
Some summer morning,

When from thy cheerful eyes a ray
Hath struck a bliss upon the day,
A bliss that would not go away,
A sweet forewarning?

JAMES HOGG.

[1772-1835.]

WHEN MAGGY GANGS AWAY.

O, WHAT will a' the lads do
When Maggy gangs away?
O, what will a' the lads do
When Maggy gangs away?
There 's no a heart in a' the glen
That disna dread the day; —
O, what will a' the lads do
When Maggy gangs away?

Young Jock has ta'en the hill for 't,
A waefu' wight is he;
Poor Harry 's ta'en the bed for 't,
An' laid him down to dee;
And Sandy 's gane unto the kirk,
And learnin fast to pray; —
O, what will a' the lads do
When Maggy gangs away?

The young laird o' the Lang Shaw
Has drunk her health in wine;
The priest has said — in confidence —
The lassie was divine;
And that is mair in maiden's praise
Than ony priest should say; —
But O, what will the lads do
When Maggy gangs away?

The wailing in our green glen
That day will quaver high,
'T will draw the redbreast frae the wood,
The laverock frae the sky;
The fairies frae their beds o' dew
Will rise and join the lay, —
An' hey! what a day 't will be
When Maggy gangs away?

THE RAPTURE OF KILMENY.

BONNY Kilmeny gaed up the glen;
But it wasna to meet Duneira's men,
Nor the rosy monk of the isle to see,
For Kilmeny was pure as pure could be.
It was only to hear the yorlin sing,
And pu' the cress-flower round the spring;
The scarlet hip and the hindberrye,
And the nut that hangs frae the hazel-tree;
For Kilmeny was pure as pure could be.
But lang may her minny look o'er the wa',
And lang may she seek i' the green-wood shaw;
Lang the laird of Duneira blame,
And lang, lang greet, or Kilmeny come hame!

When many a day had come and fled,
When grief grew calm, and hope was dead,
When mass for Kilmeny's soul had been sung,
When the bedesman had prayed, and the dead-bell rung,
Late, late in a gloamin' when all was still,
When the fringe was red on the westlin' hill,
The wood was sere, the moon i' the wane,
The reek o' the cot hung over the plain,
Like a little wee cloud in the world its lane;
When the ingle lowed with an eiry leme,
Late, late in the gloamin' Kilmeny came hame!

"Kilmeny, Kilmeny, where have you been?
Lang hae we sought baith holt and den,
By linn, by ford, by greenwood tree,
Yet you are halesome and fair to see.
Where gat you that joup o' the lily sheen?
That bonny snood o' the birk sae green?
And these roses, the fairest that ever were seen?
Kilmeny, Kilmeny, where have you been?"

Kilmeny looked up with a lovely grace,
But nae smile was seen on Kilmeny's face;
As still was her look, and as still was her e'e,
As the stillness that lay on the emerant lea,
Or the mist that sleeps on a waveless sea.

For Kilmeny had been she knew not where,
And Kilmeny had seen what she could not declare.
Kilmeny had been where the cock never crew,
Where the rain never fell, and the wind never blew;
But it seemed as the harp of the sky had rung,
And the airs of heaven played round her tongue,
When she spake of the lovely forms she had seen,
And a land where sin had never been, —
A land of love and a land of light,
Withouten sun or moon or night;
Where the river swa'd a living stream,
And the light a pure celestial beam:
The land of vision it would seem,
A still, an everlasting dream.
In yon green-wood there is a waik,
And in that waik there is a wene,
And in that wene there is a maike,
That neither has flesh, blood, nor bane;
And down in yon green-wood he walks his lane.

In that green wene Kilmeny lay,
Her bosom happed wi' the flowerets gay;
But the air was soft, and the silence deep,
And bonny Kilmeny fell sound asleep;
She kend nae mair, nor opened her e'e,
Till waked by the hymns of a far countrye.
She awaked on a couch of the silk sae slim,
All striped wi' the bars of the rainbow's rim;
And lovely beings round were rife,
Who erst had travelled mortal life;
And aye they smiled, and 'gan to speer,
"What spirit has brought this mortal here?"
They clasped her waist and her hands sae fair,
They kissed her cheek, and they kemed her hair,
And round came many a blooming fere,
Saying, "Bonny Kilmeny, ye're welcome here!

"O, would the fairest of mortal kind
Aye keep the holy truths in mind,
That kindred spirits their motions see,
Who watch their ways with anxious e'e,
And grieve for the guilt of humanitye!
O, sweet to Heaven the maiden's prayer,
And the sigh that heaves a bosom sae fair!
And dear to Heaven the words of truth,
And the praise of virtue frae beauty's mouth!
And dear to the viewless forms of air,
The minds that kythe as the body fair!
O bonny Kilmeny! free frae stain,
If ever you seek the world again, —
That world of sin, of sorrow, and fear, —
O, tell of the joys that are waiting here,
And tell of the signs you shall shortly see;
Of the times that are now, and the times that shall be."

They lifted Kilmeny, they led her away,
And she walked in the light of a sunless day:
The sky was a dome of crystal bright,
The fountain of vision, and fountain of light;
The emerald fields were of dazzling glow,
And the flowers of everlasting blow.
Then deep in the stream her body they laid,
That her youth and beauty never might fade;
And they smiled on heaven, when they saw her lie
In the stream of life that wandered by.
And she heard a song, she heard it sung,
She kend not where; but sae sweetly it rung,
It fell on her ear like a dream of the morn:
"O, blest be the day Kilmeny was born!
Now shall the land of the spirits see,
Now shall it ken what a woman may be!
The sun that shines on the world sae bright,
A borrowed gleid of the fountain of light;
And the moon that sleeks the sky sae dun,
Like a gouden bow, or a beamless sun,
Shall wear away, and be seen nae mair,
And the angels shall miss them travelling the air.
But lang, lang after baith night and day,
When the sun and the world have elyed away;
When the sinner has gane to his waesome doom,
Kilmeny shall smile in eternal bloom!"

Then Kilmeny begged again to see
The friends she had left in her own countrye,
To tell of the place where she had been,
And the glories that lay in the land unseen;

To warn the living maidens fair,
The loved of Heaven, the spirits' care,
That all whose minds unmeled remain
Shall bloom in beauty when time is gane.

With distant music, soft and deep,
They lulled Kilmeny sound asleep;
And when she awakened, she lay her lane,
All happed with flowers in the green-wood wene.
When seven long years were come and fled;
When grief was calm, and hope was dead;
When scarce was remembered Kilmeny's name,
Late, late in a gloamin' Kilmeny came hame!
And O, her beauty was fair to see,
But still and steadfast was her e'e!
Such beauty bard may never declare,
For there was no pride nor passion there;
And the soft desire of maiden's een
In that mild face could never be seen.
Her seymar was the lily flower,
And her cheek the moss-rose in the shower,
And her voice like the distant melodye,
That floats along the twilight sea.
But she loved to raike the lanely glen,
And keeped afar frae the haunts of men;
Her holy hymns unheard to sing,
To suck the flowers, and drink the spring.
But wherever her peaceful form appeared,
The wild beasts of the hill were cheered;
The wolf played blithely round the field,
The lordly bison lowed and kneeled;
The dun deer wooed with manner bland,
And cowered aneath her lily hand.
And when at even the woodlands rung,
When hymns of other worlds she sung
In ecstasy of sweet devotion,
O, then the glen was all in motion!
The wild beasts of the forest came,
Broke from their bughts and faulds the tame,
And goved around, charmed and amazed;
Even the dull cattle crooned and gazed,
And murmured, and looked with anxious pain
For something the mystery to explain.
The buzzard came with the throstle-cock;
The corby left her houf in the rock;
The blackbird alang wi' the eagle flew;
The hind came tripping o'er the dew;
The wolf and the kid their raike began,
And the tod, and the lamb, and the leveret ran;
The hawk and the hern attour them hung,
And the merl and the mavis forhooyed their young;
And all in a peaceful ring were hurled;—
It was like an eve in a sinless world!

When a month and a day had come and gane,
Kilmeny sought the green-wood wene;
There laid her down on the leaves sae green,
And Kilmeny on earth was never mair seen.
But O, the words that fell from her mouth
Were words of wonder, and words of truth!
But all the land were in fear and dread,
For they kendna whether she was living or dead.
It wasna her hame, and she couldna remain;
She left this world of sorrow and pain,
And returned to the Land of Thought again.

THOMAS MOORE.

[1779-1852.]

FLY TO THE DESERT.

Fly to the desert, fly with me,
Our Arab tents are rude for thee;
But, O, the choice what heart can doubt,
Of tents with love, or thrones without?

Our rocks are rough, but smiling there
The acacia waves her yellow hair,
Lonely and sweet, nor loved the less
For flowering in a wilderness.

Our sands are bare, but down their slope
The silvery-footed antelope
As gracefully and gayly springs
As o'er the marble courts of kings.

Then come,—thy Arab maid will be
The loved and lone acacia-tree,
The antelope, whose feet shall bless
With their light sound thy loveliness.

O, there are looks and tones that dart
An instant sunshine through the heart,
As if the soul that minute caught
Some treasure it through life had sought;

As if the very lips and eyes
Predestined to have all our sighs,
And never be forgot again,
Sparkled and spoke before us then!

So came thy every glance and tone,
When first on me they breathed and shone;
New as if brought from other spheres,
Yet welcome as if loved for years.

THE MID HOUR OF NIGHT.

At the mid hour of night, when stars are weeping, I fly
To the lone vale we loved, when life shone warm in thine eye;
And I think oft, if spirits can steal from the regions of air,
To revisit past scenes of delight, thou wilt come to me there,
And tell me our love is remembered even in the sky!

Then I sing the wild song 't was once such pleasure to hear,
When our voices, commingling, breathed like one on the ear;
And, as Echo far off through the vale my sad orison rolls,
I think, O my love! 't is thy voice, from the Kingdom of Souls,
Faintly answering still the notes that once were so dear.

THE VALE OF AVOCA.

There is not in this wide world a valley so sweet
As that vale, in whose bosom the bright waters meet;
O, the last ray of feeling and life must depart
Ere the bloom of that valley shall fade from my heart!

Yet it was not that Nature had shed o'er the scene
Her purest of crystal and brightest of green;
'T was not the soft magic of streamlet or hill, —
O, no! it was something more exquisite still.

'T was that friends, the beloved of my bosom, were near,
Who made every dear scene of enchantment more dear,
And who felt how the best charms of nature improve,
When we see them reflected from looks that we love.

Sweet Vale of Avoca! how calm could I rest
In thy bosom of shade, with the friends I love best;
Where the storms that we feel in this cold world should cease,
And our hearts, like thy waters, be mingled in peace.

O THOU WHO DRY'ST THE MOURNER'S TEAR.

O Thou who dry'st the mourner's tear!
How dark this world would be,
If, when deceived and wounded here,
We could not fly to thee.
The friends who in our sunshine live,
When winter comes, are flown;
And he who has but tears to give
Must weep those tears alone.
But thou wilt heal that broken heart
Which, like the plants that throw
Their fragrance from the wounded part,
Breathes sweetness out of woe.

When joy no longer soothes or cheers,
And e'en the hope that threw
A moment's sparkle o'er our tears
Is dimmed and vanished too,
O, who would bear life's stormy doom,
Did not thy wing of love
Come, brightly wafting through the gloom
Our peace-branch from above?
Then sorrow, touched by thee, grows bright
With more than rapture's ray;
As darkness shows us worlds of light
We never saw by day!

THOU ART, O GOD!

Thou art, O God! the life and light
Of all this wondrous world we see;
Its glow by day, its smile by night,
Are but reflections caught from thee.

Where'er we turn, thy glories shine,
And all things fair and bright are thine.

When day, with farewell beam, delays
  Among the opening clouds of even,
And we can almost think we gaze
  Through golden vistas into heaven, —
Those hues that make the sun's decline
So soft, so radiant, Lord! are thine.

When night, with wings of starry gloom,
  O'ershadows all the earth and skies,
Like some dark, beauteous bird, whose plume
  Is sparkling with unnumbered eyes, —
That sacred gloom, those fires divine,
So grand, so countless, Lord! are thine.

When youthful spring around us breathes,
  Thy spirit warms her fragrant sigh;
And every flower the summer wreathes
  Is born beneath that kindling eye.
Where'er we turn, thy glories shine,
And all things fair and bright are Thine.

LORD BYRON.

[1788 - 1824.]

SHE WALKS IN BEAUTY.

She walks in beauty, like the night
  Of cloudless climes and starry skies,
And all that 's best of dark and bright
  Meets in her aspect and her eyes,
Thus mellowed to that tender light
  Which Heaven to gaudy day denies.

One shade the more, one ray the less,
  Had half impaired the nameless grace
Which waves in every raven tress,
  Or softly lightens o'er her face,
Where thoughts serenely sweet express
  How pure, how dear their dwelling-place.

And on that cheek and o'er that brow,
  So soft, so calm, yet eloquent,
The smiles that win, the tints that glow,
  But tell of days in goodness spent,
A mind at peace with all below,
  A heart whose love is innocent!

THE DESTRUCTION OF SENNACHERIB.

The Assyrian came down like the wolf on the fold,
And his cohorts were gleaming in purple and gold;
And the sheen of their spears was like stars on the sea,
When the blue wave rolls nightly on deep Galilee.

Like the leaves of the forest when summer is green,
That host with their banners at sunset were seen;
Like the leaves of the forest when autumn hath blown,
That host on the morrow lay withered and strown.

For the Angel of Death spread his wings on the blast,
And breathed in the face of the foe as he passed;
And the eyes of the sleepers waxed deadly and chill,
And their hearts but once heaved, and forever grew still!

And there lay the steed with his nostrils all wide,
But through them there rolled not the breath of his pride:
And the foam of his gasping lay white on the turf,
And cold as the spray of the rock-beating surf.

And there lay the rider distorted and pale,
With the dew on his brow and the rust on his mail;
And the tents were all silent, the banners alone,
The lances unlifted, the trumpet unblown.

And the widows of Ashur are loud in their wail,
And the idols are broke in the temple of Baal;
And the might of the Gentile, unsmote by the sword,
Hath melted like snow in the glance of the Lord!

THE LAKE OF GENEVA.

Clear, placid Leman! thy contrasted lake,
With the wild world I dwelt in, is a thing
Which warns me, with its stillness, to forsake
Earth's troubled waters for a purer spring.
This quiet sail is as a noiseless wing
To waft me from distraction; once I loved
Torn ocean's roar, but thy soft murmuring
Sounds sweet as if a sister's voice reproved,
That I with stern delights should e'er have been so moved.

It is the hush of night, and all between
Thy margin and the mountains, dusk, yet clear,
Mellowed and mingling, yet distinctly seen,
Save darkened Jura, whose capt heights appear
Precipitously steep; and drawing near,
There breathes a living fragrance from the shore,
Of flowers yet fresh with childhood; on the ear
Drops the light drip of the suspended oar,
Or chirps the grasshopper one good-night carol more:

He is an evening reveller, who makes
His life an infancy, and sings his fill;
At intervals, some bird from out the brakes
Starts into voice a moment, then is still.
There seems a floating whisper on the hill,
But that is fancy, for the starlight dews
All silently their tears of love instil,
Weeping themselves away, till they infuse
Deep into Nature's breast the spirit of her hues.

MONT BLANC.

Mont Blanc is the monarch of mountains;
They crowned him long ago
On a throne of rocks, in a robe of clouds,
With a diadem of snow.
Around his waist are forests braced,
The avalanche in his hand;
But ere it fall, that thundering ball
Must pause for my command.

The glacier's cold and restless mass
Moves onward day by day;
But I am he who bids it pass,
Or with its ice delay.
I am the spirit of the place,
Could make the mountain bow
And quiver to his caverned base, —
And what with me wouldst *Thou?*

THE IMMORTAL MIND.

When coldness wraps this suffering clay,
Ah, whither strays the immortal mind?
It cannot die, it cannot stay,
But leaves its darkened dust behind.
Then, unembodied, doth it trace
By steps each planet's heavenly way?
Or fill at once the realms of space,
A thing of eyes, that all survey?

Eternal, boundless, undecayed,
A thought unseen, but seeing all,
All, all in earth or skies displayed,
Shall it survey, shall it recall:
Each fainter trace that memory holds
So darkly of departed years,
In one broad glance the soul beholds,
And all that was at once appears.

Before creation peopled earth,
Its eyes shall roll through chaos back;
And where the farthest heaven had birth,
The spirit trace its rising track.
And where the future mars or makes,
Its glance dilate o'er all to be,
While sun is quenched or system breaks,
Fixed in its own eternity.

Above or love, hope, hate, or fear,
It lives all passionless and pure:
An age shall fleet like earthly year;
Its years as moments shall endure.
Away, away, without a wing,
O'er all, through all, its thoughts shall fly, —
A nameless and eternal thing,
Forgetting what it was to die.

PERCY BYSSHE SHELLEY.

[1792 - 1822.]

STANZAS WRITTEN IN DEJECTION NEAR NAPLES.

The sun is warm, the sky is clear,
The waves are dancing fast and bright,
Blue isles and snowy mountains wear
The purple noon's transparent light:
The breath of the moist air is light
Around its unexpanded buds;
Like many a voice of one delight, —
The winds', the birds', the ocean-floods', —
The City's voice itself is soft like Solitude's.

I see the Deep's untrampled floor
With green and purple sea-weeds strown;
I see the waves upon the shore
Like light dissolved in star-showers thrown:
I sit upon the sands alone;
The lightning of the noontide ocean
Is flashing round me, and a tone
Arises from its measured motion, —
How sweet, did any heart now share in my emotion!

Alas! I have nor hope nor health,
Nor peace within nor calm around,
Nor that content surpassing wealth
The sage in meditation found,
And walked with inward glory crowned, —
Nor fame, nor power, nor love, nor leisure;
Others I see whom these surround, —
Smiling they live, and call life pleasure;
To me that cup has been dealt in another measure.

Yet now despair itself is mild
Even as the winds and waters are;
I could lie down like a tired child,
And weep away the life of care
Which I have borne, and yet must bear,
Till death like sleep might steal on me,
And I might feel in the warm air
My cheek grow cold, and hear the sea
Breathe o'er my dying brain its last monotony.

TO A SKYLARK.

Hail to thee, blithe spirit!
Bird thou never wert,
That from heaven, or near it,
Pourest thy full heart
In profuse strains of unpremeditated art.

Higher still and higher
From the earth thou springest
Like a cloud of fire;
The blue deep thou wingest,
And singing still dost soar, and soaring ever singest.

In the golden lightning
Of the sunken sun
O'er which clouds are brightening,
Thou dost float and run,
Like an unbodied joy whose race is just begun.

The pale purple even
Melts around thy flight;
Like a star of heaven,
In the broad daylight
Thou art unseen, but yet I hear thy shrill delight.

Keen as are the arrows
Of that silver sphere,
Whose intense lamp narrows
In the white dawn clear
Until we hardly see, we feel that it is there.

All the earth and air
With thy voice is loud,
As, when night is bare,
From one lonely cloud
The moon rains out her beams, and heaven is overflowed.

What thou art we know not;
What is most like thee?
From rainbow clouds there flow not
Drops so bright to see
As from thy presence showers a rain of melody.

Like a poet hidden
In the light of thought,
Singing hymns unbidden,
Till the world is wrought
To sympathy with hopes and fears it heeded not;

Like a high-born maiden
In a palace tower,
Soothing her love-laden
Soul in secret hour
With music sweet as love, which overflows her bower;

Like a glow-worm golden
In a dell of dew,
Scattering unbeholden
Its aerial hue
Among the flowers and grass, which screen it from the view;

Like a rose embowered
In its own green leaves,
By warm winds deflowered,
Till the scent it gives
Makes faint with too much sweet these heavy-wingéd thieves.

Sound of vernal showers
On the twinkling grass,
Rain-awakened flowers,
All that ever was
Joyous and clear and fresh thy music doth surpass.

Teach us, sprite or bird,
What sweet thoughts are thine!
I have never heard
Praise of love or wine
That panted forth a flood of rapture so divine.

Chorus hymeneal
Or triumphal chant
Matched with thine, would be all
But an empty vaunt,—
A thing wherein we feel there is some hidden want.

What objects are the fountains
Of thy happy strain?
What fields, or waves, or mountains?
What shapes of sky or plain?
What love of thine own kind? what ignorance of pain?

With thy clear, keen joyance
Languor cannot be;
Shadow of annoyance
Never came near thee:
Thou lovest, but ne'er knew love's sad satiety.

Waking or asleep,
Thou of death must deem
Things more true and deep
Than we mortals dream,
Or how could thy notes flow in such a crystal stream?

We look before and after,
And pine for what is not:
Our sincerest laughter
With some pain is fraught;
Our sweetest songs are those that tell of saddest thought.

Yet if we could scorn
Hate and pride and fear;
If we were things born
Not to shed a tear,
I know not how thy joy we ever should come near.

Better than all measures
Of delightful sound,
Better than all treasures
That in books are found,
Thy skill to poet were, thou scorner of the ground!

Teach me half the gladness
That thy brain must know
Such harmonious madness
From my lips would flow,
The world should listen then, as I am listening now!

ONE WORD IS TOO OFTEN PROFANED.

One word is too often profaned
For me to profane it,
One feeling too falsely disdained
For thee to disdain it.
One hope is too like despair
For prudence to smother,
And pity from thee is more dear
Than that from another.

I can give not what men call love;
But wilt thou accept not
The worship the heart lifts above,
And the heavens reject not,—
The desire of the moth for the star,
Of the night for the morrow,
The devotion to something afar
From the sphere of our sorrow?

JOHN KEATS.

[1796-1821.]

THE EVE OF SAINT AGNES.

SAINT AGNES' Eve, — ah, bitter chill it was!
The owl, for all his feathers, was a-cold;
The hare limped trembling through the frozen grass,
And silent was the flock in woolly fold:
Numb were the beadsman's fingers while he told
His rosary, and while his frosted breath,
Like pious incense from a censer old,
Seemed taking flight for heaven without a death,
Past the sweet virgin's picture, while his prayer he saith.

His prayer he saith, this patient, holy man;
Then takes his lamp, and riseth from his knees,
And back returneth, meagre, barefoot, wan,
Along the chapel aisle by slow degrees:
The sculptured dead, on each side, seem to freeze,
Imprisoned in black, purgatorial rails:
Knights, ladies, praying in dumb ora-t'ries,
He passeth by; and his weak spirit fails
To think how they may ache in icy hoods and mails.

Northward he turneth through a little door,
And scarce three steps, ere music's golden tongue
Flattered to tears this aged man and poor;
But no, — already had his death-bell rung;
The joys of all his life were said and sung;
His was harsh penance on Saint Agnes' Eve:
Another way he went, and soon among
Rough ashes sat he for his soul's reprieve,
And all night kept awake, for sinners' sake to grieve.

That ancient beadsman heard the prelude soft;
And so it chanced, for many a door was wide,
From hurry to and fro. Soon, up aloft,
The silver, snarling trumpets 'gan to chide;
The level chambers, ready with their pride,
Were glowing to receive a thousand guests;
The carvéd angels, ever eager-eyed,
Stared, where upon their heads the cornice rests,
With hair blown back, and wings put crosswise on their breasts.

At length burst in the argent revelry,
With plume, tiara, and all rich array,
Numerous as shadows haunting fairily
The brain, new stuffed in youth with triumphs gay
Of old romance. These let us wish away,
And turn, sole-thoughted, to one lady there,
Whose heart had brooded, all that wintry day,
On love, and winged Saint Agnes' saintly care,
As she had heard old dames full many times declare.

They told her how, upon Saint Agnes' Eve,
Young virgins might have visions of delight,
And soft adorings from their loves receive
Upon the honeyed middle of the night,
If ceremonies due they did aright;
As, supperless to bed they must retire,
And couch supine their beauties, lily white;
Nor look behind, nor sideways, but require
Of Heaven with upward eyes for all that they desire.

Full of this whim was thoughtful Madeline:
The music, yearning like a god in pain,
She scarcely heard; her maiden eyes divine,
Fixed on the floor, saw many a sweeping train
Pass by, — she heeded not at all: in vain
Came many a tiptoe, amorous cavalier,
And back retired; not cooled by high disdain.

But she saw not; her heart was otherwhere;
She sighed for Agnes' dreams, the sweetest of the year.

She danced along with vague, regardless eyes,
Anxious her lips, her breathing quick and short:
The hallowed hour was near at hand: she sighs
Amid the timbrels, and the thronged resort
Of whispers, or in anger or in sport;
Mid looks of love, defiance, hate, and scorn,
Hoodwinked with fairy fancy; all amort,
Save to Saint Agnes, and her lambs unshorn,
And all the bliss to be before to-morrow morn.

So, purposing each moment to retire,
She lingered still. Meantime, across the moors,
Had come young Porphyro, with heart on fire
For Madeline. Beside the portal doors,
Buttressed from moonlight, stands he, and implores
All saints to give him sight of Madeline,
But for one moment in the tedious hours,
That he might gaze and worship all unseen;
Perchance speak, kneel, touch, kiss, — in sooth, such things have been.

He ventures in: let no buzzed whisper tell;
All eyes be muffled, or a hundred swords
Will storm his heart, love's feverous citadel.
For him, those chambers held barbarian hordes,
Hyena foemen, and hot-blooded lords,
Whose very dogs would execrations howl
Against his lineage; not one breast affords
Him any mercy, in that mansion foul,
Save one old beldame, weak in body and in soul.

Ah, happy chance! the aged creature came,
Shuffling along with ivory-headed wand,
To where he stood, hid from the torch's flame,
Behind a broad hall-pillar, far beyond
The sound of merriment and chorus bland.
He startled her; but soon she knew his face,
And grasped his fingers in her palsied hand,
Saying, "Mercy, Porphyro! hie thee from this place;
They are all here to-night, the whole bloodthirsty race!

"Get hence! get hence! there 's dwarfish Hildebrand;
He had a fever late, and in the fit
He cursèd thee and thine, both house and land:
Then there 's that old Lord Maurice, not a whit
More tame for his gray hairs—Alas me! flit!
Flit like a ghost away." — "Ah! gossip dear,
We 're safe enough; here in this armchair sit,
And tell me how" — "Good saints! not here, not here;
Follow me, child, or else these stones will be thy bier."

He followed through a lowly archèd way,
Brushing the cobwebs with his lofty plume,
And as she muttered "Well-a—well-a-day!"
He found him in a little moonlit room,
Pale, latticed, chill, and silent as a tomb.
"Now tell me where is Madeline," said he,
"O, tell me, Angela, by the holy loom
Which none but secret sisterhood may see,
When they Saint Agnes' wool are weaving piously."

"Saint Agnes! Ah! it is Saint Agnes' Eve, —
Yet men will murder upon holy days;
Thou must hold water in a witch's sieve,
And be liege-lord of all the elves and fays,
To venture so: it fills me with amaze
To see thee, Porphyro! — Saint Agnes' Eve!

God's help! my lady fair the conjurer plays
This very night; good angels her deceive!
But let me laugh awhile, I 've mickle time to grieve."

Feebly she laugheth in the languid moon,
While Porphyro upon her face doth look,
Like puzzled urchin on an aged crone
Who keepeth closed a wondrous riddle-book,
As spectacled she sits in chimney-nook.
But soon his eyes grew brilliant, when she told
His lady's purpose; and he scarce could brook
Tears, at the thought of those enchantments cold,
And Madeline asleep in lap of legends old.

Sudden a thought came like a full-blown rose,
Flushing his brow, and in his painéd heart
Made purple riot; then doth he propose
A stratagem, that makes the beldame start:
"A cruel man and impious thou art!
Sweet lady, let her pray, and sleep, and dream
Alone with her good angels, far apart
From wicked men like thee. Go, go! —I deem
Thou canst not surely be the same that thou didst seem."

"I will not harm her, by all saints I swear!"
Quoth Porphyro; "O, may I ne'er find grace,
When my weak voice shall whisper its last prayer,
If one of her soft ringlets I displace,
Or look with ruffian passion in her face:
Good Angela, believe me by these tears;
Or I will, even in a moment's space,
Awake, with horrid shout, my foemen's ears,
And beard them, though they be more fanged than wolves and bears."

"Ah! why wilt thou affright a feeble soul?
A poor, weak, palsy-stricken, churchyard thing,
Whose passing-bell may ere the midnight toll;
Whose prayers for thee, each morn and evening,
Were never missed." Thus plaining, doth she bring
A gentler speech from burning Porphyro;
So woful, and of such deep sorrowing,
That Angela gives promise she will do
Whatever he shall wish, betide her weal or woe.

Which was to lead him, in close secrecy,
Even to Madeline's chamber, and there hide
Him in a closet, of such privacy
That he might see her beauty unespied,
And win perhaps that night a peerless bride,
While legioned fairies paced the coverlet,
And pale enchantment held her sleepy-eyed.
Never on such a night have lovers met,
Since Merlin paid his demon all the monstrous debt.

"It shall be as thou wishest," said the dame:
"All cates and dainties shall be storéd there
Quickly on this feast-night: by the tambour frame
Her own lute thou wilt see; no time to spare,
For I am slow and feeble, and scarce dare
On such a catering trust my dizzy head.
Wait here, my child, with patience; kneel in prayer
The while. Ah! thou must needs the lady wed,
Or may I never leave my grave among the dead."

So saying, she hobbled off with busy fear.
The lover's endless minutes slowly passed:
The dame returned, and whispered in his ear
To follow her; with aged eyes aghast
From fright of dim espial. Safe at last,
Through many a dusky gallery, they gain
The maiden's chamber, silken, hushed, and chaste;

Where Porphyro took covert, pleased amain.
His poor guide hurried back with agues in her brain.

Her faltering hand upon the balustrade,
Old Angela was feeling for the stair,
When Madeline, Saint Agnes' charméd maid,
Rose, like a missioned spirit, unaware;
With silver taper's light, and pious care,
She turned, and down the aged gossip led
To a safe level matting. Now prepare,
Young Porphyro, for gazing on that bed!
She comes, she comes again, like ringdove frayed and fled.

Out went the taper as she hurried in,
Its little smoke in pallid moonshine died:
She closed the door, she panted, all akin
To spirits of the air, and visions wide:
No uttered syllable, or, woe betide!
But to her heart, her heart was voluble,
Paining with eloquence her balmy side;
As though a tongueless nightingale should swell
Her throat in vain, and die, heart-stifled, in her dell.

A casement high and triple-arched there was,
All garlanded with carven imageries
Of fruits, and flowers, and bunches of knot-grass,
And diamonded with panes of quaint device,
Innumerable of stains and splendid dyes
As are the tiger-moth's deep-damasked wings;
And in the midst, 'mong thousand heraldries,
And twilight saints, and dim emblazonings,
A shielded scutcheon blushed with blood of queens and kings.

Full on this casement shone the wintry moon,
And threw warm gules on Madeline's fair breast,
As down she knelt for heaven's grace and boon:
Rose-bloom fell on her hands, together prest,
And on her silver cross soft amethyst,
And on her hair a glory, like a saint:
She seemed a splendid angel, newly drest,
Save wings, for heaven: — Porphyro grew faint:
She knelt, so pure a thing, so free from mortal taint.

Anon his heart revives: her vespers done,
Of all its wreathéd pearls her hair she frees;
Unclasps her warméd jewels one by one;
Loosens her fragrant bodice; by degrees
Her rich attire creeps rustling to her knees:
Half hidden, like a mermaid in seaweed,
Pensive awhile she dreams awake, and sees,
In fancy, fair Saint Agnes in her bed,
But dares not look behind, or all the charm is fled.

Soon, trembling in her soft and chilly nest
In sort of wakeful swoon, perplexed she lay,
Until the poppied warmth of sleep oppressed
Her soothéd limbs, and soul fatigued away;
Flown, like a thought, until the morrow-day;
Blissfully havened both from joy and pain;
Clasped like a missal where swart Paynims pray;
Blinded alike from sunshine and from rain,
As though a rose should shut, and be a bud again.

Stolen to this paradise, and so entranced,
Porphyro gazed upon her empty dress,
And listened to her breathing, if it chanced
To wake into a slumberous tenderness;

Which when he heard, that minute did he bless,
And breathed himself: then from the closet crept,
Noiseless as fear in a wide wilderness,
And over the hushed carpet, silent, stept,
And 'tween the curtains peeped, where, lo!—how fast she slept.

Then by the bedside, where the faded moon
Made a dim, silver twilight, soft he set
A table, and, half anguished, threw thereon
A cloth of woven crimson, gold, and jet:—
O for some drowsy Morphean amulet!
The boisterous, midnight, festive clarion,
The kettle-drum, and far-heard clarionet,
Affray his ears, though but in dying tone:—
The hall-door shuts again, and all the noise is gone.

And still she slept an azure-lidded sleep,
In blanchéd linen, smooth, and lavendered,
While he from forth the closet brought a heap
Of candied apple, quince, and plum, and gourd;
With jellies soother than the creamy curd,
And lucid syrops, tinct with cinnamon;
Manna and dates, in argosy transferred
From Fez; and spicéd dainties, every one,
From silken Samarcand to cedared Lebanon.

These delicates he heaped with glowing hand
On golden dishes and in baskets bright
Of wreathéd silver: sumptuous they stand
In the retired quiet of the night,
Filling the chilly room with perfume light.—
"And now, my love, my seraph fair, awake!
Thou art my heaven, and I thine eremite:
Open thine eyes, for meek Saint Agnes' sake,
Or I shall drowse beside thee, so my soul doth ache."

Thus whispering, his warm, unnervéd arm
Sank in her pillow. Shaded was her dream
By the dusk curtains:—'t was a midnight charm
Impossible to melt as icéd stream:
The lustrous salvers in the moonlight gleam;
Broad golden fringe upon the carpet lies:
It seemed he never, never could redeem
From such a steadfast spell his lady's eyes;
So mused awhile, entoiled in wooféd fantasies.

Awakening up, he took her hollow lute,—
Tumultuous,—and, in chords that tenderest be,
He played an ancient ditty, long since mute,
In Provence called, "La belle dame sans mercy";
Close to her ear touching the melody:
Wherewith disturbed, she uttered a soft moan;
He ceased—she panted quick—and suddenly
Her blue affrayéd eyes wide open shone:
Upon his knees he sank, pale as smooth-sculptured stone.

Her eyes were open, but she still beheld,
Now wide awake, the vision of her sleep:
There was a painful change, that nigh expelled
The blisses of her dream so pure and deep;
At which fair Madeline began to weep,
And moan forth witless words with many a sigh;
While still her gaze on Porphyro would keep,
Who knelt, with joinéd hands and piteous eye,
Fearing to move or speak, she looked so dreamingly.

"Ah, Porphyro!" said she, "but even now
Thy voice was at sweet tremble in mine ear,

Made tunable with every sweetest vow;
And those sad eyes were spiritual and clear;
How changed thou art! how pallid, chill, and drear!
Give me that voice again, my Porphyro,
Those looks immortal, those complainings dear!
O, leave me not in this eternal woe,
For if thou diest, my love, I know not where to go."

Beyond a mortal man impassioned far
At these voluptuous accents, he arose,
Ethereal, flushed, and like a throbbing star
Seen mid the sapphire heaven's deep repose;
Into her dream he melted, as the rose
Blendeth its odor with the violet, —
Solution sweet: meantime the frost-wind blows
Like love's alarum pattering the sharp sleet
Against the window-panes; Saint Agnes' moon hath set.

'T is dark: quick pattereth the flaw-blown sleet:
"This is no dream, my bride, my Madeline!"
'T is dark: the icéd gusts still rave and beat:
"No dream, alas! alas! and woe is mine!
Porphyro will leave me here to fade and pine. —
Cruel! what traitor could thee hither bring?
I curse not, for my heart is lost in thine,
Though thou forsakest a deceivéd thing;
A dove forlorn and lost, with sick, unpruned wing."

"My Madeline! sweet dreamer! lovely bride!
Say, may I be for aye thy vassal blest?
Thy beauty's shield, heart-shaped and vermeil dyed?
Ah, silver shrine, here will I take my rest
After so many hours of toil and quest,
A famished pilgrim, — saved by miracle.
Though I have found, I will not rob thy nest
Saving of thy sweet self; if thou think'st well
To trust, fair Madeline, to no rude infidel."

"Hark! 't is an elfin-storm from fairy-land,
Of haggard seeming, but a boon indeed:
Arise, — arise! the morning is at hand;
The bloated wassailers will never heed:
Let us away, my love, with happy speed;
There are no ears to hear, or eyes to see,
Drowned all in Rhenish and the sleepy mead:
Awake! arise! my love, and fearless be,
For o'er the southern moors I have a home for thee."

She hurried at his words, beset with fears,
For there were sleeping dragons all around,
At glaring watch, perhaps, with ready spears, —
Down the wide stairs a darkling way they found, —
In all the house was heard no human sound.
A chain-dropped lamp was flickering by each door;
The arras, rich with horseman, hawk, and hound,
Fluttered in the besieging wind's up-roar,
And the long carpets rose along the gusty floor.

They glide, like phantoms, into the wide hall;
Like phantoms to the iron porch they glide,
Where lay the porter, in uneasy sprawl,
With a huge empty flagon by his side:
The wakeful bloodhound rose, and shook his hide,
But his sagacious eye an inmate owns:
By one, and one, the bolts full easy slide;
The chains lie silent on the foot-worn stones;
The key turns, and the door upon its hinges groans.

And they are gone: ay, ages long ago
These lovers fled away into the storm.
That night the baron dreamt of many a woe,
And all his warrior-guests, with shade and form

Of witch, and demon, and large coffin-worm,
Were long be-nightmared. Angela the old,
Died palsy-twitched, with meagre face deform.
The beadsman, after thousand aves told,
For aye unsought-for slept among his ashes cold.

JAMES MONTGOMERY.

[1771-1854.]

THE COMMON LOT.

Once, in the flight of ages past,
There lived a man; and who was he?
Mortal! howe'er thy lot be cast,
That man resembled thee.

Unknown the region of his birth,
The land in which he died unknown;
His name has perished from the earth,
This truth survives alone:

That joy, and grief, and hope, and fear,
Alternate triumphed in his breast;
His bliss and woe,—a smile, a tear!
Oblivion hides the rest.

He suffered,—but his pangs are o'er;
Enjoyed,—but his delights are fled;
Had friends,—his friends are now no more;
And foes,—his foes are dead.

He saw whatever thou hast seen;
Encountered all that troubles thee:
He was—whatever thou hast been;
He is—what thou shalt be.

The rolling seasons, day and night,
Sun, moon, and stars, the earth and main,
Erewhile his portion, life, and light,
To him exist in vain.

The clouds and sunbeams, o'er his eye
That once their shades and glory threw,
Have left in yonder silent sky
No vestige where they flew.

The annals of the human race,
Their ruins, since the world began,
Of him afford no other trace
Than this,—there lived a man!

FOREVER WITH THE LORD.

Forever with the Lord!
Amen! so let it be!
Life from the dead is in that word,
And immortality.

Here in the body pent,
Absent from Him I roam,
Yet nightly pitch my moving tent
A day's march nearer home.

My Father's house on high,
Home of my soul! how near,
At times, to faith's foreseeing eye
Thy golden gates appear!

Ah! then my spirit faints
To reach the land I love,
The bright inheritance of saints,
Jerusalem above!

Yet clouds will intervene,
And all my prospect flies;
Like Noah's dove, I flit between
Rough seas and stormy skies.

Anon the clouds depart,
The winds and waters cease;
While sweetly o'er my gladdened heart
Expands the bow of peace!

Beneath its glowing arch,
Along the hallowed ground,
I see cherubic armies march,
A camp of fire around.

I hear at morn and even,
At noon and midnight hour,
The choral harmonies of heaven
Earth's Babel tongues o'erpower

Then, then I feel that He,
Remembered or forgot,
The Lord, is never far from me,
Though I perceive him not.

In darkness as in light,
Hidden alike from view,
I sleep, I wake, as in his sight
Who looks all nature through.

All that I am, have been,
All that I yet may be,
He sees at once, as he hath seen,
And shall forever see.

"Forever with the Lord":
Father, if 't is thy will,
The promise of that faithful word
Unto thy child fulfil!

So, when my latest breath
Shall rend the veil in twain,
By death I shall escape from death,
And life eternal gain.

PRAYER.

Prayer is the soul's sincere desire
Uttered or unexpressed,
The motion of a hidden fire
That trembles in the breast.

Prayer is the burden of a sigh,
The falling of a tear;
The upward glancing of an eye,
When none but God is near.

Prayer is the simplest form of speech
That infant lips can try;
Prayer the sublimest strains that reach
The Majesty on high.

Prayer is the Christian's vital breath,
The Christian's native air;
His watchword at the gates of death:
He enters heaven by prayer.

Prayer is the contrite sinner's voice
Returning from his ways;
While angels in their songs rejoice,
And say, "Behold he prays!"

O Thou, by whom we come to God,
The Life, the Truth, the Way,
The path of prayer thyself hast trod:
Lord, teach us how to pray!

HELEN MARIA WILLIAMS.

[1762–1827.]

WHILST THEE I SEEK.

Whilst Thee I seek, protecting Power,
Be my vain wishes stilled!
And may this consecrated hour
With better hopes be filled.

Thy love the power of thought bestowed;
To thee my thoughts would soar:
Thy mercy o'er my life has flowed,
That mercy I adore.

In each event of life, how clear
Thy ruling hand I see!
Each blessing to my soul more dear,
Because conferred by thee.

In every joy that crowns my days,
In every pain I bear,
My heart shall find delight in praise,
Or seek relief in prayer.

When gladness wings my favored hour,
Thy love my thoughts shall fill;
Resigned, when storms of sorrow lower,
My soul shall meet thy will.

My lifted eye, without a tear,
The gathering storm shall see;
My steadfast heart shall know no fear;
That heart shall rest on thee.

UNKNOWN.

THERE WAS SILENCE IN HEAVEN.

Can angel spirits need repose
In the full sunlight of the sky?
And can the veil of slumber close
A cherub's bright and blazing eye?

Have seraphim a weary brow,
A fainting heart, an aching breast?
No, far too high their pulses flow
To languish with inglorious rest.

O, not the death-like calm of sleep
Could hush the everlasting song;
No fairy dream or slumber deep
Entrance the rapt and holy throng.

Yet not the lightest tone was heard
From angel voice or angel hand;
And not one plumèd pinion stirred
Among the pure and blissful band.

For there was silence in the sky,
A joy not angel tongues could tell,
As from its mystic fount on high
The peace of God in stillness fell.

O, what is silence here below?
The fruit of a concealed despair;
The pause of pain, the dream of woe;—
It is the rest of rapture there.

And to the wayworn pilgrim here,
More kindred seems that perfect peace,
Than the full chants of joy to hear
Roll on, and never, never cease.

From earthly agonies set free,
Tired with the path too slowly trod,
May such a silence welcome me
Into the palace of my God.

JOHN QUINCY ADAMS.

[U. S. A., 1767-1848.]

TO A BEREAVED MOTHER.

Sure, to the mansions of the blest
When infant innocence ascends,
Some angel, brighter than the rest,
The spotless spirit's flight attends.
On wings of ecstasy they rise,
Beyond where worlds material roll,
Till some fair sister of the skies
Receives the unpolluted soul.
That inextinguishable beam,
With dust united at our birth,
Sheds a more dim, discolored gleam
The more it lingers upon earth.

But when the Lord of mortal breath
Decrees his bounty to resume,
And points the silent shaft of death
Which speeds an infant to the tomb,
No passion fierce, nor low desire,
Has quenched the radiance of the flame;
Back to its God the living fire
Reverts, unclouded as it came.
Fond mourner! be that solace thine!
Let Hope her healing charm impart,
And soothe, with melodies divine,
The anguish of a mother's heart.

O, think! the darlings of thy love,
Divested of this earthly clod,
Amid unnumbered saints, above,
Bask in the bosom of their God.
O'er thee, with looks of love, they bend;
For thee the Lord of life implore;
And oft from sainted bliss descend
Thy wounded quiet to restore.
Then dry, henceforth, the bitter tear;
Their part and thine inverted see.
Thou wert their guardian angel here,
They guardian angels now to thee.

WALTER SAVAGE LANDOR.

[1775-1864.]

LAMENT.

I loved him not; and yet, now he is gone,
I feel I am alone.
I checked him while he spoke; yet, could he speak,
Alas! I would not check.

For reasons not to love him once I sought,
And wearied all my thought
To vex myself and him: I now would give
My love, could he but live
Who lately lived for me, and, when he found
'T was vain, in holy ground
He hid his face amid the shades of death!

I waste for him my breath
Who wasted his for me! but mine returns,
And this lorn bosom burns
With stifling heat, heaving it up in sleep,
And waking me to weep
Tears that had melted his soft heart: for years
Wept he as bitter tears!

"Merciful God!" such was his latest prayer,
"These may she never share!"
Quieter is his breath, his breast more cold
Than daisies in the mould,
Where children spell, athwart the church-yard gate,
His name and life's brief date.
Pray for him, gentle souls, whoe'er you be,
And, O, pray, too, for me!

THOMAS CAMPBELL.

[1777 - 1844.]

THE LAST MAN.

All worldly shapes shall melt in gloom,
The sun himself must die,
Before this mortal shall assume
Its immortality!
I saw a vision in my sleep,
That gave my spirit strength to sweep
Adown the gulf of time!
I saw the last of human mould
That shall creation's death behold,
As Adam saw her prime!

The sun's eye had a sickly glare,
The earth with age was wan;
The skeletons of nations were
Around that lonely man!
Some had expired in fight, — the brands
Still rusted in their bony hands,
In plague and famine some!
Earth's cities had no sound nor tread;
And ships were drifting with the dead
To shores where all was dumb!

Yet, prophet-like, that lone one stood,
With dauntless words and high,
That shook the sere leaves from the wood,
As if a storm passed by,
Saying, We are twins in death, proud Sun!
Thy face is cold, thy race is run,
'T is Mercy bids thee go;
For thou ten thousand thousand years
Hast seen the tide of human tears,
That shall no longer flow.

What though beneath thee man put forth
His pomp, his pride, his skill;
And arts that made fire, flood, and earth
The vassals of his will?
Yet mourn I not thy parted sway,
Thou dim, discrownéd king of day;
For all those trophied arts
And triumphs that beneath thee sprang,
Healed not a passion or a pang
Entailed on human hearts.

Go, let oblivion's curtain fall
Upon the stage of men,
Nor with thy rising beams recall
Life's tragedy again:
Its piteous pageants bring not back,
Nor waken flesh, upon the rack
Of pain anew to writhe;
Stretched in disease's shapes abhorred,
Or mown in battle by the sword,
Like grass beneath the scythe.

Even I am weary in yon skies
To watch thy fading fire;
Test of all sumless agonies,
Behold not me expire.
My lips that speak thy dirge of death, —
Their rounded gasp and gurgling breath
To see thou shalt not boast.
The eclipse of Nature spreads my pall,
The majesty of darkness shall
Receive my parting ghost!

This spirit shall return to Him
Who gave its heavenly spark;
Yet think not, Sun, it shall be dim
When thou thyself art dark!
No! it shall live again, and shine
In bliss unknown to beams of thine,
By him recalled to breath,
Who captive led captivity,
Who robbed the grave of victory,
And took the sting from death!

Go, Sun, while mercy holds me up
On Nature's awful waste
To drink this last and bitter cup
Of grief that man shall taste, —
Go, tell the night that hides thy face,
Thou saw'st the last of Adam's race,
On earth's sepulchral clod,
The darkening universe defy
To quench his immortality,
Or shake his trust in God!

GLENARA.

O, heard ye yon pibroch sound sad in the gale,
Where a band cometh slowly with weeping and wail?
'T is the chief of Glenara laments for his dear;
And her sire, and the people, are called to her bier.

Glenara came first with the mourners and shroud;
Her kinsmen they followed, but mourned not aloud:

Their plaids all their bosoms were folded around;
They marched all in silence, — they looked on the ground.

In silence they marched over mountain and moor,
To a heath where the oak-tree grew lonely and hoar:
"Now here let us place the gray stone of her cairn:
Why speak ye no word?" — said Glenara the stern.

"And tell me, I charge you! ye clan of my spouse,
Why fold ye your mantles, why cloud ye your brows?"
So spake the rude chieftain: — no answer is made,
But each mantle unfolding, a dagger displayed.

"I dreamt of my lady, I dreamt of her shroud,"
Cried a voice from the kinsmen, all wrathful and loud;
"And empty that shroud and that coffin did seem:
Glenara! Glenara! now read me my dream!"

O, pale grew the cheek of that chieftain, I ween,
When the shroud was unclosed, and no lady was seen;
When a voice from the kinsmen spoke louder in scorn,
'T was the youth who had loved the fair Ellen of Lorn:

"I dreamt of my lady, I dreamt of her grief,
I dreamt that her lord was a barbarous chief:
On a rock of the ocean fair Ellen did seem;
Glenara! Glenara! now read me my dream!"

In dust, low the traitor has knelt to the ground,
And the desert revealed where his lady was found;
From a rock of the ocean that beauty is borne, —
Now joy to the house of fair Ellen of Lorn!

LORD ULLIN'S DAUGHTER.

A CHIEFTAIN, to the Highlands bound,
Cries, "Boatman, do not tarry!
And I 'll give thee a silver pound
To row us o'er the ferry."

"Now who be ye, would cross Lochgyle,
This dark and stormy water?"
"O, I 'm the chief of Ulva's isle,
And this Lord Ullin's daughter.

"And fast before her father's men
Three days we 've fled together,
For should he find us in the glen,
My blood would stain the heather.

"His horsemen hard behind us ride;
Should they our steps discover,
Then who will cheer my bonny bride
When they have slain her lover?"

Out spoke the hardy Highland wight:
"I 'll go, my chief, — I 'm ready;
It is not for your silver bright,
But for your winsome lady;

"And by my word! the bonny bird
In danger shall not tarry:
So, though the waves are raging white,
I 'll row you o'er the ferry."

By this the storm grew loud apace,
The water-wraith was shrieking;
And in the scowl of heaven each face
Grew dark as they were speaking.

But still, as wilder blew the wind,
And as the night grew drearer,
Adown the glen rode armèd men, —
Their trampling sounded nearer.

"O, haste thee, haste!" the lady cries,
"Though tempests round us gather;
I 'll meet the raging of the skies,
But not an angry father."

The boat has left a stormy land,
A stormy sea before her, —
When, O, too strong for human hand,
The tempest gathered o'er her!

And still they rowed amidst the roar
Of waters fast prevailing:
Lord Ullin reached that fatal shore;
His wrath was changed to wailing.

For, sore dismayed, through storm and shade,
His child he did discover;
One lovely hand she stretched for aid,
And one was round her lover.

"Come back! come back!" he cried in grief,
"Across this stormy water;
And I 'll forgive your Highland chief,
My daughter!—O my daughter!"

'T was vain;—the loud waves lashed the shore,
Return or aid preventing;
The waters wild went o'er his child,
And he was left lamenting.

HORACE SMITH.

[1779-1849.]

HYMN TO THE FLOWERS.

DAY-STARS! that ope your eyes with morn, to twinkle
From rainbow galaxies of earth's creation,
And dew-drops on her holy altars sprinkle
As a libation.

Ye matin worshippers! who, bending lowly
Before the uprisen sun, God's lidless eye,
Throw from your chalices a sweet and holy
Incense on high.

Ye bright mosaics! that with storied beauty
The floor of nature's temple tessellate,
What numerous emblems of instructive duty
Your forms create!

'Neath cloistered boughs, each floral bell that swingeth,
And tolls its perfume on the passing air,
Makes Sabbath in the fields, and ever ringeth
A call to prayer.

Not to the domes where crumbling arch and column
Attest the feebleness of mortal hand,
But to that fane, most catholic and solemn,
Which God hath planned;

To that cathedral, boundless as our wonder,
Whose quenchless lamps the sun and moon supply;
Its choir the winds and waves, its organ thunder,
Its dome the sky.

There, as in solitude and shade I wander
Through the green aisles, or stretched upon the sod,
Awed by the silence, reverently I ponder
The ways of God,

Your voiceless lips, O flowers! are living preachers,
Each cup a pulpit, and each leaf a book,
Supplying to my fancy numerous teachers
From loneliest nook.

Floral apostles! that in dewy splendor
"Weep without woe, and blush without a crime,"
O, may I deeply learn, and ne'er surrender
Your lore sublime!

"Thou wert not, Solomon, in all thy glory,
Arrayed," the lilies cry, "in robes like ours;
How vain your grandeur! ah, how transitory
Are human flowers!"

In the sweet-scented pictures, heavenly Artist,
With which thou paintest Nature's wide-spread hall,
What a delightful lesson thou impartest
Of love to all!

Not useless are ye, flowers! though made for pleasure;
Blooming o'er field and wave by day and night,
From every source your sanction bids me treasure
Harmless delight.

Ephemeral sages! what instructors hoary
For such a world of thought could furnish scope?

Each fading calyx a *memento mori*,
Yet fount of hope.

Posthumous glories! angel-like collection!
Upraised from seed or bulb interred in earth,
Ye are to me a type of resurrection,
A second birth.

Were I, O God! in churchless lands remaining,
Far from all voice of teachers or divines,
My soul would find, in flowers of thy ordaining,
Priests, sermons, shrines!

ADDRESS TO AN EGYPTIAN MUMMY.

And thou hast walked about — how strange a story! —
In Thebes's streets, three thousand years ago!
When the Memnonium was in all its glory,
And time had not begun to overthrow
Those temples, palaces, and piles stupendous,
Of which the very ruins are tremendous!

Speak! for thou long enough hast acted dummy;
Thou hast a tongue, — come, let us hear its tune!
Thou 'rt standing on thy legs, above ground, mummy!
Revisiting the glimpses of the moon, —
Not like thin ghosts or disembodied creatures,
But with thy bones, and flesh, and limbs, and features!

Tell us, — for doubtless thou canst recollect, —
To whom should we assign the Sphinx's fame?
Was Cheops or Cephrenes architect
Of either pyramid that bears his name?
Is Pompey's Pillar really a misnomer?
Had Thebes a hundred gates, as sung by Homer?

Perhaps thou wert a Mason, and forbidden,
By oath, to tell the mysteries of thy trade;
Then say, what secret melody was hidden
In Memnon's statue, which at sunrise played?
Perhaps thou wert a priest; if so, my struggles
Are vain, for priestcraft never owns its juggles!

Perchance that very hand, now pinioned flat,
Hath hob-a-nobbed with Pharaoh, glass to glass;
Or dropped a halfpenny in Homer's hat;
Or doffed thine own, to let Queen Dido pass;
Or held, by Solomon's own invitation,
A torch, at the great temple's dedication!

I need not ask thee if that hand, when armed,
Has any Roman soldier mauled and knuckled;
For thou wert dead, and buried, and embalmed,
Ere Romulus and Remus had been suckled:
Antiquity appears to have begun
Long after thy primeval race was run.

Thou couldst develop, if that withered tongue
Might tell us what those sightless orbs have seen,
How the world looked when it was fresh and young,
And the great deluge still had left it green;
Or was it then so old that history's pages
Contained no record of its early ages?

Still silent! — Incommunicative elf!
Art sworn to secrecy? Then keep thy vows!
But, prithee, tell us something of thyself, —
Reveal the secrets of thy prison-house;
Since in the world of spirits thou hast slumbered,
What hast thou seen, what strange adventures numbered?

Since first thy form was in this box extended,
We have, above ground, seen some strange mutations;
The Roman Empire has begun and ended,
New worlds have risen, we have lost old nations,
And countless kings have into dust been humbled,
While not a fragment of thy flesh has crumbled.

Didst thou not hear the pother o'er thy head,
When the great Persian conqueror, Cambyses,
Marched armies o'er thy tomb with thundering tread,
O'erthrew Osiris, Orus, Apis, Isis, —
And shook the pyramids with fear and wonder,
When the gigantic Memnon fell asunder?

If the tomb's secrets may not be confessed,
The nature of thy private life unfold!
A heart hath throbbed beneath that leathern breast,
And tears adown that dusty cheek have rolled;
Have children climbed those knees, and kissed that face?
What was thy name and station, age and race?

Statue of flesh! Immortal of the dead!
Imperishable type of evanescence!
Posthumous man, — who quitt'st thy narrow bed,
And standest undecayed within our presence!
Thou wilt hear nothing till the judgment morning,
When the great trump shall thrill thee with its warning!

Why should this worthless tegument endure,
If its undying guest be lost forever?
O, let us keep the soul embalmed and pure
In living virtue, — that when both must sever,
Although corruption may our frame consume,
The immortal spirit in the skies may bloom!

EBENEZER ELLIOTT.

[1781 - 1849.]

A GHOST AT NOON.

THE day was dark, save when the beam
Of noon through darkness broke;
In gloom I sat, as in a dream,
Beneath my orchard oak;
Lo! splendor, like a spirit, came,
A shadow like a tree!
While there I sat, and named her name
Who once sat there with me.

I started from the seat in fear;
I looked around in awe,
But saw no beauteous spirit near,
Though all that was I saw, —
The seat, the tree, where oft, in tears,
She mourned her hopes o'erthrown,
Her joys cut off in early years,
Like gathered flowers half blown.

Again the bud and breeze were met,
But Mary did not come;
And e'en the rose, which she had set,
Was fated ne'er to bloom!
The thrush proclaimed, in accents sweet,
That winter's reign was o'er;
The bluebells thronged around my feet,
But Mary came no more.

FOREST WORSHIP.

WITHIN the sunlit forest,
Our roof the bright blue sky,
Where fountains flow, and wild-flowers blow,
We lift our hearts on high:
Beneath the frown of wicked men
Our country's strength is bowing;
But, thanks to God! they can't prevent
The lone wild-flowers from blowing!

High, high above the tree-tops,
The lark is soaring free;
Where streams the light through broken clouds
His speckled breast I see:
Beneath the might of wicked men
The poor man's worth is dying;
But, thanked be God! in spite of them,
The lark still warbles flying!

The preacher prays, "Lord, bless us!"
"Lord, bless us!" echo cries;
"Amen!" the breezes murmur low;
"Amen!" the rill replies:
The ceaseless toil of woe-worn hearts
The proud with pangs are paying,
But here, O God of earth and heaven!
The humble heart is praying.

How softly, in the pauses
Of song, re-echoed wide,
The cushat's coo, the linnet's lay,
O'er rill and river glide!
With evil deeds of evil men
The affrighted land is ringing;
But still, O Lord, the pious heart
And soul-toned voice are singing!

Hush! hush! the preacher preacheth:
"Woe to the oppressor, woe!"
But sudden gloom o'ercasts the sun
And saddened flowers below;
So frowns the Lord!—but, tyrants, ye
Deride his indignation,
And see not in the gathered brow
Your days of tribulation!

Speak low, thou heaven-paid teacher!
The tempest bursts above:
God whispers in the thunder; hear
The terrors of his love!
On useful hands and honest hearts
The base their wrath are wreaking;
But, thanked be God! they can't prevent
The storm of heaven from speaking.

CORN-LAW HYMN.

Lord! call thy pallid angel,
The tamer of the strong!
And bid him whip with want and woe
The champions of the wrong!
O, say not thou to ruin's flood,
"Up, sluggard! why so slow?"
But alone let them groan,
The lowest of the low;
And basely beg the bread they curse,
Where millions curse them now!

No; wake not thou the giant
Who drinks hot blood for wine,
And shouts unto the east and west,
In thunder-tones like thine,
Till the slow to move rush all at once,
An avalanche of men,
While he raves over waves
That need no whirlwind then;
Though slow to move, moved all at once,
A sea, a sea of men!

REGINALD HEBER.

[1783-1826.]

IF THOU WERT BY MY SIDE.

If thou wert by my side, my love,
How fast would evening fail
In green Bengala's palmy grove,
Listening the nightingale!

If thou, my love, wert by my side,
My babies at my knee,
How gayly would our pinnace glide
O'er Gunga's mimic sea!

I miss thee at the dawning gray,
When, on our deck reclined,
In careless ease my limbs I lay,
And woo the cooler wind.

I miss thee when by Gunga's stream
My twilight steps I guide,
But most beneath the lamp's pale beam
I miss thee from my side.

I spread my books, my pencil try,
The lingering noon to cheer,
But miss thy kind, approving eye,
Thy meek, attentive ear.

But when of morn or eve the star
Beholds me on my knee,
I feel, though thou art distant far,
Thy prayers ascend for me.

Then on! then on! where duty leads,
My course be onward still;
O'er broad Hindostan's sultry meads,
O'er bleak Almorah's hill.

That course nor Delhi's kingly gates
Nor wild Malwah detain;
For sweet the bliss us both awaits
By yonder western main.

Thy towers, Bombay, gleam bright, they say,
Across the dark-blue sea;
But ne'er were hearts so light and gay
As then shall meet in thee!

BERNARD BARTON.

[1784–1849.]

NOT OURS THE VOWS.

NOT ours the vows of such as plight
  Their troth in sunny weather,
While leaves are green, and skies are bright,
  To walk on flowers together.

But we have loved as those who tread
  The thorny path of sorrow,
With clouds above, and cause to dread
  Yet deeper gloom to-morrow.

That thorny path, those stormy skies,
  Have drawn our spirits nearer;
And rendered us, by sorrow's ties,
  Each to the other dearer.

Love, born in hours of joy and mirth,
  With mirth and joy may perish;
That to which darker hours gave birth
  Still more and more we cherish.

It looks beyond the clouds of time,
  And through death's shadowy portal;
Made by adversity sublime,
  By faith and hope immortal.

LEIGH HUNT.

[1784–1859.]

AN ANGEL IN THE HOUSE.

  How sweet it were, if without feeble fright,
Or dying of the dreadful beauteous sight,
An angel came to us, and we could bear
To see him issue from the silent air
At evening in our room, and bend on ours
His divine eyes, and bring us from his bowers
News of dear friends, and children who have never
Been dead indeed,—as we shall know forever.
Alas! we think not what we daily see
About our hearths, angels, that are to be,
Or may be if they will, and we prepare
Their souls and ours to meet in happy air,—
A child, a friend, a wife whose soft heart sings
In unison with ours, breeding its future wings.

ABOU BEN ADHEM AND THE ANGEL.

ABOU BEN ADHEM (may his tribe increase!)
Awoke one night from a deep dream of peace,
And saw within the moonlight in his room,
Making it rich, and like a lily in bloom,
An angel, writing in a book of gold;
Exceeding peace had made Ben Adhem bold,
And to the presence in the room he said,
"What writest thou?" The vision raised its head,
And with a look made of all sweet accord,
Answered, "The names of those who love the Lord."
"And is mine one?" said Abou. "Nay, not so,"
Replied the angel. Abou spoke more low,
But cheerly still; and said, "I pray thee, then,
Write me as one that loves his fellow-men."
  The angel wrote and vanished. The next night
It came again, with a great wakening light,
And showed the names whom love of God had blessed,
And, lo! Ben Adhem's name led all the rest.

ALLAN CUNNINGHAM.

[1785–1842.]

A WET SHEET AND A FLOWING SEA.

A WET sheet and a flowing sea,
  A wind that follows fast,
And fills the white and rustling sail,
  And bends the gallant mast,—
And bends the gallant mast, my boys,
  While, like the eagle free,

Away the good ship flies, and leaves
 Old England on our lee.

O for a soft and gentle wind!
 I heard a fair one cry;
But give to me the swelling breeze,
 And white waves heaving high,—
The white waves heaving high, my lads,
 The good ship tight and free;
The world of waters is our home,
 And merry men are we.

THOU HAST SWORN BY THY GOD.

Thou hast sworn by thy God, my Jeanie,
 By that pretty white hand o' thine,
And by a' the lowing stars in heaven,
 That thou wad aye be mine;
And I hae sworn by my God, my Jeanie,
 And by that kind heart o' thine,
By a' the stars sown thick owre heaven,
 That thou shalt aye be mine.

Then foul fa' the hands that wad loose sic bands,
 An' the heart that wad part sic luve;
But there 's nae hand can loose my band,
 But the finger o' God abuve.
Though the wee, wee cot maun be my bield,
 And my claithing e'er so mean,
I wad lap me up rich i' the faulds o' luve,
 Heaven's armfu' o' my Jean.

Her white arm wad be a pillow for me
 Far safter than the down;
And Luve wad winnow owre us his kind, kind wings,
 An' sweetly I 'd sleep, an' soun'.
Come here to me, thou lass o' my luve,
 Come here, and kneel wi' me!
The morn is fu' o' the presence o' God,
 An' I canna pray without thee.

The morn-wind is sweet 'mang the beds o' new flowers,
 The wee birds sing kindlie an' hie;
Our gudeman leans owre his kale-yard dyke,
 And a blythe auld bodie is he.
The Beuk maun be taen when the carle comes hame,
 Wi' the holie psalmodie;

And thou maun speak o' me to thy God,
 And I will speak o' thee.

SHE 'S GANE TO DWALL IN HEAVEN.

She 's gane to dwall in heaven, my lassie,
 She 's gane to dwall in heaven:
Ye 're owre pure, quo' the voice o' God,
 For dwalling out o' heaven!

O, what 'll she do in heaven, my lassie?
 O, what 'll she do in heaven?
She 'll mix her ain thoughts wi' angels' sangs,
 An' make them mair meet for heaven.

She was beloved by a', my lassie,
 She was beloved by a';
But an angel fell in love wi' her,
 An' took her frae us a'.

Low there thou lies, my lassie,
 Low there thou lies;
A bonnier form ne'er went to the yird,
 Nor frae it will arise!

Fu' soon I 'll follow thee, my lassie,
 Fu' soon I 'll follow thee;
Thou left me naught to covet ahin',
 But took gudeness sel' wi' thee.

I looked on thy death-cold face, my lassie,
 I looked on thy death-cold face;
Thou seemed a lily new cut i' the bud,
 An' fading in its place.

I looked on thy death-shut eye, my lassie,
 I looked on thy death-shut eye;
An' a lovelier light in the brow of heaven
 Fell time shall ne'er destroy.

Thy lips were ruddy and calm, my lassie,
 Thy lips were ruddy and calm;
But gane was the holy breath o' heaven,
 To sing the evening psalm.

There 's naught but dust now mine, lassie,
 There 's naught but dust now mine;
My saul 's wi' thee i' the cauld grave,
 An' why should I stay behin'?

JOHN WILSON.

[1785 - 1854.]

THE EVENING CLOUD.

A CLOUD lay cradled near the setting sun,
A gleam of crimson tinged its braided snow:
Long had I watched the glory moving on
O'er the still radiance of the lake below.
Tranquil its spirit seemed, and floated slow!
Even in its very motion there was rest;
While every breath of eve that chanced to blow
Wafted the traveller to the beauteous west.
Emblem, methought, of the departed soul,
To whose white robe the gleam of bliss is given;
And by the breath of mercy made to roll
Right onwards to the golden gates of heaven,
Where to the eye of faith it peaceful lies,
And tells to man his glorious destinies.

SIR JOHN BOWRING.

[1792 - ——.]

FROM THE RECESSES.

FROM the recesses of a lowly spirit
My humble prayer ascends: O Father! hear it.
Upsoaring on the wings of fear and meekness,
Forgive its weakness.

I know, I feel, how mean and how unworthy
The trembling sacrifice I pour before thee;
What can I offer in thy presence holy,
But sin and folly?

For in thy sight, who every bosom viewest,
Cold are our warmest vows, and vain our truest;
Thoughts of a hurrying hour, our lips repeat them,
Our hearts forget them.

We see thy hand, — it leads us, it supports us;
We hear thy voice, — it counsels and it courts us;
And then we turn away, — and still thy kindness
Forgives our blindness.

And still thy rain descends, thy sun is glowing,
Fruits ripen round, flowers are beneath us blowing,
And, as if man were some deserving creature,
Joy covers nature.

O, how long-suffering, Lord! but thou delightest
To win with love the wandering; thou invitest,
By smiles of mercy, not by frowns or terrors,
Man from his errors.

Who can resist thy gentle call, appealing
To every generous thought and grateful feeling, —
That voice paternal, whispering, watching ever, —
My bosom? — never.

Father and Saviour! plant within this bosom
The seeds of holiness; and bid them blossom
In fragrance and in beauty bright and vernal,
And spring eternal!

Then place them in those everlasting gardens,
Where angels walk, and seraphs are the wardens;
Where every flower that climbs through death's dark portal
Becomes immortal.

HYMN.

FATHER, thy paternal care
Has my guardian been, my guide.
Every hallowed wish and prayer
Has thy hand of love supplied.
Thine is every thought of bliss
Left by hours and days gone by;

Every hope thy offspring is,
Beaming from futurity.

Every sun of splendid ray,
Every moon that shines serene,
Every morn that welcomes day,
Every evening's twilight scene,
Every hour that wisdom brings,
Every incense at thy shrine, —
These, and all life's holiest things,
And its fairest, all are thine.

And for all, my hymns shall rise
Daily to thy gracious throne;
Thither let my asking eyes
Turn unwearied, righteous One!
Through life's strange vicissitude,
There reposing all my care;
Trusting still, through ill and good,
Fixed, and cheered, and counselled there.

SAMUEL WOODWORTH.

[U. S. A., 1785 - 1842.]

THE BUCKET.

How dear to this heart are the scenes of my childhood,
When fond recollection presents them to view!
The orchard, the meadow, the deep-tangled wildwood,
And every loved spot which my infancy knew! —
The wide-spreading pond, and the mill that stood by it,
The bridge, and the rock where the cataract fell,
The cot of my father, the dairy-house nigh it,
And e'en the rude bucket that hung in the well, —
The old oaken bucket, the iron-bound bucket,
The moss-covered bucket, which hung in the well.

That moss-covered vessel I hailed as a treasure;
For often at noon, when returned from the field,
I found it the source of an exquisite pleasure,
The purest and sweetest that nature can yield.
How ardent I seized it, with hands that were glowing,
And quick to the white-pebbled bottom it fell;
Then soon, with the emblem of truth overflowing,
And dripping with coolness, it rose from the well, —
The old oaken bucket, the iron-bound bucket,
The moss-covered bucket, arose from the well.

How sweet from the green, mossy brim to receive it,
As, poised on the curb, it inclined to my lips!
Not a full, blushing goblet could tempt me to leave it,
Though filled with the nectar that Jupiter sips.
And now, far removed from the loved habitation,
The tears of regret will intrusively swell,
As fancy reverts to my father's plantation,
And sighs for the bucket that hangs in the well, —
The old oaken bucket, the iron-bound bucket,
The moss-covered bucket, that hangs in the well.

ANDREWS NORTON.

[U. S. A., 1786 - 1853.]

AFTER A SUMMER SHOWER.

The rain is o'er. How dense and bright
Yon pearly clouds reposing lie!
Cloud above cloud, a glorious sight,
Contrasting with the dark blue sky!

In grateful silence earth receives
The general blessing; fresh and fair,
Each flower expands its little leaves,
As glad the common joy to share.

The softened sunbeams pour around
A fairy light, uncertain, pale;

The wind flows cool; the scented ground
  Is breathing odors on the gale.

Mid yon rich clouds' voluptuous pile,
  Methinks some spirit of the air
Might rest, to gaze below awhile,
  Then turn to bathe and revel there.

The sun breaks forth; from off the scene
  Its floating veil of mist is flung;
And all the wilderness of green
  With trembling drops of light is hung.

Now gaze on Nature, — yet the same, —
  Glowing with life, by breezes fanned,
Luxuriant, lovely, as she came,
  Fresh in her youth, from God's own hand.

Hear the rich music of that voice,
  Which sounds from all below, above;
She calls her children to rejoice,
  And round them throws her arms of love.

Drink in her influence; low-born care,
  And all the train of mean desire,
Refuse to breathe this holy air,
  And mid this living light expire.

CAROLINE BOWLES SOUTHEY.

[1787 - 1854.]

MARINER'S HYMN.

LAUNCH thy bark, mariner!
  Christian, God speed thee!
Let loose the rudder-bands, —
  Good angels lead thee!
Set thy sails warily,
  Tempests will come;
Steer thy course steadily:
  Christian, steer home!

Look to the weather-bow,
  Breakers are round thee;
Let fall the plummet now,
  Shallows may ground thee.
Reef in the foresail, there!
  Hold the helm fast!
So — let the vessel wear —
  There swept the blast.

"What of the night, watchman?
  What of the night?"
"Cloudy — all quiet —
  No land yet — all 's right."
Be wakeful, be vigilant, —
  Danger may be
At an hour when all seemeth
  Securest to thee.

How! gains the leak so fast?
  Clean out the hold, —
Hoist up thy merchandise,
  Heave out thy gold;
There — let the ingots go —
  Now the ship rights;
Hurrah! the harbor 's near —
  Lo! the red lights!

Slacken not sail yet
  At inlet or island;
Straight for the beacon steer,
  Straight for the high land;
Crowd all thy canvas on,
  Cut through the foam:
Christian! cast anchor now, —
  Heaven is thy home!

LAVINIA STODDARD.

[U. S. A., 1787 - 1820.]

THE SOUL'S DEFIANCE.

I SAID to Sorrow's awful storm
  That beat against my breast,
Rage on, — thou mayst destroy this form,
  And lay it low at rest;
But still the spirit that now brooks
  Thy tempest, raging high,
Undaunted on its fury looks,
  With steadfast eye.

I said to Penury's meagre train,
  Come on, — your threats I brave;
My last poor life-drop you may drain,
  And crush me to the grave;
Yet still the spirit that endures
  Shall mock your force the while,
And meet each cold, cold grasp of yours
  With bitter smile.

I said to cold Neglect and Scorn,
  Pass on, — I heed you not;
Ye may pursue me till my form
  And being are forgot;
Yet still the spirit, which you see
  Undaunted by your wiles,
Draws from its own nobility
  Its highborn smiles.

I said to Friendship's menaced blow,
  Strike deep, — my heart shall bear;
Thou canst but add one bitter woe
  To those already there;
Yet still the spirit that sustains
  This last severe distress
Shall smile upon its keenest pains,
  And scorn redress.

I said to Death's uplifted dart,
  Aim sure, — O, why delay?
Thou wilt not find a fearful heart,
  A weak, reluctant prey;
For still the spirit, firm and free,
  Unruffled by this last dismay,
Wrapt in its own eternity,
  Shall pass away.

WILLIAM KNOX.

[1789 - 1825.]

O, WHY SHOULD THE SPIRIT OF MORTAL BE PROUD?

O, WHY should the spirit of mortal be proud?
Like a fast-flitting meteor, a fast-flying cloud,
A flash of the lightning, a break of the wave,
He passeth from life to his rest in the grave.

The leaves of the oak and the willow shall fade,
Be scattered around and together be laid;
And the young and the old, and the low and the high,
Shall moulder to dust and together shall lie.

The child that a mother attended and loved,
The mother that infant's affection who proved,
The husband that mother and infant who blessed, —
Each, all, are away to their dwellings of rest.

The maid on whose cheek, on whose brow, in whose eye,
Shone beauty and pleasure, — her triumphs are by;
And the memory of those who have loved her and praised,
Are alike from the minds of the living erased.

The hand of the king that the sceptre hath borne,
The brow of the priest that the mitre hath worn,
The eye of the sage, and the heart of the brave,
Are hidden and lost in the depths of the grave.

The peasant whose lot was to sow and to reap,
The herdsman who climbed with his goats to the steep,
The beggar who wandered in search of his bread,
Have faded away like the grass that we tread.

The saint who enjoyed the communion of heaven,
The sinner who dared to remain unforgiven,
The wise and the foolish, the guilty and just,
Have quietly mingled their bones in the dust.

So the multitude goes, like the flower and the weed,
That wither away to let others succeed;
So the multitude comes, even those we behold,
To repeat every tale that hath often been told.

For we are the same things our fathers have been;
We see the same sights that our fathers have seen, —
We drink the same stream, and we feel the same sun,
And run the same course that our fathers have run.

The thoughts we are thinking our fathers would think;
From the death we are shrinking from, they too would shrink;
To the life we are clinging to, they too would cling;
But it speeds from the earth like a bird on the wing.

They loved, but their story we cannot unfold;
They scorned, but the heart of the haughty is cold;
They grieved, but no wail from their slumbers will come;
They joyed, but the voice of their gladness is dumb.

They died, — ay! they died; and we things that are now,
Who walk on the turf that lies over their brow,
Who make in their dwellings a transient abode,
Meet the changes they met on their pilgrimage road.

Yea, hope and despondence, and pleasure and pain,
Are mingled together in sunshine and rain;
And the smile and the tear, the song and the dirge,
Still follow each other, like surge upon surge.

'T is the twink of an eye, 't is the draught of a breath,
From the blossom of health to the paleness of death,
From the gilded saloon to the bier and the shroud, —
O, why should the spirit of mortal be proud?

RICHARD H. BARHAM.

[1788-1845.]

THE JACKDAW OF RHEIMS.

THE Jackdaw sat on the Cardinal's chair;
Bishop and abbot and prior were there;
Many a monk and many a friar,
Many a knight and many a squire,
With a great many more of lesser degree, —
In sooth, a goodly company;
And they served the Lord Primate on bended knee.
Never, I ween,
Was a prouder seen,
Read of in books or dreamt of in dreams,
Than the Cardinal Lord Archbishop of Rheims!

In and out,
Through the motley rout,
The little Jackdaw kept hopping about;
Here and there,
Like a dog in a fair,
Over comfits and cates
And dishes and plates,
Cowl and cope and rochet and pall,
Mitre and crosier, he hopped upon all.
With a saucy air
He perched on the chair
Where, in state, the great Lord Cardinal sat,
In the great Lord Cardinal's great red hat;
And he peered in the face
Of his Lordship's Grace,
With a satisfied look, as if to say,
"We two are the greatest folks here to-day!"
And the priests with awe,
As such freaks they saw,
Said, "The Devil must be in that little Jackdaw!"

The feast was over, the board was cleared,
The flawns and the custards had all disappeared,
And six little singing-boys, — dear little souls! —
In nice clean faces and nice white stoles,
Came, in order due,
Two by two,
Marching that grand refectory through!
A nice little boy held a golden ewer,
Embossed, and filled with water, as pure
As any that flows between Rheims and Namur,
Which a nice little boy stood ready to catch
In a fine golden hand-basin made to match.
Two nice little boys, rather more grown,
Poured lavender-water and eau-de-Cologne;
And a nice little boy had a nice cake of soap
Worthy of washing the hands of the Pope!
One little boy more
A napkin bore
Of the best white diaper fringed with pink,
And a cardinal's hat marked in permanent ink.

The great Lord Cardinal turns at the sight
Of these nice little boys dressed all in white;
From his finger he draws
His costly turquoise:

And, not thinking at all about little Jackdaws,
Deposits it straight
By the side of his plate,
While the nice little boys on his Eminence wait;
Till, when nobody 's dreaming of any such thing,
That little Jackdaw hops off with the ring!

There 's a cry and a shout,
And a deuce of a rout,
And nobody seems to know what they 're about,
But the monks have their pockets all turned inside out;
The friars are kneeling,
And hunting and feeling
The carpet, the floor, and the walls, and the ceiling.
The Cardinal drew
Off each plum-colored shoe,
And left his red stockings exposed to the view;
He peeps, and he feels
In the toes and the heels.
They turn up the dishes, — they turn up the plates, —
They take up the poker and poke out the grates, —
They turn up the rugs,
They examine the mugs;
But, no! — no such thing, —
They can't find THE RING!
And the Abbot declared that "when nobody twigged it,
Some rascal or other had popped in and prigged it!"

The Cardinal rose with a dignified look,
He called for his candle, his bell, and his book!
In holy anger and pious grief
He solemnly cursed that rascally thief!
He cursed him at board, he cursed him in bed;
From the sole of his foot to the crown of his head;
He cursed him in sleeping, that every night
He should dream of the Devil, and wake in a fright.
He cursed him in eating, he cursed him in drinking,
He cursed him in coughing, in sneezing, in winking;
He cursed him in sitting, in standing, in lying;
He cursed him in walking, in riding, in flying;
He cursed him living, he cursed him dying! —
Never was heard such a terrible curse!
But what gave rise
To no little surprise,
Nobody seemed one penny the worse!

The day was gone,
The night came on,
The monks and the friars they searched till dawn;
When the sacristan saw,
On crumpled claw,
Come limping a poor little lame Jackdaw!
No longer gay,
As on yesterday;
His feathers all seemed to be turned the wrong way; —
His pinions drooped, — he could hardly stand, —
His head was as bald as the palm of your hand;
His eye so dim,
So wasted each limb,
That, heedless of grammar, they all cried, "THAT 'S HIM!
That 's the scamp that has done this scandalous thing,
That 's the thief that has got my Lord Cardinal's RING!"
The poor little Jackdaw,
When the monks he saw,
Feebly gave vent to the ghost of a caw;
And turned his bald head as much as to say,
"Pray be so good as to walk this way!"
Slower and slower
He limped on before,
Till they came to the back of the belfry door,
Where the first thing they saw,
Midst the sticks and the straw,
Was the RING in the nest of that little Jackdaw!

Then the great Lord Cardinal called for his book,
And off that terrible curse he took;
The mute expression
Served in lieu of confession,
And, being thus coupled with full restitution,
The Jackdaw got plenary absolution!

When those words were heard
That poor little bird
Was so changed in a moment, 't was really absurd:
He grew sleek and fat;
In addition to that,
A fresh crop of feathers came thick as a mat!
His tail waggled more
Even than before;
But no longer it wagged with an impudent air,
No longer he perched on the Cardinal's chair.
He hopped now about
With a gait devout;
At matins, at vespers, he never was out;
And, so far from any more pilfering deeds,
He always seemed telling the Confessor's beads.
If any one lied, or if any one swore,
Or slumbered in prayer-time and happened to snore,
That good Jackdaw
Would give a great "Caw!"
As much as to say, "Don't do so any more!"
While many remarked, as his manners they saw,
That they "never had known such a pious Jackdaw!"
He long lived the pride
Of that country side,
And at last in the odor of sanctity died;
When, as words were too faint
His merits to paint,
The Conclave determined to make him a Saint.
And on newly made Saints and Popes, as you know,
It 's the custom at Rome new names to bestow,
So they canonized him by the name of Jem Crow!

RICHARD HENRY WILDE.

[U. S. A., 1789-1847.]

MY LIFE IS LIKE THE SUMMER ROSE.

My life is like the summer rose
That opens to the morning sky,
But ere the shades of evening close
Is scattered on the ground — to die.
Yet on the rose's humble bed
The sweetest dews of night are shed,
As if she wept the waste to see, —
But none shall weep a tear for me!

My life is like the autumn leaf,
That trembles in the moon's pale ray;
Its hold is frail, its date is brief;
Restless, and soon to pass away!
Yet, ere that leaf shall fall and fade,
The parent tree will mourn its shade,
The winds bewail the leafless tree, —
But none shall breathe a sigh for me!

My life is like the prints which feet
Have left on Tampa's desert strand;
Soon as the rising tide shall beat,
All trace will vanish from the sand;
Yet, as if grieving to efface
All vestige of the human race,
On that lone shore loud moans the sea, —
But none, alas! shall mourn for me!

CHARLES WOLFE.

[1791-1823.]

THE BURIAL OF SIR JOHN MOORE.

Not a drum was heard, not a funeral note,
As his corse to the rampart we hurried;
Not a soldier discharged his farewell shot
O'er the grave where our hero we buried.

We buried him darkly at dead of night,
The sods with our bayonets turning;
By the struggling moonbeams' misty light,
And the lantern dimly burning.

No useless coffin enclosed his breast,
Nor in sheet nor in shroud we wound him;
But he lay like a warrior taking his rest,
With his martial cloak around him.

Few and short were the prayers we said,
And we spoke not a word of sorrow;
But we steadfastly gazed on the face that was dead,
And we bitterly thought of the morrow.

We thought, as we hollowed his narrow bed,
And smoothed down his lonely pillow,

That the foe and the stranger would tread o'er his head,
And we far away on the billow!

Lightly they'll talk of the spirit that's gone,
And o'er his cold ashes upbraid him, —
But little he'll reck, if they let him sleep on
In the grave where a Briton has laid him.

But half our heavy task was done,
When the clock struck the hour for retiring;
And we heard the distant and random gun
That the foe was sullenly firing.

Slowly and sadly we laid him down,
From the field of his fame fresh and gory;
We carved not a line, we raised not a stone, —
But we left him alone with his glory.

JOHN HOWARD PAYNE.

[U. S. A., 1792-1852.]

SWEET HOME.

MID pleasures and palaces though we may roam,
Be it ever so humble, there's no place like home!
A charm from the skies seems to hallow us here,
Which, seek through the world, is ne'er met with elsewhere.
Home, home, sweet home!
There's no place like home!

An exile from home, splendor dazzles in vain!
O, give me my lowly thatched cottage again!
The birds singing gayly that came at my call; —
O, give me sweet peace of mind, dearer than all!
Home, home, sweet home!
There's no place like home!

FELICIA HEMANS.

[1794-1835.]

THE CHILDE'S DESTINY.

No mistress of the hidden skill,
No wizard gaunt and grim,
Went up by night to heath or hill
To read the stars for him;
The merriest girl in all the land
Of vine-encircled France
Bestowed upon his brow and hand
Her philosophic glance.
"I bind thee with a spell," said she,
"I sign thee with a sign;
No woman's love shall light on thee,
No woman's heart be thine!

"And trust me, 't is not that thy cheek
Is colorless and cold,
Nor that thine eye is slow to speak
What only eyes have told;
For many a cheek of paler white
Hath blushed with passion's kiss,
And many an eye of lesser light
Hath caught its fire from bliss:
Yet while the rivers seek the sea,
And while the young stars shine,
No woman's love shall light on thee,
No woman's heart be thine!

"And 't is not that thy spirit, awed
By beauty's numbing spell,
Shrinks from the force or from the fraud
Which beauty loves so well;
For thou hast learned to watch and wake,
And swear by earth and sky,
And thou art very bold to take
What we must still deny:
I cannot tell; the charm was wrought
By other threads than mine;
The lips are lightly begged or bought,
The heart may not be thine!

"Yet thine the brightest smile shall be
That ever beauty wore,
And confidence from two or three,
And compliments from more;
And one shall give, perchance hath given,
What only is not love, —
Friendship, O, such as saints in heaven
Rain on us from above.
If she shall meet thee in the bower,
Or name thee in the shrine,

O, wear the ring, and guard the flower, —
Her heart may not be thine!

"Go, set thy boat before the blast,
Thy breast before the gun, —
The haven shall be reached at last,
The battle shall be won;
Or muse upon thy country's laws,
Or strike thy country's lute,
And patriot hands shall sound applause,
And lovely lips be mute:
Go, dig the diamond from the wave,
The treasure from the mine,
Enjoy the wreath, the gold, the grave, —
No woman's heart is thine!

"I charm thee from the agony
Which others feel or feign,
From anger and from jealousy,
From doubt and from disdain;
I bid thee wear the scorn of years
Upon the cheek of youth,
And curl the lip at passion's tears,
And shake the head at truth:
While there is bliss in revelry,
Forgetfulness in wine,
Be thou from woman's love as free
As woman is from thine!"

KINDRED HEARTS.

O, ASK not, hope thou not, too much
Of sympathy below;
Few are the hearts whence one same touch
Bids the sweet fountains flow:
Few—and by still conflicting powers
Forbidden here to meet—
Such ties would make this life of ours
Too fair for aught so fleet.

It may be that thy brother's eye
Sees not as thine, which turns
In such deep reverence to the sky
Where the rich sunset burns;
It may be that the breath of spring,
Born amidst violets lone,
A rapture o'er thy soul can bring, —
A dream, to his unknown.

The tune that speaks of other times, —
A sorrowful delight!
The melody of distant chimes,
The sound of waves by night;
The wind that, with so many a tone,
Some chord within can thrill, —
These may have language all thine own,
To *him* a mystery still.

Yet scorn thou not for this the true
And steadfast love of years;
The kindly, that from childhood grew,
The faithful to thy tears!
If there be one that o'er the dead
Hath in thy grief borne part,
And watched through sickness by thy bed,
Call *his* a kindred heart!

But for those bonds all perfect made,
Wherein bright spirits blend,
Like sister flowers of one sweet shade
With the same breeze that bend,
For that full bliss of thought allied,
Never to mortals given,
O, lay thy lovely dreams aside,
Or lift them unto heaven!

MARIA BROOKS.

[U. S. A., 1795-1845.]

MARRIAGE.

THE bard has sung, God never formed a soul
Without its own peculiar mate, to meet
Its wandering half, when ripe to crown the whole
Bright plan of bliss, most heavenly, most complete!
But thousand evil things there are that hate
To look on happiness; these hurt, impede,
And, leagued with time, space, circumstance, and fate,
Keep kindred heart from heart, to pine and pant and bleed.

And as the dove to far Palmyra flying,
From where her native founts of Antioch beam,
Weary, exhausted, longing, panting, sighing,
Lights sadly at the desert's bitter stream, —
So many a soul, o'er life's drear desert faring,
Love's pure, congenial spring unfound, unquaffed,

Suffers, recoils, — then, thirsty and despairing
Of what it would, descends and sips the nearest draught.

JAMES G. PERCIVAL.

[U. S. A., 1795-1856.]

MAY.

I FEEL a newer life in every gale;
The winds, that fan the flowers,
And with their welcome breathings fill the sail,
Tell of serener hours, —
Of hours that glide unfelt away
Beneath the sky of May.

The spirit of the gentle south-wind calls
From his blue throne of air,
And where his whispering voice in music falls,
Beauty is budding there;
The bright ones of the valley break
Their slumbers, and awake.

The waving verdure rolls along the plain,
And the wide forest weaves,
To welcome back its playful mates again,
A canopy of leaves;
And from its darkening shadow floats
A gush of trembling notes.

Fairer and brighter spreads the reign of May;
The tresses of the woods
With the light dallying of the west-wind play;
And the full-brimming floods,
As gladly to their goal they run,
Hail the returning sun.

TO SENECA LAKE.

ON thy fair bosom, silver lake,
The wild swan spreads his snowy sail,
And round his breast the ripples break
As down he bears before the gale.

On thy fair bosom, waveless stream,
The dipping paddle echoes far,
And flashes in the moonlight gleam,
And bright reflects the polar star.

The waves along thy pebbly shore,
As blows the north-wind, heave their foam,
And curl around the dashing oar,
As late the boatman hies him home.

How sweet, at set of sun, to view
Thy golden mirror spreading wide,
And see the mist of mantling blue
Float round the distant mountain's side.

At midnight hour, as shines the moon,
A sheet of silver spreads below,
And swift she cuts, at highest noon,
Light clouds, like wreaths of purest snow.

On thy fair bosom, silver lake,
O, I could ever sweep the oar,
When early birds at morning wake,
And evening tells us toil is o'er!

JOHN G. C. BRAINARD.

[U. S. A., 1796-1828.]

THE FALL OF NIAGARA.

THE thoughts are strange that crowd into my brain,
While I look upward to thee. It would seem
As if God poured thee from his hollow hand,
And hung his bow upon thine awful front;
And spoke in that loud voice, which seemed to him
Who dwelt in Patmos for his Saviour's sake,
The sound of many waters; and had bade
Thy flood to chronicle the ages back,
And notch His centuries in the eternal rocks.

Deep calleth unto deep. And what are we,
That hear the question of that voice sublime?
O, what are all the notes that ever rung

From war's vain trumpet, by thy thundering side?
Yea, what is all the riot man can make
In his short life, to thy unceasing roar?
And yet, bold babbler, what art thou to Him
Who drowned a world, and heaped the waters far
Above its loftiest mountains?—a light wave,
That breaks, and whispers of its Maker's might.

EPITHALAMIUM.

I saw two clouds at morning
  Tinged by the rising sun,
And in the dawn they floated on
  And mingled into one;
I thought that morning cloud was blessed,
It moved so sweetly to the west.

I saw two summer currents
  Flow smoothly to their meeting,
And join their course, with silent force,
  In peace each other greeting;
Calm was their course through banks of green,
While dimpling eddies played between.

Such be your gentle motion,
  Till life's last pulse shall beat;
Like summer's beam, and summer's stream,
  Float on, in joy, to meet
A calmer sea, where storms shall cease,—
A purer sky, where all is peace.

DANIEL WEBSTER.

[U. S. A., 1782-1852.]

THE MEMORY OF THE HEART.

If stores of dry and learnèd lore we gain,
We keep them in the memory of the brain;
Names, things, and facts, — whate'er we knowledge call,—
There is the common ledger for them all;
And images on this cold surface traced
Make slight impression, and are soon effaced.
But we 've a page, more glowing and more bright,
On which our friendship and our love to write;
That these may never from the soul depart,
We trust them to the memory of the heart.
There is no dimming, no effacement there;
Each new pulsation keeps the record clear;
Warm, golden letters all the tablet fill,
Nor lose their lustre till the heart stands still.

JOSEPH RODMAN DRAKE.

[U. S. A., 1795-1820.]

THE AMERICAN FLAG.

When Freedom from her mountain height
  Unfurled her standard to the air,
She tore the azure robe of night,
  And set the stars of glory there;
She mingled with its gorgeous dyes
The milky baldric of the skies,
And striped its pure, celestial white
With streakings of the morning light;
Then from his mansion in the sun
She called her eagle-bearer down,
And gave into his mighty hand
The symbol of her chosen land.

Flag of the brave, thy folds shall fly,
The sign of hope and triumph high!
When speaks the signal-trumpet tone,
And the long line comes gleaming on,
Ere yet the life-blood, warm and wet,
Has dimmed the glistening bayonet,
Each soldier's eye shall brightly turn
To where thy sky-born glories burn,
And as his springing steps advance,
Catch war and vengeance from the glance.
And when the cannon-mouthings loud
Heave in wild wreaths the battle-shroud,
And gory sabres rise and fall
Like shoots of flame on midnight's pall,
Then shall thy meteor glances glow,
  And cowering foes shall sink beneath
Each gallant arm that strikes below
  That lovely messenger of death.

Flag of the seas, on ocean wave
Thy stars shall glitter o'er the brave;
When death, careering on the gale,
Sweeps darkly round the bellied sail,

And frighted waves rush wildly back
Before the broadside's reeling rack,
Each dying wanderer of the sea
Shall look at once to heaven and thee,
And smile to see thy splendors fly
In triumph o'er his closing eye.

Flag of the free heart's hope and home,
By angel hands to valor given,
Thy stars have lit the welkin dome,
And all thy hues were born in heaven.
Forever float that standard sheet!
Where breathes the foe but falls before us,
With Freedom's soil beneath our feet,
And Freedom's banner streaming o'er us?

JOHN PIERPONT.

[U. S. A., 1785-1866.]

PASSING AWAY.

WAS it the chime of a tiny bell
That came so sweet to my dreaming ear,
Like the silvery tones of a fairy's shell
That he winds, on the beech, so mellow and clear,
When the winds and the waves lie together asleep,
And the Moon and the Fairy are watching the deep,
She dispensing her silvery light,
And he his notes as silvery quite,
While the boatman listens and ships his oar,
To catch the music that comes from the shore?
Hark! the notes on my ear that play
Are set to words; as they float, they say,
"Passing away! passing away!"

But no; it was not a fairy's shell,
Blown on the beach, so mellow and clear;
Nor was it the tongue of a silver bell,
Striking the hour, that filled my ear,
As I lay in my dream; yet was it a chime
That told of the flow of the stream of time.
For a beautiful clock from the ceiling hung,
And a plump little girl, for a pendulum, swung
(As you've sometimes seen, in a little ring
That hangs in his cage, a canary-bird swing);
And she held to her bosom a budding bouquet,
And, as she enjoyed it, she seemed to say,
"Passing away! passing away!"

O, how bright were the wheels, that told
Of the lapse of time, as they moved round slow;
And the hands, as they swept o'er the dial of gold,
Seemed to point to the girl below.
And lo! she had changed: in a few short hours
Her bouquet had become a garland of flowers,
That she held in her outstretched hands, and flung
This way and that, as she, dancing, swung
In the fulness of grace and of womanly pride,
That told me she soon was to be a bride;
Yet then, when expecting her happiest day,
In the same sweet voice I heard her say,
"Passing away! passing away!"

While I gazed at that fair one's cheek, a shade
Of thought or care stole softly over,
Like that by a cloud in a summer's day made,
Looking down on a field of blossoming clover.
The rose yet lay on her cheek, but its flush
Had something lost of its brilliant blush;
And the light in her eye, and the light on the wheels,
That marched so calmly round above her,
Was a little dimmed, — as when Evening steals
Upon Noon's hot face. Yet one could n't but love her,
For she looked like a mother whose first babe lay
Rocked on her breast, as she swung all day;
And she seemed, in the same silver tone, to say,
"Passing away! passing away!"

While yet I looked, what a change there came!
Her eye was quenched, and her cheek was wan;

Stooping and staffed was her withered frame,
Yet just as busily swung she on;
The garland beneath her had fallen to dust;
The wheels above her were eaten with rust;
The hands, that over the dial swept,
Grew crooked and tarnished, but on they kept,
And still there came that silver tone
From the shrivelled lips of the toothless crone
(Let me never forget till my dying day
The tone or the burden of her lay),
"Passing away! passing away!"

TO CONGRESS.

A WORD FROM A PETITIONER, 1837.

What! our petitions spurned! The prayer
Of thousands — tens of thousands — cast,
Unheard, beneath your Speaker's chair!
But ye will hear us, first or last.
The thousands that last year ye scorned
Are millions now. Be warned! Be warned!

"The ox that treadeth out the corn
Thou shalt not muzzle." — Thus saith God.
And will ye muzzle the free-born, —
The man, — the owner of the sod, —
Who "gives the grazing ox his meat,"
And you — his servants here — your seat?

There 's a cloud, blackening up the sky!
East, west, and north its curtain spreads;
Lift to its muttering folds your eye!
Beware! for bursting on your heads,
It hath a force to bear you down; —
'T is an insulted people's frown.

Ye may have heard of the Soultán,
And how his Janissaries fell!
Their barracks, near the Atmeidán,
He barred, and fired; and their death-yell
Went to the stars, and their blood ran
In brooks across the Atmeidán.

The despot spake; and, in one night,
The deed was done. He wields, alone,
The sceptre of the Ottomite,
And brooks no brother near his throne.
Even now, the bow-string, at his beck,
Goes round his mightiest subjects' neck;

Yet will he, in his saddle, stoop —
I 've seen him, in his palace-yard —
To take petitions from a troop
Of women, who, behind his guard,
Come up, their several suits to press,
To state their wrongs, and ask redress.

And these, into his house of prayer,
I 've seen him take; and, as he spreads
His own before his Maker there,
These women's prayers he hears or reads; —
For, while he wears the diadem,
He is instead of God to them.

And this he must do. He may grant,
Or may deny; but hear he must.
Were his Seven Towers all adamant,
They'd soon be levelled with the dust,
And "public feeling" make short work —
Should he not hear them — with the Turk.

Nay, start not from your chairs, in dread
Of cannon-shot or bursting shell!
These shall not fall upon your head,
As once upon your house they fell.
We have a weapon, firmer set
And better than the bayonet, —

A weapon that comes down as still
As snow-flakes fall upon the sod,
But executes a freeman's will
As lightning does the will of God;
And from its force nor doors nor locks
Can shield you; — 't is the ballot-box.

Black as your deed shall be the balls
That from that box shall pour like hail!
And when the storm upon you falls,
How will your craven cheeks turn pale!
For, at its coming though ye laugh,
'T will sweep you from your hall, like chaff.

Not women, now, — the people pray.
Hear us, — or from us ye will hear!
Beware! — a desperate game ye play!
The men that thicken in your rear —
Kings though ye be — may not be scorned.
Look to your move! your stake! Ye 're warned.

WILLIAM MOTHERWELL.

[1798-1835.]

JEANIE MORRISON.

I 'VE wandered east, I 've wandered west,
  Through mony a weary way;
But never, never can forget
  The luve o' life's young day!
The fire that 's blawn on Beltane e'en
  May weel be black gin Yule;
But blacker fa' awaits the heart
  Where first fond luve grows cool.

O dear, dear Jeanie Morrison,
  The thochts o' bygane years
Still fling their shadows ower my path,
  And blind my een wi' tears:
They blind my een wi' saut, saut tears,
  And sair and sick I pine,
As memory idly summons up
  The blithe blinks o' langsyne.

'T was then we luvit ilk ither weel,
  'T was then we twa did part;
Sweet time—sad time! twa bairns at scule,
  Twa bairns, and but ae heart!
'T was then we sat on ae laigh bink,
  To leir ilk ither lear;
And tones and looks and smiles were shed,
  Remembered evermair.

I wonder, Jeanie, aften yet,
  When sitting on that bink,
Cheek touchin' cheek, loof locked in loof,
  What our wee heads could think?
When baith bent doun ower ae braid page,
  Wi' ae buik on our knee,
Thy lips were on thy lesson, but
  My lesson was in thee.

O, mind ye how we hung our heads,
  How cheeks brent red wi' shame,
Whene'er the scule-weans laughin' said,
  We cleeked thegither hame?
And mind ye o' the Saturdays
  (The scule then skail't at noon)
When we ran aff to speel the braes,—
  The broomy braes o' June?

My head rins round and round about,
  My heart flows like a sea,
As ane by ane the thochts rush back
  O' scule-time and o' thee.

O mornin' life! O mornin' luve!
  O lichtsome days and lang,
When hinnied hopes around our hearts
  Like simmer blossoms sprang!

O, mind ye, luve, how aft we left
  The deavin' dinsome toun,
To wander by the green burnside,
  And hear its waters croon?
The simmer leaves hung ower our heads,
  The flowers burst round our feet,
And in the gloamin' o' the wood,
  The throssil whusslit sweet;

The throssil whusslit in the wood,
  The burn sang to the trees,
And we, with Nature's heart in tune,
  Concerted harmonies;
And on the knowe abune the burn
  For hours thegither sat
In the silentness o' joy, till baith
  Wi' very gladness grat.

Aye, aye, dear Jeanie Morrison,
  Tears trickled doun your cheek,
Like dew-beads on a rose, yet nane
  Had ony power to speak!
That was a time, a blessed time,
  When hearts were fresh and young,
When freely gushed all feelings forth,
  Unsyllabled, unsung!

I marvel, Jeanie Morrison,
  Gin I hae been to thee
As closely twined wi' earliest thochts
  As ye hae been to me?
O, tell me gin their music fills
  Thine ear as it does mine!
O, say gin e'er your heart grows grit
  Wi' dreamings o' langsyne?

I 've wandered east, I 've wandered west,
  I 've borne a weary lot;
But in my wanderings, far or near,
  Ye never were forgot.
The fount that first burst frae this heart
  Still travels on its way;
And channels deeper, as it rins,
  The luve o' life's young day.

O dear, dear Jeanie Morrison,
  Since we were sindered young,
I 've never seen your face, nor heard
  The music o' your tongue;
But I could hug all wretchedness,
  And happy could I die,
Did I but ken your heart still dreamed
  O' bygane days and me!

THOMAS HOOD.

[1798 - 1845.]

THE SONG OF THE SHIRT.

WITH fingers weary and worn,
With eyelids heavy and red,
A woman sat, in unwomanly rags,
Plying her needle and thread,—
Stitch! stitch! stitch!
In poverty, hunger, and dirt;
And still, with a voice of dolorous pitch,
She sang the "Song of the Shirt!"

"Work! work! work!
While the cock is crowing aloof!
And work—work—work,
Till the stars shine through the roof!
It s, oh! to be a slave
Along with the barbarous Turk,
Where woman has never a soul to save,
If THIS is Christian work!

"Work—work—work!
Till the brain begins to swim;
Work—work—work,
Till the eyes are heavy and dim!
Seam, and gusset, and band;
Band, and gusset, and seam;
Till over the buttons I fall asleep,
And sew them on in my dream!

"O men with sisters dear!
O men with mothers and wives!
It is not linen you 're wearing out,
But human creatures' lives!
Stitch—stitch—stitch,
In poverty, hunger, and dirt;
Sewing at once, with a double thread,
A SHROUD as well as a shirt!

"But why do I talk of death,
That phantom of grisly bone?
I hardly fear his terrible shape,
It seems so like my own!
It seems so like my own
Because of the fast I keep;
O God! that bread should be so dear,
And flesh and blood so cheap!

"Work—work—work!
My labor never flags;
And what are its wages? A bed of straw,
A crust of bread—and rags:
A shattered roof—and this naked floor—
A table—a broken chair—
And a wall so blank my shadow I thank
For sometimes falling there!

"Work—work—work!
From weary chime to chime;
Work—work—work,
As prisoners work, for crime!
Band, and gusset, and seam;
Seam, and gusset, and band;
Till the heart is sick, and the brain benumbed,
As well as the weary hand!

"Work—work—work!
In the dull December light,
And work—work—work
When the weather is warm and bright:
While underneath the eaves
The brooding swallows cling,
As if to show me their sunny backs,
And twit me with the spring.

"O, but to breathe the breath
Of the cowslip and primrose sweet,
With the sky above my head,
And the grass beneath my feet;
For only one short hour
To feel as I used to feel,
Before I knew the woes of want,
And the walk that costs a meal!

"O, but for one short hour,—
A respite, however brief!
No blessèd leisure for love or hope,
But only time for grief!
A little weeping would ease my heart;
But in their briny bed
My tears must stop, for every drop
Hinders needle and thread!"

With fingers weary and worn,
With eyelids heavy and red,
A woman sat, in unwomanly rags,
Plying her needle and thread,—
Stitch! stitch! stitch!
In poverty, hunger, and dirt;
And still with a voice of dolorous pitch—
Would that its tone could reach the rich!—
She sang this "Song of the Shirt!"

MORNING MEDITATIONS.

LET Taylor preach, upon a morning breezy,
How well to rise while nights and larks are flying,—

For my part, getting up seems not so easy
By half as *lying*.

What if the lark does carol in the sky,
Soaring beyond the sight to find him out,—
Wherefore am I to rise at such a fly?
I 'm not a trout.

Talk not to me of bees and such-like hums,
The smell of sweet herbs at the morning prime,—
Only lie long enough, and bed becomes
A bed of *time*.

To me Dan Phœbus and his car are naught,
His steeds that paw impatiently about,—
Let them enjoy, say I, as horses ought,
The first turn-out!

Right beautiful the dewy meads appear
Besprinkled by the rosy-fingered girl;
What then,—if I prefer my pillow-beer
To early pearl?

My stomach is not ruled by other men's,
And, grumbling for a reason, quaintly begs
Wherefore should master rise before the hens
Have laid their eggs?

Why from a comfortable pillow start
To see faint flushes in the east awaken?
A fig, say I, for any streaky part,
Excepting bacon.

An early riser Mr. Gray has drawn,
Who used to haste the dewy grass among,
"To meet the sun upon the upland lawn,"—
Well,—he died young.

With charwomen such early hours agree,
And sweeps that earn betimes their bit and sup;
But I 'm no climbing boy, and need not be
All up,—all up!

So here I lie, my morning calls deferring,
Till something nearer to the stroke of noon;—
A man that's fond precociously of *stirring*
Must be a spoon.

SONG.

O LADY, leave thy silken thread
And flowery tapestry—
There 's living roses on the bush,
And blossoms on the tree.
Stoop where thou wilt, thy careless hand
Some random bud will meet;
Thou canst not tread but thou wilt find
The daisy at thy feet.

'T is like the birthday of the world,
When earth was born in bloom;
The light is made of many dyes,
The air is all perfume;
There 's crimson buds, and white and blue—
The very rainbow showers
Have turned to blossoms where they fell,
And sown the earth with flowers.

There 's fairy tulips in the east,—
The garden of the sun;
The very streams reflect the hues,
And blossom as they run;
While morn opes like a crimson rose,
Still wet with pearly showers:
Then, lady, leave the silken thread
Thou twinest into flowers.

RUTH.

SHE stood breast high amid the corn,
Clasped by the golden light of morn,
Like the sweetheart of the sun,
Who many a glowing kiss had won.

On her cheek an autumn flush
Deeply ripened;—such a blush
In the midst of brown was born,
Like red poppies grown with corn.

Round her eyes her tresses fell,—
Which were blackest none could tell;
But long lashes veiled a light
That had else been all too bright.

And her hat, with shady brim,
Made her tressy forehead dim;—
Thus she stood amid the stooks,
Praising God with sweetest looks.

Sure, I said, Heaven did not mean
Where I reap thou shouldst but glean;
Lay thy sheaf adown and come,
Share my harvest and my home.

W. B. O. PEABODY.

[U. S. A., 1799 - 1848.]

HYMN OF NATURE.

God of the earth's extended plains!
The dark green fields contented lie;
The mountains rise like holy towers,
Where man might commune with the sky;
The tall cliff challenges the storm
That lowers upon the vale below,
Where shaded fountains send their streams,
With joyous music in their flow.

God of the dark and heavy deep!
The waves lie sleeping on the sands,
Till the fierce trumpet of the storm
Hath summoned up their thundering bands;
Then the white sails are dashed like foam,
Or hurry, trembling, o'er the seas,
Till, calmed by thee, the sinking gale
Serenely breathes, Depart in peace.

God of the forest's solemn shade!
The grandeur of the lonely tree,
That wrestles singly with the gale,
Lifts up admiring eyes to thee;
But more majestic far they stand,
When, side by side, their ranks they form,
To wave on high their plumes of green,
And fight their battles with the storm.

God of the light and viewless air!
Where summer breezes sweetly flow,
Or, gathering in their angry might,
The fierce and wintry tempests blow;
All — from the evening's plaintive sigh,
That hardly lifts the drooping flower,
To the wild whirlwind's midnight cry —
Breathe forth the language of thy power.

God of the fair and open sky!
How gloriously above us springs
The tented dome, of heavenly blue,
Suspended on the rainbow's rings.
Each brilliant star, that sparkles through;
Each gilded cloud, that wanders free
In evening's purple radiance, gives
The beauty of its praise to thee.

God of the rolling orbs above!
Thy name is written clearly bright
In the warm day's unvarying blaze,
Or evening's golden shower of light.
For every fire that fronts the sun,
And every spark that walks alone
Around the utmost verge of heaven,
Were kindled at thy burning throne.

God of the world! the hour must come,
And nature's self to dust return!
Her crumbling altars must decay,
Her incense fires shall cease to burn!
But still her grand and lovely scenes
Have made man's warmest praises flow;
For hearts grow holier as they trace
The beauty of the world below.

W. A. MUHLENBERG.

[U. S. A.]

I WOULD NOT LIVE ALWAY.

I would not live alway: I ask not to stay
Where storm after storm rises dark o'er the way;
Where, seeking for rest, I but hover around
Like the patriarch's bird, and no resting is found;
Where hope, when she paints her gay bow in the air,
Leaves her brilliance to fade in the night of despair,
And joy's fleeting angel ne'er sheds a glad ray,
Save the gleam of the plumage that bears him away.

I would not live alway, thus fettered by sin,
Temptation without, and corruption within;
In a moment of strength, if I sever the chain,
Scarce the victory is mine ere I'm captive again.
E'en the rapture of pardon is mingled with fears,
And the cup of thanksgiving with penitent tears.
The festival trump calls for jubilant songs,
But my spirit her own *miserere* prolongs.

I would not live alway: no, welcome the tomb;
Immortality's lamp burns there bright mid the gloom.

There, too, is the pillow where Christ bowed his head;
O, soft be my slumbers on that holy bed!
And then the glad morn soon to follow that night,
When the sunrise of glory shall burst on my sight,
And the full matin-song, as the sleepers arise
To shout in the morning, shall peal through the skies.

Who, who would live alway, away from his God,
Away from yon heaven, that blissful abode,
Where the rivers of pleasure flow o'er the bright plains,
And the noontide of glory eternally reigns;
Where the saints of all ages in harmony meet,
Their Saviour and brethren transported to greet,
While the anthems of rapture unceasingly roll,
And the smile of the Lord is the feast of the soul?

That heavenly music! what is it I hear?
The notes of the harpers ring sweet on my ear!
And see soft unfolding those portals of gold,
The King all arrayed in his beauty behold!
O, give me, O, give me the wings of a dove!
Let me hasten my flight to those mansions above:
Ay! 't is now that my soul on swift pinions would soar,
And in ecstasy bid earth adieu evermore.

LADY DUFFERIN.

[1807-1867.]

THE IRISH EMIGRANT.

I 'M sitting on the stile, Mary,
Where we sat side by side
On a bright May morning long ago,
When first you were my bride.
The corn was springing fresh and green,
And the lark sang loud and high,
And the red was on your lip, Mary,
And the love-light in your eye.

The place is little changed, Mary;
The day 's as bright as then;
The lark's loud song is in my ear,
And the corn is green again.
But I miss the soft clasp of your hand,
And your warm breath on my cheek,
And I still keep listening for the words
You nevermore may speak.

'T is but a step down yonder lane,
The village church stands near, —
The church where we were wed, Mary;
I see the spire from here.
But the graveyard lies between, Mary,
And my step might break your rest,
Where I've laid you, darling, down to sleep,
With your baby on your breast.

I 'm very lonely now, Mary,
For the poor make no new friends;
But, O, they love the better still
The few our Father sends!
And you were all I had, Mary,
My blessing and my pride;
There 's nothing left to care for now,
Since my poor Mary died.

I 'm bidding you a long farewell,
My Mary kind and true,
But I 'll not forget you, darling,
In the land I 'm going to.
They say there 's bread and work for all,
And the sun shines always there;
But I 'll not forget old Ireland,
Were it fifty times less fair.

WINTHROP MACKWORTH PRAED.

[1801-1839.]

THE BELLE OF THE BALL.

YEARS, years ago, ere yet my dreams
Had been of being wise and witty;
Ere I had done with writing themes,
Or yawned o'er this infernal Chitty, —
Years, years ago, while all my joys
Were in my fowling-piece and filly;
In short, while I was yet a boy,
I fell in love with Laura Lilly.

I saw her at a county ball;
There, when the sound of flute and fiddle

Gave signal sweet in that old hall
Of hands across and down the middle,
Hers was the subtlest spell by far
Of all that sets young hearts romancing:
She was our queen, our rose, our star;
And when she danced — O Heaven, her dancing!

Dark was her hair; her hand was white;
Her voice was exquisitely tender;
Her eyes were full of liquid light;
I never saw a waist so slender;
Her every look, her every smile,
Shot right and left a score of arrows:
I thought 't was Venus from her isle,
I wondered where she 'd left her sparrows.

She talked of politics or prayers,
Of Southey's prose or Wordsworth's sonnets,
Of daggers or of dancing bears,
Of battles or the last new bonnets;
By candle-light, at twelve o'clock,
To me it mattered not a tittle,
If those bright lips had quoted Locke,
I might have thought they murmured Little.

Through sunny May, through sultry June,
I loved her with a love eternal;
I spoke her praises to the moon,
I wrote them for the Sunday Journal.
My mother laughed; I soon found out
That ancient ladies have no feeling.
My father frowned; but how should gout
Find any happiness in kneeling?

She was the daughter of a dean,
Rich, fat, and rather apoplectic;
She had one brother, just thirteen,
Whose color was extremely hectic;
Her grandmother, for many a year,
Had fed the parish with her bounty;
Her second-cousin was a peer,
And lord-lieutenant of the county.

But titles and the three per cents,
And mortgages, and great relations,
And India bonds, and tithes and rents,
O, what are they to love's sensations?
Black eyes, fair forehead, clustering locks,
Such wealth, such honors, Cupid chooses;
He cares as little for the stocks
As Baron Rothschild for the muses.

She sketched; the vale, the wood, the beach,
Grew lovelier from her pencil's shading:
She botanized; I envied each
Young blossom in her boudoir fading:
She warbled Handel; it was grand, —
She made the Catalani jealous:
She touched the organ; I could stand
For hours and hours and blow the bellows.

She kept an album, too, at home,
Well filled with all an album's glories, —
Paintings of butterflies and Rome,
Patterns for trimming, Persian stories,
Soft songs to Julia's cockatoo,
Fierce odes to famine and to slaughter,
And autographs of Prince Leboo,
And recipes for elder water.

And she was flattered, worshipped, bored;
Her steps were watched, her dress was noted;
Her poodle dog was quite adored;
Her sayings were extremely quoted.
She laughed, — and every heart was glad,
As if the taxes were abolished;
She frowned, — and every look was sad,
As if the opera were demolished.

She smiled on many just for fun, —
I knew that there was nothing in it;
I was the first, the only one
Her heart had thought of for a minute:
I knew it, for she told me so,
In phrase which was divinely moulded;
She wrote a charming hand, and O,
How sweetly all her notes were folded!

Our love was like most other loves, —
A little glow, a little shiver;
A rosebud and a pair of gloves,
And "Fly Not Yet," upon the river;
Some jealousy of some one's heir,
Some hopes of dying broken-hearted,
A miniature, a lock of hair,
The usual vows, — and then we parted.

We parted, — months and years rolled by;
We met again four summers after.
Our parting was all sob and sigh,
Our meeting was all mirth and laughter;
For in my heart's most secret cell
There had been many other lodgers,
And she was not the ball-room belle,
But only Mrs. — Something — Rogers.

WILLIAM LEGGETT.

[U. S. A., 1802 - 1839.]

LOVE AND FRIENDSHIP.

THE birds, when winter shades the sky,
Fly o'er the seas away,
Where laughing isles in sunshine lie,
And summer breezes play;

And thus the friends that flutter near
While fortune's sun is warm
Are startled if a cloud appear,
And fly before the storm.

But when from winter's howling plains
Each other warbler 's past,
The little snow-bird still remains,
And chirrups midst the blast.

Love, like that bird, when friendship's throng
With fortune's sun depart,
Still lingers with its cheerful song,
And nestles on the heart.

EDWARD COATE PINKNEY.

[U. S. A., 1802 - 1828.]

A HEALTH.

I FILL this cup to one made up of loveliness alone,
A woman, of her gentle sex the seeming paragon;
To whom the better elements and kindly stars have given
A form so fair, that, like the air, 't is less of earth than heaven.

Her every tone is music's own, like those of morning birds,
And something more than melody dwells ever in her words;
The coinage of her heart are they, and from her lips each flows
As one may see the burdened bee forth issue from the rose.

Affections are as thoughts to her, the measures of her hours;
Her feelings have the fragrancy, the freshness of young flowers;
And lovely passions, changing oft, so fill her, she appears
The image of themselves by turns, — the idol of past years.

Of her bright face one glance will trace a picture on the brain,
And of her voice in echoing hearts a sound must long remain;
But memory such as mine of her so very much endears,
When death is nigh my latest sigh will not be life's, but hers.

I fill this cup to one made up of loveliness alone,
A woman, of her gentle sex the seeming paragon.
Her health! and would on earth there stood some more of such a frame,
That life might be all poetry, and weariness a name.

FITZ-GREENE HALLECK.

[U. S. A., 1795 - 1867.]

BURNS.

HE kept his honesty and truth,
His independent tongue and pen,
And moved in manhood as in youth,
Pride of his fellow-men.

Strong sense, deep feeling, passions strong,
A hate of tyrant and of knave,
A love of right, a scorn of wrong,
Of coward and of slave, —

A kind, true heart, a spirit high,
That could not fear and would not bow,
Were written in his manly eye
And on his manly brow.

Praise to the bard! his words are driven,
Like flower-seeds by the far winds sown,
Where'er beneath the sky of heaven
The birds of fame have flown.

Praise to the man! a nation stood
  Beside his coffin with wet eyes,
Her brave, her beautiful, her good,
  As when a loved one dies.

And still, as on his funeral day,
  Men stand his cold earth-couch around,
With the mute homage that we pay
  To consecrated ground.

And consecrated ground it is,
  The last, the hallowed home of one
Who lives upon all memories,
  Though with the buried gone.

Such graves as his are pilgrim shrines,
  Shrines to no code or creed confined, —
The Delphian vales, the Palestines,
  The Meccas of the mind.

ON A PORTRAIT OF RED JACKET,

CHIEF OF THE TUSCARORAS.

COOPER, whose name is with his country's woven,
  First in her files, her PIONEER of mind, —
A wanderer now in other climes, has proven
  His love for the young land he left behind;

And throned her in the senate-hall of nations,
  Robed like the deluge rainbow, heaven-wrought,
Magnificent as his own mind's creations,
  And beautiful as its green world of thought;

And faithful to the Act of Congress, quoted
  As law authority, it passed nem. con.:
He writes that we are, as ourselves have voted,
  The most enlightened people ever known;

That all our week is happy as a Sunday
  In Paris, full of song and dance and laugh;
And that, from Orleans to the Bay of Fundy,
  There 's not a bailiff or an epitaph;

And furthermore — in fifty years, or sooner,
  We shall export our poetry and wine;
And our brave fleet, eight frigates and a schooner,
  Will sweep the seas from Zembla to the Line.

If he were with me, King of Tuscarora!
  Gazing, as I, upon thy portrait now,
In all its medalled, fringed, and beaded glory,
  Its eye's dark beauty, and its thoughtful brow, —

Its brow, half martial and half diplomatic;
  Its eye, upsoaring like an eagle's wings, —
Well might he boast that we, the Democratic,
  Outrival Europe, even in our kings!

For thou wast monarch born. Tradition's pages
  Tell not the planting of thy parent tree,
But that the forest tribes have bent for ages
  To thee, and to thy sires, the subject knee.

Thy name is princely, — if no poet's magic
  Could make RED JACKET grace an English rhyme,
Though some one with a genius for the tragic
  Hath introduced it in a pantomime,

Yet it is music in the language spoken
  Of thine own land; and on her herald roll,
As bravely fought for, and as proud a token
  As Cœur de Lion's of a warrior's soul.

Thy garb, — though Austria's bosom-star would frighten
  That medal pale, as diamonds the dark mine,
And George the Fourth wore, at his court at Brighton,
  A more becoming evening dress than thine;

Yet 't is a brave one, scorning wind and weather,
And fitted for thy couch, on field and flood,
As Rob Roy's tartan for the Highland heather,
Or forest green for England's Robin Hood.

Is strength a monarch's merit, like a whaler's?
Thou art as tall, as sinewy, and as strong
As earth's first kings, — the Argo's gallant sailors,
Heroes in history, and gods in song.

Is beauty?—Thine has with thy youth departed;
But the love-legends of thy manhood's years,
And she who perished, young and broken-hearted,
Are— But I rhyme for smiles and not for tears.

Is eloquence?—Her spell is thine that reaches
The heart, and makes the wisest head its sport;
And there 's one rare, strange virtue in thy speeches,
The secret of their mastery, — they are short.

The monarch mind, the mystery of commanding,
The birth-hour gift, the art Napoleon,
Of winning, fettering, moulding, wielding, banding
The hearts of millions till they move as one, —

Thou hast it. At thy bidding men have crowded
The road to death as to a festival;
And minstrels, at their sepulchres, have shrouded
With banner-folds of glory the dark pall.

Who will believe, — not I; for in deceiving
Lies the dear charm of life's delightful dream:
I cannot spare the luxury of believing
That all things beautiful are what they seem, —

Who will believe that, with a smile whose blessing
Would, like the Patriarch's, soothe a dying hour;
With voice as low, as gentle, and caressing,
As e'er won maiden's lip in moonlit bower;

With look, like patient Job's, eschewing evil;
With motions graceful as a bird's in air, —
Thou art, in sober truth, the veriest devil
That e'er clenched fingers in a captive's hair!

That in thy breast there springs a poison fountain,
Deadlier than that where bathes the Upas-tree;
And in thy wrath, a nursing cat-o'-mountain
Is calm as her babe's sleep compared with thee!

And underneath that face, like summer ocean's,
Its lip as moveless, and its cheek as clear,
Slumbers a whirlwind of the heart's emotions, —
Love, hatred, pride, hope, sorrow, — all save fear.

Love—for thy land, as if she were thy daughter,
Her pipe in peace, her tomahawk in wars;
Hatred — of missionaries and cold water;
Pride—in thy rifle-trophies and thy scars;

Hope—that thy wrongs may be by the Great Spirit
Remembered and revenged when thou art gone;
Sorrow—that none are left thee to inherit
Thy name, thy fame, thy passions, and thy throne!

WILLIAM LLOYD GARRISON.

[U. S. A.]

SONNET.

WRITTEN WHILE IN PRISON FOR DENOUNCING THE DOMESTIC SLAVE-TRADE.

HIGH walls and huge the body may confine,
And iron gates obstruct the prisoner's gaze,
And massive bolts may baffle his design,
And vigilant keepers watch his devious ways;
But scorns the immortal mind such base control:
No chains can bind it and no cell enclose.
Swifter than light it flies from pole to pole,
And in a flash from earth to heaven it goes.
It leaps from mount to mount; from vale to vale
It wanders, plucking honeyed fruits and flowers;
It visits home to hear the fireside tale
And in sweet converse pass the joyous hours;
'T is up before the sun, roaming afar,
And in its watches wearies every star.

JOHN NEAL.

[U. S. A.]

AMBITION.

I LOVED to hear the war-horn cry,
And panted at the drum's deep roll,
And held my breath, when, floating high,
I saw our starry banners fly,
As, challenging the haughty sky,
They went like battle o'er my soul.
For I was so ambitious then,
I longed to be the slave of men!

I stood and saw the morning light,
A standard swaying far and free,
And loved it like the conquering flight
Of angels, floating wide and bright
Above the storm, above the fight
Where nations strove for liberty;
And heard afar the signal-cry
Of trumpets in the hollow sky.

I sailed with storm upon the deep,
I shouted to the eagle soaring;
I hung me from the rocky steep
When all but spirits were asleep,
To feel the winds about me sweep,
And hear the gallant waters roaring:
For every sound and shape of strife
To me was as the breath of life.

But I am strangely altered now:
I love no more the bugle's voice,
The rushing wave, the plunging prow,
The mountain with its clouded brow,
The thunder when the blue skies bow
And all the sons of God rejoice.
I love to dream of tears and sighs,
And shadowy hair, and half-shut eyes!

GEORGE LUNT.

[U. S. A.]

PILGRIM SONG.

OVER the mountain wave, see where they come;
Storm-cloud and wintry wind welcome them home;
Yet, where the sounding gale howls to the sea,
There their song peals along, deep-toned and free:
"Pilgrims and wanderers, hither we come;
Where the free dare to be, —this is our home."

England hath sunny dales, dearly they bloom;
Scotia hath heather-hills, sweet their perfume:
Yet through the wilderness cheerful we stray,
Native land, native land, home far away!
"Pilgrims and wanderers, hither we come;
Where the free dare to be,— this is our home!"

Dim grew the forest-path: onward they trod;
Firm beat their noble hearts, trusting in God!
Gray men and blooming maids, high rose their song;

Hear it sweep, clear and deep, ever along:
"Pilgrims and wanderers, hither we come;
Where the free dare to be, — this is our home!"

Not theirs the glory-wreath, torn by the blast;
Heavenward their holy steps, heavenward they past.
Green be their mossy graves! ours be their fame,
While their song peals along ever the same:
"Pilgrims and wanderers, hither we come;
Where the free dare to be, — this is our home!"

CHARLES SPRAGUE.

[U. S. A., 1791 – 1874.]

THE FAMILY MEETING.

We are all here,
Father, mother,
Sister, brother,
All who hold each other dear.
Each chair is filled; we 're all at home!
To-night let no cold stranger come.
It is not often thus around
Our old familiar hearth we 're found.
Bless, then, the meeting and the spot;
For once be every care forgot;
Let gentle peace assert her power,
And kind affection rule the hour.
We 're all — all here.

We 're not all here!
Some are away, — the dead ones dear,
Who thronged with us this ancient hearth,
And gave the hour to guileless mirth.
Fate, with a stern, relentless hand,
Looked in, and thinned our little band;
Some like a night-flash passed away,
And some sank lingering day by day;
The quiet graveyard, — some lie there, —
And cruel ocean has his share.
We 're not all here.

We are all here!
Even they, — the dead, — though dead, so dear, —
Fond memory, to her duty true,
Brings back their faded forms to view.
How life-like, through the mist of years,
Each well-remembered face appears!
We see them, as in times long past;
From each to each kind looks are cast;
We hear their words, their smiles behold;
They 're round us, as they were of old.
We are all here.

We are all here,
Father, mother,
Sister, brother,
You that I love with love so dear.
This may not long of us be said;
Soon must we join the gathered dead,
And by the hearth we now sit round
Some other circle will be found.
O, then, that wisdom may we know,
Which yields a life of peace below;
So, in the world to follow this,
May each repeat in words of bliss,
We 're all — all here!

HENRY SCOTT RIDDELL.

OUR MARY.

Our Mary liket weel to stray
Where clear the burn was rowin';
And troth she was, though I say sae,
As fair as aught ere made o' clay,
And pure as ony gowan.

And happy, too, as ony lark
The claud might ever carry;
She shunned the ill and sought the good,
E'en mair than weel was understood;
And a' fouk liket Mary.

But she fell sick wi' some decay,
When she was but eleven;
And as she pined frae day to day,
We grudged to see her gaun away,
Though she was gaun to Heaven.

There 's fears for them that 's far awa'
And fykes for them are flitting;
But fears and cares, baith grit and sma',
We by and by o'er-pit them a';
But death there 's nae o'er-pitting.

And nature's ties are hard to break,
When thus they maun be broken;

And e'en the form we loved to see,
We canna lang, dear though it be,
Preserve it as a token.

But Mary had a gentle heart,
Heaven did as gently free her;
Yet lang afore she reached that part,
Dear sir, it wad ha'e made ye start
Had ye been there to see her.

Sae changed, and yet sae sweet and fair,
And growing meek and meeker,
Wi' her lang locks o' yellow hair,
She wore a little angel's air,
Ere angels cam' to seek her.

And when she couldna stray out by,
The wee wild flowers to gather,
She oft her household plays wad try,
To hide her illness frae our eye,
Lest she should grieve us farther.

But ilka thing we said or did
Aye pleased the sweet wee creature;
Indeed, ye wad ha'e thought she had
A something in her made her glad
Ayont the course o' nature.

But death's cauld hour cam' on at last,
As it to a' is comin';
And may it be, whene'er it fa's,
Nae waur to others than it was
To Mary, sweet wee woman!

SAMUEL FERGUSON.

THE FORGING OF THE ANCHOR.

Come, see the Dolphin's anchor forged; 't is at a white heat now:
The bellows ceased, the flames decreased, though on the forge's brow
The little flames still fitfully play through the sable mound;
And fitfully you still may see the grim smiths ranking round,
All clad in leathern panoply, their broad hands only bare;
Some rest upon their sledges here, some work the windlass there.

The windlass strains the tackle-chains, the black mound heaves below;
And, red and deep, a hundred veins burst out at every throe:
It rises, roars, rends all outright, — O Vulcan, what a glow!
'T is blinding white, 't is blasting bright; the high sun shines not so!
The high sun sees not, on the earth, such fiery, fearful show, —
The roof-ribs swarth, the candent hearth, the ruddy, lurid row
Of smiths, that stand, an ardent band, like men before the foe;
As, quivering through his fleece of flame, the sailing monster slow
Sinks on the anvil, — all about the faces fiery grow, —
"Hurrah!" they shout, "leap out, leap out"; bang, bang, the sledges go:
Hurrah! the jetted lightnings are hissing high and low;
A hailing fount of fire is struck at every squashing blow;
The leathern mail rebounds the hail; the rattling cinders strew
The ground around; at every bound the sweltering fountains flow;
And thick and loud the swinking crowd, at every stroke, pant "Ho!"

Leap out, leap out, my masters; leap out and lay on load!
Let's forge a goodly anchor; a bower, thick and broad:
For a heart of oak is hanging on every blow, I bode,
And I see the good ship riding all in a perilous road;
The low reef roaring on her lea; the roll of ocean poured
From stem to stern, sea after sea; the mainmast by the board;
The bulwarks down; the rudder gone; the boats stove at the chains;
But courage still, brave mariners, the bower yet remains,
And not an inch to flinch he deigns save when ye pitch sky-high,
Then moves his head, as though he said, "Fear nothing, — here am I!"

Swing in your strokes in order; let foot and hand keep time,
Your blows make music sweeter far than any steeple's chime:
But while ye swing your sledges, sing; and let the burden be,
The Anchor is the Anvil King, and royal craftsmen we!

Strike in, strike in, — the sparks begin to dull their rustling red;
Our hammers ring with sharper din, our work will soon be sped:
Our anchor soon must change his bed of fiery rich array
For a hammock at the roaring bows, or an oozy couch of clay;
Our anchor soon must change the lay of merry craftsmen here,
For the yeo-heave-ho, and the heave-away, and the sighing seamen's cheer,
When, weighing slow, at eve they go far, far from love and home,
And sobbing sweethearts, in a row, wail o'er the ocean foam.

In livid and obdurate gloom he darkens down at last;
A shapely one he is, and strong as e'er from cat was cast.
O trusted and trustworthy guard, if thou hadst life like me,
What pleasures would thy toils reward beneath the deep green sea!
O deep sea-diver, who might then behold such sights as thou?
The hoary monsters' palaces! methinks what joy 't were now
To go plumb plunging down amid the assembly of the whales,
And feel the churned sea round me boil beneath their scourging tails!
Then deep in tangle-woods to fight the fierce sea unicorn,
And send him foiled and bellowing back, for all his ivory horn;
To leave the subtle sworder-fish of bony blade forlorn;
And for the ghastly-grinning shark to laugh his jaws to scorn;
To leap down on the kraken's back, where mid Norwegian isles
He lies, a lubber anchorage for sudden shallowed miles,
Till snorting, like an under-sea volcano, off he rolls;
Meanwhile to swing, a-buffeting the far-astonished shoals.
Of his back-browsing ocean calves; or, haply in a cove,
Shell-strewn, and consecrate of old to some Undine's love,
To find the long-haired mermaidens; or, hard by icy lands,
To wrestle with the sea-serpent upon cerulean sands.

O broad-armed fisher of the deep, whose sports can equal thine?
The Dolphin weighs a thousand tons that tugs thy cable line;
And night by night 't is thy delight, thy glory day by day,
Through sable sea and breaker white, the giant game to play;
But, shamer of our little sports! forgive the name I gave, —
A fisher's joy is to destroy, thine office is to save.
O lodger in the sea-king's halls, couldst thou but understand
Whose be the white bones by thy side, or who that dripping band,
Slow swaying in the heaving waves that round about thee bend,
With sounds like breakers in a dream blessing their ancient friend:
O, couldst thou know what heroes glide with larger steps round thee,
Thine iron side would swell with pride; thou 'dst leap within the sea!
Give honor to their memories who left the pleasant strand
To shed their blood so freely for the love of fatherland,
Who left their chance of quiet age and grassy churchyard grave
So freely for a restless bed amid the tossing wave;
O, though our anchor may not be all I have fondly sung,
Honor him for their memory, whose bones he goes among!

FRANCIS MAHONY (FATHER PROUT).

[1805-1865.]

THE BELLS OF SHANDON.

WITH deep affection
And recollection,
I often think of
The Shandon bells,
Whose sounds so wild would
In days of childhood
Fling round my cradle
Their magic spells.
On this I ponder,
Where'er I wander,

And thus grow fonder,
Sweet Cork, of thee;
With thy bells of Shandon,
That sound so grand on
The pleasant waters
Of the river Lee.

I 've heard bells chiming
Full many a clime in,
Tolling sublime in
Cathedral shrine,
While at a glib rate
Brass tongues would vibrate;
But all their music
Spoke naught like thine;
For memory, dwelling
On each proud swelling
Of thy belfry, knelling
Its bold notes free,
Made the bells of Shandon
Sound far more grand on
The pleasant waters
Of the river Lee.

I 've heard bells tolling
Old Adrian's Mole in,
Their thunder rolling
From the Vatican;
And cymbals glorious
Swinging uproarious
In the gorgeous turrets
Of Notre Dame:
But thy sounds were sweeter
Than the dome of Peter
Flings o'er the Tiber,
Pealing solemnly.
O, the bells of Shandon
Sound far more grand on
The pleasant waters
Of the river Lee!

There's a bell in Moscow;
While on tower and kiosk O
In St. Sophia
The Turkman gets,
And loud in air
Calls men to prayer,
From the tapering summits
Of tall minarets.
Such empty phantom
I freely grant them;
But there 's an anthem
More dear to me, —
'T is the bells of Shandon,
That sound so grand on
The pleasant waters
Of the river Lee.

NATHANIEL PARKER WILLIS.

[U. S. A., 1807–1867.]

UNSEEN SPIRITS.

THE shadows lay along Broadway, —
'T was near the twilight tide, —
And slowly there a lady fair
Was walking in her pride.
Alone walked she; but, viewlessly,
Walked spirits at her side.

Peace charmed the street beneath her feet,
And Honor charmed the air,
And all astir looked kind on her,
And called her good as fair;
For all God ever gave to her
She kept with chary care.

She kept with care her beauties rare
From lovers warm and true;
For her heart was cold to all but gold,
And the rich came not to woo:
But honored well are charms to sell,
If priests the selling do.

Now walking there was one more fair, —
A slight girl, lily-pale;
And she had unseen company
To make the spirit quail:
'Twixt Want and Scorn she walked forlorn,
And nothing could avail.

No mercy now can clear her brow
For this world's peace to pray;
For, as love's wild prayer dissolved in air,
Her woman's heart gave way!
But the sin forgiven by Christ in heaven,
By man is cursed alway.

FROM MELANIE.

A CALM and lovely paradise
Is Italy, for minds at ease;
The sadness of its sunny skies
Weighs not upon the lives of these.
The ruined aisle, the crumbling fane,
The broken columns vast and prone, —
It may be joy, it may be pain,
Amid such wrecks to walk alone.
The saddest man will sadder be,
The gentlest lover gentler there, —

As if, whate'er the spirit's key,
It strengthened in that solemn air.

The heart soon grows to mournful things;
And Italy has not a breeze
But comes on melancholy wings;
And even her majestic trees
Stand ghostlike in the Cæsars' home,
As if their conscious roots were set
In the old graves of giant Rome,
And drew their sap all kingly yet!
And every stone your feet beneath
Is broken from some mighty thought;
And sculptures in the dust still breathe
The fire with which their lines were wrought;
And sundered arch, and plundered tomb,
Still thunder back the echo, "Rome."

Yet gayly o'er Egeria's fount
The ivy flings its emerald veil,
And flowers grow fair on Numa's mount,
And light-sprung arches span the dale;
And soft, from Caracalla's baths,
The herdsman's song comes down the breeze,
While climb his goats the giddy paths
To grass-grown architraves and frieze;
And gracefully Albano's hill
Curves into the horizon's line,
And sweetly sings that classic rill,
And fairly stands that nameless shrine;
And here, O, many a sultry noon
And starry eve, that happy June,
Came Angelo and Melanie!
And earth for us was all in tune,—
For while Love talked with them,
Hope walked apart with me.

CAROLINE ELIZABETH NORTON.

BINGEN ON THE RHINE.

A soldier of the Legion lay dying in Algiers,
There was lack of woman's nursing, there was dearth of woman's tears;
But a comrade stood beside him, while his life-blood ebbed away,
And bent, with pitying glances, to hear what he might say.
The dying soldier faltered, and he took that comrade's hand,
And he said, "I nevermore shall see my own, my native land;
Take a message, and a token, to some distant friends of mine,
For I was born at Bingen,—fair Bingen on the Rhine.

"Tell my brothers and companions, when they meet and crowd around,
To hear my mournful story, in the pleasant vineyard ground,
That we fought the battle bravely, and when the day was done,
Full many a corse lay ghastly pale beneath the setting sun;
And, mid the dead and dying, were some grown old in wars,—
The death-wound on their gallant breasts, the last of many scars;
And some were young, and suddenly beheld life's morn decline,—
And one had come from Bingen,—fair Bingen on the Rhine.

"Tell my mother that her other son shall comfort her old age;
For I was still a truant bird, that thought his home a cage.
For my father was a soldier, and even as a child
My heart leaped forth to hear him tell of struggles fierce and wild;
And when he died, and left us to divide his scanty hoard,
I let them take whate'er they would, but kept my father's sword;
And with boyish love I hung it where the bright light used to shine,
On the cottage wall at Bingen,—calm Bingen on the Rhine.

"Tell my sister not to weep for me, and sob with drooping head,
When troops come marching home again with glad and gallant tread,
But to look upon them proudly, with a calm and steadfast eye,
For her brother was a soldier too, and not afraid to die;
And if a comrade seek her love, I ask her in my name
To listen to him kindly, without regret or shame,

And to hang the old sword in its place (my father's sword and mine),
For the honor of old Bingen,—dear Bingen on the Rhine.

"There 's another,— not a sister; in the happy days gone by
You 'd have known her by the merriment that sparkled in her eye;
Too innocent for coquetry,— too fond for idle scorning,—
O friend! I fear the lightest heart makes sometimes heaviest mourning!
Tell her the last night of my life (for, ere the moon be risen,
My body will be out of pain, my soul be out of prison)
I dreamed I stood with her, and saw the yellow sunlight shine
On the vine-clad hills of Bingen,—fair Bingen on the Rhine.

"I saw the blue Rhine sweep along; I heard, or seemed to hear,
The German songs we used to sing, in chorus sweet and clear;
And down the pleasant river, and up the slanting hill,
The echoing chorus sounded, through the evening calm and still;
And her glad blue eyes were on me, as we passed, with friendly talk,
Down many a path beloved of yore, and well-remembered walk!
And her little hand lay lightly, confidingly in mine,—
But we 'll meet no more at Bingen,— loved Bingen on the Rhine."

His trembling voice grew faint and hoarse, his grasp was childish weak,—
His eyes put on a dying look,—he sighed, and ceased to speak;
His comrade bent to lift him, but the spark of life had fled,—
The soldier of the Legion in a foreign land is dead!
And the soft moon rose up slowly, and calmly she looked down
On the red sand of the battle-field, with bloody corses strewn;
Yes, calmly on that dreadful scene her pale light seemed to shine,
As it shone on distant Bingen,—fair Bingen on the Rhine.

EDWARD LORD LYTTON.

THE SABBATH.

FRESH glides the brook and blows the gale,
Yet yonder halts the quiet mill;
The whirring wheel, the rushing sail,
How motionless and still!

Six days' stern labor shuts the poor
From Nature's careless banquet-hall;
The seventh an angel opes the door,
And, smiling, welcomes all!

A Father's tender mercy gave
This holy respite to the breast,
To breathe the gale, to watch the wave,
And know—the wheel may rest!

Six days of toil, poor child of Cain,
Thy strength thy master's slave must be;
The seventh the limbs escape the chain,—
A God hath made thee free!

The fields that yester-morning knew
Thy footsteps as their serf, survey;
On thee, as them, descends the dew,
The baptism of the day.

Fresh glides the brook and blows the gale,
But yonder halts the quiet mill;
The whirring wheel, the rushing sail,
How motionless and still!

So rest, O weary heart!—but, lo,
The church-spire, glistening up to heaven,
To warn thee where thy thoughts should go
The day thy God hath given!

Lone through the landscape's solemn rest,
The spire its moral points on high.
O soul, at peace within the breast,
Rise, mingling with the sky!

They tell thee, in their dreaming school,
Of power from old dominion hurled,
When rich and poor, with juster rule,
Shall share the altered world.

Alas! since time itself began,
That fable hath but fooled the hour;
Each age that ripens power in man
But subjects man to power.

Yet every day in seven, at least,
One bright republic shall be known;

Man's world awhile hath surely ceased,
  When God proclaims his own!

Six days may rank divide the poor,
  O Dives, from thy banquet-hall;
The seventh the Father opes the door,
  And holds his feast for all!

FRANCES ANNE KEMBLE.

FAITH.

Better trust all and be deceived,
And weep that trust and that deceiving,
Than doubt one heart that if believed
Had blessed one's life with true believing.

O, in this mocking world too fast
The doubting fiend o'ertakes our youth;
Better be cheated to the last
Than lose the blessed hope of truth.

JOHN STERLING.

[1806 - 1844.]

HYMN.

O unseen Spirit! now a calm divine
  Comes forth from thee, rejoicing earth and air!
Trees, hills, and houses, all distinctly shine,
  And thy great ocean slumbers everywhere.

The mountain-ridge against the purple sky
  Stands clear and strong, with darkened rocks and dells,
And cloudless brightness opens wide on high
  A home aerial, where thy presence dwells.

The chime of bells remote, the murmuring sea,
  The song of birds in whispering copse and wood,
The distant voice of children's thoughtless glee,
  And maiden's song, are all one voice of good.

Amid the leaves' green mass a sunny play
  Of flash and shadow stirs like inward life;
The ship's white sail glides onward far away,
  Unhaunted by a dream of storm or strife.

O Thou, the primal fount of life and peace,
  Who shedd'st thy breathing quiet all around,
In me command that pain and conflict cease,
  And turn to music every jarring sound!

How longs each pulse within the weary soul
  To taste the life of this benignant hour,
To be at one with thy untroubled whole,
  And in itself to know thy hushing power.

In One, who walked on earth a man of woe,
  Was holier peace than even this hour inspires;
From him to me let inward quiet flow,
  And give the might my failing will requires.

So this great All around, so he, and thou,
  The central source and awful bound of things,
May fill my heart with rest as deep as now
  To land and sea and air thy presence brings.

FRANCES S. OSGOOD.

[U. S. A., 1812 - 1850.]

LABOR.

Pause not to dream of the future before us;
Pause not to weep the wild cares that come o'er us;
Hark how Creation's deep, musical chorus,
  Unintermitting, goes up into heaven!
Never the ocean-wave falters in flowing;
Never the little seed stops in its growing;
More and more richly the rose heart keeps glowing,
  Till from its nourishing stem it is riven.

"Labor is worship!" the robin is singing;
"Labor is worship!" the wild bee is ringing:

Listen! that eloquent whisper, upspringing
Speaks to thy soul from out nature's great heart.
From the dark cloud flows the life-giving shower;
From the rough sod blows the soft-breathing flower;
From the small insect, the rich coral bower;
Only man, in the plan, shrinks from his part.

Labor is life! — 'T is the still water faileth;
Idleness ever despaireth, bewaileth;
Keep the watch wound, for the dark rust assaileth;
Flowers droop and die in the stillness of noon.
Labor is glory! — the flying cloud lightens;
Only the waving wing changes and brightens;
Idle hearts only the dark future frightens:
Play the sweet keys, wouldst thou keep them in tune!

Labor is rest from the sorrows that greet us,
Rest from all petty vexations that meet us,
Rest from sin-promptings that ever entreat us,
Rest from world-sirens that lure us to ill.
Work, — and pure slumbers shall wait on thy pillow;
Work, — thou shalt ride over Care's coming billow;
Lie not down wearied 'neath Woe's weeping willow!
Work with a stout heart and resolute will!

Labor is health! — Lo! the husbandman reaping,
How through his veins goes the life-current leaping!
How his strong arm in its stalwart pride sweeping,
True as a sunbeam the swift sickle guides.
Labor is wealth, — in the sea the pearl groweth;
Rich the queen's robe from the frail cocoon floweth;
From the fine acorn the strong forest bloweth;
Temple and statue the marble block hides.

Droop not, though shame, sin, and anguish are round thee;
Bravely fling off the cold chain that hath bound thee!
Look to yon pure heaven smiling beyond thee:
Rest not content in thy darkness, — a clod!
Work for some good, be it ever so slowly;
Cherish some flower, be it ever so lowly:
Labor! — all labor is noble and holy;
Let thy great deeds be thy prayer to thy God.

JONES VERY.

[U. S. A.]

THE PRESENT HEAVEN.

Father! thy wonders do not singly stand,
Nor far removed where feet have seldom strayed;
Around us ever lies the enchanted land,
In marvels rich to thine own sons displayed.

In finding thee are all things round us found;
In losing thee are all things lost beside;
Ears have we, but in vain sweet voices sound,
And to our eyes the vision is denied.

Open our eyes, that we that world may see!
Open our ears, that we thy voice may hear,
And in the spirit-land may ever be,
And feel thy presence with us, always near.

TO THE PAINTED COLUMBINE.

Bright image of the early years
When glowed my cheek as red as thou,

And life's dark throng of cares and fears
Were swift-winged shadows o'er my sunny brow!

Thou blushest from the painter's page,
Robed in the mimic tints of art;
But Nature's hand in youth's green age
With fairer hues first traced thee on my heart.

The morning's blush, she made it thine;
The morn's sweet breath, she gave it thee;
And in thy look, my Columbine!
Each fond-remembered spot she bade me see.

I see the hill's far-gazing head,
Where gay thou noddest in the gale;
I hear light-bounding footsteps tread
The grassy path that winds along the vale.

I hear the voice of woodland song
Break from each bush and well-known tree,
And, on light pinions borne along,
Comes back the laugh from childhood's heart of glee.

O'er the dark rock the dashing brook,
With look of anger, leaps again,
And, hastening to each flowery nook,
Its distant voice is heard far down the glen.

Fair child of art! thy charms decay,
Touched by the withered hand of Time;
And hushed the music of that day,
When my voice mingled with the streamlet's chime:

But on my heart thy cheek of bloom
Shall live when Nature's smile has fled;
And, rich with memory's sweet perfume,
Shall o'er her grave thy tribute incense shed.

There shalt thou live and wake the glee
That echoed on thy native hill;
And when, loved flower! I think of thee,
My infant feet will seem to seek thee still.

THOMAS MILLER.

EVENING SONG.

How many days with mute adieu
Have gone down yon untrodden sky,
And still it looks as clear and blue
As when it first was hung on high.
The rolling sun, the frowning cloud
That drew the lightning in its rear,
The thunder tramping deep and loud,
Have left no foot-mark there.

The village-bells, with silver chime,
Come softened by the distant shore;
Though I have heard them many a time,
They never rung so sweet before.
A silence rests upon the hill,
A listening awe pervades the air;
The very flowers are shut and still,
And bowed as if in prayer.

And in this hushed and breathless close,
O'er earth and air and sky and sea,
A still low voice in silence goes,
Which speaks alone, great God, of thee.
The whispering leaves, the far-off brook,
The linnet's warble fainter grown,
The hive-bound bee, the building rook, —
All these their Maker own.

Now Nature sinks in soft repose,
A living semblance of the grave;
The dew steals noiseless on the rose,
The boughs have almost ceased to wave;
The silent sky, the sleeping earth,
Tree, mountain, stream, the humble sod,
All tell from whom they had their birth,
And cry, "Behold a God!"

JOHN KEBLE.

[1796 - 1821.]

MORNING.

O, TIMELY happy, timely wise,
Hearts that with rising morn arise!
Eyes that the beam celestial view,
Which evermore makes all things new!

New every morning is the love
Our wakening and uprising prove,

Through sleep and darkness safely brought,
Restored to life and power and thought.

New mercies, each returning day,
Hover around us while we pray;
New perils past, new sins forgiven,
New thoughts of God, new hopes of heaven.

If, on our daily course, our mind
Be set to hallow all we find,
New treasures still, of countless price,
God will provide for sacrifice.

Old friends, old scenes, will lovelier be,
As more of Heaven in each we see;
Some softening gleam of love and prayer
Shall dawn on every cross and care.

As for some dear familiar strain
Untired we ask, and ask again,
Ever in its melodious store
Finding a spell unheard before, —

Such is the bliss of souls serene,
When they have sworn, and steadfast mean,
Counting the cost, in all to espy
Their God, in all themselves deny.

O, could we learn that sacrifice,
What lights would all around us rise!
How would our hearts with wisdom talk
Along life's dullest, dreariest walk!

We need not bid, for cloistered cell,
Our neighbor and our work farewell,
Nor strive to wind ourselves too high
For sinful man beneath the sky.

The trivial round, the common task,
Will furnish all we ought to ask;
Room to deny ourselves; a road
To bring us, daily, nearer God.

Seek we no more: content with these,
Let present rapture, comfort, ease,
As Heaven shall bid them, come and go;
The secret this of rest below.

Only, O Lord, in thy dear love
Fit us for perfect rest above;
And help us, this and every day,
To live more nearly as we pray!

INWARD MUSIC.

There are in this loud stunning tide
Of human care and crime,
With whom the melodies abide
Of the everlasting chime;
Who carry music in their heart
Through dusky lane and wrangling mart,
Plying their daily toil with busier feet,
Because their secret souls a holy strain repeat.

SIR ROBERT GRANT.

[1814–1838.]

O SAVIOUR! WHOSE MERCY.

O Saviour! whose mercy, severe in its kindness,
Hath chastened my wanderings and guided my way,
Adored be the power that illumined my blindness,
And weaned me from phantoms that smiled to betray.

Enchanted with all that was dazzling and fair,
I followed the rainbow, I caught at the toy;
And still in displeasure thy goodness was there,
Disappointing the hope and defeating the joy.

The blossom blushed bright, but a worm was below;
The moonlight shone fair, there was blight in the beam;
Sweet whispered the breeze, but it whispered of woe;
And bitterness flowed in the soft-flowing stream.

So cured of my folly, yet cured but in part,
I turned to the refuge thy pity displayed;
And still did this eager and credulous heart
Weave visions of promise that bloomed but to fade.

I thought that the course of the pilgrim to heaven
Would be bright as the summer and glad as the morn:
Thou showedst me the path; it was dark and uneven,
All rugged with rock and all tangled with thorn.

I dreamed of celestial rewards and renown,
I grasped at the triumph that blesses the brave;
I asked for the palm-branch, the robe, and the crown,
I asked, and thou showedst me a cross and a grave!

Subdued and instructed, at length to thy will
My hopes and my wishes I freely resign;
O, give me a heart that can wait and be still,
Nor know of a wish or a pleasure but thine.

There are mansions exempted from sin and from woe,
But they stand in a region by mortals untrod;
There are rivers of joy, but they roll not below;
There is rest, but 't is found in the bosom of God.

DEAN OF CANTERBURY.

TRUST.

I KNOW not if or dark or bright
Shall be my lot;
If that wherein my hopes delight
Be best, or not.

It may be mine to drag for years
Toil's heavy chain;
Or day and night my meat be tears
On bed of pain.

Dear faces may surround my hearth
With smiles and glee;
Or I may dwell alone, and mirth
Be strange to me.

My bark is wafted to the strand
By breath divine;
And on the helm there rests a hand
Other than mine.

One who has known in storms to sail
I have on board;
Above the raving of the gale
I hear my Lord.

He holds me when the billows smite, —
I shall not fall.
If sharp, 't is short; if long, 't is light, —
He tempers all.

Safe to the land, safe to the land, —
The end is this;
And then with Him go hand in hand
Far into bliss.

BRYAN WALLER PROCTER (BARRY CORNWALL).

[1787-1874.]

A PETITION TO TIME.

TOUCH us gently, Time!
Let us glide adown thy stream
Gently, — as we sometimes glide
Through a quiet dream!
Humble voyagers are we,
Husband, wife, and children three, —
(One is lost, — an angel, fled
To the azure overhead!)

Touch us gently, Time!
We 've not proud nor soaring wings;
Our ambition, our content,
Lies in simple things.
Humble voyagers are we,
O'er life's dim, unsounded sea,
Seeking only some calm clime; —
Touch us gently, gentle Time!

A PRAYER IN SICKNESS.

SEND down thy wingéd angel, God!
Amid this night so wild;
And bid him come where now we watch,
And breathe upon our child!

She lies upon her pillow, pale,
And moans within her sleep,
Or wakeneth with a patient smile,
And striveth not to weep.

How gentle and how good a child
She is, we know too well,
And dearer to her parents' hearts
Than our weak words can tell.

We love,—we watch throughout the night
To aid, when need may be;
We hope, — and have despaired, at times,
But now we turn to thee!

Send down thy sweet-souled angel, God!
Amid the darkness wild,
And bid him soothe our souls to-night,
And heal our gentle child!

RICHARD MONCKTON MILNES (LORD HOUGHTON).

THE BROOKSIDE.

I WANDERED by the brookside,
I wandered by the mill;
I could not hear the brook flow, —
The noisy wheel was still;
There was no burr of grasshopper,
No chirp of any bird,
But the beating of my own heart
Was all the sound I heard.

I sat beneath the elm-tree;
I watched the long, long shade,
And, as it grew still longer,
I did not feel afraid;
For I listened for a footfall,
I listened for a word, —
But the beating of my own heart
Was all the sound I heard.

He came not, —no, he came not, —
The night came on alone, —
The little stars sat one by one,
Each on his golden throne;
The evening wind passed by my cheek,
The leaves above were stirred, —
But the beating of my own heart
Was all the sound I heard.

Fast silent tears were flowing,
When something stood behind;
A hand was on my shoulder, —
I knew its touch was kind:
It drew me nearer, —nearer, —
We did not speak one word,
For the beating of our own hearts
Was all the sound we heard.

THE MEN OF OLD.

I KNOW not that the men of old
Were better than men now,
Of heart more kind, of hand more bold,
Of more ingenuous brow;
I heed not those who pine for force
A ghost of time to raise,
As if they thus could check the course
Of these appointed days.

Still is it true and over-true,
That I delight to close
This book of life self-wise and new,
And let my thoughts repose
On all that humble happiness
The world has since foregone, —
The daylight of contentedness
That on those faces shone!

With rights, though not too closely scanned,
Enjoyed as far as known, —
With will, by no reverse unmanned, —
With pulse of even tone, —
They from to-day and from to-night
Expected nothing more
Than yesterday and yesternight
Had proffered them before.

To them was life a simple art
Of duties to be done,
A game where each man took his part,
A race where all must run;
A battle whose great scheme and scope
They little cared to know,
Content, as men-at-arms, to cope
Each with his fronting foe.

Man now his virtue's diadem
Puts on, and proudly wears, —
Great thoughts, great feelings, came to them,
Like instincts unawares;
Blending their souls' sublimest needs
With tasks of every day,

They went about their gravest deeds,
As noble boys at play.

A man's best things are nearest him,
Lie close about his feet;
It is the distant and the dim
That we are sick to greet:
For flowers that grow our hands beneath
We struggle and aspire, —
Our hearts must die, except they breathe
The air of fresh desire.

But, brothers, who up reason's hill
Advance with hopeful cheer, —
O, loiter not, those heights are chill,
As chill as they are clear;
And still restrain your haughty gaze
The loftier that ye go,
Remembering distance leaves a haze
On all that lies below.

THE PALM AND THE PINE.

Beneath an Indian palm a girl
Of other blood reposes;
Her cheek is clear and pale as pearl,
Amid that wild of roses.

Beside a northern pine a boy
Is leaning fancy-bound,
Nor listens where with noisy joy
Awaits the impatient hound.

Cool grows the sick and feverish calm,
Relaxed the frosty twine, —
The pine-tree dreameth of the palm,
The palm-tree of the pine.

As soon shall nature interlace
Those dimly visioned boughs,
As these young lovers face to face
Renew their early vows!

MARY HOWITT.

TIBBIE INGLIS.

Bonny Tibbie Inglis!
Through sun and stormy weather,
She kept upon the broomy hills
Her father's flock together.

Sixteen summers had she seen, —
A rosebud just unsealing;
Without sorrow, without fear,
In her mountain shealing.

She was made for happy thoughts,
For playful wit and laughter;
Singing on the hills alone,
With echo singing after.

She had hair as deeply black
As the cloud of thunder;
She had brows so beautiful,
And dark eyes flashing under.

Bright and witty shepherd-girl,
Beside a mountain water,
I found her, whom a king himself
Would proudly call his daughter.

She was sitting 'mong the crags,
Wild and mossed and hoary;
Reading in an ancient book
Some old martyr story.

Tears were starting to her eyes,
Solemn thought was o'er her;
When she saw in that lone place
A stranger stand before her.

Crimson was her sunny cheek,
And her lips seemed moving
With the beatings of her heart; —
How could I help loving?

On a crag I sat me down,
Upon the mountain hoary,
And made her read again to me
That old pathetic story.

Then she sang me mountain songs,
Till the air was ringing
With her clear and warbling voice,
Like a skylark singing.

And when eve came on at length,
Among the blooming heather,
We herded on the mountain-side
Her father's flock together.

And near unto her father's house
I said "Good night!" with sorrow,
And inly wished that I might say,
"We'll meet again to-morrow."

I watched her tripping to her home;
I saw her meet her mother.

"Among a thousand maids," I cried,
"There is not such another!"

I wandered to my scholar's home,
It lonesome looked and dreary;
I took my books, but could not read,
Methought that I was weary.

I laid me down upon my bed,
My heart with sadness laden;
I dreamed but of the mountain wold,
And of the mountain maiden.

I saw her of the ancient book
The pages turning slowly;
I saw her lovely crimson cheek,
And dark eye drooping lowly.

The dream was like the day's delight,
A life of pain's o'erpayment:
I rose, and with unwonted care,
Put on my Sabbath raiment.

To none I told my secret thoughts,
Not even to my mother,
Nor to the friend who, from my youth,
Was dear as is a brother.

I got me to the hills again;
The little flock was feeding:
And there young Tibbie Inglis sat,
But not the old book reading.

She sat as if absorbing thought
With heavy spells had bound her,
As silent as the mossy crags
Upon the mountains round her.

I thought not of my Sabbath dress;
I thought not of my learning:
I thought but of the gentle maid
Who, I believed, was mourning.

Bonny Tibbie Inglis!
How her beauty brightened,
Looking at me, half abashed,
With eyes that flamed and lightened!

There was no sorrow, then I saw,
There was no thought of sadness:
O life! what after-joy hast thou
Like love's first certain gladness?

I sat me down among the crags,
Upon the mountain hoary;
But read not then the ancient book,—
Love was our pleasant story.

And then she sang me songs again,
Old songs of love and sorrow;
For our sufficient happiness
Great charm from woe could borrow.

And many hours we talked in joy,
Yet too much blessed for laughter:
I was a happy man that day,
And happy ever after!

WILLIAM HOWITT.

THE DEPARTURE OF THE SWALLOW.

And is the swallow gone?
Who beheld it?
Which way sailed it?
Farewell bade it none?

No mortal saw it go;—
But who doth hear
Its summer cheer
As it flitteth to and fro?

So the freed spirit flies!
From its surrounding clay
It steals away
Like the swallow from the skies.

Whither? wherefore doth it go?
'T is all unknown;
We feel alone
That a void is left below.

WILLIAM LAIDLAW.

[1780-1845.]

LUCY'S FLITTIN'.

'T was when the wan leaf frae the birk-tree was fa'in,
And Martinmas dowie had wound up the year,
That Lucy rowed up her wee kist wi' her a' in 't,
And left her auld maister and neibours sae dear:
For Lucy had served i' the glen a' the simmer;

She cam there afore the bloom cam on the pea;
An orphan was she, and they had been gude till her,
Sure that was the thing brocht the tear to her ee.

She gaed by the stable where Jamie was stannin';
Richt sair was his kind heart her flittin' to see.
"Fare ye weel, Lucy!" quo' Jamie, and ran in;
The gatherin' tears trickled fast frae her ee.
As down the burnside she gaed slow wi' her flittin',
"Fare ye weel, Lucy!" was ilka bird's sang;
She heard the craw sayin 't, high on the trees sittin',
And the robin was chirpin 't the brown leaves amang.

"O, what is 't that pits my puir heart in a flutter?
And what gars the tears come sae fast to my ee?
If I wasna ettled to be ony better,
Then what gars me wish ony better to be?
I 'm just like a lammie that loses its mither;
Nae mither or friend the puir lammie can see;
I fear I hae tint my puir heart a'thegither,
Nae wonder the tear fa's sae fast frae my ee.

"Wi' the rest o' my claes I hae rowed up the ribbon,
The bonnie blue ribbon that Jamie gae me;
Yestreen, when he gae me 't, and saw I was sabbin',
I 'll never forget the wae blink o' his ee.
Though now he said naething but 'Fare ye weel, Lucy!'
It made me I neither could speak, hear, nor see:
He couldna say mair but just, 'Fare ye weel, Lucy!'
Yet that I will mind till the day that I dee."

The lamb likes the gowan wi' dew when it 's droukit;
The hare likes the brake and the braird on the lea;
But Lucy likes Jamie;—she turned and she lookit,
She thocht the dear place she wad never mair see.
Ah, weel may young Jamie gang dowie and cheerless!
And weel may he greet on the bank o' the burn!
For bonnie sweet Lucy, sae gentle and peerless,
Lies cauld in her grave, and will never return!

UNKNOWN.

SUMMER DAYS.

In summer, when the days were long,
We walked together in the wood;
Our heart was light, our step was strong,
Sweet flutterings were in our blood,
In summer, when the days were long.

We strayed from morn till evening came;
We gathered flowers, and wove us crowns;
We walked mid poppies red as flame,
Or sat upon the yellow downs;
And always wished our life the same.

In summer, when the days were long,
We leaped the hedge-row, crossed the brook;
And still her voice flowed forth in song,
Or else she read some graceful book,
In summer, when the days were long.

And then we sat beneath the trees,
With shadows lessening in the noon;
And in the sunlight and the breeze
We feasted, many a gorgeous June,
While larks were singing o'er the leas.

In summer, when the days were long,
On dainty chicken, snow-white bread,
We feasted, with no grace but song;
We plucked wild strawberries, ripe and red,
In summer, when the days were long.

We loved, and yet we knew it not,—
For loving seemed like breathing then;

We found a heaven in every spot;
Saw angels, too, in all good men;
And dreamed of God in grove and grot.

In summer, when the days are long,
Alone I wander, muse alone.
I see her not; but that old song
Under the fragrant wind is blown,
In summer, when the days are long.

Alone I wander in the wood:
But one fair spirit hears my sighs;
And half I see, so glad and good,
The honest daylight of her eyes,
That charmed me under earlier skies.

In summer, when the days are long,
I love her as we loved of old.
My heart is light, my step is strong;
For love brings back those hours of gold,
In summer, when the days are long.

FRANCES BROWNE.

LOSSES.

Upon the white sea-sand
There sat a pilgrim band,
Telling the losses that their lives had known;
While evening waned away
From breezy cliff and bay,
And the strong tides went out with weary moan.

One spake, with quivering lip,
Of a fair freighted ship,
With all his household to the deep gone down;
But one had wilder woe, —
For a fair face, long ago
Lost in the darker depths of a great town.

There were who mourned their youth
With a most loving ruth,
For its brave hopes and memories ever green;
And one upon the west
Turned an eye that would not rest,
For far-off hills whereon its joys had been.

Some talked of vanished gold,
Some of proud honors told,
Some spake of friends that were their trust no more;
And one of a green grave,
Beside a foreign wave,
That made him sit so lonely on the shore.

But when their tales were done,
There spake among them one,
A stranger, seeming from all sorrow free:
"Sad losses have ye met,
But mine is heavier yet;
For a believing heart hath gone from me."

"Alas!" these pilgrims said,
"For the living and the dead, —
For fortune's cruelty, for love's sure cross,
For the wrecks of land and sea!
But, however it came to thee,
Thine, stranger, is life's last and heaviest loss."

ROBERT NICOLL.

[1814-1837.]

WE ARE BRETHREN A'.

A happy bit hame this auld world would be,
If men, when they 're here, could make shift to agree,
An' ilk said to his neighbor, in cottage an' ha',
"Come, gi'e me your hand, — we are brethren a'."

I ken na why ane wi' anither should fight,
When to 'gree would make ae body cosie an' right,
When man meets wi' man, 't is the best way ava,
To say, "Gi'e me your hand, — we are brethren a'."

My coat is a coarse ane, an' yours may be fine,
And I maun drink water, while you may drink wine;
But we baith ha'e a leal heart, unspotted to shaw:
Sae gi'e me your hand, — we are brethren a'.

The knave ye would scorn, the unfaithfu' deride;
Ye would stand like a rock, wi' the truth on your side;
Sae would I, an' naught else would I value a straw:
Then gi'e me your hand, — we are brethren a'.

Ye would scorn to do fausely by woman or man;
I haud by the right aye, as weel as I can;
We are ane in our joys, our affections, an' a':
Come, gi'e me your hand, — we are brethren a'.

Your mother has lo'ed you as mithers can lo'e;
An' mine has done for me what mithers can do;
We are ane high an' laigh, an' we shouldna be twa:
Sae gi'e me your hand, — we are brethren a'.

We love the same simmer day, sunny and fair;
Hame! O, how we love it, an' a' that are there!
Frae the pure air of heaven the same life we draw:
Come, gi'e me your hand, — we are brethren a'.

Frail shakin' auld age will soon come o'er us baith,
An' creeping alang at his back will be death;
Syne into the same mither-yird we will fa':
Come, gi'e me your hand, — we are brethren a'.

RICHARD H. DANA.

[U. S. A.]

(From "THE BUCCANEER," published in 1827.)

THE ISLAND.

THE island lies nine leagues away.
Along its solitary shore,
Of craggy rock and sandy bay,
No sound but ocean's roar,
Save, where the bold, wild sea-bird makes her home,
Her shrill cry coming through the sparkling foam.

But when the light winds lie at rest,
And on the glassy, heaving sea
The black duck, with her glossy breast,
Sits swinging silently;
How beautiful! no ripples break the reach,
And silvery waves go noiseless up the beach.

And inland rests the green, warm dell;
The brook comes tinkling down its side;
From out the trees the Sabbath bell
Rings cheerful, far and wide,
Mingling its sound with bleatings of the flocks,
That feed about the vale among the rocks.

Nor holy bell nor pastoral bleat
In former days within the vale;
Flapped in the bay the pirate's sheet;
Curses were on the gale;
Rich goods lay on the sand, and murdered men;
Pirate and wrecker kept their revels then.

But calm, low voices, words of grace,
Now slowly fall upon the ear;
A quiet look is in each face,
Subdued and holy fear:
Each motion gentle; all is kindly done; —
Come, listen, how from crime this isle was won.

THE PIRATE.

TWELVE years are gone since Matthew Lee
Held in this isle unquestioned sway;
A dark, low, brawny man was he;
His law, — "It is my way."
Beneath his thick-set brows a sharp light broke
From small gray eyes; his laugh a triumph spoke.

Cruel of heart and strong of arm,
Loud in his sport and keen for spoil,
He little recked of good or harm,
Fierce both in mirth and toil;
Yet like a dog could fawn, if need there were;
Speak mildly, when he would, or look in fear.

Amid the uproar of the storm,
And by the lightning's sharp, red glare,
Were seen Lee's face and sturdy form;
His axe glanced quick in air:
Whose corpse at morn is floating in the sedge?
There 's blood and hair, Mat, on thy axe's edge.

THE SPECTRE HORSE.

He 's now upon the spectre's back,
With rein of silk and curb of gold.
'T is fearful speed!—the rein is slack
Within his senseless hold;
Upborne by an unseen power, he onward rides,
Yet touches not the shadow-beast he strides.

He goes with speed; he goes with dread!
And now they 're on the hanging steep!
And, now! the living and the dead,
They 'll make the horrid leap!
The horse stops short;—his feet are on the verge.
He stands, like marble, high above the surge.

And, nigh, the tall ship yet burns on,
With red, hot spars, and crackling flame.
From hull to gallant, nothing 's gone.
She burns, and yet 's the same!
Her hot, red flame is beating, all the night,
On man and horse, in their cold, phosphor light.

Through that cold light the fearful man
Sits looking on the burning ship.
He ne'er again will curse and ban.
How fast he moves the lip!
And yet he does not speak, or make a sound!
What see you, Lee? the bodies of the drowned?

"I look where mortal man may not,—
Into the chambers of the deep.
I see the dead, long, long forgot;
I see them in their sleep.
A dreadful power is mine, which none can know
Save he who leagues his soul with death and woe."

Thou mild, sad mother,—waning moon,
Thy last, low, melancholy ray
Shines toward him. Quit him not so soon!
Mother, in mercy, stay!
Despair and death are with him; and canst thou,
With that kind, earthward look, go leave him now?

O, thou wast born for things of love;
Making more lovely in thy shine
Whate'er thou look'st on. Stars above,
In that soft light of thine,
Burn softer; earth, in silvery veil, seems heaven.
Thou 'rt going down!—hast left him unforgiven!

The far, low west is bright no more.
How still it is! No sound is heard
At sea, or all along the shore,
But cry of passing bird.
Thou living thing,—and dar'st thou come so near
These wild and ghastly shapes of death and fear?

Now long that thick, red light has shone
On stern, dark rocks, and deep, still bay,
On man and horse, that seem of stone,
So motionless are they.
But now its lurid fire less fiercely burns:
The night is going,—faint, gray dawn returns.

That spectre-steed now slowly pales,
Now changes like the moonlit cloud;
That cold, thin light now slowly fails,
Which wrapped them like a shroud.
Both ship and horse are fading into air.
Lost, mazed, alone,—see, Lee is standing there!

The morning air blows fresh on him;
The waves dance gladly in his sight;
The sea-birds call, and wheel, and skim,—
O blessed morning light!
He doth not hear their joyous call; he sees
No beauty in the wave, nor feels the breeze.

WILLIAM CULLEN BRYANT.

[U. S. A.]

TO A WATERFOWL.

Whither, midst falling dew,
While glow the heavens with the last steps of day,
Far, through their rosy depths, dost thou pursue
Thy solitary way?

Vainly the fowler's eye
Might mark thy distant flight to do thee wrong,
As, darkly painted on the crimson sky,
Thy figure floats along.

Seek'st thou the plashy brink
Of weedy lake, or marge of river wide,
Or where the rocking billows rise and sink
On the chafed ocean side?

There is a Power, whose care
Teaches thy way along that pathless coast, —
The desert and illimitable air, —
Lone wandering, but not lost.

All day thy wings have fanned,
At that far height, the cold, thin atmosphere;
Yet stoop not, weary, to the welcome land,
Though the dark night is near.

And soon that toil shall end;
Soon shalt thou find a summer home, and rest,
And scream among thy fellows; reeds shall bend
Soon o'er thy sheltered nest.

Thou 'rt gone, the abyss of heaven
Hath swallowed up thy form; yet on my heart
Deeply hath sunk the lesson thou hast given,
And shall not soon depart:

He who, from zone to zone,
Guides through the boundless sky thy certain flight,
In the long way that I must tread alone,
Will lead my steps aright.

THANATOPSIS.

To him who in the love of Nature holds
Communion with her visible forms, she speaks
A various language: for his gayer hours
She has a voice of gladness, and a smile
And eloquence of beauty; and she glides
Into his darker musings with a mild
And gentle sympathy that steals away
Their sharpness ere he is aware. When thoughts
Of the last bitter hour come like a blight
Over thy spirit, and sad images
Of the stern agony, and shroud, and pall,
And breathless darkness, and the narrow house,
Make thee to shudder and grow sick at heart,
Go forth under the open sky, and list
To Nature's teachings, while from all around —
Earth, and her waters, and the depths of air —
Comes a still voice, — Yet a few days, and thee
The all-beholding sun shall see no more
In all his course; nor yet in the cold ground,
Where thy pale form was laid with many tears,
Nor in the embrace of ocean, shall exist
Thy image. Earth, that nourished thee, shall claim
Thy growth, to be resolved to earth again,
And, lost each human trace, surrendering up
Thine individual being, shalt thou go
To mix forever with the elements;
To be a brother to the insensible rock,
And to the sluggish clod which the rude swain
Turns with his share and treads upon. The oak
Shall send his roots abroad, and pierce thy mould.
Yet not to thine eternal resting-place
Shalt thou retire alone, — nor couldst thou wish
Couch more magnificent. Thou shalt lie down
With patriarchs of the infant world, — with kings,
The powerful of the earth, — the wise, the good,
Fair forms, and hoary seers of ages past,
All in one mighty sepulchre. — The hills,

Rock-ribbed, and ancient as the sun; the vales
Stretching in pensive quietness between;
The venerable woods; rivers that move
In majesty, and the complaining brooks
That make the meadows green; and, poured round all,
Old ocean's gray and melancholy waste,—
Are but the solemn decorations all
Of the great tomb of man. The golden sun,
The planets, all the infinite host of heaven,
Are shining on the sad abodes of death
Through the still lapse of ages. All that tread
The globe are but a handful to the tribes
That slumber in its bosom. Take the wings
Of morning, and the Barcan desert pierce,
Or lose thyself in the continuous woods
Where rolls the Oregon, and hears no sound
Save his own dashings,—yet the dead are there!
And millions in those solitudes, since first
The flight of years began, have laid them down
In their last sleep,—the dead reign there alone!
So shalt thou rest,—and what if thou shalt fall
Unnoticed by the living, and no friend
Take note of thy departure? All that breathe
Will share thy destiny. The gay will laugh
When thou art gone, the solemn brood of care
Plod on, and each one, as before, will chase
His favorite phantom; yet all these shall leave
Their mirth and their employments, and shall come
And make their bed with thee. As the long train
Of ages glide away, the sons of men—
The youth in life's green spring, and he who goes
In the full strength of years, matron and maid,
The bowed with age, the infant in the smiles
And beauty of its innocent age cut off—
Shall one by one be gathered to thy side
By those who in their turn shall follow them.
So live, that when thy summons comes to join
The innumerable caravan that moves
To the pale realms of shade, where each shall take
His chamber in the silent halls of death,
Thou go not, like the quarry-slave at night,
Scourged to his dungeon, but, sustained and soothed
By an unfaltering trust, approach thy grave
Like one who wraps the drapery of his couch
About him, and lies down to pleasant dreams.

THE DEATH OF THE FLOWERS.

The melancholy days are come, the saddest of the year,
Of wailing winds, and naked woods, and meadows brown and sere.
Heaped in the hollows of the grove, the withered leaves lie dead;
They rustle to the eddying gust, and to the rabbit's tread.
The robin and the wren are flown, and from the shrubs the jay;
And from the wood-top calls the crow through all the gloomy day.

Where are the flowers, the fair young flowers, that lately sprang and stood,
In brighter light and softer airs, a beauteous sisterhood?
Alas! they all are in their graves; the gentle race of flowers
Are lying in their lowly beds, with the fair and good of ours.
The rain is falling where they lie; but the cold November rain
Calls not from out the gloomy earth the lovely ones again.

The wind-flower and the violet, they perished long ago;
And the brier-rose and the orchis died amid the summer glow;

But on the hill the golden-rod, and the aster in the wood,
And the yellow sunflower by the brook in autumn beauty stood,
Till fell the frost from the clear, cold heaven, as falls the plague on men,
And the brightness of their smile was gone from upland, glade, and glen.

And now, when comes the calm, mild day, as still such days will come,
To call the squirrel and the bee from out their winter home;
When the sound of dropping nuts is heard, though all the trees are still,
And twinkle in the smoky light the waters of the rill, —
The south-wind searches for the flowers whose fragrance late he bore,
And sighs to find them in the wood and by the stream no more.

And then I think of one who in her youthful beauty died,
The fair, meek blossom that grew up and faded by my side:
In the cold, moist earth we laid her when the forest cast the leaf,
And we wept that one so lovely should have a life so brief;
Yet not unmeet it was that one, like that young friend of ours,
So gentle and so beautiful, should perish with the flowers.

TO THE FRINGED GENTIAN.

Thou blossom bright with autumn dew,
And colored with the heaven's own blue,
That openest when the quiet light
Succeeds the keen and frosty night, —

Thou comest not when violets lean
O'er wandering brooks and springs unseen,
Or columbines, in purple drest,
Nod o'er the ground-bird's hidden nest.

Thou waitest late, and com'st alone,
When woods are bare, and birds are flown,
And frosts and shortening days portend
The aged year is near its end.

Then doth thy sweet and quiet eye
Look through its fringes to the sky,
Blue, blue, as if that sky let fall
A flower from its cerulean wall.

I would that thus, when I shall see
The hour of death draw near to me,
Hope, blossoming within my heart,
May look to heaven as I depart.

THE BATTLE-FIELD.

Once this soft turf, this rivulet's sands,
Were trampled by a hurrying crowd,
And fiery hearts and armèd hands
Encountered in the battle-cloud.

Ah! never shall the land forget
How gushed the life-blood of her brave, —
Gushed, warm with hope and courage yet,
Upon the soil they fought to save.

Now all is calm and fresh and still;
Alone the chirp of flitting bird,
And talk of children on the hill,
And bell of wandering kine, are heard.

No solemn host goes trailing by
The black-mouthed gun and staggering wain;
Men start not at the battle-cry, —
O, be it never heard again!

Soon rested those who fought; but thou
Who minglest in the harder strife
For truths which men receive not now,
Thy warfare only ends with life.

A friendless warfare! lingering long
Through weary day and weary year;
A wild and many-weaponed throng
Hang on thy front and flank and rear.

Yet nerve thy spirit to the proof,
And blench not at thy chosen lot;
The timid good may stand aloof,
The sage may frown, — yet faint thou not.

Nor heed the shaft too surely cast,
The foul and hissing bolt of scorn;
For with thy side shall dwell, at last,
The victory of endurance born.

Truth, crushed to earth, shall rise again, —
The eternal years of God are hers;

But Error, wounded, writhes in pain,
And dies among his worshippers.

Yea, though thou lie upon the dust,
When they who helped thee flee in fear,
Die full of hope and manly trust,
Like those who fell in battle here!

Another hand the sword shall wield,
Another hand the standard wave,
Till from the trumpet's mouth is pealed
The blast of triumph o'er thy grave.

FROM "THE RIVULET."

AND I shall sleep; and on thy side,
As ages after ages glide,
Children their early sports shall try,
And pass to hoary age, and die.
But thou, unchanged from year to year,
Gayly shalt play and glitter here:
Amid young flowers and tender grass
Thy endless infancy shalt pass;
And, singing down thy narrow glen,
Shalt mock the fading race of men.

THE BURIAL OF LOVE.

Two dark-eyed maids, at shut of day,
Sat where a river rolled away,
With calm, sad brows, and raven hair;
And one was pale, and both were fair.

Bring flowers, they sang, bring flowers unblown;
Bring forest blooms of name unknown;
Bring budding sprays from wood and wild,
To strew the bier of Love, the child.

Close softly, fondly, while ye weep,
His eyes, that death may seem like sleep;
And fold his hands in sign of rest,
His waxen hands, across his breast.

And make his grave where violets hide,
Where star-flowers strew the rivulet's side,
And bluebirds, in the misty spring,
Of cloudless skies and summer sing.

Place near him, as ye lay him low,
His idle shafts, his loosened bow,
The silken fillet that around
His waggish eyes in sport he wound.

But we shall mourn him long, and miss
His ready smile, his ready kiss,
The patter of his little feet,
Sweet frowns and stammered phrases sweet;

And graver looks, serene and high,
A light of heaven in that young eye:
All these shall haunt us till the heart
Shall ache and ache, — and tears will start.

The bow, the band, shall fall to dust;
The shining arrows waste with rust;
And all of Love that earth can claim
Be but a memory and a name.

Not thus his nobler part shall dwell,
A prisoner in this narrow cell;
But he, whom now we hide from men
In the dark ground, shall live again, —

Shall break these clods, a form of light,
With nobler mien and purer sight,
And in the eternal glory stand
Highest and nearest God's right hand.

ELIZABETH BARRETT BROWNING.

[1809-1861.]

THE SLEEP.

OF all the thoughts of God that are
Borne inward unto souls afar,
Along the Psalmist's music deep,
Now tell me if that any is
For gift or grace surpassing this, —
"He giveth His beloved sleep"?

What would we give to our beloved?
The hero's heart, to be unmoved;
The poet's star-tuned harp, to sweep;
The patriot's voice, to teach and rouse;
The monarch's crown, to light the brows?
"He giveth *His* beloved sleep."

What do we give to our beloved?
A little faith, all undisproved;
A little dust, to overweep;
And bitter memories, to make
The whole earth blasted for our sake.
"He giveth *His* beloved sleep."

"Sleep soft, beloved!" we sometimes say
But have no tune to charm away

Sad dreams that through the eyelids creep.
But never doleful dream again
Shall break the happy slumber when
"He giveth *His* beloved sleep."

O earth, so full of dreary noises!
O men, with wailing in your voices!
O delvéd gold, the wailers heap!
O strife, O curse, that o'er it fall!
God strikes a silence through you all,
And "giveth His beloved sleep."

His dews drop mutely on the hill,
His cloud above it saileth still,
Though on its slope men sow and reap.
More softly than the dew is shed,
Or cloud is floated overhead,
"He giveth His beloved sleep."

Ay, men may wonder while they scan
A living, thinking, feeling man,
Confirmed in such a rest to keep;
But angels say, and through the word
I think their happy smile is *heard*, —
"He giveth His beloved sleep."

For me, my heart, that erst did go
Most like a tired child at a show,
That see through tears the mummers leap,
Would now its wearied vision close,
Would childlike on *His* love repose
Who "giveth His beloved sleep!"

And, friends, dear friends, when it shall be
That this low breath is gone from me,
And round my bier ye come to weep,
Let one, most loving of you all,
Say, "Not a tear must o'er her fall, —
He giveth His beloved sleep."

BERTHA IN THE LANE.

Put the broidery-frame away,
For my sewing is all done!
The last thread is used to-day,
And I need not join it on.
Though the clock stands at the noon,
I am weary! I have sewn,
Sweet, for thee, a wedding-gown.

Sister, help me to the bed,
And stand near me, dearest-sweet!
Do not shrink nor be afraid,
Blushing with a sudden heat!
No one standeth in the street!—
By God's love I go to meet,
Love I thee with love complete.

Lean thy face down! drop it in
These two hands, that I may hold
'Twixt their palms thy cheek and chin,
Stroking back the curls of gold.
'T is a fair, fair face, in sooth, —
Larger eyes and redder mouth
Than mine were in my first youth!

Thou art younger by seven years —
Ah! so bashful at my gaze
That the lashes, hung with tears,
Grow too heavy to upraise!
I would wound thee by no touch
Which thy shyness feels as such—
Dost thou mind me, dear, so much?

Have I not been nigh a mother
To thy sweetness, — tell me, dear,
Have we not loved one another
Tenderly, from year to year?
Since our dying mother mild
Said, with accents undefiled,
"Child, be mother to this child!"

Mother, mother, up in heaven,
Stand up on the jasper sea,
And be witness I have given
All the gifts required of me;—
Hope that blessed me, bliss that crowned,
Love that left me with a wound,
Life itself, that turned around!

Mother, mother, thou art kind,
Thou art standing in the room,
In a molten glory shrined,
That rays off into the gloom!
But thy smile is bright and bleak,
Like cold waves, — I cannot speak;
I sob in it, and grow weak.

Ghostly mother, keep aloof
One hour longer from my soul,
For I still am thinking of
Earth's warm-beating joy and dole!
On my finger is a ring
Which I still see glittering,
When the night hides everything.

Little sister, thou art pale!
Ah, I have a wandering brain, —
But I lose that fever-bale,
And my thoughts grow calm again.
Lean down closer, closer still!

I have words thine ear to fill,
And would kiss thee at my will.

Dear, I heard thee in the spring,
Thee and Robert, through the trees,
When we all went gathering
Boughs of May-bloom for the bees.
Do not start so! think instead
How the sunshine overhead
Seemed to trickle through the shade.

What a day it was, that day!
Hills and vales did openly
Seem to heave and throb away,
At the sight of the great sky;
And the silence, as it stood
In the glory's golden flood,
Audibly did bud — and bud!

Through the winding hedge-rows green,
How we wandered, I and you, —
With the bowery tops shut in,
And the gates that showed the view;
How we talked there! thrushes soft
Sang our pauses out, or oft
Bleatings took them from the croft.

Till the pleasure, grown too strong,
Left me muter evermore;
And, the winding road being long,
I walked out of sight, before;
And so, wrapt in musings fond,
Issued (past the wayside pond)
On the meadow-lands beyond.

I sat down beneath the beech
Which leans over to the lane,
And the far sound of your speech
Did not promise any pain;
And I blessed you full and free,
With a smile stooped tenderly
O'er the May-flowers on my knee.

But the sound grew into word
As the speakers drew more near—
Sweet, forgive me that I heard
What you wished me not to hear.
Do not weep so, do not shake —
O, I heard thee, Bertha, make
Good, true answers for my sake.

Yes, and he too! let him stand
In thy thoughts, untouched by blame.
Could he help it, if my hand
He had claimed with hasty claim!
That was wrong perhaps, but then
Such things be, — and will, again!
Women cannot judge for men.

Had he seen thee, when he swore
He would love but me alone?
Thou wert absent, — sent before
To our kin in Sidmouth town.
When he saw thee, who art best
Past compare, and loveliest,
He but judged thee as the rest.

Could we blame him with grave words,
Thou and I, dear, if we might?
Thy brown eyes have looks like birds
Flying straightway to the light;
Mine are older. — Hush! — look out —
Up the street! Is none without?
How the poplar swings about!

And that hour — beneath the beech —
When I listened in a dream,
And he said, in his deep speech,
That he owed me all esteem, —
Each word swam in on my brain
With a dim, dilating pain,
Till it burst with that last strain.

I fell flooded with a dark,
In the silence of a swoon:
When I rose, still, cold, and stark,
There was night, — I saw the moon;
And the stars, each in its place,
And the May-blooms on the grass,
Seemed to wonder what I was.

And I walked as if apart
From myself when I could stand,
And I pitied my own heart,
As if I held it in my hand
Somewhat coldly, with a sense
Of fulfilled benevolence,
And a "Poor thing" negligence.

And I answered coldly too,
When you met me at the door;
And I only heard the dew
Dripping from me to the floor;
And the flowers I bade you see
Were too withered for the bee, —
As my life, henceforth, for me.

Do not weep so — dear — heart-warm!
It was best as it befell!
If I say he did me harm,
I speak wild, — I am not well.
All his words were kind and good, —
He esteemed me! Only bl od
Runs so faint in womanhood.

Then I always was too grave,
Liked the saddest ballads sung,

With that look, besides, we have
In our faces who die young.
I had died, dear, all the same, —
Life's long, joyous, jostling game
Is too loud for my meek shame.

We are so unlike each other,
Thou and I, that none could guess
We were children of one mother,
But for mutual tenderness.
Thou art rose-lined from the cold,
And meant, verily, to hold
Life's pure pleasures manifold.

I am pale as crocus grows
Close beside a rose-tree's root!
Whosoe'er would reach the rose
Treads the crocus underfoot;
I, like May-bloom on thorn-tree,
Thou, like merry summer-bee!
Fit, that I be plucked for thee.

Yet who plucks me?—no one mourns;
I have lived my season out,
And now die of my own thorns,
Which I could not live without.
Sweet, be merry! How the light
Comes and goes! If it be night,
Keep the candles in my sight.

Are there footsteps at the door?
Look out quickly. Yea or nay?
Some one might be waiting for
Some last word that I might say.
Nay? So best!—So angels would
Stand off clear from deathly road,
Not to cross the sight of God.

Colder grow my hands and feet:
When I wear the shroud I made,
Let the folds lie straight and neat,
And the rosemary be spread,
That if any friend should come,
(To see thee, sweet!) all the room
May be lifted out of gloom.

And, dear Bertha, let me keep
On my hand this little ring,
Which at nights, when others sleep,
I can still see glittering.
Let me wear it out of sight,
In the grave,—where it will light
All the dark up, day and night.

On that grave drop not a tear!
Else, though fathom-deep the place,
Through the woollen shroud I wear
I shall feel it on my face.

Rather smile there, blessed one,
Thinking of me in the sun, —
Or forget me, smiling on!

Art thou near me? nearer? so!
Kiss me close upon the eyes,
That the earthly light may go
Sweetly as it used to rise,
When I watched the morning gray
Strike, betwixt the hills, the way
He was sure to come that day.

So — no more vain words be said!
The hosannas nearer roll —
Mother, smile now on thy dead, —
I am death-strong in my soul!
Mystic Dove alit on cross,
Guide the poor bird of the snows
Through the snow-wind above loss!

Jesus, Victim, comprehending
Love's divine self-abnegation,
Cleanse my love in its self-spending,
And absorb the poor libation!
Wind my thread of life up higher,
Up through angels' hands of fire!—
I aspire while I expire!

A MUSICAL INSTRUMENT.

What was he doing, the great god Pan,
Down in the reeds by the river?
Spreading ruin and scattering ban,
Splashing and paddling with hoofs of a goat,
And breaking the golden lilies afloat
With the dragon-fly on the river?

He tore out a reed, the great god Pan,
From the deep, cool bed of the river,
The limpid water turbidly ran,
And the broken lilies a-dying lay,
And the dragon-fly had fled away,
Ere he brought it out of the river.

High on the shore sat the great god Pan,
While turbidly flowed the river,
And hacked and hewed as a great god can
With his hard, bleak steel at the patient reed,
'Till there was not a sign of a leaf indeed
To prove it fresh from the river.

He cut it short, did the great god Pan,
(How tall it stood in the river!)

Then drew the pith like the heart of a man,
Steadily from the outside ring,
Then notched the poor dry empty thing
In holes, as he sate by the river.

"This is the way," laughed the great god Pan,
(Laughed while he sate by the river!)
"The only way since gods began
To make sweet music, they could succeed."
Then dropping his mouth to a hole in the reed,
He blew in power by the river.

Sweet, sweet, sweet, O Pan,
Piercing sweet by the river!
Blinding sweet, O great god Pan!
The sun on the hill forgot to die,
And the lilies revived, and the dragon-fly
Came back to dream on the river.

Yet half a beast is the great god Pan,
To laugh, as he sits by the river,
Making a poet out of a man.
The true gods sigh for the cost and the pain, —
For the reed that grows nevermore again
As a reed with the reeds of the river.

COWPER'S GRAVE.

It is a place where poets crowned may feel the heart's decaying.
It is a place where happy saints may weep amid their praying:
Yet let the grief and humbleness, as low as silence languish!
Earth surely now may give her calm to whom she gave her anguish.

O poets! from a maniac's tongue was poured the deathless singing!
O Christians! at your cross of hope a hopeless hand was clinging!
O men! this man in brotherhood your weary paths beguiling,
Groaned inly while he taught you peace, and died while ye were smiling!

And now, what time ye all may read through dimming tears his story,
How discord on the music fell, and darkness on the glory,
And how, when one by one sweet sounds and wandering lights departed,
He wore no less a loving face because so broken-hearted;

He shall be strong to sanctify the poet's high vocation,
And bow the meekest Christian down in meeker adoration;
Nor ever shall he be, in praise, by wise or good forsaken;
Named softly as the household name of one whom God hath taken.

With quiet sadness and no gloom I learn to think upon him,
With meekness that is gratefulness to God whose heaven hath won him,—
Who suffered once the madness-cloud to His own love to blind him;
But gently led the blind along where breath and bird could find him;

And wrought within his shattered brain such quick poetic senses
As hills have language for, and stars harmonious influences!
The pulse of dew upon the grass kept his within its number;
And silent shadows from the trees refreshed him like a slumber.

Wild timid hares were drawn from woods to share his home-caresses,
Uplooking to his human eyes with sylvan tendernesses:
The very world, by God's constraint, from falsehood's ways removing,
Its women and its men became, beside him, true and loving.

But though in blindness he remained unconscious of that guiding,
And things provided came without the sweet sense of providing,
He testified this solemn truth, while frenzy desolated, —
Nor man nor nature satisfy whom only God created!

Like a sick child that knoweth not his mother while she blesses,
And drops upon his burning brow the coolness of her kisses;
That turns his fevered eyes around, "My mother! where's my mother?"—
As if such tender words and deeds could come from any other!—

The fever gone, with leaps of heart he sees her bending o'er him;
Her face all pale from watchful love, the unweary love she bore him! —
Thus woke the poet from the dream his life's long fever gave him,
Beneath those deep pathetic Eyes, which closed in death to save him!

Thus? O, not *thus!* no type of earth can image that awaking,
Wherein he scarcely heard the chant of seraphs, round him breaking,
Or felt the new immortal throb of soul from body parted;
But felt *those eyes alone*, and knew "*My* Saviour! *not* deserted!"

Deserted! who hath dreamt that when the cross in darkness rested
Upon the Victim's hidden face, no love was manifested?
What frantic hands outstretched have e'er the atoning drops averted,
What tears have washed them from the soul, that *one* should be deserted?

Deserted! God could separate from his own essence rather:
And Adam's sins *have* swept between the righteous Son and Father;
Yea, once, Immanuel's orphaned cry his universe hath shaken, —
It went up single, echoless, "My God, I am forsaken!"

It went up from the Holy's lips amid his lost creation,
That, of the lost, no son should use those words of desolation;
That earth's worst frenzies, marring hope, should mar not hope's fruition,
And I, on Cowper's grave, should see his rapture in a vision!

WILLIAM MAKEPEACE THACKERAY.

[1811-1863.]

AT THE CHURCH GATE.

Although I enter not,
Yet round about the spot
Ofttimes I hover;
And near the sacred gate,
With longing eyes I wait,
Expectant of her.

The minster bell tolls out
Above the city's rout,
And noise and humming;
They 've hushed the minster bell:
The organ 'gins to swell;
She 's coming, she 's coming!

My lady comes at last,
Timid and stepping fast,
And hastening hither,
With modest eyes downcast,
She comes, — she 's here, she 's past, —
May Heaven go with her!

Kneel undisturbed, fair saint!
Pour out your praise or plaint,
Meekly and duly;
I will not enter there,
To sully your pure prayer
With thoughts unruly.

But suffer me to pace
Round the forbidden place,
Lingering a minute
Like outcast spirits who wait
And see through heaven's gate
Angels within it.

ALFRED TENNYSON.

MARIANA.

With blackest moss the flower-plots
Were thickly crusted, one and all,
The rusted nails fell from the knots
That held the peach to the garden-wall.
The broken sheds looked sad and strange,
Unlifted was the clinking latch,
Weeded and worn the ancient thatch
Upon the lonely moated grange.
She only said, "My life is dreary,
He cometh not," she said;
She said, "I am aweary, aweary;
I would that I were dead!"

Her tears fell with the dews at even;
Her tears fell ere the dews were dried;
She could not look on the sweet heaven,
Either at morn or eventide.

After the flitting of the bats,
When thickest dark did trance the sky,
She drew her casement-curtain by,
And glanced athwart the glooming flats.
She only said, "The night is dreary,
He cometh not," she said;
She said, "I am aweary, aweary,
I would that I were dead!"

Upon the middle of the night,
Waking she heard the night-fowl crow;
The cock sung out an hour ere light:
From the dark fen the oxen's low
Came to her: without hope of change,
In sleep she seemed to walk forlorn,
Till cold winds woke the gray-eyed morn
About the lonely moated grange.
She only said, "The day is dreary,
He cometh not," she said;
She said, "I am aweary, aweary,
And I would that I were dead!"

About a stone-cast from the wall
A sluice with blackened waters slept,
And o'er it many, round and small,
The clustered marish-mosses crept.
Hard by a poplar shook alway,
All silver-green with gnarlèd bark,
For leagues no other tree did dark
The level waste, the rounding gray.
She only said, "My life is dreary,
He cometh not," she said;
She said, "I am aweary, aweary,
I would that I were dead!"

And ever when the moon was low,
And the shrill winds were up and away,
In the white curtain, to and fro,
She saw the gusty shadow sway.
But when the moon was very low,
And wild winds bound within their cell,
The shadow of the poplar fell
Upon her bed, across her brow.
She only said, "The night is dreary,
He cometh not," she said;
She said, "I am aweary, aweary,
I would that I were dead!"

All day within the dreamy house,
The doors upon their hinges creaked,
The blue fly sung i' the pane; the mouse
Behind the mouldering wainscot shrieked,
Or from the crevice peered about.
Old faces glimmered through the doors,
Old footsteps trod the upper floors,
Old voices called her from without.
She only said, "My life is dreary,
He cometh not," she said;
She said, "I am aweary, aweary,
I would that I were dead!"

The sparrow's chirrup on the roof,
The slow clock ticking, and the sound
Which to the wooing wind aloof
The poplar made, did all confound
Her sense; but most she loathed the hour
When the thick-moted sunbeam lay
Athwart the chambers, and the day
Was sloping toward his western bower.
Then, said she, "I am very dreary,
He will not come," she said;
She wept, "I am aweary, aweary,
O God, that I were dead!"

"BREAK, BREAK, BREAK!"

Break, break, break,
On thy cold gray stones, O Sea!
And I would that my tongue could utter
The thoughts that arise in me.

O well for the fisherman's boy,
That he shouts with his sister at play!
O well for the sailor lad,
That he sings in his boat on the bay!

And the stately ships go on
To their haven under the hill;
But O for the touch of a vanished hand,
And the sound of a voice that is still!

Break, break, break,
At the foot of thy crags, O Sea!
But the tender grace of a day that is dead
Will never come back to me.

MEMORY.

I climb the hill: from end to end
Of all the landscape underneath,
I find no place that does not breathe
Some gracious memory of my friend;

No gray old grange, or lonely fold,
Or low morass and whispering reed,
Or simple stile from mead to mead,
Or sheepwalk up the windy wold;

Nor hoary knoll of ash and haw
That hears the latest linnet trill,
Nor quarry trenched along the hill,
And haunted by the wrangling daw.

Unwatched, the garden bough shall sway,
The tender blossom flutter down;
Unloved, that beech will gather brown,
This maple burn itself away;

Unloved, the sunflower, shining fair,
Ray round with flames her disk of seed,
And many a rose-carnation feed
With summer spice the humming air;

Unloved, by many a sandy bar,
The brook shall babble down the plain,
At noon or when the lesser Wain
Is twisting round the polar star;

Uncared for, gird the windy grove,
And flood the haunts of hern and crake;
Or into silver arrows break
The sailing moon in creek and cove;

Till from the garden and the wild
A fresh association blow,
And year by year the landscape grow
Familiar to the stranger's child;

As year by year the laborer tills
His wonted glebe, or lops the glades;
And year by year our memory fades
From all the circle of the hills.

DOUBT.

You say, but with no touch of scorn,
Sweet-hearted, you, whose light-blue eyes
Are tender over drowning flies,
You tell me, doubt is Devil-born.

I know not: one indeed I knew
In many a subtle question versed,
Who touched a jarring lyre at first,
But ever strove to make it true:

Perplext in faith, but pure in deeds,
At last he beat his music out.
There lives more faith in honest doubt,
Believe me, than in half the creeds.

He fought his doubts and gathered strength,
He would not make his judgment blind,
He faced the spectres of the mind
And laid them: thus he came at length

To find a stronger faith his own;
And Power was with him in the night,
Which makes the darkness and the light,
And dwells not in the light alone,

But in the darkness and the cloud,
As over Sinai's peaks of old,
While Israel made their gods of gold,
Although the trumpet blew so loud.

THE LARGER HOPE.

O YET we trust that somehow good
Will be the final goal of ill,
To pangs of nature, sins of will,
Defects of doubt, and taints of blood;

That nothing walks with aimless feet;
That not one life shall be destroyed,
Or cast as rubbish to the void,
When God hath made the pile complete;

That not a worm is cloven in vain;
That not a moth with vain desire
Is shrivelled in a fruitless fire,
Or but subserves another's gain.

Behold, we know not anything;
I can but trust that good shall fall
At last—far off—at last, to all,
And every winter change to spring.

So runs my dream: but what am I?
An infant crying in the night:
An infant crying for the light:
And with no language but a cry.

THE wish, that of the living whole
No life may fail beyond the grave,
Derives it not from what we have
The likest God within the soul?

Are God and Nature, then, at strife,
That Nature lends such evil dreams?
So careful of the type she seems,
So careless of the single life;

That I, considering everywhere
Her secret meaning in her deeds,
And finding that of fifty seeds
She often brings but one to bear,

I falter where I firmly trod,
And falling with my weight of cares

Upon the great world's altar-stairs
That slope through darkness up to God,

I stretch lame hands of faith, and grope,
And gather dust and chaff, and call
To what I feel is Lord of all,
And faintly trust the larger hope.

"So careful of the type?" but no.
From scarpèd cliff and quarried stone
She cries, "A thousand types are gone:
I care for nothing, all shall go.

"Thou makest thine appeal to me:
I bring to life, I bring to death:
The spirit does but mean the breath:
I know no more." And he, shall he,

Man, her last work, who seemed so fair,
Such splendid purpose in his eyes,
Who rolled the psalm to wintry skies,
Who built him fanes of fruitless prayer,

Who trusted God was love indeed
And love Creation's final law, —
Though Nature, red in tooth and claw
With ravin, shrieked against his creed, —

Who loved, who suffered countless ills,
Who battled for the True, the Just,
Be blown about the desert dust,
Or sealed within the iron hills?

No more? A monster then, a dream,
A discord. Dragons of the prime,
That tare each other in their slime,
Were mellow music matched with him.

O life as futile, then, as frail!
O for thy voice to soothe and bless!
What hope of answer, or redress?
Behind the veil, behind the veil.

GARDEN SONG.

Come into the garden, Maud,
For the black bat, night, has flown,
Come into the garden, Maud,
I am here at the gate alone;
And the woodbine spices are wafted abroad,
And the musk of the roses blown.

For a breeze of morning moves,
And the planet of Love is on high,
Beginning to faint in the light that she loves
On a bed of daffodil sky,
To faint in the light of the sun she loves,
To faint in his light, and to die.

All night have the roses heard
The flute, violin, bassoon;
All night has the casement jessamine stirred
To the dancers dancing in tune;
Till a silence fell with the waking bird,
And a hush with the setting moon.

I said to the lily, "There is but one
With whom she has heart to be gay.
When will the dancers leave her alone?
She is weary of dance and play."
Now half to the setting moon are gone,
And half to the rising day;
Low on the sand and loud on the stone
The last wheel echoes away.

I said to the rose, "The brief night goes
In babble and revel and wine.
O young lord-lover, what sighs are those,
For one that will never be thine?
But mine, but mine," so I sware to the rose,
"For ever and ever, mine."

And the soul of the rose went into my blood,
As the music clashed in the hall;
And long by the garden lake I stood,
For I heard your rivulet fall
From the lake to the meadow and on to the wood,
Our wood, that is dearer than all;

From the meadow your walks have left so sweet
That whenever a March-wind sighs
He sets the jewel-print of your feet
In violets blue as your eyes,
To the woody hollows in which we meet
And the valleys of Paradise.

The slender acacia would not shake
One long milk-bloom on the tree;
The white lake-blossom fell into the lake
As the pimpernel dozed on the lea;
But the rose was awake all night for your sake,

Knowing your promise to me;
The lilies and roses were all awake,
They sighed for the dawn and thee.

Queen rose of the rosebud garden of girls,
Come hither, the dances are done,
In gloss of satin and glimmer of pearls,
Queen lily and rose in one;
Shine out, little head, sunning over with curls,
To the flowers, and be their sun.

There has fallen a splendid tear
From the passion-flower at the gate.
She is coming, my dove, my dear;
She is coming, my life, my fate;
The red rose cries, "She is near, she is near";
And the white rose weeps, "She is late";
The larkspur listens, "I hear, I hear";
And the lily whispers, "I wait."

She is coming, my own, my sweet;
Were it ever so airy a tread,
My heart would hear her and beat,
Were it earth in an earthy bed;
My dust would hear her and beat,
Had I lain for a century dead;
Would start and tremble under her feet,
And blossom in purple and red.

BUGLE SONG.

The splendor falls on castle walls
And snowy summits old in story:
The long light shakes across the lakes,
And the wild cataract leaps in glory.
Blow, bugle, blow, set the wild echoes flying,
Blow, bugle; answer, echoes, dying, dying, dying.

O hark, O hear! how thin and clear,
And thinner, clearer, farther going!
O sweet and far from cliff and scar
The horns of Elfland faintly blowing!
Blow, let us hear the purple glens replying:
Blow, bugle; answer, echoes, dying, dying, dying.

O love, they die in yon rich sky,
They faint on hill or field or river:
Our echoes roll from soul to soul,
And grow forever and forever.
Blow, bugle, blow, set the wild echoes flying,
And answer, echoes, answer, dying, dying, dying.

RALPH WALDO EMERSON.

[U. S. A.]

THE APOLOGY.

Think me not unkind and rude,
That I walk alone in grove and glen;
I go to the god of the wood
To fetch his word to men.

Tax not my sloth that I
Fold my arms beside the brook;
Each cloud that floated in the sky
Writes a letter in my book.

Chide me not, laborious band,
For the idle flowers I brought;
Every aster in my hand
Goes home loaded with a thought.

There was never mystery
But 't is figured in the flowers;
Was never secret history
But birds tell it in the bowers.

One harvest from thy field
Homeward brought the oxen strong;
A second crop thy acres yield,
Which I gather in a song.

TO EVA.

O fair and stately maid, whose eyes
Were kindled in the upper skies
At the same torch that lighted mine;
For so I must interpret still
Thy sweet dominion o'er my will,
A sympathy divine.

Ah, let me blameless gaze upon
Features that seem at heart my own;
Nor fear those watchful sentinels,
Who charm the more their glance forbids,
Chaste-glowing, underneath their lids,
With fire that draws while it repels.

THINE EYES STILL SHONE.

THINE eyes still shone for me, though far
I lonely roved the land or sea:
As I behold yon evening star,
Which yet beholds not me.

This morn I climbed the misty hill,
And roamed the pastures through;
How danced thy form before my path,
Amidst the deep-eyed dew!

When the red-bird spread his sable wing,
And showed his side of flame, —
When the rosebud ripened to the rose, —
In both I read thy name.

EACH AND ALL.

LITTLE thinks, in the field, yon red-cloaked clown
Of thee from the hill-top looking down;
The heifer that lows in the upland farm,
Far-heard, lows not thine ear to charm;
The sexton, tolling his bell at noon,
Deems not that great Napoleon
Stops his horse, and lists with delight,
Whilst his files sweep round yon Alpine height;
Nor knowest thou what argument
Thy life to thy neighbor's creed has lent.
All are needed by each one;
Nothing is fair or good alone.
I thought the sparrow's note from heaven,
Singing at dawn on the alder bough;
I brought him home, in his nest, at even;
He sings the song, but it pleases not now,
For I did not bring home the river and sky;—
He sang to my ear,—they sang to my eye.
The delicate shells lay on the shore;
The bubbles of the latest wave
Fresh pearls to their enamel gave;
And the bellowing of the savage sea
Greeted their safe escape to me.
I wiped away the weeds and foam,
I fetched my sea-born treasures home;
But the poor, unsightly, noisome things
Had left their beauty on the shore,
With the sun and the sand and the wild uproar.
The lover watched his graceful maid,
As mid the virgin train she strayed,
Nor knew her beauty's best attire
Was woven still by the snow-white choir.
At last she came to his hermitage,
Like the bird from the woodlands to the cage;—
The gay enchantment was undone,
A gentle wife, but fairy none.
Then I said, "I covet truth;
Beauty is unripe childhood's cheat;
I leave it behind with the games of youth."
As I spoke, beneath my feet
The ground-pine curled its pretty wreath,
Running over the club-moss burrs;
I inhaled the violet's breath;
Around me stood the oaks and firs;
Pine-cones and acorns lay on the ground;
Over me soared the eternal sky,
Full of light and of deity;
Again I saw, again I heard,
The rolling river, the morning bird;—
Beauty through my senses stole;
I yielded myself to the perfect whole.

THE PROBLEM.

I LIKE a church, I like a cowl,
I love a prophet of the soul,
And on my heart monastic aisles
Fall like sweet strains or pensive smiles,
Yet not for all his faith can see
Would I that cowléd churchman be.
Why should the vest on him allure,
Which I could not on me endure?
Not from a vain or shallow thought
His awful Jove young Phidias brought;
Never from lips of cunning fell
The thrilling Delphic oracle;
Out from the heart of nature rolled
The burdens of the Bible old;
The litanies of nations came,
Like the volcano's tongue of flame,
Up from the burning core below, —
The canticles of love and woe.
The hand that rounded Peter's dome,
And groined the aisles of Christian Rome,
Wrought in a sad sincerity.
Himself from God he could not free;
He builded better than he knew;
The conscious stone to beauty grew.
Know'st thou what wove yon wood-bird's nest
Of leaves, and feathers from her breast;
Or how the fish outbuilt her shell,
Painting with morn each annual cell;
Or how the sacred pine-tree adds

To her old leaves new myriads?
Such and so grew these holy piles,
Whilst love and terror laid the tiles.
Earth proudly wears the Parthenon
As the best gem upon her zone;
And morning opes with haste her lids
To gaze upon the Pyramids;
O'er England's Abbeys bends the sky
As on its friends with kindred eye;
For, out of Thought's interior sphere
These wonders rose to upper air,
And Nature gladly gave them place,
Adopted them into her race,
And granted them an equal date
With Andes and with Ararat.
These temples grew as grows the grass;
Art might obey, but not surpass.
The passive Master lent his hand
To the vast Soul that o'er him planned,
And the same power that reared the shrine,
Bestrode the tribes that knelt within.
Ever the fiery Pentecost
Girds with one flame the countless host,
Trances the heart through chanting choirs,
And through the priest the mind inspires.
The word unto the prophet spoken
Was writ on tables yet unbroken;
The word by seers or sibyls told,
In groves of oak or fanes of gold,
Still floats upon the morning wind,
Still whispers to the willing mind.
One accent of the Holy Ghost
The heedless world hath never lost.
I know what say the Fathers wise,—
The book itself before me lies,—
Old Chrysostom, best Augustine,
And he who blent both in his line,
The younger *Golden Lips* or mines,
Taylor, the Shakespeare of divines;
His words are music in my ear,
I see his cowléd portrait dear,
And yet, for all his faith could see,
I would not the good bishop be.

BOSTON HYMN.

The word of the Lord by night
To the watching Pilgrims came,
As they sat by the seaside,
And filled their hearts with flame.

God said, I am tired of kings,
I suffer them no more;
Up to my ear the morning brings
The outrage of the poor.

Think ye I made this ball
A field of havoc and war,
Where tyrants great and tyrants small
Might harry the weak and poor?

My angel,—his name is Freedom,—
Choose him to be your king;
He shall cut pathways east and west,
And fend you with his wing.

Lo! I uncover the land,
Which I hid of old time in the West,
As the sculptor uncovers the statue
When he has wrought his best;

I show Columbia, of the rocks
Which dip their foot in the seas,
And soar to the air-borne flocks
Of clouds, and the boreal fleece.

I will divide my goods;
Call in the wretch and the slave:
None shall rule but the humble,
And none but Toil shall have.

I will have never a noble,
No lineage counted great;
Fishers and choppers and ploughmen
Shall constitute a state.

Go, cut down trees in the forest,
And trim the straightest boughs;
Cut down trees in the forest,
And build me a wooden house.

Call the people together,
The young men and the sires,
The digger in the harvest-field,
Hireling, and him that hires;

And here in a pine state-house
They shall choose men to rule
In every needful faculty,
In church and state and school.

Lo, now! if these poor men
Can govern the land and sea,
And make just laws below the sun,
As planets faithful be.

And ye shall succor men;
'T is nobleness to serve;
Help them who cannot help again:
Beware from right to swerve.

I break your bonds and masterships,
And I unchain the slave:
Free be his heart and hand henceforth
As wind and wandering wave.

I cause from every creature
His proper good to flow;
As much as he is and doeth,
So much he shall bestow.

But, laying hands on another,
To coin his labor and sweat,
He goes in pawn to his victim
For eternal years in debt.

To-day unbind the captive,
So only are ye unbound;
Lift up a people from the dust,
Trump of their rescue, sound!

Pay ransom to the owner,
And fill the bag to the brim.
Who is the owner? The slave is owner,
And ever was. Pay him.

O North! give him beauty for rags,
And honor, O South! for his shame;
Nevada! coin thy golden crags
With Freedom's image and name.

Up! and the dusky race
That sat in darkness long, —
Be swift their feet as antelopes,
And as behemoth strong.

Come, East and West and North,
By races, as snowflakes,
And carry my purpose forth,
Which neither halts nor shakes.

My will fulfilled shall be,
For, in daylight or in dark,
My thunderbolt has eyes to see
His way home to the mark.

THE SOUL'S PROPHECY.

All before us lies the way;
Give the past unto the wind;
All before us is the day,
Night and darkness are behind.

Eden with its angels bold,
Love and flowers and coolest sea,
Is less an ancient story told
Than a glowing prophecy.

In the spirit's perfect air,
In the passions tame and kind,
Innocence from selfish care,
The real Eden we shall find.

When the soul to sin hath died,
True and beautiful and sound,
Then all earth is sanctified,
Upsprings paradise around.

From the spirit-land afar
All disturbing force shall flee;
Stir, nor toil, nor hope shall mar
Its immortal unity.

EDGAR A. POE.

[U. S. A., 1811 – 1849.]

THE BELLS.

Hear the sledges with the bells, —
Silver bells, —
What a world of merriment their melody foretells!
How they tinkle, tinkle, tinkle,
In the icy air of night!
While the stars that oversprinkle
All the heavens seem to twinkle
With a crystalline delight;
Keeping time, time, time,
In a sort of Runic rhyme,
To the tintinnabulation that so musically wells
From the bells, bells, bells, bells,
Bells, bells, bells, —
From the jingling and the tinkling of the bells.

Hear the mellow wedding bells,
Golden bells!
What a world of happiness their harmony foretells!
Through the balmy air of night
How they ring out their delight!
From the molten-golden notes,
And all in tune,
What a liquid ditty floats
To the turtle-dove that listens, while she gloats
On the moon!
O, from out the sounding cells,
What a gush of euphony voluminously wells!

How it swells!
How it dwells
On the Future! how it tells
Of the rapture that impels
To the swinging and the ringing
Of the bells, bells, bells,
Of the bells, bells, bells, bells,
Bells, bells, bells, —
To the rhyming and the chiming of the bells!

Hear the loud alarum bells, —
Brazen bells!
What a tale of terror, now, their turbulency tells!
In the startled ear of night
How they scream out their affright!
Too much horrified to speak,
They can only shriek, shriek,
Out of tune,
In a clamorous appealing to the mercy of the fire,
In a mad expostulation with the deaf and frantic fire.
Leaping higher, higher, higher,
With a desperate desire,
And a resolute endeavor
Now—now to sit or never,
By the side of the pale-faced moon.
O, the bells, bells, bells,
What a tale their terror tells
Of Despair!
How they clang, and clash, and roar!
What a horror they outpour
On the bosom of the palpitating air!
Yet the ear it fully knows,
By the twanging,
And the clanging,
How the danger ebbs and flows;
Yet the ear distinctly tells,
In the jangling,
And the wrangling,
How the danger sinks and swells,
By the sinking or the swelling in the anger of the bells—
Of the bells—
Of the bells, bells, bells, bells,
Bells, bells, bells, —
In the clamor and the clangor of the bells!

Hear the tolling of the bells, —
Iron bells!
What a world of solemn thought their monody compels!
In the silence of the night,
How we shiver with affright
At the melancholy menace of their tone!
For every sound that floats
From the rust within their throats
Is a groan.
And the people, — ah, the people, —
They that dwell up in the steeple,
All alone,
And who, tolling, tolling, tolling,
In that muffled monotone,
Feel a glory in so rolling
On the human heart a stone, —
They are neither man nor woman, —
They are neither brute nor human, —
They are Ghouls:
And their king it is who tolls;
And he rolls, rolls, rolls,
Rolls
A pæan from the bells!
And his merry bosom swells
With the pæan of the bells!
And he dances and he yells;
Keeping time, time, time,
In a sort of Runic rhyme,
To the pæan of the bells, —
Of the bells:
Keeping time, time, time,
In a sort of Runic rhyme,
To the throbbing of the bells, —
Of the bells, bells, bells, —
To the sobbing of the bells;
Keeping time, time, time,
As he knells, knells, knells,
In a happy Runic rhyme,
To the rolling of the bells, —
Of the bells, bells, bells, —
To the tolling of the bells,
Of the bells, bells, bells, bells, —
Bells, bells, bells, —
To the moaning and the groaning of the bells.

ROBERT BROWNING.

EVELYN HOPE.

Beautiful Evelyn Hope is dead!
Sit and watch by her side an hour.
That is her book-shelf, this her bed;
She plucked that piece of geranium-flower,
Beginning to die, too, in the glass.
Little has yet been changed, I think, —

The shutters are shut, no light may pass
  Save two long rays through the hinge's
    chink.

Sixteen years old when she died!
  Perhaps she had scarcely heard my
    name, —
It was not her time to love: beside,
  Her life had many a hope and aim,
Duties enough and little cares,
  And now was quiet, now astir, —
Till God's hand beckoned unawares,
  And the sweet white brow is all of her.

Is it too late then, Evelyn Hope?
  What, your soul was pure and true,
The good stars met in your horoscope,
  Made you of spirit, fire, and dew, —
And just because I was thrice as old,
  And our paths in the world diverged
    so wide,
Each was naught to each, must I be told?
  We were fellow mortals, naught beside?

No, indeed! for God above
  Is great to grant as mighty to make,
And creates the love to reward the love, —
  I claim you still, for my own love's sake!
Delayed it may be for more lives yet,
  Through worlds I shall traverse, not a
    few, —
Much is to learn and much to forget
  Ere the time be come for taking you.

But the time will come, — at last it will,
  When, Evelyn Hope, what meant, I
    shall say,
In the lower earth, in the years long still,
  That body and soul so pure and gay?
Why your hair was amber, I shall divine,
  And your mouth of your own gera-
    nium's red, —
And what you would do with me, in fine,
  In the new life come in the old one's
    stead.

I have lived, I shall say, so much since
    then,
  Given up myself so many times,
Gained me the gains of various men,
  Ransacked the ages, spoiled the
    climes;
Yet one thing, one, in my soul's full scope,
  Either I missed or itself missed me —
And I want and find you, Evelyn Hope!
  What is the issue? let us see!

I loved you, Evelyn, all the while;
  My heart seemed full as it could hold, —
There was place and to spare for the frank
    young smile
  And the red young mouth and the
    hair's young gold.
So, hush, — I will give you this leaf to
    keep, —
  See, I shut it inside the sweet cold hand.
There, that is our secret! go to sleep;
  You will wake, and remember, and
    understand.

—

RABBI BEN EZRA.

Grow old along with me!
The best is yet to be,
The last of life, for which the first was
    made:
Our times are in His hand
Who saith, "A whole I planned,
Youth shows but half; trust God: see
    all, nor be afraid!"

Not that, amassing flowers,
Youth sighed, "Which rose make ours,
Which lily leave and then as best recall?"
Not that, admiring stars,
It yearned, "Nor Jove, nor Mars;
Mine be some figured flame which blends,
    transcends them all!"

Not for such hopes and fears,
Annulling youth's brief years,
Do I remonstrate, — folly wide the mark!
Rather I prize the doubt
Low kinds exist without,
Finished and finite clods, untroubled by
    a spark.

Poor vaunt of life indeed,
Were man but formed to feed
On joy, to solely seek and find and feast:
Such feasting ended, then
As sure an end to men;
Irks care the crop-full bird? Frets doubt
    the maw-crammed beast?

Rejoice we are allied
To That which doth provide
And not partake, effect and not receive!
A spark disturbs our clod;
Nearer we hold of God
Who gives, than of his tribes that take,
    I must believe.

Then, welcome each rebuff
That turns earth's smoothness rough,
Each sting that bids nor sit nor stand, but go!
Be our joys three parts pain!
Strive, and hold cheap the strain;
Learn, nor account the pang; dare, never grudge the throe!

For thence— a paradox
Which comforts while it mocks—
Shall life succeed in that it seems to fail:
What I aspired to be,
And was not, comforts me:
A brute I might have been, but would not sink i' the scale.

What is he but a brute
Whose flesh hath soul to suit,
Whose spirit works lest arms and legs want play?
To man, propose this test, —
Thy body at its best,
How far can that project thy soul on its lone way?

Yet gifts should prove their use:
I own the Past profuse
Of power each side, perfection every turn:
Eyes, ears took in their dole,
Brain treasured up the whole;
Should not the heart beat once, "How good to live and learn?"

Not once beat, "Praise be Thine!
I see the whole design,
I, who saw Power, shall see Love perfect too:
Perfect I call Thy plan:
Thanks that I was a man!
Maker, remake, complete, — I trust what thou shalt do!"

For pleasant is this flesh;
Our soul, in its rose-mesh
Pulled ever to the earth, still yearns for rest:
Would we some prize might hold
To match those manifold
Possessions of the brute, — gain most, as we did best!

Let us not always say,
"Spite of this flesh to-day
I strove, made head, gained ground upon the whole!"
As the bird wings and sings,
Let us cry, "All good things
Are ours, nor soul helps flesh more, now, than flesh helps soul!"

Therefore I summon age
To grant youth's heritage,
Life's struggle having so far reached its term:
Thence shall I pass, approved
A man, for aye removed
From the developed brute; a God though in the germ.

And I shall thereupon
Take rest, ere I be gone
Once more on my adventure brave and new:
Fearless and unperplexed,
When I wage battle next,
What weapons to select, what armor to indue.

Youth ended, I shall try
My gain or loss thereby;
Be the fire ashes, what survives is gold:
And I shall weigh the same,
Give life its praise or blame:
Young, all lay in dispute; I shall know, being old.

For note, when evening shuts,
A certain moment cuts
The deed off, calls the glory from the gray:
A whisper from the west
Shoots, "Add this to the rest,
Take it and try its worth: here dies another day."

So, still within this life,
Though lifted o'er its strife,
Let me discern, compare, pronounce at last,
"This rage was right i' the main,
That acquiescence vain:
The Future I may face now I have proved the Past."

For more is not reserved
To man, with soul just nerved
To act to-morrow what he learns to-day:
Here, work enough to watch
The Master work, and catch
Hints of the proper craft, tricks of the tool's true play.

As it was better, youth
Should strive, through acts uncouth,

Toward making, than repose on aught found made;
So, better, age, exempt
From strife, should know, than tempt
Further. Thou waitedst age; wait death nor be afraid!

Enough now, if the Right
And Good and Infinite
Be named here, as thou callest thy hand thine own,
With knowledge absolute,
Subject to no dispute
From fools that crowded youth, nor let thee feel alone.

Be there, for once and all,
Severed great minds from small,
Announced to each his station in the Past!
Was I, the world arraigned,
Were they, my soul disdained,
Right? Let age speak the truth and give us peace at last!

Now, who shall arbitrate?
Ten men love what I hate,
Shun what I follow, slight what I receive;
Ten, who in ears and eyes
Match me: we all surmise,
They, this thing, and I, that: whom shall my soul believe?

Not on the vulgar mass
Called "work," must sentence pass,
Things done, that took the eye and had the price;
O'er which, from level stand,
The low world laid its hand,
Found straightway to its mind, could value in a trice:

But all, the world's coarse thumb
And finger failed to plumb,
So passed in making up the main account;
All instincts immature,
All purposes unsure,
That weighed not as his work, yet swelled the man's amount:

Thoughts hardly to be packed
Into a narrow act,
Fancies that broke through language and escaped;
All I could never be,
All men ignored in me,
This I was worth to God, whose wheel the pitcher shaped.

Ay, note that Potter's wheel,
That metaphor! and feel
Why time spins fast, why passive lies our clay, —
Thou, to whom fools propound,
When the wine makes its round,
"Since life fleets, all is change; the Past gone, seize to-day!"

Fool! All that is, at all,
Lasts ever, past recall;
Earth changes, but thy soul and God stand sure:
What entered into thee,
That was, is, and shall be:
Time's wheel runs back or stops: Potter and clay endure.

He fixed thee mid this dance
Of plastic circumstance,
This Present, thou, forsooth, wouldst fain arrest:
Machinery just meant
To give thy soul its bent,
Try thee and turn thee forth, sufficiently impressed.

What though the earlier grooves
Which ran the laughing loves
Around thy base, no longer pause and press?
What though, about thy rim,
Skull-things in order grim
Grow out, in graver mood, obey the sterner stress?

Look not thou down, but up!
To uses of a cup,
The festal board, lamp's flash, and trumpet's peal,
The new wine's foaming flow,
The Master's lips aglow!
Thou, heaven's consummate cup, what needst thou with earth's wheel?

But I need, now as then,
Thee, God, who mouldest men;
And since, not even while the whirl was worst,
Did I — to the wheel of life
With shapes and colors rife,
Bound dizzily — mistake my end, to slake Thy thirst:

So, take and use Thy work!
Amend what flaws may lurk,
What strain o' the stuff, what warpings past the aim!
My times be in Thy hand!
Perfect the cup as planned!
Let age approve of youth, and death complete the same!

THE LOST LEADER.

Just for a handful of silver he left us;
Just for a ribbon to stick in his coat, —
Found the one gift of which fortune bereft us,
Lost all the others she lets us devote.
They, with the gold to give, doled him out silver,
So much was theirs who so little allowed.
How all our copper had gone for his service!
Rags — were they purple, his heart had been proud!
We that had loved him so, followed him, honored him,
Lived in his mild and magnificent eye,
Learned his great language, caught his clear accents,
Made him our pattern to live and to die!
Shakespeare was of us, Milton was for us,
Burns, Shelley, were with us, — they watch from their graves!
He alone breaks from the van and the freemen;
He alone sinks to the rear and the slaves!
We shall march prospering, — not through his presence;
Songs may inspirit us, — not from his lyre;
Deeds will be done, — while he boasts his quiescence,
Still bidding crouch whom the rest bade aspire.
Blot out his name, then, — record one lost soul more,
One task more declined, one more footpath untrod,
One more triumph for devils, and sorrow for angels,
One wrong more to man, one more insult to God!
Life's night begins; let him never come back to us!
There would be doubt, hesitation, and pain,
Forced praise on our part, — the glimmer of twilight,
Never glad, confident morning again!
Best fight on well, for we taught him, — strike gallantly,
Aim at our heart ere we pierce through his own;
Then let him receive the new knowledge and wait us,
Pardoned in Heaven, the first by the throne!

HENRY W. LONGFELLOW.

[U. S. A.]

PAUL REVERE'S RIDE.

Listen, my children, and you shall hear
Of the midnight ride of Paul Revere,
On the eighteenth of April, in Seventy-five;
Hardly a man is now alive
Who remembers that famous day and year.

He said to his friend, "If the British march
By land or sea from the town to-night,
Hang a lantern aloft in the belfry arch
Of the North Church tower as a signal light, —
One, if by land, and two, if by sea;
And I on the opposite shore will be,
Ready to ride and spread the alarm
Through every Middlesex village and farm,
For the country folk to be up and to arm."

Then he said, "Good night!" and with muffled oar
Silently rowed to the Charlestown shore,
Just as the moon rose over the bay,
Where swinging wide at her moorings lay
The Somerset, British man-of-war;
A phantom ship, with each mast and spar
Across the moon like a prison bar,
And a huge black hulk, that was magnified
By its own reflection in the tide.

Meanwhile, his friend, through alley and street,
Wanders and watches with eager ears,

Till in the silence around him he hears
The muster of men at the barrack door,
The sound of arms, and the tramp of feet,
And the measured tread of the grenadiers,
Marching down to their boats on the shore.

Then he climbed the tower of the Old North Church,
By the wooden stairs, with stealthy tread,
To the belfry-chamber overhead,
And startled the pigeons from their perch
On the sombre rafters, that round him made
Masses and moving shapes of shade, —
By the trembling ladder, steep and tall,
To the highest window in the wall,
Where he paused to listen and look down
A moment on the roofs of the town,
And the moonlight flowing over all.

Beneath, in the churchyard, lay the dead,
In their night-encampment on the hill,
Wrapped in silence so deep and still
That he could hear, like a sentinel's tread,
The watchful night-wind, as it went
Creeping along from tent to tent,
And seeming to whisper, "All is well!"
A moment only he feels the spell
Of the place and the hour, and the secret dread
Of the lonely belfry and the dead;
For suddenly all his thoughts are bent
On a shadowy something far away,
Where the river widens to meet the bay, —
A line of black that bends and floats
On the rising tide, like a bridge of boats.

Meanwhile, impatient to mount and ride,
Booted and spurred, with a heavy stride
On the opposite shore walked Paul Revere.
Now he patted his horse's side,
Now gazed at the landscape far and near,
Then, impetuous, stamped the earth,
And turned and tightened his saddle-girth;
But mostly he watched with eager search
The belfry-tower of the Old North Church,
As it rose above the graves on the hill,
Lonely and spectral and sombre and still.
And lo! as he looks, on the belfry's height
A glimmer, and then a gleam of light!
He springs to the saddle, the bridle he turns,
But lingers and gazes, till full on his sight
A second lamp in the belfry burns!

A hurry of hoofs in a village street,
A shape in the moonlight, a bulk in the dark,
And beneath, from the pebbles, in passing, a spark
Struck out by a steed flying fearless and fleet:
That was all! And yet, through the gloom and the light,
The fate of a nation was riding that night;
And the spark struck out by that steed, in his flight,
Kindled the land into flame with its heat.

He has left the village and mounted the steep,
And beneath him, tranquil and broad and deep,
Is the Mystic, meeting the ocean tides;
And under the alders, that skirt its edge,
Now soft on the sand, now loud on the ledge,
Is heard the tramp of his steed as he rides.

It was twelve by the village clock
When he crossed the bridge into Medford town.
He heard the crowing of the cock,
And the barking of the farmer's dog,
And felt the damp of the river fog,
That rises after the sun goes down.

It was one by the village clock,
When he galloped into Lexington.
He saw the gilded weathercock
Swim in the moonlight as he passed,
And the meeting-house windows, blank and bare,
Gaze at him with a spectral glare,
As if they already stood aghast
At the bloody work they would look upon.

It was two by the village clock
When he came to the bridge in Concord town.
He heard the bleating of the flock,
And the twitter of birds among the trees,
And felt the breath of the morning breeze
Blowing over the meadows brown.
And one was safe and asleep in his bed
Who at the bridge would be first to fall,
Who that day would be lying dead,
Pierced by a British musket-ball.

You know the rest. In the books you have read,
How the British Regulars fired and fled, —

How the farmers gave them ball for ball,
From behind each fence and farm-yard wall,
Chasing the redcoats down the lane,
Then crossing the fields to emerge again
Under the trees at the turn of the road,
And only pausing to fire and load.

So through the night rode Paul Revere;
And so through the night went his cry of alarm
To every Middlesex village and farm, —
A cry of defiance and not of fear,
A voice in the darkness, a knock at the door,
And a word that shall echo forevermore!
For, borne on the night-wind of the Past,
Through all our history, to the last,
In the hour of darkness and peril and need,
The people will waken and listen to hear
The hurrying hoof-beats of that steed
And the midnight message of Paul Revere.

MAIDENHOOD.

MAIDEN! with the meek, brown eyes,
In whose orbs a shadow lies
Like the dusk in evening skies!

Thou whose locks outshine the sun,
Golden tresses, wreathed in one,
As the braided streamlets run!

Standing, with reluctant feet,
Where the brook and river meet,
Womanhood and childhood fleet!

Gazing, with a timid glance,
On the brooklet's swift advance,
On the river's broad expanse!

Deep and still, that gliding stream
Beautiful to thee must seem,
As the river of a dream.

Then why pause with indecision,
When bright angels in thy vision
Beckon thee to fields Elysian?

Seest thou shadows sailing by,
As the dove, with startled eye,
Sees the falcon's shadow fly?

Hearest thou voices on the shore,
That our ears perceive no more,
Deafened by the cataract's roar?

O, thou child of many prayers!
Life hath quicksands, — Life hath snares!
Care and age come unawares!

Like the swell of some sweet tune,
Morning rises into noon,
May glides onward into June.

Childhood is the bough, where slumbered
Birds and blossoms many-numbered;—
Age, that bough with snows encumbered.

Gather, then, each flower that grows,
When the young heart overflows,
To embalm that tent of snows.

Bear a lily in thy hand;
Gates of brass cannot withstand
One touch of that magic wand.

Bear through sorrow, wrong, and ruth,
In thy heart the dew of youth,
On thy lips the smile of truth.

O, that dew, like balm, shall steal
Into wounds that cannot heal,
Even as sleep our eyes doth seal;

And that smile, like sunshine, dart
Into many a sunless heart,
For a smile of God thou art.

A PSALM OF LIFE.

WHAT THE HEART OF THE YOUNG MAN SAID TO THE PSALMIST.

TELL me not, in mournful numbers,
  Life is but an empty dream!
For the soul is dead that slumbers,
  And things are not what they seem.

Life is real! Life is earnest!
  And the grave is not its goal;
Dust thou art, to dust returnest,
  Was not spoken of the soul.

Not enjoyment, and not sorrow,
  Is our destined end or way;
But to act, that each to-morrow
  Find us farther than to-day.

Art is long, and Time is fleeting,
  And our hearts, though stout and brave,
Still, like muffled drums, are beating
  Funeral marches to the grave.

In the world's broad field of battle,
  In the bivouac of Life,
Be not like dumb, driven cattle!
  Be a hero in the strife!

Trust no Future, howe'er pleasant!
  Let the dead Past bury its dead!
Act,—act in the living Present!
  Heart within, and God o'erhead!

Lives of great men all remind us
  We can make our lives sublime,
And, departing, leave behind us
  Footprints on the sands of time;—

Footprints, that perhaps another,
  Sailing o'er life's solemn main,
A forlorn and shipwrecked brother,
  Seeing, shall take heart again.

Let us, then, be up and doing,
  With a heart for any fate,
Still achieving, still pursuing,
  Learn to labor and to wait.

RESIGNATION.

THERE is no flock, however watched and tended,
  But one dead lamb is there!
There is no fireside, howsoe'er defended,
  But has one vacant chair!

The air is full of farewells to the dying,
  And mournings for the dead;
The heart of Rachel, for her children crying,
  Will not be comforted!

Let us be patient! These severe afflictions
  Not from the ground arise,
But oftentimes celestial benedictions
  Assume this dark disguise.

We see but dimly through the mists and vapors;
  Amid these earthly damps
What seem to us but sad, funereal tapers
  May be heaven's distant lamps.

There is no Death! What seems so is transition;
  This life of mortal breath
Is but a suburb of the life elysian,
  Whose portal we call Death.

She is not dead,—the child of our affection,—
  But gone unto that school
Where she no longer needs our poor protection,
  And Christ himself doth rule.

In that great cloister's stillness and seclusion,
  By guardian angels led,
Safe from temptation, safe from sin's pollution,
  She lives, whom we call dead.

Day after day we think what she is doing
  In those bright realms of air;
Year after year, her tender steps pursuing,
  Behold her grown more fair.

Thus do we walk with her, and keep unbroken
  The bond which nature gives,
Thinking that our remembrance, though unspoken,
  May reach her where she lives.

Not as a child shall we again behold her:
  For when with raptures wild
In our embraces we again enfold her,
  She will not be a child;

But a fair maiden, in her Father's mansion,
  Clothed with celestial grace;
And beautiful with all the soul's expansion
  Shall we behold her face.

And though at times impetuous with emotion
  And anguish long suppressed,
The swelling heart heaves moaning like the ocean,
  That cannot be at rest,—

We will be patient, and assuage the feeling
  We may not wholly stay;
By silence sanctifying, not concealing,
  The grief that must have way.

SANTA FILOMENA.

WHENE'ER a noble deed is wrought,
Whene'er is spoken a noble thought,
Our hearts, in glad surprise,
To higher levels rise.

The tidal wave of deeper souls
Into our inmost being rolls,
And lifts us unawares
Out of all meaner cares.

Honor to those whose words or deeds
Thus help us in our daily needs,
And by their overflow
Raise us from what is low!

Thus thought I, as by night I read
Of the great army of the dead,
The trenches cold and damp,
The starved and frozen camp, —

The wounded from the battle-plain,
In dreary hospitals of pain,
The cheerless corridors,
The cold and stony floors.

Lo! in that house of misery
A lady with a lamp I see
Pass through the glimmering gloom,
And flit from room to room.

And slow, as in a dream of bliss,
The speechless sufferer turns to kiss
Her shadow, as it falls
Upon the darkening walls.

As if a door in heaven should be
Opened and then closed suddenly,
The vision came and went,
The light shone and was spent.

On England's annals, through the long
Hereafter of her speech and song,
That light its rays shall cast
From portals of the past.

A Lady with a Lamp shall stand
In the great history of the land,
A noble type of good,
Heroic womanhood.

Nor even shall be wanting here
The palm, the lily, and the spear,
The symbols that of yore
Saint Filomena bore.

HAWTHORNE.

MAY 23, 1864.

How beautiful it was, that one bright day
In the long week of rain!
Though all its splendor could not chase away
The omnipresent pain.

The lovely town was white with apple-blooms,
And the great elms o'erhead
Dark shadows wove on their aerial looms
Shot through with golden thread.

Across the meadows, by the gray old manse,
The historic river flowed;
I was as one who wanders in a trance,
Unconscious of his road.

The faces of familiar friends seemed strange;
Their voices I could hear,
And yet the words they uttered seemed to change
Their meaning to my ear.

For the one face I looked for was not there,
The one low voice was mute;
Only an unseen presence filled the air,
And baffled my pursuit.

Now I look back, and meadow, manse, and stream
Dimly my thought defines;
I only see — a dream within a dream —
The hill-top hearsed with pines.

I only hear above his place of rest
Their tender undertone,
The infinite longings of a troubled breast,
The voice so like his own.

There in seclusion and remote from men
The wizard hand lies cold,
Which at its topmost speed let fall the pen,
And left the tale half told.

Ah! who shall lift that wand of magic power,
And the lost clew regain?
The unfinished window in Aladdin's tower
Unfinished must remain!

GERALD MASSEY.

TO-DAY AND TO-MORROW.

High hopes that burned like stars sublime
  Go down the heavens of Freedom,
And true hearts perish in the time
  We bitterliest need them!
But never sit we down, and say
  There 's nothing left but sorrow;
We walk the wilderness to-day,
  The promised land to-morrow.

Our birds of song are silent now,
  There are no flowers blooming;
Yet life beats in the frozen bough,
  And Freedom's spring is coming!
And Freedom's tide comes up alway,
  Though we may stand in sorrow;
And our good bark aground to-day
  Shall float again to-morrow.

Through all the long, dark nights of years
  The people's cry ascendeth,
And earth is wet with blood and tears;
  But our meek sufferance endeth!
The few shall not forever sway,
  The many toil in sorrow;
The powers of earth are strong to-day,
  But Heaven shall rule to-morrow.

Though hearts brood o'er the past, our eyes
  With smiling features glisten!
For lo! our day bursts up the skies:
  Lean out your souls and listen!
The world rolls Freedom's radiant way
  And ripens with her sorrow;
Keep heart! who bear the cross to-day
  Shall wear the crown to-morrow.

O Youth! flame earnest, still aspire,
  With energies immortal!
To many a heaven of desire
  Our yearning opes a portal:
And though age wearies by the way,
  And hearts break in the furrow,
We 'll sow the golden grain to-day,
  And harvest comes to-morrow.

Build up heroic lives, and all
  Be like a sheathen sabre,
Ready to flash out at God's call,
  O chivalry of labor!
Triumph and toil are twins; and aye,
  Joy suns the cloud of sorrow;
And 't is the martyrdom to-day
  Brings victory to-morrow.

JOHN G. WHITTIER.

[U. S. A.]

THE GRAVE BY THE LAKE.

Where the Great Lake's sunny smiles
Dimple round its hundred isles,
And the mountain's granite ledge
Cleaves the water like a wedge,
Ringed about with smooth, gray stones,
Rest the giant's mighty bones.

Close beside, in shade and gleam,
Laughs and ripples Melvin stream;
Melvin water, mountain-born,
All fair flowers its banks adorn;
All the woodland's voices meet,
Mingling with its murmurs sweet.

Over lowlands forest-grown,
Over waters island-strown,
Over silver-sanded beach,
Leaf-locked bay and misty reach,
Melvin stream and burial-heap,
Watch and ward the mountains keep.

Who that Titan cromlech fills?
Forest-kaiser, lord o' the hills?
Knight who on the birchen tree
Carved his savage heraldry?
Priest o' the pine-wood temples dim,
Prophet, sage, or wizard grim?

Rugged type of primal man,
Grim utilitarian,
Loving woods for hunt and prowl,
Lake and hill for fish and fowl,
As the brown bear blind and dull
To the grand and beautiful:

Not for him the lesson drawn
From the mountains smit with dawn.
Star-rise, moon-rise, flowers of May,
Sunset's purple bloom of day, —
Took his life no hue from thence,
Poor amid such affluence?

Haply unto hill and tree
All too near akin was he:

Unto him who stands afar
Nature's marvels greatest are;
Who the mountain purple seeks
Must not climb the higher peaks.

Yet who knows in winter tramp,
Or the midnight of the camp,
What revealings faint and far,
Stealing down from moon and star,
Kindled in that human clod
Thought of destiny and God?

Stateliest forest patriarch,
Grand in robes of skin and bark,
What sepulchral mysteries,
What weird funeral-rites, were his?
What sharp wail, what drear lament,
Back scared wolf and eagle sent?

Now, whate'er he may have been,
Low he lies as other men;
On his mound the partridge drums,
There the noisy blue-jay comes;
Rank nor name nor pomp has he
In the grave's democracy.

Part thy blue lips, Northern lake!
Moss-grown rocks, your silence break!
Tell the tale, thou ancient tree!
Thou, too, slide-worn Ossipee!
Speak, and tell us how and when
Lived and died this king of men!

Wordless moans the ancient pine;
Lake and mountain give no sign;
Vain to trace this ring of stones;
Vain the search of crumbling bones:
Deepest of all mysteries,
And the saddest, silence is.

Nameless, noteless, clay with clay
Mingles slowly day by day;
But somewhere, for good or ill,
That dark soul is living still;
Somewhere yet that atom's force
Moves the light-poised universe.

Strange that on his burial-sod
Harebells bloom, and golden-rod,
While the soul's dark horoscope
Holds no starry sign of hope!
Is the Unseen with sight at odds?
Nature's pity more than God's?

Thus I mused by Melvin's side,
While the summer eventide
Made the woods and inland sea
And the mountains mystery;
And the hush of earth and air
Seemed the pause before a prayer, —

Prayer for him, for all who rest,
Mother Earth, upon thy breast, —
Lapped on Christian turf, or hid
In rock-cave or pyramid:
All who sleep, as all who live,
Well may need the prayer, "Forgive!"

Desert-smothered caravan,
Knee-deep dust that once was man,
Battle-trenches ghastly piled,
Ocean-floors with white bones tiled,
Crowded tomb and mounded sod,
Dumbly crave that prayer to God.

O the generations old
Over whom no church-bells tolled,
Christless, lifting up blind eyes
To the silence of the skies!
For the innumerable dead
Is my soul disquieted.

Where be now these silent hosts?
Where the camping-ground of ghosts?
Where the spectral conscripts led
To the white tents of the dead?
What strange shore or chartless sea
Holds the awful mystery?

Then the warm sky stooped to make
Double sunset in the lake;
While above I saw with it,
Range on range, the mountains lit;
And the calm and splendor stole
Like an answer to my soul.

Hear'st thou, O of little faith,
What to thee the mountain saith,
What is whispered by the trees? —
"Cast on God thy care for these;
Trust him, if thy sight be dim:
Doubt for them is doubt of him.

"Blind must be their close-shut eyes
Where like night the sunshine lies,
Fiery-linked the self-forged chain
Binding ever sin to pain,
Strong their prison-house of will,
But without He waiteth still.

"Not with hatred's undertow
Doth the Love Eternal flow;

Every chain that spirits wear
Crumbles in the breath of prayer;
And the penitent's desire
Opens every gate of fire.

"Still thy love, O Christ arisen!
Yearns to reach these souls in prison?
Through all depths of sin and loss
Drops the plummet of thy cross!
Never yet abyss was found
Deeper than that cross could sound!"

Therefore well may Nature keep
Equal faith with all who sleep,
Set her watch of hills around
Christian grave and heathen mound,
And to cairn and kirkyard send
Summer's flowery dividend.

Keep, O pleasant Melvin stream,
Thy sweet laugh in shade and gleam!
On the Indian's grassy tomb
Swing, O flowers, your bells of bloom!
Deep below, as high above,
Sweeps the circle of God's love.

MY BIRTHDAY.

Beneath the moonlight and the snow
  Lies dead my latest year;
The winter winds are wailing low
  Its dirges in my ear.

I grieve not with the moaning wind
  As if a loss befell;
Before me, even as behind,
  God is, and all is well!

His light shines on me from above,
  His low voice speaks within, —
The patience of immortal love
  Outwearying mortal sin.

Not mindless of the growing years
  Of care and loss and pain,
My eyes are wet with thankful tears
  For blessings which remain.

If dim the gold of life has grown,
  I will not count it dross,
Nor turn from treasures still my own
  To sigh for lack and loss.

The years no charm from Nature take;
  As sweet her voices call,
As beautiful her mornings break,
  As fair her evenings fall.

Love watches o'er my quiet ways,
  Kind voices speak my name,
And lips that find it hard to praise
  Are slow, at least, to blame.

How softly ebb the tides of will!
  How fields, once lost or won,
Now lie behind me green and still
  Beneath a level sun!

How hushed the hiss of party hate,
  The clamor of the throng!
How old, harsh voices of debate
  Flow into rhythmic song!

Methinks the spirit's temper grows
  Too soft in this still air,
Somewhat the restful heart foregoes
  Of needed watch and prayer.

The bark by tempest vainly tossed
  May founder in the calm,
And he who braved the polar frost
  Faint by the isles of balm.

Better than self-indulgent years
  The outflung heart of youth,
Than pleasant songs in idle ears
  The tumult of the truth.

Rest for the weary hands is good,
  And love for hearts that pine,
But let the manly habitude
  Of upright souls be mine.

Let winds that blow from heaven refresh,
  Dear Lord, the languid air;
And let the weakness of the flesh
  Thy strength of spirit share.

And, if the eye must fail of light,
  The ear forget to hear,
Make clearer still the spirit's sight,
  More fine the inward ear!

Be near me in mine hours of need
  To soothe, to cheer, or warn,
And down these slopes of sunset lead
  As up the hills of morn!

THE VANISHERS.

SWEETEST of all childlike dreams
In the simple Indian lore
Still to me the legend seems
Of the shapes who flit before.

Flitting, passing, seen and gone,
Never reached nor found at rest,
Baffling search, but beckoning on
To the Sunset of the Blest.

From the clefts of mountain rocks,
Through the dark of lowland firs,
Flash the eyes and flow the locks
Of the mystic Vanishers!

And the fisher in his skiff,
And the hunter on the moss,
Hear their call from cape and cliff,
See their hands the birch-leaves toss.

Wistful, longing, through the green
Twilight of the clustered pines,
In their faces rarely seen
Beauty more than mortal shines.

Fringed with gold their mantles flow
On the slopes of westering knolls;
In the wind they whisper low
Of the Sunset Land of Souls.

Doubt who may, O friend of mine!
Thou and I have seen them too;
On before with beck and sign
Still they glide, and we pursue.

More than clouds of purple trail
In the gold of setting day;
More than gleams of wing or sail
Beckon from the sea-mist gray.

Glimpses of immortal youth,
Gleams and glories seen and flown,
Far-heard voices sweet with truth,
Airs from viewless Eden blown, —

Beauty that eludes our grasp,
Sweetness that transcends our taste,
Loving hands we may not clasp,
Shining feet that mock our haste, —

Gentle eyes we closed below,
Tender voices heard once more,
Smile and call us, as they go
On and onward, still before.

Guided thus, O friend of mine!
Let us walk our little way,
Knowing by each beckoning sign
That we are not quite astray.

Chase we still, with baffled feet,
Smiling eye and waving hand,
Sought and seeker soon shall meet,
Lost and found, in Sunset Land!

IN SCHOOL-DAYS.

STILL sits the school-house by the road,
A ragged beggar sunning;
Around it still the sumachs grow,
And blackberry-vines are running.

Within, the master's desk is seen,
Deep scarred by raps official;
The warping floor, the battered seats,
The jack-knife's carved initial;

The charcoal frescos on its wall;
Its door's worn sill, betraying
The feet that, creeping slow to school,
Went storming out to playing!

Long years ago a winter sun
Shone over it at setting;
Lit up its western window-panes,
And low eaves' icy fretting.

It touched the tangled golden curls,
And brown eyes full of grieving,
Of one who still her steps delayed
When all the school were leaving.

For near her stood the little boy
Her childish favor singled;
His cap pulled low upon a face
Where pride and shame were mingled.

Pushing with restless feet the snow
To right and left, he lingered;—
As restlessly her tiny hands
The blue-checked apron fingered.

He saw her lift her eyes; he felt
The soft hand's light caressing,
And heard the tremble of her voice,
As if a fault confessing.

"I'm sorry that I spelt the word:
I hate to go above you,

Because," — the brown eyes lower fell, —
"Because, you see, I love you!"

Still memory to a gray-haired man
That sweet child-face is showing.
Dear girl! the grasses on her grave
Have forty years been growing!

He lives to learn, in life's hard school,
How few who pass above him
Lament their triumph and his loss,
Like her, — because they love him.

LAUS DEO!

ON HEARING THE BELLS RING ON THE PASSAGE OF THE CONSTITUTIONAL AMENDMENT ABOLISHING SLAVERY.

It is done!
Clang of bell and roar of gun
Send the tidings up and down.
How the belfries rock and reel!
How the great guns, peal on peal,
Fling the joy from town to town!

Ring, O bells!
Every stroke exulting tells
Of the burial hour of crime.
Loud and long, that all may hear,
Ring for every listening ear
Of Eternity and Time!

Let us kneel:
God's own voice is in that peal,
And this spot is holy ground.
Lord, forgive us! What are we,
That our eyes this glory see,
That our ears have heard the sound!

For the Lord
On the whirlwind is abroad;
In the earthquake he has spoken;
He has smitten with his thunder
The iron walls asunder,
And the gates of brass are broken!

Loud and long
Lift the old exulting song;
Sing with Miriam by the sea
He has cast the mighty down;
Horse and rider sink and drown;
"He hath triumphed gloriously!"

Did we dare,
In our agony of prayer,
Ask for more than He has done?
When was ever his right hand
Over any time or land
Stretched as now beneath the sun?

How they pale,
Ancient myth and song and tale,
In this wonder of our days,
When the cruel rod of war
Blossoms white with righteous law,
And the wrath of man is praise!

Blotted out!
All within and all about
Shall a fresher life begin;
Freer breathe the universe
As it rolls its heavy curse
On the dead and buried sin!

It is done!
In the circuit of the sun
Shall the sound thereof go forth.
It shall bid the sad rejoice,
It shall give the dumb a voice,
It shall belt with joy the earth!

Ring and swing,
Bells of joy! On morning's wing
Send the song of praise abroad!
With a sound of broken chains
Tell the nations that He reigns,
Who alone is Lord and God!

THE EVE OF ELECTION.

From gold to gray
Our mild sweet day
Of Indian summer fades too soon;
But tenderly
Above the sea
Hangs, white and calm, the hunter's moon.

In its pale fire,
The village spire
Shows like the zodiac's spectral lance:
The painted walls
Whereon it falls
Transfigured stand in marble trance!

O'er fallen leaves
The west-wind grieves,
Yet comes a seed-time round again;
And morn shall see
The State sown free
With baleful tares or healthful grain.

Along the street
The shadows meet
Of Destiny, whose hands conceal
The moulds of fate
That shape the state,
And make or mar the common weal.

Around I see
The powers that be;
I stand by Empire's primal springs;
And princes meet
In every street,
And hear the tread of uncrowned kings!

Hark! through the crowd
The laugh runs loud,
Beneath the sad, rebuking moon.
God save the land
A careless hand
May shake or swerve ere morrow's noon!

No jest is this;
One cast amiss
May blast the hope of Freedom's year.
O, take me where
Are hearts of prayer,
And foreheads bowed in reverent fear!

Not lightly fall
Beyond recall
The written scrolls a breath can float;
The crowning fact
The kingliest act
Of Freedom is the freeman's vote!

For pearls that gem
A diadem
The diver in the deep sea dies;
The regal right
We boast to-night
Is ours through costlier sacrifice;

The blood of Vane,
His prison pain
Who traced the path the Pilgrim trod,
And hers whose faith
Drew strength from death,
And prayed her Russell up to God!

Our hearts grow cold,
We lightly hold
A right which brave men died to gain;
The stake, the cord,
The axe, the sword,
Grim nurses at its birth of pain.

The shadow rend,
And o'er us bend,
O martyrs, with your crowns and palms,—
Breathe through these throngs
Your battle songs,
Your scaffold prayers, and dungeon psalms!

Look from the sky,
Like God's great eye,
Thou solemn moon, with searching beam;
Till in the sight
Of thy pure light
Our mean self-seekings meaner seem.

Shame from our hearts
Unworthy arts,
The fraud designed, the purpose dark;
And smite away
The hands we lay
Profanely on the sacred ark.

To party claims
And private aims,
Reveal that august face of Truth,
Whereto are given
The age of heaven,
The beauty of immortal youth.

So shall our voice
Of sovereign choice
Swell the deep bass of duty done,
And strike the key
Of time to be,
When God and man shall speak as one!

WILLIAM ALLINGHAM.

THE TOUCHSTONE.

A MAN there came, whence none could tell,
Bearing a touchstone in his hand;
And tested all things in the land
By its unerring spell.

Quick birth of transmutation smote
The fair to foul, the foul to fair;
Purple nor ermine did he spare,
Nor scorn the dusty coat.

Of heirloom jewels, prized so much,
Were many changed to chips and clods,
And even statues of the gods
Crumbled beneath its touch.

Then angrily the people cried,
"The loss outweighs the profit far;
Our goods suffice us as they are;
We will not have them tried."

And since they could not so avail
To check this unrelenting guest,
They seized him, saying, "Let him test
How real is our jail!"

But, though they slew him with the sword,
And in a fire his touchstone burned,
Its doings could not be o'erturned,
Its undoings restored.

And when, to stop all future harm,
They strewed its ashes on the breeze;
They little guessed each grain of these
Conveyed the perfect charm.

CHARLES MACKAY.

SMALL BEGINNINGS.

A traveller through a dusty road strewed acorns on the lea;
And one took root and sprouted up, and grew into a tree.
Love sought its shade, at evening time, to breathe his early vows;
And age was pleased, in heats of noon, to bask beneath its boughs;
The dormouse loved its dangling twigs, the birds sweet music bore;
It stood a glory in its place, a blessing evermore.

A little spring had lost its way amid the grass and fern,
A passing stranger scooped a well, where weary men might turn;
He walled it in, and hung with care a ladle at the brink;
He thought not of the deed he did, but judged that toil might drink.
He passed again, and lo! the well, by summers never dried,
Had cooled ten thousand parchéd tongues, and saved a life beside.

A dreamer dropped a random thought; 't was old, and yet 't was new;
A simple fancy of the brain, but strong in being true.
It shone upon a genial mind, and, lo! its light became
A lamp of life, a beacon ray, a monitory flame:
The thought was small; its issue great; a watch-fire on the hill;
It sheds its radiance far adown, and cheers the valley still.

A nameless man, amid a crowd that thronged the daily mart,
Let fall a word of Hope and Love, unstudied, from the heart;
A whisper on the tumult thrown,—a transitory breath,—
It raised a brother from the dust; it saved a soul from death.
O germ! O fount! O word of love! O thought at random cast!
Ye were but little at the first, but mighty at the last.

TUBAL CAIN.

Old Tubal Cain was a man of might
In the days when Earth was young;
By the fierce red light of his furnace bright
The strokes of his hammer rung;
And he lifted high his brawny hand
On the iron glowing clear,
Till the sparks rushed out in scarlet showers,
As he fashioned the sword and spear.
And he sang, "Hurrah for my handiwork!
Hurrah for the spear and sword!
Hurrah for the hand that shall wield them well,
For he shall be king and lord!"

To Tubal Cain came many a one,
As he wrought by his roaring fire,
And each one prayed for a strong steel blade
As the crown of his desire:
And he made them weapons sharp and strong,
Till they shouted loud for glee,
And gave him gifts of pearl and gold,
And spoils of the forest free.
And they sang, "Hurrah for Tubal Cain,
Who hath given us strength anew!
Hurrah for the smith, hurrah for the fire,
And hurrah for the metal true!"

But a sudden change came o'er his heart
  Ere the setting of the sun,
And Tubal Cain was filled with pain
  For the evil he had done;
He saw that men, with rage and hate,
  Made war upon their kind,
That the land was red with the blood they shed
  In their lust for carnage blind.
And he said, "Alas! that ever I made,
  Or that skill of mine should plan,
The spear and the sword for men whose joy
  Is to slay their fellow-man."

And for many a day old Tubal Cain
  Sat brooding o'er his woe;
And his hand forbore to smite the ore,
  And his furnace smouldered low.
But he rose at last with a cheerful face,
  And a bright, courageous eye,
And bared his strong right arm for work,
  While the quick flames mounted high.
And he sang, "Hurrah for my handicraft!"
  And the red sparks lit the air;
"Not alone for the blade was the bright steel made";
  And he fashioned the first ploughshare.

OLIVER WENDELL HOLMES.

[U. S. A.]

THE LIVING TEMPLE.

NOT in the world of light alone,
Where God has built his blazing throne,
Nor yet alone in earth below,
With belted seas that come and go,
And endless isles of sunlit green,
Is all thy Maker's glory seen:
Look in upon thy wondrous frame,—
Eternal wisdom still the same!

The smooth, soft air with pulse-like waves
Flows murmuring through its hidden caves,
Whose streams of brightening purple rush,
Fired with a new and livelier blush,
While all their burden of decay
The ebbing current steals away,
And red with Nature's flame they start
From the warm fountains of the heart.

No rest that throbbing slave may ask,
Forever quivering o'er his task,
While far and wide a crimson jet
Leaps forth to fill the woven net
Which in unnumbered crossing tides
The flood of burning life divides,
Then, kindling each decaying part,
Creeps back to find the throbbing heart.

But warmed with that unchanging flame
Behold the outward moving frame,
Its living marbles jointed strong
With glistening band and silvery thong,
And linked to reason's guiding reins
By myriad rings in trembling chains,
Each graven with the threaded zone
Which claims it as the master's own.

See how yon beam of seeming white
Is braided out of seven-hued light,
Yet in those lucid globes no ray
By any chance shall break astray.
Hark how the rolling surge of sound,
Arches and spirals circling round,
Wakes the hushed spirit through thine ear
With music it is heaven to hear.

Then mark the cloven sphere that holds
All thought in its mysterious folds,
That feels sensation's faintest thrill,
And flashes forth the sovereign will;
Think on the stormy world that dwells
Locked in its dim and clustering cells!
The lightning gleams of power it sheds
Along its hollow glassy threads!

O Father! grant thy love divine
To make these mystic temples thine!
When wasting age and wearying strife
Have sapped the leaning walls of life,
When darkness gathers over all,
And the last tottering pillars fall,
Take the poor dust thy mercy warms,
And mould it into heavenly forms!

DOROTHY Q.

A FAMILY PORTRAIT.

GRANDMOTHER's mother; her age, I guess,
Thirteen summers, or something less;
Girlish bust, but womanly air,
Smooth, square forehead, with uprolled hair,
Lips that lover has never kissed,
Taper fingers and slender wrist,

Hanging sleeves of stiff brocade,—
So they painted the little maid.

On her hand a parrot green
Sits unmoving and broods serene;
Hold up the canvas full in view,—
Look! there's a rent the light shines through,
Dark with a century's fringe of dust,—
That was a Redcoat's rapier-thrust!
Such is the tale the lady old,
Dorothy's daughter's daughter, told.

Who the painter was none may tell,—
One whose best was not over well;
Hard and dry, it must be confessed,
Flat as a rose that has long been pressed;
Yet in her cheek the hues are bright,
Dainty colors of red and white;
And in her slender shape are seen
Hint and promise of stately mien.

Look not on her with eyes of scorn,—
Dorothy Q. was a lady born!
Ay! since the galloping Normans came,
England's annals have known her name;
And still to the three-hilled rebel town
Dear is that ancient name's renown,
For many a civic wreath they won,
The youthful sire and the gray-haired son.

O damsel Dorothy! Dorothy Q.!
Strange is the gift that I owe to you;
Such a gift as never a king
Save to daughter or son might bring,—
All my tenure of heart and hand,
All my title to house and land;
Mother and sister, and child and wife,
And joy and sorrow, and death and life!

What if a hundred years ago
Those close-shut lips had answered, No,
When forth the tremulous question came
That cost the maiden her Norman name;
And under the folds that look so still
The bodice swelled with the bosom's thrill?
Should I be I, or would it be
One tenth another to nine tenths me?

Soft is the breath of a maiden's Yes:
Not the light gossamer stirs with less;
But never a cable that holds so fast
Through all the battles of wave and blast,
And never an echo of speech or song
That lives in the babbling air so long!
There were tones in the voice that whispered then
You may hear to-day in a hundred men!

O lady and lover, how faint and far
Your images hover, and here we are,
Solid and stirring in flesh and bone,—
Edward's and Dorothy's—all their own—
A goodly record for time to show
Of a syllable spoken so long ago!—
Shall I bless you, Dorothy, or forgive,
For the tender whisper that bade me live?

It shall be a blessing, my little maid!
I will heal the stab of the Redcoat's blade,
And freshen the gold of the tarnished frame,
And gild with a rhyme your household name,
So you shall smile on us brave and bright
As first you greeted the morning's light,
And live untroubled by woes and fears
Through a second youth of a hundred years.

THE VOICELESS.

We count the broken lyres that rest
Where the sweet wailing singers slumber,
But o'er their silent sister's breast
The wild-flowers who will stoop to number?
A few can touch the magic string,
And noisy Fame is proud to win them:—
Alas for those that never sing,
But die with all their music in them!

Nay, grieve not for the dead alone
Whose song has told their hearts' sad story,—
Weep for the voiceless, who have known
The cross without the crown of glory!
Not where Leucadian's breezes sweep
O'er Sappho's memory-haunted billow,
But where the glistening night-dews weep
On nameless sorrow's churchyard pillow.

O hearts that break and give no sign
Save whitening lip and fading tresses,
Till Death pours out his cordial wine
Slow-dropped from Misery's crushing presses,—
If singing breath or echoing chord
To every hidden pang were given,
What endless melodies were poured,
As sad as earth, as sweet as heaven!

ROBINSON OF LEYDEN.

He sleeps not here; in hope and prayer
His wandering flock had gone before,
But he, the shepherd, might not share
Their sorrows on the wintry shore.

Before the Speedwell's anchor swung,
Ere yet the Mayflower's sail was spread,
While round his feet the Pilgrims clung,
The pastor spake, and thus he said:—

"Men, brethren, sisters, children dear!
God calls you hence from over sea;
Ye may not build by Haerlem Meer,
Nor yet along the Zuyder-Zee.

"Ye go to bear the saving word
To tribes unnamed and shores untrod:
Heed well the lessons ye have heard
From those old teachers taught of God.

"Yet think not unto them was lent
All light for all the coming days,
And Heaven's eternal wisdom spent
In making straight the ancient ways:

"The living fountain overflows
For every flock, for every lamb,
Nor heeds, though angry creeds oppose,
With Luther's dike or Calvin's dam."

He spake: with lingering, long embrace,
With tears of love and partings fond,
They floated down the creeping Maas,
Along the isle of Ysselmond.

They passed the frowning towers of Briel,
The "Hook of Holland's" shelf of sand,
And grated soon with lifting keel
The sullen shores of Fatherland.

No home for these!—too well they knew
The mitred king behind the throne;—
The sails were set, the pennons flew,
And westward ho! for worlds unknown.

—And these were they who gave us birth,
The Pilgrims of the sunset wave,
Who won for us this virgin earth,
And freedom with the soil they gave.

The pastor slumbers by the Rhine,—
In alien earth the exiles lie,—
Their nameless graves our holiest shrine,
His words our noblest battle-cry!

Still cry them, and the world shall hear,
Ye dwellers by the storm-swept sea!
Ye *have* not built by Haerlem Meer,
Nor on the land-locked Zuyder-Zee!

THE DEACON'S MASTERPIECE;

OR, THE WONDERFUL "ONE-HOSS SHAY."

A LOGICAL STORY.

Have you heard of the wonderful one-hoss shay,
That was built in such a logical way
It ran a hundred years to a day,
And then, of a sudden, it—ah, but stay,
I'll tell you what happened without delay,
Scaring the parson into fits,
Frightening people out of their wits,—
Have you ever heard of that, I say?

Seventeen hundred and fifty-five.
Georgius Secundus was then alive,—
Snuffy old drone from the German hive.
That was the year when Lisbon-town
Saw the earth open and gulp her down,
And Braddock's army was done so brown,
Left without a scalp to its crown.
It was on the terrible Earthquake-day
That the Deacon finished the one-hoss shay.

Now in building of chaises, I tell you what,
There is always *somewhere* a weakest spot,—
In hub, tire, felloe, in spring or thill,
In panel, or crossbar, or floor, or sill,
In screw, bolt, thoroughbrace,—lurking still,
Find it somewhere you must and will,—
Above or below, or within or without,—
And that's the reason, beyond a doubt,
A chaise *breaks down*, but does n't *wear out*.

But the Deacon swore (as Deacons do,
With an "I dew vum," or an "I tell *yeou*")
He would build one shay to beat the taown
'n' the keounty 'n' all the kentry raoun';
It should be so built that it *could n'* break daown:
—"Fur," said the Deacon, "'t 's mighty plain

Thut the weakes' place mus' stan' the strain;
'n' the way t' fix it, uz I maintain,
Is only jest
T' make that place uz strong uz the rest."

So the Deacon inquired of the village folk
Where he could find the strongest oak,
That could n't be split nor bent nor broke, —
That was for spokes and floor and sills;
He sent for lancewood to make the thills;
The crossbars were ash, from the straightest trees,
The panels of white-wood, that cuts like cheese,
But lasts like iron for things like these;
The hubs of logs from the "Settler's ellum," —
Last of its timber, — they could n't sell 'em,
Never an axe had seen their chips,
And the wedges flew from between their lips,
Their blunt ends frizzled like celery-tips;
Step and prop-iron, bolt and screw,
Spring, tire, axle, and linchpin too,
Steel of the finest, bright and blue;
Thoroughbrace bison-skin, thick and wide;
Boot, top, dasher, from tough old hide
Found in the pit when the tanner died.
That was the way he "put her through." —
"There!" said the Deacon, "naow she'll dew!"

Do! I tell you, I rather guess
She was a wonder, and nothing less!
Colts grew horses, beards turned gray,
Deacon and deaconess dropped away,
Children and grandchildren, — where were they?
But there stood the stout old one-hoss shay
As fresh as on Lisbon-earthquake-day!

Eighteen hundred; — it came and found
The Deacon's masterpiece strong and sound.
Eighteen hundred increased by ten; —
"Hahnsum kerridge" they called it then.
Eighteen hundred and twenty came; —
Running as usual; much the same.
Thirty and forty at last arrive,
And then come fifty, and fifty-five.

Little of all we value here
Wakes on the morn of its hundredth year
Without both feeling and looking queer.
In fact, there 's nothing that keeps its youth,
So far as I know, but a tree and truth.
(This is a moral that runs at large;
Take it. — You 're welcome. — No extra charge.)

First of November, — the Earthquake-day. —
There are traces of age in the one-hoss shay,
A general flavor of mild decay,
But nothing local as one may say.
That could n't be, — for the Deacon's art
Had made it so like in every part
That there was n't a chance for one to start.
For the wheels were just as strong as the thills,
And the floor was just as strong as the sills,
And the panels just as strong as the floor,
And the whippletree neither less nor more,
And the back-crossbar as strong as the fore,
And spring and axle and hub *encore*.
And yet, *as a whole*, it is past a doubt
In another hour it will be *worn out!*

First of November, 'Fifty-five!
This morning the parson takes a drive.
Now, small boys, get out of the way!
Here comes the wonderful one-hoss shay.
Drawn by a rat-tailed, ewe-necked bay.
"Huddup!" said the parson. — Off went they.

The parson was working his Sunday's text, —
Had got to *fifthly*, and stopped perplexed
At what the — Moses — was coming next.
All at once the horse stood still,
Close by the meet'n'-house on the hill.
— First a shiver, and then a thrill,
Then something decidedly like a spill, —
And the parson was sitting upon a rock,
At half past nine by the meet'n'-house clock, —
Just the hour of the Earthquake shock!
— What do you think the parson found,
When he got up and stared around?
The poor old chaise in a heap or mound,
As if it had been to the mill and ground!
You see, of course, if you 're not a dunce,
How it went to pieces all at once, —

All at once, and nothing first,
Just as bubbles do when they burst.

End of the wonderful one-hoss shay.
Logic is logic. That's all I say.

THE CHAMBERED NAUTILUS.

This is the ship of pearl, which, poets feign,
Sails the unshadowed main, —
The venturous bark that flings
On the sweet summer wind its purpled wings
In gulfs enchanted, where the Siren sings,
And coral reefs lie bare,
Where the cold sea-maids rise to sun their streaming hair.

Its webs of living gauze no more unfurl;
Wrecked is the ship of pearl!
And every chambered cell,
Where its dim dreaming life was wont to dwell,
As the frail tenant shaped his growing shell,
Before thee lies revealed, —
Its irised ceiling rent, its sunless crypt unsealed!

Year after year beheld the silent toil
That spread his lustrous coil;
Still, as the spiral grew,
He left the past year's dwelling for the new,
Stole with soft step its shining archway through,
Built up its idle door,
Stretched in his last-found home, and knew the old no more.

Thanks for the heavenly message brought by thee,
Child of the wandering sea,
Cast from her lap, forlorn!
From thy dead lips a clearer note is born
Than ever Triton blew from wreathèd horn!
While on mine ear it rings,
Through the deep caves of thought I hear a voice that sings: —

Build thee more stately mansions, O my soul,
As the swift seasons roll!
Leave thy low-vaulted past!
Let each new temple, nobler than the last,
Shut thee from heaven with a dome more vast,
Till thou at length art free,
Leaving thine outgrown shell by life's unresting sea!

UNDER THE VIOLETS.

Her hands are cold; her face is white;
No more her pulses come and go;
Her eyes are shut to life and light; —
Fold the white vesture, snow on snow,
And lay her where the violets blow.

But not beneath a graven stone,
To plead for tears with alien eyes;
A slender cross of wood alone
Shall say, that here a maiden lies
In peace beneath the peaceful skies.

And gray old trees of hugest limb
Shall wheel their circling shadows round
To make the scorching sunlight dim
That drinks the greenness from the ground,
And drop their dead leaves on her mound.

When o'er their boughs the squirrels run,
And through their leaves the robins call,
And, ripening in the autumn sun,
The acorns and the chestnuts fall,
Doubt not that she will heed them all.

For her the morning choir shall sing
Its matins from the branches high,
And every minstrel-voice of Spring,
That trills beneath the April sky,
Shall greet her with its earliest cry.

When, turning round their dial-track,
Eastward the lengthening shadows pass,
Her little mourners, clad in black,
The crickets, sliding through the grass,
Shall pipe for her an evening mass.

At last the rootlets of the trees
Shall find the prison where she lies,
And bear the buried dust they seize
In leaves and blossoms to the skies.
So may the soul that warmed it rise!

If any, born of kindlier blood,
  Should ask, What maiden lies below?
Say only this: A tender bud,
  That tried to blossom in the snow,
  Lies withered where the violets blow.

JAMES RUSSELL LOWELL.

[U. S. A.]

THE HERITAGE.

The rich man's son inherits lands,
  And piles of brick, and stone, and gold,
And he inherits soft, white hands,
  And tender flesh that fears the cold,
  Nor dares to wear a garment old;
A heritage, it seems to me,
One scarce would wish to hold in fee.

The rich man's son inherits cares;
  The bank may break, the factory burn,
A breath may burst his bubble shares,
  And soft, white hands could hardly earn
  A living that would serve his turn;
A heritage, it seems to me,
One scarce would wish to hold in fee.

The rich man's son inherits wants,
  His stomach craves for dainty fare;
With sated heart, he hears the pants
  Of toiling hinds with brown arms bare,
  And wearies in his easy chair;
A heritage, it seems to me,
One scarce would wish to hold in fee.

What doth the poor man's son inherit?
  Stout muscles and a sinewy heart,
A hardy frame, a hardier spirit;
  King of two hands, he does his part
  In every useful toil and art;
A heritage, it seems to me,
A king might wish to hold in fee.

What doth the poor man's son inherit?
  Wishes o'erjoyed with humble things,
A rank adjudged by toil-won merit,
  Content that from employment springs,
  A heart that in his labor sings;
A heritage, it seems to me,
A king might wish to hold in fee.

What doth the poor man's son inherit?
  A patience learned by being poor,
Courage, if sorrow come, to bear it,
  A fellow-feeling that is sure
  To make the outcast bless his door;
A heritage, it seems to me,
A king might wish to hold in fee.

O rich man's son! there is a toil,
  That with all others level stands;
Large charity doth never soil,
  But only whiten, soft, white hands,—
  This is the best crop from thy lands;
A heritage, it seems to me,
Worth being rich to hold in fee.

O poor man's son! scorn not thy state;
  There is worse weariness than thine,
In merely being rich and great;
  Toil only gives the soul to shine,
  And makes rest fragrant and benign;
A heritage, it seems to me,
Worth being poor to hold in fee.

Both, heirs to some six feet of sod,
  Are equal in the earth at last;
Both, children of the same dear God,
  Prove title to your heirship vast
  By record of a well-filled past;
A heritage, it seems to me,
Well worth a life to hold in fee.

NEW ENGLAND SPRING.

(From "The Biglow Papers.")

I, country-born an' bred, know where to find
Some blooms thet make the season suit the mind,
An' seem to metch the doubtin' bluebird's notes,—
Half-vent'rin' liverworts in furry coats,
Blood-roots, whose rolled-up leaves ef fur oncurl,
Each on em 's cradle to a baby-pearl,—
But these are jes' Spring's pickets; sure ez sin,
The rebble frosts 'll try to drive 'em in;
For half our May 's so awfully like May n't
'T would rile a Shaker or an evrige saint;
Though I own up I like our back'ard springs
Thet kind o' haggle with their greens an' things,
An' when you 'most give up, 'ithout more words,
Toss the fields full o' blossoms, leaves, an' birds:

Thet 's Northun natur', slow an' apt to doubt,
But when it does git stirred, there 's no gin-out!

Fust come the blackbirds clatt'rin' in tall trees,
An' settlin' things in windy Congresses, —
Queer politicians, though, for I 'll be skinned
Ef all on 'em don't head against the wind.
'Fore long the trees begin to show belief,
The maple crimsons to a coral-reef,
Then saffron swarms swing off from all the willers,
So plump they look like yaller caterpillars,
Then gray hosschesnuts leetle hands unfold
Softer 'n a baby's be a' three days old:
Thet 's robin-redbreast's almanick; he knows
Thet arter this ther' 's only blossom-snows;
So, choosin' out a handy crotch an' spouse,
He goes to plast'rin' his adobë house.

Then seems to come a hitch, — things lag behind,
Till some fine mornin' Spring makes up her mind,
An' ez, when snow-swelled rivers cresh their dams
Heaped up with ice thet dovetails in an' jams,
A leak comes spirtin' thru some pin-hole cleft,
Grows stronger, fercer, tears out right an' left,
Then all the waters bow themselves an' come,
Suddin, in one gret slope o' shedderin foam,
Jes' so our Spring gits everythin' in tune
An' gives one leap from April into June;
Then all comes crowdin' in; afore you think,
Young oak-leaves mist the side-hill woods with pink;
The cat-bird in the laylock-bush is loud;
The orchards turn to heaps o' rosy cloud;
Red-cedars blossom tu, though few folks know it,
An' look all dipt in sunshine like a poet;
The lime-trees pile their solid stacks o' shade
An' drows'ly simmer with the bees' sweet trade;
In ellum shrouds the flashin' hang-bird clings,
An' for the summer vy'ge his hammock slings;
All down the loose-walled lanes in archin' bowers
The barb'ry droops its strings o' golden flowers,
Whose shrinkin' hearts the school-gals love to try
With pins — they 'll worry yourn so, boys, bimeby!
But I don't love your cat'logue style, — do you? —
Ez ef to sell off Natur' by vendoo;
One word with blood in 't 's twice ez good ez two:
Nuff sed, June 's bridesman, poet of the year,
Gladness on wings, the bobolink, is here;
Half hid in tip-top apple-blooms he swings,
Or climbs aginst the breeze with quiverin' wings,
Or, givin' way to 't in a mock despair,
Runs down, a brook o' laughter, thru the air.

THE COURTIN'.

God makes sech nights, all white an' still
Fur 'z you can look or listen,
Moonshine an' snow on field an' hill,
All silence an' all glisten.

Zekle crep' up quite unbeknown
An' peeked in thru the winder,
An' there sot Huldy all alone,
'Ith no one nigh to hender.

A fireplace filled the room's one side
With half a cord o' wood in —
There warnt no stoves (tell comfort died)
To bake ye to a puddin'.

The wa'nut logs shot sparkles out
Towards the pootiest, bless her,
An' leetle flames danced all about
The chiny on the dresser.

Agin the chimbley crook-necks hung,
An' in amongst 'em rusted
The ole queen's-arm thet gran'ther Young
Fetched back from Concord busted.

The very room, coz she was in,
Seemed warm from floor to ceilin',

An' she looked full ez rosy agin
  Ez the apples she was peelin'.

'T was kin' o' kingdom-come to look
  On sech a blessed cretur,
A dogrose blushin' to a brook
  Ain't modester nor sweeter.

He was six foot o' man, A 1,
  Clean grit an' human natur';
None could n't quicker pitch a ton
  Nor dror a furrer straighter.

He 'd sparked it with full twenty gals,
  Hed squired 'em, danced 'em, druv 'em,
Fust this one, an' then thet, by spells —
  All is, he could n't love 'em.

But long o' her his veins 'ould run
  All crinkly like curled maple,
The side she breshed felt full o' sun
  Ez a south slope in Ap'il.

She thought no v'ice hed sech a swing
  Ez hisn in the choir;
My! when he made Ole Hunderd ring,
  She *knowed* the Lord was nigher.

An' she 'd blush scarlit, right in prayer,
  When her new meetin'-bunnet
Felt somehow thru its crown a pair
  O' blue eyes sot upon it.

Thet night, I tell ye, she looked *some!*
  She seemed to 've gut a new soul,
For she felt sartin-sure he 'd come,
  Down to her very shoe-sole.

She heered a foot, an' knowed it tu,
  A-raspin' on the scraper, —
All ways to once her feelins flew
  Like sparks in burnt-up paper.

He kin' o' l'itered on the mat,
  Some doubtfle o' the sekle,
His heart kep' goin' pity-pat,
  But hern went pity Zekle.

An' yit she gin her cheer a jerk
  Ez though she wished him furder,
An' on her apples kep' to work,
  Parin' away like murder.

"You want to see my Pa, I s'pose?"
  "Wal . . . . no . . . . I come da-
  signin'" —
"To see my Ma? She 's sprinklin' clo'es
  Agin to-morrer's i'nin'."

To say why gals act so or so,
  Or don't, 'ould be presumin';
Mebby to mean *yes* an' say *no*
  Comes nateral to women.

He stood a spell on one foot fust,
  Then stood a spell on t' other,
An' on which one he felt the wust
  He could n't ha' told ye nuther.

Says he, "I 'd better call agin";
  Says she, "Think likely, Mister";
Thet last word pricked him like a pin,
  An' . . . . Wal, he up an' kist her.

When Ma bimeby upon 'em slips,
  Huldy sot pale ez ashes,
All kin' o' smily roun' the lips
  An' teary roun' the lashes.

For she was jes' the quiet kind
  Whose naturs never vary,
Like streams that keep a summer mind
  Snowhid in Jenooary.

The blood clost roun' her heart felt glued
  Too tight for all expressin',
Tell mother see how metters stood,
  An' gin 'em both her blessin'.

Then her red come back like the tide
  Down to the Bay o' Fundy,
An' all I know is they was cried
  In meetin' come nex' Sunday.

AMBROSE.

NEVER, surely, was holier man
Than Ambrose, since the world began;
With diet spare and raiment thin
He shielded himself from the father of sin;
With bed of iron and scourgings oft,
His heart to God's hand as wax made soft.

Through earnest prayer and watchings long
He sought to know 'twixt right and wrong,
Much wrestling with the blessed Word
To make it yield the sense of the Lord,
That he might build a storm-proof creed
To fold the flock in at their need.

At last he builded a perfect faith,
Fenced round about with *The Lord thus saith;*
To himself he fitted the doorway's size,
Meted the light to the need of his eyes,

And knew, by a sure and inward sign,
That the work of his fingers was divine.

Then Ambrose said, "All those shall die
The eternal death who believe not as I";
And some were boiled, some burned in fire,
Some sawn in twain, that his heart's desire,
For the good of men's souls, might be satisfied,
By the drawing of all to the righteous side.

One day, as Ambrose was seeking the truth
In his lonely walk, he saw a youth
Resting himself in the shade of a tree;
It had never been given him to see
So shining a face, and the good man thought
'T were pity he should not believe as he ought.

So he set himself by the young man's side,
And the state of his soul with questions tried;
But the heart of the stranger was hardened indeed,
Nor received the stamp of the one true creed,
And the spirit of Ambrose waxed sore to find
Such face the porch of so narrow a mind.

"As each beholds in cloud and fire
The shape that answers his own desire,
So each," said the youth, "in the Law shall find
The figure and features of his mind;
And to each in his mercy hath God allowed
His several pillar of fire and cloud."

The soul of Ambrose burned with zeal
And holy wrath for the young man's weal:
"Believest thou then, most wretched youth,"
Cried he, "a dividual essence in Truth?
I fear me thy heart is too cramped with sin
To take the Lord in his glory in."

Now there bubbled beside them where they stood
A fountain of waters sweet and good;
The youth to the streamlet's brink drew near
Saying, "Ambrose, thou maker of creeds, look here!"

Six vases of crystal then he took,
And set them along the edge of the brook.

"As into these vessels the water I pour,
There shall one hold less, another more,
And the water unchanged, in every case,
Shall put on the figure of the vase;
O thou, who wouldst unity make through strife,
Canst thou fit this sign to the Water of Life?"

When Ambrose looked up, he stood alone,
The youth and the stream and the vases were gone;
But he knew, by a sense of humbled grace,
He had talked with an angel face to face,
And felt his heart change inwardly,
As he fell on his knees beneath the tree.

AFTER THE BURIAL.

Yes, faith is a goodly anchor;
When skies are sweet as a psalm,
At the bows it lolls so stalwart,
In bluff, broad-shouldered calm.

And when over breakers to leeward
The tattered surges are hurled,
It may keep our head to the tempest,
With its grip on the base of the world.

But, after the shipwreck, tell me
What help in its iron thews,
Still true to the broken hawser,
Deep down among sea-weed and ooze?

In the breaking gulfs of sorrow,
When the helpless feet stretch out
And find in the deeps of darkness
No footing so solid as doubt,

Then better one spar of Memory,
One broken plank of the Past,
That our human heart may cling to,
Though hopeless of shore at last!

To the spirit its splendid conjectures,
To the flesh its sweet despair,
Its tears o'er the thin-worn locket
With its anguish of deathless hair!

Immortal? I feel it and know it,
Who doubts it of such as she?
But that is the pang's very secret,—
Immortal away from me.

There 's a narrow ridge in the graveyard
Would scarce stay a child in his race,
But to me and my thought it is wider
Than the star-sown vague of Space.

Your logic, my friend, is perfect,
Your morals most drearily true;
But, since the earth clashed on *her* coffin,
I keep hearing that, and not you.

Console if you will, I can bear it;
'T is a well-meant alms of breath;
But not all the preaching since Adam
Has made Death other than Death.

It is pagan; but wait till you feel it, —
That jar of our earth, that dull shock
When the ploughshare of deeper passion
Tears down to our primitive rock.

Communion in spirit! Forgive me,
But I, who am earthy and weak,
Would give all my incomes from dream-
land
For a touch of her hand on my cheek.

That little shoe in the corner,
So worn and wrinkled and brown,
With its emptiness confutes you,
And argues your wisdom down.

COMMEMORATION ODE.

HARVARD UNIVERSITY, JULY 21, 1865.

. . . . . .

LIFE may be given in many ways,
And loyalty to Truth be sealed
As bravely in the closet as the field,
So generous is Fate;
But then to stand beside her,
When craven churls deride her,
To front a lie in arms, and not to yield, —
This shows, methinks, God's plan
And measure of a stalwart man,
Limbed like the old heroic breeds,
Who stand self-poised on manhood's
solid earth,
Not forced to frame excuses for his
birth,
Fed from within with all the strength he
needs.
Such was he, our Martyr-Chief,
Whom late the Nation he had led,
With ashes on her head,
Wept with the passion of an angry grief:
Forgive me, if from present things I
turn
To speak what in my heart will beat and
burn,
And hang my wreath on his world-hon-
ored urn.
Nature, they say, doth dote,
And cannot make a man
Save on some worn-out plan,
Repeating us by rote:
For him her Old-World moulds aside
she threw,
And, choosing sweet clay from the
breast
Of the unexhausted West,
With stuff untainted shaped a hero new,
Wise, steadfast in the strength of God,
and true.
How beautiful to see
Once more a shepherd of mankind indeed,
Who loved his charge, but never loved
to lead;
One whose meek flock the people joyed
to be,
Not lured by any cheat of birth,
But by his clear-grained human
worth,
And brave old wisdom of sincerity!
They knew that outward grace is
dust;
They could not choose but trust
In that sure-footed mind's unfaltering
skill,
And supple-tempered will
That bent like perfect steel to spring
again and thrust.
His was no lonely mountain-peak
of mind,
Thrusting to thin air o'er our cloudy
bars,
A seamark now, now lost in vapors
blind;
Broad prairie rather, genial, level-
lined,
Fruitful and friendly for all human
kind,
Yet also nigh to Heaven and loved of
loftiest stars.
Nothing of Europe here,
Or, then, of Europe fronting mornward
still,
Ere any names of Serf and Peer
Could Nature's equal scheme deface;
Here was a type of the true elder
race,
And one of Plutarch's men talked with
us face to face.

I praise him not; it were too late;
And some innative weakness there must be
In him who condescends to victory
Such as the Present gives, and cannot wait,
Safe in himself as in a fate.
So always firmly he:
He knew to bide his time,
And can his fame abide,
Still patient in his simple faith sublime,
Till the wise years decide.
Great captains, with their guns and drums,
Disturb our judgment for the hour,
But at last silence comes:
These all are gone, and, standing like a tower,
Our children shall behold his fame,
The kindly-earnest, brave, foreseeing man,
Sagacious, patient, dreading praise, not blame,
New birth of our new soil, the first American.

. . . . .

We sit here in the Promised Land
That flows with Freedom's honey and milk:
But 't was they won it, sword in hand,
Making the nettle danger soft for us as silk.
We welcome back our bravest and our best;—
Ah, me! not all! some come not with the rest,
Who went forth brave and bright as any here!
I strive to mix some gladness with my strain,
But the sad strings complain,
And will not please the ear;
I sweep them for a pæan, but they wane
Again and yet again
Into a dirge, and die away in pain.
In these brave ranks I only see the gaps,
Thinking of dear ones whom the dumb turf wraps,
Dark to the triumph which they died to gain:
Fitlier may others greet the living,
For me the past is unforgiving;
I with uncovered head
Salute the sacred dead,
Who went, and who return not.—
Say not so!
'T is not the grapes of Canaan that repay,
But the high faith that failed not by the way;
Virtue treads paths that end not in the grave;
No bar of endless night exiles the brave;
And to the saner mind
We rather seem the dead that stayed behind.
Blow, trumpets, all your exultations blow!
For never shall their aureoled presence lack:
I see them muster in a gleaming row,
With ever-youthful brows that nobler show;
We find in our dull road their shining track;
In every nobler mood
We feel the orient of their spirit glow,
Part of our life's unalterable good,
Of all our saintlier aspiration;
They come transfigured back,
Secure from change in their high-hearted ways,
Beautiful evermore, and with the rays
Of morn on their white Shields of Expectation!

MARIA WHITE LOWELL.

[U. S. A., 1821-1853.]

THE ALPINE SHEEP.

When on my ear your loss was knelled,
And tender sympathy upburst,
A little spring from memory welled,
Which once had quenched my bitter thirst.

And I was fain to bear to you
A portion of its mild relief,
That it might be as healing dew,
To steal some fever from your grief.

After our child's untroubled breath
Up to the Father took its way,
And on our home the shade of Death
Like a long twilight haunting lay,

And friends came round, with us to weep
Her little spirit's swift remove,
The story of the Alpine sheep
Was told to us by one we love.

They, in the valley's sheltering care,
Soon crop the meadow's tender prime,
And when the sod grows brown and bare,
The shepherd strives to make them climb

To airy shelves of pasture green,
That hang along the mountain's side,
Where grass and flowers together lean,
And down through mist the sunbeams slide.

But naught can tempt the timid things
The steep and rugged paths to try,
Though sweet the shepherd calls and sings,
And seared below the pastures lie,

Till in his arms their lambs he takes,
Along the dizzy verge to go;
Then, heedless of the rifts and breaks,
They follow on, o'er rock and snow.

And in those pastures, lifted fair,
More dewy-soft than lowland mead,
The shepherd drops his tender care,
And sheep and lambs together feed.

This parable, by Nature breathed,
Blew on me as the south-wind free
O'er frozen brooks, that flow unsheathed
From icy thraldom to the sea.

A blissful vision, through the night,
Would all my happy senses sway,
Of the good Shepherd on the height,
Or climbing up the starry way,

Holding our little lamb asleep, —
While, like the murmur of the sea,
Sounded that voice along the deep,
Saying, "Arise and follow me!"

THOMAS W. PARSONS.

[U. S. A.]

CAMPANILE DE PISA.

Snow was glistening on the mountains, but the air was that of June,
Leaves were falling, but the runnels playing still their summer tune,
And the dial's lazy shadow hovered nigh the brink of noon.
On the benches in the market, rows of languid idlers lay,
When to Pisa's nodding belfry, with a friend, I took my way.

From the top we looked around us, and as far as eye might strain,
Saw no sign of life or motion in the town, or on the plain,
Hardly seemed the river moving, through the willows to the main;
Nor was any noise disturbing Pisa from her drowsy hour,
Save the doves that fluttered 'neath us, in and out and round the tower.

Not a shout from gladsome children, or the clatter of a wheel,
Nor the spinner of the suburb, winding his discordant reel,
Nor the stroke upon the pavement of a hoof or of a heel.
Even the slumberers, in the churchyard of the Campo Santo seemed
Scarce more quiet than the living world that underneath us dreamed.

Dozing at the city's portal, heedless guard the sentry kept,
More than oriental dulness o'er the sunny farms had crept,
Near the walls the ducal herdsman by the dusty roadside slept;
While his camels, resting round him, half alarmed the sullen ox,
Seeing those Arabian monsters pasturing with Etruria's flocks.

Then it was, like one who wandered, lately, singing by the Rhine,
Strains perchance to maiden's hearing sweeter than this verse of mine,
That we bade Imagination lift us on her wing divine.
And the days of Pisa's greatness rose from the sepulchral past,
When a thousand conquering galleys bore her standard at the mast.

Memory for a moment crowned her sovereign mistress of the seas,
When she braved, upon the billows, Venice and the Genoese,
Daring to deride the Pontiff, though he shook his angry keys.

When her admirals triumphant, riding o'er the Soldan's waves,
Brought from Calvary's holy mountain fitting soil for knightly graves.

When the Saracen surrendered, one by one, his pirate isles,
And Ionia's marbled trophies decked Lungarno's Gothic piles,
Where the festal music floated in the light of ladies' smiles;
Soldiers in the busy court-yard, nobles in the hall above,
O, those days of arms are over,—arms and courtesy and love!

Down in yonder square at sunrise, lo! the Tuscan troops arrayed,
Every man in Milan armor, forged in Brescia every blade:
Sigismondi is their captain—Florence! art thou not dismayed?
There 's Lanfranchi! there the bravest of Gherardesca stem,
Hugolino—with the bishop; but enough, enough of them.

Now, as on Achilles' buckler, next a peaceful scene succeeds;
Pious crowds in the cathedral duly tell their blessed beads;
Students walk the learned cloister; Ariosto wakes the reeds;
Science dawns; and Galileo opens to the Italian youth,
As he were a new Columbus, new discovered realms of truth.

Hark; what murmurs from the million in the bustling market rise!
All the lanes are loud with voices, all the windows dark with eyes;
Black with men the marble bridges, heaped the shores with merchandise;
Turks and Greeks and Libyan merchants in the square their councils hold,
And the Christian altars glitter gorgeous with Byzantine gold.

Look! anon the masqueraders don their holiday attire;
Every palace is illumined,—all the town seems built of fire,—
Rainbow-colored lanterns dangle from the top of every spire.
Pisa's patron saint hath hallowed to himself the joyful day,
Never on the thronged Rialto showed the Carnival more gay.

Suddenly the bell beneath us broke the vision with its chime;
"Signors," quoth our gray attendant, "it is almost vesper time";
Vulgar life resumed its empire,—down we dropt from the sublime.
Here and there a friar passed us, as we paced the silent streets,
And a cardinal's rumbling carriage roused the sleepers from the seats.

ON A BUST OF DANTE.

SEE, from this counterfeit of him
Whom Arno shall remember long,
How stern of lineament, how grim
The father was of Tuscan song.
There but the burning sense of wrong,
Perpetual care and scorn abide;
Small friendship for the lordly throng;
Distrust of all the world beside.

Faithful if this wan image be,
No dream his life was,—but a fight;
Could any BEATRICE see
A lover in that anchorite?
To that cold Ghibeline's gloomy sight
Who could have guessed the visions came
Of beauty, veiled with heavenly light,
In circles of eternal flame?

The lips, as Cumæ's cavern close,
The cheeks, with fast and sorrow thin,
The rigid front, almost morose,
But for the patient hope within,
Declare a life whose course hath been
Unsullied still, though still severe,
Which, through the wavering days of sin,
Keep itself icy-chaste and clear.

Not wholly such his haggard look
When wandering once, forlorn he strayed,
With no companion save his book,
To Corvo's hushed monastic shade:
Where, as the Benedictine laid
His palm upon the pilgrim-guest,
The single boon for which he prayed
The convent's charity was rest.

Peace dwells not here, —this rugged face
 Betrays no spirit of repose;
The sullen warrior sole we trace,
 The marble man of many woes.
Such was his mien when first arose
 The thought of that strange tale divine,
When hell he peopled with his foes,
 The scourge of many a guilty line.

War to the last he waged with all
 The tyrant canker-worms of earth;
Baron and duke, in hold and hall,
 Cursed the dark hour that gave him birth;
He used Rome's harlot for his mirth;
 Plucked bare hypocrisy and crime;
But valiant souls of knightly worth
 Transmitted to the rolls of Time.

O Time! whose verdicts mock our own,
 The only righteous judge art thou;
That poor old exile, sad and lone,
 Is Latium's other Virgil now:
Before his name the nations bow:
 His words are parcel of mankind,
Deep in whose hearts, as on his brow,
 The marks have sunk of DANTE'S mind.

JOHN G. SAXE.

[U. S. A.]

WISHING.

OF all amusements for the mind,
 From logic down to fishing,
There is n't one that you can find
 So very cheap as "wishing."
A very choice diversion too,
 If we but rightly use it,
And not, as we are apt to do,
 Pervert it, and abuse it.

I wish — a common wish, indeed —
 My purse were somewhat fatter,
That I might cheer the child of need,
 And not my pride to flatter;
That I might make Oppression reel,
 As only gold can make it,
And break the Tyrant's rod of steel,
 As only gold can break it.

I wish — that Sympathy and Love,
 And every human passion
That has its origin above,
 Would come and keep in fashion;
That Scorn and Jealousy and Hate,
 And every base emotion,
Were buried fifty fathom deep
 Beneath the waves of Ocean!

I wish — that friends were always true,
 And motives always pure;
I wish the good were not so few,
 I wish the bad were fewer;
I wish that parsons ne'er forgot
 To heed their pious teaching;
I wish that practising was not
 So different from preaching!

I wish — that modest worth might be
 Appraised with truth and candor;
I wish that innocence were free
 From treachery and slander;
I wish that men their vows would mind;
 That women ne'er were rovers;
I wish that wives were always kind,
 And husbands always lovers!

I wish — in fine — that Joy and Mirth,
 And every good Ideal,
May come erewhile throughout the earth
 To be the glorious Real;
Till God shall every creature bless
 With his supremest blessing,
And Hope be lost in Happiness,
 And Wishing in Possessing!

SLEEP AND DEATH.

Two wandering angels, Sleep and Death,
 Once met in sunny weather:
And while the twain were taking breath,
 They held discourse together.

Quoth Sleep (whose face, though twice as fair,
 Was strangely like the other's, —
So like, in sooth, that anywhere
 They might have passed for brothers):

"A busy life is mine, I trow;
 Would I were omnipresent!
So fast and far have I to go;
 And yet my work is pleasant.

"I cast my potent poppies forth,
 And lo! — the cares that cumber

The toiling, suffering sons of earth
Are drowned in sweetest slumber.

"The student rests his weary brain,
And waits the fresher morrow;
I ease the patient of his pain,
The mourner of his sorrow.

"I bar the gates where cares abide,
And open Pleasure's portals
To visioned joys; thus, far and wide,
I earn the praise of mortals."

"Alas!" replied the other, "mine
Is not a task so grateful;
Howe'er to mercy I incline,
To mortals I am hateful.

"They call me 'Kill-joy,' every one,
And speak in sharp detraction
Of all I do; yet have I done
Full many a kindly action."

"True!" answered Sleep, "but all the while
Thine office is berated,
'T is only by the vile and weak
That thou art feared and hated.

"And though thy work on earth has given
To all a shade of sadness;
Consider — every saint in heaven
Remembers thee with gladness!"

SARAH HELEN WHITMAN.

[U. S. A.]

A STILL DAY IN AUTUMN.

I LOVE to wander through the woodlands hoary
In the soft light of an autumnal day,
When Summer gathers up her robes of glory,
And like a dream of beauty glides away.

How through each loved, familiar path she lingers,
Serenely smiling through the golden mist,
Tinting the wild grape with her dewy fingers
Till the cool emerald turns to amethyst:

Kindling the faint stars of the hazel, shining
To light the gloom of Autumn's mouldering halls
With hoary plumes the clematis entwining
Where o'er the rock her withered garland falls.

Warm lights are on the sleepy uplands waning
Beneath soft clouds along the horizon rolled,
Till the slant sunbeams through their fringes raining
Bathe all the hills in melancholy gold.

The moist winds breathe of crispéd leaves and flowers
In the damp hollows of the woodland sown,
Mingling the freshness of autumnal showers
With spicy airs from cedarn alleys blown.

Beside the brook and on the umbered meadow,
Where yellow fern-tufts fleck the faded ground,
With folded lids beneath their palmy shadow
The gentian nods, in dewy slumbers bound.

Upon those soft, fringed lids the bee sits brooding,
Like a fond lover loath to say farewell,
Or with shut wings, through silken folds intruding,
Creeps near her heart his drowsy tale to tell.

The little birds upon the hillside lonely
Flit noiselessly along from spray to spray,
Silent as a sweet wandering thought that only
Shows its bright wings and softly glides away.

ALFRED B. STREET.

[U. S. A.]

THE SETTLER.

His echoing axe the settler swung
Amid the sea-like solitude,
And, rushing, thundering, down were flung
The Titans of the wood;
Loud shrieked the eagle, as he dashed
From out his mossy nest, which crashed
With its supporting bough,
And the first sunlight, leaping, flashed
On the wolf's haunt below.

Rude was the garb, and strong the frame
Of him who plied his ceaseless toil:
To form that garb the wild-wood game
Contributed their spoil;
The soul that warmed that frame disdained
The tinsel, gaud, and glare, that reigned
Where men their crowds collect;
The simple fur, untrimmed, unstained,
This forest-tamer decked.

The paths which wound mid gorgeous trees,
The stream whose bright lips kissed their flowers,
The winds that swelled their harmonies
Through those sun-hiding bowers,
The temple vast, the green arcade,
The nestling vale, the grassy glade,
Dark cave, and swampy lair:
These scenes and sounds majestic made
His world, his pleasures, there.

His roof adorned a pleasant spot,
Mid the black logs green glowed the grain,
And herbs and plants the woods knew not
Throve in the sun and rain.
The smoke-wreath curling o'er the dell,
The low, the bleat, the tinkling bell,
All made a landscape strange,
Which was the living chronicle
Of deeds that wrought the change.

The violet sprung at spring's first tinge,
The rose of summer spread its glow,
The maize hung out its autumn fringe,
Rude winter brought his snow;
And still the lone one labored there,
His shout and whistle broke the air,
As cheerily he plied
His garden-spade, or drove his share
Along the hillock's side.

He marked the fire-storm's blazing flood
Roaring and crackling on its path,
And scorching earth, and melting wood,
Beneath its greedy wrath;
He marked the rapid whirlwind shoot,
Trampling the pine-tree with its foot,
And darkening thick the day
With streaming bough and severed root,
Hurled whizzing on its way.

His gaunt hound yelled, his rifle flashed,
The grim bear hushed his savage growl;
In blood and and foam the panther gnashed
His fangs, with dying howl;
The fleet deer ceased its flying bound,
Its snarling wolf-foe bit the ground,
And, with its moaning cry,
The beaver sank beneath the wound
Its pond-built Venice by.

Humble the lot, yet his the race,
When Liberty sent forth her cry,
Who thronged in conflict's deadliest place,
To fight, —to bleed, —to die!
Who cumbered Bunker's height of red,
By hope through weary years were led,
And witnessed Yorktown's sun
Blaze on a nation's banner spread,
A nation's freedom won.

CHRISTOPHER P. CRANCH.

[U. S. A.]

STANZAS.

Thought is deeper than all speech,
Feeling deeper than all thought;
Souls to souls can never teach
What unto themselves was taught.

We are spirits clad in veils;
Man by man was never seen;
All our deep communing fails
To remove the shadowy screen.

Heart to heart was never known,
Mind with mind did never meet;

We are columns left alone
  Of a temple once complete.

Like the stars that gem the sky,
  Far apart, though seeming near,
In our light we scattered lie;
  All is thus but starlight here.

What is social company
  But a babbling summer stream?
What our wise philosophy
  But the glancing of a dream?

Only when the sun of love
  Melts the scattered stars of thought;
Only when we live above
  What the dim-eyed world hath taught;

Only when our souls are fed
  By the Fount which gave them birth,
And by inspiration led,
  Which they never drew from earth.

We like parted drops of rain
  Swelling till they meet and run,
Shall be all absorbed again,
  Melting, flowing into one.

WILLIAM E. CHANNING.

[U. S. A.]

SLEEPY HOLLOW.

No abbey's gloom, nor dark cathedral stoops,
  No winding torches paint the midnight air;
Here the green pines delight, the aspen droops
  Along the modest pathways, and those fair
Pale asters of the season spread their plumes
  Around this field, fit garden for our tombs.

And shalt thou pause to hear some funeral bell
  Slow stealing o'er thy heart in this calm place,
Not with a throb of pain, a feverish knell,
  But in its kind and supplicating grace,
It says, Go, pilgrim, on thy march, be more
  Friend to the friendless than thou wast before;

Learn from the loved one's rest serenity;
  To-morrow that soft bell for thee shall sound,
And thou repose beneath the whispering tree,
  One tribute more to this submissive ground;—
Prison thy soul from malice, bar out pride,
  Nor these pale flowers nor this still field deride:

Rather to those ascents of being turn,
  Where a ne'er-setting sun illumes the year
Eternal, and the incessant watch-fires burn
  Of unspent holiness and goodness clear,—
Forget man's littleness, deserve the best,
  God's mercy in thy thought and life confest.

JULIA WARD HOWE.

[U. S. A.]

FROM "A TRIBUTE TO A SERVANT."

Not often to the parting soul
Does Life in dreary grimness show;
Earth's captive, leaving prison-walls,
Beholds them touched with sunset glow.

And she forgot her sleepless nights,
Her weary tasks of foot and hand,
And, soothed with thoughts of pleasantness,
Lay floating towards the silent land.

The talk of comfortable hours,
The merry dancing tunes I played,
Gay banquets with the children shared,
And summer days in greenwood shade,—

They lay far scattered in the past,
Through the dim vista of disease;
But when I spake, and held her hand,
The parting cloud showed things like these.

I questioned not her peace with God,
Nor pried into her guiltless mind,
Like those unskilful surgeon-priests
Who rack the soul with probings blind.

For I 've seen men who meant not ill
Compelling doctrine out of Death,
With Hell and Heaven acutely poised
Upon the turning of a breath;

While agonizing judgments hung
Ev'n on the Saviour's helpful name;
As mild Madonna's form, of old,
A hideous torture-tool became.

I could but say, with faltering voice
And eyes that glanced aside to weep,
"Be strong in faith and hope, my child;
He giveth his belovéd sleep.

"And though thou walk the shadowy vale
Whose end we know not, He will aid;
His rod and staff shall stay thy steps."
"I know it well," she smiled and said.

She knew it well, and knew yet more
My deepest hope, though unexprest,
The hope that God's appointed sleep
But heightens ravishment with rest.

My children, living flowers, shall come
And strew with seed this grave of thine,
And bid the blushing growths of Spring
Thy dreary painted cross entwine.

Thus Faith, cast out of barren creeds,
Shall rest in emblems of her own;
Beauty still springing from Decay,
The cross-wood budding to the crown.

BATTLE HYMN OF THE REPUBLIC.

MINE eyes have seen the glory of the coming of the Lord:
He is trampling out the vintage where the grapes of wrath are stored;
He hath loosed the fateful lightning of his terrible swift sword;
His truth is marching on.

I have seen him in the watch-fires of a hundred circling camps;
They have builded him an altar in the evening dews and damps;
I can read his righteous sentence by the dim and flaring lamps.
His day is marching on.

I have read a fiery gospel, writ in burnished rows of steel:
"As ye deal with my contemners, so with you my grace shall deal;
Let the Hero, born of woman, crush the serpent with his heel,
Since God is marching on."

He has sounded forth the trumpet that shall never call retreat;
He is sifting out the hearts of men before his judgment-seat:
O, be swift, my soul, to answer him! be jubilant, my feet!
Our God is marching on.

In the beauty of the lilies Christ was born across the sea,
With a glory in his bosom that transfigures you and me:
As he died to make men holy, let us die to make men free,
While God is marching on.

H. D. THOREAU.

[U. S. A.]

INSPIRATION.

IF with light head erect I sing,
Though all the Muses lend their force,
From my poor love of anything,
The verse is weak and shallow as its source.

But if with bended neck I grope,
Listening behind me for my wit,
With faith superior to hope,
More anxious to keep back than forward it;

Making my soul accomplice there
Unto the flame my heart hath lit,
Then will the verse forever wear, —
Time cannot bend the line which God has writ.

I hearing get, who had but ears,
And sight, who had but eyes before;

I moments live, who lived but years,
And truth discern, who knew but learning's lore.

Now chiefly is my natal hour,
And only now my prime of life,
Of manhood's strength it is the flower,
'T is peace's end, and war's beginning strife.

It comes in summer's broadest noon,
By a gray wall, or some chance place,
Unseasoning time, insulting June,
And vexing day with its presuming face.

I will not doubt the love untold
Which not my worth nor want hath bought,
Which wooed me young, and wooed me old,
And to this evening hath me brought.

ELIZABETH LLOYD HOWELL.

[U. S. A.]

MILTON'S PRAYER IN BLINDNESS.

I AM old and blind!
Men point at me as smitten by God's frown;
Afflicted and deserted of my kind;
Yet I am not cast down.

I am weak, yet strong;
I murmur not that I no longer see;
Poor, old, and helpless, I the more belong,
Father supreme! to thee.

O merciful One!
When men are farthest, then thou art most near;
When friends pass by me, and my weakness shun,
Thy chariot I hear.

Thy glorious face
Is leaning toward me; and its holy light
Shines in upon my lonely dwelling-place, —
And there is no more night.

On my bended knee
I recognize thy purpose clearly shown:
My vision thou hast dimmed, that I may see
Thyself, — thyself alone.

I have naught to fear;
This darkness is the shadow of thy wing;
Beneath it I am almost sacred; here
Can come no evil thing.

O, I seem to stand
Trembling, where foot of mortal ne'er hath been,
Wrapped in the radiance of thy sinless land,
Which eye hath never seen!

Visions come and go:
Shapes of resplendent beauty round me throng;
From angel lips I seem to hear the flow
Of soft and holy song.

It is nothing now,
When heaven is opening on my sightless eyes? —
When airs from paradise refresh my brow,
The earth in darkness lies.

In a purer clime
My being fills with rapture, — waves of thought
Roll in upon my spirit, — strains sublime
Break over me unsought.

Give me my lyre!
I feel the stirrings of a gift divine:
Within my bosom glows unearthly fire,
Lit by no skill of mine.

C. F. ALEXANDER.

THE BURIAL OF MOSES.

BY Nebo's lonely mountain
On this side Jordan's wave,
In a vale in the land of Moab
There lies a lonely grave.
And no man knows that sepulchre,
And no man saw it e'er,
For the angels of God upturned the sod,
And laid the dead man there.

That was the grandest funeral
That ever passed on earth ;
But no man heard the trampling,
Or saw the train go forth :
Noiselessly as the daylight
Comes back when night is done,
And the crimson streak on ocean's cheek
Grows into the great sun.

Noiselessly as the spring-time
Her crown of verdure weaves,
And all the trees on all the hills
Open their thousand leaves ;
So without sound of music
Or voice of them that wept,
Silently down from the mountain's crown
The great procession swept.

Perchance the bald old eagle
On gray Beth-Peor's height,
Out of his lonely eyrie
Looked on the wondrous sight ;
Perchance the lion, stalking,
Still shuns that hallowed spot,
For beast and bird have seen and heard
That which man knoweth not.

But when the warrior dieth,
His comrades in the war,
With arms reversed and muffled drum,
Follow his funeral car ;
They show the banners taken,
They tell his battles won,
And after him lead his masterless steed,
While peals the minute-gun.

Amid the noblest of the land,
We lay the sage to rest,
And give the bard an honored place
With costly marble drest,
In the great minster transept
Where lights like glories fall,
And the organ rings and the sweet choir sings
Along the emblazoned wall.

This was the truest warrior
That ever buckled sword,
This the most gifted poet
That ever breathed a word ;
And never earth's philosopher
Traced with his golden pen,
On the deathless page, truths half so sage
As he wrote down for men.

And had he not high honor, —
The hillside for a pall
To lie in state while angels wait
With stars for tapers tall,
And the dark rock-pines like tossing plumes
Over his bier to wave,
And God's own hand, in that lonely land,
To lay him in the grave ?

In that strange grave without a name
Whence his uncoffined clay
Shall break again, O wondrous thought !
Before the judgment-day,
And stand with glory wrapt around
On the hills he never trod,
And speak of the strife that won our life
With the Incarnate Son of God.

O lonely grave in Moab's land !
O dark Beth-Peor's hill !
Speak to these cúrious hearts of ours,
And teach them to be still.
God hath his mysteries of grace,
Ways that we cannot tell ;
He hides them deep, like the hidden sleep
Of him he loved so well.

E. H. SEARS.

[U. S. A.]

CHRISTMAS HYMN.

Calm on the listening ear of night
Come Heaven's melodious strains,
Where wild Judæa stretches far
Her silver-mantled plains !

Celestial choirs, from courts above,
Shed sacred glories there ;
And angels, with their sparkling lyres,
Make music on the air.

The answering hills of Palestine
Send back the glad reply ;
And greet, from all their holy heights,
The dayspring from on high.

On the blue depths of Galilee
There comes a holier calm,
And Sharon waves, in solemn praise,
Her silent groves of palm.

"Glory to God!" the sounding skies
Loud with their anthems ring;
Peace to the earth, good-will to men,
From heaven's Eternal King!

Light on thy hills, Jerusalem!
The Saviour now is born!
And bright on Bethlehem's joyous plains
Breaks the first Christmas morn.

THEODORE PARKER.

[U. S. A., 1812–1860.]

THE WAY, THE TRUTH, AND THE LIFE.

O THOU great Friend to all the sons of men,
Who once appeared in humblest guise below,
Sin to rebuke, to break the captive's chain,
And call thy brethren forth from want and woe, —

We look to thee! thy truth is still the Light
Which guides the nations, groping on their way,
Stumbling and falling in disastrous night,
Yet hoping ever for the perfect day.

Yes; thou art still the Life, thou art the Way
The holiest know; Light, Life, the Way of heaven!
And they who dearest hope and deepest pray
Toil by the Light, Life, Way, which thou hast given.

FREDERIC WILLIAM FABER.

[1815–1863.]

THE WILL OF GOD.

I WORSHIP thee, sweet Will of God!
And all thy ways adore,
And every day I live I seem
To love thee more and more.

When obstacles and trials seem
Like prison-walls to be,
I do the little I can do,
And leave the rest to thee.

I have no cares, O blessed Will!
For all my cares are thine;
I live in triumph, Lord! for thou
Hast made thy triumphs mine.

And when it seems no chance or change
From grief can set me free,
Hope finds its strength in helplessness,
And gayly waits on thee.

Man's weakness waiting upon God
Its end can never miss,
For men on earth no work can do
More angel-like than this.

He always wins who sides with God,
To him no chance is lost;
God's will is sweetest to him when
It triumphs at his cost.

Ill that he blesses is our good,
And unblest good is ill;
And all is right that seems most wrong,
If it be his sweet Will!

THE RIGHT MUST WIN.

O, IT is hard to work for God,
To rise and take his part
Upon this battle-field of earth,
And not sometimes lose heart!

He hides himself so wondrously,
As though there were no God;
He is least seen when all the powers
Of ill are most abroad.

Or he deserts us at the hour
The fight is all but lost;
And seems to leave us to ourselves
Just when we need him most.

Ill masters good, good seems to change
To ill with greatest ease;
And, worst of all, the good with good
Is at cross-purposes.

Ah! God is other than we think;
His ways are far above,
Far beyond reason's height, and reached
Only by childlike love.

Workman of God! O, lose not heart,
But learn what God is like;
And in the darkest battle-field
Thou shalt know where to strike.

Thrice blest is he to whom is given
The instinct that can tell
That God is on the field when he
Is most invisible.

Blest, too, is he who can divine
Where real right doth lie,
And dares to take the side that seems
Wrong to man's blindfold eye.

For right is right, since God is God;
And right the day must win;
To doubt would be disloyalty,
To falter would be sin!

DAVID A. WASSON.

[U. S. A.]

SEEN AND UNSEEN.

The wind ahead, the billows high,
A whited wave, but sable sky,
And many a league of tossing sea,
Between the hearts I love and me.

The wind ahead: day after day
These weary words the sailors say;
To weeks the days are lengthened now, —
Still mounts the surge to meet our prow.

Through longing day and lingering night
I still accuse Time's lagging flight,
Or gaze out o'er the envious sea,
That keeps the hearts I love from me.

Yet, ah, how shallow is all grief!
How instant is the deep relief!
And what a hypocrite am I,
To feign forlorn, to 'plain and sigh!

The wind ahead? The wind is free!
Forevermore it favoreth me, —
To shores of God still blowing fair,
O'er seas of God my bark doth bear.

The surging brine *I* do not sail,
This blast adverse is not my gale;
'T is here I only seem to be,
But really sail another sea, —

Another sea, pure sky its waves,
Whose beauty hides no heaving graves, —
A sea all haven, whereupon
No hapless bark to wreck hath gone.

The winds that o'er my ocean run,
Reach through all heavens beyond the sun;
Through life and death, through fate, through time,
Grand breaths of God they sweep sublime.

Eternal trades, they cannot veer,
And blowing, teach us how to steer;
And well for him whose joy, whose care,
Is but to keep before them fair.

O, thou God's mariner, heart of mine,
Spread canvas to the airs divine!
Spread sail! and let thy Fortune be
Forgotten in thy Destiny!

For Destiny pursues us well,
By sea, by land, through heaven or hell;
It suffers Death alone to die,
Bids life all change and chance defy.

Would earth's dark ocean suck thee down?
Earth's ocean thou, O Life, shalt drown,
Shalt flood it with thy finer wave,
And, sepulchred, entomb thy grave!

Life loveth life and good: then trust
What most the spirit would, it must;
Deep wishes, in the heart that be,
Are blossoms of necessity.

A thread of Law runs through thy prayer,
Stronger than iron cables are;
And Love and Longing toward her goal,
Are pilots sweet to guide the soul.

So Life must live, and Soul must sail,
And Unseen over Seen prevail,
And all God's argosies come to shore,
Let ocean smile, or rage and roar.

And so, mid storm or calm, my bark
With snowy wake still nears her mark;
Cheerly the trades of being blow,
And sweeping down the wind I go.

ALL 'S WELL.

SWEET-VOICÉD Hope, thy fine discourse
Foretold not half life's good to me:
Thy painter, Fancy, hath not force
To show how sweet it is to Be!
Thy witching dream
And pictured scheme
To match the fact still want the power;
Thy promise brave
From birth to grave
Life's boon may beggar in an hour.

Ask and receive, —'t is sweetly said;
Yet what to plead for know I not;
For Wish is worsted, Hope o'ersped,
And aye to thanks returns my thought.
If I would pray,
I 've naught to say
But this, that God may be God still;
For Him to live
Is still to give,
And sweeter than my wish His will.

O wealth of life, beyond all bound!
Eternity each moment given!
What plummet may the Present sound?
Who promises a *future* heaven?
Or glad, or grieved,
Oppressed, relieved,
In blackest night, or brightest day,
Still pours the flood
Of golden good,
And more than heart-full fills me aye.

My wealth is common; I possess
No petty province, but the whole;
What 's mine alone is mine far less
Than treasure shared by every soul.
Talk not of store,
Millions or more, —
Of values which the purse may hold, —
But this divine!
I own the mine
Whose grains outweigh a planet's gold.

I have a stake in every star,
In every beam that fills the day;
All hearts of men my coffers are,
My ores arterial tides convey;
The fields, the skies,
And sweet replies
Of thought to thought are my gold dust, —
The oaks, the brooks,
And speaking looks
Of lovers' faith and friendship's trust.

Life's youngest tides joy-brimming flow
For him who lives above all years,
Who all-immortal makes the Now,
And is not ta'en in Time's arrears:
His life 's a hymn
The seraphim
Might hark to hear or help to sing,
And to his soul
The boundless whole
Its bounty all doth daily bring.

"All mine is thine," the sky-soul saith:
"The wealth I am, must thou become:
Richer and richer, breath by breath, —
Immortal gain, immortal room!"
And since all his
Mine also is,
Life's gift outruns my fancies far,
And drowns the dream
In larger stream,
As morning drinks the morning star.

ROYALTY.

THAT regal soul I reverence, in whose eyes
Suffices not all worth the city knows
To pay that debt which his own heart he owes;
For less than level to his bosom rise
The low crowd's heaven and stars: above their skies
Runneth the road his daily feet have pressed;
A loftier heaven he beareth in his breast,
And o'er the summits of achieving hies
With never a thought of merit or of meed;
Choosing divinest labors through a pride
Of soul, that holdeth appetite to feed
Ever on angel-herbage, naught beside;
Nor praises more himself for hero-deed
Than stones for weight, or open seas for tide.

RICHARD CHENEVIX TRENCH.

THE KINGDOM OF GOD.

I SAY to thee, do thou repeat
To the first man thou mayest meet,
In lane, highway, or open street, —

That he, and we, and all men move
Under a canopy of Love,
As broad as the blue sky above:

That doubt and trouble, fear and pain,
And anguish, all are sorrows vain;
That death itself shall not remain:

That weary deserts we may tread,
A dreary labyrinth may thread,
Through dark ways underground be led;

Yet, if we will our Guide obey,
The dreariest path, the darkest way,
Shall issue out in heavenly day.

And we, on divers shores now cast,
Shall meet, our perilous voyage past,
All in our Father's home at last.

And ere thou leave them, say thou this,
Yet one word more: They only miss
The winning of that final bliss

Who will not count it true that Love,
Blessing, not cursing, rules above,
And that in it we live and move.

And one thing further make him know,
That to believe these things are so,
This firm faith never to forego,—

Despite of all which seems at strife
With blessing, and with curses rife,—
That this *is* blessing, this *is* life.

ARTHUR HUGH CLOUGH.

[1819-1861.]

THE NEW SINAI.

Lo, here is God, and there is God!
  Believe it not, O man!
In such vain sort to this and that
  The ancient heathen ran;
Though old Religion shake her head,
  And say, in bitter grief,
The day behold, at first foretold,
  Of atheist unbelief:
Take better part, with manly heart,
  Thine adult spirit can;
Receive it not, believe it not,
  Believe it not, O Man!

As men at dead of night awaked
  With cries, "The king is here,"
Rush forth and greet whome'er they meet,
  Whoe'er shall first appear;
And still repeat, to all the street,
  "'T is he,—the king is here";
The long procession moveth on,
  Each nobler form they see,
With changeful suit they still salute,
  And cry, "'T is he! 't is he!"

So, even so, when men were young,
  And earth and heaven was new,
And His immediate presence he
  From human hearts withdrew,
The soul perplexed and daily vexed
  With sensuous False and True,
Amazed, bereaved, no less believed,
  And fain would see Him too.
"He is!" the prophet-tongues proclaimed;
  In joy and hasty fear,
"He is!" aloud replied the crowd,
  "Is, here, and here, and here."

"He is! They are!" in distance seen
  On yon Olympus high,
In those Avernian woods abide,
  And walk this azure sky:
"They are! They are!" to every show
  Its eyes the baby turned,
And blazes sacrificial, tall,
  On thousand altars burned:
"They are! They are!"—On Sinai's top
  Far seen the lightning's shone,
The thunder broke, a trumpet spoke,
  And God said, "I am One."

God spake it out, "I, God, am One";
  The unheeding ages ran,
And baby thoughts again, again,
  Have dogged the growing man:
And as of old from Sinai's top
  God said that God is One,
By Science strict so speaks he now
  To tell us, There is None!
Earth goes by chemic forces; Heaven 's
  A Mécanique Céleste!
And heart and mind of human kind
  A watch-work as the rest!

Is this a Voice, as was the Voice
  Whose speaking told abroad,
When thunder pealed, and mountain reeled,
  The ancient truth of God?
Ah, not the Voice; 't is but the cloud,
  The outer darkness dense,
Where image none, nor e'er was seen
  Similitude of sense.

'T is but the cloudy darkness dense,
That wrapt the Mount around;
While in amaze the people stays,
To hear the Coming Sound.

Some chosen prophet-soul the while
Shall dare, sublimely meek,
Within the shroud of blackest cloud
The Deity to seek:
Mid atheistic systems dark,
And darker hearts' despair,
That soul has heard perchance his word,
And on the dusky air,
His skirts, as passed He by, to see
Hath strained on their behalf,
Who on the plain, with dance amain,
Adore the Golden Calf.

'T is but the cloudy darkness dense;
Though blank the tale it tells,
No God, no Truth! yet He, in sooth,
Is there, — within it dwells;
Within the sceptic darkness deep
He dwells that none may see,
Till idol forms and idol thoughts
Have passed and ceased to be:
No God, no Truth! ah though, in sooth,
So stand the doctrine's half;
On Egypt's track return not back,
Nor own the Golden Calf.

Take better part, with manlier heart,
Thine adult spirit can:
No God, no Truth, receive it ne'er—
Believe it ne'er—O Man!
But turn not then to seek again
What first the ill began;
No God, it saith; ah, wait in faith
God's self-completing plan;
Receive it not, but leave it not,
And wait it out, O man!

The Man that went the cloud within
Is gone and vanished quite;
"He cometh not," the people cries,
"Nor bringeth God to sight":
"Lo these thy gods, that safety give,
Adore and keep the feast!"
Deluding and deluded cries
The Prophet's brother-Priest:
And Israel all bows down to fall
Before the gilded beast.

Devout, indeed! that priestly creed,
O Man, reject as sin!
The clouded hill attend thou still,
And him that went within.
He yet shall bring some worthy thing
For waiting souls to see;
Some sacred word that he hath heard
Their light and life shall be;
Some lofty part, than which the heart
Adopt no nobler can,
Thou shalt receive, thou shalt believe,
And thou shalt do, O Man!

FROM THE "BOTHIE OF TOBER-NA-VUOLICH."

WHERE does Circumstance end, and Providence, where begins it?
What are we to resist, and what are we to be friends with?
If there is battle 't is battle by night; I stand in the darkness,
Here in the midst of men, Ionian and Dorian on both sides,
Signal and password known; which is friend, which is foeman?
Is it a friend? I doubt, though he speak with the voice of a brother.
O that the armies indeed were arrayed! O joy of the onset!
Sound, thou trumpet of God, come forth Great Cause, and array us!
King and leader appear, thy soldiers answering seek thee.
Would that the armies indeed were arrayed. O where is the battle!
Neither battle I see, nor arraying, nor King in Israel,
Only infinite jumble and mess and dislocation,
Backed by a solemn appeal, "For God's sake do not stir there!"

THE STREAM OF LIFE.

O STREAM descending to the sea,
Thy mossy banks between,
The flow'rets blow, the grasses grow,
The leafy trees are green.

In garden plots the children play,
The fields the laborers till,
The houses stand on either hand.
And thou descendest still.

O life descending into death,
Our waking eyes behold,

Parent and friend thy lapse attend,
Companions young and old.

Strong purposes our minds possess,
Our hearts affections fill,
We toil and earn, we seek and learn,
And thou descendest still.

O end to which our currents tend,
Inevitable sea,
To which we flow, what do we know,
What shall we guess of thee?

A roar we hear upon thy shore,
As we our course fulfil;
Scarce we divine a sun will shine
And be above us still.

QUA CURSUM VENTUS.

As ships becalmed at eve, that lay
With canvas drooping, side by side,
Two towers of sail at dawn of day
Are scarce, long leagues apart, descried;

When fell the night, upsprung the breeze,
And all the darkling hours they plied,
Nor dreamt but each the selfsame seas
By each was cleaving, side by side:

E'en so, — but why the tale reveal
Of those whom, year by year unchanged,
Brief absence joined anew to feel,
Astounded, soul from soul estranged?

At dead of night their sails were filled,
And onward each rejoicing steered:
Ah, neither blame, for neither willed,
Or wist, what first with dawn appeared!

To veer, how vain! On, onward strain,
Brave barks! In light, in darkness too,
Through winds and tides one compass guides, —
To that, and your own selves, be true.

But O blithe breeze, and O great seas,
Though ne'er, that earliest parting past,
On your wide plain they join again,
Together lead them home at last!

One port, methought, alike they sought,
One purpose hold where'er they fare, —
O bounding breeze, O rushing seas,
At last, at last, unite them there

SAMUEL LONGFELLOW.

[U. S. A.]

THE GOLDEN SUNSET.

THE golden sea its mirror spreads
Beneath the golden skies,
And but a narrow strip between
Of land and shadow lies.

The cloud-like rocks, the rock-like clouds,
Dissolved in glory float,
And, midway of the radiant flood,
Hangs silently the boat.

The sea is but another sky,
The sky a sea as well,
And which is earth, and which the heavens,
The eye can scarcely tell.

So when for us life's evening hour
Soft passing shall descend,
May glory born of earth and heaven,
The earth and heavens blend;

Flooded with peace the spirit float,
With silent rapture glow,
Till where earth ends and heaven begins
The soul shall scarcely know.

UNKNOWN.

QUIET FROM GOD.

QUIET from God! It cometh not to still
The vast and high aspirings of the soul,
The deep emotions which the spirit fill,
And speed its purpose onward to the goal;
It dims not youth's bright eye,
Bends not joy's lofty brow,
No guiltless ecstasy
Need in its presence bow.

It comes not in a sullen form, to place
Life's greatest good in an inglorious rest;
Through a dull, beaten track its way to trace,
And to lethargic slumber lull the breast;
Action may be its sphere,
Mountain paths, boundless fields,
O'er billows its career:
This is the power it yields.

To sojourn in the world, and yet apart;
To dwell with God, yet still with man to feel;
To bear about forever in the heart
The gladness which His spirit doth reveal;
Not to deem evil gone
From every earthly scene;
To see the storm come on,
But feel His shield between.

It giveth not a strength to human kind,
To leave all suffering powerless at its feet,
But keeps within the temple of the mind
A golden altar, and a mercy-seat;
A spiritual ark,
Bearing the peace of God
Above the waters dark,
And o'er the desert's sod.

How beautiful within our souls to keep
This treasure, the All-Merciful hath given;
To feel, when we awake, and when we sleep,
Its incense round us, like a breeze from heaven!
Quiet at hearth and home,
Where the heart's joys begin;
Quiet where'er we roam,
Quiet around, within.

Who shall make trouble?—not the evil minds
Which like a shadow o'er creation lower,
The spirit peace hath so attunéd, finds
There feelings that may own the Calmer's power;
What may she not confer,
E'en where she must condemn?
They take not peace from her,
She may speak peace to them!

ELIZA SCUDDER.

[U. S. A.]

THE LOVE OF GOD.

Thou Grace Divine, encircling all,
A soundless, shoreless sea!
Wherein at last our souls must fall,
O Love of God most free!

When over dizzy heights we go,
One soft hand blinds our eyes,
The other leads us, safe and slow,
O Love of God most wise!

And though we turn us from thy face,
And wander wide and long,
Thou hold'st us still in thine embrace,
O Love of God most strong!

The saddened heart, the restless soul,
The toil-worn frame and mind,
Alike confess thy sweet control,
O Love of God most kind!

But not alone thy care we claim,
Our wayward steps to win;
We know thee by a dearer name,
O Love of God within!

And filled and quickened by thy breath,
Our souls are strong and free
To rise o'er sin and fear and death,
O Love of God, to thee!

SARAH F. ADAMS.

NEARER, MY GOD, TO THEE.

Nearer, my God, to thee,
Nearer to thee!
E'en though it be a cross
That raiseth me;
Still all my song shall be,
Nearer, my God, to thee,
Nearer to thee!

Though like the wanderer,
The sun gone down,
Darkness be over me,
My rest a stone;
Yet in my dreams I 'd be
Nearer, my God, to thee,
Nearer to thee!

There let the way appear
Steps unto Heaven;
All that thou send'st to me
In mercy given;
Angels to beckon me
Nearer, my God, to thee,
Nearer to thee!

Then with my waking thoughts
  Bright with thy praise,
Out of my stony griefs
  Bethel I 'll raise;
So by my woes to be
Nearer, my God, to thee,
  Nearer to thee!

Or if on joyful wing
  Cleaving the sky,
Sun, moon, and stars forgot,
  Upwards I fly,
Still all my song shall be,
Nearer, my God, to thee,
  Nearer to thee!

ANNA L. WARING.

MY TIMES ARE IN THY HAND.

Father, I know that all my life
  Is portioned out for me,
And the changes that will surely come,
  I do not fear to see;
But I ask thee for a present mind
  Intent on pleasing thee.

I ask thee for a thoughtful love,
  Through constant watching wise,
To meet the glad with joyful smiles,
  And to wipe the weeping eyes;
And a heart at leisure from itself,
  To soothe and sympathize.

I would not have the restless will
  That hurries to and fro,
Seeking for some great thing to do,
  Or secret thing to know;
I would be treated as a child,
  And guided where I go.

Wherever in the world I am,
  In whatsoe'er estate,
I have a fellowship with hearts
  To keep and cultivate;
And a work of lowly love to do,
  For the Lord on whom I wait.

So I ask thee for the daily strength,
  To none that ask denied.
And a mind to blend with outward life,
  While keeping at thy side,
Content to fill a little space,
  If thou be glorified.

And if some things I do not ask
  In my cup of blessing be,
I would have my spirit filled the more
  With grateful love to thee;
And careful, less to serve thee much,
  Than to please thee perfectly.

There are briers besetting every path,
  Which call for patient care;
There is a cross in every lot,
  And an earnest need for prayer;
But a lowly heart that leans on thee
  Is happy anywhere.

In a service which thy love appoints,
  There are no bonds for me;
For my secret heart is taught "the truth"
  That makes thy children "free";
And a life of self-renouncing love
  Is a life of liberty.

JAMES FREEMAN CLARKE.

[U. S. A.]

CANA.

Dear Friend! whose presence in the house,
  Whose gracious word benign,
Could once, at Cana's wedding feast,
  Change water into wine;

Come, visit us! and when dull work
  Grows weary, line on line,
Revive our souls, and let us see
  Life's water turned to wine.

Gay mirth shall deepen into joy,
  Earth's hopes grow half divine,
When Jesus visits us, to make
  Life's water glow as wine.

The social talk, the evening fire,
  The homely household shrine,
Grow bright with angel visits, when
  The Lord pours out the wine.

For when self-seeking turns to love,
  Not knowing mine nor thine,
The miracle again is wrought,
  And water turned to wine.

HORATIUS BONAR.

THE INNER CALM.

Calm me, my God, and keep me calm,
While these hot breezes blow ;
Be like the night-dew's cooling balm
Upon earth's fevered brow.

Calm me, my God, and keep me calm,
Soft resting on thy breast ;
Soothe me with holy hymn and psalm,
And bid my spirit rest.

Calm me, my God, and keep me calm ;
Let thine outstretchéd wing
Be like the shade of Elim's palm
Beside her desert spring.

Yes, keep me calm, though loud and rude
The sounds my ear that greet,
Calm in the closet's solitude,
Calm in the bustling street ;

Calm in the hour of buoyant health,
Calm in my hour of pain,
Calm in my poverty or wealth,
Calm in my loss or gain ;

Calm in the sufferance of wrong,
Like Him who bore my shame,
Calm mid the threatening, taunting throng,
Who hate Thy holy name ;

Calm when the great world's news with power
My listening spirit stir ;
Let not the tidings of the hour
E'er find too fond an ear ;

Calm as the ray of sun or star
Which storms assail in vain,
Moving unruffled through earth's war,
The eternal calm to gain.

THE MASTER'S TOUCH.

In the still air the music lies unheard ;
In the rough marble beauty hides unseen :
To make the music and the beauty, needs
The master's touch, the sculptor's chisel keen.

Great Master, touch us with thy skilful hand ;
Let not the music that is in us die !
Great Sculptor, hew and polish us ; nor let,
Hidden and lost, thy form within us lie !

Spare not the stroke ! do with us as thou wilt !
Let there be naught unfinished, broken, marred ;
Complete thy purpose, that we may become
Thy perfect image, thou our God and Lord !

W. ALEXANDER.

UP ABOVE.

Down below, the wild November whistling
Through the beech's dome of burning red,
And the Autumn sprinkling penitential
Dust and ashes on the chestnut's head.

Down below, a pall of airy purple
Darkly hanging from the mountain-side ;
And the sunset from his eyebrow staring
O'er the long roll of the leaden tide.

Up above, the tree with leaf unfading,
By the everlasting river's brink ;
And the sea of glass, beyond whose margin
Never yet the sun was known to sink.

Down below, the white wings of the sea-bird
Dashed across the furrows, dark with mould,
Flitting, like the memories of our childhood,
Through the trees, now waxen pale and old.

Down below, imaginations quivering
Through our human spirits like the wind;
Thoughts that toss, like leaves about the woodland ;
Hope, like sea-birds, flashed across the mind.

Up above, the host no man can number,
In white robes, a palm in every hand,
Each some work sublime forever working,
In the spacious tracts of that great land.

Up above, the thoughts that know not anguish;
Tender care, sweet love for us below;
Noble pity, free from anxious terror;
Larger love, without a touch of woe.

Down below, a sad, mysterious music
Wailing through the woods and on the shore,
Burdened with a grand majestic secret,
That keeps sweeping from us evermore.

Up above, a music that entwineth
With eternal threads of golden sound,
The great poem of this strange existence,
All whose wondrous meaning hath been found.

HARRIET BEECHER STOWE.

[U. S. A.]

THE OTHER WORLD.

It lies around us like a cloud, —
A world we do not see;
Yet the sweet closing of an eye
May bring us there to be.

Its gentle breezes fan our cheek;
Amid our worldly cares
Its gentle voices whisper love,
And mingle with our prayers.

Sweet hearts around us throb and beat,
Sweet helping hands are stirred,
And palpitates the veil between
With breathings almost heard.

The silence — awful, sweet, and calm —
They have no power to break;
For mortal words are not for them
To utter or partake.

So thin, so soft, so sweet they glide,
So near to press they seem, —
They seem to lull us to our rest,
And melt into our dream.

And in the hush of rest they bring
'T is easy now to see
How lovely and how sweet a pass
The hour of death may be.

To close the eye, and close the ear,
Wrapped in a trance of bliss,
And gently dream in loving arms
To swoon to that — from this.

Scarce knowing if we wake or sleep,
Scarce asking where we are,
To feel all evil sink away,
All sorrow and all care.

Sweet souls around us! watch us still,
Press nearer to our side,
Into our thoughts, into our prayers,
With gentle helpings glide.

Let death between us be as naught,
A dried and vanished stream;
Your joy be the reality,
Our suffering life the dream.

MRS. LEWES (GEORGE ELIOT).

O MAY I JOIN THE CHOIR INVISIBLE!

O may I join the choir invisible
Of those immortal dead who live again
In minds made better by their presence; live
In pulses stirred to generosity,
In deeds of daring rectitude, in scorn
Of miserable aims that end with self,
In thoughts sublime that pierce the night like stars,
And with their mild persistence urge men's minds
To vaster issues.
So to live is heaven:
To make undying music in the world,
Breathing a beauteous order, that controls
With growing sway the growing life of man.
So we inherit that sweet purity
For which we struggled, failed, and agonized
With widening retrospect that bred despair.
Rebellious flesh that would not be subdued,

A vicious parent shaming still its child,
Poor anxious penitence, is quick dissolved;
Its discords quenched by meeting harmonies,
Die in the large and charitable air.
And all our rarer, better, truer self,
That sobbed religiously in yearning song,
That watched to ease the burden of the world,
Laboriously tracing what must be,
And what may yet be better, — saw within
A worthier image for the sanctuary,
And shaped it forth before the multitude,
Divinely human, raising worship so
To higher reverence more mixed with love, —
That better self shall live till human Time
Shall fold its eyelids, and the human sky
Be gathered like a scroll within the tomb,
Unread forever.
This is life to come,
Which martyred men have made more glorious
For us, who strive to follow.
May I reach
That purest heaven, — be to other souls
The cup of strength in some great agony,
Enkindle generous ardor, feed pure love,
Beget the smiles that have no cruelty,
Be the sweet presence of a good diffused,
And in diffusion ever more intense!
So shall I join the choir invisible,
Whose music is the gladness of the world.

CHARLES KINGSLEY.

[1819 - 1874.]

THE THREE FISHERS.

Three fishers went sailing out into the west,
Out into the west as the sun went down;
Each thought on the woman who loved him the best,
And the children stood watching them out of the town;
For men must work, and women must weep,
And there's little to earn, and many to keep,
Though the harbor bar be moaning.

Three wives sat up in the lighthouse tower,
And they trimmed the lamps as the sun went down,
They looked at the squall, and they looked at the shower,
And the night rack came rolling up ragged and brown!
But men must work, and women must weep,
Though storms be sudden, and waters deep,
And the harbor bar be moaning.

Three corpses lay out on the shining sands
In the morning gleam as the tide went down,
And the women are weeping and wringing their hands
For those who will never come back to the town;
For men must work, and women must weep,
And the sooner it's over, the sooner to sleep, —
And good by to the bar and its moaning.

THE SANDS OF DEE.

"O Mary, go and call the cattle home,
And call the cattle home,
And call the cattle home,
Across the sands of Dee";
The western wind was wild and dank wi' foam,
And all alone went she.

The western tide crept up along the sand,
And o'er and o'er the sand,
And round and round the sand,
As far as eye could see.
The rolling mist came down and hid the land, —
And never home came she.

"O, is it weed, or fish, or floating hair, —
A tress o' golden hair,
A drownéd maiden's hair
Above the nets at sea?
Was never salmon yet that shone so fair
Among the stakes on Dee."

They rowed her in across the rolling foam,
The cruel crawling foam,

The cruel hungry foam,
To her grave beside the sea:
But still the boatmen hear her call the cattle home
Across the sands of Dee!

A MYTH.

A FLOATING, a floating
Across the sleeping sea,
All night I heard a singing bird
Upon the topmast tree.

"O, came you from the isles of Greece,
Or from the banks of Seine,
Or off some tree in forests free,
Which fringe the Western main?"

"I came not off the old world, —
Nor yet from off the new, —
But I am one of the birds of God
Which sing the whole night through."

"O sing and wake the dawning,
O whistle for the wind;
The night is long, the current strong,
My boat it lags behind."

"The current sweeps the old world,
The current sweeps the new;
The wind will blow, the dawn will glow
Ere thou hast sailed them through."

DINAH MULOCK CRAIK.

COMING HOME.

THE lift is high and blue,
And the new moon glints through
The bonnie corn-stooks o' Strathairly;
My ship 's in Largo Bay,
And I ken it weel, — the way
Up the steep, steep brae of Strathairly.

When I sailed ower the sea, —
A laddie bold and free, —
The corn sprang green on Strathairly;
When I come back again,
'T is an auld man walks his lane,
Slow and sad through the fields o' Strathairly.

Of the shearers that I see,
Ne'er a body kens me,
Though I kent them a' at Strathairly;
And this fisher-wife I pass,
Can she be the braw lass
That I kissed at the back of Strathairly?

O, the land 's fine, fine!
I could buy it a' for mine,
My gowd 's yellow as the stooks o' Strathairly;
But I fain yon lad wad be,
That sailed ower the salt sea,
As the dawn rose gray on Strathairly.

TOO LATE.

COULD ye come back to me, Douglas, Douglas,
In the old likeness that I knew,
I would be so faithful, so loving, Douglas,
Douglas, Douglas, tender and true.

Never a scornful word should grieve ye,
I 'd smile on ye sweet as the angels do; —
Sweet as your smile on me shone ever,
Douglas, Douglas, tender and true.

O to call back the days that are not!
My eyes were blinded, your words were few:
Do you know the truth now up in heaven,
Douglas, Douglas, tender and true?

I never was worthy of you, Douglas;
Not half worthy the like of you:
Now all men beside seem to me like shadows, —
I love *you*, Douglas, tender and true.

Stretch out your hand to me, Douglas, Douglas,
Drop forgiveness from heaven like dew;
As I lay my heart on your dead heart, Douglas,
Douglas, Douglas, tender and true.

OUTWARD BOUND.

OUT upon the unknown deep,
Where the unheard oceans sound,
Where the unseen islands sleep, —
Outward bound.

Following towards the silent west
O'er the horizon's curvéd rim,
On, to islands of the blest;
He with me and I with him,
Outward bound.

Nothing but a speck we seem
In the waste of waters round;
Floating, floating like a dream,
Outward bound.
But within that tiny speck
Two brave hearts with one accord,
Past all tumult, pain, and wreck,
Look up calm, and praise the Lord,
Outward bound.

ELIZABETH A. ALLEN.

[U. S. A.]

UNTIL DEATH.

Make me no vows of constancy, dear friend,
To love me, though I die, thy whole life long,
And love no other till thy days shall end,—
Nay, it were rash and wrong.

If thou canst love another, be it so;
I would not reach out of my quiet grave
To bind thy heart, if it should choose to go;—
Love should not be a slave.

My placid ghost, I trust, will walk serene
In clearer light than gilds those earthly morns,
Above the jealousies and envies keen
Which sow this life with thorns.

Thou wouldst not feel my shadowy caress,
If, after death, my soul should linger here;
Men's hearts crave tangible, close tenderness,
Love's presence, warm and near.

It would not make me sleep more peacefully
That thou wert wasting all thy life in woe
For my poor sake; what love thou hast for me,
Bestow it ere I go!

Carve not upon a stone when I am dead
The praises which remorseful mourners give
To women's graves, — a tardy recompense, —
But speak them while I live.

Heap not the heavy marble on my head
To shut away the sunshine and the dew;
Let small blooms grow there, and let grasses wave,
And rain-drops filter through.

Thou wilt meet many fairer and more gay
Than I; but, trust me, thou canst never find
One who will love and serve thee night and day
With a more single mind.

Forget me when I die! The violets
Above my rest will blossom just as blue,
Nor miss thy tears; e'en Nature's self forgets;—
But while I live, be true!

HARRIET WINSLOW SEWALL.

[U. S. A.]

WHY THUS LONGING?

Why thus longing, thus forever sighing
For the far off, unattained, and dim,
While the beautiful, all round thee lying,
Offers up its low perpetual hymn!

Wouldst thou listen to its gentle teaching
All thy restless yearnings it would still,
Leaf and flower and laden bee are preaching
Thine own sphere, though humble, first to fill.

Poor indeed thou must be, if around thee
Thou no ray of light and joy canst throw,
If no silken chord of love hath bound thee
To some little world through weal and woe;

If no dear eyes thy fond love can brighten,
No fond voices answer to thine own,

If no brother's sorrow thou canst lighten
By daily sympathy and gentle tone.

Not by deeds that gain the world's applauses,
Not by works that win thee world renown,
Not by martyrdom or vaunted crosses,
Canst thou win and wear the immortal crown.

Daily struggling, though unloved and lonely,
Every day a rich reward will give;
Thou wilt find by hearty striving only,
And truly loving, thou canst truly live.

Dost thou revel in the rosy morning
When all nature hails the Lord of light,
And his smile, nor low nor lofty scorning,
Gladdens hall and hovel, vale and height?

Other hands may grasp the field and forest,
Proud proprietors in pomp may shine,
But with fervent love if thou adorest,
Thou art wealthier, — all the world is thine.

Yet if through earth's wide domains thou rovest,
Sighing that they are not thine alone,
Not those fair fields, but thyself thou lovest,
And their beauty and thy wealth are gone.

COVENTRY PATMORE.

WOMAN.

All powers of the sea and air,
All interests of hill and plain,
I so can sing, in seasons fair,
That who hath felt may feel again:
Nay, more; the gracious muses bless
At times my tongue, until I can
With moving emphasis express
The likeness of the perfect man:
Elated oft with such free songs,
I think with utterance free to raise
That hymn for which the whole world longs, —
A worthy hymn in woman's praise;
The best half of creation's best,
Its heart to feel, its eye to see,
The crown and complex of the rest,
Its aim and its epitome.

Yet now it is my chosen task
To sing her worth as maid and wife;
And were such post to seek, I 'd ask
To live her laureate all my life.
On wings of love uplifted free,
And by her gentleness made great,
I 'd teach how noble man should be,
To match with such a lovely mate;
Until (for who may hope too much
From her who wields the powers of love),
Our lifted lives at last should touch
That lofty goal to which they move:
Until we find, as darkness rolls
Far off, and fleshly mists dissolve,
That nuptial contrasts are the poles
On which the heavenly spheres revolve.

THE CHASE.

She wearies with an ill unknown;
In sleep she sobs and seems to float,
A water-lily, all alone
Within a lonely castle-moat;
And as the full moon, spectral, lies
Within the crescent's gleaming arms,
The present shows her heedless eyes
A future dim with vague alarms:
She sees, and yet she scarcely sees;
For, life-in-life not yet begun,
Too many are life's mysteries
For thought to fix t'ward any one.

She 's told that maidens are by youths
Extremely honored and desired;
And sighs, "If those sweet tales be truths,
What bliss to be so much admired!"
The suitors come; she sees them grieve;
Her coldness fills them with despair:
She 'd pity if she could believe;
She 's sorry that she cannot care.

Who 's this that meets her on her way?
Comes he as enemy, or friend;
Or both? Her bosom seems to say
He cannot pass, and there an end.
Whom does he love? Does he confer
His heart on worth that answers his?

Perhaps he's come to worship her:
She fears, she hopes, she thinks he is.

Advancing stepless, quick, and still,
As in the grass a serpent glides,
He fascinates her fluttering will,
Then terrifies with dreadful strides:
At first, there's nothing to resist:
He fights with all the forms of peace;
He comes about her like a mist,
With subtle, swift, unseen increase;
And then, unlooked for, strikes amain
Some stroke that frightens her to death;
And grows all harmlessness again,
Ere she can cry, or get her breath.
At times she stops, and stands at bay;
But he, in all more strong than she,
Subdues her with his pale dismay,
Or more admired audacity.

All people speak of him with praise:
How wise his talk; how sweet his tone;
What manly worship in his gaze!
It nearly makes her heart his own.
With what an air he speaks her name:
His manner always recollects
Her sex: and still the woman's claim
Is taught its scope by his respects.
Her charms, perceived to prosper first
In his beloved advertencies,
When in her glass they are rehearsed,
Prove his most powerful allies.

Ah, whither shall a maiden flee,
When a bold youth so swift pursues,
And siege of tenderest courtesy,
With hope perseverant, still renews!
Why fly so fast? Her flattered breast
Thanks him who finds her fair and good;
She loves her fears; veiled joys arrest
The foolish terrors of her blood;
By secret, sweet degrees, her heart,
Vanquished, takes warmth from his desire:
She makes it more, with bashful art,
And fuels love's late dreaded fire.

The gallant credit he accords
To all the signs of good in her,
Redeems itself; his praiseful words
What they attribute still confer.
Her heart is thrice as rich in bliss,
She's three times gentler than before:
He gains a right to call her his,
Now she through him is so much more!
Ah, might he, when by doubts aggrieved,
Behold his tokens next her breast,
At all his words and sighs perceived
Against its blithe upheaval pressed.
But still she flies: should she be won,
It must not be believed or thought
She yields: she's chased to death, undone,
Surprised, and violently caught.

THE LOVER.

He meets, by heavenly chance express,
His destined wife; some hidden hand
Unveils to him that loveliness
Which others cannot understand.
No songs of love, no summer dreams
Did e'er his longing fancy fire
With vision like to this; she seems
In all things better than desire.
His merits in her presence grow,
To match the promise in her eyes,
And round her happy footsteps blow
The authentic airs of Paradise.

The least is well, yet nothing's light
In all the lover does; for he
Who pitches hope at such a height
Will do all things with dignity.
She is so perfect, true, and pure,
Her virtue all virtue so endears,
That often, when he thinks of her,
Life's meanness fills his eyes with tears.

LETITIA E. LANDON.

THE SHEPHERD-BOY.

Like some vision olden
Of far other time,
When the age was golden,
In the young world's prime
Is thy soft pipe ringing,
O lonely shepherd-boy,
What song art thou singing,
In thy youth and joy?

Or art thou complaining
Of thy lowly lot,
And thine own disdaining,
Dost ask what thou hast not?
Of the future dreaming,
Weary of the past,
For the present scheming,
All but what thou hast.

No, thou art delighting
  In thy summer home,
Where the flowers inviting
  Tempt the bee to roam;
Where the cowslip bending
  With its golden bells,
Of each glad hour's ending
  With a sweet chime tells.

All wild creatures love him
  When he is alone,
Every bird above him
  Sings its softest tone,
Thankful to high Heaven,
  Humble in thy joy,
Much to thee is given,
  Lowly shepherd-boy.

DEATH AND THE YOUTH.

"NOT yet, the flowers are in my path,
  The sun is in the sky;
Not yet, my heart is full of hope,
  I cannot bear to die.

"Not yet, I never knew till now
  How precious life could be;
My heart is full of love, O Death!
  I cannot come with thee!"

But Love and Hope, enchanted twain,
  Passed in their falsehood by;
Death came again, and then he said,
  "I 'm ready now to die!"

AUBREY DE VERE.

THE SISTERS.

"I KNOW not how to comfort thee;
  Yet dare not say, Weep on!
I know how little life is worth
  When love itself is gone.

"The mighty with the weak contend;
  The many with the few:
The hard and heavy hearts oppress
  The tender and the true.

"Had he been capable of love,
  His love had clung to thee;
He was too weak a thing to bear
  That noble energy.

"Lift, lift your forehead from my lap,
  And lay it on my breast:
I too have wept; but you I deemed
  Still safe within your nest."

Her words were vain, but not her tears;
  The mourner raised her eyes,
Subdued by the atoning power
  Of pitying sympathies:

Subdued at first, erelong consoled,
  At last she ceased to moan;
For those who feel another's pain
  Will soon forget their own.

O ye whom broken vows bereave,
  Your vows to heaven restore;
O ye for blighted love who grieve,
  Love deeper and love more!

The arrow cannot wound the air,
  Nor thunder rend the sea,
Nor injury long afflict the heart
  That rests, O Love, in thee!

The winds may blow, the waves may swell;
  But soon those tumults cease,
And the pure element subsides
  Into its native peace.

ALICE CAREY.

[U. S. A.]

KRUMLEY.

O BLUSHING flowers of Krumley!
  'T is she who makes you sweet.
I envy every silver wave
  That laughs about her feet.
How dare the waves, how dare the flowers,
  Rise up and kiss her feet?

Ye wanton woods of Krumley!
  Ye clasp her with your boughs,
And stoop to kiss her all the way
  Beside her homeward cows.
I hate ye, woods of Krumley,
  I 'm jealous of your boughs!

I tell ye, banks of Krumley,
'T is not your sunny days
That set your meadows up and down
With blossoms all ablaze.
The flowers that love her crowd to bloom
Along her trodden ways.

O dim and dewy Krumley,
'T is not your birds at all
That make the air one warble
From rainy spring to fall.
They only mock the sweeter songs
That from her sweet lips fall.

O bold, bold winds of Krumley,
Do ye mean my heart to break,
So light ye lift her yellow hair,
So lightly kiss her cheek?
O flower and bird, O wave and wind,
Ye mean my heart to break!

THE SURE WITNESS.

The solemn wood had spread
Shadows around my head, —
"Curtains they are," I said,
"Hung dim and still about the house of prayer";
Softly among the limbs,
Turning the leaves of hymns,
I hear the winds, and ask if God were there.
No voice replied, but while I listening stood,
Sweet peace made holy hushes through the wood.

With ruddy, open hand,
I saw the wild rose stand
Beside the green gate of the summer hills,
And pulling at her dress,
I cried, "Sweet hermitess,
Hast thou beheld Him who the dew distils?"
No voice replied, but while I listening bent,
Her gracious beauty made my heart content.

The moon in splendor shone, —
"She walketh Heaven alone,
And seeth all things," to myself I mused;
"Hast thou beheld Him, then,
Who hides himself from men
In that great power through nature interfused?"
No speech made answer, and no sign appeared,
But in the silence I was soothed and cheered.

Waking one time, strange awe
Thrilling my soul, I saw
A kingly splendor round about the night;
Such cunning work the hand
Of spinner never planned, —
The finest wool may not be washed so white.
"Hast thou come out of Heaven?"
I asked; and lo!
The snow was all the answer of the snow.

Then my heart said, Give o'er;
Question no more, no more!
The wind, the snow-storm, the wild hermit flower,
The illuminated air,
The pleasure after prayer,
Proclaim the unoriginated Power!
The mystery that hides him here and there.
Bears the sure witness he is everywhere.

HER LAST POEM.

Earth with its dark and dreadful ills,
Recedes and fades away;
Lift up your heads, ye heavenly hills;
Ye gates of death, give way!

My soul is full of whispered song, —
My blindness is my sight;
The shadows that I feared so long
Are full of life and light.

My pulses faint and fainter beat,
My faith takes wider bounds;
I feel grow firm beneath my feet
The green, immortal grounds.

The faith to me a courage gives.
Low as the grave to go, —
I know that my Redeemer lives, —
That I shall live I know.

The palace walls I almost see
Where dwells my Lord and King.
O grave, where is thy victory?
O death, where is thy sting?

PHEBE CAREY.

[U. S. A.]

FIELD PREACHING.

I HAVE been out to-day in field and wood,
Listening to praises sweet and counsel good
Such as a little child had understood,
That, in its tender youth,
Discerns the simple eloquence of truth.

The modest blossoms, crowding round my way,
Though they had nothing great or grand to say,
Gave out their fragrance to the wind all day;
Because His loving breath,
With soft persistence, won them back from death.

And the right royal lily, putting on
Her robes, more rich than those of Solomon,
Opened her gorgeous missal in the sun,
And thanked Him, soft and low,
Whose gracious, liberal hand had clothed her so.

When wearied, on the meadow-grass I sank;
So narrow was the rill from which I drank,
An infant might have stepped from bank to bank;
And the tall rushes near
Lapping together, hid its waters clear.

Yet to the ocean joyously it went;
And rippling in the fulness of content,
Watered the pretty flowers that o'er it leant;
For all the banks were spread
With delicate flowers that on its bounty fed.

The stately maize, a fair and goodly sight,
With serried spear-points bristling sharp and bright,
Shook out his yellow tresses, for delight,
To all their tawny length,
Like Samson, glorying in his lusty strength.

And every little bird upon the tree,
Ruffling his plumage bright, for ecstasy,
Sang in the wild insanity of glee;
And seemed, in the same lays,
Calling his mate and uttering songs of praise.

The golden grasshopper did chirp and sing;
The plain bee, busy with her housekeeping,
Kept humming cheerfully upon the wing,
As if she understood
That, with contentment, labor was a good.

I saw each creature, in his own best place,
To the Creator lift a smiling face,
Praising continually his wondrous grace;
As if the best of all
Life's countless blessings was to live at all!

So with a book of sermons, plain and true,
Hid in my heart, where I might turn them through,
I went home softly, through the falling dew,
Still listening, rapt and calm,
To Nature giving out her evening psalm.

While, far along the west, mine eyes discerned,
Where, lit by God, the fires of sunset burned,
The tree-tops, unconsumed, to flame were turned;
And I, in that great hush,
Talked with His angels in each burning bush!

NEARER HOME.

ONE sweetly welcome thought,
Comes to me o'er and o'er;
I 'm nearer home to-day
Than I 've ever been before;

Nearer my Father's house
Where the many mansions be;
Nearer the Great White Throne,
Nearer the Jasper Sea;

Nearer that bound of life,
Where we lay our burdens down,—
Nearer leaving the cross,
Nearer gaining the crown.

But lying dimly between,
Winding down through the night,
Lies the dark and uncertain stream
That leads us at length to the light.

Closer and closer my steps
  Come to the dark abysm,
Closer Death to my lips
  Presses the awful chrism;

Father, perfect my trust!
  Strengthen my feeble faith!
Let me feel as I shall, when I stand
  On the shores of the river of death:—

Feel as I would, were my feet
  Even now slipping over the brink,—
For it may be I am nearer home,
  Nearer now, than I think!

PEACE.

O LAND, of every land the best,—
  O Land, whose glory shall increase;
Now in your whitest raiment drest
  For the great festival of peace:

Take from your flag its fold of gloom,
  And let it float undimmed above,
Till over all our vales shall bloom
  The sacred colors that we love.

On mountain high, in valley low,
  Set Freedom's living fires to burn;
Until the midnight sky shall show
  A redder glory than the morn.

Welcome, with shouts of joy and pride,
  Your veterans from the war-path's track;
You gave your boys, untrained, untried;
  You bring them men and heroes back!

And shed no tear, though think you must
  With sorrow of the martyred band;
Not even for him whose hallowed dust
  Has made our prairies holy land.

Though by the places where they fell,
  The places that are sacred ground,
Death, like a sullen sentinel,
  Paces his everlasting round.

Yet when they set their country free,
  And gave her traitors fitting doom,
They left their last great enemy,
  Baffled, beside an empty tomb.

Not there, but risen, redeemed, they go
  Where all the paths are sweet with flowers;
They fought to give us peace, and lo!
  They gained a better peace than ours.

SYDNEY DOBELL.

KEITH OF RAVELSTON.

O HAPPY, happy maid,
In the year of war and death
She wears no sorrow!
By her face so young and fair,
By the happy wreath
That rules her happy hair,
She might be a bride to-morrow!
She sits and sings within her moonlit bower,
Her moonlit bower in rosy June,
Yet ah, her bridal breath,
Like fragrance from some sweet night-blowing flower,
Moves from her moving lips in many a mournful tune!
She sings no song of love's despair,
She sings no lover lowly laid,
No fond peculiar grief
Has ever touched or bud or leaf
Of her unblighted spring.
She sings because she needs must sing;
She sings the sorrow of the air
Whereof her voice is made.
That night in Britain howsoe'er
On any chords the fingers strayed
They gave the notes of care.
A dim sad legend old
Long since in some pale shade
Of some far twilight told,
She knows not when or where,
She sings, with trembling hand on trembling lute-strings laid:—

The murmur of the mourning ghost
  That keeps the shadowy kine,
"O Keith of Ravelston,
  The sorrows of thy line!"

Ravelston, Ravelston,
  The merry path that leads
Down the golden morning hill,
  And through the silver meads;

Ravelston, Ravelston,
  The stile beneath the tree,

The maid that kept her mother's kine,
The song that sang she !

She sang her song, she kept her kine,
She sat beneath the thorn
When Andrew Keith of Ravelston
Rode through the Monday morn ;

His henchmen sing, his hawk-bells ring,
His belted jewels shine !
O Keith of Ravelston,
The sorrows of thy line !

Year after year, where Andrew came,
Comes evening down the glade,
And still there sits a moonshine ghost
Where sat the sunshine maid.

Her misty hair is faint and fair,
She keeps the shadowy kine;
O Keith of Ravelston,
The sorrows of thy line!

I lay my hand upon the stile,
The stile is lone and cold,
The burnie that goes babbling by
Says naught that can be told.

Yet, stranger! here, from year to year,
She keeps her shadowy kine;
O Keith of Ravelston,
The sorrows of thy line!

Step out three steps, where Andrew stood:
Why blanch thy cheeks for fear?
The ancient stile is not alone,
'T is not the burn I hear!

She makes her immemorial moan,
She keeps her shadowy kine;
O Keith of Ravelston,
The sorrows of thy line!

THOMAS BURBIDGE.

EVENTIDE.

COMES something down with eventide,
Beside the sunset's golden bars,
Beside the floating scents, beside
The twinkling shadows of the stars.

Upon the river's rippling face,
Flash after flash the white
Broke up in many a shallow place;
The rest was soft and bright.

By chance my eye fell on the stream;
How many a marvellous power
Sleeps in us, — sleeps, and doth not dream!
This knew I in that hour.

For then my heart, so full of strife,
No more was in me stirred;
My life was in the river's life,
And I nor saw nor heard.

I and the river, we were one:
The shade beneath the bank,
I felt it cool; the setting sun
Into my spirit sank.

A rushing thing in power serene
I was; the mystery
I felt of having ever been
And being still to be.

Was it a moment or an hour?
I knew not; but I mourned
When, from that realm of awful power
I to these fields returned.

ROSE TERRY COOKE.

[U. S. A.]

THE ICONOCLAST.

A THOUSAND years shall come and go,
A thousand years of night and day,
And man, through all their changing show,
His tragic drama still shall play.

Ruled by some fond ideal's power,
Cheated by passion or despair,
Still shall he waste life's trembling hour,
In worship vain, and useless prayer.

Ah! where are they who rose in might,
Who fired the temple and the shrine,
And hurled, through earth's chaotic night,
The helpless gods it deemed divine?

Cease, longing soul, thy vain desire!
What idol, in its stainless prime,
But falls, untouched of axe or fire,
Before the steady eyes of Time?

He looks, and lo! our altars fall,
The shrine reveals its gilded clay,
With decent hands we spread the pall,
And, cold with wisdom, glide away.

O, where were courage, faith, and truth,
If man went wandering all his day
In golden clouds of love and youth,
Nor knew that both his steps betray?

Come, Time, while here we sit and wait,
Be faithful, spoiler, to thy trust!
No death can further desolate
The soul that knows its god was dust.

"IT IS MORE BLESSED."

GIVE! as the morning that flows out of heaven;
Give! as the waves when their channel is riven;
Give! as the free air and sunshine are given;
Lavishly, utterly, carelessly give.
Not the waste drops of thy cup overflowing,
Not the faint sparks of thy hearth ever glowing,
Not a pale bud from the June rose's blowing;
Give as He gave thee, who gave thee to live.

Pour out thy love like the rush of a river
Wasting its waters, for ever and ever,
Through the burnt sands that reward not the giver;
Silent or songful, thou nearest the sea.
Scatter thy life as the Summer shower's pouring!
What if no bird through the pearl-rain is soaring?
What if no blossom looks upward adoring?
Look to the life that was lavished for thee!

Give, though thy heart may be wasted and weary,
Laid on an altar all ashen and dreary;
Though from its pulses a faint miserere
Beats to thy soul the sad presage of fate,
Bind it with cords of unshrinking devotion;
Smile at the song of its restless emotion;
'T is the stern hymn of eternity's ocean;
Hear! and in silence thy future await.

So the wild wind strews its perfumed caresses,
Evil and thankless the desert it blesses,
Bitter the wave that its soft pinion presses,
Never it ceaseth to whisper and sing.
What if the hard heart give thorns for thy roses?
What if on rocks thy tired bosom reposes?
Sweetest is music with minor-keyed closes,
Fairest the vines that on ruin will cling.

Almost the day of thy giving is over;
Ere from the grass dies the bee-haunted clover,
Thou wilt have vanished from friend and from lover.
What shall thy longing avail in the grave?
Give as the heart gives whose fetters are breaking,
Life, love, and hope, all thy dreams and thy waking.
Soon, heaven's river thy soul-fever slaking,
Thou shalt know God and the gift that he gave.

ANNE C. (LYNCH) BOTTA.

[U. S. A.]

LOVE.

Go forth in life, O friend! not seeking love,
A mendicant that with imploring eye
And outstretched hand asks of the passers-by
The alms his strong necessities may move:
For such poor love, to pity near allied,
Thy generous spirit may not stoop and wait,
A suppliant whose prayer may be denied
Like a spurned beggar's at a palace-gate:
But thy heart's affluence lavish uncontrolled, —
The largess of thy love give full and free,
As monarchs in their progress scatter gold;
And be thy heart like the exhaustless sea,
That must its wealth of cloud and dew bestow,
Though tributary streams or ebb or flow.

LYDIA H. SIGOURNEY.

[U. S. A., 1791-1865.]

INDIAN NAMES.

Ye say they all have passed away,
 That noble race and brave;
That their light canoes have vanished
 From off the crested wave;
That mid the forests where they roamed
 There rings no hunter's shout;
But their name is on your waters,
 Ye may not wash it out.

'T is where Ontario's billow
 Like ocean's surge is curled,
Where strong Niagara's thunders wake
 The echo of the world.
Where red Missouri bringeth
 Rich tribute from the West,
And Rappahannock sweetly sleeps,
 On green Virginia's breast.

Ye say their cone-like cabins,
 That clustered o'er the vale,
Have fled away like withered leaves
 Before the autumn gale;
But their memory liveth on your hills,
 Their baptism on your shore,
Your everlasting rivers speak
 Their dialect of yore.

Old Massachusetts wears it
 Upon her lordly crown,
And broad Ohio bears it
 Amid his young renown;
Connecticut hath wreathed it
 Where her quiet foliage waves;
And bold Kentucky breathed it hoarse
 Through all her ancient caves.

Wachusett hides its lingering voice
 Within his rocky heart,
And Alleghany graves its tone
 Throughout his lofty chart;
Monadnock on his forehead hoar
 Doth seal the sacred trust;
Your mountains build their monument,
 Though ye destroy their dust.

Ye call these red-browed brethren
 The insects of an hour,
Crushed like the noteless worm amid
 The regions of their power;
Ye drive them from their fathers' lands,
 Ye break of faith the seal,
But can ye from the court of Heaven
 Exclude their last appeal?

Ye see their unresisting tribes,
 With toilsome step and slow,
On through the trackless desert pass,
 A caravan of woe;
Think ye the Eternal Ear is deaf?
 His sleepless vision dim?
Think ye the *soul's blood* may not cry
 From that far land to him?

WILLIAM H. FURNESS.

[U. S. A.]

ETERNAL LIGHT.

Slowly, by God's hand unfurled,
Down around the weary world,
Falls the darkness; O, how still
Is the working of his will!

Mighty Spirit, ever nigh,
Work in me as silently;
Veil the day's distracting sights,
Show me heaven's eternal lights.

Living stars to view be brought
In the boundless realms of thought;
High and infinite desires,
Flaming like those upper fires.

Holy Truth, Eternal Right,
Let them break upon my sight;
Let them shine serene and still,
And with light my being fill.

JAMES T. FIELDS.

[U. S. A.]

WORDSWORTH.

The grass hung wet on Rydal banks,
 The golden day with pearls adorning,
When side by side with him we walked
 To meet midway the summer morning.

The west-wind took a softer breath,
 The sun himself seemed brighter shin-
  ing,

As through the porch the minstrel stepped,—
His eye sweet Nature's look enshrining.

He passed along the dewy sward,
The bluebird sang aloft "good morrow!"
He plucked a bud, the flower awoke,
And smiled without one pang of sorrow.

He spoke of all that graced the scene,
In tones that fell like music round us;
We felt the charm descend, nor strove
To break the rapturous spell that bound us.

We listened with mysterious awe,
Strange feelings mingling with our pleasure;
We heard that day prophetic words,
High thoughts the heart must always treasure.

Great Nature's Priest! thy calm career
With that sweet morn on earth has ended:
But who shall say thy mission died
When, winged for Heaven, thy soul ascended!

HENRY HOWARD BROWNELL.

[U. S. A., 1820-1872.]

THE BURIAL OF THE DANE.

BLUE gulf all around us,
Blue sky overhead,—
Muster all on the quarter,
We must bury the dead!

It is but a Danish sailor,
Rugged of front and form;
A common son of the forecastle,
Grizzled with sun and storm.

His name and the strand he hailed from
We know,—and there 's nothing more!
But perhaps his mother is waiting
In the lonely island of Fohr.

Still, as he lay there dying,
Reason drifting awreck,
"'T is my watch," he would mutter,
"I must go upon deck!"

Ay, on deck,—by the foremast!—
But watch and lookout are done;
The Union-Jack laid o'er him,
How quiet he lies in the sun!

Slow the ponderous engine,
Stay the hurrying shaft!
Let the roll of the ocean
Cradle our giant craft,—
Gather around the grating,
Carry your messmate aft!

Stand in order, and listen
To the holiest page of prayer!
Let every foot be quiet,
Every head be bare,—
The soft trade-wind is lifting
A hundred locks of hair.

Our captain reads the service
(A little spray on his cheeks),
The grand old words of burial,
And the trust a true heart seeks,—
"We therefore commit his body
To the deep,"—and, as he speaks,

Launched from the weather-railing,
Swift as the eye can mark,
The ghastly, shotted hammock
Plunges, away from the shark,
Down, a thousand fathoms,
Down into the dark!

A thousand summers and winters
The stormy Gulf shall roll
High o'er his canvas coffin,—
But, silence to doubt and dole!
There's a quiet harbor somewhere
For the poor a-weary soul.

Free the fettered engine,
Speed the tireless shaft!
Loose to'gallant and topsail,
The breeze is fair abaft!

Blue sea all around us,
Blue sky bright o'erhead,—
Every man to his duty!
We have buried our dead.

BAYARD TAYLOR.

[U. S. A.]

THE MOUNTAINS.

(From "THE MASQUE OF THE GODS.")

HOWE'ER the wheels of Time go round,
We cannot wholly be discrowned.
We bind, in form, and hue, and height,
The Finite to the Infinite,
And, lifted on our shoulders bare,
The races breathe an ampler air.
The arms that clasped, the lips that kissed,
Have vanished from the morning mist;
The dainty shapes that flashed and passed
In spray the plunging torrent cast,
Or danced through woven gleam and shade,
The vapors and the sunbeams braid,
Grow thin and pale: each holy haunt
Of gods or spirits ministrant
Hath something lost of ancient awe;
Yet from the stooping heavens we draw
A beauty, mystery, and might,
Time cannot change nor worship slight.
The gold of dawn and sunset sheds
Unearthly glory on our heads;
The secret of the skies we keep;
And whispers, round each lonely steep,
Allure and promise, yet withhold,
What bard and prophet never told.
While Man's slow ages come and go,
Our dateless chronicles of snow
Their changeless old inscription show,
And men therein forever see
The unread speech of Deity.

AN ORIENTAL IDYL.

A SILVER javelin which the hills
Have hurled upon the plain below,
The fleetest of the Pharpar's rills,
Beneath me shoots in flashing flow.

I hear the never-ending laugh
Of jostling waves that come and go,
And suck the bubbling pipe, and quaff
The sherbet cooled in mountain snow.

The flecks of sunshine gleam like stars
Beneath the canopy of shade;
And in the distant, dim bazaars,
I scarcely hear the hum of trade.

No evil fear, no dream forlorn,
Darkens my heaven of perfect blue;
My blood is tempered to the morn,—
My very heart is steeped in dew.

What Evil is I cannot tell;
But half I guess what Joy may be;
And, as a pearl within its shell,
The happy spirit sleeps in me.

I feel no more the pulse's strife,—
The tides of Passion's ruddy sea,—
But live the sweet, unconscious life
That breathes from yonder jasmine-tree.

Upon the glittering pageantries
Of gay Damascus streets I look
As idly as a babe that sees
The painted pictures of a book.

Forgotten now are name and race;
The Past is blotted from my brain;
For Memory sleeps, and will not trace
The weary pages o'er again.

I only know the morning shines,
And sweet the dewy morning air,
But does it play with tendrilled vines?
Or does it lightly lift my hair?

Deep-sunken in the charmed repose,
This ignorance is bliss extreme;
And whether I be Man, or Rose,
O, pluck me not from out my dream!

THE VOYAGERS.

No longer spread the sail!
No longer strain the oar!
For never yet has blown the gale
Will bring us nearer shore.

The swaying keel slides on,
The helm obeys the hand;
Fast we have sailed from dawn to dawn,
Yet never reach the land.

Each morn we see its peaks,
Made beautiful with snow;
Each eve its vales and winding creeks,
That sleep in mist below.

At noon we mark the gleam
Of temples tall and fair;
At midnight watch its bonfires stream
In the auroral air.

And still the keel is swift,
  And still the wind is free,
And still as far its mountains lift
  Beyond the enchanted sea.

Yet vain is all return,
  Though false the goal before;
The gale is ever dead astern,
  The current sets to shore.

O shipmates, leave the ropes;
  And what though no one steers,
We sail no faster for our hopes,
  No slower for our fears.

THE SONG OF THE CAMP.

"Give us a song!" the soldiers cried,
  The outer trenches guarding,
When the heated guns of the camps allied
  Grew weary of bombarding.

The dark Redan, in silent scoff,
  Lay, grim and threatening, under;
And the tawny mound of the Malakoff
  No longer belched its thunder.

There was a pause. A guardsman said:
  "We storm the forts to-morrow;
Sing while we may, another day
  Will bring enough of sorrow."

They lay along the battery's side,
  Below the smoking cannon:
Brave hearts, from Severn and from Clyde,
  And from the banks of Shannon.

They sang of love, and not of fame;
  Forgot was Britain's glory:
Each heart recalled a different name,
  But all sang "Annie Laurie."

Voice after voice caught up the song,
  Until its tender passion
Rose like an anthem, rich and strong, —
  Their battle-eve confession.

Dear girl, her name he dared not speak,
  But, as the song grew louder,
Something upon the soldier's cheek
  Washed off the stains of powder.

Beyond the darkening ocean burned
  The bloody sunset's embers,
While the Crimean valleys learned
  How English love remembers.

And once again a fire of hell
  Rained on the Russian quarters,
With scream of shot, and burst of shell,
  And bellowing of the mortars!

And Irish Nora's eyes are dim
  For a singer, dumb and gory;
And English Mary mourns for him
  Who sang of "Annie Laurie."

Sleep, soldiers! still in honored rest
  Your truth and valor wearing;
The bravest are the tenderest, —
  The loving are the daring.

SARA J. LIPPINCOTT (GRACE GREENWOOD).

[U. S. A.]

THE POET OF TO-DAY.

More than the soul of ancient song is given
  To thee, O poet of to-day! — thy dower
Comes, from a higher than Olympian heaven,
  In holier beauty and in larger power.

To thee Humanity, her woes revealing,
  Would all her griefs and ancient wrongs rehearse;
Would make thy song the voice of her appealing,
  And sob her mighty sorrows through thy verse.

While in her season of great darkness sharing,
  Hail thou the coming of each promise-star
Which climbs the midnight of her long despairing,
  And watch for morning o'er the hills afar.

Wherever Truth her holy warfare wages,
  Or Freedom pines, there let thy voice be heard;
Sound like a prophet-warning down the ages
  The human utterance of God's living word.

But bring not thou the battle's stormy chorus,
The tramp of armies, and the roar of fight,
Not war's hot smoke to taint the sweet morn o'er us,
Nor blaze of pillage, reddening up the night.

O, let thy lays prolong that angel-singing,
Girdling with music the Redeemer's star,
And breathe God's peace, to earth 'glad tidings' bringing
From the near heavens, of old so dim and far!

ALEXANDER SMITH.

[1830-1867.]

LADY BARBARA.

Earl Gawain wooed the Lady Barbara,
High-thoughted Barbara, so white and cold!
'Mong broad-branched beeches in the summer shaw,
In soft green light his passion he has told.
When rain-beat winds did shriek across the wold,
The Earl to take her fair reluctant ear
Framed passion-trembled ditties manifold;
Silent she sat his amorous breath to hear,
With calm and steady eyes; her heart was otherwhere.

He sighed for her through all the summer weeks;
Sitting beneath a tree whose fruitful boughs
Bore glorious apples with smooth, shining cheeks,
Earl Gawain came and whispered, "Lady, rouse!
Thou art no vestal held in holy vows;
Out with our falcons to the pleasant heath."
Her father's blood leapt up unto her brows, —
He who, exulting on the trumpet's breath,
Came charging like a star across the lists of death,

Trembled, and passed before her high rebuke:
And then she sat, her hands clasped round her knee:
Like one far-thoughted was the lady's look,
For in a morning cold as misery
She saw a lone ship sailing on the sea;
Before the north 't was driven like a cloud,
High on the poop a man sat mournfully:
The wind was whistling through mast and shroud.
And to the whistling wind thus did he sing aloud: —

"Didst look last night upon my native vales,
Thou Sun! that from the drenching sea hast clomb?
Ye demon winds! that glut my gaping sails,
Upon the salt sea must I ever roam,
Wander forever on the barren foam?
O, happy are ye, resting mariners!
O Death, that thou wouldst come and and take me home!
A hand unseen this vessel onward steers,
And onward I must float through slow, moon-measured years.

"Ye winds! when like a curse ye drove us on,
Frothing the waters, and along our way,
Nor cape nor headland through red mornings shone,
One wept aloud, one shuddered down to pray,
One howled 'Upon the deep we are astray.'
On our wild hearts his words fell like a blight:
In one short hour my hair was stricken gray,
For all the crew sank ghastly in my sight
As we went driving on through the cold starry night.

"Madness fell on me in my loneliness,
The sea foamed curses, and the reeling sky

Became a dreadful face which did oppress
Me with the weight of its unwinking eye.
It fled, when I burst forth into a cry,—
A shoal of fiends came on me from the deep;
I hid, but in all corners they did pry,
And dragged me forth, and round did dance and leap;
They mouthed on me in dream, and tore me from sweet sleep.

"Strange constellations burned above my head,
Strange birds around the vessel shrieked and flew,
Strange shapes, like shadows, through the clear sea fled,
As our lone ship, wide-winged, came rippling through,
Angering to foam the smooth and sleeping blue."
The lady sighed, "Far, far upon the sea,
My own Sir Arthur, could I die with you!
The wind blows shrill between my love and me."
Fond heart! the space between was but the apple-tree.

There was a cry of joy, with seeking hands
She fled to him, like worn bird to her nest;
Like washing water on the figured sands,
His being came and went in sweet unrest,
As from the mighty shelter of his breast
The Lady Barbara her head uprears
With a wan smile, "Methinks I'm but half blest:
Now when I've found thee, after weary years,
I cannot see thee, love! so blind I am with tears."

MATTHEW ARNOLD.

THE TERRACE AT BERNE.

TEN years!—and to my waking eye
Once more the roofs of Berne appear;
The rocky banks, the terrace high,
The stream,—and do I linger here?

The clouds are on the Oberland,
The Jungfrau snows look faint and far;
But bright are those green fields at hand,
And through those fields comes down the Aar,

And from the blue twin lakes it comes,
Flows by the town, the churchyard fair,
And 'neath the garden-walk it hums,
The house,—and is my Marguerite there?

Ah, shall I see thee, while a flush
Of startled pleasure floods thy brow,
Quick through the oleanders brush,
And clap thy hands, and cry, '*T is thou?*

Or hast thou long since wandered back,
Daughter of France! to France, thy home;
And flitted down the flowery track
Where feet like thine too lightly come?

Doth riotous laughter now replace
Thy smile, and rouge, with stony glare,
Thy cheek's soft hue and fluttering lace
The kerchief that enwound thy hair?

Or is it over?—art thou dead?—
Dead?—and no warning shiver ran
Across my heart, to say thy thread
Of life was cut, and closed thy span!

Could from earth's ways that figure slight
Be lost, and I not feel 't was so?
Of that fresh voice the gay delight
Fail from earth's air, and I not know?

Or shall I find thee still, but changed,
But not the Marguerite of thy prime?
With all thy being rearranged,
Passed through the crucible of time;

With spirit vanished, beauty waned,
And hardly yet a glance, a tone,
A gesture,—anything,—retained
Of all that was my Marguerite's own?

I will not know!—for wherefore try
To things by mortal course that live
A shadowy durability
For which they were not meant to give?

Like driftwood spars which meet and pass
Upon the boundless ocean-plain,

So on the sea of life, alas!
  Man nears man, meets, and leaves again.

I knew it when my life was young,
  I feel it still, now youth is o'er!
The mists are on the mountain hung,
  And Marguerite I shall see no more.

URANIA.

She smiles and smiles, and will not sigh,
While we for hopeless passion die;
Yet she could love, those eyes declare,
Were but men nobler than they are.

Eagerly once her gracious ken
Was turned upon the sons of men;
But light the serious visage grew, —
She looked, and smiled, and saw them through.

Our petty souls, our strutting wits,
Our labored puny passion-fits, —
Ah, may she scorn them still, till we
Scorn them as bitterly as she!

Yet O, that Fate would let her see
One of some worthier race than we, —
One for whose sake she once might prove
How deeply she who scorns can love.

His eyes be like the starry lights, —
His voice like sounds of summer nights, —
In all his lovely mien let pierce
The magic of the universe!

And she to him will reach her hand,
And gazing in his eyes will stand,
And know her friend, and weep for glee!
And cry, Long, long I've looked for thee!

Then will she weep, — with smiles, till then,
Coldly she mocks the sons of men.
Till then her lovely eyes maintain
Their gay, unwavering, deep disdain.

THE LAST WORD.

Creep into thy narrow bed,
Creep, and let no more be said!
Vain thy onset! all stands fast;
Thou thyself must break at last.

Let the long contention cease!
Geese are swans, and swans are geese.
Let them have it how they will!
Thou art tired; best be still!

They out-talked thee, hissed thee, tore thee.
Better men fared thus before thee;
Fired their ringing shot and passed,
Hotly charged, — and broke at last.

Charge once more, then, and be dumb!
Let the victors, when they come,
When the forts of folly fall,
Find thy body by the wall.

ROBERT LORD LYTTON.

THE ARTIST.

O Artist, range not over-wide:
  Lest what thou seek be haply hid
In bramble-blossoms at thy side,
  Or shut within the daisy-lid.

God's glory lies not out of reach.
  The moss we crush beneath our feet,
The pebbles on the wet sea-beach,
  Have solemn meanings strange and sweet.

The peasant at his cottage door
  May teach thee more than Plato knew;
See that thou scorn him not: adore
  God in him, and thy nature too.

Know well thy friends. The woodbine's breath,
  The woolly tendril on the vine,
Are more to thee than Cato's death,
  Or Cicero's words to Catiline.

The wild rose is thy next in blood:
  Share Nature with her, and thy heart.
The kingcups are thy sisterhood:
  Consult them duly on thine art.

The Genius on thy daily ways
  Shall meet, and take thee by the hand:
But serve him not as who obeys:
  He is thy slave if thou command:

And blossoms on the blackberry-stalks
  He shall enchant as thou dost pass,

Till they drop gold upon thy walks,
And diamonds in the dewy grass.

Be quiet. Take things as they come:
Each hour will draw out some surprise.
With blessing let the days go home:
Thou shalt have thanks from evening skies.

Lean not on one mind constantly:
Lest, where one stood before, two fall.
Something God hath to say to thee
Worth hearing from the lips of all.

All things are thine estate: yet must
Thou first display the title-deeds,
And sue the world. Be strong: and trust
High instincts more than all the creeds.

The world of Thought is packed so tight,
If thou stand up another tumbles:
Heed it not, though thou have to fight
With giants; whoso follows stumbles.

Assert thyself: and by and by
The world will come and lean on thee.
But seek not praise of men: thereby
Shall false shows cheat thee. Boldly be.

Each man was worthy at the first:
God spake to us ere we were born:
But we forget. The land is curst:
We plant the brier, reap the thorn.

Remember, every man He made
Is different: has some deed to do,
Some work to work. Be undismayed,
Though thine be humble: do it too.

Not all the wisdom of the schools
Is wise for thee. Hast thou to speak?
No man hath spoken for thee. Rules
Are well: but never fear to break

The scaffolding of other souls:
It was not meant for thee to mount;
Though it may serve thee. Separate wholes
Make up the sum of God's account.

Earth's number-scale is near us set;
The total God alone can see;
But each some fraction: shall I fret
If you see Four where I saw Three?

A unit's loss the sum would mar;
Therefore if I have One or Two,
I am as rich as others are,
And help the whole as well as you.

This wild white rosebud in my hand
Hath meanings meant for me alone,
Which no one else can understand:
To you it breathes with altered tone:

We go to Nature, not as lords,
But servants; and she treats us thus:
Speaks to us with indifferent words,
And from a distance looks at us.

Let us go boldly, as we ought,
And say to her, "We are a part
Of that supreme original Thought
Which did conceive thee what thou art.

"We will not have this lofty look:
Thou shalt fall down, and recognize
Thy kings: we will write in thy book;
Command thee with our eyes."

She hath usurpt us. She should be
Our model; but we have become
Her miniature-painters. So when we
Entreat her softly, she is dumb.

Nor serve the subject overmuch:
Nor rhythm and rhyme, nor color and form.
Know Truth hath all great graces, such
As shall with these thy work inform.

We ransack History's tattered page:
We prate of epoch and costume:
Call this, and that, the Classic Age:
Choose tunic now, now helm and plume:

But while we halt in weak debate
'Twixt that and this appropriate theme,
The offended wild-flowers stare and wait,
The bird hoots at us from the stream.

Next, as to laws. What 's beautiful
We recognize in form and face:
And judge it thus, and thus, by rule,
As perfect law brings perfect grace:

If through the effect we drag the cause,
Dissect, divide, anatomize,
Results are lost in loathsome laws,
And all the ancient beauty dies:

Till we, instead of bloom and light,
See only sinews, nerves, and veins;
Nor will the effect and cause unite,
For one is lost if one remains:

But from some higher point behold
  This dense, perplexing complication;
And laws involved in laws unfold,
  And orb into thy contemplation.

God, when he made the seed, conceived
  The flower; and all the work of sun
And rain, before the stem was leaved,
  In that prenatal thought was done;

The girl who twines in her soft hair
  The orange-flower, with love's devotion,
By the mere act of being fair
  Sets countless laws of life in motion;

So thou, by one thought thoroughly great,
  Shalt, without heed thereto, fulfil
All laws of art. Create! create!
  Dissection leaves the dead dead still.

Burn catalogues. Write thine own books.
  What need to pore o'er Greece and Rome?
When whoso through his own life looks
  Shall find that he is fully come,

Through Greece and Rome, and Middle Age:
  Hath been by turns, ere yet full-grown,
Soldier, and Senator, and Sage,
  And worn the tunic and the gown.

Cut the world thoroughly to the heart.
  The sweet and bitter kernel crack.
Have no half-dealings with thine art.
  All heaven is waiting: turn not back.

If all the world for thee and me
  One solitary shape possessed,
What shall I say? a single tree,
  Whereby to type and hint the rest,

And I could imitate the bark
  And foliage, both in form and hue,
Or silvery-gray, or brown and dark,
  Or rough with moss, or wet with dew,

But thou, with one form in thine eye,
  Couldst penetrate all forms: possess
The soul of form: and multiply
  A million like it, more or less,—

Which were the Artist of us twain?
  The moral 's clear to understand.
Where'er we walk, by hill or plain,
  Is there no mystery on the land?

The osiered, oozy water, ruffled
  By fluttering swifts that dip and wink:
Deep cattle in the cowslips muffled,
  Or lazy-eyed upon the brink:

Or, when—a scroll of stars—the night
  (By God withdrawn) is rolled away,
The silent sun, on some cold height,
  Breaking the great seal of the day:

Are these not words more rich than ours?
  O, seize their import if you can!
Our souls are parched like withering flowers,
  Our knowledge ends where it began.

While yet about us fall God's dews,
  And whisper secrets o'er the earth
Worth all the weary years we lose
  In learning legends of our birth,

Arise, O Artist! and restore
  Their music to the moaning winds,
Love's broken pearls to life's bare shore,
  And freshness to our fainting minds.

ANNE WHITNEY.

[U. S. A.]

BERTHA.

THE leaves have fallen from the trees;
For under them grew the buds of May,
And such is Nature's constant way;
  Let us accept the work of her hand.
Still, if the winds sweep bare the height,
Something is left for hearts' delight,
  Let us but know and understand.

Bertha looked down from the rocky cliff,
Whose feet the tender foam-wreaths kist,
Toward the outer circle of mist
  That hedged the old and wonderful sea.
Below her, as if with endless hope,
Up the beach's marbled slope,
  The waters clomb eternally.

Many a long-bleached sail in sight
Hovered awhile, then flitted away,
Beyond the opening of the bay;
  Fair Bertha entered her cottage late;
"He does not come," she said, and smiled,

"But the shore is dark, and the sea is wild,
And, dearest father, we still must wait."

She hastened to her inner room,
And silently mused there alone;
"Three springs have come, three winters gone,
And still we wait from hour to hour;
But earth waits long for her harvest-time,
And the aloe, in the northern clime,
Waits an hundred years for its flower.

"Under the apple-boughs as I sit
In May-time, when the robin's song
Thrills the odorous winds along,
The innermost heaven seems to ope;
I think, though the old joys pass from sight,
Still something is left for hearts' delight,
For life is endless, and so is hope.

"If the aloe waits an hundred years,
And God's times are so long indeed
For simple things, as flower and weed,
That gather only the light and gloom,
For what great treasures of joy and dole,
Of life and death, perchance, must the soul,
Ere it flower in heavenly peace, find room?

"I see that all things wait in trust,
As feeling afar God's distant ends,
And unto every creature he sends
That measure of good that fills its scope;
The marmot enters the stiffening mould,
And the worm its dark sepulchral fold,
To hide there with its beautiful hope."

Still Bertha waited on the cliff,
To catch the gleam of a coming sail,
And the distant whisper of the gale,
Winging the unforgotten home;
And hope at her yearning heart would knock,
When a sunbeam on a far-off rock
Married a wreath of wandering foam.

Was it well? you ask—(nay, was it ill?)—
Who sat last year by the old man's hearth;
The sun had passed below the earth,
And the first star locked its western gate,
When Bertha entered his darkening home,
And smiling said, "He does not come,
But, dearest father, we still can wait!"

J. H. PERKINS.

[U. S. A.]

THE UPRIGHT SOUL.

LATE to our town there came a maid,
A noble woman, true and pure,
Who, in the little while she stayed,
Wrought works that shall endure.

It was not anything she said, —
It was not anything she did:
It was the movement of her head,
The lifting of her lid.

Her little motions when she spoke,
The presence of an upright soul,
The living light that from her broke,
It was the perfect whole:

We saw it in her floating hair,
We saw it in her laughing eye;
For every look and feature there
Wrought works that cannot die.

For she to many spirits gave
A reverence for the true, the pure,
The perfect, that has power to save,
And make the doubting sure.

She passed, she went to other lands,
She knew not of the work she did;
The wondrous product of her hands
From her is ever hid.

Forever, did I say? O, no!
The time must come when she will look
Upon her pilgrimage below,
And find it in God's book,

That, as she trod her path aright,
Power from her very garments stole;
For such is the mysterious might
God grants the upright soul.

A deed, a word, our careless rest,
A simple thought, a common feeling,
If He be present in the breast,
Has from him powers of healing.

Go, maiden, with thy golden tresses,
Thine azure eye and changing cheek,
Go, and forget the one who blesses
Thy presence through the week.

Forget him: he will not forget,
But strive to live and testify
Thy goodness, when earth's sun has set,
And Time itself rolled by.

GEORGE MACDONALD.

O LASSIE AYONT THE HILL!

O LASSIE ayont the hill!
Come ower the tap o' the hill,
Or roun' the neuk o' the hill,
For I want ye sair the nicht,
I 'm needin' ye sair the nicht,
For I 'm tired and sick o' mysel',
A body's sel' 's the sairest weicht,—
O lassie, come ower the hill!

Gin a body could be a thocht o' grace,
And no a sel' ava!
I 'm sick o' my heid, and my han's and my face,
An' my thochts and mysel' and a';
I 'm sick o' the warl' and a';
The licht gangs by wi' a hiss;
For thro' my een the sunbeams fa',
But my weary heart they miss.
O lassie ayont the hill!
Come ower the tap o' the hill,
Or roun' the neuk o' the hill;
Bidena ayont the hill!

For gin ance I saw yer bonnie heid,
And the sunlicht o' yer hair,
The ghaist o' mysel' wad fa' doun deid;
I wad be mysel' nae mair.
I wad be mysel' nae mair.
Filled o' the sole remeid;
Slain by the arrows o' licht frae yer hair.
Killed by yer body and heid.
O lassie ayont the hill, etc.

But gin ye lo'ed me ever sae sma',
For the sake o' my bonnie dame,
Whan I cam' to life, as she gaed awa',
I could bide my body and name,
I micht bide by mysel' the weary same;
Aye setting up its heid
Till I turn frae the claes that cover my frame,
As gin they war roun' the deid.
O lassie ayont the hill, etc.

But gin ye lo'ed me as I lo'e you,
I wad ring my ain deid knell;
Mysel' wad vanish, shot through and through
Wi' the shine o' yer sunny sel',
By the licht aneath yer broo,
I wad dee to mysel', and ring my bell,
And only live in you.

O lassie ayont the hill!
Come ower the tap o' the hill,
Or roun' the neuk o' the hill,
For I want ye sair the nicht,
I 'm needin' ye sair the nicht,
For I 'm tired and sick o' mysel',
A body's sel' 's the sairest weicht,—
O lassie, come ower the hill!

HYMN FOR THE MOTHER.

MY child is lying on my knees;
The signs of heaven she reads;
My face is all the heaven she sees,
Is all the heaven she needs.

And she is well, yea, bathed in bliss,
If heaven is in my face,—
Behind it is all tenderness
And truthfulness and grace.

I mean her well so earnestly,
Unchanged in changing mood;
My life would go without a sigh
To bring her something good.

I also am a child, and I
Am ignorant and weak;
I gaze upon the starry sky,
And then I must not speak;

For all behind the starry sky,
Behind the world so broad,
Behind men's hearts and souls doth lie
The Infinite of God.

Ay, true to her, though troubled sore,
I cannot choose but be:
Thou who art peace forevermore
Art very true to me.

If I am low and sinful, bring
More love where need is rife;
Thou knowest what an awful thing
It is to be a life.

Hast thou not wisdom to enwrap
My waywardness about,
In doubting safety on the lap
Of Love that knows no doubt?

Lo! Lord, I sit in thy wide space,
My child upon my knee;
She looketh up into my face,
And I look up to thee.

ELIZA SPROAT TURNER.

[U. S. A.]

AN ANGEL'S VISIT.

SHE stood in the harvest-field at noon,
And sang aloud for the joy of living.
She said: "'T is the sun that I drink like wine,
To my heart this gladness giving."

Rank upon rank the wheat fell slain;
The reapers ceased. "'T is sure the splendor
Of sloping sunset light that thrills
My breast with a bliss so tender."

Up and up the blazing hills
Climbed the night from the misty meadows.
"Can they be stars, or living eyes
That bend on me from the shadows?"

"Greeting!" "And may you speak, indeed?"
All in the dark her sense grew clearer;
She knew that she had, for company,
All day an angel near her.

"May you tell us of the life divine,
To us unknown, to angels given?"
"Count me your earthly joys, and I
May teach you those of heaven."

"They say the pleasures of earth are vain;
Delusions all, to lure from duty;
But while God hangs his bow in the rain,
Can I help my joy in beauty?

"And while he quickens the air with song,
My breaths with scent, my fruits with flavor,
Will he, dear angel, count as sin
My life in sound and savor?

"See, at our feet the glow-worm shines,
Lo! in the east a star arises;
And thought may climb from worm to world
Forever through fresh surprises:

"And thought is joy. . . . And, hark! in the vale
Music, and merry steps pursuing;
They leap in the dance, — a soul in my blood
Cries out, Awake, be doing!

"Action is joy; or power at play,
Or power at work in world or emprises:
Action is life; part from the deed,
More from the doing rises."

"And are these all?" She flushed in the dark.
"These are not all. I have a lover;
At sound of his voice, at touch of his hand,
The cup of my life runs over.

"Once, unknowing, we looked and neared,
And doubted, and neared, and rested never,
Till life seized life, as flame meets flame,
To escape no more forever.

"Lover and husband; then was love
The wine of my life, all life enhancing:
Now 't is my bread, too needful and sweet
To be kept for feast-day chancing.

"I have a child." She seemed to change;
The deep content of some brooding creature
Looked from her eyes. "O, sweet and strange!
Angel, be thou my teacher:

"When He made us one in a babe,
Was it for joy, or sorest proving?
For now I fear no heaven could win
Our hearts from earthly loving.

"I have a friend. Howso I err,
I see her uplifting love bend o'er me;
Howso I climb to my best, I know
Her foot will be there before me.

"Howso parted, we must be nigh,
Held by old years of every weather;
The best new love would be less than ours
Who have lived our lives together.

"Now, lest forever I fail to see
Right skies, through clouds so bright and tender,
Show me true joy." The angel's smile
Lit all the night with splendor.

"Save that to Love and Learn and Do
In wondrous measure to us is given;
Save that we see the face of God,
You have named the joys of heaven."

CHRISTINA ROSSETTI.

AFTER DEATH.

The curtains were half drawn, the floor was swept
And strewn with rushes; rosemary and may
Lay thick upon the bed on which I lay,
Where through the lattice ivy-shadows crept.
He leaned above me, thinking that I slept,
And could not hear him; but I heard him say,
"Poor child! poor child!" and as he turned away,
Came a deep silence, and I knew he wept.
He did not touch the shroud, or raise the fold
That hid my face, or take my hand in his,
Or ruffle the smooth pillows for my head.
He did not love me living: but once dead
He pitied me; and very sweet it is
To know he still is warm, though I am cold.

WEARY.

I would have gone; God bade me stay:
I would have worked; God bade me rest.
He broke my will from day to day;
He read my yearnings unexpressed,
And said me nay.

Now I would stay; God bids me go:
Now I would rest; God bids me work.
He breaks my heart tossed to and fro;
My soul is wrung with doubts that lurk
And vex it so!

I go, Lord, where thou sendest me;
Day after day I plod and moil;
But, Christ my Lord, when will it be
That I may let alone my toil
And rest with thee?

DORA GREENWELL.

THE SUNFLOWER.

Till the slow daylight pale,
A willing slave, fast bound to one above,
I wait; he seems to speed, and change, and fail;
I know he will not move.

I lift my golden orb
To his, unsmitten when the roses die,
And in my broad and burning disk absorb
The splendors of his eye.

His eye is like a clear
Keen flame that searches through me; I must droop
Upon my stalk, I cannot reach his sphere;
To mine he cannot stoop.

I win not my desire,
And yet I fail not of my guerdon; lo!
A thousand flickering darts and tongues of fire
Around me spread and glow;

All rayed and crowned, I miss
No queenly state until the summer wane,
The hours flit by; none knoweth of my bliss,
And none has guessed my pain;

I follow one above,
I track the shadow of his steps, I grow
Most like to him I love
Of all that shines below.

VESPERS.

WHEN I have said my quiet say,
When I have sung my little song,
How sweetly, sweetly dies the day
The valley and the hill along;
How sweet the summons, "Come away,"
That calls me from the busy throng!

I thought beside the water's flow
Awhile to lie beneath the leaves,
I thought in Autumn's harvest glow
To rest my head upon the sheaves;
But, lo! methinks the day was brief
And cloudy; flower, nor fruit, nor leaf
I bring, and yet accepted, free,
And blest, my Lord, I come to thee.

What matter now for promise lost,
Through blast of spring or summer rains!
What matter now for purpose crost,
For broken hopes and wasted pains;
What if the olive little yields,
What if the grape be blighted? Thine
The corn upon a thousand fields,
Upon a thousand hills the vine.

Thou lovest still the poor; O, blest
In poverty beloved to be!
Less lowly is my choice confessed,
I love the rich in loving Thee!
My spirit bare before thee stands,
I bring no gift, I ask no sign,
I come to thee with empty hands,
The surer to be filled from thine!

ELIZABETH H. WHITTIER.

[U. S. A., 1816-1848.]

CHARITY.

THE pilgrim and stranger, who, through the day,
Holds over the desert his trackless way,
Where the terrible sands no shade have known,
No sound of life save his camel's moan,
Hears, at last, through the mercy of Allah to all,
From his tent-door, at evening, the Bedouin's call:
"Whoever thou art, whose need is great,
In the name of God, the Compassionate
And Merciful One, for thee I wait!"

For gifts, in his name, of food and rest,
The tents of Islam of God are blest.
Thou, who hast faith in the Christ above,
Shall the Koran teach thee the Law of Love?
O Christian!—open thy heart and door,—
Cry, east and west, to the wandering poor,—
"Whoever thou art, whose need is great,
In the name of Christ, the Compassionate
And Merciful One, for thee I wait!"

THE MEETING WATERS.

CLOSE beside the meeting waters,
Long I stood as in a dream,
Watching how the little river
Fell into the broader stream.

Calm and still the mingled current
Glided to the waiting sea;
On its breast serenely pictured
Floating cloud and skirting tree.

And I thought, "O human spirit!
Strong and deep and pure and blest,
Let the stream of my existence
Blend with thine, and find its rest!"

I could die as dies the river,
In that current deep and wide;
I would live as live its waters,
Flashing from a stronger tide!

ELIZABETH AKERS ALLEN.

WHEN THE GRASS SHALL COVER ME.

WHEN the grass shall cover me,
Head to foot where I am lying;
When not any wind that blows,
Summer bloom or winter snows,
Shall awake me to your sighing:
Close above me as you pass,
You will say, "How kind she was,"
You will say, "How true she was,"
When the grass grows over me.

When the grass shall cover me,
Holden close to earth's warm bosom;
While I laugh, or weep, or sing,
Nevermore for anything

You will find in blade and blossom,
Sweet small voices, odorous,
Tender pleaders of my cause,
That shall speak me as I was, —
When the grass grows over me.

When the grass shall cover me!
Ah, beloved in my sorrow,
Very patient can I wait;
Knowing that or soon or late,
There will dawn a clearer morrow:
When your heart will moan, "Alas,
Now I know how true she was;
Now I know how dear she was," —
When the grass grows over me.

UNKNOWN.

AGAIN.

O, SWEET and fair! O, rich and rare!
That day so long ago.
The autumn sunshine everywhere,
The heather all aglow,
The ferns were clad in cloth of gold,
The waves sang on the shore.
Such suns will shine, such waves will sing
Forever evermore.

O, fit and few! O, tried and true!
The friends who met that day.
Each one the other's spirit knew,
And so in earnest play
The hours flew past, until at last
The twilight kissed the shore.
We said, "Such days shall come again
Forever evermore."

One day again, no cloud of pain
A shadow o'er us cast;
And yet we strove in vain, in vain,
To conjure up the past;
Like, but unlike, — the sun that shone,
The waves that beat the shore,
The words we said, the songs we sung,
Like, — unlike, — evermore.

For ghosts unseen crept in between,
And, when our songs flowed free,
Sang discords in an undertone,
And marred our harmony.
"The past is ours, not yours," they said:
"The waves that beat the shore,
Though like the same, are not the same,
O, never, never more!"

LUCY LARCOM.

[U. S. A.]

A STRIP OF BLUE.

I DO not own an inch of land,
But all I see is mine, —
The orchard and the mowing-fields,
The lawns and gardens fine.
The winds my tax-collectors are,
They bring me tithes divine, —
Wild scents and subtle essences,
A tribute rare and free:
And more magnificent than all,
My window keeps for me
A glimpse of blue immensity, —
A little strip of sea.

Richer am I than he who owns
Great fleets and argosies;
I have a share in every ship
Won by the inland breeze
To loiter on yon airy road
Above the apple-trees.
I freight them with my untold dreams,
Each bears my own picked crew;
And nobler cargoes wait for them
Than ever India knew, —
My ships that sail into the East
Across that outlet blue.

Sometimes they seem like living shapes, —
The people of the sky, —
Guests in white raiment coming down
From Heaven, which is close by:
I call them by familiar names,
As one by one draws nigh,
So white, so light, so spirit-like,
From violet mists they bloom!
The aching wastes of the unknown
Are half reclaimed from gloom,
Since on life's hospitable sea
All souls find sailing-room.

The ocean grows a weariness
With nothing else in sight;
Its east and west, its north and south,
Spread out from morn to night:
We miss the warm, caressing shore,
Its brooding shade and light.
A part is greater than the whole;
By hints are mysteries told;
The fringes of eternity, —
God's sweeping garment-fold,
In that bright shred of glimmering sea,
I reach out for, and hold.

The sails, like flakes of roseate pearl,
Float in upon the mist;
The waves are broken precious stones, —
Sapphire and amethyst,
Washed from celestial basement walls
By suns unsetting kissed.
Out through the utmost gates of space,
Past where the gay stars drift,
To the widening Infinite, my soul
Glides on, a vessel swift;
Yet loses not her anchorage
In yonder azure rift.

Here sit I, as a little child:
The threshold of God's door
Is that clear band of chrysoprase;
Now the vast temple floor,
The blinding glory of the dome
I bow my head before:
The universe, O God, is home,
In height or depth, to me;
Yet here upon thy footstool green
Content am I to be;
Glad, when is opened to my need
Some sea-like glimpse of thee.

BY THE FIRESIDE.

What is it fades and flickers in the fire,
Mutters and sighs, and yields reluctant breath,
As if in the red embers some desire,
Some word prophetic burned, defying death?

Lords of the forests, stalwart oak and pine,
Lie down for us in flames of martyrdom:
A human, household warmth, their death-fires shine;
Yet fragrant with high memories they come;

Bringing the mountain-winds that in their boughs
Sang of the torrent, and the plashy edge
Of storm-swept lakes; and echoes that arouse
The eagles from a splintered eyrie-ledge;

And breath of violets sweet about their roots;
And earthy odors of the moss and fern;
And hum of rivulets; smell of ripening fruits;
And green leaves that to gold and crimson turn.

What clear Septembers fade out in a spark!
What rare Octobers drop with every coal!
Within these costly ashes, dumb and dark,
Are hid spring's budding hope, and summer's soul.

Pictures far lovelier smoulder in the fire,
Visions of friends who walked among these trees,
Whose presence, like the free air, could inspire
A wingéd life and boundless sympathies.

Eyes with a glow like that in the brown beech,
When sunset through its autumn beauty shines;
Or the blue gentian's look of silent speech,
To heaven appealing as earth's light declines;

Voices and steps forever fled away
From the familiar glens, the haunted hills, —
Most pitiful and strange it is to stay
Without you in a world your lost love fills.

Do you forget us, — under Eden trees,
Or in full sunshine on the hills of God, —
Who miss you from the shadow and the breeze,
And tints and perfumes of the woodland sod?

Dear for your sake the fireside where we sit
Watching these sad, bright pictures come and go
That waning years are with your memory lit,
Is the one lonely comfort that we know.

Is it all memory? Lo, these forest-boughs
Burst on the hearth into fresh leaf and bloom;

Waft a vague, far-off sweetness through the house,
And give close walls the hillside's breathing-room.

A second life, more spiritual than the first,
They find, a life won only out of death.—
O sainted souls, within you still is nursed
For us a flame not fed by mortal breath!

Unseen, ye bring to us, who love and wait,
Wafts from the heavenly hills, immortal air;
No flood can quench your hearts' warmth, or abate;
Ye are our gladness, here and everywhere.

CHARLOTTE P. HAWES.

[U. S. A.]

DOWN THE SLOPE.

WHO knoweth life but questions death
With guessings of that dimmer day
When one is slowly lift from clay
On wingéd breath?

But man advances: far and high
His forces fly with lightning stroke:
Till, worn with years, his vigor broke,
He turns to die:

When lo! he finds it still a life;
New ministration and new trust;
Along a happy way that 's just
Aside from strife.

And all day following friendly feet
That lead on bravely to the light,
As one walks downward, strong and bright,
The slanted street,—

And feels earth's benedictions wide,
Alike on forest, lake, or town;
Nor marks the slope,—he going down
The sunniest side.

O, bounteous natures everywhere!
Perchance at least one need not fear
A change to cross from your love here
To God's love there.

UNKNOWN.

THE TWO WORLDS.

Two worlds there are. To one our eyes we strain,
Whose magic joys we shall not see again:
Bright haze of morning veils its glimmering shore.
Ah, truly breathed we there
Intoxicating air,—
Glad were our hearts in that sweet realm of
Nevermore.

The lover there drank her delicious breath
Whose love has yielded since to change or death;
The mother kissed her child whose days are o'er.
Alas! too soon have fled
The irreclaimable dead:
We see them—visions strange—amid the
Nevermore.

The merry song some maiden used to sing,
The brown, brown hair that once was wont to cling
To temples long clay-cold: to the very core
They strike our weary hearts
As some vexed memory starts
From that long faded land,—the realm of
Nevermore.

It is perpetual summer there. But here
Sadly we may remember rivers clear,
And harebells quivering on the meadow-floor.
For brighter bells and bluer,
For tenderer hearts and truer,
People that happy land—the realm of
Nevermore.

Upon the frontier of this shadowy land
We, pilgrims of eternal sorrow, stand:
What realm lies forward, with its happier store
Of forests green and deep,
Of valleys hushed in sleep,
And lakes most peaceful? 'T is the land of
Evermore.

Very far off its marble cities seem, —
Very far off — beyond our sensual dream —
Its woods, unruffled by the wild winds' roar:
Yet does the turbulent surge
Howl on its very verge.
One moment, — and we breathe within the
Evermore.

They whom we loved and lost so long ago,
Dwell in those cities, far from mortal woe,
Haunt those fresh woodlands, whence sweet carollings soar.
Eternal peace have they:
God wipes their tears away:
They drink that river of life which flows for
Evermore.

Thither we hasten through these regions dim,
But lo! the wide wings of the seraphim
Shine in the sunset! On that joyous shore
Our lightened hearts shall know
The life of long ago:
The sorrow-burdened past shall fade for
Evermore.

ADELINE D. T. WHITNEY.

[U. S. A.]

SUNLIGHT AND STARLIGHT.

God sets some souls in shade, alone;
They have no daylight of their own:
Only in lives of happier ones
They see the shine of distant suns.

God knows. Content thee with thy night,
Thy greater heaven hath grander light.
To-day is close; the hours are small;
Thou sit'st afar, and hast them all.

Lose the less joy that doth but blind;
Reach forth a larger bliss to find.
To-day is brief: the inclusive spheres
Rain raptures of a thousand years.

"I WILL ABIDE IN THINE HOUSE."

Among so many, can He care?
Can special love be everywhere?
A myriad homes, — a myriad ways, —
And God's eye over every place.

Over; but *in?* The world is full;
A grand omnipotence must rule;
But is there life that doth abide
With mine own living, side by side?

So many, and so wide abroad:
Can any heart have all of God?
From the great spaces, vague and dim,
May one small household gather Him?

I asked: my soul bethought of this:—
In just that very place of his
Where He hath put and keepeth you,
God hath no other thing to do!

NANCY A. W. PRIEST.

[U. S. A.]

OVER THE RIVER.

Over the river they beckon to me, —
Loved ones who 've crossed to the farther side;
The gleam of their snowy robes I see,
But their voices are drowned in the rushing tide.
There 's one with ringlets of sunny gold,
And eyes, the reflection of heaven's own blue;
He crossed in the twilight, gray and cold,
And the pale mist hid him from mortal view.
We saw not the angels who met him there;
The gates of the city we could not see;
Over the river, over the river,
My brother stands waiting to welcome me!

Over the river, the boatman pale
Carried another, — the household pet:
Her brown curls waved in the gentle gale —
Darling Minnie! I see her yet.
She crossed on her bosom her dimpled hands,
And fearlessly entered the phantom bark;

We watched it glide from the silver sands,
And all our sunshine grew strangely dark.
We know she is safe on the farther side,
Where all the ransomed and angels be;
Over the river, the mystic river,
My childhood's idol is waiting for me.

For none return from those quiet shores,
Who cross with the boatman cold and pale;
We hear the dip of the golden oars,
And catch a gleam of the snowy sail,—
And lo! they have passed from our yearning heart;
They cross the stream, and are gone for aye;
We may not sunder the veil apart,
That hides from our vision the gates of day.
We only know that their barks no more
May sail with us o'er life's stormy sea;
Yet somewhere, I know, on the unseen shore,
They watch, and beckon, and wait for me.

And I sit and think, when the sunset's gold,
Is flushing river, and hill, and shore,
I shall one day stand by the water cold,
And list for the sound of the boatman's oar;
I shall watch for a gleam of the flapping sail;
I shall hear the boat as it gains the strand;
I shall pass from sight, with the boatman pale,
To the better shore of the spirit land;
I shall know the loved who have gone before,—
And joyfully sweet will the meeting be,
When over the river, the peaceful river,
The Angel of Death shall carry me.

ADELAIDE A. PROCTER.

JUDGE NOT.

Judge not; the workings of his brain
And of his heart thou canst not see;
What looks to thy dim eyes a stain,
In God's pure light may only be
A scar, brought from some well-won field,
Where thou wouldst only faint and yield.

The look, the air, that frets thy sight
May be a token that below
The soul has closed in deadly fight
With some infernal fiery foe,
Whose glance would scorch thy smiling grace,
And cast thee shuddering on thy face!

The fall thou darest to despise,—
May be the angel's slackened hand
Has suffered it, that he may rise
And take a firmer, surer stand;
Or, trusting less to earthly things,
May henceforth learn to use his wings.

And judge none lost; but wait and see,
With hopeful pity, not disdain;
The depth of the abyss may be
The measure of the height of pain
And love and glory that may raise
This soul to God in after days!

FRIEND SORROW.

Do not cheat thy heart, and tell her,
"Grief will pass away;
Hope for fairer times in future,
And forget to-day."
Tell her, if you will, that Sorrow
Need not come in vain;
Tell her that the lesson taught her
Far outweighs the pain.

Cheat her not with the old comfort
(Soon she will forget);—
Bitter truth,—alas! but matter
Rather for regret.
Bid her not seek other pleasures,
Turn to other things;
Rather, nurse her cagéd Sorrow
Till the captive sings.

Bid her rather go forth bravely,
And the stranger greet,
Not as foe, with shield and buckler,
But as dear friends meet.
Bid her with a strong grasp hold her
By the dusky wings,
And she'll whisper, low and gently,
Blessings that she brings.

THOMAS BUCHANAN READ.

[U. S. A.]

THE CLOSING SCENE.

WITHIN his sober realm of leafless trees
The russet year inhaled the dreamy air;
Like some tanned reaper in his hour of ease,
When all the fields are lying brown and bare.

The gray barns looking from their hazy hills
O'er the dim waters widening in the vales,
Sent down the air a greeting to the mills,
On the dull thunder of alternate flails.

All sights were mellowed and all sounds subdued,
The hills seemed farther and the streams sang low;
As in a dream the distant woodman hewed
His winter log with many a muffled blow.

The embattled forests, erewhile armed in gold,
Their banners bright with every martial hue,
Now stood, like some sad beaten host of old,
Withdrawn afar in Time's remotest blue.

On slumb'rous wings the vulture held his flight;
The dove scarce heard its sighing mate's complaint;
And like a star slow drowning in the light,
The village church-vane seemed to pale and faint.

The sentinel-cock upon the hillside crew,
Crew thrice, and all was stiller than before, —
Silent till some replying warder blew
His alien horn, and then was heard no more.

Where erst the jay, within the elm's tall crest,
Made garrulous trouble round her unfledged young,
And where the oriole hung her swaying nest,
By every light wind like a censer swung: —

Where sang the noisy masons of the eaves,
The busy swallows circling ever near,
Foreboding, as the rustic mind believes,
An early harvest and a plenteous year; —

Where every bird which charmed the vernal feast,
Shook the sweet slumber from its wings at morn,
To warn the reaper of the rosy east, —
All now was songless, empty, and forlorn.

Alone from out the stubble piped the quail,
And croaked the crow through all the dreamy gloom;
Alone the pheasant, drumming in the vale,
Made echo to the distant cottage loom.

There was no bud, no bloom, upon the bowers;
The spiders wove their thin shrouds night by night;
The thistle-down, the only ghost of flowers,
Sailed slowly by, passed noiseless out of sight.

Amid all this, in this most cheerless air,
And where the woodbine shed upon the porch
Its crimson leaves, as if the Year stood there
Firing the floor with his inverted torch;

Amid all this, the centre of the scene,
The white-haired matron with monotonous tread,
Plied the swift wheel, and with her joyless mien,
Sat, like a Fate, and watched the flying thread.

She had known Sorrow, — he had walked with her,
Oft supped and broke the bitter ashen crust;
And in the dead leaves still he heard the stir
Of his black mantle trailing in the dust.

While yet her cheek was bright with summer bloom,
Her country summoned and she gave her all;
And twice War bowed to her his sable plume, —
Regave the swords to rust upon her wall.

Regave the swords, — but not the hand that drew
And struck for Liberty its dying blow,
Nor him who, to his sire and country true,
Fell mid the ranks of the invading foe.

Long, but not loud, the droning wheel went on,
Like the low murmur of a hive at noon;
Long, but not loud, the memory of the gone
Breathed through her lips a sad and tremulous tune.

At last the thread was snapped: her head was bowed;
Life dropt the distaff through his hands serene;
And loving neighbors smoothed her careful shroud,
While death and winter closed the autumn scene.

JEAN INGELOW.

THE HIGH TIDE ON THE COAST OF LINCOLNSHIRE.

(1571.)

The old mayor climbed the belfry tower,
The ringers ran by two, by three;
"Pull, if ye never pulled before;
Good ringers, pull your best," quoth he.
"Play uppe, play uppe, O Boston bells!
Ply all your changes, all your swells,
Play uppe 'The Brides of Enderby.'"

Men say it was a stolen tyde —
The Lord that sent it, he knows all;
But in myne ears doth still abide
The message that the bells let fall:
And there was naught of strange, beside
The flights of mews and peewits pied
By millions crouched on the old sea-wall.

I sat and spun within the doore,
My thread brake off, I raised myne eyes;
The level sun, like ruddy ore,
Lay sinking in the barren skies;
And dark against day's golden death
She moved where Lindis wandereth,
My sonne's faire wife, Elizabeth.

"Cusha! Cusha! Cusha!" calling,
Ere the early dews were falling,
Farre away I heard her song.
"Cusha! Cusha!" all along;
Where the reedy Lindis floweth,
Floweth, floweth,
From the meads where melick groweth
Faintly came her milking song.

"Cusha! Cusha! Cusha!" calling,
"For the dews will soon be falling;
Leave your meadow grasses mellow,
Mellow, mellow;
Quit your cowslips, cowslips yellow;
Comme uppe Whitefoot, come uppe Lightfoot,
Quit the stalks of parsley hollow,
Hollow, hollow;
Come uppe Jetty, rise and follow,
From the clovers lift your head;
Come uppe Whitefoot, come uppe Lightfoot,
Come uppe Jetty, rise and follow,
Jetty, to the milking-shed."

If it be long, aye, long ago,
When I beginne to think howe long,
Againe I hear the Lindis flow,
Swift as an arrowe, sharp and strong;
And all the aire it seemeth me
Bin full of floating bells (sayth shee),
That ring the tune of Enderby.

Alle fresh the level pasture lay,
And not a shadowe mote be seene,
Save where full fyve good miles away
The steeple towered from out the greene.
And lo! the great bell farre and wide
Was heard in all the country side
That Saturday at eventide.

The swannerds where their sedges are
Moved on in sunset's golden breath,
The shepherde lads I heard afarre,
And my sonne's wife, Elizabeth;
Till floating o'er the grassy sea
Came downe that kyndly message free,
The "Brides of Mavis Enderby."

Then some looked uppe into the sky,
  And all along where Lindis flows
To where the goodly vessels lie,
  And where the lordly steeple shows.
They sayde, "And why should this thing be,
What danger lowers by land or sea?
They ring the tune of Enderby!

"For evil news from Mablethorpe,
  Of pyrate galleys warping down;
For shippes ashore beyond the scorpe,
  They have not spared to wake the towne;
But while the west bin red to see,
And storms be none, and pyrates flee,
Why ring 'The Brides of Enderby'?"

I looked without, and lo! my sonne
  Came riding downe with might and main,
He raised a shout as he drew on,
  Till all the welkin rang again,
"Elizabeth! Elizabeth!"
(A sweeter woman ne'er drew breath
Than my sonne's wife, Elizabeth.)

"The olde sea-wall (he cried) is downe,
  The rising tide comes on apace,
And boats adrift in yonder towne
  Go sailing uppe the market-place."
He shook as one that looks on death:
"God save you, mother!" straight he saith;
"Where is my wife, Elizabeth?"

"Good sonne, where Lindis winds away
  With her two bairns I marked her long;
And ere yon bells beganne to play
  Afar I heard her milking song."
He looked across the grassy sea,
To right, to left, "Ho Enderby!"
They rang, "The Brides of Enderby!"

With that he cried and beat his breast;
  For lo! along the river's bed
A mighty eygre reared his crest,
  And uppe the Lindis raging sped.
It swept with thunderous noise, loud;
Shaped like a curling snow-white cloud,
Or like a demon in a shroud.

And rearing Lindis backward pressed,
  Shook all her trembling bankes amaine;
Then madly at the eygre's breast
  Flung uppe her weltering walls again.
Then bankes came downe with ruin and rout, —
Then beaten foam flew round about, —
Then all the mighty floods were out.

So farre, so fast the eygre drave,
  The heart had hardly time to beat,
Before a shallow seething wave
  Sobbed in the grasses at our feet:
The feet had hardly time to flee
Before it brake against the knee,
And all the world was in the sea.

Upon the roofe we sate that night,
  The noise of bells went sweeping by:
I marked the lofty beacon-light
  Stream from the church-tower, red and high, —
A lurid mark and dread to see;
And awesome bells they were to mee,
That in the dark rang "Enderby."

They rang the sailor-lads to guide
  From roofe to roofe who fearless rowed;
And I — my sonne was at my side,
  And yet the ruddy beacon glowed:
And yet he moaned beneath his breath,
"O come in life, or come in death!
O lost! my love, Elizabeth."

And didst thou visit him no more?
  Thou didst, thou didst, my daughter deare;
The waters laid thee at his doore,
  Ere yet the early dawn was clear.
The pretty bairns in fast embrace,
The lifted sun shone on thy face,
Downe drifted to thy dwelling-place.

That flow strewed wrecks about the grass,
  That ebbe swept out the flocks to sea;
A fatal ebbe and flow, alas!
  To manye more than myne and me:
But each will mourn his own (she saith).
And sweeter woman ne'er drew breath
Than my sonne's wife, Elizabeth.

I shall never hear her more
By the reedy Lindis shore,
"Cusha, Cusha, Cusha!" calling,
Ere the early dews be falling;
I shall never hear her song,
"Cusha, Cusha!" all along,
Where the sunny Lindis floweth,
    Goeth, floweth;
From the meads where melick groweth,

When the water winding down
Onward floweth to the town.

I shall never see her more
Where the reeds and rushes quiver,
Shiver, quiver;
Stand beside the sobbing river,
Sobbing, throbbing, in its falling,
To the sandy lonesome shore:
I shall never hear her calling,
"Leave your meadow grasses mellow;
Mellow, mellow;
Quit your cowslips, cowslips yellow;
Come uppe Whitefoot, come uppe Lightfoot;
Quit your pipes of parsley hollow,
Hollow, hollow;
Come uppe Lightfoot, rise and follow;
Lightfoot, Whitefoot;
From your clovers lift the head;
Come uppe Jetty, follow, follow,
Jetty, to the milking-shed."

SEVEN TIMES FOUR.

MATERNITY.

Heigh-ho! daisies and buttercups!
Fair yellow daffodils, stately and tall!
When the wind wakes how they rock in the grasses,
And dance with the cuckoo-buds slender and small!
Here's two bonny boys, and here's mother's own lasses,
Eager to gather them all.

Heigh-ho! daisies and buttercups!
Mother shall thread them a daisy chain;
Sing them a song of the pretty hedge-sparrow,
That loved her brown little ones, loved them full fain;
Sing, "Heart, thou art wide though the house be but narrow,"
Sing once, and sing it again.

Heigh-ho! daisies and buttercups!
Sweet wagging cowslips, they bend and they bow;
A ship sails afar over warm ocean waters,
And haply one musing doth stand at her prow.
O bonny brown sons, and O sweet little daughters,
Maybe he thinks on you now.

Heigh-ho! daisies and buttercups!
Fair yellow daffodils stately and tall!
A sunshiny world full of laughter and leisure,
And fresh hearts unconscious of sorrow and thrall!
Send down on their pleasure smiles passing its measure,
God that is over us all!

SEVEN TIMES SEVEN.

LONGING FOR HOME.

A song of a boat:—
There was once a boat on a billow:
Lightly she rocked to her port remote,
And the foam was white in her wake like snow,
And her frail mast bowed when the breeze would blow,
And bent like a wand of willow.

I shaded mine eyes one day when a boat
Went curtsying over the billow,
I marked her course till, a dancing mote,
She faded out on the moonlit foam,
And I stayed behind in the dear-loved home;
And my thoughts all day were about the boat,
And my dreams upon the pillow.

I pray you hear my song of a boat,
For it is but short:—
My boat you shall find none fairer afloat,
In river or port.
Long I looked out for the lad she bore,
On the open desolate sea,
And I think he sailed to the heavenly shore,
For he came not back to me—
Ah me!

A song of a nest:—
There was once a nest in a hollow;
Down in the mosses and knot-grass pressed,
Soft and warm and full to the brim.
Vetches leaned over it purple and dim,
With buttercup-buds to follow.

I pray you hear my song of a nest,
For it is not long:
You shall never light in a summer quest
The bushes among,—

Shall never light on a prouder sitter,
  A fairer nestful, nor ever know
A softer sound than their tender twitter,
  That wind-like did come and go.

I had a nestful once of my own,
  Ah, happy, happy I!
Right dearly I loved them; but when they were grown
  They spread out their wings to fly.
O, one after one they flew away,
  Far up to the heavenly blue,
To the better country, the upper day,
  And — I wish I was going too.

I pray you, what is the nest to me,
  My empty nest?
And what is the shore where I stood to see
  My boat sail down to the west?
Can I call that home where I anchor yet,
  Though my good man has sailed?
Can I call that home where my nest was set,
  Now all its hope hath failed?

Nay, but the port where my sailor went,
  And the land where my nestlings be:
There is the home where my thoughts are sent,
  The only home for me—
            Ah me!

THOMAS BAILEY ALDRICH.

[U. S. A.]

BEFORE THE RAIN.

We knew it would rain, for all the morn,
  A spirit on slender ropes of mist
Was lowering its golden buckets down
  Into the vapory amethyst

Of marshes and swamps and dismal fens,—
  Scooping the dew that lay in the flowers,
Dipping the jewels out of the sea,
  To sprinkle them over the land in showers.

We knew it would rain, for the poplars showed
  The white of their leaves, the amber grain
Shrunk in the wind, — and the lightning now
  Is tangled in tremulous skeins of rain!

AFTER THE RAIN.

The rain has ceased, and in my room
The sunshine pours an airy flood;
And on the church's dizzy vane
The ancient Cross is bathed in blood.

From out the dripping ivy-leaves,
Antiquely carven, gray and high,
A dormer, facing westward, looks
Upon the village like an eye:

And now it glimmers in the sun,
A square of gold, a disk, a speck:
And in the belfry sits a Dove
With purple ripples on her neck.

PISCATAQUA RIVER.

Thou singest by the gleaming isles,
  By woods, and fields of corn,
Thou singest, and the heaven smiles
  Upon my birthday morn.

But I within a city, I,
  So full of vague unrest,
Would almost give my life to lie
  An hour upon thy breast!

To let the wherry listless go,
  And, wrapt in dreamy joy,
Dip, and surge idly to and fro,
  Like the red harbor-buoy;

To sit in happy indolence,
  To rest upon the oars,
And catch the heavy earthy scents
  That blow from summer shores;

To see the rounded sun go down,
  And with its parting fires
Light up the windows of the town
  And burn the tapering spires;

And then to hear the muffled tolls
  From steeples slim and white,
And watch, among the Isles of Shoals,
  The Beacon's orange light.

O River! flowing to the main
  Through woods, and fields of corn,

Hear thou my longing and my pain
  This sunny birthday morn;

And take this song which sorrow shapes
  To music like thine own,
And sing it to the cliffs and capes
  And crags where I am known!

ROBERT BUCHANAN.

THE GREEN GNOME.

A MELODY.

RING, sing! ring, sing! pleasant Sabbath bells!
Chime, rhyme! chime, rhyme! through dales and dells!
Rhyme, ring! chime, sing! pleasant Sabbath bells!
Chime, sing! rhyme, ring! over fields and fells!

And I galloped and I galloped on my palfrey white as milk,
My robe was of the sea-green woof, my serk was of the silk;
My hair was golden-yellow, and it floated to my shoe;
My eyes were like two harebells bathed in little drops of dew;
My palfrey, never stopping, made a music sweetly blent
With the leaves of autumn dropping all around me as I went;
And I heard the bells, grown fainter, far behind me peal and play,
Fainter, fainter, fainter, till they seemed to die away;
And beside a silver runnel, on a little heap of sand,
I saw the green gnome sitting, with his cheek upon his hand.
Then he started up to see me, and he ran with a cry and bound,
And drew me from my palfrey white and set me on the ground.
O crimson, crimson were his locks, his face was green to see,
But he cried, "O light-haired lassie, you are bound to marry me!"
He clasped me round the middle small, he kissed me on the cheek,
He kissed me once, he kissed me twice, I could not stir or speak;
He kissed me twice, he kissed me thrice; but when he kissed again,
I called aloud upon the name of Him who died for men.

Sing, sing! ring, ring! pleasant Sabbath bells!
Chime, rhyme! chime, rhyme! through dales and dells!
Rhyme, ring! chime, sing! pleasant Sabbath bells!
Chime, sing! rhyme, ring! over fields and fells!

O faintly, faintly, faintly, calling men and maids to pray,
So faintly, faintly, faintly rang the bells far away;
And as I named the Blessed Name, as in our need we can,
The ugly green gnome became a tall and comely man:
His hands were white, his beard was gold, his eyes were black as sloes,
His tunic was of scarlet woof, and silken were his hose;
A pensive light from faëryland still lingered on his cheek,
His voice was like the running brook when he began to speak:
"O, you have cast away the charm my step-dame put on me,
Seven years have I dwelt in Faëryland, and you have set me free.
O, I will mount thy palfrey white, and ride to kirk with thee,
And, by those dewy little eyes, we twain will wedded be!"

Back we galloped, never stopping, he before and I behind,
And the autumn leaves were dropping, red and yellow in the wind;
And the sun was shining clearer, and my heart was high and proud,
As nearer, nearer, nearer rang the kirk-bells sweet and loud,
And we saw the kirk, before us, as we trotted down the fells,
And nearer, clearer, o'er us, rang the welcome of the bells.

Ring, sing! ring, sing! pleasant Sabbath bells!
Chime, rhyme! chime, rhyme! through dales and dells!

Rhyme, ring! chime, sing! pleasant Sabbath bells!
Chime, sing! rhyme, ring! over fields and fells!

E. C. STEDMAN.

[U. S. A.]

THE DOORSTEP.

THE conference-meeting through at last,
We boys around the vestry waited
To see the girls come tripping past,
Like snowbirds willing to be mated.

Not braver he that leaps the wall
By level musket-flashes litten,
Than I, who stepped before them all,
Who longed to see me get the mitten.

But no; she blushed, and took my arm!
We let the old folks have the highway,
And started toward the Maple Farm
Along a kind of lover's by-way.

I can't remember what we said,
'T was nothing worth a song or story,
Yet that rude path by which we sped
Seemed all transformed, and in a glory.

The snow was crisp beneath our feet,
The moon was full, the fields were gleaming;
By hood and tippet sheltered sweet,
Her face with youth and health was beaming.

The little hand outside her muff—
O sculptor, if you could but mould it!—
So lightly touched my jacket-cuff,
To keep it warm I had to hold it.

To have her with me there alone,—
'T was love and fear and triumph blended.
At last we reached the foot-worn stone
Where that delicious journey ended.

The old folks, too, were almost home;
Her dimpled hand the latches fingered,
We heard the voices nearer come,
Yet on the doorstep still we lingered.

She shook her ringlets from her hood,
And with a "Thank you, Ned," dissembled;
But yet I knew she understood
With what a daring wish I trembled.

A cloud passed kindly overhead,
The moon was slyly peeping through it,
Yet hid its face, as if it said,
"Come, now or never! do it! *do it!*"

My lips till then had only known
The kiss of mother and of sister,
But somehow, full upon her own
Sweet, rosy, darling mouth,—I kissed her!

Perhaps 't was boyish love, yet still,
O listless woman, weary lover!
To feel once more that fresh, wild thrill
I 'd give— But who can live youth over?

PAN IN WALL STREET.

A. D. 1867.

JUST where the Treasury's marble front
Looks over Wall Street's mingled nations,—
Where Jews and Gentiles most are wont
To throng for trade and last quotations,—
Where, hour by hour, the rates of gold
Outrival, in the ears of people,
The quarter-chimes, serenely tolled
From Trinity's undaunted steeple;—

Even there I heard a strange, wild strain
Sound high above the modern clamor,
Above the cries of greed and gain,
The curbstone war, the auction's hammer,—
And swift, on Music's misty ways,
It led, from all this strife for millions,
To ancient, sweet-do-nothing days
Among the kirtle-robed Sicilians.

And as it stilled the multitude,
And yet more joyous rose, and shriller,
I saw the minstrel where he stood
At ease against a Doric pillar:
One hand a droning organ played,
The other held a Pan's-pipe (fashioned
Like those of old) to lips that made
The reeds give out that strain impassioned.

'T was Pan himself had wandered here
  A-strolling through this sordid city,
And piping to the civic ear
  The prelude of some pastoral ditty!
The demigod had crossed the seas, —
  From haunts of shepherd, nymph, and satyr,
And Syracusan times, — to these
  Far shores and twenty centuries later.

A ragged cap was on his head:
  But — hidden thus — there was no doubting
That, all with crispy locks o'erspread,
  His gnarlèd horns were somewhere sprouting;
His club-feet, cased in rusty shoes,
  Were crossed, as on some frieze you see them,
And trousers, patched of divers hues,
  Concealed his crooked shanks beneath them.

He filled the quivering reeds with sound,
  And o'er his mouth their changes shifted,
And with his goat's-eyes looked around
  Where'er the passing current drifted;
And soon, as on Trinacrian hills
  The nymphs and herdsmen ran to hear him,
Even now the tradesmen from their tills,
  With clerks and porters, crowded near him.

The bulls and bears together drew
  From Jauncey Court and New Street Alley,
As erst, if pastorals be true,
  Came beasts from every wooded valley;
The random passers stayed to list, —
  A boxer Ægon, rough and merry, —
A Broadway Daphnis, on his tryst
  With Nais at the Brooklyn Ferry.

A one-eyed Cyclops halted long
  In tattered cloak of army pattern,
And Galatea joined the throng, —
  A blowsy, apple-vending slattern;
While old Silenus staggered out
  From some new-fangled lunch-house handy,
And bade the piper, with a shout,
  To strike up Yankee Doodle Dandy!

A newsboy and a peanut-girl
  Like little Fauns began to caper:
His hair was all in tangled curl,
  Her tawny legs were bare and taper;
And still the gathering larger grew,
  And gave its pence and crowded nigher,
While aye the shepherd-minstrel blew
  His pipe, and struck the gamut higher.

O heart of Nature, beating still
  With throbs her vernal passion taught her, —
Even here, as on the vine-clad hill,
  Or by the Arethusan water!
New forms may fold the speech, new lands
  Arise within these ocean-portals,
But Music waves eternal wands, —
  Enchantress of the souls of mortals!

So thought I, — but among us trod
  A man in blue, with legal baton,
And scoffed the vagrant demigod,
  And pushed him from the step I sat on.
Doubting I mused upon the cry,
  "Great Pan is dead!" — and all the people
Went on their ways: — and clear and high
  The quarter sounded from the steeple.

ALGERNON CHARLES SWINBURNE.

A MATCH.

If love were what the rose is,
  And I were like the leaf,
Our lives would grow together
In sad or singing weather,
Blown fields or flowerful closes,
  Green pleasure or gray grief;
If love were what the rose is,
  And I were like the leaf.

If I were what the words are,
  And love were like the tune,
With double sound and single
Delight our lips would mingle,
With kisses glad as birds are
  That get sweet rain at noon;
If I were what the words are
  And love were like the tune.

If you were life, my darling,
  And I your love were death,
We 'd shine and snow together
Ere March made sweet the weather

With daffodil and starling
  And hours of fruitful breath;
If you were life, my darling,
  And I your love were death.

If you were thrall to sorrow,
  And I were page to joy,
We 'd play for lives and seasons,
With loving looks and treasons,
And tears of night and morrow,
  And laughs of maid and boy;
If you were thrall to sorrow,
  And I were page to joy.

If you were April's lady,
  And I were lord in May,
We 'd throw with leaves for hours,
And draw for days with flowers,
Till day like night were shady,
  And night were bright like day;
If you were April's lady,
  And I were lord in May.

If you were queen of pleasure,
  And I were king of pain,
We 'd hunt down love together,
Pluck out his flying-feather,
And teach his feet a measure,
  And find his mouth a rein;
If you were queen of pleasure,
  And I were king of pain.

R. H. STODDARD.

[U. S. A.]

NEVER AGAIN.

THERE are gains for all our losses,
  There are balms for all our pain:
But when youth, the dream, departs,
It takes something from our hearts,
  And it never comes again.

We are stronger, and are better,
  Under manhood's sterner reign:
Still we feel that something sweet
Followed youth, with flying feet,
  And will never come again.

Something beautiful is vanished,
  And we sigh for it in vain:
We seek it everywhere,
On the earth and in the air,
  But it never comes again!

LANDWARD.

THE sky is thick upon the sea,
  The sea is sown with rain,
And in the passing gusts we hear
  The clanging of the crane.

The cranes are flying to the south;
  We cut the northern foam:
The dreary land they leave behind
  Must be our future home.

Its barren shores are long and dark,
  And gray its autumn sky;
But better these than this gray sea,
  If but to land — and die!

NOVEMBER.

THE wild November comes at last
  Beneath a veil of rain;
The night-wind blows its folds aside,
  Her face is full of pain.

The latest of her race, she takes
  The Autumn's vacant throne:
She has but one short moon to live,
And she must live alone.

A barren realm of withered fields:
  Bleak woods of fallen leaves:
The palest morns that ever dawned:
  The dreariest of eves:

It is no wonder that she comes,
  Poor month! with tears of pain:
For what can one so hopeless do
  But weep, and weep again!

J. T. TROWBRIDGE.

[U. S. A.]

AT SEA.

THE night was made for cooling shade,
  For silence, and for sleep;
And when I was a child, I laid
My hands upon my breast, and prayed,
  And sank to slumbers deep.
Childlike, as then, I lie to-night,
And watch my lonely cabin-light.

Each movement of the swaying lamp
  Shows how the vessel reels,
And o'er her deck the billows tramp,
And all her timbers strain and cramp
  With every shock she feels;
It starts and shudders, while it burns,
And in its hingéd socket turns.

Now swinging slow, and slanting low,
  It almost level lies:
And yet I know, while to and fro
I watch the seeming pendule go
  With restless fall and rise,
The steady shaft is still upright,
Poising its little globe of light.

O hand of God! O lamp of peace!
  O promise of my soul!
Though weak and tossed, and ill at ease
Amid the roar of smiting seas, —
  The ship's convulsive roll, —
I own, with love and tender awe,
Yon perfect type of faith and law.

A heavenly trust my spirit calms, —
  My soul is filled with light;
The ocean sings his solemn psalms;
The wild winds chant; I cross my palms;
  Happy, as if to-night,
Under the cottage roof again,
I heard the soothing summer rain.

ELIZABETH AKERS ALLEN (FLORENCE PERCY).

[U. S. A.]

IN THE DEFENCES.

AT WASHINGTON.

Along the ramparts which surround the town
  I walk with evening, marking all the while
How night and autumn, closing softly down,
  Leave on the land a blessing and a smile.

In the broad streets the sounds of tumult cease,
  The gorgeous sunset reddens roof and spire,
The city sinks to quietude and peace,
  Sleeping, like Saturn, in a ring of fire;

Circled with forts, whose grim and threatening walls
  Frown black with cannon, whose abated breath
Waits the command to send the fatal balls
  Upon their errands of dismay and death.

And see, directing, guiding, silently
  Flash from afar the mystic signal-lights,
As gleamed the fiery pillar in the sky
  Leading by night the wandering Israelites.

The earthworks, draped with summer weeds and vines,
  The rifle-pits, half hid with tangled briers,
But wait their time; for see, along the lines
  Rise the faint smokes of lonesome picket-fires,

Where sturdy sentinels on silent beat
  Cheat the long hours of wakeful loneliness
With thoughts of home, and faces dear and sweet,
  And, on the edge of danger, dream of bliss.

Yet at a word, how wild and fierce a change
  Would rend and startle all the earth and skies
With blinding glare, and noises dread and strange,
  And shrieks, and shouts, and deathly agonies.

The wide-mouthed guns would war, and hissing shells
  Would pierce the shuddering sky with fiery thrills,
The battle rage and roll in thunderous swells,
  And war's fierce anguish shake the solid hills.

But now how tranquilly the golden gloom
  Creeps up the gorgeous forest-slopes, and flows
Down valleys blue with fringy aster-bloom, —
  An atmosphere of safety and repose.

Against the sunset lie the darkening hills,
Mushroomed with tents, the sudden growth of war;
The frosty autumn air, that blights and chills,
Yet brings its own full recompense therefor;

Rich colors light the leafy solitudes,
And far and near the gazer's eyes behold
The oak's deep scarlet, warming all the woods,
And spendthrift maples scattering their gold.

The pale beech shivers with prophetic woe,
The towering chestnut ranks stand blanched and thinned,
Yet still the fearless sumach dares the foe,
And waves its bloody guidons in the wind.

Where mellow haze the hill's sharp outline dims,
Bare elms, like sentinels, watch silently,
The delicate tracery of their slender limbs
Pencilled in purple on the saffron sky.

Content and quietude and plenty seem
Blessing the place, and sanctifying all;
And hark! how pleasantly a hidden stream
Sweetens the silence with its silver fall!

The failing grasshopper chirps faint and shrill,
The cricket calls, in massy covert hid,
Cheery and loud, as stoutly answering still
The soft persistence of the katydid.

With dead moths tangled in its blighted bloom,
The golden-rod swings lonesome on its throne,
Forgot of bees; and in the thicket's gloom,
The last belated peewee cries alone.

The hum of voices, and the careless laugh
Of cheerful talkers, fall upon the ear;
The flag flaps listlessly adown its staff;
And still the katydid pipes loud and near.

And now from far the bugle's mellow throat
Pours out, in rippling flow, its silver tide;
And up the listening hills the echoes float
Faint and more faint and sweetly multiplied.

Peace reigns; not now a soft-eyed nymph that sleeps
Unvexed by dreams of strife or conqueror,
But Power, that, open-eyed and watchful, keeps
Unwearied vigil on the brink of war.

Night falls; in silence sleep the patriot bands;
The tireless cricket yet repeats its tune,
And the still figure of the sentry stands
In black relief against the low full moon.

EDNA DEAN PROCTOR.

[U. S. A.]

OUR HEROES.

THE winds that once the Argo bore
Have died by Neptune's ruined shrines,
And her hull is the drift of the deep sea floor,
Though shaped of Pelion's tallest pines.
You may seek her crew in every isle,
Fair in the foam of Ægean seas,
But out of their sleep no charm can wile
Jason and Orpheus and Hercules.

And Priam's voice is heard no more
By windy Ilium's sea-built walls;
From the washing wave and the lonely shore
No wail goes up as Hector falls.
On Ida's mount is the shining snow,
But Jove has gone from its brow away,
And red on the plain the poppies grow
Where Greek and Trojan fought that day.

Mother Earth! Are thy heroes dead?
Do they thrill the soul of the years no more?
Are the gleaming snows and the poppies red
All that is left of the brave of yore?
Are there none to fight as Theseus fought,
Far in the young world's misty dawn?
Or teach as the gray-haired Nestor taught,
Mother Earth! Are thy heroes gone?

Gone?—in a nobler form they rise;
Dead?—we may clasp their hands in ours,
And catch the light of their glorious eyes,
And wreathe their brows with immortal flowers.
Wherever a noble deed is done,
There are the souls of our heroes stirred;
Wherever a field for truth is won,
There are our heroes' voices heard.

Their armor rings on a fairer field
Than Greek or Trojan ever trod,
For Freedom's sword is the blade they wield,
And the light above them the smile of God!
So, in his isle of calm delight,
Jason may dream the years away,
But the heroes live, and the skies are bright,
And the world is a braver world to-day.

GEORGE H. BOKER.

[U. S. A.]

DIRGE FOR A SOLDIER.

Close his eyes; his work is done!
What to him is friend or foeman,
Rise of moon, or set of sun,
Hand of man, or kiss of woman?
Lay him low, lay him low,
In the clover or the snow!
What cares he? he cannot know:
Lay him low!

As man may, he fought his fight,
Proved his truth by his endeavor;
Let him sleep in solemn night,
Sleep forever and forever.
Lay him low, lay him low,
In the clover or the snow!
What cares he? he cannot know:
Lay him low!

Fold him in his country's stars,
Roll the drum and fire the volley!
What to him are all our wars,
What but death-bemocking folly?
Lay him low, lay him low,
In the clover or the snow!
What cares he? he cannot know:
Lay him low!

Leave him to God's watching eye,
Trust him to the hand that made him.
Mortal love weeps idly by:
God alone has power to aid him.
Lay him low, lay him low,
In the clover or the snow!
What cares he? he cannot know:
Lay him low!

LOUISE CHANDLER MOULTON.

[U. S. A.]

THE HOUSE IN THE MEADOW.

It stands in a sunny meadow,
The house so mossy and brown,
With its cumbrous old stone chimneys,
And the gray roof sloping down.

The trees fold their green arms round it,—
The trees a century old;
And the winds go chanting through them,
And the sunbeams drop their gold.

The cowslips spring in the marshes,
The roses bloom on the hill,
And beside the brook in the pasture
The herds go feeding at will.

Within, in the wide old kitchin,
The old folks sit in the sun,
That creeps through the sheltering woodbine,
Till the day is almost done.

Their children have gone and left them;
They sit in the sun alone!
And the old wife's ears are failing
As she harks to the well-known tone

That won her heart in her girlhood,
That has soothed her in many a care,
And praises her now for the brightness
Her old face used to wear.

She thinks again of her bridal,—
How, dressed in her robe of white,
She stood by her gay young lover
In the morning's rosy light.

O, the morning is rosy as ever,
But the rose from her cheek is fled;

And the sunshine still is golden,
But it falls on a silvered head.

And the girlhood dreams, once vanished,
Come back in her winter-time,
Till her feeble pulses tremble
With the thrill of spring-time's prime.

And looking forth from the window,
She thinks how the trees have grown
Since, clad in her bridal whiteness,
She crossed the old door-stone.

Though dimmed her eyes' bright azure,
And dimmed her hair's young gold,
The love in her girlhood plighted
Has never grown dim or old.

They sat in peace in the sunshine
Till the day was almost done,
And then, at its close, an angel
Stole over the threshold stone.

He folded their hands together, —
He touched their eyelids with balm,
And their last breath floated outward,
Like the close of a solemn psalm!

Like a bridal pair they traversed
The unseen, mystical road
That leads to the Beautiful City,
Whose builder and maker is God.

Perhaps in that miracle country
They will give her lost youth back,
And the flowers of the vanished spring-time
Will bloom in the spirit's track.

One draught from the living waters
Shall call back his manhood's prime;
And eternal years shall measure
The love that outlasted time.

But the shapes that they left behind them,
The wrinkles and silver hair, —
Made holy to us by the kisses
The angel had printed there, —

We will hide away 'neath the willows,
When the day is low in the west,
Where the sunbeams cannot find them,
Nor the winds disturb their rest.

And we'll suffer no telltale tombstone,
With its age and date, to rise
O'er the two who are old no longer,
In the Father's house in the skies.

THE LATE SPRING.

She stood alone amidst the April fields, —
Brown, sodden fields, all desolate and bare.
"The spring is late," she said, "the faithless spring,
That should have come to make the meadows fair.

"Their sweet South left too soon, among the trees
The birds, bewildered, flutter to and fro;
For them no green boughs wait, — their memories
Of last year's April had deceived them so."

She watched the homeless birds, the slow, sad spring,
The barren fields, and shivering, naked trees.
"Thus God has dealt with me, his child," she said;
"I wait my spring-time, and am cold like these.

"To them will come the fulness of their time;
Their spring, though late, will make the meadows fair;
Shall I, who wait like them, like them be blessed?
I am His own, — doth not my Father care?"

NORA PERRY.

[U. S. A.]

IN JUNE.

So sweet, so sweet the roses in their blowing,
So sweet the daffodils, so fair to see;
So blithe and gay the humming-bird agoing
From flower to flower, a hunting with the bee.

So sweet, so sweet the calling of the thrushes,
The calling, cooing, wooing, everywhere;

So sweet the water's song through reeds and rushes,
The plover's piping note, now here, now there.

So sweet, so sweet from off the fields of clover,
The west-wind blowing, blowing up the hill;
So sweet, so sweet with news of some one's lover,
Fleet footsteps, ringing nearer, nearer still.

So near, so near, now listen, listen, thrushes;
Now plover, blackbird, cease, and let me hear;
And, water, hush your song through reeds and rushes,
That I may know whose lover cometh near.

So loud, so loud the thrushes kept their calling,
Plover or blackbird never heeding me;
So loud the mill-stream too kept fretting, falling,
O'er bar and bank, in brawling, boisterous glee.

So loud, so loud; yet blackbird, thrush, nor plover,
Nor noisy mill-stream, in its fret and fall,
Could drown the voice, the low voice of my lover,
My lover calling through the thrushes' call.

"Come down, come down!" he called, and straight the thrushes
From mate to mate sang all at once, "Come down!"
And while the water laughed through reeds and rushes,
The blackbird chirped, the plover piped, "Come down!"

Then down and off, and through the fields of clover,
I followed, followed, at my lover's call;
Listening no more to blackbird, thrush, or plover,
The water's laugh, the mill-stream's fret and fall.

AFTER THE BALL.

THEY sat and combed their beautiful hair,
Their long, bright tresses, one by one,
As they laughed and talked in the chamber there,
After the revel was done.

Idly they talked of waltz and quadrille,
Idly they laughed, like other girls,
Who over the fire, when all is still,
Comb out their braids and curls.

Robe of satin and Brussels lace,
Knots of flowers and ribbons, too,
Scattered about in every place,
For the revel is through.

And Maud and Madge in robes of white,
The prettiest nightgowns under the sun,
Stockingless, slipperless, sit in the night,
For the revel is done, —

Sit and comb their beautiful hair,
Those wonderful waves of brown and gold,
Till the fire is out in the chamber there,
And the little bare feet are cold.

Then out of the gathering winter chill,
All out of the bitter St. Agnes weather,
While the fire is out and the house is still,
Maud and Madge together, —

Maud and Madge in robes of white,
The prettiest nightgowns under the sun,
Curtained away from the chilly night,
After the revel is done, —

Float along in a splendid dream,
To a golden gittern's tinkling tune,
While a thousand lustres shimmering stream
In a palace's grand saloon.

Flashing of jewels and flutter of laces,
Tropical odors sweeter than musk,
Men and women with beautiful faces,
And eyes of tropical dusk, —

And one face shining out like a star,
One face haunting the dreams of each,
And one voice, sweeter than others are,
Breaking into silvery speech, —

Telling, through lips of bearded bloom,
An old, old story over again,

As down the royal bannered room,
To the golden gittern's strain,

Two and two, they dreamily walk,
While an unseen spirit walks beside,
And all unheard in the lovers' talk,
He claimeth one for a bride.

O, Maud and Madge, dream on together,
With never a pang of jealous fear!
For, ere the bitter St. Agnes weather
Shall whiten another year,

Robed for the bridal, and robed for the tomb,
Braided brown hair and golden tress,
There 'll be only one of you left for the bloom
Of the bearded lips to press, —

Only one for the bridal pearls,
The robe of satin and Brussels lace, —
Only one to blush through her curls
At the sight of a lover's face.

O beautiful Madge, in your bridal white,
For you the revel has just begun;
But for her who sleeps in your arms to-night
The revel of Life is done!

But robed and crowned with your saintly bliss,
Queen of heaven and bride of the sun,
O beautiful Maud, you 'll never miss
The kisses another hath won!

G. W. THORNBURY.

THE JESTER'S SERMON.

THE Jester shook his head and bells, and leaped upon a chair,
The pages laughed, the women screamed, and tossed their scented hair;
The falcon whistled, staghounds bayed, the lapdog barked without,
The scullion dropped the pitcher brown, the cook railed at the lout!
The steward, counting out his gold, let pouch and money fall,
And why? because the Jester rose to say grace in the hall!

The page played with the heron's plume, the steward with his chain,
The butler drummed upon the board, and laughed with might and main;
The grooms beat on their metal cans, and roared till they were red,
But still the Jester shut his eyes and rolled his witty head;
And when they grew a little still, read half a yard of text,
And, waving hand, struck on the desk, then frowned like one perplexed.

"Dear sinners all," the fool began, "man's life is but a jest,
A dream, a shadow, bubble, air, a vapor at the best,
In a thousand pounds of law I find not a single ounce of love;
A blind man killed the parson's cow in shooting at the dove;
The fool that eats till he is sick must fast till he is well;
The wooer who can flatter most will bear away the belle.

"Let no man halloo he is safe till he is through the wood;
He who will not when he may, must tarry when he should;
He who laughs at crooked men should need walk very straight;
O, he who once has won a name may lie abed till eight!
Make haste to purchase house and land, be very slow to wed;
True coral needs no painter's brush, nor need be daubed with red.

"The friar, preaching, cursed the thief (the pudding in his sleeve),
To fish for sprats with golden hooks is foolish, by your leave, —
To travel well, — an ass's ears, ape's face, hog's mouth, and ostrich legs.
He does not care a pin for thieves who limps about and begs.
Be always first man at a feast and last man at a fray;
The short way round, in spite of all, is still the longest way.
When the hungry curate licks the knife, there 's not much for the clerk;
When the pilot, turning pale and sick, looks up, — the storm grows dark."

Then loud they laughed, the fat cook's tears ran down into the pan:
The steward shook, that he was forced to drop the brimming can;
And then again the women screamed, and every staghound bayed,—
And why? because the motley fool so wise a sermon made.

ANNIE FIELDS.

[U. S. A.]

CLIMBING.

He said, "O brother, where 's the use of climbing?
Come rather to the shade beside me here,
And break the bread, and pour the plenteous wine!

"Why thus forever climbing one sad way?
Rather burn cedar on the marble hearth,
And sleep, and wake, and hear the singers pass.

"Come! Stay thy feet, and pant and climb no more!
Stay Jollity, stay Wit, and Grace, and Ease,
Nor spend your strength of days in scaling heights!"

But Wit had clomb full well, and passed beyond,
While he who stayed, cried, "Brother, where 's the use?"
And Jollity went mingling with the sad,

Still passing onward, up the difficult road,
While Grace accompanied,—and all, but Ease;
And Ease and he two dull companions made.

Forever after said he not, "What use!"
Grew weary of sweet cedar and soft couch;
And wistful gazed to watch those climbing feet.

HELEN HUNT.

[U. S. A.]

CORONATION.

At the king's gate the subtle noon
Wove filmy yellow nets of sun;
Into the drowsy snare too soon
The guards fell one by one.

Through the king's gate, unquestioned then,
A beggar went, and laughed, "This brings
Me chance, at last, to see if men
Fare better, being kings."

The king sat bowed beneath his crown,
Propping his face with listless hand;
Watching the hour-glass sifting down
Too slow its shining sand.

"Poor man, what wouldst thou have of me?"
The beggar turned, and, pitying,
Replied, like one in a dream, "Of thee,
Nothing. I want the king."

Uprose the king, and from his head
Shook off the crown and threw it by.
"O man, thou must have known," he said,
"A greater king than I!"

Through all the gates, unquestioned then,
Went king and beggar hand in hand.
Whispered the king, "Shall I know when
Before *his* throne I stand?"

The beggar laughed. Free winds in haste
Were wiping from the king's hot brow
The crimson lines the crown had traced.
"This is his presence now."

At the king's gate, the crafty noon
Unwove its yellow nets of sun;
Out of their sleep in terror soon
The guards waked one by one.

"Ho here! Ho there! Has no man seen
The king?" The cry ran to and fro;
Beggar and king, they laughed, I ween,
The laugh that free men know.

On the king's gate the moss grew gray:
The king came not. They called him dead;
And made his eldest son one day
Slave in his father's stead.

THE WAY TO SING.

The birds must know. Who wisely sings
Will sing as they;
The common air has generous wings,
Songs make their way.
No messenger to run before,
Devising plan;
No mention of the place or hour
To any man;
No waiting till some sound betrays
A listening ear;
No different voice, no new delays,
If steps draw near.

"What bird is that? Its song is good."
And eager eyes
Go peering through the dusky wood,
In glad surprise;
Then late at night, when by his fire
The traveller sits,
Watching the flame grow brighter, higher,
The sweet song flits
By snatches through his weary brain
To help him rest;
When next he goes that road again,
An empty nest
On leafless bough will make him sigh,
"Ah me! last spring
Just here I heard, in passing by,
That rare bird sing!"

But while he sighs, remembering
How sweet the song,
The little bird, on tireless wing,
Is borne along
In other air, and other men
With weary feet,
On other roads, the simple strain
Are finding sweet.
The birds must know. Who wisely sings
Will sing as they;
The common air has generous wings,
Songs make their way.

DANTE GABRIEL ROSSETTI.

THE SEA-LIMITS.

Consider the sea's listless chime;
Time's self it is made audible, —
The murmur of the earth's own shell,
Secret continuance sublime
Is the era's end. Our sight may pass
No furlong farther. Since time was,
This sound hath told the lapse of time.

No quiet which is death's, — it hath
The mournfulness of ancient life,
Enduring always at dull strife.
As the world's heart of rest and wrath,
Its painful pulse is on the sands.
Lost utterly, the whole sky stands
Gray and not known along its path.

Listen alone beside the sea,
Listen alone among the woods;
Those voices of twin solitudes
Shall have one sound alike to thee.
Hark where the murmurs of thronged men
Surge and sink back and surge again, —
Still the one voice of wave and tree.

Gather a shell from the strewn beach,
And listen at its lips; they sigh
The same desire and mystery,
The echo of the whole sea's speech.
And all mankind is thus at heart
Not anything but what thou art;
And earth, sea, man, are all in each.

CELIA THAXTER.

[U. S. A.]

A SUMMER DAY.

At daybreak in the fresh light, joyfully
The fishermen drew in their laden net;
The shore shone rosy purple, and the sea
Was streaked with violet.

And pink with sunrise, many a shadowy sail
Lay southward, lighting up the sleeping bay;
And in the west the white moon, still and pale,
Faded before the day.

Silence was everywhere. The rising tide
Slowly filled every cove and inlet small;
A musical low whisper, multiplied,
You heard, and that was all.

No clouds at dawn, but as the sun climbed higher,
White columns, thunderous, splendid, up the sky
Floated and stood, heaped in his steady fire,
A stately company.

Stealing along the coast from cape to cape
The weird mirage crept tremulously on,
In many a magic change and wondrous shape,
Throbbing beneath the sun.

At noon the wind rose, swept the glassy sea
To sudden ripple, thrust against the clouds
A strenuous shoulder, gathering steadily
Drove them before in crowds;

Till all the west was dark, and inky black
The level-ruffled water underneath,
And up the wind-cloud tossed, —a ghostly rack, —
In many a ragged wreath.

Then sudden roared the thunder, a great peal
Magnificent, that broke and rolled away;
And down the wind plunged, like a furious keel,
Cleaving the sea to spray;

And brought the rain sweeping o'er land and sea.
And then was tumult! Lightning sharp and keen,
Thunder, wind, rain, —a mighty jubilee
The heaven and earth between!

Loud the roused ocean sang, a chorus grand;
A solemn music rolled in undertone
Of waves that broke about on either hand
The little island lone;

Where, joyful in his tempest as his calm,
Held in the hollow of that hand of his,
I joined with heart and soul in God's great psalm,
Thrilled with a nameless bliss.

Soon lulled the wind, the summer storm soon died;
The shattered clouds went eastward, drifting slow;
From the low sun the rain-fringe swept aside,
Bright in his rosy glow,

And wide a splendor streamed through all the sky;
O'er sea and land one soft, delicious blush,
That touched the gray rocks lightly, tenderly;
A transitory flush.

Warm, odorous gusts blew off the distant land,
With spice of pine-woods, breath of hay new-mown,
O'er miles of waves and sea-scents cool and bland,
Full in our faces blown.

Slow faded the sweet light, and peacefully
The quiet stars came out, one after one:
The holy twilight fell upon the sea,
The summer day was done.

Such unalloyed delight its hours had given,
Musing, this thought rose in my grateful mind,
That God, who watches all things, up in heaven,
With patient eyes and kind,

Saw and was pleased, perhaps, one child of his
Dared to be happy like the little birds,
Because He gave his children days like this,
Rejoicing beyond words;

Dared, lifting up to Him untroubled eyes
In gratitude that worship is, and prayer,
Sing and be glad with ever new surprise,
He made his world so fair!

SUBMISSION.

The sparrow sits and sings, and sings;
Softly the sunset's lingering light
Lies rosy over rock and turf,
And reddens where the restless surf
Tosses on high its plumes of white.

Gently and clear the sparrow sings,
While twilight steals across the sea,

And still and bright the evening star
Twinkles above the golden bar
That in the west lies quietly.

O, steadfastly the sparrow sings,
And sweet the sound; and sweet the touch
Of wooing winds; and sweet the sight
Of happy Nature's deep delight
In her fair spring, desired so much!

But while so clear the sparrow sings
A cry of death is in my ear;
The crashing of the riven wreck,
Breakers that sweep the shuddering deck,
And sounds of agony and fear.

How is it that the birds can sing?
Life is so full of bitter pain;
Hearts are so wrung with hopeless grief;
Woe is so long and joy so brief;
Nor shall the lost return again.

Though rapturously the sparrow sings,
No bliss of Nature can restore
The friends whose hands I clasped so warm,
Sweet souls that through the night and storm
Fled from the earth forevermore.

Yet still the sparrow sits and sings,
Till longing, mourning, sorrowing love,
Groping to find what hope may be
Within death's awful mystery,
Reaches its empty arms above;

And listening, while the sparrow sings,
And soft the evening shadows fall,
Sees, through the crowding tears that blind,
A little light, and seems to find
And clasp God's hand, who wrought it all.

WILLIAM MORRIS.

MARCH.

SLAYER of winter, art thou here again?
O welcome, thou that bring'st the summer nigh!
The bitter wind makes not thy victory vain,
Nor will we mock thee for thy faint blue sky.
Welcome, O March! whose kindly days and dry
Make April ready for the throstle's song,
Thou first redresser of the winter's wrong!

Yea, welcome, March! and though I die ere June,
Yet for the hope of life I give thee praise,
Striving to swell the burden of the tune
That even now I hear thy brown birds raise,
Unmindful of the past or coming days;
Who sing, "O joy! a new year is begun!
What happiness to look upon the sun!"

O, what begetteth all this storm of bliss,
But Death himself, who, crying solemnly,
Even from the heart of sweet Forgetfulness,
Bids us, "Rejoice! lest pleasureless ye die.
Within a little time must ye go by.
Stretch forth your open hands, and, while ye live,
Take all the gifts that Death and Life may give"?

HARRIET McEWEN KIMBALL.

[U. S. A.]

THE CRICKETS.

PIPE, little minstrels of the waning year,
In gentle concert pipe!
Pipe the warm noons; the mellow harvest near;
The apples dropping ripe;

The tempered sunshine, and the softened shade;
The trill of lonely bird;
The sweet, sad hush on Nature's gladness laid;
The sounds through silence heard!

Pipe tenderly the passing of the year;
The summer's brief reprieve;
The dry husk rustling round the yellow ear;
The chill of morn and eve!

Pipe the untroubled trouble of the year;
Pipe low the painless pain;
Pipe your unceasing melancholy cheer;
The year is in the wane.

ALL 'S WELL.

The day is ended. Ere I sink to sleep,
My weary spirit seeks repose in thine;
Father! forgive my trespasses, and keep
This little life of mine.

With loving-kindness curtain thou my bed,
And cool in rest my burning pilgrim feet;
Thy pardon be the pillow for my head,—
So shall my sleep be sweet.

At peace with all the world, dear Lord, and thee,
No fears my soul's unwavering faith can shake;
All 's well, whichever side the grave for me
The morning light may break!

HARRIET W. PRESTON.

[U. S. A.]

THE SURVIVORS.

In this sad hour, so still, so late,
When flowers are dead, and birds are flown,
Close-sheltered from the blasts of Fate,
Our little love burns brightly on,

Amid the wrecks of dear desire
That ride the waves of life no more;
As stranded voyagers light their fire
Upon a lonely island shore.

And though we deem that soft and fair,
Beyond the tempest and the sea,
Our heart's true homes are smiling, where
In life we never more shall be,—

Yet we are saved, and we may rest;
And, hearing each the other's voice,
We cannot hold ourselves unblest,
Although we may not quite rejoice.

We 'll warm our hearts, and softly sing
Thanks for the shore whereon we 're driven;
Storm-tossed no more, we 'll fold the wing,
And dream forgotten dreams of heaven.

HIRAM RICH.

[U. S. A.]

IN THE SEA.

The salt wind blows upon my cheek,
As it blew a year ago,
When twenty boats were crushed among
The rocks of Norman's Woe.
'T was dark then; 't is light now,
And the sails are leaning low.

In dreams, I pull the sea-weed o'er,
And find a face not his,
And hope another tide will be
More pitying than this:
The wind turns, the tide turns,—
They take what hope there is.

My life goes on as life must go,
With all its sweetness spilled:
My God, why should one heart of two
Beat on, when one is stilled?
Through heart-wreck, or home-wreck,
Thy happy sparrows build.

Though boats go down, men build again
Whatever wind may blow;
If blight be in the wheat one year,
They trust again, and sow.
The grief comes, the change comes,
The tides run high or low.

Some have their dead, where, sweet and calm,
The summers bloom and go;
The sea withholds my dead,—I walk
The bar when tides are low,
And wonder how the grave-grass
Can have the heart to grow!

Flow on, O unconsenting sea,
And keep my dead below;
The night-watch set for me is long,
But, through it all, I know,
Or life comes or death comes,
God leads the eternal flow.

FRANCIS BRET HARTE.

[U. S. A.]

CONCHA.

PRESIDIO DE SAN FRANCISCO.

1800.

I.

Looking seaward, o'er the sand-hills stands the fortress, old and quaint,
By the San Francisco friars lifted to their patron saint, —

Sponsor to that wondrous city, now apostate to the creed,
On whose youthful walls the Padre saw the angel's golden reed;

All its trophies long since scattered, all its blazon brushed away,
And the flag that flies above it but a triumph of to-day.

Never scar of siege or battle challenges the wandering eye, —
Never breach of warlike onset holds the curious passer-by;

Only one sweet human fancy interweaves its threads of gold
With the plain and homespun present, and a love that ne'er grows old;

Only one thing holds its crumbling walls above the meaner dust, —
Listen to the simple story of a woman's love and trust.

II.

Count von Resanoff, the Russian, envoy of the mighty Czar,
Stood beside the deep embrasures where the brazen cannon are.

He with grave provincial magnates long had held serene debate
On the Treaty of Alliance and the high affairs of state;

He, from grave provincial magnates, oft had turned to talk apart
With the Comandante's daughter, on the questions of the heart,

Until points of gravest import yielded slowly, one by one,
And by Love was consummated what Diplomacy begun;

Till beside the deep embrasures, where the brazen cannon are,
He received the twofold contract for approval of the Czar;

Till beside the brazen cannon the betrothèd bade adieu,
And, from sally-port and gateway, north the Russian eagles flew.

III.

Long beside the deep embrasures, where the brazen cannon are,
Did they wait the promised bridegroom and the answer of the Czar;

Day by day on wall and bastion beat the hollow empty breeze, —
Day by day the sunlight glittered on the vacant, smiling seas;

Week by week the near hills whitened in their dusty leather cloaks, —
Week by week the far hills darkened from the fringing plain of oaks;

Till the rains came, and far-breaking, on the fierce southwester tost,
Dashed the whole long coast with color, and then vanished and were lost.

So each year the seasons shifted; wet and warm and drear and dry;
Half a year of clouds and flowers, — half a year of dust and sky.

Still it brought no ship nor message, — brought no tidings ill nor meet
For the statesmanlike Commander, for the daughter fair and sweet.

Yet she heard the varying message, voiceless to all ears beside:
"He will come," the flowers whispered; "Come no more," the dry hills sighed.

Still she found him with the waters lifted by the morning breeze,—
Still she lost him with the folding of the great white-tented seas;

Until hollows chased the dimples from her cheeks of olive brown,
And at times a swift, shy moisture dragged the long sweet lashes down;

Or the small mouth curved and quivered as for some denied caress,
And the fair young brow was knitted in an infantine distress.

Then the grim Commander, pacing where the brazen cannon are,
Comforted the maid with proverbs,—wisdom gathered from afar;

Bits of ancient observation by his fathers garnered, each
As a pebble worn and polished in the current of his speech:

"'Those who wait the coming rider travel twice as far as he';
'Tired wench and coming butter never did in time agree.'

"'He that getteth himself honey, though a clown, he shall have flies';
'In the end God grinds the miller'; 'In the dark the mole has eyes.'

"'He whose father is Alcalde, of his trial hath no fear,'—
And be sure the Count has reasons that will make his conduct clear."

Then the voice sententious faltered, and the wisdom it would teach
Lost itself in fondest trifles of his soft Castilian speech;

And on "Concha," "Conchitita," and "Conchita," he would dwell
With the fond reiteration which the Spaniard knows so well.

So with proverbs and caresses, half in faith and half in doubt,
Everv day some hope was kindled, flickered, faded, and went out.

IV.

Yearly, down the hillside sweeping, came the stately cavalcade,
Bringing revel to vaquero, joy and comfort to each maid;

Bringing days of formal visit, social feast and rustic sport;
Of bull-baiting on the plaza, of love-making in the court.

Vainly then at Concha's lattice,—vainly as the idle wind
Rose the thin high Spanish tenor that bespoke the youth too kind;

Vainly, leaning from their saddles, caballeros, bold and fleet,
Plucked for her the buried chicken from beneath their mustang's feet;

So in vain the barren hillsides with their gay serapes blazed,
Blazed and vanished in the dust-cloud that their flying hoofs had raised.

Then the drum called from the rampart, and once more with patient mien
The Commander and his daughter each took up the dull routine,—

Each took up the petty duties of a life apart and lone,
Till the slow years wrought a music in its dreary monotone.

V.

Forty years on wall and bastion swept the hollow idle breeze,
Since the Russian eagle fluttered from the California seas.

Forty years on wall and bastion wrought its slow but sure decay;
And St. George's cross was lifted in the port of Monterey.

And the citadel was lighted, and the hall
was gayly drest,
All to honor Sir George Simpson, famous
traveller and guest.

Far and near the people gathered to the
costly banquet set,
And exchanged congratulation with the
English baronet;

Till the formal speeches ended, and
amidst the laugh and wine
Some one spoke of Concha's lover, —
heedless of the warning sign.

Quickly then cried Sir George Simpson:
"Speak no ill of him, I pray.
He is dead. He died, poor fellow, forty
years ago this day.

"Died while speeding home to Russia,
falling from a fractious horse.
Left a sweetheart too, they tell me.
Married, I suppose, of course!

"Lives she yet?" A death-like silence
fell on banquet, guests, and hall,
And a trembling figure rising fixed the
awe-struck gaze of all.

Two black eyes in darkened orbits gleamed
beneath the nun's white hood;
Black serge hid the wasted figure, bowed
and stricken where it stood.

"Lives she yet?" Sir George repeated.
All were hushed as Concha drew
Closer yet her nun's attire. "Señor,
pardon, she died too!"

DICKENS IN CAMP.

Above the pines the moon was slowly
drifting,
The river sang below;
The dim Sierras, far beyond, uplifting
Their minarets of snow.

The roaring camp-fire, with rude humor,
painted
The ruddy tints of health
On haggard face, and form that drooped
and fainted
In the fierce race for wealth;

Till one arose, and from his pack's scant
treasure
A hoarded volume drew,
And cards were dropped from hands of
listless leisure
To hear the tale anew;

And then, while round them shadows
gathered faster,
And as the firelight fell,
He read aloud the book wherein the
Master
Had writ of "Little Nell."

Perhaps 't was boyish fancy, — for the
reader
Was youngest of them all, —
But, as he read, from clustering pine and
cedar
A silence seemed to fall;

The fir-trees, gathering closer in the
shadows,
Listened in every spray,
While the whole camp, with "Nell" on
English meadows,
Wandered and lost their way.

And so in mountain solitudes — o'ertaken
As by some spell divine —
Their cares dropped from them like the
needles shaken
From out the gusty pine.

Lost is that camp, and wasted all its fire:
And he who wrought that spell?
Ah, towering pine, and stately Kentish
spire,
Ye have one tale to tell!

Lost is that camp! but let its fragrant
story
Blend with the breath that thrills
With hop-vines' incense all the pensive
glory
That fills the Kentish hills.

And on that grave where English oak
and holly
And laurel wreaths entwine,
Deem it not all a too presumptuous
folly, —
This spray of Western pine!

ANNIE D. GREEN (MARIAN DOUGLAS).

[U. S. A.]

THE PURITAN LOVERS.

Drawn out, like lingering bees, to share
The last, sweet summer weather,
Beneath the reddening maples walked
Two Puritans together, —

A youth and maiden, heeding not
The woods which round them brightened,
Just conscious of each other's thoughts,
Half happy and half frightened.

Grave were their brows, and few their words,
And coarse their garb and simple;
The maiden's very cheek seemed shy
To own its worldly dimple.

For stern the time; they dwelt with Care;
And Fear was oft a comer;
A sober April ushered in
The Pilgrim's toilful summer.

And stern their creed; they tarried here
Mere desert-land sojourners:
They must not dream of mirth or rest,
God's humble lesson-learners.

The temple's sacred perfume round
Their week-day robes was clinging;
Their mirth was but the golden bells
On priestly garments ringing.

But as to-day they softly talked,
That serious youth and maiden,
Their plainest words strange beauty wore,
Like weeds with dewdrops laden.

The saddest theme had something sweet,
The gravest, something tender,
While with slow steps they wandered on,
Mid summer's fading splendor.

He said, "Next week the church will hold
A day of prayer and fasting";
And then he stopped, and bent to pick
A white life-everlasting, —

A silvery bloom, with fadeless leaves;
He gave it to her, sighing;
A mute confession was his glance,
Her blush a mute replying.

"Mehetabel!" (at last he spoke),
"My fairest one and dearest!
One thought is ever to my heart
The sweetest and the nearest.

"You read my soul; you know my wish;
O, grant me its fulfilling!"
She answered low, "If Heaven smiles,
And if my father 's willing!"

No idle passion swayed her heart,
This quaint New England beauty!
Faith was the guardian of her life, —
Obedience was a duty.

Too truthful for reserve, she stood,
Her brown eyes earthward casting,
And held with trembling hand the while
Her white life-everlasting.

Her sober answer pleased the youth, —
Frank, clear, and gravely cheerful;
He left her at her father's door,
Too happy to be fearful.

She looked on high, with earnest plea,
And Heaven seemed bright above her;
And when she shyly spoke his name,
Her father praised her lover.

And when, that night, she sought her couch,
With head-board high and olden,
Her prayer was praise, her pillow down,
And all her dreams were golden.

And still upon her throbbing heart,
In bloom and breath undying,
A few life-everlasting flowers,
Her lover's gift, were lying.

O Venus' myrtles, fresh and green!
O Cupid's blushing roses!
Not on your classic flowers alone
The sacred light reposes;

Though gentler care may shield your buds
From north-winds rude and blasting,
As dear to Love, those few, pale flowers
Of white life-everlasting.

WILLIAM D. HOWELLS.

[U. S. A.]

BEFORE THE GATE.

THEY gave the whole long day to idle laughter,
To fitful song and jest,
To moods of soberness as idle, after,
And silences, as idle too as the rest.

But when at last upon their way returning,
Taciturn, late, and loath,
Through the broad meadow in the sunset burning,
They reached the gate, one fine spell hindered them both.

Her heart was troubled with a subtile anguish
Such as but women know
That wait, and lest love speak or speak not languish,
And what they would, would rather they would not so;

Till he said, — man-like nothing comprehending
Of all the wondrous guile
That women won win themselves with, and bending
Eyes of relentless asking on her the while, —

"Ah, if beyond this gate the path united
Our steps as far as death,
And I might open it! —" His voice, affrighted
At its own daring, faltered under his breath.

Then she — whom both his faith and fear enchanted
Far beyond words to tell,
Feeling her woman's finest wit had wanted
The art he had that knew to blunder so well —

Shyly drew near, a little step, and mocking,
"Shall we not be too late
For tea?" she said. "I'm quite worn out with walking:
Yes, thanks, your arm. And will you — open the gate?"

S. M. B. PIATT.

[U. S. A.]

MY OLD KENTUCKY NURSE.

I KNEW a Princess: she was old,
Crisp-haired, flat-featured, with a look
Such as no dainty pen of gold
Would write of in a Fairy Book.

So bent she almost crouched, her face
Was like the Sphinx's face, to me,
Touched with vast patience, desert grace,
And lonesome, brooding mystery.

What wonder that a faith so strong
As hers, so sorrowful, so still,
Should watch in bitter sands so long,
Obedient to a burdening will!

This Princess was a Slave, — like one
I read of in a painted tale;
Yet free enough to see the sun,
And all the flowers, without a vail.

Not of the Lamp, not of the Ring,
The helpless, powerful Slave was she,
But of a subtler, fiercer Thing:
She was the Slave of Slavery.

Court-lace nor jewels had she seen:
She wore a precious smile, so rare
That at her side the whitest queen
Were dark, — her darkness was so fair.

Nothing of loveliest loveliness
This strange, sad Princess seemed to lack;
Majestic with her calm distress
She was, and beautiful though black:

Black, but enchanted black, and shut
In some vague Giant's tower of air,
Built higher than her hope was. But
The True Knight came and found her there.

The Knight of the Pale Horse, he laid
His shadowy lance against the spell
That hid her Self: as if afraid,
The cruel blackness shrank and fell.

Then, lifting slow her pleasant sleep,
He took her with him through the night,
And swam a River cold and deep,
And vanished up an awful Height.

And, in her Father's House beyond,
They gave her beauty, robe, and crown,
—On me, I think, far, faint, and fond,
Her eyes to-day look, yearning, down.

B. F. TAYLOR.

[U. S. A.]

THE OLD-FASHIONED CHOIR.

I HAVE fancied sometimes, the old Bethel-bent beam,
That trembled to earth in the Patriarch's dream,
Was a ladder of song in that wilderness rest
From the pillow of stone to the Blue of the Blest,
And the angels descending to dwell with us here,
"Old Hundred" and "Corinth" and "China" and "Mear."

All the hearts are not dead, nor under the sod,
That those breaths can blow open to Heaven and God!
Ah, "Silver Street" leads by a bright golden road,
—O, not to the hymns that in harmony flowed,—
But those sweet human psalms in the old-fashioned choir,
To the girl that sang alto,—the girl that sang air!
"Let us sing in His praise," the good minister said,
All the psalm-books at once fluttered open at "York,"
Sunned their long dotted wings in the words that he read,
While the leader leaped into the tune just ahead,
And politely picked up the key-note with a fork,
And the vicious old viol went growling along,
At the heels of the girls, in the rear of the song.

I need not a wing,—bid no genii come,
With a wonderful web from Arabian loom,
To bear me again up the river of Time,
When the world was in rhythm and life was its rhyme;
Where the stream of the years flowed so noiseless and narrow,
That across it there floated the song of the sparrow;
For a sprig of green caraway carries me there,
To the old village church and the old village choir,
When clear of the floor my feet slowly swung
And timed the sweet pulse of the praise as they sung
Till the glory aslant from the afternoon sun
Seemed the rafters of gold in God's temple begun!
You may smile at the nasals of old Deacon Brown,
Who followed by scent till he ran the tune down,—
And dear sister Green, with more goodness than grace,
Rose and fell on the tunes as she stood in her place,
And where "Coronation" exultantly flows,
Tried to reach the high notes on the tips of her toes!
To the land of the leal they have gone with their song,
Where the choir and the chorus together belong.
O, be lifted, ye Gates! Let me hear them again,—
Blessed song, blessed Sabbath, forever Amen!

LAURA C. REDDEN.

[U. S. A.]

MAZZINI.

A LIGHT is out in Italy,
A golden tongue of purest flame.
We watched it burning, long and lone,
And every watcher knew its name,
And knew from whence its fervor came:
That one rare light of Italy,
Which put self-seeking souls to shame!

This light which burnt for Italy
Through all the blackness of her night,

She doubted, once upon a time,
  Because it took away her sight,
She looked and said, "There is no light!"
  It was thine eyes, poor Italy!
That knew not dark apart from bright.

This flame which burnt for Italy,
  It would not let her haters sleep.
They blew at it with angry breath,
  And only fed its upward leap,
And only made it hot and deep.
  Its burning showed us Italy,
And all the hopes she had to keep.

This light is out in Italy,
  Her eyes shall seek for it in vain!
For her sweet sake it spent itself,
  Too early flickering to its wane, —
Too long blown over by her pain.
  Bow down and weep, O Italy,
Thou canst not kindle it again!

UNAWARES.

The wind was whispering to the vines
The secret of the summer night;
The tinted oriel window gleamed
But faintly in the misty light;
Beneath it we together sat
In the sweet stillness of content.

Till from a slow-consenting cloud
Came forth Diana, bright and bold,
And drowned us, ere we were aware,
In a great shower of liquid gold;
And, shyly lifting up my eyes,
I made acquaintance with your face.

And sudden something in me stirred,
And moved me to impulsive speech,
With little flutterings between,
And little pauses to beseech,
From your sweet graciousness of mind,
Indulgence and a kindly ear.

Ah! glad was I as any bird
That softly pipes a timid note,
To hear it taken up and trilled
Out cheerily by a stronger throat,
When, free from discord and constraint,
Your thought responded to my thought.

I had a carven missal once,
With graven scenes of "Christ, his Woe."
One picture in that quaint old book
Will never from my memory go,
Though merely in a childish wise
I used to search for it betimes.

It showed the face of God in man
Abandoned to his watch of pain,
And given of his own good-will
To every weaker thing's disdain;
But from the darkness overhead
Two pitying angel eyes looked down.

How often in the bitter night
Have I not fallen on my face,
Too sick and tired of heart to ask
God's pity in my grievous case;
Till the dank deadness of the dark,
Receding, left me, pitiless.

Then have I said: "Ah! Christ the Lord!
God sent his angel unto thee;
But both ye leave me to myself, —
Perchance ye do not even see!"
Then was it as a mighty stone
Above my sunken heart were rolled.

Now, in the moon's transfiguring light,
I seemed to see you in a dream;
Your listening face was silvered o'er
By one divinely radiant beam;
I leant towards you, and my talk
Was dimly of the haunting past.

I took you through deep soundings where
My freighted ships went down at noon, —
Gave glimpses of deflowered plains,
Blown over by the hot Simoon;
Then I was silent for a space:
"God sends no angel unto me!"

My heart withdrew into itself,
When lo! a knocking at the door:
"Am I so soon a stranger here,
Who was an honored guest before?"
Then looking in your eyes, I knew
You were God's angel sent to me!

JOHN HAY.

[U. S. A.]

A WOMAN'S LOVE.

A sentinel angel sitting high in glory
Heard this shrill wail ring out from Purgatory:
"Have mercy, mighty angel, hear my story!

"I loved, — and, blind with passionate love, I fell.
Love brought me down to death, and death to Hell.
For God is just, and death for sin is well.

"I do not rage against his high decree,
Nor for myself do ask that grace shall be;
But for my love on earth who mourns for me.

"Great Spirit! Let me see my love again
And comfort him one hour, and I were fain
To pay a thousand years of fire and pain."

Then said the pitying angel, "Nay, repent
That wild vow! Look, the dial-finger's bent
Down to the last hour of thy punishment!"

But still she wailed, "I pray thee, let me go!
I cannot rise to peace and leave him so.
O, let me soothe him in his bitter woe!"

The brazen gates ground sullenly ajar,
And upward, joyous, like a rising star,
She rose and vanished in the ether far.

But soon adown the dying sunset sailing,
And like a wounded bird her pinions trailing,
She fluttered back, with broken-hearted wailing.

She sobbed, "I found him by the summer sea
Reclined, his head upon a maiden's knee, —
She curled his hair and kissed him. Woe is me!"

She wept, "Now let my punishment begin!
I have been fond and foolish. Let me in
To expiate my sorrow and my sin."

The angel answered, "Nay, sad soul, go higher!
To be deceived in your true heart's desire
Was bitterer than a thousand years of fire!"

ELIZABETH STUART PHELPS.

[U. S. A.]

ON THE BRIDGE OF SIGHS.

It chanceth once to every soul,
Within a narrow hour of doubt and dole,

Upon Life's Bridge of Sighs to stand,
A palace and a prison on each hand.

O palace of the rose-heart's hue!
How like a flower the warm light falls from you!

O prison with the hollow eyes!
Beneath your stony stare no flowers arise.

O palace of the rose-sweet sin!
How safe the heart that does not enter in!

O blessed prison-walls! how true
The freedom of the soul that chooseth you!

ALL THE RIVERS.

"All the rivers run into the sea."
Like the pulsing of a river,
The motion of a song,
Wind the olden words along
The tortuous windings of my thought, whenever
I sit beside the sea.

All the rivers run into the sea.
O you little leaping river,
Laugh on beneath your breath!
With a heart as deep as death,
Strong stream, go patient, brave and hasting never,
I sit beside the sea.

All the rivers run into the sea.
Why the striving of a river,
The passion of a soul?
Calm the eternal waters roll
Upon the eternal shore. Somewhere, whatever
Seeks it finds the sea.

All the rivers run into the sea.
O thou bounding, burning river,
Hurrying heart! — I seem
To know (so one knows in a dream)
That in the waiting heart of God forever
Thou too shalt find the sea.

REBECCA S. PALFREY.

[U. S. A.]

WHITE UNDERNEATH.

INTO a city street,
Narrow and noisome, chance had led my feet;
Poisonous to every sense; and the sun's rays
Loved not the unclean place.

It seemed that no pure thing
Its whiteness here would ever dare to bring;
Yet even into this dark place and low,
God had sent down his snow.

Here, too, a little child
Stood by the drift, now blackened and defiled;
And with his rosy hands, in earnest play,
Scraped the dark crust away.

Checking my hurried pace,
To watch the busy hands and earnest face,
I heard him laugh aloud in pure delight,
That underneath, 't was white.

Then, through a broken pane,
A woman's voice summoned him in again,
With softened mother-tones, that half excused
The unclean words she used.

And as I lingered near,
His baby accents fell upon my ear:
"See, I can make the snow again for you,
All clean and white and new!"

Ah! surely God knows best.
Our sight is short; faith trusts to him the rest.
Sometimes, we know, he gives to human hands
To work out his commands.

Perhaps he holds apart,
By baby fingers, in that mother's heart,
One fair, clean spot that yet may spread and grow,
Till all be white as snow.

WILLIAM C. GANNETT.

[U. S. A.]

LISTENING FOR GOD.

I HEAR it often in the dark,
  I hear it in the light, —
Where *is* the voice that calls to me
  With such a quiet might?
It seems but echo to my thought,
  And yet beyond the stars;
It seems a heart-beat in a hush,
  And yet the planet jars.

O, may it be that far within
  My inmost soul there lies
A spirit-sky, that opens with
  Those voices of surprise?
And can it be, by night and day,
  That firmament serene
Is just the heaven where God himself,
  The Father, dwells unseen?

O God within, so close to me
  That every thought is plain,
Be judge, be friend, be Father still,
  And in thy heaven reign!
Thy heaven is mine, — my very soul!
  Thy words are sweet and strong;
They fill my inward silences
  With music and with song.

They send me challenges to right,
  And loud rebuke my ill;
They ring my bells of victory,
  They breathe my "Peace, be still!"
They ever seem to say, "My child,
  Why seek me so all day?
Now journey inward to thyself,
  And listen by the way."

MARY G. BRAINERD.

[U. S. A.]

GOD KNOWETH.

I KNOW not what shall befall me,
  God hangs a mist o'er my eyes,
And so, each step of my onward path,
  He makes new scenes to rise,
And every joy he sends me comes
  As a sweet and glad surprise.

I see not a step before me,
As I tread on another year;
But the past is still in God's keeping,
The future his mercy shall clear,
And what looks dark in the distance
May brighten as I draw near.

For perhaps the dreaded future
Has less bitter than I think;
The Lord may sweeten the waters
Before I stoop to drink,
Or, if Marah must be Marah,
He will stand beside its brink.

It may be he keeps waiting
Till the coming of my feet
Some gift of such rare blessedness,
Some joy so strangely sweet,
That my lips shall only tremble
With the thanks they cannot speak.

O restful, blissful ignorance!
'T is blessed not to know,
It holds me in those mighty arms
Which will not let me go,
And hushes my soul to rest
On the bosom which loves me so!

So I go on not knowing;
I would not if I might;
I would rather walk in the dark with God,
Than go alone in the light;
I would rather walk with Him by faith,
Than walk alone by sight.

My heart shrinks back from trials
Which the future may disclose,
Yet I never had a sorrow
But what the dear Lord chose;
So I send the coming tears back,
With the whispered word, "HE knows."

JOHN W. CHADWICK.

[U. S. A.]

A SONG OF TRUST.

O LOVE DIVINE, of all that is
The sweetest still and best,
Fain would I come and rest to-night
Upon thy tender breast;

As tired of sin as any child
Was ever tired of play,
When evening's hush has folded in
The noises of the day;

When just for very weariness
The little one will creep
Into the arms that have no joy
Like holding him in sleep;

And looking upward to thy face,
So gentle, sweet, and strong,
In all its looks for those who love,
So pitiful of wrong,

I pray thee turn me not away,
For, sinful though I be,
Thou knowest everything I need,
And all my need of thee.

And yet the spirit in my heart
Says, Wherefore should I pray
That thou shouldst seek me with thy love,
Since thou dost seek alway;

And dost not even wait until
I urge my steps to thee;
But in the darkness of my life
Art coming still to me?

I pray not, then, because I would;
I pray because I must;
There is no meaning in my prayer
But thankfulness and trust.

I would not have thee otherwise
Than what thou ever art:
Be still thyself, and then I know
We cannot live apart.

But still thy love will beckon me,
And still thy strength will come,
In many ways to bear me up
And bring me to my home.

And thou wilt hear the thought I mean,
And not the words I say;
Wilt hear the thanks among the words
That only seem to pray;

As if thou wert not always good,
As if thy loving care
Could ever miss me in the midst
Of this thy temple fair.

For, if I ever doubted thee,
How could I any more!

This very night my tossing bark
Has reached the happy shore;

And still, for all my sighs, my heart
Has sung itself to rest,
O Love Divine, most far and near,
Upon thy tender breast.

PAUL H. HAYNE.

[U. S. A.]

PRE-EXISTENCE.

WHILE sauntering through the crowded street,
Some half-remembered face I meet,

Albeit upon no mortal shore
That face, methinks, has smiled before.

Lost in a gay and festal throng,
I tremble at some tender song,—

Set to an air whose golden bars
I must have heard in other stars.

In sacred aisles I pause to share
The blessings of a priestly prayer,—

When the whole scene which greets mine eyes
In some strange mode I recognize

As one whose every mystic part
I feel prefigured in my heart.

At sunset, as I calmly stand,
A stranger on an alien strand,

Familiar as my childhood's home
Seems the long stretch of wave and foam.

One sails toward me o'er the bay,
And what he comes to do and say

I can foretell. A prescient lore
Springs from some life outlived of yore.

O swift, instinctive, startling gleams
Of deep soul-knowledge! not as *dreams*

For aye ye vaguely dawn and die,
But oft with lightning certainty

Pierce through the dark, oblivious brain,
To make old thoughts and memories plain,—

Thoughts which perchance must travel back
Across the wild, bewildering track

Of countless æons; memories far,
High-reaching as yon pallid star,

Unknown, scarce seen whose flickering grace
Faints on the outmost rings of space!

FROM THE WOODS.

WHY should I, with a mournful, morbid spleen,
Lament that here, in this half-desert scene,
My lot is placed?
At least the poet-winds are bold and loud,—
At least the sunset glorifies the cloud,
And forests old and proud
Rustle their verdurous banners o'er the waste.

Perchance 't is best that I, whose Fate's eclipse
Seems final,—I, whose sluggish life-wave slips
Languid away,—
Should here, within these lowly walks, apart
From the fierce throbbings of the populous mart,
Commune with mine own heart,
While Wisdom blooms from buried Hope's decay.

Nature, though wild her forms, sustains me still;
The founts are musical,—the barren hill
Glows with strange lights;
Through solemn pine-groves the small rivulets fleet
Sparkling, as if a Naiad's silvery feet,
In quick and coy retreat,
Glanced through the star-gleams on calm summer nights;

And the great sky, the royal heaven above,
Darkens with storms or melts in hues of love;
While far remote,
Just where the sunlight smites the woods with fire,
Wakens the multitudinous sylvan choir;
Their innocent love's desire
Poured in a rill of song from each harmonious throat.

My walls are crumbling, but immortal looks
Smile on me here from faces of rare books:
Shakespeare consoles
My heart with true philosophies; a balm
Of spiritual dews from humbler song or psalm
Fills me with tender calm,
Or through hushed heavens of soul Milton's deep thunder rolls!

And more than all, o'er shattered wrecks of Fate,
The relics of a happier time and state,
My nobler life
Shines on unquenched! O deathless love that lies
In the clear midnight of those passionate eyes!
Joy waneth! Fortune flies!
What then? Thou still art here, soul of my soul, my Wife!

ISA CRAIG KNOX.

BALLAD OF THE BRIDES OF QUAIR.

A STILLNESS crept about the house,
At evenfall, in noontide glare;
Upon the silent hills looked forth
The many-windowed House of Quair.

The peacock on the terrace screamed;
Browsed on the lawn the timid hare;
The great trees grew i' the avenue,
Calm by the sheltered House of Quair.

The pool was still; around its brim
The alders sickened all the air;
There came no murmur from the streams,
Though nigh flowed Leither, Tweed, and Quair.

The days hold on their wonted pace,
And men to court and camp repair,
Their part to fill, of good or ill,
While women keep the House of Quair.

And one is clad in widow's weeds,
And one is maiden-like and fair,
And day by day they seek the paths
About the lonely fields of Quair.

To see the trout leap in the streams,
The summer clouds reflected there,
The maiden loves in pensive dreams
To hang o'er silver Tweed and Quair.

Within, in pall-black velvet clad,
Sits stately in her oaken chair—
A stately dame of ancient name—
The mother of the House of Quair.

Her daughter broiders by her side,
With heavy drooping golden hair,
And listens to her frequent plaint,—
"Ill fare the brides that come to Quair.

"For more than one hath lived in pine,
And more than one hath died of care,
And more than one hath sorely sinned,
Left lonely in the House of Quair.

"Alas! and ere thy father died
I had not in his heart a share,
And now—may God forfend her ill—
Thy brother brings his bride to Quair."

She came; they kissed her in the hall,
They kissed her on the winding stair,
They led her to the chamber high,
The fairest in the House of Quair.

They bade her from the window look,
And mark the scene how passing fair,
Among whose ways the quiet days
Would linger o'er the wife of Quair.

"'T is fair," she said on looking forth,
"But what although 't were bleak and bare—"
She looked the love she did not speak,
And broke the ancient curse of Quair.

"Where'er he dwells, where'er he goes,
His dangers and his toils I share."
What need be said,—she was not one
Of the ill-fated brides of Quair.

HENRY TIMROD.

[U. S. A.]

SPRING IN CAROLINA.

SPRING, with that nameless pathos in the air
Which dwells with all things fair,
Spring, with her golden suns and silver rain,
Is with us once again.

Out in the lonely woods the jasmine burns
Its fragrant lamps, and turns
Into a royal court with green festoons
The banks of dark lagoons.

In the deep heart of every forest tree
The blood is all aglee,
And there 's a look about the leafless bowers
As if they dreamed of flowers.

Yet still on every side we trace the hand
Of Winter in the land,
Save where the maple reddens on the lawn,
Flushed by the season's dawn;

Or where, like those strange semblances we find
That age to childhood bind,
The elm puts on, as if in Nature's scorn,
The brown of autumn corn.

As yet the turf is dark, although you know
That, not a span below,
A thousand germs are groping through the gloom,
And soon will burst their tomb.

In gardens you may note amid the dearth,
The crocus breaking earth;
And near the snowdrop's tender white and green,
The violet in its screen.

But many gleams and shadows need must pass
Along the budding grass,
And weeks go by, before the enamored South
Shall kiss the rose's mouth.

Still there 's a sense of blossoms yet unborn
In the sweet airs of morn;
One almost looks to see the very street
Grow purple at his feet.

At times a fragrant breeze comes floating by,
And brings, you know not why,
A feeling as when eager crowds await
Before a palace gate

Some wondrous pageant; and you scarce would start,
If from a beech's heart,
A blue-eyed Dryad, stepping forth, should say,
"Behold me! I am May!"

WALTER F. MITCHELL.

[U. S. A.]

TACKING SHIP OFF SHORE.

THE weather-leech of the topsail shivers,
The bow-lines strain, and the lee-shrouds slacken,
The braces are taut, the lithe boom quivers,
And the waves with the coming squall-cloud blacken.

Open one point on the weather-bow,
Is the lighthouse tall on Fire Island Head?
There 's a shade of doubt on the captain's brow,
And the pilot watches the heaving lead.

I stand at the wheel, and with eager eye
To sea and to sky and to shore I gaze,
Till the muttered order of "*Full and by!*"
Is suddenly changed for "*Full for stays!*"

The ship bends lower before the breeze,
As her broadside fair to the blast she lays,
And she swifter springs to the rising seas,
As the pilot calls, "*Stand by for stays!*"

It is silence all, as each in his place,
With the gathered coil in his hardened hands,
By tack and bowline, by sheet and brace,
Waiting the watchword impatient stands.

And the light on Fire Island Head draws near,
As, trumpet-winged, the pilot's shout
From his post on the bowsprit's heel I hear,
With the welcome call of, "*Ready! About!*"

No time to spare! It is touch and go;
And the captain growls, "Down, helm! hard down!"
As my weight on the whirling spokes I throw,
While heaven grows black with the storm-cloud's frown.

High o'er the knight-heads flies the spray,
As we meet the shock of the plunging sea;
And my shoulder stiff to the wheel I lay,
As I answer, "*Ay, ay, sir! Ha-a-rd a lee!*"

With the swerving leap of a startled steed
The ship flies fast in the eye of the wind,
The dangerous shoals on the lee recede,
And the headland white we have left behind.

The topsails flutter, the jibs collapse,
And belly and tug at the groaning cleats;
The spanker slats, and the mainsail flaps;
And thunders the order, "*Tacks and sheets!*"

Mid the rattle of blocks and the tramp of the crew,
Hisses the rain of the rushing squall:
The sails are aback from clew to clew,
And now is the moment for, "Mainsail, haul!"

And the heavy yards, like a baby's toy,
By fifty strong arms are swiftly swung:
She holds her way, and I look with joy
For the first white spray o'er the bulwarks flung.

"*Let go, and haul!*" 'T is the last command,
And the head-sails fill to the blast once more;
Astern and to leeward lies the land,
With its breakers white on the shingly shore.

What matters the reef, or the rain, or the squall?
I steady the helm for the open sea;
The first mate clamors, "Belay there, all!"
And the captain's breath once more comes free.

And so off shore let the good ship fly;
Little care I how the gusts may blow,
In my fo'castle bunk, in a jacket dry,
Eight bells have struck, and my watch is below.

HARRIET PRESCOTT SPOFFORD.

[U. S. A.]

HEREAFTER.

Love, when all these years are silent, vanished quite and laid to rest,
When you and I are sleeping, folded breathless breast to breast,
When no morrow is before us, and the long grass tosses o'er us,
And our grave remains forgotten, or by alien footsteps pressed, —

Still that love of ours will linger, that great love enrich the earth,
Sunshine in the heavenly azure, breezes blowing joyous mirth;
Fragrance fanning off from flowers, melody of summer showers,
Sparkle of the spicy wood-fires round the happy autumn hearth.

That's our love. But you and I, dear, — shall we linger with it yet,
Mingled in one dewdrop, tangled in one sunbeam's golden net, —
On the violet's purple bosom, I the sheen, but you the blossom,
Stream on sunset winds and be the haze with which some hill is wet?

Or, beloved, — if ascending, — when we have endowed the world
With the best bloom of our being, whither will our way be whirled,
Through what vast and starry spaces, toward what awful holy places,
With a white light on our faces, spirit over spirit furled?

Only this our yearning answers, — where-
so'er that way defile,
Not a film shall part us through the æons
of that mighty while,
In the fair eternal weather, even as
phantoms still together,
Floating, floating, one forever, in the
light of God's great smile!

SONG.

In the summer twilight,
While yet the dew was hoar,
I went plucking purple pansies
Till my love should come to shore.
The fishing-lights their dances
Were keeping out at sea,
And, "Come," I sang, "my true love,
Come hasten home to me!"

But the sea it fell a-moaning,
And the white gulls rocked thereon,
And the young moon dropped from heaven,
And the lights hid, one by one.
All silently their glances
Slipped down the cruel sea,
And, "Wait," cried the night and wind
and storm, —
"Wait till I come to thee."

WILLIAM WINTER.

[U. S. A.]

AZRAEL.

Come with a smile, when come thou must,
Evangel of the world to be,
And touch and glorify this dust, —
This shuddering dust that now is me, —
And from this prison set me free!

Long in those awful eyes I quail,
That gaze across the grim profound:
Upon that sea there is no sail,
Nor any light, nor any sound,
From the far shore that girds it round.

Only — two still and steady rays,
That those twin orbs of doom o'ertop;
Only — a quiet, patient gaze
That drinks my being, drop by drop,
And bids the pulse of nature stop.

Come with a smile, auspicious friend,
To usher in the eternal day!
Of these weak terrors make an end,
And charm the paltry chains away
That bind me to this timorous clay!

And let me know my soul akin
To sunrise and the winds of morn,
And every grandeur that has been
Since this all-glorious world was born,
Nor longer droop in my own scorn.

Come, when the way grows dark and chill,
Come, when the baffled mind is weak,
And in the heart that voice is still
Which used in happier days to speak,
Or only whispers sadly meek.

Come with a smile that dims the sun!
With pitying heart and gentle hand!
And waft me, from a work that 's done,
To peace that waits on thy command,
In God's mysterious better land!

JOAQUIN MILLER.

[U. S. A.]

FROM "WALKER IN NICARAGUA."

Success had made him more than king;
Defeat made him the vilest thing
In name, contempt or hate can bring:
So much the loaded dice of war
Do make or mar of character.
Speak ill who will of him, he died
In all disgrace; say of the dead
His heart was black, his hands were
red, —
Say this much, and be satisfied.

. . . . .

I lay this crude wreath on his dust,
Inwove with sad, sweet memories
Recalled here by these colder seas.
I leave the wild bird with his trust,
To sing and say him nothing wrong;
I wake no rivalry of song.

He lies low in the levelled sand,
Unsheltered from the tropic sun,
And now of all he knew, not one
Will speak him fair, in that far land.
Perhaps 't was this that made me seek,
Disguised, his grave one winter-tide;

A weakness for the weaker side,
A siding with the helpless weak.

A palm not far held out a hand;
Hard by a long green bamboo swung,
And bent like some great bow unstrung,
And quivered like a willow wand;
Beneath a broad banana's leaf,
Perched on its fruits that crooked hung,
A bird in rainbow splendor sung
A low, sad song of tempered grief.

No sod, no sign, no cross nor stone,
But at his side a cactus green
Upheld its lances long and keen;
It stood in hot red sands alone,
Flat-palmed and fierce with lifted spears;
One bloom of crimson crowned its head,
A drop of blood, so bright, so red,
Yet redolent as roses' tears.
In my left hand I held a shell,
All rosy lipped and pearly red;
I laid it by his lowly bed,
For he did love so passing well
The grand songs of the solemn sea.
O shell! sing well, wild, with a will,
When storms blow hard and birds be still,
The wildest sea-song known to thee!

I said some things, with folded hands,
Soft whispered in the dim sea-sound,
And eyes held humbly to the ground,
And frail knees sunken in the sands.
He had done more than this for me,
And yet I could not well do more:
I turned me down the olive shore,
And set a sad face to the sea.

SUNRISE IN VENICE.

Night seems troubled and scarce asleep;
Her brows are gathered in broken rest;
Sullen old lion of dark St. Mark,
And a star in the east starts up from the deep;
White as my lilies that grow in the west.
Hist! men are passing hurriedly.
I see the yellow wide wings of a bark
Sail silently over my morning-star.
I see men move in the moving dark,
Tall and silent as columns are, —
Great sinewy men that are good to see,
With hair pushed back and with open breasts;
Barefooted fishermen seeking their boats,
Brown as walnuts and hairy as goats, —
Brave old water-dogs, wed to the sea,
First to their labors and last to their rests.

Ships are moving! I hear a horn;
A silver trumpet it sounds to me,
Deep-voiced and musical, far a-sea . . .
Answers back, and again it calls.
'T is the sentinel boats that watch the town
All night, as mounting her watery walls,
And watching for pirate or smuggler. Down
Over the sea, and reaching away,
And against the east, a soft light falls, —
Silvery soft as the mist of morn,
And I catch a breath like the breath of day.

The east is blossoming! Yea, a rose,
Vast as the heavens, soft as a kiss,
Sweet as the presence of woman is,
Rises and reaches and widens and grows
Right out of the sea, as a blossoming tree;
Richer and richer, so higher and higher,
Deeper and deeper it takes its hue;
Brighter and brighter it reaches through
The space of heaven and the place of stars,
Till all is as rich as a rose can be,
And my rose-leaves fall into billows of fire.
Then beams reach upward as arms from a sea;
Then lances and arrows are aimed at me.
Then lances and spangles and spars and bars
Are broken and shivered and strown on the sea;
And around and about me tower and spire
Start from the billows like tongues of fire.

UNKNOWN.

DIFFERENT POINTS OF VIEW.

Saith the white owl to the martin folk,
In the belfry tower so grim and gray:
"Why do they deafen us with these bells?
Is any one dead or born to-day?"

A martin peeped over the rim of its nest,
And answered crossly: "Why, ain't you heard
That an heir is coming to the great estate?"
"I 'ave n't," the owl said, "'pon my word."

"Are men born so, with that white cockade?"
Said the little field-mouse to the old brown rat.
"Why, you silly child," the sage replied,
"This is the bridegroom, — they know him by that."

Saith the snail so snug in his dappled shell,
Slowly stretching one cautious horn,
As the beetle was hurrying by so brisk,
Much to his snailship's inward scorn:

"Why does that creature ride by so fast?
Has a fire broke out to the east or west?"
"Your Grace, he rides to the wedding-feast," —
"Let the madman go. What I want 's rest."

The swallows around the woodman skimmed,
Poising and turning on flashing wing;
One said: "How liveth this lump of earth?
In the air, he can neither soar nor spring.

"Over the meadows we sweep and dart,
Down with the flowers, or up in the skies;
While these poor lumberers toil and slave,
Half starved, *for how can they catch their flies?*"

Quoth the dry-rot worm to his artisans
In the carpenter's shop, as they bored away:
"Hark to the sound of the saw and file!
What are these creatures at work at, — say?"

From his covered passage a worm looked out,
And eyed the beings so busy o'erhead:
"I scarcely know, my lord; but I think
They 're making a box to bury their dead!"

Says a butterfly with his wings of blue
All in a flutter of careless joy,
As he talks to a dragon-fly over a flower:
"Ours is a life, sir, with no alloy.

"What are those black things, row and row,
Winding along by the new-mown hay?"
"That is a funeral," says the fly:
"The carpenter buries his son to-day."

ANNA BOYNTON AVERILL.

[U. S. A.]

BIRCH STREAM.

At noon, within the dusty town,
Where the wild river rushes down,
And thunders hoarsely all day long,
I think of thee, my hermit stream,
Low singing in thy summer dream,
Thine idle, sweet, old, tranquil song.

Northward, Katahdin's chasmed pile
Looms through thy low, long, leafy aisle,
Eastward, Olamon's summit shines;
And I upon thy grassy shore,
The dreamful, happy child of yore,
Worship before mine olden shrines.

Again the sultry noontide hush
Is sweetly broken by the thrush,
Whose clear bell rings and dies away
Beside thy banks, in coverts deep,
Where nodding buds of orchis sleep
In dusk, and dream not it is day.

Again the wild cow-lily floats
Her golden-freighted, tented boats,
In thy cool coves of softened gloom,
O'ershadowed by the whispering reed,
And purple plumes of pickerel-weed,
And meadow-sweet in tangled bloom.

The startled minnows dart in flocks
Beneath thy glimmering amber rocks,
If but a zephyr stirs the brake;
The silent swallow swoops, a flash
Of light, and leaves, with dainty plash,
A ring of ripples in her wake.

— Without, the land is hot and dim;
The level fields in languor swim,
Their stubble-grasses brown as dust;
And all along the upland lanes,
Where shadeless noon oppressive reigns,
Dead roses wear their crowns of rust.

Within, is neither blight nor death,
The fierce sun woos with ardent breath,
But cannot win thy sylvan heart.
Only the child who loves thee long,
With faithful worship pure and strong,
Can know how dear and sweet thou art.

So loved I thee in days gone by,
So love I yet, though leagues may lie
  Between us, and the years divide;—
A breath of coolness, dawn, and dew,—
A joy forever fresh and true,
  Thy memory doth with me abide.

KATE PUTNAM OSGOOD.

[U. S. A.]

DRIVING HOME THE COWS.

Out of the clover and blue-eyed grass
  He turned them into the river lane;
One after another he let them pass,
  Then fastened the meadow bars again.

Under the willows, and over the hill,
  He patiently followed their sober pace;
The merry whistle for once was still,
  And something shadowed the sunny face.

Only a boy! and his father had said
  He never could let his youngest go:
Two already were lying dead,
  Under the feet of the trampling foe.

But after the evening work was done,
  And the frogs were loud in the meadow-swamp,
Over his shoulder he slung his gun,
  And stealthily followed the footpath damp.

Across the clover, and through the wheat,
  With resolute heart and purpose grim,
Though cold was the dew on his hurrying feet,
  And the blind bat's flitting startled him.

Thrice since then had the lanes been white,
  And the orchards sweet with apple-bloom;
And now, when the cows came back at night,
  The feeble father drove them home.

For news had come to the lonely farm
  That three were lying where two had lain;
And the old man's tremulous, palsied arm
  Could never lean on a son's again.

The summer day grew cool and late:
  He went for the cows when the work was done;
But down the lane, as he opened the gate,
  He saw them coming, one by one:

Brindle, Ebony, Speckle, and Bess,
  Shaking their horns in the evening wind;
Cropping the buttercups out of the grass,—
  But who was it following close behind?

Loosely swung in the idle air
  The empty sleeve of army blue;
And worn and pale, from the crisping hair,
  Looked out a face that the father knew.

For Southern prisons will sometimes yawn,
  And yield their dead unto life again:
And the day that comes with a cloudy dawn
  In golden glory at last may wane.

The great tears sprang to their meeting eyes;
  For the heart must speak when the lips are dumb:
And under the silent evening skies
  Together they followed the cattle home.

LIZZIE G. PARKER.

[U. S. A.]

WAITING.

For a foot that will not come,
  For a song that will not sound,
I hearken, wait and moan alway,
  And weary months go round.

Never again in the world
  Shall that lost footstep be;
Nor sea, nor bird, nor reedy wind
  Can match that song to me.

But in the chants of heaven,
  And down the golden street,
My heart shall single out that song
  And know that touch of feet.

EDWIN ARNOLD.

"HE AND SHE."

"SHE is dead!" they said to him.
"Come away;
Kiss her and leave her, thy love is clay!"

They smoothed her tresses of dark brown
hair;
On her forehead of stone they laid it fair;

Over her eyes that gazed too much
They drew the lids with a gentle touch;

With a tender touch they closed up well
The sweet thin lips that had secrets to
tell;

About her brows and beautiful face
They tied her veil and her marriage lace,

And drew on her white feet her white
silk shoes —
Which were the whitest no eye could
choose —

And over her bosom they crossed her
hands.
"Come away!" they said; "God under-
stands."

And there was silence, and nothing there
But silence, and scents of eglantere,

And jasmine, and roses, and rosemary;
And they said, "As a lady should lie,
lies she."

And they held their breath till they left
the room,
With a shudder, to glance at its still-
ness and gloom.

But he who loved her too well to dread
The sweet, the stately, the beautiful
dead,

He lit his lamp and took the key
And turned it, —alone again—he and she.

He and she; but she would not speak,
Though he kissed, in the old place, the
quiet cheek.

He and she; yet she would not smile,
Though he called her the name she loved
erewhile.

He and she; still she did not move
To any one passionate whisper of love.

Then he said: "Cold lips and breasts
without breath,
Is there no voice, no language of death?

"Dumb to the ear and still to the sense,
But to heart and to soul distinct, intense?

"See now; I will listen with soul, not ear;
What was the secret of dying, dear?

"Was it the infinite wonder of all
That you ever could let life's flower fall?

"Or was it a greater marvel to feel
The perfect calm o'er the agony steal?

"Was the miracle greater to find how deep
Beyond all dreams sank downward that
sleep?

"Did life roll back its records, dear,
And show, as they say it does, past
things clear?

"And was it the innermost heart of the
bliss
To find out so, what a wisdom love is?

"O perfect dead! O dead most dear,
I hold the breath of my soul to hear!

"I listen as deep as to horrible hell,
As high as to heaven, and you do not tell.

"There must be pleasure in dying, sweet,
To make you so placid from head to feet!

"I would tell you, darling, if I were dead,
And 't were your hot tears upon my brow
shed;

"I would say, though the Angel of Death
had laid
His sword on my lips to keep it unsaid.

"You should not ask vainly, with stream-
ing eyes,
Which of all deaths was the chiefest sur-
prise,

"The very strangest and suddenest thing
Of all the surprises that dying must
bring."

Ah, foolish world! O most kind dead!
Though he told me, who will believe it
was said?

Who will believe that he heard her say,
With the sweet, soft voice, in the dear
old way:

"The utmost wonder is this, — I hear
And see you, and love you, and kiss
you, dear;

"And am your angel, who was your
bride,
And know that, though dead, I have
never died."

AFTER DEATH IN ARABIA.

He who died at Azan sends
This to comfort all his friends:

Faithful friends! It lies, I know,
Pale and white and cold as snow;
And ye say, "Abdallah's dead!"
Weeping at the feet and head,
I can see your falling tears,
I can hear your sighs and prayers;
Yet I smile and whisper this, —
"*I* am not the thing you kiss;
Cease your tears, and let it lie;
It *was* mine, it is not I."

Sweet friends! What the women lave,
For its last bed of the grave,
Is but a hut which I am quitting,
Is a garment no more fitting,
Is a cage from which, at last,
Like a hawk my soul hath passed.
Love the inmate, not the room, —
The wearer, not the garb, — the plume
Of the falcon, not the bars
Which kept him from those splendid
stars.

Loving friends! Be wise and dry
Straightway every weeping eye, —
What ye lift upon the bier
Is not worth a wistful tear.
'T is an empty sea-shell, — one
Out of which the pearl is gone;
The shell is broken, it lies there;
The pearl, the all, the soul, is here.
'T is an earthen jar, whose lid
Allah sealed, the while it hid
That treasure of his treasury,
A mind that loved him; let it lie!
Let the shard be earth's once more,
Since the gold shines in his store!

Allah glorious! Allah good!
Now thy world is understood;
Now the long, long wonder ends;
Yet ye weep, my erring friends,
While the man whom ye call dead,
In unspoken bliss, instead,
Lives and loves you; lost, 't is true,
By such light as shines for you;
But in the light ye cannot see
Of unfulfilled felicity, —
In enlarging paradise,
Lives a life that never dies.

Farewell, friends! Yet not farewell;
Where I am, ye, too, shall dwell.
I am gone before your face,
A moment's time, a little space.
When ye come where I have stepped,
Ye will wonder why ye wept;
Ye will know, by wise love taught,
That here is all, and there is naught.
Weep awhile, if ye are fain, —
Sunshine still must follow rain;
Only not at death, — for death,
Now I know, is that first breath
Which our souls draw when we enter
Life, which is of all life centre.

Be ye certain all seems love,
Viewed from Allah's throne above;
Be ye stout of heart, and come
Bravely onward to your home!
La Allah illa Allah! yea!
Thou love divine! Thou love alway!

He that died at Azan gave
This to those who made his grave.

UNKNOWN.

UNSEEN.

At the spring of an arch in the great
north tower,
High up on the wall, is an angel's head;
And beneath it is carved a lily flower,
With delicate wings at the side out-
spread.

They say that the sculptor wrought from the face
Of his youth's lost love, of his promised bride,
And when he had added the last sad grace
To the features, he dropped his chisel and died.

And the worshippers throng to the shrine below,
And the sight-seers come with their curious eyes,
But deep in the shadow, where none may know
Its beauty, the gem of his carving lies.

Yet at early morn on a midsummer's day,
When the sun is far to the north, for the space
Of a few short minutes, there falls a ray
Through an amber pane on the angel's face.

It was wrought for the eye of God, and it seems
That he blesses the work of the dead man's hand
With a ray of the golden light that streams
On the lost that are found in the deathless land.

HARRIET O. NELSON.

[U. S. A.]

THE QUIET MEETING.

DEAR friend of old, whom memory links
With sunny hour and summer weather,
Do you with me remember yet
That Sabbath morn together,

When straying from our wonted ways,
From prayer and song and priestly teacher,
Those kind, sweet helps by which the Lord
Stoops to his yearning creature,

And led by some faint sense of need
Which each in each perceived unuttered,
Some craving for an unknown good,
That in the spirit fluttered,

Our footsteps sought the humble house
Unmarked by cross or towering steeple,
Where for their First-day gathering came
God's plain and simple people?

The air was soft, the sky was large,
The grass as gay with golden flowers
As if the last night's sky had fallen
On earth in starry showers.

And, as we walked, the apple-trees
Shed their late bloom for every comer;
Our souls drank deep of joy and peace,
For it was youth and summer.

Yet through the doorway, rude and low,
The plain-robed folk we followed after,
Our steps, like theirs, demure and slow,
Our lips as free from laughter.

We sat apart, but still were near
As souls may draw unto each other
Who seek through stronger love to God
A nobler love to brother.

How deep the common silence was;
How pure and sweet those woman faces,
Which patience, gentleness, and peace
Had stamped with heavenly graces.

No noise of prayer came through the hush,
No praise sang through the portals lowly,
Save merry bird-songs from without,
And even those seemed holy.

Then daily toil was glorified,
And love was something rarer, finer;
The whole earth, sanctified through Christ,
And human life, diviner.

And when at length, by lips of age,
The silent hour was fitly broken,
Our hearts found echo in the words
From wise experience spoken.

Then at the elder's clasp of hand
We rose and met beneath the portal;
Some earthly dust our lives had lost,
And something gained immortal.

Since then, when sermon, psalm, and rite,
And solemn organ's tuneful pealing,

All fail to raise my sluggish sense
  To higher thought and feeling,

My mind goes back the winding track
  Of years whose flight hath left me lonely,
Once more my soul is upward drawn,
  And hears the spirit only.

W. J. LINTON.

MIDWINTER.

MIDWINTER comes to-morrow
  My welcome guest to be;
White-haired, wide-wingéd sorrow,
  With Christmas gifts for me.
Thy angel, God!—I thank thee still,
Thy will be done, thy better will!

I thank thee, Lord!—the whiteness
  Of winter on my heart
Shall keep some glint of brightness,
  Though sun and stars depart.
Thou smilest on the snow; thy will
Is dread and drear, but lovely still.

DEFINITIONS.

WISDOM.

THE perfect sight of duty; thought which moulds
A rounded life, and its true aims beholds.

REVERENCE.

Obeisance unto greatness understood;
The first step of a human life toward good.

SERVICE.

Think what God doth for man; so mayst thou know
How godlike service is, and serve also.

DESPAIR.

The shadow of a slave who turns his back
On the light, and cries, "The universe is black!"

DOUBT.

The mountain's image trembling in the lake:
Look up. Perhaps the mountain does not quake.

DEFEAT.

One of the stairs to heaven. Halt not to count
What you have trampled on. Look up, and mount.

FAILURE.

Who knows?—Each year, as does the wheat-seed, dies;
And so God harvests his eternities.

FORGIVENESS.

The condonation of a wrong. What then?
Even the wrong-doers are our brother-men!

OBSTINACY.

A mule with blinkers. Ay, he goes quite straight,
Runs at the gate-post, and will miss the gate.

PRUDENCE.

The saddle-girth of valor. Thou art wise
To gird it well, but not around thy eyes.

PATRIOTISM.

Not the mere holding a great flag unfurled,
But making it the goodliest in the world.

NARROWNESS.

Be narrow!—as the bud, the flame, the dart;
But narrow in thy aim, not at thy heart.

WEALTH.

Cornelia's jewels; blind old Milton's thought;
Job's patience; and the lesson Lazarus taught.

MARGARET J. PRESTON.

[U. S. A.]

READY.

I WOULD be ready, Lord,
My house in order set,
None of the work thou gavest me
To do, unfinished yet.

I would be watching, Lord,
With lamp well trimmed and clear,
Quick to throw open wide the door,
What time thou drawest near.

I would be waiting, Lord,
Because I cannot know
If in the night or morning watch,
I may be called to go.

I would be working, Lord,
Each day, each hour, for thee;
Assured that thus I wait thee well,
Whene'er thy coming be.

I would he living, Lord,
As ever in thine eye;
For whoso lives the nearest thee
The fittest is to die.

A BIRD'S MINISTRY.

FROM his home in an Eastern bungalow,
In sight of the everlasting snow
Of the grand Himalayas, row on row,

Thus wrote my friend: —
"I had travelled far
From the Afghan towers of Candahar,
Through the sand-white plains of Sinde-Sagar;

"And once, when the daily march was o'er,
As tired I sat in my tented door,
Hope failed me, as never it failed before.

"In swarming city, at wayside fane,
By the Indus' bank, on the scorching plain,
I had taught, — and my teaching all seemed vain.

"'No glimmer of light (I sighed) appears;
The Moslem's Fate and the Buddhist's fears
Have gloomed their worship this thousand years.

"'For Christ and his truth I stand alone
In the midst of millions: a sand-grain blown
Against yon temple of ancient stone

"'As soon may level it!' Faith forsook
My soul, as I turned on the pile to look:
Then rising, my saddened way I took

"To its lofty roof, for the cooler air:
I gazed, and marvelled; — how crumbled were
The walls I had deemed so firm and fair!

"For, wedged in a rift of the massive stone,
Most plainly rent by its roots alone,
A beautiful peepul-tree had grown:

"Whose gradual stress would still expand
The crevice, and topple upon the sand
The temple, while o'er its wreck should stand

"The tree in its living verdure! — Who
Could compass the thought? — The bird that flew
Hitherward, dropping a seed that grew,

"Did more to shiver this ancient wall
Than earthquake, — war, — simoon, — or all
The centuries, in their lapse and fall!

"Then I knelt by the riven granite there,
And my soul shook off its weight of care,
As my voice rose clear on the tropic air: —

"'The living seeds I have dropped remain
In the cleft: Lord, quicken with dew and rain,
Then temple and mosque shall be rent in twain!'"

ERASTUS W. ELLSWORTH.

[U. S. A.]

WHAT IS THE USE?

I SAW a man, by some accounted wise,
For some things said and done before their eyes,

Quite overcast, and in a restless muse,
Pacing a path about,
And often giving out:
"What is the use?"

Then I, with true respect: What meanest thou
By those strange words, and that unsettled brow?
Health, wealth, the fair esteem of ample views,
To these things thou art born
But he, as one forlorn:
"What is the use?"

"I have surveyed the sages and their books,
Man, and the natural world of woods and brooks,
Seeking that perfect good that I would choose;
But find no perfect good,
Settled and understood.
What is the use?

"Life, in a poise, hangs trembling on the beam,
Even in a breath bounding to each extreme
Of joy and sorrow; therefore I refuse
All beaten ways of bliss,
And only answer this:
What is the use?

"The hoodwinked world is seeking happiness.
'Which way!' they cry, 'here?' 'no!' 'there?' 'who can guess?'
And so they grope, and grope, and grope, and cruise
On, on, till life is lost,
At blindman's with a ghost.
What is the use?

"Love first, with most, then wealth, distinction, fame,
Quicken the blood and spirit on the game.
Some try them all, and all alike accuse:
'I have been all,' said one,
'And find that all is none.'
What is the use?

"In woman's love we sweetly are undone,
Willing to attract, but harder to be won,
Harder to keep is she whose love we choose.
Loves are like flowers that grow
In soils on fire below.
What is the use?

"Some pray for wealth, and seem to pray aright;
They heap until themselves are out of sight;
Yet stand, in charities, not over shoes,
And ask of their old age
As an old ledger page,
What is the use? . . . .

"The strife for fame and the high praise of power,
Is as a man, who, panting up a tower,
Bears a great stone, then, straining all his thews,
Heaves it, and sees it make
A splashing in a lake.
What is the use? . . . .

"Should some new star, in the fair evening sky,
Kindle a blaze, startling so keen an eye
Of flamings eminent, athwart the dews,
Our thoughts would say, No doubt
That star will soon burn out.
What is the use?

"Who'll care for me, when I am dead and gone?
Not many now, and surely, soon, not one;
And should I sing like an immortal Muse,
Men, if they read the line,
Read for their good, not mine;
What is the use? . . . .

"Spirit of Beauty! Breath of golden lyres!
Perpetual tremble of immortal wires!
Divinely torturing rapture of the Muse!
Conspicuous wretchedness!
Thou starry, sole success!—
What is the use?

"Doth not all struggle tell, upon its brow,
That he who makes it is not easy now,
But hopes to be? Vain hope that dost abuse!
Coquetting with thine eyes,
And fooling him who sighs.
What is the use?

"Go pry the lintels of the pyramids;
Lift the old kings' mysterious coffin-lids—
This dust was theirs whose names these stones confuse,
These mighty monuments
Of mighty discontents.
What is the use?

"Did not he sum it all, whose Gate of Pearls
Blazed royal Ophir, Tyre, and Syrian girls, —
The great, wise, famous monarch of the Jews?
Though rolled in grandeur vast,
He said of all, at last:
What is the use?

"O, but to take, of life, the natural good,
Even as a hermit caverned in a wood,
More sweetly fills my sober-suited views,
Than sweating to attain
Any luxurious pain.
What is the use?

"Give me a hermit's life, without his beads, —
His lantern-jawed, and moral-mouthing creeds;
Systems and creeds the natural heart abuse.
What need of any book,
Or spiritual crook?
What is the use?

"I love, and God is love; and I behold
Man, Nature, God, one triple chain of gold, —
Nature in all sole oracle and muse.
What should I seek, at all,
More than is natural?
What is the use?"

Seeing this man so heathenly inclined, —
So wilted in the mood of a good mind,
I felt a kind of heat of earnest thought;
And studying in reply,
Answered him, eye to eye:

Thou dost amaze me that thou dost mistake
The wandering rivers for the fountain lake.
What is the end of living?—happiness?
An end that none attain,
Argues a purpose vain.

Plainly, this world is not a scope for bliss,
But duty. Yet we see not all that is,
Or may be, some day, if we love the light.
What man is, in desires,
Whispers where man aspires.

But what and where are we? what now —to-day?
Souls on a globe that spins our lives away, —
A multitudinous world, where Heaven and Hell,
Strangely in battle met,
Their gonfalons have set.

Dust though we are, and shall return to dust,
Yet being born to battles, fight we must;
Under which ensign is our only choice.
We know to wage our best,
God only knows the rest.

Then since we see about us sin and dole,
And some things good, why not, with hand and soul,
Wrestle and succor out of wrong and sorrow, —
Grasping the swords of strife,
Making the most of life?

Yea, all that we can wield is worth the end,
If sought as God's and man's most loyal friend.
Naked we come into the world, and take
Weapons of various skill, —
Let us not use them ill.

As for the creeds, Nature is dark at best;
And darker still is the deep human breast.
Therefore consider well of creeds and books,
Lest thou mayst somewhat fail
Of things beyond the vail.

Nature was dark to the dim starry age
Of wistful Job: and that Athenian sage,
Pensive in piteous thought of Faith's distress;
For still she cried, with tears:
"More light, ye crystal spheres!"

But rouse thee, man! Shake off this hideous death!
Be man! Stand up! Draw in a mighty breath!
This world has quite enough emasculate hands,
Dallying with doubt and sin.
Come—here is work—begin!

Come, here is work—and a rank field—begin.
Put thou thine edge to the great weeds of sin;

So shalt thou find the use of life, and see
Thy Lord, at set of sun,
Approach and say, "Well done!"

This at the last: They clutch the sapless fruit,
Ashes and dust of the Dead Sea, who suit
Their course of life to compass happiness;
But be it understood
That, to be greatly good,
All is the use.

TOM TAYLOR.

ABRAHAM LINCOLN.

(From "The London Punch.")

You lay a wreath on murdered Lincoln's bier,
You, who with mocking pencil wont to trace,
Broad for the self-complacent British sneer,
His length of shambling limb, his furrowed face.

His gaunt, gnarled hands, his unkempt, bristling hair,
His garb uncouth, his bearing ill at ease,
His lack of all we prize as debonair,
Of power or will to shine, of art to please.

You, whose smart pen backed up the pencil's laugh,
Judging each step, as though the way were plain;
Reckless, so it could point its paragraph,
Of chief's perplexity or people's pain.

Beside this corpse, that bears for winding-sheet
The stars and stripes he lived to rear anew,
Between the mourners at his head and feet,
Say, scurril-jester, is there room for you?

Yes, he had lived to shame me from my sneer,
To lame my pencil, and confute my pen, —
To make me own this hind of princes peer,
This rail-splitter a true-born king of men.

My shallow judgment I had learned to rue,
Noting how to occasion's height he rose,
How his quaint wit made home-truth seem more true,
How, iron-like, his temper grew by blows.

How humble, yet how hopeful he could be:
How in good fortune and in ill the same:
Nor bitter in success, nor boastful he,
Thirsty for gold, nor feverish for fame.

He went about his work, — such work as few
Ever had laid on head and heart and hand, —
As one who knows, where there 's a task to do,
Man's honest will must Heaven's good grace command;

Who trusts the strength will with the burden grow,
That God makes instruments to work his will,
If but that will we can arrive to know,
Nor tamper with the weights of good and ill.

So he went forth to battle on the side
That he felt clear was Liberty's and Right's,
As in his peasant boyhood he had plied
His warfare with rude Nature's thwarting mights, —

The uncleared forest, the unbroken soil,
The iron bark that turns the lumberers axe,
The rapid that o'erbears the boatman's toil,
The prairie, hiding the mazed wanderer's tracks.

The ambushed Indian, and the prowling bear, —
Such were the needs that helped his youth to train:

Rough culture, -- but such trees large fruit may bear,
If but their stocks be of right girth and grain.

So he grew up, a destined work to do,
And lived to do it; four long-suffering years'
Ill-fate, ill-feeling, ill-report, lived through,
And then he heard the hisses change to cheers.

The taunts to tribute, the abuse to praise,
And took both with the same unwavering mood:
Till, as he came on light, from darkling days,
And seemed to touch the goal from where he stood,

A felon had, between the goal and him,
Reached from behind his back, a trigger prest, —
And those perplexed and patient eyes were dim,
Those gaunt, long-laboring limbs were laid to rest!

The words of mercy were upon his lips,
Forgiveness in his heart and on his pen,
When this vile murderer brought swift eclipse
To thoughts of peace on earth, good-will to men.

The Old World and the New, from sea to sea,
Utter one voice of sympathy and shame!
Sore heart, so stopped when it at last beat high;
Sad life, cut short just as its triumph came.

A deed accurst! Strokes have been struck before
By the assassin's hand, whereof men doubt
If more of horror or disgrace they bore;
But thy foul crime, like Cain's, stands darkly out.

Vile hand, that brandest murder on a strife,
Whate'er its grounds, stoutly and nobly striven;
And with the martyr's crown crownest a life
With much to praise, little to be forgiven.

MRS. MILES.

HYMN TO CHRIST.

Thou, who didst stoop below
To drain the cup of woe,
Wearing the form of frail mortality,
Thy blessed labors done,
Thy crown of victory won,
Hast passed from earth, — passed to thy throne on high.

Our eyes behold thee not,
Yet hast thou not forgot
Those who have placed their hope, their trust, in thee:
Before thy Father's face
Thou hast prepared a place,
That where thou art, there may they also be.

It was no path of flowers,
Through this dark world of ours,
Belovéd of the Father, thou didst tread;
And shall we in dismay
Shrink from the narrow way,
When clouds and darkness are around it spread?

O Thou who art our life,
Be with us through the strife;
Was not thy head by earth's fierce tempests bowed?
Raise thou our eyes above
To see a Father's love
Beam, like a bow of promise, through the cloud.

E'en through the awful gloom,
Which hovers o'er the tomb,
That light of love our guiding star shall be;
Our spirits shall not dread
The shadowy way to tread,
Friend! Guardian! Saviour! which doth lead to thee!

F. M. FINCH.

[U. S. A.]

THE BLUE AND THE GRAY.

By the flow of the inland river,
Whence the fleets of iron have fled,
Where the blades of the grave-grass quiver,
Asleep are the ranks of the dead;—
Under the sod and the dew,
Waiting the judgment day;—
Under the one, the Blue;
Under the other, the Gray.

From the silence of sorrowful hours
The desolate mourners go,
Lovingly laden with flowers
Alike for the friend and the foe;—
Under the sod and the dew,
Waiting the judgment day;—
Under the roses, the Blue;
Under the lilies, the Gray.

So with an equal splendor
The morning sun-rays fall,
With a touch, impartially tender,
On the blossoms blooming for all;—
Under the sod and the dew,
Waiting the judgment day;—
'Broidered with gold, the Blue;
Mellowed with gold, the Gray.

So, when the summer calleth,
On forest and field of grain
With an equal murmur falleth
The cooling drip of the rain;—
Under the sod and the dew,
Waiting the judgment day;—
Wet with the rain, the Blue;
Wet with the rain, the Gray.

Sadly, but not with upbraiding,
The generous deed was done;
In the storm of the years that are fading,
No braver battle was won;—
Under the sod and the dew,
Waiting the judgment day;—
Under the blossoms, the Blue;
Under the garlands, the Gray.

No more shall the war-cry sever,
Or the winding rivers be red;
They banish our anger forever
When they laurel the graves of our dead!
Under the sod and the dew,
Waiting the judgment day;—
Love and tears for the Blue,
Tears and love for the Gray.

HENRY ABBEY.

THE STATUE.

In Athens, when all learning centred there,
Men reared a column of surpassing height
In honor of Minerva, wise and fair,
And on the top, that dwindled to the sight,
A statue of the goddess was to stand,
That wisdom might obtain in all the land.

And he who, with the beauty in his heart,
Seeking in faultless work immortal youth,
Would mould this statue with the finest art,
Making the wintry marble glow with truth,
Should gain the prize. Two sculptors sought the fame;
The prize they craved was an enduring name.

Alcamenes soon carved his little best;
But Phidias, beneath a dazzling thought
That like a bright sun in a cloudless west
Lit up his wide, great soul, with pure love wrought
A statue, and its face of changeless stone
With calm, far-sighted wisdom towered and shone.

Then to be judged the labors were unveiled;
But at the marble thought, that by degrees
Of hardship Phidias cut, the people railed.
"The lines are coarse; the form too large," said these;
"And he who sends this rough result of haste
Sends scorn, and offers insult to our taste."

Alcamenes' praised work was lifted high
Upon the capital where it might stand;
But there it seemed too small, and 'gainst the sky
Had no proportion from the uplooking land;
So it was lowered, and quickly put aside,
And the scorned thought was mounted to be tried.

Surprise swept o'er the faces of the crowd,
And changed them as a sudden breeze may change
A field of fickle grass, and long and loud
Their mingled shouts to see a sight so strange.
The statue stood completed in its place,
Each coarse line melted to a line of grace.

So bold, great actions, that are seen too near,
Look rash and foolish to unthinking eyes;
They need the past for distance to appear
In their true grandeur. Let us yet be wise
And not too soon our neighbor's deed malign,
For what seems coarse is often good and fine.

JOHN BURROUGHS.

[U. S. A.]

WAITING.

SERENE, I fold my hands and wait,
Nor care for wind, or tide, or sea;
I rave no more 'gainst time or fate,
For lo! my own shall come to me.

I stay my haste, I make delays,
For what avails this eager pace?
I stand amid the eternal ways,
And what is mine shall know my face.

Asleep, awake, by night or day,
The friends I seek are seeking me;
No wind can drive my bark astray,
Nor change the tide of destiny.

What matter if I stand alone?
I wait with joy the coming years;
My heart shall reap where it has sown,
And garner up its fruit of tears.

The waters know their own and draw
The brook that springs in yonder height;
So flows the good with equal law
Unto the soul of pure delight.

The stars come nightly to the sky;
The tidal wave unto the sea;
Nor time, nor space, nor deep, nor high,
Can keep my own away from me.

SARAH WOOLSEY.

[U. S. A.]

IN THE MIST.

SITTING all day in a silver mist,
In silver silence all the day,
Save for the low, soft hiss of spray
And the lisp of sands by waters kissed,
As the tide draws up the bay.

Little I hear and nothing I see,
Wrapped in that veil by fairies spun;
The solid earth is vanished for me
And the shining hours speed noiselessly,
A woof of shadow and sun.

Suddenly out of the shifting veil
A magical bark, by the sunbeams lit,
Flits like a dream — or seems to flit —
With a golden prow and a gossamer sail,
And the waves make room for it.

A fair, swift bark from some radiant realm,
Its diamond cordage cuts the sky
In glittering lines, all silently
A seeming spirit holds the helm
And steers. Will he pass me by?

Ah! not for me is the vessel here,
Noiseless and swift as a sea-bird's flight
She swerves and vanishes from the sight;
No flap of sail, no parting cheer, —
She has passed into the light.

Sitting some day in a deeper mist,
Silent, alone, some other day,

An unknown bark, from an unknown bay,
By unknown waters lapped and kissed,
Shall near me through the spray.

No flap of sail, no scraping of keel,
Shadowy, dim, with a banner dark,
It will hover, will pause, and I shall feel
A hand which grasps me, and shivering steal
To the cold strand, and embark.

Embark for that far, mysterious realm
Where the fathomless, trackless waters flow.
Shall I feel a Presence dim, and know
Thy dear hand, Lord, upon the helm,
Nor be afraid to go?
And through black waves and stormy blast
And out of the fog-wreaths, dense and dun,
Guided by thee, shall the vessel run,
Gain the fair haven, night being past,
And anchor in the sun?

JOHN JAMES PIATT.

[U. S. A.]

THE MORNING STREET.

Alone I walk the morning street,
Filled with the silence vague and sweet:
All seems as strange, as still, as dead,
As if unnumbered years had fled,
Letting the noisy Babel lie
Breathless and dumb against the sky;
The light wind walks with me alone
Where the hot day flame-like was blown,
Where the wheels roared, the dust was beat;
The dew is in the morning street.

Where are the restless throngs that pour
Along this mighty corridor
While the noon shines?—the hurrying crowd
Whose footsteps make the city loud,—
The myriad faces,—hearts that beat
No more in the deserted street?
Those footsteps in their dreaming maze
Cross thresholds of forgotten days;
Those faces brighten from the years
In rising suns long set in tears;
Those hearts,—far in the Past they beat,
Unheard within the morning street.

A city of the world's gray prime,
Lost in some desert far from Time,
Where noiseless ages, gliding through,
Have only sifted sand and dew,—
Yet a mysterious hand of man
Lying on all the haunted plan,
The passions of the human heart
Quickening the marble breast of Art,—
Were not more strange to one who first
Upon its ghostly silence burst
Than this vast quiet where the tide
Of life, upheaved on either side,
Hangs trembling, ready soon to beat
With human waves the morning street.
Ay, soon the glowing morning flood
Breaks through the charmèd solitude:
This silent stone, to music won,
Shall murmur to the rising sun;
The busy place, in dust and heat,
Shall rush with wheels and swarm with feet;
The Arachne-threads of Purpose stream
Unseen within the morning gleam;
The life shall move, the death be plain;
The bridal throng, the funeral train,
Together, face to face, shall meet
And pass within the morning street.

RICHARD W. GILDER.

[U. S. A.]

DAWN.

The night was dark, though sometimes a faint star
A little while a little space made bright.
The night was long and like an iron bar
Lay heavy on the land: till o'er the sea
Slowly, within the East, there grew a light
Which half was starlight, and half seemed to be
The herald of a greater. The pale white
Turned slowly to pale rose, and up the height
Of heaven slowly climbed. The gray sea grew

Rose-colored like the sky. A white gull flew
Straight toward the utmost boundary of the East,
Where slowly the rose gathered and increased.
It was as on the opening of a door
By one that in his hand a lamp doth hold,
Whose flame is hidden by the garment's fold, —
The still air moves, the wide room is less dim.

More bright the East became, the ocean turned
Dark and more dark against the brightening sky, —
Sharper against the sky the long sea line.
The hollows of the breakers on the shore
Were green like leaves whereon no sun doth shine,
Though white the outer branches of the tree.
From rose to red the level heaven burned;
Then sudden, as if a sword fell from on high,
A blade of gold flashed on the horizon's rim.

THE SOWER.

I.

A Sower went forth to sow,
His eyes were wild with woe;
He crushed the flowers beneath his feet,
Nor smelt the perfume, warm and sweet,
That prayed for pity everywhere.
He came to a field that was harried
By iron, and to heaven laid bare:
He shook the seed that he carried
O'er that brown and bladeless place.
He shook it, as God shakes hail
Over a doomed land,
When lightnings interlace
The sky and the earth, and his wand
Of love is a thunder-flail.
Thus did that Sower sow;
His seed was human blood,
And tears of women and men.
And I, who near him stood,
Said: When the crop comes, then
There will be sobbing and sighing,
Weeping and wailing and crying,
And a woe that is worse than woe.

II.

It was an autumn day
When next I went that way.
And what, think you, did I see?
What was it that I heard?
The song of a sweet-voiced bird?
Nay, — but the songs of many,
Thrilled through with praising prayer.
Of all those voices not any
Were sad of memory:
And a sea of sunlight flowed,
And a golden harvest glowed!
On my face I fell down there;
I hid my weeping eyes,
I said: O God, thou art wise!
And I thank thee, again and again,
For the Sower whose name is Fain.

WILLIAM BELL SCOTT.

THE DANCE.

(From "The Witch's Ballad.")

O, I hae come from far away,
From a warm land far away,
A southern land ayont the sea,
With sailor lads about the mast
Merry and canny and kind to me.

And I hae been to yon town,
To try my luck in yon town:
Nort, and Mysie, Elspie too,
Right braw we were to pass the gate
Wi' gowden clasps on girdles blue.

Mysie smiled wi' miming mouth,
Innocent mouth, miming mouth;
Elspie wore her scarlet gown,
Nort's gray eyes were unco' gleg,
My Castile comb was like a crown.

We walked abreast all up the street,
Into the market up the street:
Our hair wi' marygolds was wound,
Our bodices wi' love-knots laced,
Our merchandise wi' tansy bound.

Nort had chickens, I had cocks,
Gamesome cocks, loud-crowing cocks;
Mysie ducks, and Elspie drakes.
For a wee groat or a pound,
We lost nae time wi' gives and takes.

Lost nae time, for weel we knew,
In our sleeves fu' weel we knew,
When the gloaming came that night,
Duck nor drake, nor hen nor cock,
Would be found by candlelight.

When our chaffering a' was done,
All was paid for, sold and done,
We drew a glove on ilka hand,
We sweetly curtsied each to each,
And deftly danced a saraband.

The market lasses looked and laughed,
Left their gear and looked and laughed;
They made as they would join the game,
But soon their mithers, wild and wud,
Wi' whack and screech they stopped the same.

Sae loud the tongues o' raudies grew,
The flitin' and the skirlin' grew,
At a' the windows i' the place,
Wi' spoons and knives, wi' needle or awl,
Was thrust out ilka hand and face.

And down each stair they thronged anon;
Gentle, simple, thronged anon;
Souter and tailor, frowzy Nan,
The ancient widow young again
Simpering behind her fan.

Without choice, against their will,
Doited, dazed against their will,
The market lassie and her mither,
The farmer and his husbandman,
Hand in hand danced a' thegether.

Slow at first, but faster soon,
Still increasin' wild and fast,
Hoods and mantles, hats and hose,
Blindly doffed, and frae them cast,
Left them naked, heads and toes.

They would hae torn us limb frae limb,
Dainty limb frae dainty limb;
But never ane o' them could win
Across the line that I had drawn
Wi' bleeding thumb a-witherskin.

There was Jeff the provost's son,
Jeff the provost's only son;
There was Father Auld himsel',
The Lombard frae the hostelrie,
And the lawyer Peter Fell.

All goodly men we singled out,
Waled them well and singled out,
And drew them by the left hand in, —
Mysie the priest, and Elspie won
The Lombard, Nort the lawyer curle,
And I my mysel' the provost's son.

Then wi' cantrip kisses seven,
Three times round wi' kisses seven,
Warped and woven there spun we,
Arms and legs and flaming hair,
Like a whirlwind on the sea.

Like the wind that sucks the sea,
Over and in and on the sea,
Good sooth, it was a mad delight:
And ilka man o' all the four
Shut his eyes and laughed outright, —

Laughed as long as they had breath,
Laughed while they had sense or breath;
And close about us coiled a mist
Of gnats and midges, wasps and flies;
Like the whirlwind shaft it rist.

Drawn up was I right off my feet,
Into the mist and off my feet;
And, dancing on each chimney-top,
I saw a thousand darling imps
Keeping time wi' skip and hop.

We 'll gang ance mair to yon town,
Wi' better luck to yon town:
We 'll walk in silk and cramoisie,
And I shall wed the prevost's son;
My lady o' the town I 'll be!

For I was born a crowned king's child,
Born and nursed a king's child,
King o' a land ayont the sea,
Where the Blackamoor kissed me first
And taught me art and glamourie.

The Lombard shall be Elspie's man,
Elspie's gowden husbandman;
Nort shall take the lawyer's hand;
The priest shall swear another vow.
We 'll dance again the saraband!

JOSEPH BRENNAN.

COME TO ME, DEAREST.

Come to me, dearest, I 'm lonely without thee,
Day-time and night-time, I 'm thinking about thee;

Night-time and day-time, in dreams I behold thee;
Unwelcome the waking which ceases to fold thee.
Come to me, darling, my sorrows to lighten,
Come in thy beauty to bless and to brighten;
Come in thy womanhood, meekly and lowly,
Come in thy lovingness, queenly and holy.

Swallows will flit round the desolate ruin,
Telling of spring and its joyous renewing
And thoughts of thy love, and its manifold treasure,
Are circling my heart with a promise of pleasure.
O Spring of my spirit, O May of my bosom,
Shine out on my soul, till it bourgeon and blossom;
The waste of my life has a rose-root within it.
And thy fondness alone to the sunshine can win it.

Figure that moves like a song through the even,
Features lit up by a reflex of heaven;
Eyes like the skies of poor Erin, our mother,
Where shadow and sunshine are chasing each other;
Smiles coming seldom, but childlike and simple,
Planting in each rosy cheek a sweet dimple;—
O, thanks to the Saviour, that even thy seeming
Is left to the exile to brighten his dreaming.

You have been glad when you knew I was gladdened;
Dear, are you sad now to hear I am saddened?
Our hearts ever answer in tune and in time, love,
As octave to octave, and rhyme unto rhyme, love:
I cannot weep but your tears will be flowing,
You cannot smile but my cheek will be glowing;
I would not die without you at my side, love,
You will not linger when I shall have died, love.

Come to me, dear, ere I die of my sorrow,
Rise on my gloom like the sun of to-morrow;
Strong, swift, and fond as the words which I speak, love,
With a song on your lip and a smile on your cheek, love.
Come, for my heart in your absence is weary, —
Haste, for my spirit is sickened and dreary, —
Come to the arms which alone should caress thee,
Come to the heart that is throbbing to press thee!

CHARLES G. LELAND.

[U. S. A.]

THE MUSIC-LESSON OF CONFUCIUS.

THE music-lesson of Koung-tseu the wise,
Known as Confucius in the western world.

Of all the sages of the Flowery Land
None knew so well as great Confucius
The ancient rites; and when his mother died,
Three years he mourned alone beside her tomb
As the Old Custom bade, nor did he miss
A single detail of the dark old forms
Required of the bereaved, for he had made
Himself a model for all living men:
A mirror and a pattern of the Past.

Now when the years of mourning with their rites
Were at an end, Confucius came forth
And wandered as of old with other men,
Giving his counsel unto many kings;
But still the hand of grief was on his heart,
And his dark hue set forth his darkened hours.
To drive away these sorrows from his soul,

Remembering that music had been made
A moral motive in the golden books
Of wisdom by the sacred ancestors,
He played upon the Kin — the curious lute
Invented by Fou-Hi in days of old;
Fou-Hi of the bull's head and dragon's form,
The Lord of Learning who upraised mankind
From being silent brutes to singing men.

In vain Confucius played upon the lute;
He found that music would not be to him
What it had been of old, — a pastime gay:
For he had borne through three long years of grief
Stupendous knowledge, and his mighty soul,
Grasping the lines which link all earthly lore,
Had been by suffering raised to greater power:
For he who *knows* and suffers, if he will
May raise himself unnumbered scales o'er man.

The music spoke no more its wonted sounds,
But whispered mysteries in a broken tongue
Which urged him sorely. Then Confucius said:
"O secret Music! sacred tongue of God!
I hear thee calling to me, and I come!
Of old I did but know thy outer form,
And dreamed not of the spirit hid within;
The Goddess in the Lotus. Yes, I come,
And will not rest, — nor will I calm my doubt
Till I have seen thee plainly with mine eyes,
And palpably have touched thee with my hand,
Then shall I know thee, — raised to life for me
For what thou truly art.
Lo! I have heard
That in the land of Kin a master lives,
So deeply skilled in music, that mankind
Begin again to give a glowing faith
Unto the golden stories which are told
Of the strange harmonies which built the world,
And of the melody whose key is God.
Now I will travel to the land of Kin,
And know this sage of music, great Siang,
And learn the secret lore which hides within
All sweet well-ordered sounds." He went his way,
Nor rested till he stood before the man.

Thus spoke Siang unto Confucius:
"Of all the arts, great Music is the art
To raise the soul above all earthly storms;
For in it lies that purest harmony
Which lifts us over self and up to God.
Thou who hast studied deeply the *Koua*—
The eight great symbols of created things —
Knowest the sacred power of the line
Which when unbroken flies to all the worlds
As light unending, — but in broken forms
Falls short as sky and earth, clouds, winds, and fire,
The deep blue ocean and the mountain high,
And the red lightning hissing in the wave.
The mighty law which formed what thou canst see,
As clearly lives in all that thou canst hear,
And more than this, in all that thou canst feel.
Here, take thy lute in hand. I teach the air
Made by the sage Wen Wang of ancient days."

Confucius took the lute and played the air
Till all his soul seemed passing into song;
Then he fell deep into the solemn chords
As though his body and the lute were one,
And every chord a wave which bore him on
Through the great sea of ecstasy. His hands
Then ceased to play, — but in his raptured look
They saw him following out the harmony.

Five days went by, and still Confucius
Played all day long the ancient simple air;

And when Siang would teach him more, he said:
"Not yet, my master, I would seize the *thought*,
The subtle thought which hides within the tune."
To which the master answered: "It is well.
Take five days more!" And when the time was passed
Unto Siang thus spoke Confucius:
"I do begin to see, — yet what I see
Is very dim. I am as one who looks
And nothing sees except a luminous cloud:
Give me but five more days, and at the end
If I have not attained the great idea
Hidden of old within the melody,
I will leave music as beyond my power."
"Do as thou wilt, O pupil!" cried Siang
In deepest admiration; "never yet
Had I a scholar who was like to thee."

And on the fifteenth day Confucius rose
And stood before Siang, and cried aloud:
"The mist which shadowed me is blown away,
I am as one who stands upon a cliff
And gazes far and wide upon the world,
For I have mastered every secret thought,
Yea, every shadow of a feeling dim
Which flitted through the spirit of Wen Wang
When he composed that air. I speak to him,
I hear him clearly answer me again;
And more than that, I see his very form:
A man of middle stature, with a hue
Half blended with the dark and with the fair;
His features long, and large sweet eyes which beam
With great benevolence, — a noble face!
His voice is deep and full, and all his air
Inspires a sense of virtue and of love.
I know that I behold the very man,
The sage of ancient days, Wen Wang the just."

Then good Siang lay down upon the dust,
And said: "Thou art my master. Even thus
The ancient legend, known to none but me,
Describes our first great sire. And thou hast seen
That which I never yet myself beheld,
Though I have played the sacred song for years,
Striving with all my soul to penetrate
Its mystery unto the master's form,
Whilst thou hast reached it at a single bound: —
Henceforth the gods alone can teach thee tune."

MINE OWN.

And O, the longing, burning eyes!
And O, the gleaming hair
Which waves around me, night and day,
O'er chamber, hall, and stair!

And O, the step, half dreamt, half heard!
And O, the laughter low!
And memories of merriment
Which faded long ago!

O, art thou Sylph, — or truly Self, —
Or either at thy choice?
O, speak in breeze or beating heart,
But let me hear thy voice!

"O, some do call me Laughter, love;
And some do call me Sin": —
"And they may call thee what they will,
So I thy love may win.

"And some do call me Wantonness,
And some do call me Play": —
"O, they might call thee what they would
If thou wert mine alway!"

"And some do call me Sorrow, love,
And some do call me Tears,
And some there be who name me Hope,
And some that name me Fears.

"And some do call me Gentle Heart,
And some Forgetfulness": —
"And if thou com'st as one or all,
Thou comest but to bless!"

"And some do call me Life, sweetheart,
And some do call me Death;
And he to whom the two are one
Has won my heart and faith."

She twined her white arms round his neck: —
The tears fell down like rain.
"And if I live or if I die,
We'll never part again."

HELEN BARRON BOSTWICK.

[U. S. A.]

URVASI.

'T is a story told by Kalidasa, —
Hindoo poet, —in melodious rhyme,
How with train of maidens, young Urvasi
Came to keep great Indra's festal time.

'T was her part in worshipful confession
Of the god-name on that sacred day,
Walking flower-crowned in the long procession,
"I love Puru-shotta-ma" to say.

Pure as snow on Himalayan ranges,
Heaven-descended, soon to heaven withdrawn,
Fairer than the moon-flower of the Ganges,
Was Urvasi, Daughter of the Dawn.

But it happened that the gentle maiden
Loved one Puru-avas,—fateful name!—
And her heart, with its sweet secret laden,
Faltered when her time of utterance came.

"I love"—then she stopped, and people wondered;
"I love"—she must guard her secret well;
Then from sweetest lips that ever blundered,
"I love Puru-avas," trembling fell.

Ah, what terror seized on poor Urvasi!
Misty grew the violets of her eyes,
And her form bent like a broken daisy,
While around her rose the mocking cries.

But great Indra said, "The maid shall marry
Him whose image in her faithful heart
She so near to that of God doth carry,
Scarce her lips can keep their names apart."

Call it then not weakness or dissembling,
If, in striving the high name to reach,
Through our voices runs the tender trembling
Of an earthly name too dear for speech!

Ever dwells the lesser in the greater;
In God's love the human: we by these
Know he holds Love's simplest stammering sweeter
Than cold praise of wordy Pharisees.

UNKNOWN.

THE FISHERMAN'S FUNERAL.

Up on the breezy headland the fisherman's grave they made,
Where, over the daisies and clover bells, the birchen branches swayed;
Above us the lark was singing in the cloudless skies of June,
And under the cliffs the billows were chanting their ceaseless tune:
For the creamy line was curving along the hollow shore,
Where the dear old tides were flowing that he would ride no more.
The dirge of the wave, the note of the bird, and the priest's low tone were blent
In the breeze that blew from the moorland, all laden with country scent;
But never a thought of the new-mown hay tossing on sunny plains,
Or of lilies deep in the wild-wood, or roses gemming the lanes,
Woke in the hearts of the stern bronzed men who gathered around the grave,
Where lay the mate who had fought with them the battle of wind and wave.

How boldly he steered the coble across the foaming bar,
When the sky was black to the eastward and the breakers white on the Scar!
How his keen eye caught the squall ahead, how his strong hand furled the sail,
As we drove o'er the angry waters before the raging gale!
How cheery he kept all the long dark night; and never a parson spoke
Good words, like those he said to us, when at last the morning broke!

So thought the dead man's comrades, as silent and sad they stood,
While the prayer was prayed, the blessing said, and the dull earth struck the wood;

And the widow's sob and the orphan's wail jarred through the joyous air;
How could the light wind o'er the sea, blow on so fresh and fair?
How could the gay waves laugh and leap, landward o'er sand and stone,
While he, who knew and loved them all lay lapped in clay alone?

But for long, when to the beetling heights the snow-tipped billows roll,
When the cod, and skate, and dogfish dart around the herring shoal;
When gear is sorted, and sails are set, and the merry breezes blow,
And away to the deep sea-harvest the stalwart reapers go,
A kindly sigh, and a hearty word, they will give to him who lies
Where the clover springs, and the heather blooms, beneath the northern skies.

JOHN C. FREMONT.

ON RECROSSING THE ROCKY MOUNTAINS IN WINTER, AFTER MANY YEARS.

Long years ago I wandered here,
In the midsummer of the year, —
Life's summer too;
A score of horsemen here we rode,
The mountain world its glories showed,
All fair to view.

These scenes in glowing colors drest,
Mirrored the life within my breast,
Its world of hopes;
The whispering woods and fragrant breeze
That stirred the grass in verdant seas
On billowy slopes,

And glistening crag in sunlit sky,
Mid snowy clouds piled mountains high,
Were joys to me;
My path was o'er the prairie wide,
Or here on grander mountain-side,
To choose, all free.

The rose that waved in morning air,
And spread its dewy fragrance there
In careless bloom,
Gave to my heart its ruddiest hue,
O'er my glad life its color threw
And sweet perfume.

Now changed the scene and changed the eyes,
That here once looked on glowing skies,
Where summer smiled;
These riven trees, this wind-swept plain
Now show the winter's dread domain,
Its fury wild.

The rocks rise black from storm-packed snow,
All checked the river's pleasant flow,
Vanished the bloom;
These dreary wastes of frozen plain
Reflect my bosom's life again,
Now lonesome gloom.

The buoyant hopes and busy life
Have ended all in hateful strife,
And thwarted aim.
The world's rude contact killed the rose,
No more its radiant color shows
False roads to fame.

Backward, amidst the twilight glow
Some lingering spots yet brightly show
On hard roads won,
Where still some grand peaks mark the way
Touched by the light of parting day
And memory's sun.

But here thick clouds the mountains hide,
The dim horizon bleak and wide
No pathway shows,
And rising gusts, and darkening sky,
Tell of "the night that cometh," nigh,
The brief day's close.

UNKNOWN.

JULY DAWNING.

We left the city, street and square,
With lamplights glimmering through and through,
And turned us toward the suburb, where—
Full from the east—the fresh wind blew.

One cloud stood overhead the sun, —
A glorious trail of dome and spire, —
The last star flickered, and was gone;
The first lark led the matin choir.

Wet was the grass beneath our tread,
  Thick-dewed the bramble by the way;
The lichen had a lovelier red,
  The elder-flower a fairer gray.

And there was silence on the land,
  Save when, from out the city's fold,
Stricken by Time's remorseless wand,
  A bell across the morning tolled.

The beeches sighed through all their boughs;
  The gusty pennons of the pine
Swayed in a melancholy drowse,
  But with a motion sternly fine.

One gable, full against the sun,
  Flooded the garden-space beneath
With spices, sweet as cinnamon,
  From all its honeysuckled breath.

Then crew the cocks from echoing farms,
  The chimney-tops were plumed with smoke,
The windmill shook its slanted arms,
  The sun was up, the country woke!

And voices sounded mid the trees
  Of orchards red with burning leaves,
By thick hives, sentinelled by bees,—
  From fields which promised tented sheaves;

Till the day waxed into excess,
  And on the misty, rounding gray,—
One vast, fantastic wilderness,
  The glowing roofs of London lay.

UNKNOWN.

THE FISHERMAN'S SUMMONS.

The sea is calling, calling.
Wife, is there a log to spare?
Fling it down on the hearth and call them in,
The boys and girls with their merry din,
I am loth to leave you all just yet,
In the light and the noise I might forget,
The voice in the evening air.

The sea is calling, calling,
Along the hollow shore.
I know each nook in the rocky strand,
And the crimson weeds on the golden sand,
And the worn old cliff where the sea-pinks cling,
And the winding caves where the echoes ring.
I shall wake them nevermore.

How it keeps calling, calling,
It is never a night to sail.
I saw the "sea-dog" over the height,
As I strained through the haze my failing sight,
And the cottage creaks and rocks, well-nigh,
As the old "Fox" did in the days gone by,
In the moan of the rising gale.

Yet it is calling, calling.
It is hard on a soul, I say,
To go fluttering out in the cold and the dark,
Like the bird they tell us of, from the ark;
While the foam flies thick on the bitter blast,
And the angry waves roll fierce and fast,
Where the black buoy marks the bay.

Do you hear it calling, calling?
And yet, I am none so old.
At the herring fishery, but last year,
No boat beat mine for tackle and gear,
And I steered the coble past the reef,
When the broad sail shook like a withered leaf,
And the rudder chafed my hold.

Will it never stop calling, calling?
Can't you sing a song by the hearth?
A heartsome stave of a merry glass,
Or a gallant fight, or a bonnie lass?
Don't you care for your grand-dad just so much?
Come near then, give me a hand to touch,
Still warm with the warmth of earth.

You hear it calling, calling?
Ask her why she sits and cries.
She always did when the sea was up,
She would fret, and never take bit or sup
When I and the lads were out at night,
And she saw the breakers cresting white
Beneath the low black skies.

But, then, it is calling, calling,
No summons to soul was sent.
Now— Well, fetch the parson, find the book,
It is up on the shelf there if you look;

The sea has been friend, and fire, and bread;
Put me, where it will tell of me, lying dead,
How It called, and I rose and went.

MARY N. PRESCOTT.

[U. S. A.]

WORK.

SWEET wind, fair wind, where have you been?
"I 've been sweeping the cobwebs out of the sky;
I've been grinding a grist in the mill hard by;
I 've been laughing at work while others sigh;
Let those laugh who win!"

Sweet rain, soft rain, what are you doing?
"I 'm urging the corn to fill out its cells;
I 'm helping the lily to fashion its bells;
I 'm swelling the torrent and brimming the wells;
Is that worth pursuing?"

Redbreast, redbreast, what have you done?
"I 've been watching the nest where my fledgelings lie;
I 've sung them to sleep with a lullaby;
By and by I shall teach them to fly,
Up and away, every one!"

Honey-bee, honey-bee, where are you going?
"To fill my basket with precious pelf;
To toil for my neighbor as well as myself;
To find out the sweetest flower that grows,
Be it a thistle or be it a rose, —
A secret worth the knowing!"

Each content with the work to be done,
Ever the same from sun to sun:
Shall you and I be taught to work
By the bee and the bird, that scorn to shirk?

Wind and rain fulfilling His word!
Tell me, was ever a legend heard
Where the wind, commanded to blow, deferred;
Or the rain, that was bidden to fall, demurred?

TWO MOODS.

I PLUCKED the harebells as I went
Singing along the river-side;
The skies above were opulent
Of sunshine. "Ah! whate'er betide,
The world is sweet, is sweet," I cried,
That morning by the river-side.

The curlews called along the shore;
The boats put out from sandy beach;
Afar I heard the breakers' roar,
Mellowed to silver-sounding speech;
And still I sang it o'er and o'er,
"The world is sweet forevermore!"

Perhaps, to-day, some other one,
Loitering along the river-side,
Content beneath the gracious sun,
May sing, again, "Whate'er betide,
The world is sweet." I shall not chide,
Although *my* song is done.

ARTHUR O'SHAUGHNESSY.

SONG OF A FELLOW-WORKER.

I FOUND a fellow-worker when I deemed I toiled alone:
My toil was fashioning thought and sound, and his was hewing stone;
I worked in the palace of my brain, he in the common street,
And it seemed his toil was great and hard, while mine was great and sweet.

I said, "O fellow-worker, yea, for I am a worker too,
The heart nigh fails me many a day, but how is it with you?
For while I toil great tears of joy will sometimes fill my eyes,
And when I form my perfect work it lives and never dies.

"I carve the marble of pure thought until the thought takes form,
Until it gleams before my soul and makes the world grow warm;
Until there comes the glorious voice and words that seem divine,
And the music reaches all men's hearts and draws them into mine.

"And yet for days it seems my heart shall blossom never more,
And the burden of my loneliness lies on me very sore:
Therefore, O hewer of the stones that pave base human ways,
How canst thou bear the years till death, made of such thankless days?"

Then he replied: "Ere sunrise, when the pale lips of the day
Sent forth an earnest thrill of breath at warmth of the first ray,
A great thought rose within me, how, while men asleep had lain,
The thousand labors of the world had grown up once again.

"The sun grew on the world, and on my soul the thought grew too, —
A great appalling sun, to light my soul the long day through.
I felt the world's whole burden for a moment, then began
With man's gigantic strength to do the labor of one man.

"I went forth hastily, and lo! I met a hundred men,
The worker with the chisel and the worker with the pen, —
The restless toilers after good, who sow and never reap,
And one who maketh music for their souls that may not sleep.

"Each passed me with a dauntless look, and my undaunted eyes
Were almost softened as they passed with tears that strove to rise
At sight of all those labors, and because that every one,
Ay, the greatest, would be greater if my little were undone.

"They passed me, having faith in me, and in our several ways,
Together we began to-day as on the other days:
I felt their mighty hands at work, and, as the day wore through,
Perhaps they felt that even I was helping somewhat too:

"Perhaps they felt, as with those hands they lifted mightily
The burden once more laid upon the world so heavily,
That while they nobly held it as each man can do and bear,
It did not wholly fall my side as though no man were there.

"And so we toil together many a day from morn till night,
I in the lower depths of life, they on the lovely height;
For though the common stones are mine, and they have lofty cares,
Their work begins where this leaves off, and mine is part of theirs.

"And 't is not wholly mine or theirs I think of through the day,
But the great eternal thing we make together, I and they;
Far in the sunset I behold a city that man owns,
Made fair with all their nobler toil, built of my common stones.

"Then noonward, as the task grows light with all the labor done,
The single thought of all the day becomes a joyous one:
For, rising in my heart at last where it has lain so long,
It thrills up seeking for a voice, and grows almost a song.

"But when the evening comes, indeed, the words have taken wing,
The thought sings in me still, but I am all too tired to sing;
Therefore, O you my friend, who serve the world with minstrelsy,
Among our fellow-workers' songs make that one song for me."

ARCHDEACON HARE.

ITALY. A PROPHECY.

1818.

Strike the loved harp; let the prelude be,
Italy! Italy!
That chord again, again that note of glee,—
Italy! Italy!
Italy! O Italy! the very sound it charmeth:
Italy! O Italy! the name my bosom warmeth.
High thought of self-devotions,
Compassionate emotions,

Soul-stirring recollections,
With hopes, their bright reflections.
Rush to my troubled heart at thought of thee,
My own illustrious, injured Italy.

Dear queen of snowy mountains,
And consecrated fountains,
Within whose rocky, heaven-aspiring pale
Beauty has fixed a dwelling
All others so excelling
To praise it right, thine own sweet tones would fail;
Hail to thee! hail!
How rich art thou in lakes to poet dear,
And those broad pines amid the sunniest glade
So reigning through the year,
Within the magic circle of their shade
No sunbeam may appear!
How fair thy double sea!
In blue celestially
Glittering and circling! but I may not dwell
On gifts, which, decking thee too well,
Allured the spoiler. Let me fix my ken
Rather upon thy godlike men,
The good, the wise, the valiant, and the free,
On history's pillars towering gloriously,
A trophy reared on high upon thy strand,
That every people, every clime
May mark and understand,
What memorable courses may be run,
What golden never-failing treasures won,
From time,
In spite of chance,
And worser ignorance,
If men be ruled by Duty's firm decree,
And wisdom hold her paramount mastery.

What art thou now? Alas! Alas!
Woe, woe!
That strength and virtue thus should pass
From men below!
That so divine, so beautiful a Maid
Should in the withering dust be laid,
As one that— Hush! who dares with impious breath
To speak of death?
The fool alone and unbeliever weepeth.
We know she only sleepeth;
And from the dust,
At the end of her correction,
Truth hath decreed her joyous resurrection:
She shall arise, she must.
For can it be that wickedness hath power
To undermine or topple down the tower
Of virtue's edifice?
And yet that vice
Should be allowed on sacred ground to plant
A rock of adamant?
It is of ice,
That rock soon destined to dissolve away
Before the righteous sun's returning ray.

But who shall bear the dazzling radiancy,
When first the royal Maid awaking
Darteth around her wild indignant eye,
When first her bright spear shaking,
Fixing her feet on earth, her looks on sky,
She standeth like the Archangel prompt to vanquish,
Yet still imploring succor from on high?
O days of weary hope and passionate anguish,
When will ye end!
Until that end be come, until I hear
The Alps their mighty voices blend,
To swell and echo back the sound most dear
To patriot hearts, the cry of Liberty,
I must live on. But when the glorious Queen
As erst is canopied with Freedom's sheen,
When I have prest, with salutation meet,
With reverent love to kiss her honored feet,
I then may die,
Die how well satisfied!
Conscious that I have watched the second birth
Of her I've loved the most upon the earth,
Conscious beside
That no more beauteous sight can here be given:
Sublimer visions are reserved for heaven.

T. K. HERVEY.

EPITAPH.

Farewell! since never more for thee
The sun comes up our eastern skies,
Less bright henceforth shall sunshine be
To some fond hearts and saddened eyes.

There are who for thy last, long sleep
Shall sleep as sweetly nevermore, —
Shall weep because thou canst not weep,
And grieve that all thy griefs are o'er.

Sad thrift of love! the loving breast
On which the aching head was thrown,
Gave up the weary head to rest,
But kept the aching for its own.

FREDERICK TENNYSON.

THE BLACKBIRD.

How sweet the harmonies of afternoon!
The Blackbird sings along the sunny breeze
His ancient song of leaves, and summer boon;
Rich breath of hayfields streams through whispering trees;
And birds of morning trim their bustling wings,
And listen fondly—while the Blackbird sings.

How soft the lovelight of the west reposes
On this green valley's cheery solitude,
On the trim cottage with its screen of roses,
On the gray belfry with its ivy hood,
And murmuring mill-race, and the wheel that flings
Its bubbling freshness—while the Blackbird sings.

The very dial on the village church
Seems as 't were dreaming in a dozy rest;
The scribbled benches underneath the porch
Bask in the kindly welcome of the west:
But the broad casements of the old Three Kings
Blaze like a furnace—while the Blackbird sings.

And there beneath the immemorial elm
Three rosy revellers round a table sit,
And through gray clouds give laws unto the realm,
Curse good and great, but worship their own wit,
And roar of fights, and fairs, and junketings,
Corn, colts, and curs—the while the Blackbird sings.

Before her home, in her accustomed seat,
The tidy grandam spins beneath the shade
Of the old honeysuckle, at her feet
The dreaming pug, and purring tabby laid;
To her low chair a little maiden clings,
And spells in silence—while the Blackbird sings.

Sometimes the shadow of a lazy cloud
Breathes o'er the hamlet with its gardens green,
While the far fields with sunlight overflowed
Like golden shores of Fairyland are seen;
Again the sunshine on the shadow springs,
And fires the thicket—where the Blackbird sings.

The woods, the lawn, the peakèd manor-house,
With its peach-covered walls, and rookery loud,
The trim, quaint garden-alleys, screened with boughs,
The lion-headed gates, so grim and proud,
The mossy fountain with its murmurings,
Lie in warm sunshine—while the Blackbird sings.

The ring of silver voices, and the sheen
Of festal garments, —and my lady streams
With her gay court across the garden green;
Some laugh, and dance, some whisper their love-dreams;
And one calls for a little page; he strings
Her lute beside her—while the Blackbird sings.

A little while—and lo! the charm is heard;
A youth, whose life has been all summer, steals
Forth from the noisy guests around the board,
Creeps by her softly; at her footstool kneels;
And, when she pauses, murmurs tender things
Into her fond ear—while the Blackbird sings.

The smoke-wreaths from the chimneys curl up higher,
And dizzy things of eve begin to float
Upon the light; the breeze begins to tire.
Half-way to sunset with a drowsy note
The ancient clock from out the valley swings;
The grandam nods—and still the Blackbird sings.

Far shouts and laughter from the farmstead peal,
Where the great stack is piling in the sun;
Through narrow gates o'erladen wagons reel,
And barking curs into the tumult run;
While the inconstant wind bears off, and brings
The merry tempest—and the Blackbird sings.

On the high wold the last look of the sun
Burns, like a beacon, over dale and stream;
The shouts have ceased, the laughter and the fun;
The grandam sleeps, and peaceful be her dream;
Only a hammer on an anvil rings;
The day is dying—still the Blackbird sings.

Now the good vicar passes from his gate,
Serene, with long white hair; and in his eye
Burns the clear spirit that hath conquered Fate,
And felt the wings of immortality;
His heart is thronged with great imaginings,
And tender mercies—while the Blackbird sings.

Down by the brook he bends his steps, and through
A lowly wicket; and at last he stands
Awful beside the bed of one who grew
From boyhood with him, — who with lifted hands
And eyes seems listening to far welcomings
And sweeter music — than the Blackbird sings.

Two golden stars, like tokens from the blest,
Strike on his dim orbs from the setting sun;
His sinking hands seem pointing to the west;
He smiles as though he said, "Thy will be done!"
His eyes, they see not those illuminings;
His ears, they hear not — what the Blackbird sings.

JOHN A. DORGAN.

[U. S. A.]

FATE.

These withered hands are weak,
But they shall do my bidding, though so frail;
These lips are thin and white, but shall not fail
The appointed words to speak.

Thy sneer I can forgive,
Because I know the strength of destiny;
Until my task is done, I cannot die;
And then, I would not live.

MARY BOLLES BRANCH.

[U. S. A.]

THE PETRIFIED FERN.

In a valley, centuries ago,
Grew a little fern-leaf, green and slender,
Veining delicate and fibres tender;
Waving when the wind crept down so low;

Rushes tall, and moss, and grass grew round it,
Playful sunbeams darted in and found it,
Drops of dew stole in by night, and crowned it,
But no foot of man e'er trod that way;
Earth was young and keeping holiday.

Monster fishes swam the silent main,
Stately forests waved their giant branches,
Mountains hurled their snowy avalanches,
Mammoth creatures stalked across the plain;
Nature revelled in grand mysteries;
But the little fern was not of these,
Did not number with the hills and trees,
Only grew and waved its wild sweet way,—
No one came to note it day by day.

Earth, one time, put on a frolic mood,
Heaved the rocks and changed the mighty motion
Of the deep, strong currents of the ocean;
Moved the plain and shook the haughty wood,
Crushed the little fern in soft moist clay,
Covered it, and hid it safe away.
O, the long, long centuries since that day!
O, the agony, O, life's bitter cost,
Since that useless little fern was lost!

Useless! Lost! There came a thoughtful man
Searching Nature's secrets, far and deep;
From a fissure in a rocky steep
He withdrew a stone, o'er which there ran
Fairy pencillings, a quaint design,
Veinings, leafage, fibres clear and fine,
And the fern's life lay in every line!
So, I think, God hides some souls away,
Sweetly to surprise us the last day.

INDEX OF FIRST LINES.

INDEX OF SUBJECTS.

THE END.

www.ingramcontent.com/pod-product-compliance
Lightning Source LLC
LaVergne TN
LVHW020128110826
845151LV00001B/305

* 9 7 8 1 4 2 5 5 4 0 3 7 1 *